George I. Sánchez

THE LAMAR SERIES IN WESTERN HISTORY

The Lamar Series in Western History includes scholarly books of general public interest that enhance the understanding of human affairs in the American West and contribute to a wider understanding of the West's significance in the political, social, and cultural life of America. Comprising works of the highest quality, the series aims to increase the range and vitality of Western American history, focusing on frontier places and people, Indian and ethnic communities, the urban West and the environment, and the art and illustrated history of the American West.

Recent Titles

George I. Sánchez: The Long Fight for Mexican American Integration, by Carlos Kevin Blanton
The Yaquis and the Empire: Violence, Spanish Imperial Power, and Native Resilience in Colonial Mexico, by Raphael Brewster Folsom
Gathering Together: The Shawnee People through Diaspora and Nationhood, 1600–1870, by Sami Lakomäki
Nature's Noblemen: Transatlantic Masculinities and the Nineteenth-Century American West, by Monica Rico
Rush to Gold: The French and the California Gold Rush, 1848–1854, by Malcolm J. Rohrbough
Sun Chief: The Autobiography of a Hopi Indian, by Don C. Talayesva, edited by Leo Simmons, Second Edition
Before L.A.: Race, Space, and Municipal Power in Los Angeles, 1781–1894, by David Samuel Torres-Rouff
Geronimo, by Robert M. Utley

Forthcoming Titles

American Genocide: The California Indian Catastrophe, 1846–1873, by Benjamin Madley
The Cherokee Diaspora, by Gregory Smithers
Ned Kelly and Billy the Kid, by Robert Utley

GEORGE I. SÁNCHEZ

*The Long Fight for
Mexican American Integration*

Carlos Kevin Blanton

Yale
UNIVERSITY
PRESS
New Haven & London

Published with assistance of the foundation established in memory of
Philip Hamilton McMillan of the Class of 1894, Yale College.

Yale University Press books may be purchased in quantity for educational,
business, or promotional use. For information, please e-mail sales.press@yale.edu
(U.S. office) or sales@yaleup.co.uk (U.K. office).

Set in Postscript Electra and Trajan type by Westchester Book Group.
Printed in the United States of America.

Library of Congress Cataloging-in-Publication Data

Blanton, Carlos Kevin, 1970–. George I. Sánchez : the long fight for Mexican American
integration / Carlos Kevin Blanton.
pages   cm—(The Lamar series in Western history)
Includes bibliographical references and index.
ISBN 978-0-300-19032-8 (hardback)
1. Sánchez, George Isidore, 1906–1972.   2. Mexican Americans—Biography.
3. Intellectuals—United States—Biography.   4. Social reformers—United States—
Biography.   5. Political activists—United States—Biography.   6. Educators—
Texas—Biography.   7. Mexican Americans—Civil rights—Southwest,
New—History—20th century.   8. Mexican Americans—Segregation—
Southwest, New—History—20th century.   9. Education, Bilingual—
Southwest, New—History—20th century.   10. Southwest,
New—Race relations—History—20th century.   I. Title.
E184.M5B555 2015
970.92—dc23
[B]
2014018632

A catalogue record for this book is available from the British Library.

This paper meets the requirements of ANSI/NISO Z39.48-1992 (Permanence of Paper).

10 9 8 7 6 5 4 3 2 1

Dedicated with love to Kristine

Contents

PREFACE

Nearly twenty years ago I began a dissertation on the history of bilingual education in the United States. Among the most useful secondary sources on this topic were decades-old works by George I. Sánchez of the University of Texas, a figure with whom I was only slightly familiar. Though he had been dead since I was a toddler, Sánchez's writings from the 1930s through the 1960s crackled with sharp insight into the complex issues I attempted to fathom. Though most historical actors in this dissertation and later in a monograph were confined to a chapter or two, Sánchez was a transgressive force who, had I allowed it, could have haunted the pages of every chapter. My publications from that project in some way address issues Sánchez first raised decades ago and that I further explore in this book.

But this background only partially explains my connection to the project. After receiving my doctorate at Rice University in 1999, I gratefully accepted a tenure-track position with the Chicano/Latino Studies program at Portland State University. In the fall of 1999, my first term as a full-time professor, I experienced an epiphany in my Chicano studies introductory class. In my lecture on pre-Chicano leaders Sánchez completely took over most of the class. The good professor had once again monopolized my energies quite against my will. As I lamented Sánchez's unanticipated prominence in the lecture, a freshman asked an innocent question that momentarily stunned me with possibilities: if you know all this about Sánchez and if he's as important as you say, why don't *you* write a book about him? I recall stammering out some nonreply, a thinly disguised cover for the sparks going off within. I had never thought of taking on such a research project and ruminated on it for the next few years. Since that moment I have obtained a new job, published a book and several articles, found myself promoted to associate professor with tenure, and, not least, have started a family. In all that time this project has been a part of my life. The conclusion of a long, consuming project like this creates ambivalence—feelings of pride, joy, exhaustion, reticence, and relief unevenly mingle. Yet, having to briefly summarize these years is, without a doubt, a joyless exercise. It feels like cheating the pages to come. So I will be brief here. In a sentence, George I. Sánchez of the University of Texas is the single most important Mexican American intellectual between the Great Depression and the Great Society.

But before I explain where this topic fits in Chicana/o history and what that is, I must begin with more personal observations. I must admit it has been very difficult for me to immerse myself in another life. My role as a biographer is to impart understanding, sympathy, and empathy, while maintaining a critical gaze. Establishing any ideal sense of distance or objectivity is impossible. Prior experience has taught me how much the writing of history is a personal undertaking from the perspective of the historian. But writing biography feels even more personal. Studying Sánchez has forced me to be more critical of my own career and to realize how different my own academic reality is from his. For example, Sánchez lived and worked at a time when the notion that Mexican American children could be educated at all was revolutionary. For those of us who have grown up with Mexican American, Chicana/o or Latina/o studies and such programs' message of equality and pride, who were never told we were deficient and could not succeed, who came of age given the opportunity to celebrate difference instead of being forced to hide it, we can never truly walk in Sánchez's shoes. Like his Spanish colonial ancestors of New Mexico, Sánchez was a pioneer—he encountered the strange new world of academia at a time when much of it was hostile to those of his ethnicity and working-class background. Though there was no one else like him, his successes would ensure that in many small and large ways all Chicana/o scholars after him would cross his well-worn path and fight many of his battles. Whether he speaks to one's ethnic heritage, one's modest upbringing, one's political passions, or one's interest in a fascinating life well lived, Sánchez's story is the stuff heroes are made of.

This book adheres to some basic guidelines with regard to use of terms, style, and citations. They too are personal and need explanation. With regard to terms of identity, Sánchez most consistently used *Mexican American* in his letters and publications. Accordingly, that term appears most often in this book. Sánchez was very connected to the activist ethos of his community at that time, and, not coincidentally, scholars have since referred to this as the *Mexican American Generation*. Additional terms—*Spanish-speaking, Latin American,*

Latino, Mexicano, more regional terms such as *Tejano* and *Hispano,* and finally *Chicano*—crop up in this book because Sánchez utilized them, and they provide an occasional dose of variety. With regard to style, the above terms will appear as I prefer to write them rather than follow Sánchez's sense of grammar and punctuation. For example, he used the hyphen in Mexican American; I do not. He did not capitalize Spanish terms of identity such as *Mexicano* or *Latino,* though he did underscore or italicize the terms; I do both. This book makes frequent reference to grants and salaries, though the value of money has changed considerably in the passage of several decades. I use the U.S. Bureau of Labor and Statistics' online cost price index (CPI) calculator to estimate dollar amounts from the past to the present (July 2013). I present these modern equivalents parenthetically in the text at the end of sentences. In cases where the amount is cumulative over a period of time I specify usually the earliest yearly calculation.

I have silently corrected misspellings and typographical errors in the citations and, when minor, in quotations. George I. Sánchez is the only name abbreviated in the notes (GIS). In brackets I estimate a date for archival sources that have no clear date. In my archival citations I refrain from specifying page numbers in letters and memos, though not in manuscripts. Where a series of related materials appear as a packet (whether grouped as such by archivists or by the historical actors who produced them), I have respected this intent by treating such materials as a unitary file and imposing my own sequential page numbering. And as of the final submission of the manuscript to press, a very small fragment of the source material from the Sánchez Papers bears the moniker, in brackets, of "old system," indicating when I accessed them before or during a major reorganization of the collection several years ago. All other documents in the Sánchez Papers bear the box and file numbers of the current organization.

ACKNOWLEDGMENTS

I would be perpetrating a gross falsity if I did not share the credit for this book with many brilliant, loving, generous people in my life. Whether family, friends, or colleagues, they have contributed to this project in ways I can never fully acknowledge. For those I may have neglected in what follows, my deepest apologies and warmest regards for your support.

Any historical project involving a great deal of research is dependent first of all on the goodwill and good humor of librarians and archivists who tirelessly enable the search for evidence. Thank you, Joel Kitchens and the ILL/document delivery staff at Texas A&M University Evans Library. I would also like to thank Ann Massman of the Center for Southwest Research at the University of New Mexico at Albuquerque, Vanessa Smith and Janet Walsh of the Franklin Library and Special Collections-Archives at Fisk University in Nashville, Tennessee, Sarah Haldeman and Allen Fisher of the LBJ Presidential Library in Austin, Texas, Grace Olivarez and Tom Kreneck of the Mary and Jeff Bell Library at Texas A&M University–Corpus Christi, Daniel Rooney of the National Archives and Records Administration II at College Park, Maryland, Charlotte Sturm and Ken Rose at the Rockefeller Archive Center in Sleepy Hollow, New York, Dave Smith of the Walt Disney Company Archives in Burbank, California, Kelly Haigh and Lilace Hatayama of the Young Research Library at the University of California at Los Angeles, Ryder Kouba and Gregory Yerke of the Special Collections of the University of Houston Library, Bill Frank of the Huntington Library in San Marino, California, and of course Christian Kelleher, Margo Gutiérrez, and the entire staff of the Nettie Lee Benson Latin American Collection at the University of Texas at Austin, where the incredibly rich and voluminous George I. Sánchez Papers reside. In particular, Christian labored above and beyond the call of duty to help me update box and folder numbers for research I conducted before and during the major reorganization of the Sán-chez Papers.

I would like to thank Yale University Press for its support of this project at every step of the way. Throughout this process Ash Lago, Dan Heaton, and Lawrence Kenney have made sure the project was on time, complete, and of high quality. I especially thank my editor, Laura Davulis, for her excitement about this work and its potential and for helping me make this a far better manu-script than I could have made it on my own. For the generosity of spirit and willingness to answer any and all questions with unflinching completeness and honesty, I would like to thank my interview subjects Mark Sprague, Cynthia Kennedy, Billy Cowart, and Bob Sánchez. I hope what follows captures what you all so eloquently remember and love about George I. Sánchez. I greatly ben-efited from the medical expertise of Professor and Chair Dr. Roger J. Lewis of the Department of Emergency Medicine and Professor and Associate Chief Dr. Mallory Witt of the Division of Infectious Diseases and HIV Medicine, both at the Harbor-UCLA Medical Center of Torrance, California; and Assistant Pro-fessors of the Department of Internal Medicine Drs. Lucas Blanton and Megan Berman, both at the University of Texas Medical Branch, Galveston, Texas.

This book could not have gotten off the ground without essential support from Texas A&M University. In particular, the Department of History has sup-ported the project with regular funds for summer research and conference travel. The College of Liberal Arts through its College Enhancement grant in 2005 and the Vice President of Research through its Program for Scholarly and Creative Activity grant in 2002 and 2007 have been of immense help. During this time the encouragement and support of the then–History Department Head Walter Buenger and Dean of the College of Liberal Arts Charlie Johnson were crucial. And Texas A&M University provided me with a much-needed faculty development leave in the fall of 2007 to finish exploring the Sánchez Papers and begin the writing process.

I want to thank so many colleagues in my department, some of whom are still here while others have moved on to other places. I would especially like to single out those who have read parts of this project over the past decade: R. J. Q. Adams, Armando Alonzo, Jovita Baber, Dale Baum, Julia Kirk Blackwelder, Cynthia Bouton, Al Broussard, Walter Buenger, Glenn Chambers, Leah Devun, Tom Dunlap, Kate Engel, April Hatfield, Felipe Hinojosa, Sylvia Hof-fert, Angela Hudson, Walter Kamphoefner, Harold Livesay, Anthony Mora, Jason Parker, Lisa Ramos, Jim Rosenheim, Brian Rouleau, Rebecca Schloss, Adam Seipp, Ernest Starks, David Vaught, Molly Warsh, and Larry Yarak. My col-leagues at the Glasscock Center for Humanities Research, Texas A&M University Press, and elsewhere in the Aggie community have lent incredible support: Victor Arizpe, Michael Benedik, Lynn Burlbaw, Terah Venzant Chambers, Shannon Davies, Mary Lenn Dixon, Joseph Jewell, Antonio LaPastina, Ken Meier, Pixey Mosley, Irene Moyna, Larry Oliver, Marco Portales, Rogelio Saenz, Simon Sheather, José Villalobos, and Karen Watson. My students at all levels inspire me daily, especially my graduate students: David Cameron, Rainlilly Elizondo, Joel Kitchens, Sara Leimon, Ralph Morales, and Cassie Rincones. Friends and colleagues throughout the profession have been incredible to me along the way and I thank you: Barbara Beatty, John Boles, Rick and Jeny Burrell, Carl Caldwell and Lora Wildenthal, Gregg Cantrell, Jason Connor, Jeanice Davis, Arnoldo DeLeón, Michelle Detry and Chris Schacherer, Ignacio García, David Gutiérrez, Randal and Naomi Hall, Allen Matusow, David Montejano, Michael Olivas, Cynthia Orozco, Julie Leininger Pycior, Vicki Ruiz, J. J. and Angela Saenz, Steve Schloss, Richard Valencia, Kelton Williams, Steve Wilson and Cheryl Matherly, and Emilio Zamora. Mario García and Ben Johnson read the entire manuscript and provided invaluable as well as marvelously constructive and supportive suggestions. You have my deepest appreciation and gratitude.

Many wonderful people form my extended family. My thanks go to all my uncles, aunts, cousins, and their children. You put up with many years of my incessant talking about this person and his life through holiday football games, meals, vacations, and the like without ever seeming to tire. Tío Juan and Tía Gloria, I miss you both and wish you were here to read these words. Dennis and Joyce Broglio, thank you for being great in-laws and for always asking about the book. To my parents, Lee and Belia, and my siblings, Celina and Lucas, and my sister-in-law Megan and nephew Brice and niece Emily, I love you all dearly and would not be here without your affection and encouragement. And now (unless you want me to continue) I really can stop talking about George I. Sánchez.

The big difference between the acknowledgments in my first book and in this one is that I have started my own family. My daughter Isabel Renée Blanton and son Thomas Benjamin Blanton are among the greatest joys of my life, and I treasure every moment with them. They tried their best to keep Dad from finishing this book in loving, insistent, and creative ways. And were it not for the fact that they make me a better, more hopeful person every day, I might not have finished this book. And to their mother, my wife, Kristine Renée Broglio, to whom this book is dedicated, you have all my love always and forever. Though my words here fall short, as they always do, of expressing how very incomprehensibly much I feel about you, this book is a monument to one of the greatest gifts I have ever been given—each day of your love.

INTRODUCTION

This book is more than a chronicle of George I. Sánchez's life. In discovering the surprising depth and breadth and very human flaws of one brilliant Mexican American intellectual and activist, I arrive at an approximation of the entire twentieth-century Chicana/o experience. Biography can draw out larger themes of an era or specific topics in an academic field as effectively as any other kind of historical study. And delving into the personal as well as the professional can enliven the sometimes dry, academic subjects scholars devote themselves to in ways that are elegant and inspiring. There is, I realize, a certain amount of verisimilitude involved. There are topics Sánchez's life cannot adequately convey, owing either to their particulars or to my own intellectual limits. Nevertheless, this book aims to do just that.

The field of Chicana/o history is a relatively recent product of student activism. It was founded in the late 1960s as students on college campuses organized for Chicano studies content, courses, and programs at all levels of schooling.[1] They supported what one historian recently referred to as "utopian nationalist ideals embedded in the theory of internal colonialism," such as an end to racism and community autonomy from white power. Another credits the rise in Marxist-Leninist ideals associated with cultural nationalism. Yet another scholar remarks that the movement was tied to a youth-centered "culture of resistance" seeking "self-determination" through a variety of "national liberation and anti-colonial struggles" around the globe. In 1969 this ferment spurred a conference at the University of California at Santa Barbara that produced *El Plan de Santa Barbara*, calling for the programmatic institutionalization of Chicano studies throughout higher education in ways connected to exploited barrio communities. College and high school students around the country agitated for a greater knowledge of self through Chicano studies in their schools.

Younger scholars, inspired by *el movimiento*, viewed Chicano history as a part of the larger intellectual and cultural politics of liberation from oppression.[2]

This heightened, self-conscious connection of scholarship with activism had the unfortunate effect of blurring the focus and depth of historical perception. Among early Chicano scholars it created what one historian has termed a "them versus us" kind of historical sensibility. And it led to one-size-fits-all interpretations that flattened the Chicana/o community's internal diversity. One such historian, in an essay collection in honor of George Sánchez, remarked, "Chicano history emerged as a product of the Chicano Movement because of our people's social and psychic need to gain self-knowledge" that would help disenthrall them from "such a degree of deranged assimilation that it had produced a monstrous distortion of our true past." This early work found outlets in the pages of interdisciplinary academic journals such as *Aztlán* and *El Grito* as well as in Rodolfo Acuña's pathbreaking *Occupied America: The Chicano's Struggle Toward Liberation* (1972).[3]

The study of Chicana/o peoples was certainly older than *el movimiento*, however. As the historian David Gutiérrez demonstrates, Chicano scholars of the late 1960s and 1970s, whether they were fully appreciative of it or not, stood atop pioneering work on their subject. George I. Sánchez was one of those pioneers. In fact, the historian quoted in the paragraph above noted that in a visit he had with an elderly, ailing Sánchez, the old professor's eagerness to engage Chicanismo still fell short. This is because throughout Sánchez's career he stressed the heterogeneity of Mexican peoples, of their full educational and civic potential, of their loyalty and love of country, and of their desire for integration into the mainstream of society as equals. He was not alone in this. Other scholars, such as the historian Carlos Castañeda of the University of Texas and the folklorist Arthur Campa of the University of Denver, maintained similar kinds of projects that got at the same themes. These very integrationist notions eventually became fodder for more militant scholars. But such militant perspectives did not last. Chicana/o history by the end of the 1970s and 1980s moderated; it came to a greater appreciation of the internal diversity of the Chicana/o population as well as more nuanced ways of analyzing race, class, gender, and identity.[4]

These developments gained further traction in the 1990s and 2000s. Like scholars in other academic disciplines, recent Chicana/o historians emphasize new avenues of agency, of cultural production, of multiple, contested, and constructed identities as well as a greater appreciation of gendered and transnational perspectives. In short, Chicana/o history today has a recent but vibrant intellectual heritage. And its trajectory pushes past an exclusionary looking inward and toward broader concepts and interpretations at the center of other major fields of U.S. history. And given the demographic trends in this country, I believe that the extension of Chicana/o history's reach toward new and different audiences can only be positive.

Chicana/o history still has underdeveloped areas. Biography is one such relatively neglected area. Recently, however, some biographies with interdisciplinary appeal have emerged. Tom Kreneck's biography of the businessman and member of the League of United Latin American Citizens (LULAC) Felix Tijerina is as influential as it is illuminating. Works on the founder of the American G.I. Forum (AGIF), Hector P. Garcia, by Ignacio García and Michelle Hall Kells explore the cohesiveness and contradictions of his long decades of activism. Biographies of the scholars Carlos Castañeda by Félix Almaráz and Américo Paredes by Ramón Saldívar and José Limón, both of whom were at the University of Texas, set a high bar in interpretive engagement. And Mario T. García has produced several *testimonios* that allow labor leaders, journalists, politicians, scholars, priests, and legendary teachers to speak for themselves.[5]

Despite the attraction of George I. Sánchez as a historical figure, a full-length biography of him has had to wait until now. Seemingly everyone consults his papers and, given his precociousness as an intellectual and activist, many Chicana/o scholars discuss Sánchez substantially in their works on other topics. Sánchez's wide range of activity has perhaps inhibited scholars from approaching him as a topic of study in his own right. Wrapping one's arms around the totality of George Sánchez is difficult. Two dissertations of the 1970s are the earliest attempts to grapple with his life and career.[6] In the 1980s, 1990s, and 2000s Sánchez became an essential part of other works on immigration, education, identity, politics, and Chicano historiography.[7] During this period Mario García appraised Sánchez in a chapter of his landmark monograph *Mexican Americans* and in his foreword to the reissue of Sánchez's *Forgotten People* by the University of New Mexico Press.[8] Other works, notably articles, analyze Sánchez through a larger focus on a period or subtheme of his activism.[9] My own publications over the past decade interpret Sánchez through such topics as intelligence testing, civil rights, immigration restrictionism, and opposition to compensatory education in journals with different topical specialties and disciplinary orientations.[10]

This book heavily engages one of the major interpretive paradigms in Chicana/o history: the generational theme. Early Chicana/o historians triumphantly wrote of their particular historical moment in the late 1960s and 1970s as a time of breaking away from self-limiting conceptions of self. To them, Chicano history elevated the present as a sharp, liberating, progressive rupture from the sad, narrow past. And, after all, they were baby boomers, so a great deal of their triumphalism was couched in a generational framework. Scholars of that time, despite some variation, imposed a generational understanding of Chicano history and consciousness that reified presentist ideas. Since the late 1980s and 1990s, however, the generational theme has taken a more sophisticated shape. It now emphasizes three basic cohorts that define the twentieth-century Chicana/o experience: the Mexicanist Generation, the Mexican American Generation, and the Chicano Generation. But before proceeding, a word of caution is in order. The best work on this concept holds to looser constructions of these generational lines with plenty of overlap, exceptions, and some commonality. And the generational portrayal in this introduction is drawn starkly for the purposes of contrast. For example, Sánchez's life in the biography that follows is not so monochromatic in interpretation.[11]

The Mexicanist Generation spans the late nineteenth century through the late 1920s and is the least documented of the three. Emilio Zamora's *The World of the Mexican Worker in Texas* analyzes how this cohort embraced a Mexican identity. Up through the twenties, most Mexican peoples in the United States considered themselves outsiders to the nation, literally and figuratively; this included those whose ancestors had resided for centuries in what is now the United States. This interpretational construction explains why many nineteenth- and early-twentieth-century Mexican peoples sought to reinforce their ethnic identity with Mexico through *mutualistas* (mutual aid societies) whether they were immigrants or not and often looked to Mexico for news, business, and cultural belonging. Through its consular service the Mexican government reinforced this posture.[12]

The Mexican American Generation, dominant from the 1930s to the 1960s, receives the most attention. García's *Mexican Americans* is especially influential with this cohort, which was shaped by military service in the First World War, patriotism, borderlands violence, and nativism in the 1910s and 1920s and by the repatriation of nearly half a million Mexican and U.S. citizens in the 1930s. These young Mexican Americans sought a deeper identification with the United States and stressed patriotism, citizenship, middle-class aspirations, external validation, assimilation to mainstream norms and institutions, less confrontational forms of protest, and a hyphenated ethnic existence. And they regarded their generational perspective vis-à-vis their predecessors as triumphantly and as chauvinistically as the Chicano Generation did with regard to them decades later. Inherent in their worldview was the idea of using civic engagement to challenge racial discrimination as well as economic injustice.[13]

The Chicano Generation stems from the late 1960s through at least the 1990s, if not into the twenty-first century. Though critical works did not exist in the early years of the field, scholars, led by Ignacio García's *Chicanismo*, have rediscovered this period. By the late sixties, as twentieth-century liberalism unraveled owing to the centrifugal forces of Vietnam and unease with the Great Society's antipoverty and civil rights agenda, a group of young intellectuals and activists—the children of the Mexican American Generation—reversed the ideological sacred cows of their parents in crafting their own ideological paradigm. Embracing New Left intellectual currents, Chicanos adopted confrontational aspects of the counterculture protests of the era and were more critical of the U.S. government and society. In addition, the Chicano Generation rejected traditional middle-class norms, sought internal validation, deemphasized assimilation, and abandoned a hyphenated existence for a more culturally nationalistic conceptualization of themselves as a separate race. And they sought to institutionalize these perspectives through Chicana/o studies programs.[14]

This is the basic structure, drawn in purposely stark terms, of the generational theme in Chicana/o history. It is not without its critics. The historian Cynthia Orozco argues that while the generational theme can be quite useful, "the heterogeneity of the Raza community must be considered as well," alleging that it too often leaves out women, immigrants, a broader spectrum of political ideologies, and regional differences. And all these generations—mothers and daughters, fathers and sons—often lived in the same communities, went to the same underperforming public schools, struggled with dead-end jobs, and experienced discrimination, though they may have differed in how they addressed such problems and in what context they saw them. This commonality is important. Local studies in particular find far greater intergenerational cohesiveness. For example, in one such study Felipe Hinojosa writes, "In the end, the Chicano Movement was more reformist than revolutionary." This makes it less of a break from the Mexican American Generation than an updated extension of it. The generational theme, it seems, is inherently problematical, even when loosely defined. It has two important points to its credit, however, points that weigh like bricks upon any rival interpretations attempting to take off: first, it offers more explanatory power than any other competing theory that explains the broad sweep of twentieth-century Chicana/o history; second, historical actors themselves recognized generational differences in ways not dissimilar to the actual historical model. So there is a there, there.[15]

Where does Sánchez fit in terms of the generational interpretation? He belonged to the middle group, the Mexican American Generation. Compared to that of other intellectuals of this cohort, such as the historian Castañeda, the folklorist Arthur Campa, and the labor economist Ernesto Galarza, Sánchez's work is the most intellectually vibrant after these many decades. This is not to say he had no connection to the Chicano movement. In fact, he badly wanted to embrace it. I do not view Sánchez as a transitional generational figure, however, as I do his colleague Paredes, whose magnificent *With His Pistol in His Hand* from 1958 is "the ur-text of Chicano studies," according to one recent scholar. Sánchez's Chicanismo was always affected and hesitant. Nevertheless, the issues he raised about Mexican American schooling, about Mexican Americans' political possibilities, and about the fact that their contributions to American life went unrecognized consumed the attention of later Chicana/o intellectuals. It still does today. Of Mexican American Generation thinkers, George Sánchez was the most concerned with disseminating otherwise scholarly ideas among the general public in easily digestible form. He held so strongly to popularizing knowledge that he intentionally sabotaged his own academic publishing time and again. In doing so he ignored professional and financial considerations that might have been more helpful to him personally. And of the Mexican American Generation intellectuals Sánchez was the most politically active in advancing the civil and socioeconomic rights of the Mexican American community.[16]

These are admirable qualities. But George I. Sánchez was also a real person with faults and limitations. Right or wrong, he was not always likeable. He struggled throughout his life, as many people do, to align the way things are with how they should be. Cosmopolitan, witty, highly professional, and scrupulous, Sánchez was capable of a stormy passion that could boil over into righteous, yet counterproductive anger; he could be a giving teacher and collaborator, yet a caustic colleague; he was generous to those he agreed with, yet bullying to those he disagreed with. It was a bitter pill for Sánchez to swallow that he had come so far in his life and overcome such large obstacles to then be mostly ignored. Early in his career he rarely allowed feelings of despair or cynicism to show through his scholarly work and correspondence, even in letters to those close to him. But as he aged he found it harder to bottle the edge caused by his unending, daily confrontations with the shadow of racial discrimination. Its burden wearied him by the end. He was no saint and sometimes quite a bit to take. But he was beloved by friends and allies, who never saw him duck a fight when the honor, dignity, or well-being of Mexican Americans were on the line. Sánchez was a fighter, and that quality, while readily admired from a distance, is harder to live with day in and day out.

Connected to the generational theme are institutional studies that focus on the most important activist groups in each cohort. For the Mexican American Generation, especially in Sánchez's New Mexico and Texas, they were LULAC and AGIF. Sánchez was heavily involved in both. LULAC was the premier activist group of the Mexican American Generation in the 1930s and 1940s. AGIF challenged LULAC's hegemony within the Mexican American Generation by the 1950s and 1960s, but they were more alike than different. For example, both LULAC and AGIF typified this generation's ideological core: middle-class values and aspirations, even if they were not yet a reality for many, the importance of U.S. citizenship and patriotism, self-improvement through education, and growing confrontations with racial discrimination. The broader aim of all these beliefs was the full incorporation of Mexican Americans into national life. In this way, LULAC and AGIF were not far removed from their generational predecessors or successors, although there are some differences. The Mexican American Generation groups advocated more internalized aspects of cultural assimilation, such as speaking English in public and professional settings and emphasizing racial otherness, but these differences are often magnified to the exclusion of the all-important integrationist commonality.[17]

This book is organized into twelve chapters. Chapter 1, "Early Life and Education, 1906–1930," deals with the very real structural obstacles inhibiting educational success for the young George I. Sánchez and children like him in the early twentieth century. Sánchez grew up destitute in grimy, southwestern mining towns. Yet he became a rural schoolteacher immediately after graduating from high school in the early 1920s. By the end of the decade he had earned a college degree from the University of New Mexico, taking classes during the summer, at night, and by correspondence. The Rockefeller-funded General Education Board (GEB) supported Sánchez's master's and doctoral degrees at the University of Texas at Austin and the University of California at Berkeley, respectively, in the 1930s. Chapter 2, "New Mexico Schools and New Deal Politics, 1930–1935," examines the understudied connection between New Deal liberalism and the Mexican American mind. Sánchez was profoundly shaped by the New Deal and became a reformer in New Mexico's educational politics. His position in the state bureaucracy, funded by the GEB, was to advocate on behalf of rural Hispano children and poor districts. He lost his job because of political retaliation. Chapter 3, "Exile, Recognition, and Underemployment, 1935–1940," expands on recent studies of the transnational realities of the Mexican American Generation. Sánchez wrote a book on Mexican education for the GEB and Rosenwald Fund and worked, first, on African American education in the U.S. South for the Rosenwald Fund and then as the administrator of a national teacher-training project in Venezuela. In 1940, while an adjunct instructor at the University of New Mexico, Sánchez wrote his magnum opus, *Forgotten People: A Study of New Mexicans.*

Sánchez spent the Second World War advancing Good Neighborism through education—his war of ideas—and advancing civil rights for Mexican Americans from behind the scenes—his war of activism. Chapter 4, "Sánchez's War of Ideas, 1940–1944," begins with his acquiring a tenured position at the University of Texas in 1940. Sánchez wrote about the treatment of Mexican Americans as a domestic corollary of the Good Neighbor policy toward Latin America and unsuccessfully sought to enlist in the armed forces as an intelligence officer. Chapter 5, "Sánchez's War of Activism, 1940–1944," documents how, in the midst of a horrific global conflict, challenging the system could become a dangerous game. Sánchez contested Jim Crow, collaborated with the American Civil Liberties Union (ACLU), directed the Good Neighbor committee of his university, and worked with federal agencies like the Fair Employment Practices Commission, the Office of Civilian Defense, and Coordinator of Inter-American Affairs. Chapter 6, "Sánchez's War of Survival and His Transformations, 1944–1949," analyzes his fundamentally academic life. It deals with the deadly bout of tuberculosis that almost killed him in 1944, his return in 1945 to a more conservative University of Texas, where his activist scholarship was now considered passé, and his divorce and remarriage in 1946 and 1947. In spite of acrimonious disputes over his salary, Sánchez embarked on the study of racial discrimination with major GEB support, setting the stage for his activism of the 1950s, explored in the next four chapters.

Chapter 7, "Politics and the Mexican American Generation," examines the Mexican American Generation's liberalism, enacted through groups like LULAC and AGIF. Sánchez was a cold war liberal who was red-baited and experienced retaliation by his employer. Chapter 8, "Mexican Americans and the Immigration Issue," interprets the most controversial issue with respect to Sánchez and the Mexican American Generation. His restrictionism, particularly over undocumented labor, was divisive and ineffective but not nativist. Chapter 9, "Segregated Schools and Perceptions of Inequality," explores how education was the lifeblood of Mexican American Generation activism and how Sánchez's integrationist perspectives fueled it. Sánchez helped challenge the racial segregation of Mexican American schoolchildren through the *Bastrop v. Delgado* (1948) and *Hernández v. Driscoll* (1957) cases. Ultimately, he was an integration purist. Chapter 10, "Mexican American Racial Identity, Whiteness, and Civil Rights," is a comparative civil rights history. I analyze Sánchez's affiliation with the ACLU, his little-known civil rights group called the American Council of Spanish-Speaking People (ACSSP), and his connections to other civil rights movements. Sánchez offers an excellent test case of what whiteness meant to civil rights activists beyond strategy and rhetoric.

Chapter 11, "Sánchez in Camelot and the Great Society, 1960–1967," adds greater context to Mexican American activism and politics during the 1960s. It begins with Sánchez's involvement in the John F. Kennedy administration's efforts in Latin America. Though he was invited to consult with the White House more frequently than ever during Lyndon Johnson's Great Society, he was a liberal in the mold of the Texas senator Ralph Yarborough and disliked Johnson. In 1967 he helped shape the Bilingual Education Act and was briefly considered for an appointment to the Equal Employment Opportunity Commission (EEOC). Despite a brief scholarly resurgence early in the sixties, Sánchez's productivity declined as the decade progressed. Chapter 12, "Chicanismo and Old Age, 1967–1972," investigates Sánchez's view of the Chicano movement as seen through older, experienced, tired eyes from the late 1960s to the early 1970s. Sánchez became ill. His writing dropped off, and teaching his classes became trying. He was in constant pain, and his drinking began to take a toll. He engaged young, radical Chicanos in the late 1960s and early 1970s, but his Old Left perspective made him tragically unhip. He remained a symbol and institution to the students; he stood among them, but not of them. Nevertheless, he played a role in his university's halting embrace of the Center for Mexican American Studies just before his death in the spring of 1972. In a brief epilogue I discuss how Sánchez is remembered and why and summarize the contributions of this book. This is a story that needs to be told.

Part One

1906–1930s

EARLY LIFE AND EDUCATION
1906–1930

I do not claim to be the proud descendant of the *conquistadores*. That would be claiming that I am an unadulterated bastard. I do claim that my Indo-hispanic ancestors were not foreigners—or immigrants in the sense that the Italians, or the Poles, or the Irish and others were immigrants. We were here first—as Indians, then as Spaniards, and then as *mestizos*. The genetic contribution of the fabled conquistadores was minimal, *machos* though they probably were. This is *my* country.

—*George I. Sánchez*

George I. Sánchez was born in New Mexico as the state shed its frontier status. At the turn of the nineteenth to the twentieth century rural New Mexico seemed not so altered from the frontier days of the Spanish colonial era, especially for its native Spanish-speakers. Life was hard; little economic or educational opportunity existed. However, the rustic land and ancient people that produced George Sánchez were undergoing rapid, tumultuous change, including an industrial revolution and a demographic revolution. As new industries devoured natural resources, an influx of immigrants arrived from across the United States and around the world. Large-scale ranching, mining, and railroad enterprises in the late nineteenth century transformed the region. Unlike the massive Mexican immigration of the early twentieth century in California and Texas, the Hispano presence in New Mexico was a far older, native population. While other parts of the Southwest boasted of Spanish settlement during the eighteenth and early nineteenth centuries, New Mexico's dated to the late sixteenth and early seventeenth centuries. The young Sánchez was pulled toward two worlds—one, the revered, sacred, New Mexican past of glory and bounty of his ancestors, he imagined; the other, the depressing circumstances of his meager, grimy, industrial youth, he lived.[1]

I present here a narrative of educational triumph at a time when things were bad and getting worse for Chicanas/os. The increasing systematization of educational segregation, unequal facilities, and demeaning curricular practices of the era encouraged Mexican American children to drop out of public school at an early age to work in factories and fields. Despite these potentially debilitating obstacles, Sánchez survived and even thrived. Though it is difficult to generalize across the entire Southwest, it is commonly understood that Mexican American children in the early twentieth century attended the public schools at half the rate of Anglos with retention rates well above 50 percent in the early grades. Educational histories often expend greater energy analyzing the structure of such educational oppression at the expense of delving into the personal experiences of schooling. But those experiences exist. One cannot read Alonso Perales's classic *Are We Good Neighbors?* from the 1940s, for example, without learning, through the numerous affidavits of the victims of racial discrimination, several of them from children in and out of school, how it felt to be taught to be inferior and less than normal. The theme of George Sánchez's childhood is the constant struggle to succeed and be recognized. For him this manifested itself in a thirst for knowledge and ever-higher levels of educational attainment. George I. Sánchez beat the odds.[2]

IMAGINING A BRIGHTER PAST AND FUTURE

A critical aspect of Sánchez's identity was his sense of Spanish heritage. Nearly all Sánchez scholars have mentioned, unsurprisingly since he constantly dwelled on it, his claim that he descended from the original seventeenth-century Spanish pioneers of New Mexico. It was an integral part of his identity. As forward thinking as his reformist ideas might have been, their motivations sprang from Sánchez's projections backward in time to a cherished, idealized past in which speaking Spanish, constructing a new society on the frontier, being a proud *Mexicano* carried no stigma. In Sánchez's mind, he was the child of centuries-old aristocratic Spanish families that had, by his own time, fallen into dire straits. Late in life Sánchez corrected a sociologist who operated, he felt, with overly rigid definitions of class among Mexican Americans, insisting that his own family had been relatively well off until recent generations. This notion of being descended from past greatness, as trivial or fussy as it might seem today, was a serious matter to Sánchez. His lengthy curriculum vitae from his first to his final years at the University of Texas highlighted this dusty heritage by parenthetically noting that his family dated to the earliest colonial days. Such restoration constructions by Sánchez, while ridiculously fastidious in today's professional atmosphere, illustrate at least one of the deeply personal motivations that drove his career. They also explain the righteous anger he flashed throughout his life when his abilities or the abilities of his people were questioned.[3]

Scholars speculate on the meaning of such identities. Laura Gómez writes of the elite and middling *Nuevo Mexicano* families in the last half of the nineteenth century that their veneration of the Spanish past served to negate Native American and African American roots. She argues that New Mexicans' construction of a mythic, heroic Spanish past is also an embrace of whiteness. Such interpretations are complicated in Sánchez's case by the fact that his articulation of that kind of past depended on who his audience was. He emphasized Hispanicity to professional, mostly Anglo audiences. To *Mexicanos*, however (as indicated by the epigraph above), Sánchez discussed his heritage quite differently. Throughout his life Sánchez made multiple, contradictory claims to larger identities such as whiteness, Mexican-ness, and *mestizaje*. For a Mexican American then and now to so flexibly define his or her identity to others is not especially rare. U.S. Sen. Dennis Chávez of New Mexico also shifted definitions of himself in order to advance his political agenda. And Sánchez variously defined himself to multiple audiences provided it advanced his agenda of integrating Mexican Americans into all facets of national life. An important theme in Sánchez's identity was realism. Carey McWilliams memorably blamed a Spanish "fantasy heritage" for creating a historical fog that obscured the brutal oppression native *Mexicanos* faced. No one decried that fantasy myth as much as Sánchez, who in 1940 urged abandoning "easy and pleasant" exercises of thinking of the Spanish colonial era in terms of "robes of pomp and splendor" and "the blowing of trumpets, the glistening of armor, the tramping of steeds, the manly deeds of swashbuckling adventurers." Though Sánchez's pivot away from a romanticized past is perhaps insufficient by many post-1960s perspectives, he and his generational cohort were the first Chicanas/os to challenge Anglos' assertions of their inferiority. The Spanish past was crucial to Sánchez, but as a point of attacking the injustices of the present, not of escaping or forgetting them.[4]

George Isidoro Sánchez y Sánchez was born on October 4, 1906, in Bernalillo County, New Mexico. His parents, Telesforo and Juliana Sánchez (they were both surnamed Sánchez), raised young George and his older brother Juan and younger brother Telesforo in a working-class hamlet a few miles west of Albuquerque. His mother was young when George was born, likely only nineteen, and his father probably twenty-four. George Sánchez remembered his neighborhood of Los Nuanes as being a slum. This little community just north of the larger suburb of Barelas contained many families who originally possessed New Mexico's Atrisco land grant dating to the seventeenth century. Sánchez proudly noted that his family were official heirs to the land and that his New Mexico lineage went back to 1602. His brothers stayed in New Mexico for their entire lives. Juan became a butcher in Albuquerque, and Telesforo became an educator, eventually rising to assistant director of vocational education for the New Mexico State Department of Education in Santa Fe.[5]

Sánchez's family were hardworking Catholics, although, as was true of many Mexican Americans and Mexican immigrants of the era, they seem to have exhibited some anticlericalism. Perhaps it was simply an impatience with excessive religiosity. This was especially manifested in the family patriarch, as Sánchez recalled: "My father who, supposedly, was a Catholic (and I was once a Knight of Columbus) used to say (in Spanish): Go out and do all that you possibly can, until you are practically dead—then pray like hell." By all accounts the elder Telesforo Sánchez was an irascible character. He was a miner who moved the family throughout New Mexico and Arizona during the 1910s and 1920s. He also ran a regular poker game at local saloons to supplement the family income. According to Sánchez, his father exuded a palpable, physical presence among men; he was a formidable person, respected and maybe even feared in his community. Though Sánchez hardly spoke of his mother (an intriguing silence), he idolized his father.[6]

As was the case in many poor, yet proud and ambitious families, education for the Sánchez family became *the* means for advancement. Telesforo and Juliana were not schooled beyond the third grade, but both were resolute that their children be educated. Throughout Sánchez's life he constantly drove himself to battle losing odds, embrace seemingly impossible goals, and stretch his abilities. He remembered his father this way: "My father, who didn't go beyond a poor third grade, would monopolize my elementary school textbooks in the evening. He progressed to books on the war (World War I still in progress kthen [sic]), to *Ivanhoe*, to the *Leather-Stocking Tales*, etc." Not only did Sánchez's father labor under a limited educational background to keep up with his son's work, he did so in a second language, as the family spoke only Spanish at home.[7]

Another part of George Sánchez's education from his father involved the development of a political consciousness, of an unshakable faith in the political action of and solidarity among working men and women. Telesforo Sánchez was a fierce union man. A half-century removed from events, Sánchez vividly reminisced about the Arizona mines his father worked in, relating how radical anarcho-syndicalist recruiters were run out of Jerome, Arizona, by baseball bat–wielding members of his father's local and union wives physically harassed the scabs who crossed the picket line during strikes. He remembered how as a child he emulated these brawny, righteous union men. The elder Telesforo Sánchez's union was likely Jerome's Local 101 of the International Union of Mine, Mill, and Smelter Workers (IUMMSW). In the Jerome strike of 1917 this was the moderate option; a more radical option, the anarcho-syndicalist International Workers of the World (IWW), disagreed with the settlement reached by the IUMMSW and disrupted mine production. This led to the dubious deportation of the IWW by a combination of union miners and company agents calling themselves the Jerome Loyalty League. Some seventy-five IWW members, including a few chagrined company spies, were railroaded from Jerome to the middle of the California desert, foreshadowing a larger deportation at the Bisbee mines later that year. This was serious business. Being tied to the IWW was dangerous for union supporters during the wartime repression of anything remotely radical. The most important Mexican American group in Arizona at the time, the *mutualista* called La Alianza Hispano-Americana, declined to involve itself in these disputes, citing an unwillingness to oppose the wartime interests of the U.S. government. So the Sánchez family was more leftist than the Alianza, just not as much as the IWW. In this bareknuckled, pro-union, pro-education, secular upbringing of the 1910s and early 1920s, the young George learned never to separate education from activism.[8]

HARD TIMES AND THE ESCAPE OF SCHOOL

Sánchez attended small public schools in New Mexico and Arizona. In 1913, when he was seven, the family moved from the Los Nuanes slums near Albuquerque to the boomtown of Jerome, where his father worked as a miner; they also lived briefly in Winslow, Arizona. The mining communities of that era teemed with immigrants from Europe and Mexico, all engaged in backbreaking physical labor and forming a veritable Babel of languages. These schools, though poor, did not segregate grades or individual classrooms by ethnicity, remembered Sánchez. As a result, Sánchez, a bright child, learned English rapidly and enjoyed early academic success. Though mired in poverty and enduring substandard housing, diet, and health in the raucous mining communities, Sánchez avoided the progressive educational techniques of segregation and English-only instruction that were just then being foisted on schools across the nation. In a study of the racial politics of the nearby town of Clifton-Morenci, the historian Linda Gordon notes that European immigrants were not yet viewed as white by Anglo elites, though that definition would soon change. Such a background may have given the young Sánchez a greater sense of connection to different peoples.[9]

Sánchez spent much of his youth, from 1913 to 1921, in the central Arizona mining town of Jerome. As a Jerome High School freshman and sophomore Sánchez excelled in academics and music (fig. 1.1). He played coronet for the school band and orchestra while his older brother, Juan, played saxophone and was a class officer. By 1920 an economic recession ended the copper-mining boom of Jerome, and Sánchez's father was laid off. Mexican and Mexican American miners, usually relegated to menial, lower-paying tasks, were especially hard hit. Sánchez spent his junior year of high school in Winslow, Arizona, where his father found occasional work. He recalled that his Winslow neighborhood was nicknamed Dogtown and was on the wrong side of the tracks. Finally, in 1922 the family moved back to the Albuquerque area for good, living in a small community, Barelas, between the Los Nuanes neighborhood of his early childhood and the city. By this time George Sánchez was a senior in high school and fortunate to still live in a part of the Southwest where the racial segregation of Mexican children did not ensnare him. It was at Albuquerque High School that he met his future wife, Virginia Romero, and lifelong friend and fellow Mexican American intellectual Arthur Campa.[10]

Sánchez graduated in May 1923 from high school at the precocious age of sixteen, though he seemed too busy to even take stock of this achievement. In Sánchez's very active senior year his academic success was overshadowed by his many extracurricular activities. The teenaged Sánchez, in the midst of the roaring twenties, caught the bustling spirit of the times. He played jazz coronet in an orchestra, worked as a dance promoter, prospected in the mountains near Albuquerque and in southern Colorado, and worked as a clerk and a janitor. In the most interesting job of his teenage years Sánchez boxed professionally in the Albuquerque area under the name Kid Feliz at the slender build of five feet seven and 112 pounds. Sadly, his fight record remains unrecovered.[11]

Though these odd jobs sound almost literary in their exotic, hucksterish nature, Sánchez's sole motivation was to help his family. He did much of this work during summers and after school, and, in fact, this was how he was able to justify staying in school while his family went hungry. Sánchez recalled that gnawing hunger was an issue for him at this time; sorting through spoiled vegetables and fruit in alleys behind buildings for something to salvage was a common occurrence for the brilliant young student. Sánchez took pains to stress that these experiences were adventures only from the perspective of looking back and that at the time they were undesirable compromises that permitted his continued education. And not all of these jobs were safe. Even the musical sideline, while innocent sounding, had a darker side. Years later Sánchez indirectly described to a fellow New Mexican some aspects of the lifestyle during

1.1. George I. Sánchez as a freshman at Jerome
High School in Arizona. Box 95, Folder 1, SP.
Reproduction by permission of Benson
Latin American Center.

his jazz orchestra years: "Are you related to the Marcos Lovato who was a member of our jazz orchestra (coronet) and who died some thirty years ago? He lived at Ranchos de Atrisco. He drank heavily (we all did in those days!), developed tuberculosis (I did, too, later) and died." Adventurous though his experiences may have been, Sánchez's youthful exertions were trying, unhealthy, and based primarily on necessity.[12]

THE TEENAGE SCHOOLTEACHER

After his high school graduation in 1923 the sixteen-year-old Sánchez, no doubt to the overwhelming pride of his parents, secured a teaching position in the rural, hilly outposts of Bernalillo County. These were segregated Hispano schools, and his pupils suffered economic distress and cultural isolation to such a degree that they made his own background seem almost privileged. Sánchez started out in the education profession as roughly as one could possibly imagine—an ungraded, one-room school in the rural hamlet of Yrrisarri, south-east of Albuquerque at the edge of Bernalillo County. The young Lyndon Baines Johnson repeated this same kind of initial teaching experience several years later in Texas. Sánchez recollected borrowing an uncle's mare to ride out to school on snowy or rainy days, when the dirt roads made automobile trans-portation impossible. And he was reckless. Sánchez and the county superinten-dent, Atanasio Montoya, hotly disagreed over the young man's habit of giving weekend automobile rides back to Albuquerque to young, unattached female teachers from neighboring schools. After one such row that ended with the spirited teenager threatening to wrap the physically handicapped superinten-dent's crutches around his neck, Sánchez was reassigned in the 1924–25 aca-demic year to a more remote school at the other edge of Bernalillo County in the far west. It was near a Navajo reservation at a place called El Ojo Hediondo (Stink-Eye).[13]

Though these teaching assignments were in areas where he had no personal ties, Sánchez made friends quickly and strove to earn the community's trust. Occasionally his efforts created precarious situations that he compounded through his engaging personality. According to one story, an area man he knew asked for a ride to Albuquerque for the weekend. After loading up his old jalopy and starting down the dirt roads, the older man asked his youthful driver if he wanted a drink. Sánchez later related, "I said the usual, 'Don't mind if I do,' expecting a flask or bottle. To my immense surprise and consternation, to say nothing of my horror, he lifted the blanket and there, big as all get out, was a thirty-five gallon keg of white mule—from which he drew out 'one-for-the-road.' I needed that drink! Prohibition laws could have landed me in jail, my car con-fiscated, my job lost—and all calamity could have been my lot. However, that drink (maybe it was plural!) was powerful medicine—and we made it into town without incident. I unloaded my cargo on the edge of Albuquerque and went home to sleep it off. Community relations can be quite strenuous."[14]

Sánchez excelled at these stints in the most marginal areas of the county and soon began a rapid career ascent. Showing that there must not have been terri-bly hard feelings over their prior altercation, Superintendent Montoya assigned Sánchez to become principal of a school near Albuquerque called Los Padillas for the 1925–26 academic year. According to Sánchez, this reversal of fortune probably owed something to his marriage to Virginia (Virgie) Romero on June 15, 1925, after his stint at El Ojo Hediondo. The politically well-connected Vir-gie Romero was his senior year sweetheart at Albuquerque High; her grandfa-ther, Don Andrés Romero, was a powerful, wealthy figure in Bernalillo County. In addition to now being married and suddenly on a fast track of career advancement within the Bernalillo schools, the ever-entrepreneurial Sánchez took advantage of the proximity of Los Padillas to also direct the Spanish department of Albuquerque's night school in 1925 and 1926.[15]

Sánchez excelled as a diligent, dedicated public school teacher who could handle difficult conditions. His salary rose commensurately with his rise in responsibilities. In his two years as a rural schoolteacher at Yrrisarri and El Ojo Hediondo, Sánchez had annual salaries of $1,035 and $1,125 ($14,099.30 and $15,325.33). Once he married and transferred to positions closer to town as a teacher-principal, it rose to $1,440 and then to $1,620 ($19,168.05 and $21,320.39) by the end of the 1920s. In his seven years in the public schools of Bernalillo County, the ambitious Sánchez became a highly sought-after, polished professional. Also of interest is how he taught. Between 1925 and 1930 Sánchez was a teacher-principal at Los Padillas as well as a county supervisor for Superintendent Montoya. Sánchez introduced policies such as urging five-year-olds to informally (and freely) visit the school for pre–first grade instruction, what modern observers might generously call a loose, informal kind of kindergarten. Another innovation Sánchez introduced was getting away from rote learning. He tried, in his own words, "to isolate the various handicaps that each child had (non-attendance, ill-health, poor language development, etc.) and then we tried to apply the remedy that was appropriate to each handicap." Though it sounds somewhat basic to educators today, this attempt to individualize as much of the curriculum as possible to each student's needs was very much part of the new progressive education movement. Individualization depended on a sharp, trained eye for diagnosing learning challenges that all too frequently bled into deeper issues outside the classroom.[16]

THE ORIGINAL NONTRADITIONAL STUDENT

The attentiveness to pedagogy and innovation stemmed from the fact that Sánchez took his teaching profession with the utmost seriousness. While teaching during the twenties he took not only courses by correspondence, by extension at remote locations, at night, and on weekends, but also a constant full load of summer courses. By the end of the decade he graduated from the University of New Mexico with distinction without ever having matriculated for a regular term or taken a full-time course load. Between 1923 and 1926, reacting to Superintendent Montoya's desire that his county teachers obtain out-of-state training, Sánchez took nineteen courses toward his bachelor's degree through the University of California (1925), Colorado State Teachers College (1926), New Mexico Normal University (1924–26), and the New Mexico State Teachers College

(1925). These courses were in history, Spanish, science, education, sociology, and psychology. By 1926 he focused his energy on obtaining his bachelor of arts degree in education at the University of New Mexico. Sánchez finished the degree in 1930 and earned selection to Phi Kappa Phi, an academic honor society.[17]

This early phase of Sánchez's academic career with its catch-as-catch-can approach to taking courses at the limited times available to him resulted in a chaotic-looking transcript. In November 1926, for example, Sánchez had to abandon either a correspondence or extension course with New Mexico State University because he was too busy teaching adult night classes in the Albuquerque schools. His transcript at the University of New Mexico demonstrates that his earliest courses were in education, likely the continuing education courses teachers could get during weekends and summers. Therefore, he ended up taking a large part of his core curriculum late in his academic career. Though Sánchez was mostly an A student, the lowest scores of his undergraduate career were in educational psychology. At the time, such courses stressed the uncritical acceptance of and instruction in intelligence tests that held nonwhite races in the United States to be mentally handicapped. Sánchez's C and B performances in five such classes during his undergraduate career may explain his later criticism of the validity of the concept of IQ and other forms of testing. In the early 1930s Sánchez challenged psychometric experts within academia in several devastating articles. This was not long after taking courses taught by the very proponents of such racialized pseudoscience. It is tempting to imagine a strident Sánchez's vigorous objections to such notions of Mexican American inferiority as being the cause of his uncharacteristically mediocre grades in educational psychology.[18]

Sánchez graduated from the University of New Mexico, as he later mentioned, "without having attended a single regular semester in any college—at the same time working as a teacher, principal, and supervisor in both urban and rural elementary schools." Though it certainly makes Sánchez's intellectual odyssey all the more admirable to those who today have an array of higher educational opportunities, for him it must have made for a lonely, socially isolated experience. As is often the case with many nontraditional students who take classes while working demanding jobs, Sánchez absorbed little of the social atmosphere of university life. Racial prejudice likely influenced this experience as well. He and Virgie are hardly mentioned in the University of New Mexico yearbooks. When they do appear it is only as names in the freshman class or, in George's case, as a member of Phi Kappa Phi. To the extent that Sánchez recalled his undergraduate days in later years with any fondness, the memories often centered on those summer sessions when he had more time to simply be a student. Rarely did this young, ambitious, married man with a rapidly ascending career in local educational circles have time for levity or college high jinks with fellow classmates.[19]

Sánchez kept taking courses at the University of New Mexico in the summer of 1930 after his graduation, diligently working toward a master's degree in education. He spent the next academic year, 1930–31, at the University of Texas. This was the first time since high school that Sánchez was able to be a full-time student, and he made the most of the opportunity. Adding his course credits from the University of New Mexico, he obtained his master's degree in education at the University of Texas in June 1931 after only one academic year and a summer. Unlike his record during his undergraduate career, Sánchez's performance at the University of Texas was spotless, with twelve A's in education, Spanish, and government. Sánchez financed his yearlong stay at Texas with a fellowship from the General Education Board (GEB). He later credited the GEB officials Jackson Davis and Leo Favrot as key mentors for their support of his graduate study (fig. 1.2).[20]

Sánchez formed lasting academic attachments at the University of Texas. He fondly remembered his government professor, J. Alton Burdine, who later became the university's dean of arts and sciences. One important connection he made was with the education professor Herschel T. Manuel, who became his advisor. Manuel was an early opponent of IQ testing and decried how it justified the racial segregation of Mexican American children. Sánchez found in Manuel

1.2. Sánchez as a graduate student at the University of Texas, as he appeared in the school's yearbook, *The Cactus*, for the academic year 1930–31. Box 95, Folder 1, SP. Reproduction by permission of Benson Latin American Center.

an intellectual mentor who could train him to demolish such pseudoscientific findings. Years later Manuel wrote to Sánchez to thank him "for the opportunity of having had you as a gifted student and later as a productive colleague and sincere friend." Sánchez also developed a warm friendship with the young Carlos E. Castañeda, who was then working as a librarian at the university, and later became one of the history department's most productive and influential colleagues as a national expert on the Spanish Southwest. The Sánchez and Castañeda families were close for years. At this time Sánchez also engaged Alonso S. Perales, the founder of LULAC, about challenging racially segregated schools through expert pedagogical testimony.[21]

After graduating from the University of Texas with his master's degree in education and then working a few years as a crusading New Mexico state education bureaucrat, Sánchez pursued a doctorate in education at the University of California at Berkeley with another GEB fellowship. After some graduate course work there in the summers of 1932 and 1933, he enrolled for the 1933–34 academic year and finished his doctorate in the spring of 1934. Sánchez confessed to his mentor at the University of New Mexico, President James F. Zimmerman, that he would be hard-pressed to manage a full complement of courses, his comprehensive exams, and a completed dissertation by May 1934. He did, however. Taking courses in administration, psychology, theory, and elementary education, Sánchez passed his comprehensive exams that February and in late April successfully defended his thesis, "The Education of Bilinguals in a State School System" under the direction of Frank William Hart. The self-directed Sánchez was tightly focused during these years. In the GEB renewal application for support at Berkeley, Sánchez pinpointed that his training prepared him to occupy a specific niche: "There is a crying need for specialization in [the] field of bilingual education. The Southwest, as well as other sections, [are] about ready for departures from current educational practices in this respect but need specialized, trained leadership. This leadership can best come from bilinguals themselves." Decades later, in somewhat different language, young Chicano scholars would make essentially the same argument.[22]

Sánchez obtained all A's with the exception of two courses his first semester. And his personal life expanded when his and Virgie's first child, a son named George Eugene, arrived in 1930 as Sánchez graduated with his bachelor's degree and began work on his master's at the University of Texas. Two years later they had a daughter, Julienne Consuelo (Connie). While spending the minimum of one year in residence at Berkeley, taking a full graduate load, keeping up with the educational politics of New Mexico, and juggling to care for two children aged three and one, George and Virgie Sánchez managed as best they could. George's mother, Juliana, was deceased by this time, and his father, Telesforo, was sick and living with relatives in a small home George had purchased. The senior Telesforo Sánchez died during the Second World War at around the age of sixty. The reasons for his father's ailments and his mother's early death have not survived in Sánchez's archival records. To a long-lost cousin who had lived near his father as a child, Sánchez later reminisced, "Against doctor's orders, I used to take him a bottle of whiskey every time I went there (I am sure he must have shared them with your father!)."[23]

Hardly any Mexican Americans matriculated through the public schools of the United States at this time. Few ever moved beyond grade school, much less graduated from high school or succeeded in higher education. At a time when Mexican American experiences in the U.S. educational system were ridden with the hard bigotry of racial segregation and the soft bigotry of minuscule expectations, George I. Sánchez beat the odds. He shattered them. How? His family background of hard work and the memory, even if entirely imagined, of familial past glory, meaning, and purpose drove him. Aside from a select number of politicians who achieved local or statewide success, mostly in New Mexico and Texas, no prominent Mexican Americans were involved in the formation of state and national policy at this time. Few Mexican Americans contributed to the scholarly community as anything other than exoticized subjects of study. Even fewer Mexican Americans had their research supported by national foundations. The only Mexican American of the era to whom these descriptions could possibly apply is George I. Sánchez. It was this fascinating, admirable struggle to become a highly trained educational professional—among other, more basic struggles of supporting himself and his family—that propelled Sánchez's equally fascinating career.

———— •⟨∞⟩• ————

NEW MEXICO SCHOOLS AND
NEW DEAL POLITICS
1930–1935

The frequent prostitution of democratic ideals to the cause of expediency, politics, vested interests, ignorance, class and "race" prejudice, and to indifference and inefficiency is a sad commentary on the intelligence and justice of a society that makes claims to those very progressive democratic ideals.

George I. Sánchez was a New Deal man. The Great Depression of the 1930s and the Roosevelt administration's New Deal response—with its tensions between radicalism and conservatism, between thought and action—greatly influenced Sánchez. It was a political attitude, if not quite an outright ideology, espousing experimentalism and reform that most shaped the young Sánchez. Decades later he still believed the lessons of the New Deal were the primary lessons all activists and scholars should learn. Sánchez's career during the first half of the thirties took as many twists and turns as a protagonist in an up-from-the bootstraps novel. Beginning the decade as a rural schoolteacher and principal in Bernalillo County, he soon obtained his master's degree at the University of Texas at Austin and his doctorate at the University of California at Berkeley; he fathered two children with Virgie; he carved out a prestigious position within the New Mexico State Department of Education intended to be autonomous from the vicious politics of race. And he lost that job precisely because of those politics.

If New Deal ethnic voters in Chicago had their origins in the pre-Depression, as documented by the historian Lizbeth Cohen in her groundbreaking *Making a New Deal*, so the Mexican American Generation too had begun to gel ideologically before Roosevelt's presidency, much as they vigorously championed it.

The ideological ferment during the crucial decade of the thirties did, however, give the Mexican American Generation greater cohesiveness. Though this generation was conservative socially and in its religion, for the most part the "Mexican American mind," as the historian Richard A. García has written, coalesced around "the U.S. liberal consensus of the New Deal and Fair Deal politics of statism, centralism, McCarthyism, and Keynesianism." Few scholars have written of Mexican Americans in terms of New Deal policy and politics, however. Mostly, Mexican Americans appear in scholarship as an element of other national problems of the period. And in these circumstances, particularly in California and Texas, New Deal policymakers primarily commodified Mexican Americans and Mexican immigrants as a source of farm labor in need of greater control and stability for growers' benefit.[1]

PROGRESSIVE EDUCATION AND THE NEW DEAL

In terms of his professional socialization in the field of education, Sánchez was a disciple of the progressive education movement. Progressive ideas had infused his teaching practices in those rural New Mexico classrooms of the 1920s, but in addition the array of theorists and reformers who collectively identified themselves with the progressive education movement gave Sánchez the professional socialization and training to channel the attitude of New Deal experimentalism into educational policy. Progressive education was a house divided, however. It encompassed a variety of ideological impulses, some bent on replicating the existing social order and others on challenging it. Herbert Kliebard creates a typology of progressive education reformers: traditional humanists, curricular developmentalists, social efficiency adherents, and social reconstructionists (or social meliorists). Sánchez best fits into social reconstructionism. If, to state things entirely too baldly, humanists attempted to preserve as much of the traditional forms of schooling as possible and fetishized the Western tradition, if curricular reformers attempted to atomize curriculum to reach every individual child's identifiable potential as the schools' central goal, and if social efficiency adherents desired smooth-running schools that harmonized social inequalities rather than challenged them, then social reconstructionists used education to address societal injustice and inequality through an activist pedagogy.[2]

Social reconstructionism peaked during the 1930s, feeding off the public's widespread dissatisfaction with the status quo during the Depression. It and Sánchez arrived on the national education scene at the same time. This type of progressive education valued the teaching of critical thinking and democratic citizenship through the study of controversial issues in American life. This pedagogy conceived of itself as an agent for social change. Sánchez continued to teach in this inquiry-based (not results-based) mode throughout his career. This fed Sánchez's New Deal inclinations, which in turn shaped a lifelong conceptualization of how reform could and should happen. Sánchez remained eternally convinced that a little more political daring and a few more studies would spur the necessary reforms to make possible the full integration of his people in American life. This simple, perhaps even naïve predisposition, itself a kind of secular faith that channeled FDR's breezy optimism and confidence for his immense, inchoate New Deal, was as much a legacy of the era for Sánchez as were specific policies. In fact, as schoolteachers, both George and Virgie Sánchez participated in bringing the New Deal to New Mexico through the New Mexico Educational Association (NMEA), an important statewide network of activists. In the late 1920s and early 1930s the Sánchezes were part of a liberal block within NMEA clamoring for increased funding of rural New Mexico schools (*rural* was a coded reference for Hispanos). Because of the efforts of the NMEA the state of New Mexico earned a reputation for positive innovation during the worst days of the Depression.[3]

Even before completing his graduate degrees, Sánchez carved out a reputation as an academic activist. Scholars have coined the term *service intellectuals* for New Deal academics who utilized government agencies and private philanthropies to advance their political agenda. The name fits Sánchez nicely. The service intellectual model of academic activism brought his work to a wider, more public audience. Such hybridity was a double-edged sword, however. Sánchez was too much for some and never enough for others. For example, in the early 1940s one of his GEB mentors, Jackson Davis, had confidentially remarked of Sánchez in a background check to a potential federal employer that while in New Mexico he "worked best in single harness and sometimes I had the feeling that he was inclined to put first his own studies and writings." Davis damningly implied that the young Sánchez was a careerist unwilling "to help the people and to get under the load." Davis nurtured and championed Sánchez's development, yet even he wondered how much his GEB got out of its star pupil. A far worse problem for Sánchez's academic backers, however, was that his writings were couched in the same provocative language as his political pieces. His master's thesis at the University of Texas under Herschel T. Manuel, the innocently titled "A Study of the Scores of Spanish-Speaking Children of Repeated Tests," is a case in point.[4]

The thesis challenged the work of hereditarian IQ scholars, then dominant in the field. Sánchez administered a battery of intelligence tests to his students in the Bernalillo county schools for the 1928–29 and 1929–30 academic years. The grades ranged from three to eight, with a stable sample under controlled conditions. There was no coaching of the tests or deviation from New Mexico's state-approved curriculum, which was lacking in terms of content for these tests anyway. Sánchez found that scores increased after each testing despite the fact that the Haggerty and Stanford intelligence tests were designed to measure innate ability. He challenged the implication of hereditary intellectual inferiority by positing environmental issues as the reason for low test performance by Mexican American students; poor home environments, language limitations, and improper test conditions were more determinative than heredity. Sánchez even commented on allegations of intellectual inferiority stemming from Native American genetic inheritance in a long, defensive digression about the Spanish background of New Mexicans. Given that Jim Crow closely followed racial otherness, it is unsurprising that the young scholar ludicrously denied the obvious Native American inheritance of Hispanos. Not much later he would proudly claim, in print, the Native American heritage of his people. Sánchez's takeaway point in the thesis was that supposedly inviolable, inert IQ tests really measured only general educational opportunity. The carefully couched academic terminology of the thesis belied its defiant content. By 1931 there were not many successful academic challenges to the hereditarian camp; in the subfield of Mexican American testing Manuel and Sánchez were in fact the sole dissenters. The mentor–pupil pair sought to raise supposedly stable IQ levels by following the state curriculum to the letter and then simply retesting until the process ceased to be intimidating. Apparently, good teaching and greater familiarity with the tests resulted in a twenty-point rise in IQ. This proved Sánchez's point that the general conviction of the ineducability of Mexican American children was owing to a clumsy pseudoscience that valued bold, half-baked claims over careful research.[5]

Between his master's and doctoral degrees in 1931 and 1934, Sánchez published pathbreaking articles debunking claims that Mexican American children were mentally incapable of regular schooling. In such respected venues as the *Journal of Applied Psychology*, *Journal of Genetic Psychology*, and *Journal of Social Psychology*, he published passionate, engaged criticisms of the old IQ science, then just beginning to crack under a sustained assault from across the intellectual spectrum. He blamed low scores on the racism, neglect, and poverty daily visited upon Mexican American children. Sánchez was not against all testing, however. At this time such radical skepticism went too far for him. It was the application of tests that drew his ire, as the above epigraph illustrates.[6]

Sánchez nevertheless took the idea of educational testing seriously. He was trained as a progressive educator, after all. He advanced an interpretation, something of a middle path, that he and others hoped would preserve Chicana/o educability while acknowledging low educational performance. It went something like this: though the lack of English vocabulary hampered Mexican American schoolchildren, their poor development of Spanish was doubly detrimental. This deadly combination, according to Sánchez, was a dual language handicap, an idea pioneered by Manuel. Thus, early in his career Sánchez advocated a more specialized, English-intensive curriculum for Mexican Americans, believing it would cause, in a very short time, the pedagogical justification for racial segregation to vanish (fig. 2.1). This was wishful thinking, although LULAC and his progressive education colleagues in New Mexico joined Sánchez in taking this view. For example, Sánchez's recommendation of a language-intensive kindergarten class for Spanish-speakers, while helpful, could never counteract stark levels of inequality. On this point Sánchez underestimated the

2.1. Sánchez as a very young man in New
Mexico, in a photograph probably from
the 1920s or early 1930s. Box 75, Folder 1,
SP. Reproduction by permission of
Benson Latin American Center.

stubbornness of racism and overestimated the ability of less exceptional instructors than himself to bridge the gap between remedial and standard work in a normal school day. Not all teachers could have done what he did as a young man in the Bernalillo County schools. So while Sánchez's challenges to the IQ establishment are quite remarkable, his efforts to provide an alternative explanation for poor Mexican American test scores reflected a young, optimistic scholar's mistake born not of any lack of nerve but of a professional fidelity to the world of scholarship. It was the kind of mistake he repeated throughout his career. Becoming resigned to cynicism or capitulating to racial discrimination was never an option for Sánchez.[7]

AN EDUCATIONAL POLITICO FOR THE GEB

George I. Sánchez was most fortunate that his academic ability got him noticed by the president of the University of New Mexico, James Zimmerman, and the education professor Lloyd Tireman as well as Bronson Cutting, the Republican U.S. Senator of New Mexico who championed progressive and Hispano causes. To help with Tireman's experimental schools for Spanish-speaking children and other reforms to New Mexico's educational system, Zimmerman and Cutting urged the GEB to further Sánchez's career by giving him a fellowship in 1930–31 to study with Manuel at the University of Texas. They also influenced Sánchez's becoming the director of information and statistics for the New Mexico State Department of Education, a division funded entirely by the GEB. His prestigious foundation support gave him, in theory, the protection to take bold actions around Mexican American educational reform. It also guaranteed political controversy. And he would have to give up the position of Bernalillo County superintendent of schools, which had been offered him after his supervisor, Atanasio Montoya, was promoted to the state bureaucracy.[8]

Sánchez chose the more exciting, uncertain route of academic activism over the comfort of the local administrative position his career had built toward. One wonders how Virgie felt at this choice given that her own family was much more settled and prominent in the area. There was always tension between George Sánchez's willingness to explore meaningful, exciting jobs anywhere and Virgie Sánchez's desire to stay close to home and to live a quieter, more conventional life. But George Sánchez loved New Mexico politics and its rough edges. The chairman of the New Mexico Democratic Party in 1932, for example, angrily spat out that Sánchez and his fellow teacher-lobbyists were "educational politicos." Sánchez applied for a permit to carry a weapon to protect himself at school budget meetings. New Mexico school politics was contentious during this heightened period of economic hardship and racial animosity, a fact constantly worrying to Virgie.[9]

Virginia Romero Sánchez, a descendent of Don Andrés Romero, a territorial governor of New Mexico, was as remarkable and assertive as her husband. She was active in her husband's political battles and advanced his career. During one controversy in 1933 Virgie, concerned about her husband's safety, pleaded with Zimmerman not to allow him to travel home alone. In this incident she also minimized his controversial work in an attempt to relieve what she felt was immense pressure against him. She defended and advanced her husband vehemently and at times, one suspects, without his full consent. She copublished an article with him glorifying Spanish education in sixteenth-century Mexico. Arguing against the traditional narrative that North American education derived from sober New England Puritans or aristocratic Chesapeake planters, the Sánchez duo overenthusiastically argued that the conquistadors in Mexico were positive influences in the creation of schools shortly after the initial conquest in the 1520s. George and Virgie had a rollicking kind of relationship: a young, public, relatively coequal couple, brilliant and brassy, trying to positively change their world and raise a family at full speed.[10]

Sánchez's job as the director of the Division of Information and Statistics in the New Mexico State Department of Education was unique in that it was funded entirely, as noted, by a four-year GEB grant beginning in 1931. His salary was $2,700 a year with $1,800 a year budgeted for clerical support and $1,500 for travel ($41,378.39, $27,585.59, and $22,987.99 today). Zimmerman and Sánchez midwifed the negotiations between the GEB and the Department of Education. The foundation expected that sometime in 1934 or 1935 the state would assume the support of the division permanently. The GEB created this agency because it distrusted the level of educational professionalism in New Mexico. The negotiations began while Sánchez was still on GEB fellowship and finishing his master's degree at the University of Texas in 1930. The GEB desired its division to be independent of politics and have the ultimate goal of perhaps evolving into a hybrid university/state research cooperative. The GEB trusted the small number of people it knew best—Sánchez, Zimmerman, and Tireman—far more than anyone else in the state. Sánchez's job involved a supervisory connection to Tireman's San José school, undertaking research, coordinating with agencies interested in education, and shaping state policy. His influential division created a wealth of statistics for policymakers and scholars.[11]

Sánchez's publications during this era are fascinating. His autonomous position within the state educational bureaucracy allowed him to be very bold, perhaps even reckless. For example, in a series of articles he authored and coauthored in the *New Mexico School Review* of 1932, in the depths of the Depression, Sánchez charged that the state of New Mexico failed its students through educational waste, inefficiency, and misplaced priorities. These articles countered calls for trimming school budgets. One article, "A Source of School Revenue Fails Us," charged local county treasurers with creatively dodging the state's constitutional requirement to supplement local schools through court fees and fines. Another article, "Teachers' Salaries Cost Less Today Than They Did a Decade Ago," argued that real wages had fallen for teachers even as their professional obligations and workloads increased. These publications had awfully sharp points to them. In a coauthored article in 1932, Sánchez and NMEA Executive Secretary Paul Fickinger blasted efforts to roll back teachers' salaries. They found that the average monthly salary of a rural public school teacher in New Mexico was almost nine dollars lower than state employees performing common labor. High school teachers in larger districts were paid less than state stenographers and clerks. They located a presumably well-connected janitor at one state office who received $1,800 a year while the seven other janitors in the same building doing the same work received not even $900 a year ($30,605.91 and $15,302.96 today). While these reports may have pleased educators, their allies, and citizens who felt closer to their local schools than to high-ranking Santa Fe officials (or elite janitors!), they assuredly angered the political establishment.[12]

Sánchez's directorship involved a little bit of everything: crafting educational statistics, preparing state reports, cheerleading for educational reform, coordinating political activity by pressure groups like the NMEA, and spending a great deal of time visiting all corners of the state to spread the gospel of school professionalism and reform. Sánchez worked at a breakneck pace. He gave innumerable speeches to local civic and educational groups. From the summer of 1931 to the summer of 1932, his first year as director, he visited 90 towns, made 42 formal public addresses, met with 31 teacher conferences and 39 administrator conferences, attended 21 local and state board meetings, and logged 11,065 miles crisscrossing the state. And he cranked out seventeen publications in academic and nonacademic venues. The next year's report to the GEB listed almost as many publications and even more miles logged.[13]

RACE AND SCHOOLS / OIL AND WATER

For nearly two years Sánchez led a charmed existence. The external support of his division protected him. But the hard times were getting harder, and his brash advocacy got entangled in a lively political issue: the school equalization bill of 1933. This legislation wound its way through both chambers of the state legislature that year and was championed by the NMEA's teacher activists, who sought a more serious state commitment of resources to education. Sánchez was intimately involved in drafting the bill in 1932 at the NMEA meeting. He reported to the GEB as follows: "The Convention promises to be a most important gathering for the school people of this state for at that time will be crystalized the bulk of our proposals for legislative enactment. I am to present the bills which we have developed in regards to school finance and new sources of school revenue." In a subsequent update to the GEB, Sánchez explained the bill's particulars: "We hope to realize about three million dollars for the operation of the Equalization Bill from revenues derived from a gross receipts tax, graduated income tax, and a corporation tax." He went on, "This means that the Spanish-speaking child, who as a rule lives in the poorer districts, will have advantages that he hasn't had here before."[14]

The effort failed. The real opposition to the equalization bill (House Bill 183) was not so much the taxpayers' association or business groups, though they were predictably opposed; it came from Governor Arthur Seligman, Sánchez's ultimate supervisor. After the bill passed the House overwhelmingly and the Senate with only slight opposition, it came to Governor Seligman for his signature. Although Seligman had assured Sánchez and the NMEA of his support, he vetoed it at the last moment with explanations that Sánchez found insubstantial. Sánchez let his feelings of anger and betrayal get the best of him. He remembered years later, "I had the cold comfort of being asked (by Representative Tony Fernández—later Congressman) to refute the Governor's veto message. Before the House of Representatives, I tore the hide off the Governor—I was mad. As a consequence, I was blacklisted by the Administration." Even the GEB would have blanched at this impolitic bluntness had they been fully apprised. Perhaps anticipating a negative reaction to his very public challenge of the state's chief executive, Sánchez soft-pedaled the address in a report to the GEB. He did not need to hide it. The fallout from his remarks had an immediate impact.[15]

In early April 1933, while Sánchez was preoccupied with equalization, the psychology professor Richard Page of the University of New Mexico approached him regarding a study to quantify Anglo racism toward Mexican Americans via a Thurstone scale. Page wanted to distribute the scale to high school students throughout the state. Zimmerman had cautioned Page that this kind of research could blow up in his face. At that time, for example, racial tensions at the University of New Mexico were high. Zimmerman specifically worried about the questions on the scale that were designed to elicit a racist response. Therefore Zimmerman asked Page to consult with Sánchez before proceeding.

Sánchez, who later admitted he had not read the scale thoroughly, overconfi-
dently predicted little or no difficulty and offered Page his mailing list of school
officials for distribution purposes. He even took the extraordinary step of guaran-
teeing that "if such criticism would arise I would be glad to accept full responsibility in order that the University might not be embroiled in some non-sensical
difficulty, which would re-act unfavorably to the institution." Page was excited
to proceed though he fretted, "I have found that this study is somehow a thing
that is very easily misunderstood and needs patient and careful explanation."[16]

Page and Zimmerman were right to be cautious, and Sánchez was not only
wrong but also foolish to think that the scale would not spark outrage. Some of
the questions, modified by Page from scales designed to measure the degree of
white prejudice toward African Americans, went as follows: "2. It is glaringly obvious that the Spanish-speaking people are inferior," and "7. No matter how much
you educate Spanish-speaking people, they are nothing but greasers." Respon-
dents were to put a check mark in the left margin next to the question if they
agreed with the statements. Other questions, for example, "3. They [Spanish-
speaking people] are a helpful and kindly people" and "9. I would be glad to
accept a social invitation from a Spanish-speaking family," teased out sympathetic responses. The questions fell into seven categories: three sympathetic to
varying degrees, three antagonistic to varying degrees, and one neutral.[17]

Hispano leaders, simmering in anger over recently failed efforts to grapple
with discrimination at the University of New Mexico through antifraternity
legislation, turned on Page and Sánchez with ferocity. And Governor Seligman
was out for blood, specifically Sánchez's. Seligman got wind of the scale's intended mass distribution before it went out, halted it, and formed an investigative committee headed by the University of New Mexico's Board of Regent
Henry Coors to discover those responsible. Seligman wasted little time in publicly demanding that Zimmerman fire Page and that the GEB fire or reassign
Sánchez. The survey was denounced as racist in a public meeting in the Old
Town section of Albuquerque, a heavily Hispano neighborhood. Community
leaders called for action against the university and those responsible for the
survey. A. A. Sena, the leader of a mass protest, incited the crowd by saying that
"Page ought to be lynched" and volunteered to carry out the act; E. A. Perrault,
a former New Mexico secretary of state and at the time a director in the New
Mexico Department of Labor, dismissed the twenty-six-year-old Sánchez as
well meaning but in need of a grownup to oversee him. One state senator
threatened to introduce a bill abolishing the University of New Mexico.[18]

As promised, Sánchez jumped into the fray to take responsibility. If he thought
this might spare Zimmerman some political heat, he was sorely mistaken.

Governor Seligman pounced on this opening to settle a score. Sánchez had apparently cut Seligman deeply with his comments over the veto of the equalization bill weeks before. Telegramming and writing to John D. Rockefeller, the founder of the GEB, that Sánchez was planting "the seeds of race hatred" in the minds of New Mexico's schoolchildren, Seligman asked that the GEB replace Sánchez. Unwilling to fire a protégé they had invested so much in, the GEB deflected any action back to the governor to repudiate the grant or not. At this point an important benefactor, Senator Cutting, spoke on Sánchez's behalf, defending his work to Seligman and to Rockefeller, who was likely confused by the flurry of mail sent directly to him instead of to his foundation: "I have already written Mr. Rockefeller requesting that no action be taken about George Sánchez pending a full investigation of the affair. I also stated that I felt Mr. Sánchez had done most valuable work in the state and that I did not believe drastic action should be taken on account of what was no doubt a mistake of judgment." This was enough to get the Democratic governor Seligman, who was dependent on the Progressive Republican Cutting's support, to back off. Cutting commanded too many Hispano votes, and Seligman, who hurt himself with Hispanos by opposing equalization, needed the race survey issue to rebuild support. Getting even with Sánchez by further pursuing his dismissal was ultimately less important to him than that.[19]

Zimmerman pleaded with Cutting to keep Sánchez from being sacrificed, calling him "a most unusual student" who possessed "a wonderful personality" and who was important to the state's future. Interestingly, Zimmerman was much more willing to defend Sánchez, a GEB employee with the state, than his own psychology professor. He and other university officials scapegoated Page. Several academic colleagues and students in the extended hearings scurried to portray Page as unmindful of their concerns all along. In his defense before the investigating committee, Page contextualized the Thurstone scale, explained its scientific validity, and defended his motives. He also admitted to badly misjudging the reaction. Page's brief to the investigating committee recorded personal slurs, death threats voiced in public meetings, and death threats that came to his home anonymously via telephone or mail. One read, "We are giving you 24 hours to leave town[.] Take your choice Rat[.] The Duce II." After saddling him with the majority of the blame, the committee sought Page's resignation. They also criticized Zimmerman and Sánchez for having tin ears.[20]

As the controversy unfolded, Sánchez's reports to the GEB took on greater intensity. The incident rattled him, and he wanted to assure the GEB that he and his staff were taking the matter seriously. He reiterated that the controversy was wildly unpredictable and contrary to logic, assuring Leo Favrot he was "making every effort to smooth over the rift." Favrot responded with condolences and a bit of perspective: "I trust that you and your friends will be successful in convincing the people of New Mexico that whatever error has been made was an error of the head and not of the heart." Sánchez reflected quite a bit about the controversy and how he, one of the most passionate Mexican American activists in the state, could be so effectively tarred by a weak, conservative, anti-Mexican politician to such an extent that members of his own community whom he had known all his life could become whipped up in a rage against him. The controversy was hard on the Sánchezes. When George was to begin his trip to return home from testifying before the investigatory committee, Virgie frantically pleaded with Zimmerman not to let her husband travel unaccompanied for fear he might be attacked or their child kidnapped. George Sánchez later recalled the scary time: "Oh brother! Police had to patrol my home, I had to carry a gun in my pocket. I was a dirty dog with the *mexicanos* who held mass meetings over the state urging that I be hanged, etc." The story was being carried by newspapers as far away as *La Prensa* in San Antonio. Page's academic career never recovered, and Sánchez felt terrible about it: "I want to assure you that in spite of the adverse results of the recent controversy I believe that the only mistake made was a political one and that academically and professionally there was absolutely no ground for the conclusions arrived at. I want to assure you that I sympathize with you and regret sincerely the position in which you have been placed. I can not but think that you were forced to be the unhappy Christian that was thrown to the lions for the greater glory of God."[21]

Sánchez took a leave of absence during the academic year of 1933–34 at the University of California at Berkeley to complete his doctorate. The GEB supported his year on leave at Berkeley to the tune of $1,900 ($34,045.31 today). Sánchez's time in California did not mean disengagement from New Mexico educational issues, however. He continued to rail about the fiscal mismanagement of school funds and equalization in reports and public addresses that were every bit as stinging as before. While he reflected on his awkward situation after these setbacks, he did not allow them to alter his basic approach. But the race controversy was a blemish on Sánchez's reputation in New Mexico and, in part, accounted for his tremendous difficulty in maintaining meaningful employment later in the decade.[22]

MAKING A NEW DEAL FOR MEXICAN AMERICANS

Sánchez sought to weave Mexican Americans into the national fabric of American life through academic research. To borrow a turn of phrase from an iconic history of this period, Sánchez intended to "make a New Deal" for Mexican Americans. Those activists most beholden to the ideology and tactics of the Mexican American Generation tended to conceive of solutions to their community's plight in New Deal terms; the more idiosyncratic the activists of this generation were, the less dependably liberal they were. No one was more representative of the Mexican American Generation and no Mexican American Generation activist was quite so self-consciously indebted to the New Deal as George I. Sánchez. Getting away from his Division of Information of Statistics to become a University of California graduate student in the summer of 1933 shortly after Roosevelt's first one hundred days of activity, Sánchez thought more expansively about his work and how it might focus the government's attention on Mexican Americans' plight. The atmosphere at Berkeley was conducive to innovative, antiestablishment thinking. The campus was embroiled in pro-labor and antidiscrimination student activism. Indeed, Sánchez's doctoral dissertation at Berkeley bears a more freewheeling style of writing and interpretation. What the master's thesis at the University of Texas suggested, Sánchez's doctoral dissertation spelled out with brio. While admitting to dangerous problems in the field of educating Mexican Americans, the ambitious graduate student did not hold these problems to be in any way insurmountable. He wrote that shoddy, inefficient, wasteful, bigoted educational practices denigrated the nation's democratic ideals. Sánchez included the studies of the Berkeley economist Paul Taylor on the racial and economic exploitation of Mexican agricultural workers in Texas and California to further ground his work in recent, cutting-edge social science.[23]

He acknowledged that not all Chicanas/os took full advantage of the educational opportunities available, but that those opportunities were mostly of such an inferior and degrading quality that the community's distrust was excusable. Sánchez placed the responsibility for this dilemma not on Mexican Americans struggling to survive in a hostile, racist world; rather, he blamed an unengaged, ill-informed government. Many of Sánchez's recommended reforms came out of the familiar progressive education playbook: increasing educational professionalism, decreasing local school politics in educational decision making, and equalizing public school funds to benefit those children, mostly Hispanos, at the bottom of the socioeconomic ladder. Though the race scale controversy of 1933 may have clipped his wings, Sánchez did not back down from his dreams for bettering education in his state. In fact, he seemed even more optimistic about achieving them in those exciting early days of the New Deal.[24]

Sánchez thought deeply about incorporating the needs of Mexican Americans into the national policy conversation. If the New Deal made an effort to reach so many more classes of Americans directly—farmers, sharecroppers, union members, consumers, the unemployed, students, and African Americans (the latter quietly and indirectly)—why not spur it to reach Mexican Americans? The attention Sánchez had in mind involved studying and acting against Mexican American poverty, exploitation, and neglect. In his first term at Berkeley Sánchez wrote to Zimmerman that in his spare time he conceived of a plan for a New Deal–style agency for Mexican American education he intended to propose to the GEB. He wrote that Arizona, California, Colorado, New Mexico, and Texas were home to over two million Mexican Americans who faced severe racial segregation in the schools. Another hindrance to solving such problems was that the small but growing body of research on Mexican American education was scattered. Sánchez felt the field could benefit from some coordination, especially an academic journal to allow isolated researchers throughout the country to arrive at more effective solutions. The twenty-seven-year-old doctoral student recommended that "a Division of Bilingual Education be established in the National Office of Education for coordinating, supervising, and field research purposes." He went on, "I believe firmly that such a division would be supported by a bloc of congressmen from the southwestern states. If I could be released for the purpose, I would gladly attempt to secure enough interest and popular and professional support to interest the congressmen and the Office of Education."[25]

A lack of confidence or bravado was never a weakness for George I. Sánchez. To Chicana/o scholars and intellectuals steeped in traditional assumptions that Mexican Americans of this period were ignored and stoically removed themselves from decision-making authority as opposed to the succeeding Chicano Generation of the late 1960s and 1970s who were the first Mexican Americans to have the imagination to dream of national attention, Sánchez's proposal from the early days of the New Deal might seem fantastical. While not quite like discovering a cell phone in a stratum of ancient undisturbed rock, this is nevertheless jarring to those trained in the field. This proposal came three and a half decades before young Chicanas/os bandied about similar ideas in various plans and manifestos. One difference is apparent, however. Unlike the Chicanos of the late sixties and seventies whose plans were far removed from any locus of power, Sánchez involved not only Zimmerman, a state university president, the GEB's Favrot, a representative of one of the most important educational philanthropies in the country pertaining to minorities, but also Cutting, a sitting U.S. senator. Zimmerman enthusiastically approved of Sánchez's rough proposal and set up a meeting with Cutting over the Thanksgiving holiday in 1933, when Sánchez was in town. Leveraging the senator's enthusiasm, Sánchez and Zimmerman then lobbied Favrot.[26]

Sánchez insisted that his proposal for a national research center at the University of New Mexico build on the GEB's commitment of resources to fund his directorship within the New Mexico education bureaucracy. This new center he would direct, pitched Sánchez, required an outlay of $20,000 a year to be shared by the university, the state, the national office of education, and the GEB and through an individual contribution by the wealthy Cutting ($358,376.92 today). Sánchez planned on much of the research at the center being carried out by University of New Mexico faculty and graduate students. It would begin in late 1935 at the termination of the original GEB grant supporting his state division. While intrigued, the GEB, without whose participation the proposed national division would go nowhere, passed on the idea. Favrot was hesitant about transferring GEB's support, near the end of the grant, to what he viewed as an entirely different purpose. He reiterated that while the GEB had no problem with the impressive proposal, their "purpose in the awarding of fellowships to you and in setting up the division in the State Department of Education was to set up the administrative division in the State Department that would be professional and not political." He reminded Sánchez that the current grant was not yet completed and would not be until the state officially adopted Sánchez's small division. Favrot delicately hinted that neither he nor the rest of the GEB really trusted the state of New Mexico in the absence of Sánchez and his independent division applying pressure. Sánchez's thrashing over equalization and the race survey the prior spring gave the GEB pause about the ultimate viability of its division after the grant ended.[27]

Neither Sánchez nor Zimmerman took Favrot's initial no as final. In 1934 Zimmerman wrangled from Cutting a commitment to personally contribute at or in excess of the $5,000 he gave for the original GEB-funded San José experimental school project ($86,919.78 today). Perceptively shifting their argument, Zimmerman and Sánchez assured Favrot that the Division of Information and Statistics already did in a small, incidental way the very kind of research that a University of New Mexico center could specialize in. They stressed that the newer proposal organically grew from the former effort and should be seen as strengthening it. But internal considerations at the philanthropy worked against Sánchez's idea. The GEB was getting out of the practice of funding state divisions for minority (African American) education throughout the South. Favrot felt that with the current mood of his board, any alteration in the grant might jeopardize the entire GEB foray in New Mexico.[28]

The GEB did not budge from its position, and eventually Senator Cutting came to believe that the new project might detract from the existing programs he already sponsored. At any rate, the senator was distracted by a major political challenge that year from the liberal Democrat Dennis Chávez. So Sánchez and Zimmerman again recast their project in such a way that would place most of the burden on the University of New Mexico. Zimmerman was confident that outside funding would eventually come if they began the work on their own. This required the soon-to-be-titled Dr. Sánchez to be a member of the University of New Mexico faculty for the 1935–36 year once the GEB grant for the state division expired. Both were jittery about the prospect that the state would assume responsibility for the division. Throughout 1934 Sánchez kept the idea of the project alive and recast it in ways he felt might appeal to the GEB. However, the GEB remained unmoved, and Senator Cutting died the next year in a tragic plane crash shortly after narrowly winning a contentious reelection bid.[29]

Sánchez never fully gave up on the project and neither did Zimmerman, who was eager for any opportunity to raise the profile of the University of New Mexico. He realized that Sánchez's academic prowess and his ambition ensured the potential for external recognition. In the later 1930s, when the university's participation was no longer feasible, Sánchez reworked the proposal for the University of California at Berkeley. Citing the interdisciplinary synergy of university service intellectuals, New Deal agencies, and philanthropic organizations, Sánchez argued that education colleges at most research universities still maintained an ossified perspective: "There is also a feeling that the traditional teachers college curriculum needs enrichment in fields which heretofore had been considered the province of sociology, economics, anthropology, public welfare, and political science departments alone." Sánchez outlined areas of study for such a division of rural education within a college of education, including courses on diverse minority groups in the United States.[30]

Sánchez would not give up on the project. While working abroad in South America later in the decade, he brainstormed to Zimmerman about the comparison between the U.S. Southwest and the U.S. South. Profoundly affected by working for the Rosenwald Fund in Chicago on southern African American education and enthusiastic about the service intellectual research coming from the southern regionalists at the University of North Carolina and Fisk University, Sánchez stressed that such a proposal "should stress rural sociology, southwestern economics, the local share-cropping mess, culture contacts and the incorporation of the Spanish-speaking population into the New Deal type of

modern agrarianism, etc. Its chief function should be research and field studies. Much should be made out of the fact that practically nothing is now available in printed form about Southwestern Culture. Stress should be placed upon
the need of studies like that of Howard Odum on *Southern Regions;* of Alexander, Embree, and Johnson on *Cotton Tenancy;* mine on *Mexico;* and of the
need for activities like that of resettlement in backward New Mexico villages."
Sánchez reiterated to Zimmerman that such an agency was crucial for the University of New Mexico if it was serious about becoming an academic powerhouse: "I suggest that the University make a bid to establish a Southwestern
Institute and seek to develop this field much as the George Peabody Research
and Field Studies Division and the U. of North Carolina Sociology Department have developed their respective fields." He concluded, "Personally, I
would like nothing better than to have a chance to organize such a project."[31]

POLITICAL SUCCESS AND FAILURE IN NEW MEXICO

Upon completing his doctorate in the spring of 1934, Dr. George I. Sánchez
came back to Santa Fe on a full-time basis to head his division for its final year
of GEB funding. He also accepted an invitation from Yale University to give a
series of lectures that August. His agency was very pleased with the external
recognition. The University of New Mexico alumni magazine ran a story on
Sánchez and his Yale jaunt a month later. The press came at an opportune time
and was not accidental as Zimmerman had suggested to the magazine's editor
that he spotlight his protégé. Zimmerman soon received a note from Virgie asking him to talk up her husband for the story because it might boost his campaign for the presidency of NMEA, "As you probably know George would like
to get the nomination for the presidency of the N.M.E.A. this year, if no one
from the University is going to try. . . . I think we can give George a good boost
by giving him a nice write-up now that he is at Yale. Etiquette books do say that
nice people don't brag about themselves. That is just the point. George wouldn't
think of publicizing himself so I'm taking the opportunity of doing it while he
is away. That article that Mr. Hall wants to write seems to me to be the solution.
What do you think?" Virgie ended the note, "Do forgive my nerve. My only
excuse is that I love George and I'll do anything for him." After letting Virgie
know that the interview was his idea, the bemused President Zimmerman acknowledged her influence in successfully garnering support for George. He
won the presidency that fall by a significant majority.[32]

Sánchez rebounded from the setbacks of 1933. As president of NMEA he
came to determine more directly its political course for the legislative session of

1935. To the GEB Sánchez argued that his election validated their entire endeavor: "The election for the presidency was hotly contested and amounted to a battle between liberal and conservative educational forces. The largest vote ever polled in a New Mexico Educational Association [contest] gave me a very large majority and elected officers who were considered advocates of the liberal program which I have sponsored during the last four years." Sánchez assured Favrot this was an endorsement of the Division of Information and Statistics' efforts and meant big reform in the next session. Davis and Favrot were happy for Sánchez, though they were still eager for the state to pick up the support of their division. For Sánchez, this was building to another equalization crusade on behalf of poor, Hispano children.[33]

Sánchez worked harder on equalization in the New Mexico legislative session of 1935 and made sure he was not distracted by side issues. He championed the equalization bill from his position as the elected president of the NMEA rather than as an unelected bureaucrat. He urged audiences to consider raising the bar of educational attainment in the state by targeting those at the bottom: "In New Mexico half of our population is Spanish-speaking. Over half of our school census is Spanish-speaking and whether we want to or not we must realize that the fact remains that New Mexico is going to progress just as rapidly and only as rapidly as this 50 per cent of our population progresses." Sánchez repeated an educational mantra not so dissimilar to popular ones today, namely, that children did not fail schools so much as schools failed children. The equalization bill passed, and Sánchez and NMEA had their moment of glory. He reminded the GEB that he now worked under a new regime at the State Department of Education, as H. R. Rogers succeeded Georgia Lusk. While Lusk was never quite in his, Zimmerman's, or the GEB's full confidence, she was an ally nonetheless. Rogers, a more conservative Democrat, was noncommittal about a permanent, independent division of his agency, and he was not the political maverick Lusk was. At the very time Sánchez was publicly lobbying for educational reform in the state legislature, that body also considered whether or not to permanently fund his division.[34]

This period marked a turning point in Sánchez's career. The New Mexico state legislature refused to continue Sánchez's division within the State Department of Education when the grant ran out in the summer of 1935. The losses of 1933—the equalization bill and the race scale controversy—were temporary. This was not. Sánchez was now out of a job. He had burned through his once-considerable political capital. The refusal was also a rejection of the GEB's vision of educational reform. Ultimately, New Mexico decided it did not need to alter in a meaningful way how it delivered education. The Division of Information and Statistics withered away. Consequently, having had his position cut out from beneath him, Sánchez felt his only course of action was to resign immediately, despite the fact that a month remained on the grant. Officially, the disappointed Sánchez justified his decision to the Board of Education as a need for rest since he estimated he had taken only two weeks' vacation in four years. While unhappy with this final result, the GEB was positive in its assessment of Sánchez's performance and perseverance in a place they felt was a wasteland of educational professionalism.[35]

Privately, Sánchez was less constrained. To Favrot he wrote that Rogers disliked him because of his activism. Rogers was so anti-Sánchez he would not even commit to retaining Sánchez's two administrative assistants elsewhere in the bureaucracy: "A great deal of resentment was aroused by my active part in drafting and securing the passage of the Equalization Act, the Transportation Act, and the Proposal for a constitutional amendment providing for an appointive State Commissioner of Education. Our agitation, over a period of four years, for educational reforms has naturally tread on many toes." Sánchez urged the GEB to sit on further requests from the state. According to Sánchez, Rogers was a throwback to the old style of New Mexico educational politics, which meant future reformers "will have to run the gamut of the political patronage system now in effect in the rest of the Department." Zimmerman shared Sánchez's pessimism. The Democratic sweep in New Mexico and the senatorial election narrowly won by Cutting, then in the midst of a divisive legal challenge from his Democratic opponent, Chávez, who had President Roosevelt's support, signaled that the independent, Progressive Republican faction in New Mexico politics built on strong Mexican American support was losing steam. Days after Sánchez left his division Cutting perished. This simply underscored the point that the political makeup of New Mexico was realigning along different ideological and partisan divisions. Zimmerman dismissed the idea that anything could be expected of Rogers and urged the GEB to hold off on further grant applications from the state. He and Favrot felt Sánchez had been ridden hard and put up wet. Zimmerman was "convinced that the progressive legislation which we have secured in New Mexico is due almost entirely to the earnest and determined efforts of Dr. Sánchez."[36]

George I. Sánchez would not change his ideals or his activist scholarship; his commitment to them in fact only deepened. What did change was the venue from which he employed his talents. Up to this point, Sánchez was known in some small circles nationally as a New Mexico *wunderkind*. But from this point forward he deepened his academic reputation as a scholar of Mexican Americans, Latin America, and the action pedagogy becoming popular in the United States and Mexico. His defeats set him on the path to national and international prestige through exciting, albeit brief, jobs as an educational expert for foundations and foreign governments. Zimmerman, a visionary with regard to his university who had a knack for nurturing local talent, was nevertheless wrong in predicting his protégé's future: "He has worked like a beaver for four years, and has accomplished more than many men have been able to accomplish in a lifetime. It is my sincere belief that when temporary political considerations have passed, there will be a much clearer recognition of the fundamental work which George has done for New Mexico." In fact, the opposite happened. Sánchez's career in New Mexico never recovered from the damage caused between 1933 and 1935. It took New Mexicans decades to come to terms with his brief but dramatic impact on their state. This historical recovery is still in progress.[37]

3

EXILE, RECOGNITION, AND UNDEREMPLOYMENT
1935–1940

Girded with good health, economic security, social self-sufficiency, education, and the ability to compete for a living wherever he may be, the New Mexican can set forth from the limited prospects of his present environment and embark towards new horizons. Released from the handicaps of his present situation, he need no longer be a problem child, a culturally unassimilated subject, but a respected and self-respecting American. Thus, armed with the culture of his country, incorporated into the American fold, he is no longer the stepchild of a nation. Freed from cultural bondage and from the despair of dire poverty, the New Mexicans will have harvested the true fruits of their conquest and will cease to exist as forgotten people.

After the demise of his position in the New Mexico State Department of Education, what was to become of George I. Sánchez? The GEB and President Zimmerman agreed that he needed to get away from New Mexico for a while. They wanted him to publish more in order to reenter educational politics from the vantage point of a safe, tenured professorship at the University of New Mexico. Sánchez had exciting experiences from 1935 to 1940. He left the State Department of Education as a victim of politics, became an employee of major national foundations and then an educational administrator in a foreign country, and reemerged in New Mexico as an adjunct, nontenured professor. By the end of the decade Sánchez parlayed his career's bright promise into a plum position at a major university. His reputation, mostly a local one in the first half of the decade, by the second half of the decade was national and international.

Traditional historical interpretations hold the Mexican American Generation to be isolated and narrowly provincial in its worldview. In reality, however, these were a transnational, global people despite however much they may have stressed U.S. citizenship for strategic and ideological reasons through organizations like LULAC. Recent work in Chicana/o history stresses the early-twentieth-century immigrant experience in the origins of the Mexican American Generation, especially the influence of Mexican consulates or of revolutionary ideas flowing from Mexico to the United States. The historians Emilio Zamora and Ben Johnson examine how Mexican American leaders—the loyalist, nationalistic people who created LULAC—maintained a far more global and cosmopolitan perspective than previously thought. The rich diversity of George I. Sánchez's experiences in the U.S. Southwest, the U.S. South, and Latin America with numerous philanthropies, levels of government, and higher education adds to this interpretive current. During the late 1930s Sánchez was everywhere as a fiery academic activist.[1]

MEXICO: A REVOLUTION BY EDUCATION

In 1935, as his position with the State of New Mexico crumbled, Sánchez looked forward to a career change. Performing academic research for national philanthropic foundations like the GEB and the Chicago-based Julius Rosenwald Fund enhanced his nascent professional reputation. This career change did not mean he would stop contributing to social change, but now he would do so from behind the scenes and with his pen. Embracing the change with his usual aplomb, Sánchez jauntily wrote to a colleague, "In the meantime, maybe there is a revolution or two needing a corporal (they've already got plenty of generals) and my talents may come in good stead!" In the weeks leading up to his resignation from the State Department of Education in March 1935, Sánchez serendipitously came into contact with Rosenwald representatives who were touring New Mexico. The Rosenwald Fund director, Edwin R. Embree, visited the University of New Mexico, the GEB's San José Training School, Indian Bureau offices, various public officials, cultural arts specialists, and educators like Sánchez. Weeks before Sánchez's resignation Embree congratulated the GEB for having "found and maintained as good a man as Sánchez." Embree marked Sánchez as a potential asset for his own foundation.[2]

Once Sánchez resigned, the GEB and Rosenwald Fund began a friendly negotiation over him. Embree began by writing to the GEB about obtaining Sánchez's services. GEB continued to pay Sánchez's salary for a few months after his resignation—a soft landing for valued talent who they felt had gotten a raw deal—and also considered subsidizing him for a possible position at the University of New Mexico. This was tentative, however, and would not be decided

until well into the fall. What about the rest of 1935? Sánchez needed employment, and Zimmerman had difficulty finding, on such short notice, an ade-
quate living for his protégé at his cash-strapped school. He did not anticipate
having a spot for Sánchez until the spring of 1936, meaning nine months of
unemployment. Embree proposed that during that time Sánchez write a long-
planned book for the Rosenwald Fund on Mexican education: "We had expected Frank Tannenbaum to make this Mexican study for us but so many
obligations have accumulated about him that I see no likelihood of his doing
this work for us within the next year or two. . . . In many ways I think he [Sán-
chez] would be a better man than Tannenbaum." Embree reported that Sánchez was anxious to get started because it allowed him to save face by acquiring
a prestigious academic position after having received "a rather ignominious
kick out of office." The GEB officials Hill and Favrot endorsed the maneuver.
Embree made it a point to solicit Zimmerman's input on the move. Zimmerman was hesitant about it since he had plans for Sánchez to help him transform
the University of New Mexico into an academic powerhouse in Mexican American research. Embree justified the action as giving Sánchez additional professional experience should he seek a future appointment. Zimmerman was
ultimately persuaded it was the best move at the time and expected the political
enmity toward Sánchez to soon dissipate. Embree walked a tightrope; it benefited Rosenwald to employ Sánchez for a year on the Mexico book project, but
for the long term they were limited to African American education in the South.[3]

Sánchez began work with the Rosenwald Fund while still on the payroll of
the GEB. In 1935 the Rosenwald Fund spent $6,565 on Sánchez's study of
Mexican education, a subject that fascinated them for the comparative light it
might shed on African American education in the U.S. South ($111,626.56 to-
day). One of Sánchez's first duties involved acting as an interpreter on a
Rosenwald–GEB tour of Mexico. The trip resulted in an oddly ritualized evening interview (accompanied by fireworks and singing schoolchildren) with
Secretary of Public Education Ignacio García Téllez, who discoursed at length
on the principles of socialistic education in rural Mexican schools. It was these
rural schools Sánchez and the Rosenwald Fund found most interesting. Indeed, Sánchez was collecting research material for the project even before the
trip and coauthored with Moisés Sáenz a report of his experiences called "A
Brief Review of the New Education in Mexico." Sánchez was in good company.
Sáenz had studied under the progressive education luminary John Dewey. He
was also briefly Mexico's secretary of public education in the late twenties.
Sáenz urged American writers to realize Mexican education's revolutionary potential for achieving Dewey's ideals.[4]

Though he admitted it was rushed, Sánchez viewed this report as the beginning of a book on Mexico's cultural missions to its rural population. Sánchez felt, as did his Rosenwald colleagues, that the Mexican educational scene offered a valuable experience for American educators. He said of the cultural missions, "It seems that there the U.S. may find an institution that might well be transplanted into our rural areas with profit. The present program of Rural Rehabilitation under the F.E.R.A. and similar federal agencies would probably do well to adopt this method of procedure." Sánchez's research would keep him in Mexico City through most of the summer and early fall, aflame with the prospect of transplanting the Mexican approach to the American Southwest. Sánchez stressed to the GEB and to Zimmerman that this job was merely further training for the kind of work he would come back to perform in New Mexico.[5]

His research in Mexico expanded Sánchez intellectually. For example, he visited the famed Mayan archeologist (and spy) Sylvanus G. Morley at his Chichén Itzá dig in Yucatán. Morley's lectures at the University of New Mexico in the 1920s had fired Sánchez's imagination as a young man. Sánchez later remembered that his conversations with Morley in Mexico inspired a lifetime interest in Mayan mathematics. Mexican postrevolutionary ideology also stimulated him. He was clearly in awe of rural Mexican schoolteachers, particularly with respect to how they dealt with the everyday violence that could be visited on them by antigovernment partisans. He remembered fifteen-year-old women who were threatened with mutilation should they continue to teach but who went on doing so, often armed in the classroom. In writing to Zimmerman, Sánchez could hardly contain his enthusiasm for the topic while, in his own words, avoiding "malaria, snakes, dysentery, and attractive señoritas!" Zimmerman must have been alarmed that research in Mexico seemed to be further radicalizing his already combustible young protégé. Indeed, the political waters in New Mexico were not calming. Sánchez would not let them. His farewell address to the NMEA publicly called out State Superintendent Rogers for turning the state agency into a site of patronage for antireform educators. As to their efforts to broaden the grant idea for a university program, Sánchez insisted that it have the same kind of policy impact as his old bureaucratic division: "As you can see, while I believe in sound research, I insist that scientific study be made practical and effective. A social project at the U. must have as its aim the improvement of actual situations—not research for research's sake, but dynamic field research and active social participation."[6]

Zimmerman's efforts to secure Sánchez's services at the university in 1936 were frustrated by several factors. First, the GEB disliked sinking more money into a state they felt disregarded their efforts. Second, Zimmerman overshot his pitch. He requested an additional GEB grant of $9,350 to fund a planned Division of Statistics and Research in Bilingual Problems for three years, of which $7,100 went toward the salary of Sánchez ($156,693.22 and $118,986.29 today). Nearly tripling Sánchez's salary gave the GEB pause, even after negotiating Zimmerman down to $7,500 for two years and finally $5,000 for two and one-half years ($125,689.75 and $83,793.17 today). Third, the GEB felt the proposal did not sufficiently share the burden of financing the research agency. Fourth, and perhaps most important, both discovered in the middle of the negotiations that they were losing Sánchez to the Rosenwald Fund indefinitely. Rosenwald offered Sánchez an opportunity to work for their foundation full-time as a pedagogical expert on African American education in the South. An upset Zimmerman recalled the entire proposal once Sánchez made it clear he was not immediately returning. Influencing Sánchez was the problem he had with Zimmerman's proposal. His original plan had been to direct an independent, interdisciplinary university agency involving coordinated research all over campus. Anyone affiliated with Chicano studies programs that arose out of the late 1960s and 1970s will be struck by the parallels in content, scope, and administrative focus with Sánchez's proposal of the mid-1930s. Zimmerman, though, instead slotted Sánchez as an untenured research professor within the College of Education. Sánchez balked. In a long, handwritten letter to Zimmerman, he fretted about being thrust into an education college. He desired interdisciplinarity and autonomy.[7]

So in the fall of 1936 Sánchez made the momentous decision to uproot his family from New Mexico in order to take a full-time position with the Rosenwald Fund in Chicago. Despite his reassurances of returning soon, Zimmerman remained unhappy. At the time of this shift, Sánchez's *Mexico: A Revolution by Education* came out. Today this book might very well be considered an apologia for the Mexican Revolution, the leftist tendencies of the Lázaro Cárdenas administration of the thirties, and the long-serving governing party known as the PRI, or Partido Revolucionario Institucional. Sánchez traveled hundreds of miles across Mexico visiting the cultural missions of Mexican socialistic education; these were revolutionary training institutes for rural teachers. Given his own social reconstructionism, it is understandable why Sánchez so enthusiastically took to the topic. To Sánchez, this was Mexico's version of the New Deal, arguing that they "stand for what is new in education, in agrarian reforms, in economic practices, in political policies, and in social relationships. Born of dire need, they represent all the elements that distinguish modern Mexico from old Mexico. They symbolize the change from feudalism to socialism, from exploitation to co-operation, from slavery to freedom. They wage a revolution by education."[8]

Not all of these schools fulfilled their lofty goals, however. Sánchez condemned the violence and intimidation waged by some education reformers against the Catholic Church; but he also blamed church supporters for "fanaticism." He was mostly impressed with it all and drew comparisons to social reconstructionism in the United States: "The pupils of the school, then, are the Mexican masses and the curriculum is based on the life problems of the Mexican peoples. These ideals have been expressed many times before by those who would co-ordinate the life of the school with the life of the community in which the school operates. In the United States we have proposed this doctrine often but, except in rare instances, have not achieved the success desired." The historian Mary Kay Vaughan depicts Mexican education of this era as a fascinating intellectual, ideological, and nationalistic project. At this time Mexican educators were inculcating the Mexican Revolution through the classroom in a pedagogy that promoted redistributive economic policies and political participation as an integral part of Mexican citizenship. Such practices would have made social reconstructionists in the Unites States green with envy. Mexican educators such as Sáenz and Rafael Ramírez, who wrote the glowing foreword of *Mexico: A Revolution by Education* and directed rural education for the cultural missions, supported these ideas. Sánchez was as close to real decision-making power as an outside observer in Mexico as he would ever be in his career in the United States. He reveled in that insider's knowledge. Scholarly reviews were mostly positive, with some slight criticism of Sánchez's relentlessly upbeat analysis. *Mexico: A Revolution by Education* was Sánchez's first book and established him as a recognized scholar of education and, although he had no formal training in the region, of Latin America.[9]

THE ROSENWALD FUND

Sánchez's work for the Rosenwald Fund in Chicago involved a wide range of tasks pertaining to his pedagogical expertise and administrative background. He consulted extensively with the Progressive Education Association over experimental Rosenwald activities, visited and inspected Rosenwald-supported K–12 and higher education institutions, and lobbied southern state bureaucrats, politicians, and local officials for funds. All the while, Sánchez promoted his idea of borrowing the cultural mission idea from Mexico and transplanting it to the United States. Many educators believed the lessons learned in Mexico could help in the education of minorities in the United States, particularly African Americans. This was an eye-opening experience. Later in the 1940s Sánchez reminisced that he knew little of African Americans before joining the Rosenwald Fund and learned a great deal in his limited time there.[10]

One of Sánchez's projects at Rosenwald was shaping its teacher-training program at the Louisiana Negro Normal and Industrial Institute at Grambling, now Grambling University. The sociologist Charles S. Johnson of Fisk University, who, like Sánchez, remained stubbornly optimistic about the possibility of gradual, progressive change in society, lauded this program as one of the most innovative efforts on behalf of African American education. Until the summer of 1937 Sánchez oversaw this program. He established its curriculum, its budget, and its specialized staff of nurses, agricultural instructors, home economists, and rural school supervisors; he even busied himself in the purchase of a bus for making school inspections. Getting things done required collaborating with African American educators and with white, segregationist Louisiana bureaucrats charged with overseeing the school. Sánchez, the Rosenwald Fund, and Grambling personnel expended much time and energy on this experimental teaching program, the larger story of which remains untold.[11]

How children in rural schools learned was Sánchez's professional niche. For example, the Rosenwald Fund's "Rote Learning Study," which originated with the sociologist Robert Park of the University of Chicago and his protégé Johnson sought to culturally enrich impoverished, rural African Americans more quickly and effectively than standard textbooks and pedagogies designed for more privileged white students. While not quite Ebonics, or African American vernacular English, of the late sixties and seventies, this project demonstrates how far reformers of the period took their social reconstructionist pedagogy. The investigators wanted to affiliate their study with the Tennessee Valley Authority, the ultimate symbol of the New Deal's modernizing impulse for rural America. Reputable scholars like Park, Johnson, the anthropologist Robert Redfield, and the noted African American historian Horace Mann Bond also joined the project.[12]

Sánchez's expertise with the bilingual schools of New Mexico and the socialistic schools of postrevolutionary Mexico vitally informed the study, which regarded its subjects as so untouched by modernity as to resemble peasants in distant locales speaking exotic languages. In theory, this project for rural southerners was as modernizing and nationalizing an endeavor as the cultural centers of Mexico. Johnson referenced Mexican education as a model for reforming the educational experience of African Americans. In the 1930s Sánchez argued that the cooperation between local communities and government could transform education. Like Johnson, he naïvely believed in the ability of society to educate away racial prejudice. Also like Johnson, he embraced more confrontational stances later. Johnson, then the director of Fisk University's Race Relations Institute and later the school's president, was quite taken by the implications this study had with regard to mitigating the poor school conditions rural African Americans experienced. To avoid the development of an alleged cultural deficiency stemming from hopelessness and despair, Johnson sought to enhance black schooling by beginning with the rural African American child's own personal matrix of experiences with discrimination and exploitation as a means of Americanizing them since, he postulated, "the Negro child in his present setting in the rural South is neither American, in terms of the democratic ideal, nor African, in terms of his cultural heritage."[13]

To most people today such an exoticized portrayal of African Americans rankles. Even by the late 1960s and 1970s, such evocative language rightly came to be regarded as offensive and condescending. Sánchez discussed the concept of race similarly. In describing his time at the Rosenwald Fund years later, he remarked in especially graphic language, "The community mores in most of the South then are beyond description to me. The miserable, stinking, stomach-turning schools offered the Negro (and the poor White, by the way) still haunt me in my nightmares. The repression, the abandonment, the lack of humaneness, was unbelievable. Here, indeed, was a community become animalistic. No longer a slave, the Negro was thrown on the dung heap—to fester, and to rot, and to stink. His community had become insane, criminally insane. And the end is not yet. Nor is that of the American of Mexican descent in the Southwest." Sánchez used such language not to humiliate African Americans but to attack the conditions forced on them by racists. What he meant by "animalistic" is clarified later, as is which "community" he referenced: "As I've indicated earlier, I got to know the U.S. American South—the Negro, the poor White, the White power structure. *¡Miserable!* How can one describe animalistic policy and practice? I can only reiterate the title of the great novel by the great Venezuelan writer, Rómulo Gallegos: *Pobre Negro.*" Elaborating on the spiritual toll of "White power," Sánchez echoed Frederick Douglass: "The poor whites, some poor economically, some better off, but all of them poor in their heads and in their souls—have paid, and are paying the price of bigotry, of racism. And they are paying more than is the Negro. If there ever was a sick community, that is it."[14]

One of Sánchez's duties was to lobby public officials over school funding equalization. The Rosenwald Fund actively supported schools for African Americans hit hard by the Depression. Yet they still needed southern state legislatures to raise levels of funding for these schools to survive. In November and December 1936 Sánchez spent two weeks in Louisiana, where he lobbied the state's education agency. He worked within the Jim Crow segregationist system instead of challenging it. But at that time equalization represented the pinnacle of the African American civil rights movement, culminating in the *Gaines v. Canada* decision of 1938, which mandated the University of Missouri to either admit black law students or create a separate state school for them. Equalization was the first step the NAACP took in challenging *Plessey v. Ferguson*. Most African American leaders, including Roosevelt's Black Cabinet, accepted segregation during the thirties as an unfortunate temporary reality to be ameliorated as much as possible. Thus working within Jim Crow in the decade was as far as the African American civil rights movement had pushed, and George I. Sánchez was right there with them.[15]

Begging on behalf of destitute African American schools during the Depression must have been frustrating for Sánchez, a feeling perhaps heightened by his own place in the racial hierarchy of the South. As a Mexican American with a somewhat exotic appearance, his own status in the minds of the audiences he lobbied likely gave him pause. Lynching in the South was, after all, still an ever-present reality and not limited to African Americans. He later reminisced about this experience: "I went into work with two fantastic communities— that of the southern Whites, and that of the Southern Negroes. As far apart as the poles. To them, fortunately, I was neither a White or a Negro—but a little of both." However he played his racial identity—whether it was to shade into whiteness for certain audiences or to emphasize racial otherness elsewhere— Sánchez occupied a racial no-man's-land in the deep South due to his Mexicanness. Little is know of black–brown relations of the thirties. One notable study documents Mexican American hostility to racial otherness, while another portrays a more ambivalent stance. Sánchez's experience seems mostly strategic.[16]

He nevertheless felt a calling to return to the Southwest. Despite his gratitude at being rescued from a difficult situation in New Mexico and his pride in the fascinating work he did for Rosenwald, Sánchez lamented that his employer was "virtually prohibited from extending its interests and experiments into the Southwest. This is the only disappointment I feel in connection to my present work. I feel it keenly, however, as you know how deeply I am bound up with that area and its peoples." Perhaps because Rosenwald expanded his horizons, Sánchez's ideas for a center on the education of bilinguals in the Southwest grew grander and went beyond the University of New Mexico, whose ability to construct such a program Sánchez began to doubt. He felt that schools of education were too unwieldy for the program he had in mind and that disciplines like sociology, economics, history, and anthropology needed inclusion in such a center.[17]

VENEZUELA

In the spring of 1937 Sánchez accepted, with the Rosenwald Fund's encouragement, what he thought would be a brief leave from the fund to consult for the Republic of Venezuela on overhauling its national educational system. He was excited about being a personal advisor to the government's minister of education. Originally planned for three months, the offer quickly expanded. Sánchez would eventually stay in Venezuela for a year as the director of the national teacher-training institute and as a technical advisor to the ministry. He accepted the offer with some trepidation at how unpredictably his career moved. In one revealing letter to the GEB's Favrot, Sánchez admitted things were not working out as planned. He offhandedly remarked, "Sometimes I get a little discouraged at the situation under which I work. Maybe I'm just hard to satisfy!" Perhaps this anxiousness had to do with marital difficulties. Sánchez's family left Chicago for Albuquerque ahead of him as he finished his work at Rosenwald. The official story was that they were to spend extra time in New Mexico before they all left for Venezuela. But Sánchez privately asked his old friend Carlos Castañeda, who was teaching at the University of New Mexico that year, if he and his family could check in on Virgie and the kids. Sánchez wrote, "She is quite ill and has to stay in New Mexico to convalesce before I can send for her. She has had a recurrence of an old trouble and has been undergoing a complete nervous breakdown." Castañeda earnestly assured his friend that he and his family would call on them as soon as possible, praying that the "relapse of her former malady" would soon end.[18]

Mental illness of any kind, if this is indeed what it was (there are no medical records to consult), is rarely discussed in an open, free manner today, much less three-quarters of a century ago. Whatever Virgie's "breakdown" as described by George was—the result of a debilitating aspect of her psyche, acute depression from an unhappy marriage to a workaholic spouse who uprooted her and her children from New Mexico, or possibly an overreaction by an unhappy husband in an increasingly quarrelsome union—correspondence indicates that Virgie Sánchez was reputed to be in fragile health. As Sánchez wrote his mentors for advice on the Venezuela job, Virgie vented her fears about her husband's career to Favrot. Though her original letter went unrecorded, Favrot wrote a long, indulgent response (he seemed to like Virgie very much) insisting that Rosenwald was not dismissing George, that they were quite happy with his

work, and that they encouraged the move. Favrot assured Virgie that they
would eventually make their way back to the Southwest and that a change might
be healthy. He closed, "I hope the children are well and that before long you
will be relieved of the temporary handicap from which you are suffering." The
Sánchez family's embarkation to Venezuela, like their departure from Chicago,
took place in phases and separately. While Virgie and the children went to New
Mexico in mid-June, George stayed in Chicago to tie up loose ends at work. He
spent hardly any time at all with his family in New Mexico before going to New
York City to ship out to Venezuela in the waning days of July. Virgie, George Jr.,
and Connie left from New Orleans in mid-September, assisted by the Rosenwald staff. As much as the office staff missed George, they missed Virgie
equally and thanked her for her kind wishes and parting gifts.[19]

Sánchez described to Embree his new role in setting up the national teacher-
training institute in Venezuela as "a 26-hour-a-day job!" The national educational
system was being overhauled during a brief period of liberal reform. Sánchez
claimed that of the 140,000 children enrolled in the public schools, 113,000
were in the first grade. And of 4,500 schools, only 5 percent were actually fit for
classroom purposes and 98 percent of the buildings were privately owned. He
addressed the dearth of trained teachers and administrators through his institutionalization of Mexican-style cultural missions. Adopting a colonizing perspective, Sánchez dismissively remarked to Embree that his efforts involved
"breaking down social prejudices, traditional apathy, obstructive habits (political and personal), and in-bred aimlessness." To Castañeda he was more blunt:
"The job here is interesting. It is like creating a nation—everything yet to be
done. Still, it is most challenging. My immediate task is that of organizing this
'Sala Técnica' and that of establishing a National Teachers College. As Director
of both of these enterprises, I have my hands full." He declared to Favrot, "This
task of acting 'little God' to a country just 'abornin' is most trying! Fascinating,
nevertheless." Sánchez's paternalistic perspective of Venezuela, compared to his
more sophisticated outlook on Mexico, is interesting. Because he went to Venezuela as an outsider, he perhaps stressed his Americanness in ways he would
have considered improper in Mexico. But his own nation soon complicated
such chauvinism. Sánchez controlled large sums of government funds to purchase school equipment and sought help from the U.S. consulate in identifying
an American firm. After making an appointment he was asked to wait in the
hall for over an hour while, in plain sight, the consulate read his morning newspaper. Sánchez blew his top. Apparently the official thought he was a Venezuelan
native. That such condescension followed the flag galled Sánchez no end and
possibly checked his own colonial predispositions.[20]

Sánchez developed contacts in Venezuela that he maintained for the rest of his life. In many respects Venezuela's educational overhaul was something of a Pan-Latino effort, a kind of Foreign Legion of Latin American educators converging in Venezuela at that time. The educators then in Sánchez's milieu later worked as faculty and administrators in Chile, Puerto Rico, Panama, the United States, Venezuela, and the Pan American Union. Though the model of educational reform Sánchez pursued was inherited from postrevolutionary Mexico, it developed a Pan-Latino patina in Venezuela.[21]

Sánchez stepped into a flush political context. He remarked to Embree, "This country is truly a paradox of financial super-abundance and popular starvation (literally). While the national budget is always much 'in the black' (no foreign debt, no taxes) and any department can overspend its budget by large sums, there is an astonishing lack of efficacy in the government's program. Teachers are on starvation wages, what passes for education is purely academic gymnastics." He requested of the Venezuelan cabinet approximately one-third more than the original education appropriation from before his arrival and was partially successful. Sánchez was proud that his schools instituted a free lunch program in Caracas, the nation's capital. He hoped to expand it nationally and to address the lack of access to medical care and health information in rural areas of the country. Sánchez talked about publishing an account of his work titled "Release from Tyranny." But Venezuela was merely transitioning from one authoritarian government to another; the political situation that had been so rosy in 1937 rapidly dissipated as the government tacked to the right. The Venezuelan Ministry of Education wanted Sánchez to stay for another year, but he confided to Embree, "The Venezuelan setup has been muddled again. The Cabinet under which I worked was considered too progressive so a more conservative one has been named. The Ministry of Education is in a bad state. While I hear that I'm to be called back, I haven't had an official call and doubt very much that it will be made. As a matter of fact, I'm not even counting on it as I can't reconcile the change in Ministers with a desire to carry out the program which I had inaugurated. So that is probably just that. It was a fine experience and no bones broken."[22]

However, this explanation rings hollow. Sánchez was never so doctrinaire a leftist as to be unable to accommodate a more conservative governing philosophy. Personal issues also played a role. Virgie's health collapsed. If her husband's correspondence is accurate, Virgie had a relapse of the vaguely asserted breakdown of before. Sánchez wrote to Embree about leaving Venezuela: "Virgie and the children are with me and are well. We had an enjoyable trip [back home to New Mexico by way of Cuba and Central America]—it did Virgie a great deal of good. The voyage was a fine remedy for another breakdown she suffered during our last month in Venezuela." Perhaps indicative that this was an emotional or psychological breakdown, Embree's immediate response pointedly refused to broach the subject. The timeline here is also instructive. Before May 1938 Sánchez only mentioned he would negotiate a new contract, not leave Venezuela. But the letters from May on are more about family than politics. To the GEB's Davis, with whom he was always more guarded, Sánchez discussed possibly returning to Venezuela without his family: "On June 10th my family and I are returning to New Mexico, via Colombia, Panama, and California. I expect to be in Albuquerque on July 12 to arrange for my family to stay there as, even though I return to Venezuela, my wife's health and the children's education demand that they stay on home grounds." To Zimmerman he cryptically mentioned his family was "rather tired of living in quiet isolation down here" and that "even if I return to Venezuela I shall leave the family in New Mexico— Virgie's health is to [sic] insecure to risk the inevitable stress and strain which results from life in the tropics." Zimmerman, who liked Virgie a great deal, oddly refused to comment on her condition. To Ruth Warren, a secretary at the Rosenwald Fund, Sánchez reported that Virgie had gained fifteen pounds since returning to New Mexico and that his family's happiness was his determining factor to forgo another year in Venezuela.[23]

Separation was painful for Sánchez. He joked with Castañeda that he was a bachelor for nearly four months at the end of his time with Rosenwald. After Venezuela became untenable, Sánchez remarked to Embree that his own health was better in New Mexico since he was freed from that stress: "The fishing in New Mexico has certain charms that are hard to resist—besides, I haven't been feeling quite up to par so have been trying to take the cure (between fishing trips, of course). I am just now beginning to feel more like myself than I have felt for six months—so anything can happen now!" "The cure" may have simply referred to rest and relaxation; but in the context of the letter, particularly with its reference to the usual drinking that can accompany fishing, that seems overly cautious. Virgie Sánchez's voice is not entirely absent with respect to this time. A year later she was prevailed upon to write of her experiences traveling around Latin America for the *LULAC News*. In two brief articles she complained of patriarchal customs, sassy servants, poor health, poorer food, outrageous prices, lazy and bewildered natives, and exasperation with husbands. She advised ladies, "Don't question hubby too closely when the bell-hop lugs him in at 3 a.m. He might tell the truth and hurt your feelings." The column was meant to be funny in that rollicking way George and Virgie had, but, in light of the backdrop of her health and unhappiness the year before, these columns take on an edgier tone with a coded exposition of long-simmering hurts and resentments.[24]

UNDEREMPLOYMENT IN NEW MEXICO

The demise of the Venezuelan position stalled Sánchez's career. Back in New Mexico he hustled from one speaking engagement to the next, shuffling between adjunct teaching jobs, grant proposals, and commissioned writing and dabbling in educational politics in a way that was just as controversial as before but without any semblance of protection. During this time Sánchez unsuccessfully sought the presidency of New Mexico Normal University in Las Vegas. Scheming for the big job was standard operating procedure for Sánchez. He was young, brash, and ambitious enough to turn heads; and if not always a serious candidate, he at least generated attention. While in Venezuela he plotted with Embree over administrative positions in the Puerto Rican Department of Education and at the University of Puerto Rico. The pair went so far as to urge Will Alexander, a longtime Rosenwald associate and prominent New Dealer, to discuss a possible Sánchez appointment with President Roosevelt (fig. 3.1).[25]

These schemes never came to anything, nor did a proposed book based on his Venezuelan experiences. Sánchez was treading water in a number of impermanent jobs between 1938 and 1940. To a friend he mentioned consulting opportunities, such as leading a Progressive Education Association tour of Latin America and other jobs: "Not doing much else—teach at the U. here and odd research jobs (Res. Associate for the State NYA) while I plan on what to do next. . . . There are two or three prospects for a satisfactory permanent position around here but, so far, I'm just marking time. Maybe I'll go into sheep herdin' one of these days. I have the 'dope' for a book on Venezuela—but can't take time off to do it (these part time jobs are bad—two ½ time jobs add up to 2 jobs except in salary!)" Sánchez is expressing in the thirties the common complaint of the adjunct instructor today. During these years Sánchez was without major foundation support. He pestered the GEB for what he referred to as "an independent research agency or a 'Public Conscience, Inc.' in this neck of the woods." Like the southern regionalists he admired, Sánchez sought rational social planning by enlightened governmental officials. Underscoring the point that the GEB was done with New Mexico, Favrot responded, "I don't think I agree with you that an independent research agency could help to improve the situation that you describe. I think improvements have to come from within, and through pressure exerted by a man like yourself who is competent to analyze the situation and point out defects."[26]

3.1. Sánchez early in his career, perhaps in
the late 1930s or early 1940s. Reproduction
by permission of Cynthia Kennedy from
her private family photo collection.

Sánchez plugged away. A long, dense essay he wrote while at Rosenwald, "The Community School in the Rural Scene," emerged in a national collection, *The Community School*, and advanced his academic reputation. In an article on the same theme for the Progressive Education Association, he criticized the nation for inadequately preparing rural schoolteachers. And he asserted himself more formally as a Mexican American leader. In 1939 his address to the national LULAC convention in San Antonio, titled "Minority Groups and Democracy," foreshadowed the loyalist tack of Mexican American civil rights groups during the Second World War. He lamented the forgotten plight of Mexican Americans: "No one is undertaking to pave the way for the work of these institutions. The schools, the agricultural agencies, the health bureaus, the 'New Deal' programs—all governmental services find their efforts handicapped by conditions that are outside their understanding or that are just beyond the fringe of their scope of action. In this region, as in other rural areas but in a more pronounced degree, there is a 'no man's land' in cultural rehabilitation." Another public venue for Sánchez was New Mexico's Coronado Cuarto Centennial Celebration of 1940, where he challenged the state's over-romanticizing of the past. Sánchez also worked with the U.S. State Department in its emphasis on the Good Neighbor policy. He hoped the State Department's Division of Cultural Relations would sponsor a Latin American institute at the University of New Mexico.[27]

Sánchez participated as well in planning a large gathering of activists in Albuquerque in March 1939 under the auspices of the Los Angeles–based Congreso del Pueblo de Habla Española. While the Congreso's labor activist founders, Josefina Fierro de Bright and Luisa Moreno, represented a more radical left perspective, Sánchez and others, such as his colleague Arthur Campa and the California labor activist Eduardo Quevedo, represented a more liberal position. The Albuquerque meeting never happened owing to local red-baiting of the organization. Realizing that some members might be communists or sensing an opportunity to curry favor with the more conservative voices in the Mexican American community, Sánchez loudly withdrew from his organizing role as the meeting inched closer. A few years later Sánchez urged the leftist writer Louis Adamic to be cautious in writing about the Congreso. Quevedo recalled years later that Sánchez and Campa resigned from the planning committee under duress from red-baiters. Decades later in a less than lucid letter, Sánchez remarked he had planned to infiltrate and destroy the Congreso from the beginning, though this fanciful notion is doubtful.[28]

But New Mexico politics beckoned to Sánchez like a siren's call. In late 1938 he argued that the equalization law of 1935 was sloppily administered or, as he personally suspected, applied in such a way as to shortchange Mexican American schoolchildren. Sánchez confessed to Favrot about having a "half-way regret that someone else didn't uncover this mess—but what can a fellow do? I may survive the animosities that will, of course, arise over the matter. Otherwise, I'll be looking for a hole to crawl into elsewhere!" Favrot, much as he liked Sánchez, could not bring himself to encourage yet another self-destructive crusade. In the *New Mexico Business Review* in January 1939 Sánchez charged that nearly one million dollars of surplus state funds generated through a combination of sales and income taxes were misappropriated by the Board of Education in ways that discriminated against Mexican Americans. The state board hastily arranged for a hearing, at which Sánchez presented his case, the result of which was the board's acknowledgment of their legal responsibility to more actively manage the minimum foundation requirement of the equalization law. Sánchez was victorious and soon published his findings academically. However, this episode likely rekindled distrust of him among the political establishment.[29]

FORGOTTEN PEOPLE

Without a doubt the single most important activity of Sánchez's final years in New Mexico was obtaining the support of the Carnegie Foundation for the book that eventually became his magnum opus, *Forgotten People: A Study of New Mexicans*. Nearly a decade's worth of New Deal–oriented, service intellectual life came together in this book. In it Sánchez dealt with the history of New Mexicans, what he argued was their cultural and economic stagnation at the time of the Great Depression, and his vision of changing the status quo through a more responsive government and a more educated citizenry. Anticipating the internal colonial model of Chicana/o scholars decades later, Sánchez insisted in *Forgotten People* that Mexican Americans did not choose poverty and discrimination for themselves; rather, they were forced upon them by a brutal, exploitive colonial past in which Spanish, Mexican, and then American rule consistently championed the wealthy and powerful over the poor and powerless. Whatever success some Hispanos achieved, he claimed, was more than offset by the fact that "the great masses of the people constitute a severely handicapped social and economic minority."[30]

Today it is obvious that Sánchez discounted human agency. Overemphasizing victimization was very much the new style of social science research which, in the United States during the 1930s, moved away from harsh, direct, hereditarian assessments of minority groups to more paternalistic, indirect, environmental assessments. Low minority educational achievement was thus attributed to flawed culture, which was deemed correctible, as opposed to flawed genetics, which was not. Sánchez was no stranger to applying these models, condescending as they appear today, to his own beloved *gente*. But to Sánchez this supposed backwardness of culture was the sad legacy of a lack of inclusion, of race prejudice, and of neglect by society and government. The answer was integration: "The New Mexican often carries on inferior and obsolete practices and beliefs because he has been permitted, and forced, to remain in isolation. Of necessity, he has persisted in a traditional way of life that is below current standards. His language has suffered disuse, yet he has had little chance to learn to use English effectively. His social status reflects his economic insufficiency. His lack of education handicaps him in the exercise of his political power. That same lack makes him a public charge once he has lost his land, his traditional source of livelihood. Midst the wreckage of his economy and his culture, and unprepared for the new order of things, he is pathetic in his helplessness—a stranger in his own home." Sánchez was still optimistic about Mexican Americans' future, however, as indicated by the epigraph above. To Sánchez, the culture that most needed reforming, according to *Forgotten People,* was the culture of poverty, neglect, and hopelessness. In this sense he articulates a modernist voice in Chicano thought that presciently anticipates later perspectives on discrimination, exploitation, and struggle.[31]

The background to *Forgotten People* was the Carnegie Foundation's desire to undertake a socioeconomic and educational study of Mexican Americans in the Southwest. It contracted with the University of New Mexico about such a project, and President Zimmerman turned to his underemployed protégé, who secured the grant. Sánchez was teaching courses as a part-time associate professor of education and a part-time university research associate. He was earning a living, but it was a living at Zimmerman's discretion without tenure or a stable academic niche. Sánchez took leave of his courses between February and October of 1939 to travel north to the impoverished Taos County along the upper Rio Grande and on the state's border with Colorado. Carnegie's $4,000 grant was sizeable enough to relieve Sánchez of teaching for a yearlong research project ($67,034.53 today).[32]

Sánchez believed his study was no mere report to be freely distributed without fanfare. The Carnegie Foundation, though their attention at that time was occupied by another study they sponsored, Gunnar Myrdal's future blockbuster *An American Dilemma: The Negro Problem and Modern Democracy,* which was published a few years later, agreed with Sánchez. Carnegie's motivation in this project was to sponsor adult education in New Mexico's poor communities. The project application called for $42,000 from Carnegie over three years to be spent on adult community education to be administered by the University of New Mexico and tied into cooperative work arrangements with state and county health and agricultural agencies, officials of the National Youth Administration and Works Progress Administration, the American Association for Adult Education, and a local philanthropy, the Harwood Foundation ($698,835.00 today). The book Sánchez wrote grew out of this action project report for Carnegie. It was vintage Sánchez: reform through effective coordination of various efforts did not necessitate ideological innovation, just a can-do attitude by existing entities. Once again Zimmerman enhanced the university's national profile by teaming with a major foundation for another cooperative venture. And once again, his young protégé Sánchez, only thirty-two years old at the beginning of the study, helmed the effort with skill and flair. Carnegie was so impressed with the report that its director, Francis Keppel, authorized an additional $1,000 beyond the grant as a subvention to be applied to the cost of publishing *Forgotten People* through an academic press ($16,638.93 today).[33]

THE UNIVERSITY OF TEXAS

Forgotten People opened doors for the ambitious Sánchez. Zimmerman, who one suspects toiled long and hard to find the funds to keep Sánchez around after his return from Venezuela, had promised Sánchez a tenured professorship. A professorship, however, was a far cry from directing an independent, national research agency to study Mexican Americans, the idea they had once brainstormed. But even this lowered expectation was no longer viable by 1940. Apparently, the best Zimmerman could do after two years of adjunct duty on Sánchez's part was to offer him a nonfaculty assistantship to the dean of the College of Education, Simon P. Naninga. Sánchez felt terribly let down. Immediately after Venezuela, Sánchez's academic career was still gelling—one book and some articles and book chapters. But now Sánchez's prestigious work with Carnegie and forthcoming *Forgotten People* no longer fit his unglamorous day job and made him a target of a wealthier, ambitious school.[34]

That school was the University of Texas. Its new president, Homer P. Rainey, sought to turn his bucolic southern state school into a national academic powerhouse by following the model of the University of California at Berkeley during the twenties and thirties. This meant hiring young academic stars. Sánchez, with his Berkeley doctorate, fit the bill. He was on the market for any offers involving a faculty line with academic rank, preferably tenure and promotion beyond the assistant level, and a decent salary. Castañeda hinted strongly in the summer of 1939 of Texas's interest. These hints evolved into conversations that fall when Sánchez's old professors Frederick Eby, Clarence T. Gray, and Herschel T. Manuel began assembling a position from which to attract their former pupil. In informal negotiations Sánchez indicated to Castañeda he wanted $4,000 in salary and a tenured faculty line, though he was willing to give on salary (Castañeda's suggestion) for a more senior professorship ($66,555.71 today). In January 1940 the University of Texas finalized a contract for Sánchez, and he signed it on April 1, 1940. He began his official employment on September 15 that next fall. The position Sánchez accepted was a joint one at $3,600 salary, half from the History and Philosophy of Education Department and half from the Educational Psychology Department ($59,900.14 today). But to offset the lower salary he started as a full professor and was expected to be highly involved with the university's new Institute of Latin American Studies. His title was Professor of Latin American Education and he often referred to being the chair of Latin American education, though that designation was entirely honorific.[35]

After Castañeda, the person at the University of Texas most excited to have Sánchez as a colleague had to be Manuel. Since the late 1920s Manuel had led an informally organized research project on Latin American children at the University of Texas. He produced a legion of graduate students and early environmentalist studies on Mexican American testing and school performance. He sat on over sixty master's theses from the late 1920s to the end of the Second World War on Mexican American education. Sánchez was the obvious choice to complement and eventually succeed Manuel. Sánchez later remarked, "When I came here it was with the understanding that I would take over the work in the education of Spanish-speaking children previously done by Dr. Manuel, and to inaugurate the new field of Education in Latin America." That a Chicana/o scholar was the subject of a faculty raid within academia in that era of obvious structural racism toward minorities is a phenomenal achievement.[36]

Leaving New Mexico was difficult. Sánchez's allies viewed his departure as a blow. Albuquerque LULAC council number 34 put forward a resolution on May 7, 1940, to "strongly recommend and urge the Board of Regents of the University of New Mexico to do everything within their power, and if possible establish a policy, with the end of creating a position for Dr. Sánchez, worthy of his ability, so that he may return to the Educational System of the State of New Mexico at the end of his contract year with the University of Texas." The board responded that Zimmerman kept Sánchez on unpaid leave for a year to retain his junior, untenured position for him in order to facilitate a quick, easy return should he have a change of heart. Undated petitions to keep Sánchez bore over two hundred names. Many, but not all, were Spanish and came from Hispano areas. Whatever Sánchez's impatience in challenging an entrenched, racist political system, he was clearly well liked by professional educators throughout the state and by students and faculty at the University of New Mexico. He quickly left town to teach summer school at the University of Southern California from mid-June to the end of August and then traveled straight to Austin for the fall term. A letter to the *Albuquerque Tribune* lamented New Mexico's loss. The writer asked, "Why has he not received the recognition from New Mexico that he has received elsewhere? Why does he hold only a professorship at this University? The answer is a disgrace. There are a sufficient number of so-called educators on the faculty and connected with the University otherwise, 'outsiders' saturated with jealousy and intolerance, who have prevented Dr. Sánchez and others of his caliber from being honored as they deserve." Sánchez always considered moving back. In his first year in Austin, Zimmerman floated the idea that he direct a planned Latin American studies program. This possibility hinged on the usual stingy legislative appropriations as well as on hoped-for GEB subsidies. It came to nothing. The initiative to go back to New Mexico always rested with Sánchez, and professionally he always stood to lose more than to gain by doing so.[37]

The late 1930s were a momentous time for George I. Sánchez. After being pushed out of a high-profile state job, he published books and articles, obtained major grants, and worked far and wide as an educational expert. By the end of this decade he had built a national and international reputation as an activist-scholar for all peoples, regardless of race, class, language, or nation. Sadly, in order to be recognized for his accomplishments he was forced to leave his beloved New Mexico. Sánchez's career in the 1930s opens a window into the world of academic activism at the high tide of leftist reform during the New Deal as seen through the eyes of a Chicana/o pioneer in academia. Sánchez was neither insular nor unsophisticated. He ranged near and far as an academic activist, working in a variety of communities in the United States and around the world. Early Mexican American leaders and activists, as George I. Sánchez exemplifies, are far more interesting than we once realized.

Part Two

1940s

4

SÁNCHEZ'S WAR OF IDEAS
1940–1944

I can't emphasize this too much. Every day I am under pressure to bring the matter [racial discrimination] into the open for a public airing—a procedure fraught with danger to all concerned. I am resisting this pressure and will continue to do so even to the point of losing the goodwil [*sic*] of the group which, for many years, I have defended and sponsored. Already there are elements that despair of governmental attention except through the creation of an unsavory public "scene." Personally, I view these tendencies with both fear and deep sorrow. These people are fundamentally loyal and well-meaning but, after all, they are becoming desperate at a seemingly impossible and unjust situation.

The Second World War was one of the busiest and most damaging times of George I. Sánchez's life. He took advantage of opportunities to expand his burgeoning national reputation through government service. Yet he experienced the limits of that civic participation in that the nation he loved was not willing to lay aside racism in order to achieve wartime unity. The war almost destroyed Sánchez. When the war began he was an up-and-coming academic with a young family and a bright future at a university that regarded him highly; by war's end he was emotionally burned out, physically disabled, distressed by a broken marriage, and working at a university that no longer valued his activist scholarship. Scholars often discuss the Mexican American military experience of the Second World War and postwar activism, but, apart from labor and immigration topics, the wartime home front remains understudied. The world of education is especially understudied. What public schools taught about Latin America and, more specifically, Mexican Americans became a key element of Chicana/o organization and activism during the Second World War. Recent works provide a framework for understanding this vein of activism, but none is as instructive as George I. Sánchez's war of ideas.[1]

I analyze here how Sánchez the scholar fought over the war's meaning. Inserting Mexican Americans into the national understanding of the wartime Good Neighbor policy and advancing the idea that Mexican Americans represented a domestic corollary to the Good Neighbor policy became Sánchez's central goal. The fight against racist, fascist, imperial powers abroad did not end there. How Latin Americans were treated at home was an extension of it. Sánchez pushed this notion by editing a children's textbook series with a prestigious national publishing company and through his presidency of LULAC. He wrote a monograph on Mexican higher education for the Carnegie Foundation as a way to advance Good Neighborism. And he sought to take his war of ideas into a military domain that, crushingly, exposed the limits of how far someone like him was allowed to participate.

THE FLEETING ACADEMIC LIFE

Sánchez's first year at the University of Texas was a purely academic existence for the first time in his career. He enjoyed the fellowship of his colleagues while the academic rhythm of teaching and research filled his days. He had finally found the position of top rank and tenure that had long eluded him. During his first semester Sánchez wrote to Embree at the Rosenwald Fund that his initial service work at the university—inaugurating a field school in the South Texas border town of Laredo for local teachers—was a good candidate for Rosenwald funding. Surprisingly, Sánchez knew little about the South Texas borderlands and was impressed by its potential for intercultural education and research. Embree was delighted that his protégé had finally found a home, though he remained uninterested in picking up where they had left off.[2]

Sánchez was happy. He held a split appointment in the Department of Educational Psychology under Clarence T. Gray and the Department of History and Philosophy of Education under Frederick Eby. In the 1890s Eby had studied under John Dewey at the University of Chicago and G. Stanley Hall at Clark University, two luminaries of the progressive education movement. He obtained his doctorate from Clark in 1900. Sánchez fondly regarded Eby's "intellectualism, his independence, his forthrightness, and his fearlessness." These qualities could be mistaken for "coldness and belligerence," Sánchez remembered decades later. The two must have cut quite a contrast, a topic Sánchez dwelled on in a memorial in 1968: "He brought me to the University of Texas in 1940. He was a devout Baptist, I a so-so Catholic. His tendency was towards pacifism, mine was militant. He saw history one way, I another. It would appear that we were absolutely incompatible intellectually. However, in our association of twenty-eight years we did not have one even minor disagreement." While not paid at the same rate as older, senior professors in either department, Sánchez was satisfied. His total salary was $3,600 for his first academic year, 1940–41, and it remained there until he was given a $400 increase in the 1942–43 academic year ($59,900.14 and $5,716.44 today). Through parts of 1943 and 1944 Sánchez was on unpaid leave while serving the government in various administrative capacities. This was one of the most productive periods in his career and resulted in a monograph, textbooks, academic articles, and outstanding professional service. He had use of a full-time secretary and an administrative assistant as a part of his start-up package. His specialty was the study of education in Latin America and of Latin Americans in the United States, subjects he took over in 1940 from Manuel and continued until his death in 1972 (fig. 4.1).[3]

4.1. Sánchez, smiling broadly, assumes his new position as a professor at the University of Texas in the 1940s. Reproduction by permission of Cynthia Kennedy.

As happy as Sánchez was at the University of Texas, he had not forfeited his ambition. In his second year there he explored becoming chancellor of the University of Puerto Rico. He consulted with Embree and James Shotwell of Carnegie over the matter. Embree was close to Rexford Tugwell, the Columbia University professor and prominent New Dealer who was elevated to the governorship of Puerto Rico from his previous post as chancellor at the University of Puerto Rico. In 1941 and 1942 Sánchez and Pedro Cebollero, a former colleague from Venezuela and then at the University of Puerto Rico's College of Education, traded gossip about the job, informally debated a media campaign, and discussed how best to navigate the sensitive issue of Puerto Rican independence. Sánchez's contacts with foundations, prominent New Dealers, and local and national educators indicate that he was at least a plausible candidate.[4]

Sánchez fit quite well with respect to one of the great concerns of the University of Texas at that time, their new Institute for Latin American Studies. In 1940 the Office of Coordinator of Inter-American Affairs (CIAA), headed by Nelson Rockefeller, allocated up to $37,500 for the creation of the institute ($623,959.82 today). That Sánchez was an intimate of the Rockefeller-derived GEB made his fit within the new institute that much more cozy. Sánchez led a bifurcated existence as a genial, cheerleading sort of scholar with regard to educational trends in Latin America while simultaneously switching to a more critical, activist perspective where the treatment of Latinas/os in the United States was concerned.[5]

The Second World War engulfed all this. There is little in his correspondence to indicate Sánchez's personal reaction to the attack on Pearl Harbor. His professional reaction, though, is very clear. As the events unfolded, Sánchez and his LULAC allies sprang into action, adopting a manner similar to that of the NAACP's two-front strategy—the Double V campaign—which simultaneously targeted fascism abroad and racism at home. Days after Pearl Harbor Sánchez and other Mexican American leaders traveled to Washington to meet with government officials to pledge their loyalty and willingness to sacrifice and also to propose a plan for the federal government to ensure their rights as citizens. Sánchez urged the creation of a Latin American Research and Policies Commission to focus on what he argued were the three million "orphan people" subject to "discriminatory practices in wage scales and employment procedures, in education, [and] in the exercise of civil rights." Claiming that Mexican Americans "live in a veritable concentration camp," Sánchez complained that New Deal federal policy was used primarily "to heighten their isolation and ostracism and to accentuate inequalities and their position of underprivilege." Sánchez applied directly to Rockefeller's new CIAA on December 31 of that year, weeks after he and his delegation of LULACers met with Rockefeller, Undersecretary of the Interior John Dempsey, Assistant Secretary of the Interior Oscar Chapman, Will Alexander of the Office of Production Management, and Vice President Henry Wallace. Sánchez and the LULAC delegation wanted government support for such a commission to the tune of $71,000 ($1,125,108.50 today). The CIAA did not act on this bold proposal.[6]

Sánchez increased his already heavy university service commitment during the war as well as his teaching duties. During his first two years at the University of Texas Sánchez had teaching assistants every semester for his largest classes and, in his first year, no summer teaching. His service during the 1941–42 academic year, his second year, involved a full load of departmental committee work, an active role on the executive committee of the new Institute of Latin American Studies, and directing the Laredo field school in the summer. By his reckoning this accounted for 240 hours of his time during the academic year. His administrative load in 1942–43, however, more than tripled to 870 hours owing to his role as director of the university's new Inter-American Relations Committee. That year he also carried additional coursework without teaching assistants. By the fall of 1943 Sánchez took a paid leave from teaching to work on his many governmental obligations as part of the war effort; at the end of 1943 he turned that limited leave into a longer, open-ended, unpaid leave for civilian wartime administration with the federal government. After pining for a traditional academic post for almost a decade, Sánchez had finally gotten one at the University of Texas only to enjoy just one normal academic year before the war effectively froze his salary, increased his workload, and led him away from those treasured academic rhythms.[7]

THE INTER-AMERICAN SERIES

George Sánchez contributed to the war effort through a school textbook series with the Macmillan Publishing Company. In fighting the war with his pen, Sánchez decried the nefarious influence of fascism in Mexico, proclaimed the importance of hemispheric solidarity, and elevated the role of education in advancing freedom and democracy. Many educators and authors in the United States felt a duty to promote social change during the war. And emphasizing cultural equality, often called intercultural education, resonated with the need for hemispheric solidarity. One intercultural education advocate articulated its goals as first learning about concepts of race, class, culture, democracy, and religion, then confronting intolerance in the classroom, and finally emphasizing intercultural education in all content areas. This was about making more and better citizens. And it encouraged the study of foreign languages, a casualty of the First World War. The seeds of this movement were manifest in the 1930s with Roosevelt's Good Neighbor Policy. In 1938 the State Department created a whole division to promote such notions. What some called Pan Americanism, inter-Americanism, and Good Neighborism were hemispheric cousins to the domestically centered intercultural movement. Sánchez eagerly sought to engage this intellectual mood. Before the end of his first year at the University of Texas, Sánchez and P. A. Knowlton, the editor in chief at Macmillan, were in contact about capitalizing on the Good Neighbor mood. Knowlton felt that Sánchez was exactly the person Macmillan needed to successfully publish a national textbook series "in the field of Spanish and the still larger but less well-defined area of inter-American relations," the Inter-American Series. The national influence of Texas's textbook adoption process opened doors for Sánchez, as Knowlton had already been working on the Texas market.[8]

Sánchez recruited university instructors and K–12 teachers and administrators, taking care to ensure that each book maintained a diversity of authors and editing all the manuscripts for a general 1 percent royalty apart from any specific royalties he received for personal authorship. President Rainey encouraged Sánchez to pursue this opportunity. Macmillan advertised the initial run of four books for grades three through six as furnishing a foundational basis of Latin American life and geography. The Inter-American Series involved *The Day Before Yesterday in America* by A. O. Bowden, Carmen González de Porter, Prudence Cutright, and W. W. Charters for grade three, *The Lands of Middle America* by Carlos E. Castañeda and Eleanor C. Delaney for grade four, *Spanish Gold* by Delaney, Sánchez, Cutright, and Charters for grade five, and *Our Friends in South America* by Glenn Ross Barr, Willis K. Jones, and Delaney for grade six. *The Day Before Yesterday in America* dealt with Native American anthropology and history, *The Lands of Middle America* surveyed the geography of Mexico, Central America, and the Caribbean, and *Our Friends in South America* was a geographic survey of South America. The series additionally generated a high school textbook by Samuel Guy Inman and Castañeda, *A History of Latin America for Schools*. The authors firmly believed their work furthered the wartime ethos of Pan Americanism.[9]

In addition to his general editing duties, two books involving Sánchez as an author stand out as fascinating interpretations of the national wartime mood. *Latin America: Twenty Friendly Nations* emphasized multiculturalism in its social studies content. The history section on the independence period, for example, predictably compared Latin America with the United States in a negative light, though the authors' explanations stressed the legacies of poverty, oppression, isolation, and the persistence of warfare as the root causes. As far as Macmillan was concerned, however, the most controversial aspect of the Inter-American Series was its extension of Good Neighborism to the United States. This theme is best exemplified in *Spanish Gold*. The gold in this book was the thriving Hispanic culture already present in the United States and discovered by two young cousins, John and Patty, who traveled the nation with their Uncle Jim, an artist. Journeying from Puerto Rico to Florida, then Texas, New Mexico, and California, John and Patty meet Latino children, ride burros, and engage in all manner of intercultural interactions that relentlessly hammer the point that Latin Americans already lived within the United States and that they were all right. *Spanish Gold* transcends the wartime mood. It is about dispelling racial prejudice and bridging social and cultural difference. Sánchez had to fight to get this book approved because Macmillan sensed it would generate controversy in Jim Crow states.[10]

The Inter-American Series was plagued with problems. An administrator for the Corpus Christi Independent School District, Edmundo E. Mireles, was a key author for the series. He had a manuscript in hand that was perfect for the all-important Texas public school textbook market. However, Mireles reneged on his commitment once a quicker, local publishing option emerged. Sánchez had counted on his old friend Arthur L. Campa of the University of New Mexico to helm grammar textbooks Macmillan had already commissioned. Campa energetically threw himself into the project and did not balk when Sánchez, apologetically and under orders from Macmillan, asked him to accept additional coauthors on his manuscript and inserted him as a coauthor of another one. But Campa was soon drafted into the military. Castañeda, a workhorse originally slotted for multiple books, ended up having little time for the project after becoming an investigator for the Roosevelt administration's Fair Employment Practices Commission (FEPC). As Sánchez and the young James Michener, the future best-selling novelist then working as an associate editor at Macmillan and assigned to the Inter-American Series, dealt with the usual cranky authors, deadlines, excuses, revisions, and disputes inherent to such a large publishing enterprise, they traded brief asides about volunteering for the military, which Michener did in 1942. One big concern was a paper shortage. The official contracts to the authors issued in the spring of 1942 contained a war clause that obliged the publisher to curtail the production or sale of any book owing to paper rationing mandates. Macmillan exercised its war clause powers to slow down production on the series. The publisher had to cut its paper use in 1944 to 75 percent of 1942 levels; in 1945 that target hovered between 60 and 65 percent. The delay was most unfortunate for the

Inter-American Series. Despite some good reviews, the multicultural mood quickly burned out.[11]

LULAC

George I. Sánchez was the national president of the League of United Latin American Citizens (LULAC) for a yearlong term in 1941–42. LULAC was the largest Mexican American activist organization during these years. The war gave the league an unprecedented opportunity to articulate its message of self-help, patriotism, and civic engagement; and it was one of their lowest membership ebbs because of Mexican Americans' military service and internal migration to wartime industries. Many LULAC councils disbanded, bringing to a sharp end the first mobilization stage of the organization's history, during which it grew without pause since its founding in 1929. Even Sánchez's successor as national president, Benjamin Osuna of New Mexico, had his term disrupted by military service. LULAC was quite active despite its small, perilous state. And LULAC's agenda during the war owed much to Sánchez's planning and vision.[12]

Mexican Americans everywhere took action. Shortly after Pearl Harbor, Sánchez and his fellow LULAC officers M. C. Gonzales and Perales visited with the Washington officials Rockefeller, Alexander, and others to discuss the idea of a Latin American Research and Policies Commission. Speaking officially as the president general of LULAC on that occasion, Sánchez alerted Rockefeller and other U.S. officials of Mexican Americans' willingness to serve their country. As unmoved as many of these federal officials were on the commission idea, their participation in this meeting was an acknowledgment of how global conflict gave Mexican Americans a newfound importance. In one letter (from which the epigraph above is taken), Sánchez had to explain to Rockefeller that he walked a tightrope in trying to satisfy Mexican Americans' demands for equality on the one hand and avoiding divisiveness that might hamper the war effort on the other. As Sánchez sounded the attentive, gracious Uncle Tom for officials in Washington in this communication, he simultaneously forwarded a protest by three Mexican American veterans of the First World War who met with discrimination at a restaurant in Texas. Sánchez walked a fine line playing both the mediator and the instigator.[13]

Sánchez imbued Mexican American experiences with global realities by stressing Good Neighborism. Sánchez had been energetically making this link for some time. In 1938, during the planning of the 400th anniversary celebration of Coronado in New Mexico, he wrote that the American Southwest "is unusually well equipped to participate in any cultural open door program with our southern neighbors." Sánchez was not alone in pairing internal and external concerns of the United States. Older LULAC leaders like José de la Luz Sáenz joined him in this. So did Virgie Sánchez, as LULAC's first lady. She visited women's club meetings such as the Pan American Roundtable and the League of Women Voters. To the latter group Virgie gave a speech urging Texans to stand together in the national crisis. She drily noted that the Civil War and the War with Mexico had been over for many years. Virgie also spearheaded activities sponsored by LULAC, such as benefit teas, toy drives, and dinners. She and George often spoke together at such events.[14]

The U.S. State Department sought to meet wartime labor demands through the bracero agreement with Mexico in 1942. In this agreement Mexico supplied the United States with provisional laborers in an environment regulated by both nations. Incidents of racial discrimination, particularly in Texas, which was blacklisted by Mexico from the agreement, complicated that mission. In an effort to placate Mexico and a nervous State Department, Governor Coke Stevenson of Texas in 1942 responded to the blacklist by creating the Texas Good Neighbor Commission (GNC), the aim of which was to placate the Mexican government enough that it would lift its ban. Sánchez and other LULACers, despite their emphasis on citizenship for organizing the Mexican American community, worked hard to utilize the Mexican government's newfound and, from the perspective of many Anglo Texans, shocking assertiveness regarding the treatment of its citizens. William P. Blocker, the U.S. consulate general for Ciudad Juárez, regarded LULAC with hostility and suspicion. He reported to Washington his suspicions that Sánchez and other LULAC officials like Gonzales, the organization's secretary and an attorney for the Mexican consulate in San Antonio, manufactured outrage with the ultimate aim of discrediting the U.S. government during the wartime crisis. Blocker nursed a deep resentment over Gonzales's dual role as Mexican American activist and Mexico's legal counsel. Blocker intimated that LULAC leaked sensitive FEPC investigative information in order to rile Mexico. For Sánchez and his allies this was a tricky, dangerous game of playing off the concerns of a foreign government against one's own government in a time of war.[15]

In response to Blocker's lengthy report on the first meeting of Governor Stevenson's GNC, Assistant Secretary of State Adolph Berle Jr. wrote that he hoped LULAC would begin to back off complaints after gaining some attention: "It is gratifying to note that Dr. Sánchez hopes to change the attitude of the LULAC society from one of agitation and criticism to one of cooperation and encouragement of those concerned to accept the responsibilities of citizenship and to do everything possible to avoid inviting discrimination." Berle hoped that LULAC would just sit down and clap louder, that their complaints had caused enough fuss, and that they would refrain from taking offense or, at the very least, from publicizing it. Blocker's elaborations on the "Latin psychology" were even more insulting. He felt that Texans should mend Jim Crow, not end it: "I pointed out that some cases that had been presented to us were pure and simple cases of class distinction, although they had been classed as racial discrimination, and I felt that if the committee could succeed in convincing not only the Mexican consular service, but the LULAC society and other societies of Latin-American citizens to draw a line between racial discrimination and class distinction as is customarily applied in Mexico and other Latin-American countries, I felt that it would assist the committee in ironing out a large number of grievances that will, unfortunately, be presented to it from time to time." Blocker's desire that Latinos more precisely understand their feudal vassalage in a Texan *herrenvolk* democracy turns the issue of discrimination back on its victims.[16]

Complaints by Mexican Americans to the GNC, particularly those of Gonzales and Perales, were routinely forwarded to the State Department. As LULAC had intended, this internationalized what were really domestic civil rights. When a restaurant near an East Texas refining company refused to serve the LULAC attorney John J. Herrera and the Mexican consul of Houston Adolfo Dominguez as they investigated factory complaints, the laconic Governor Stevenson actually exerted himself to defuse the situation. Undersecretary of State Sumner Welles, arguably the most powerful shaper of U.S. foreign policy early in the war, expressed frustration over this incident. Stevenson denied any discrimination at the plant or anywhere else in the area and apologized for the fact that the waitress at the Blue Moon Café did not recognize the Mexican dignitary's status. Like Blocker, Stevenson did not necessarily want ill treatment of the right sort of higher-class *Mexicanos*.[17]

The State Department was uniformly unsympathetic to the plight of Mexican Americans and Mexican workers. U.S. Consul of Monterrey Henry S. Waterman excitedly reported that a Mexican consul of Galveston, Texas, in a speech at a Rotary Club in Monterrey lambasted the zoot suiters of Los Angeles. Waterman pressed the sly official to allow his remarks to be printed, but to no avail. Blocker constantly wrote to Washington with dark assessments, among them the following: "More and more I am convinced that Mr. M. C. Gonzales and Mr. Alonso S. Perales, and probably Dr. George Isidore Sánchez, of the University of Texas, are responsible for the majority of the cases that have been filed by the Mexican Embassy with the Department." He was convinced that

LULAC pursued racial agitation over national unity. Other officials at the State Department belittled and mocked LULAC members as little more than nuisances with overactive imaginations.[18]

And they spied on Mexican Americans. One of Sánchez's research assistants at the University of Texas was a mole for the State Department. Pauline Kibbe, who later published a book on the subject, reported on Sánchez and Gonzales to Blocker. She complained to him that Gonzales masterminded the Mexican consul incident at the café and that Sánchez allowed Gonzales, who, she sniffed, was "the most heartily hated man in Texas" and also "in complete disfavor with the Governor," to speak at public meetings about Good Neighborism. Kibbe claimed to have threatened to resign unless Sánchez replaced Gonzales on Good Neighbor programs. To Blocker she urged that Gonzales be "removed" from the issue and LULAC be "discouraged" by the federal government. While she spied on Sánchez, Kibbe wrote reports for him on discriminatory conditions throughout Texas that deemphasized the severity and impact of racism and seemed more concerned with black–brown fraternization than with the prejudicial conditions both experienced.[19]

Sánchez and LULAC officials were brokers between the government and the governed. Though LULAC is axiomatically criticized for their caution, one must realize that they were in dangerous positions. To exert pressure on civil rights, they enlisted a foreign government—and a not always friendly one at that—in the middle of a terrible conflict. This had the potential to expose them to the kinds of attacks that could destroy lives and careers. They knew this and still took action. Contrary to scholars who criticize LULAC and other Mexican American Generation activists as overly deferential to white power and to maintaining a privileged status within their communities, they did transmit the discrimination complaints of working-class Chicanas/os throughout the country. This is reflected by the complaints Sánchez forwarded. The notes sent to the professor—some typed, others not; some in English, others in Spanish—illustrate how LULAC, during the Second World War, acted on complaints made by the entire Chicana/o community, no matter how small the place or unknown *la gente*. Their people needed no badges.[20]

Sánchez constantly confronted officials who were practicing or presiding over racial discrimination. He gave talks to national education conferences about the racial segregation of Mexican American children in the schools as doing "more harm to Pan-Americanism than a shipload of Nazi agents." The Zoot Suit situation in Los Angeles especially drew his ire. Before the severe disturbances broke out he wrote to the Office of War Information of his concern that the racist proceedings of the Sleepy Lagoon case in Los Angeles sent a horrible message. He complained that press accounts of the "blood lust" of "Aztec forebears" indicated that the Los Angeles grand jury was going "off on a tangent" and "witch hunting." Sánchez protested to the City of Austin that its selective service board classified Mexicans as a separate race rather than as an ethnicity; in any case, the process was flawed, he argued, because officials just went by the sound of the name anyway. Some complaints, however, Sánchez turned back. To one LULACer from California angry about braceros, Sánchez responded that the cooperation of Mexico in leveraging civil rights at home was too important to risk via impolitic protests over its bracero deal.[21]

THE DEVELOPMENT OF HIGHER EDUCATION IN MEXICO

Between 1943 and 1945 Sánchez published on the state of Mexican education. In one article he argued that higher education in Mexico suffered from curricular backwardness and administrative anarchy, though recent sensible reforms bore positive effects. Despite the need to continue embracing modernity, Sánchez felt that Mexican universities needed to also maintain the humanistic glory inherited from the sixteenth century. He was unsatisfied with articles, however. Only two years removed from *Forgotten People*, Sánchez went back to the Carnegie Endowment for International Peace with a book project on Mexican higher education. James Shotwell, the director of Carnegie's Division of Economics and History, wanted Sánchez for an entirely research-oriented project. In May 1941 he approved a $2,500 grant for Sánchez to conduct three months of research in Mexico leading to a report in March 1942 ($39,616.50 today). Sánchez used the grant to pay for a teaching assistant to cover his classes in the summer and fall of 1941, to pay for clerical assistance, and to travel to libraries in Morelia, Guadalajara, and Mexico City. Carnegie felt the report encouraged Good Neighborism in the academic community.[22]

Sánchez was excited about the Mexican intellectual scene in 1941 and 1942. He used his Carnegie research to inject himself more fully into that world and wrote to President Rainey in January 1942 that the immediate postrevolutionary ideological chasm between left and right was dissipating, a wartime response that aided Pan Americanism. Sánchez confessed that his prior fears of "facistic [sic] tendencies in the educational and political sphere" were eased after his participation in the First Congress on National Education in Mexico City. He gleefully noted, "Such men as José Vasconcelos, notorious for his dissatisfaction with us and exponent of what might be regarded as un-American ideas took the lead in supporting the position that, in terms of ideals and cultural purposes, we are one." He was tickled to participate in a roundtable discussion he felt represented the conference's intellectual aspirations on "the thought that *mestizaje* (amalgamation, fusion, reciprocal incorporation), sometimes in the biological sense but always in the spiritual sense, is a dominant and worthwhile characteristic of Americanism. At the same time, cultural pluralism and the rights of minority groups to form a part of and to contribute to society was supported as an American ideal and as a worthwhile educational motive." Older historical interpretations that leaders in the Mexican American Generation internalized a harsh, self-loathing cultural assimilation do not resonate with how Sánchez in the thirties and forties borrowed from Latin American intellectuals to arrive at conceptions of cultural pluralism and *mestizaje*.[23]

After submitting his report to Carnegie in 1942, Sánchez formally asked about turning it into a small book. The project's central tension was between Sánchez's desire to more deeply explore the left–right political divide in Mexican higher education and Shotwell's preference to keep a lid on any potentially explosive ideological disputes that might spoil the intended goodwill. Though one manuscript reporter, Irving Kandel of Columbia University's Teachers College, was very positive, the other, the Mexican scholar Silvio Zavala, reacted negatively to Sánchez's critique of the Catholic Church. So Shotwell insisted the study limit itself to extolling the virtues and glorious past of Mexican universities. While not exactly what he wanted to write, this was not entirely beyond Sánchez's interests. Sánchez accordingly softened his interpretations, and Shotwell sent the manuscript, *The Development of Higher Education in Mexico*, to King's Crown Press, a division of Columbia University Press. The Carnegie Foundation provided a small subvention of $500 to cover the cost of a limited printing of four hundred copies, one hundred of which went directly to Carnegie ($7,145.55 today).[24]

The Development of Higher Education in Mexico came out in 1944 to limited distribution. It described the creation of Mexican higher education at a time when the Spanish renaissance was cresting in sunny brilliance and the New World was scarcely a gleam in the eyes of dour Englishmen in their dark, dank castles who were coming off a dismal century-long civil war and massive territorial losses on the continent. Mexico needed some reform. But, sensitive to the long centuries of humanistic instruction in its centers of higher learning, Sánchez stipulated that such reform was "neither a denial of Mexico's cultural heritage nor an attempt to inject some foreign 'ism' into Mexican policy." And far too defensively, though one imagines in a silent nod to the negative report, Sánchez stiltedly stated, "Mexico can be a Catholic country and still be a modern, progressive, and intelligent country." *The Development of Higher Education in Mexico*, while a useful narrative about a neglected topic, was not

Sánchez's best work. It was hastily written with a heavy editorial hand by its sponsor. Nevertheless, it was positively reviewed and represented the third monograph of Sánchez's first decade beyond the doctorate—a very good professional start in any era.[25]

"NO VACANCIES" IN THE NAVY

The war galvanized Sánchez and many of his colleagues to do more for their country. Even Sánchez's contact from the Carnegie Endowment for International Peace wrote bellicosely. By 1942 several friends volunteered for service or were drafted. The recently divorced Campa was drafted into the army in the middle of applying for a commission, which meant he went in as a private. Campa lamented his bad luck and the fact that in Albuquerque there were no deferments for thirty-seven-year-old professors of Spanish folklore: "Kerch[eville] is already in the army and so is Lopes. We hired La Casa and Reindorph [sic], but we did not replace Kerch. Good Profs are getting scarcer and scarcer." Sánchez seriously considered volunteering. He regularly met high-level military personnel in his wartime activities; they urged him to apply for an intelligence post given his background in Latin America. Finally, on September 16, 1942 (Diez y Seis de Septiembre, or Mexican Independence Day, no less, as if he was trying to make a point), nine months after Pearl Harbor, Sánchez wrote to the navy to apply for a position in intelligence. In a long, typed letter describing his personal and professional attributes, he dropped the name of a lieutenant colonel who had persuaded him to offer the Office of Naval Intelligence (ONI) his services. The navy's officer procurement division in New Orleans promptly forwarded the application forms. Sánchez turned them around in a few days with several required letters of recommendation soon after.[26]

Sánchez's application seemed well founded. Historians note the shockingly poor state of ONI in Latin America at the beginning of the war. Undersecretary Welles felt these postings were the navy's least desirable ones. Reports of drunkenness, licentiousness, and basic ignorance about the countries in which intelligence officers served created a vacuum of accurate information. FDR's executive order in 1941 authorized the FBI to act as intelligence gatherers in the Americas. Given the ONI's bureaucratic losses to the FBI, who also performed poorly, and the State Department, one wonders if Sánchez's application was not doomed from the start. At any rate, the navy still needed officers, particularly those with advanced educations. In fact C. Vann Woodward, then a young historian of the U.S. South, successfully attained a naval commission to write small, quick books on naval battles, a subject in which he had no professional training. Even if Sánchez's expertise in Latin America was unnecessary, his ability to write large projects and quickly would seem to have fit the navy's needs.[27]

Sánchez's recommendation letters came from Director Shotwell, U.S. Commissioner of Indian Affairs John Collier, Director Embree, and Favrot. His colleague Charles Arrowood at the University of Texas recommended Sánchez as well suited for the job: "Dr. Sánchez is a man of complete probity, courteous manners, even and firm disposition, and capacity for strong and decisive action. He is a gentleman and a strong man. You can repose complete confidence in his character." However, despite having passed his physical exam and two early stages of the application process, things went sideways for Sánchez. By late November the navy responded that he was too young. He turned thirty-six on October 4 but needed to be thirty-seven at the date of his application to serve as a lieutenant commander in the navy for intelligence. The procurement office offered to consider him for lieutenant, a shade higher than the usual rank of lieutenant, junior grade, the rank of most officer appointments to the Naval Reserve directly from civil life. But Sánchez was annoyed. He quickly replied that he would prefer his application to be considered on its merits without reference to age. And if not, he could wait a few more months for his age to round up to thirty-seven instead of down to thirty-six to then be considered for the position he desired. The reaction from New Orleans was immediate and negative. Commander E. D. Walbridge replied that age was simply one issue, and he was disinclined to support Sánchez's application anyway. Beyond naval intelligence, Walbridge wrote, "It is obvious that your qualifications are not appropriate to any other type of billet in the Navy." The naval procurement officer then remarked, "The Navy needs men now and not later" and concluded, "It has been my observation that citizens from civil life who have been appointed in the Naval Reserve have, in a great majority of cases made personal sacrifices to enter the service."[28]

This was a stinging rebuke. Sánchez proposed giving up his 3-A classification (family hardship), which protected him from the draft. Did they feel Sánchez was trying to apply out of his league in a cynical effort to claim a good faith effort to enlist before being turned away? Were they peeved at his questioning of the application process? Did these local officers in Jim Crow Louisiana dislike Sánchez's affiliation with pro–African American foundations such as the GEB and Rosenwald Fund? Or did they simply not want a Mexican serving as a naval officer, particularly in intelligence? One thing seems definite. If this was a ruse by Sánchez to convince others he was no coward, then the episode should have stopped there. He offered and was turned down. Instead, it went on and on. A few days after declining to be considered for lieutenant (something Walbridge's letter ruled out and Sánchez silently ignored), the professor abruptly changed course. Between December 4 and December 8, coinciding with the one-year anniversary of Pearl Harbor, Sánchez, perhaps chagrined at the turn of events, changed his mind about the lesser appointment. As he explained, "The new War Manpower ruling, and the realization that there will probably be no further opportunities to enter the armed services unless I complete my present application, changes this situation radically. Since I am sincerely interested in rendering personal service during the present emergency, I feel that I should complete that application and avoid being 'frozen' out of the armed forces." He heard nothing back from New Orleans and within weeks wrote another naval procurement office in Dallas about applying for government service in occupied countries. This also went unanswered.[29]

In the spring Sánchez again pestered naval officials, who refused to further process his application for the more carefully stated reason that "your particular qualifications are excellent for one in your field of endeavor. However, the Bureau regrets that there are no vacancies for a person with your abilities. . . . Your interest in the Naval Reserve is appreciated and it is regretted that you have failed to meet the requirements for appointment therein." Undaunted, Sánchez replied within a week to the New Orleans office that he would consider any junior officer rank in any other naval division, presumably including combat duty. Walbridge agreed to review the application one more time in Washington. A month later Walbridge issued his final rejection, noting, "It is regretted that the patriotic offer of your services cannot be accepted."[30]

Whatever anger or shame he felt at this constant stream of rejections, Sánchez persisted in trying to obtain other military commissions. In April 1943, as his last round of rejections arrived from New Orleans and Washington, he was approached by Major General Allen Gullion of the Provost Marshal General to become a governance expert for occupied areas. He immediately applied but within two weeks was told there was "no suitable vacancy for your selection and admittance to the School of Military Government at the present time." Again, Sánchez asked to be reconsidered and was told it was not going to happen. Later applications also failed. His friend Irving Melbo, who was teaching at training facilities in Newfoundland and England, requested that Sánchez join his unit. He had the backing of his commanding officer, and Sánchez was willing to drop all of his commitments. But this too failed.[31]

This was Sánchez's last attempt to join the armed forces. After this he accepted a prestigious civilian assignment with the CIAA in Washington in late 1943, after serving as a part-time civilian consultant on Latin American issues with the Office of Civilian Defense and directing a University of Texas Inter-American committee. His draft status was 3-A from March 1941 to December 1943, when he entered the CIAA. At that time his classification briefly changed to 1-A (eligible for military service) and then to 2-A (not to be drafted for important civilian work) before being labeled 4-A (not to be drafted after discharging wartime service) for much of 1944 and early 1945, when he was deathly ill and convalescing in New Mexico. Sánchez was unhappy about the entire situation. He recounted to a friend, "The Navy turned down my application on the ground of 'no vacancies.' That refusal made me mad and I am still trying." Even more galling, government agencies continued to contact Sánchez to inquire if he knew of any bright young men interested in military service.[32]

From the beginning of his first year at the University of Texas in September 1940 to February 1944, George I. Sánchez championed better understanding between Anglos and Latinos in the United States and abroad. Whether it went by the name of Good Neighborism, inter-Americanism, inter-cultural relations, or Pan Americanism, the ultimate cause was the same. Sánchez's war of ideas involved his publishing venture with Macmillan, his efforts against discrimination while with LULAC, his grant and eventual monograph with Carnegie, and his efforts to join the Office of Naval Intelligence. This war of ideas was an important part of the Mexican American response to the Second World War. Sánchez believed that despite the irritant of racial discrimination, the cause of the United States was just and the world would be a far safer, better place with an Allied victory against fascism. He only wished to add to this common sentiment his yearning for the nation to live up to its ideals in how it treated all its people.

5

SÁNCHEZ'S WAR OF ACTIVISM
1940–1944

Protests reach me about such matters as employment in war industries, infringement of civil rights and similar conflicts, which constitute a threat to our civilian defense. [I] take these up with the appropriate agencies, giving whatever guidance I can. You will be interested to know that, to avoid complications, I make these contacts without referring to or in any other way committing OCD [Office of Civilian Defense]. . . . You will note from the above that I am employing my time in "trouble-shooting" activities and in stimulating leadership to more active efforts in getting the Spanish-speaking people to greater participation in the war effort and to encourage greater cooperative action on the part of English-speaking and Spanish-speaking people.

The pseudo-science of the Los Angeles official who is quoted as reporting to the Grand Jury on the Sleepy Lagoon murder case that "Mexican" youths are motivated to crime by certain biological or "racial" characteristics would be laughable if it were not so tragic, so dangerous, and, worse still, so typical of biased attitudes and misguided thinking which are reflected in the practices not only of California communities but also elsewhere in this country.

During the Second World War George I. Sánchez advanced Mexican American civil rights. This much might seem predictable. After all, I have documented how Sánchez fought the war against racism and fascism with his pen. However, rather than limiting himself to such an academic direction, Sánchez also took on Jim Crow more confrontationally. With a few exceptions this record is hidden from historical memory. These few exceptions, however, represent a rapidly growing and important trend in Chicana/o historiography. If the Mexican American war of ideas through education is scantily documented and

underappreciated, then its war of activism for civil rights is booming. Recent
studies by Emilio Zamora, Thomas Guglielmo, and Lisa Ramos intensely focus on the obscured yet fascinating strategies and activities of the long Mexican
American civil rights movement during the Second World War.[1]

In the midst of a horrific global conflict, directly challenging the system was
dangerous. But Sánchez and other Mexican American activists of this era—in
a story that historians are still discovering—seized their opportunity in much
the same way as the African American civil rights leadership did through their
wartime Double V campaign. Sánchez's actions with regard to the Charles
Bunn Fund, the Texas Civil Rights Fund, the University of Texas Inter-American
Committee, and the Fair Employment Practices Commission represented a
more assertive phase of Mexican American civil rights than ever before. Like his
war of ideas, Sánchez's war of activism brought tantalizing opportunity and frustrating failure. Though all this effort on his part did not permanently alter the
racial discrimination his people faced on a daily basis, the war permanently altered him. George I. Sánchez was never the same after the war.

WARTIME CIVIL RIGHTS

The key to this burst of civil rights activity in the middle of the Second World
War was a surprising influx of cash. In January or February 1942 a law professor
at the University of Wisconsin then working as a special assistant to Undersecretary Sumner Welles in the State Department, Charles A. Bunn, and his
spouse, Harriet Bunn, contacted Sánchez about unexpectedly coming into
$10,000 ($142,911.04 today). Moved by Sánchez's *Forgotten People*, the Bunns
wanted to anonymously aid Mexican Americans. They prioritized donating to
real people who toiled without aid over supporting existing cultural programs.
After a few weeks of cheerful negotiations, Sánchez obtained control of the
donation, which he deposited in an Austin bank to be drawn out only by him
for expenditures aiding Mexican Americans in Texas and New Mexico. Officially called the Latin American Fund, the donation was privately referred to
by Sánchez as the Bunn Fund. He requested formal permission from the University of Texas to administer it, though they seemed to care not a whit. They
blandly congratulated their new hire for engaging in what they termed charitable activities. The Bunns trusted Sánchez completely. Charles Bunn and Sánchez met in Washington later in 1942 as Sánchez conferred with the Office of
War Information on Mexican American issues. One Bunn project was a fascinating training program affiliated with a local LULAC in the little New Mexico
village of Santa Cruz. It involved the state director of vocational instruction,

Sánchez's friend Brice Sewell. The program trained young rural women for the wartime aircraft industry on the West Coast, producing a cohort of Rosita the Riveters. Years later Sánchez chauvinistically recalled, "Some good (Anglo) soul, and a poor Mexican American organization [LULAC] placed a sum of money in my trust. . . . I doled this out to . . . New Mexico mountain village girls who were doomed to marry the 'culls' after the best young men volunteered or were drafted for service in World War II. While some of them went to college, most of the girls received specialized vocational education and 'graduated' to the airplane industry in California (and to marriages to men much better than the village clods and rejects). I am very proud of the results."[2]

One of the benefits of being a law professor was the free advice Bunn could give his fund. Sánchez asked Bunn about test cases over racial discrimination. Sánchez brimmed with excitement over arousing the ACLU's interest and seeking the NAACP's advice, though Bunn cautioned him against challenging discrimination too directly. They became friends and discussed politics, the war, their health, and their lives as much as they did the disbursement of the fund. When most of the $10,000 had been spent by war's end, Sánchez sent Bunn an accounting that neatly summarized the fund's activities. He spent nearly $900 on the Austin Community Center, $175 on the Austin Pan-American Roundtable, $350 on a community center in Santa Cruz, New Mexico, $200 for office expenses, $550 on the vocational training program in Santa Cruz, over $2,000 on travel expenses to (somewhat inefficiently, one might add) investigate other sources of funding, $2,200 on the Texas Civil Rights Fund for legal cases challenging racial discrimination, over $600 to LULAC's Austin council for a clubhouse, $1,000 for the Inter-American House in Austin, and nearly $600 in direct financial aid to students in danger of dropping out of school ($12,892.86, $2,506.94, $5,013.89, $2,865.08, $7,878.97, $28,650.80, $31,515.88, $8,595.24, and $14,325.40 today). By war's end, Sánchez had spent $8,635 of the $10,000 Bunn Fund.[3]

The largest expenditure from the Bunn Fund was generating wartime civil rights cases in Texas. Sánchez was under tremendous pressure from LULACers to end racial discrimination. The LULAC cofounder and former state legislator J. T. Canales of Brownsville urged Sánchez to take on issues such as segregated swimming pools and the like, issues that Canales feverishly imagined had to be not the usual racists practicing the usual racism but "the under hand work of some persons, who are masquerating [sic] under the cloaks of loyal American citizens, but who, in fact are either spies or traitors to our Country." Sánchez contacted the civil rights division of the U.S. Department of Justice alleging that police in Karnes County created a state of terror by physically brutalizing

Mexicans. Sánchez urged a federal investigation and passed along other complaints. These officials thanked Sánchez and assured him of the "proper consideration" of the "carefully noted" problem. No action was ever taken.[4]

Sánchez made contact with the ACLU over Mexican American discrimination in 1942. Sánchez indicated to Roger Baldwin, the national ACLU director, that it was an opportune moment to highlight how racial discrimination against Mexican Americans was a drag on wartime morale and contradictory to Pan Americanism. Sánchez felt that with just a little effort the ACLU could do a terrific amount of good. At this time he was open to various kinds of alliances. Sánchez brought up a recent conversation with the New Dealer Will Alexander, who had suggested Mexican Americans turn to the NAACP for advice. Baldwin, who was intimately connected with the African American civil rights movement, doused these hopes: "I think it would be unwise to involve the NAACP except as consultant. The race discrimination laws have a considerable history and a recognized status, while no such arguments can be invoked for discrimination against Spanish Americans." This was no ordinary disagreement. Baldwin's opinion carried a great deal of weight, especially as Sánchez looked to the ACLU for organizational and financial assistance.[5]

Baldwin and the ACLU recommended that Sánchez work only with ACLU-affiliated, white attorneys in Texas to undertake litigation rather than with his civil rights partner, M. C. Gonzales of San Antonio. Sánchez and Gonzales, perhaps discouraged by Baldwin's lack of confidence in their abilities, briefly dropped the effort. But in the end Mexican Americans needed the ACLU far more than autonomy. By late 1942 as these efforts took firmer shape, Sánchez confessed to Baldwin, "I have had no experience in this type of procedure so am at a loss about plans and arrangements." A Bunn Fund allocation of $2,200 combined with some undefined ACLU support gave the needed impetus to the formation of an organization Sánchez founded in September 1943, unoriginally called the Texas Civil Rights Fund. It consisted of several sympathetic Anglos, including L. W. Fox, a school administrator in San Antonio; G. Louis Joughin, a professor of English at the University of Texas; J. O. Loftin, the president of San Antonio Junior College; and Harry Moore, a professor of Sociology at the University of Texas. Others joined later. The committee eschewed publicity and deferred to Sánchez, its chairman. He went out of his way to retain Gonzales as the fund's attorney despite Baldwin's heavy-handed hints to seek other expertise. Sánchez's inability to interest federal agencies in Mexican American discrimination prodded him in 1942 to presciently remark to Baldwin, "It seems to me that the only mandatory action which we can get in these matters will have to come from court decisions." This was a far cry from Sánchez's belief of the 1930s that the right dose of self-help and government sponsorship of modernization efforts would alleviate Mexican Americans' plight. This realization did not diminish his efforts. It enlarged them via a heightened conviction to seek more confrontational means to obtain justice.[6]

The Texas Civil Rights Fund sponsored a jury discrimination case in New Braunfels, challenges to police brutality in Karnes County and Kerr County, a public accommodations case over a segregated swimming pool tied to a state legislative resolution declaring Mexican peoples to be white, and county primaries that excluded Mexican Americans on the basis of race. They planned to challenge racist real estate clauses and segregated schools too, but indecision and losses in personnel stunted this brief venture. Sánchez was no longer intimately connected to the Texas Civil Rights Fund by the end of 1943, when he left the university to take a civilian post in Washington. The remaining members were hesitant and quarrelsome without him. Joughin and Moore exerted themselves questioning Gonzales on the finer points of law. They confessed to Baldwin that the organization was in a state of paralysis in Sánchez's absence. After one bout of pointed questioning by Joughin that resulted in Gonzales's defensive review of the legal points at stake as well as his urgent request that the committee authorize him to proceed, Moore decided to resign owing to his discomfort with the whole civil rights enterprise and with Gonzales. That Gonzales investigated a Texas Ranger for police brutality was likely not lost on these junior professors at the state's flagship university, where the senior history professor Walter Prescott Webb had just written a highly popular deification of that police force. The Texas Civil Rights Fund stopped its work in 1944 as several members quietly left the group in Sánchez's absence. However, this short-lived experiment was the basis for a more extensive collaboration in the 1950s between Sánchez and the ACLU.[7]

THE UNIVERSITY OF TEXAS INTER-AMERICAN
RELATIONS COMMITTEE

If the Texas Civil Rights Fund was the quiet underground of Chicana/o wartime activism in Texas, then a more public phase of this activism was the University of Texas Inter-American Relations Committee (IARC). The idea of the IARC came from David Saposs, an official with the Coordinator of Inter-American Affairs Office (CIAA) in Washington. This was a godsend for Sánchez, who for years encouraged the idea that Good Neighborism began at home, not abroad. CIAA authorized a $17,000 grant to the eight-person committee of faculty and administrators at the university ($228,905.49 today). They crafted conferences on Latin American issues, developed contacts among civic groups, studied the education of Spanish-speaking minorities, and disbursed small matching grants to local Good Neighbor efforts from the Girl Scouts to woodworking classes in rural Texas towns. IARC was a part of CIAA's collaboration in 1942 with the Department of State in an endeavor called the Program for Cooperation with Spanish-Speaking Minorities in the United States. Concerned with Mexican Americans' ability to withstand subversive propaganda from communists and *sinarquistas*, the program was budgeted $80,000 and six employees to spread Good Neighborism domestically ($1,143,288.34 today). Though State Department bureaucrats blanched at Mexican Americans' civil rights assertiveness, Nelson Rockefeller's CIAA was more willing to secure Mexican American cooperation. The CIAA was enthusiastic about Sánchez's participation, covering up to one-third of his salary for part of 1943 to allow him to serve as IARC's full-time director. The University of Texas covered the rest of Sánchez's salary and eased his teaching duties.[8]

Once the IARC emerged, the GEB searched for study projects they could sponsor through it. In late 1942, for example, GEB rejected a proposal from Herschel Manuel to compare test scores among children from the American Southwest, Mexico, and Puerto Rico. The GEB felt that wartime action studies should be more tightly focused on the Southwest and should engage popular audiences. Silently, they negatively compared Manuel to Sánchez in this internal debate. Though unfair, it demonstrates how the pupil (Sánchez) had eclipsed the master (Manuel) by the 1940s, at least to the GEB. After rejecting Manuel's project and visiting Austin, it took Sánchez only a few weeks before taking the hint and supplying a proposal of his own. In spring 1943 Sánchez capitalized on his relationships at the GEB by allowing them to shape his proposal. That Sánchez, a former fellow and researcher at the Rockefeller-endowed GEB, was the director of this study project and this committee, funded by both GEB and CIAA money authorized by Rockefeller, made the arrangement so cozy that it must have seemed criminal.[9]

Sánchez was "in like Flynn," to use the parlance of the time. Internal GEB memoranda suggest that even before he submitted his $10,000 proposal they planned to accept it ($134,650.29 today). The end result was the monograph *Spanish-Speaking Children in Texas* (1944), by Wilson Little. Though this was originally his project, Sánchez had left the University of Texas to join the war effort through federal agencies by late 1943 and 1944. So the project passed to his research assistant, Little, who analyzed the data and wrote the book once Sánchez's initial surveys were returned. Though *Spanish-Speaking Children in Texas* did not get his full attention, Sánchez's interpretive stamp was on it. Little decried the intellectual sham that passed for pedagogical segregation. It took place in the same substandard, dilapidated material conditions and with the same lowered expectations. The book was published in the fall of 1944 shortly after Little left to work in the Oklahoma City public schools and while Sánchez was away. The IARC chair passed to Robert Sutherland of the university's Hogg Foundation. But in the absence of Sánchez, the GEB felt uncomfortable sponsoring other planned antidiscrimination studies or funding parts of state agencies to alleviate discrimination. Sadly, everyone seemed to disengage from the effort just as State Superintendent L. A. Woods pledged his support. So much hinged on Sánchez's involvement, and in 1943 and 1944 there was far too little of him to go around.[10]

One episode in Sánchez's plethora of wartime activities has generated debate among historians of late: the passage of House Concurrent Resolution 105 in the Texas legislature on May 6, 1943, the so-called Caucasian Race Resolution. Was this an example of Mexican Americans claiming whiteness and embracing the bigotry of a more perfect Jim Crow system that targeted African Americans and not them? Or was it simply another exercise in strategic positioning in their long, constant effort to force racists to honor their civil rights? Were one to focus simply on the Caucasian Race Resolution's passage as an end in itself, as does one recent historian, then one might reasonably conclude the former. However, the importance of this legislation lay in how it could be used. Sánchez was relatively uninvolved in the creation of the resolution and spent little of his time lobbying for it. He was enthusiastic about its possibilities, however, and viewed it as leverage in the nation's symbolic attempt to appease an increasingly angry Mexico. It represented for him a new line of attack in bolder, more confrontational challenges to racism. The resolution vaguely concluded, "All persons of the Caucasian Race within the jurisdiction of this State are entitled to the full and equal accommodations, advantages, facilities, and privileges of all public places of business or amusement." Since state and federal courts had long defined Mexican Americans as Caucasian, this was a weak, narrow antidiscrimination statement.[11]

Sánchez viewed the resolution as fodder for a lawsuit by his Texas Civil Rights Fund. He puckishly wrote to one ally that while he was aware "the passage of this act is nothing more than a very fine gesture," he felt it might be utilized in a way that "gives the lie to our black reputation." To the ACLU's Baldwin he was more specific: "You are probably aware that the last session of the Texas Legislature passed a concurrent resolution establishing a good neighbor state policy which provides that equal treatment shall be given to Latin Americans in all public places and businesses. After due deliberation we have decided to test this in court." Though Sánchez believed such legal action would fail because a house resolution was not as binding as statutory law, he saw it as a means of exposing the hypocrisy of the state's claim to be non-discriminatory. The Texas Civil Rights Fund supplied Gonzales with $1,000 to test the Caucasian Race Resolution over public swimming pools and restaurants, areas Baldwin regarded as trivial ($13,465.03 today). While he seems to have had little to do with crafting it, the existence of the Caucasian Race Resolution was, for Sánchez, one more wedge with which to pry open civil rights. It was not a statement of belief in white supremacy; it did not scare off the ACLU, then one of the most prominent champions of African American civil rights that had already urged a separate civil rights path for Mexican Americans.[12]

THE FAIR EMPLOYMENT PRACTICES COMMISSION

Sánchez's involvement with the federal government's Fair Employment Practices Commission (FEPC) was far more meaningful in his fight for Mexican American equality than the Caucasian Race Resolution. The FEPC was created in 1942 shortly after FDR's Executive Order Number 8802, which dealt with discrimination in the workplace. At the time, FEPC's executive secretary, Lawrence Cramer, asked Sánchez for the names of experts on Mexican American labor and discrimination who could serve as field investigators. Sánchez recommended a number of people, such as Gonzales, several University of Texas personnel, including his IARC colleagues Manuel and Rex Hopper, his graduate students Reginald Reindorp and Alfredo Vásquez, and New Mexicans Arthur Campa and Antonio M. Fernández. Despite his enthusiasm, by the summer of 1942 Sánchez was already spread too thin to commit to the agency more fully.[13]

In early 1943 Cramer contacted Sánchez about a conference to reorganize the FEPC. This time Sánchez attended at his own expense. Though FEPC regarded him as a representative of LULAC and, by extension, of Mexican Americans (his presidential term ended months before), Sánchez asked that he also represent the university's IARC and the Office of Civilian Defense. At a three-hour meeting on February 19, 1943, in the Social Security Building, with twenty-five representatives of minority groups in attendance, U.S. Attorney General Francis Biddle, Paul McNutt of the War Manpower Commission, and FEPC personnel charted a course to expand and strengthen the agency. Invited participants included Walter White of the NAACP, Roger Baldwin of the ACLU, the Roman Catholic theologian Rev. John A. Ryan, Rabbi Israel Goldstein of the National Conference of Christians and Jews, and A. Phillip Randolph of the Brotherhood of Sleeping Car Porters. Sánchez was in exactly the company he felt he belonged—a mixed group of activists representing various constituencies and jointly lobbying the federal government for reforms.[14]

At this meeting Sánchez engaged in a process instantly familiar to many minorities in academia, business, and other professional endeavors today: speaking for a larger group one is perceived to represent, whether one has the authority to do so or not. It is a tricky business to separate a personal agenda from a larger agenda others expect. Sánchez's remarks acknowledged this awkward role. He boldly commented on the proposed changes to FEPC, hesitated, and then started over by explaining why it was difficult for him to represent his people rather than the narrower, more recognized pressure groups the other speakers represented: "So the position that our group takes is—and by the way, I should clarify this—the Spanish-speaking citizens of the United States are only loosely organized. They have no paid workers, no official representatives, no financed representatives of any sort, but I think that I can speak [for] the consensus of that group when I say that we are in full agreement with the statement of the principles already made." He noted there were millions of Spanish-speaking citizens who faced daily racial discrimination resembling that experienced by African Americans: "Now, while we would not by any extreme stretch of the imagination support Jim Crowism for the Negro, we are particularly susceptible to a Jim Crowism among the Spanish-speaking groups, and obviously object vigorously to the extension of Jim Crowism to the Spanish-speaking citizens of the United States."[15]

Sánchez and others were in a hurry for President Roosevelt to enact the proposed FEPC reforms. Three weeks after the conference, White and Randolph sent the participants a chain telegram urging immediate action. Sánchez authorized his signature that day, wishing both men well in prodding the government. In a confidential memo to his IARC colleague Robert Sutherland, College of Education supervisors Frederick Eby and Clarence T. Gray, his civil rights ally Gonzales, and the supervisor at the Office of Civilian Defense, Robert E. Smith, Sánchez enthusiastically related the broad base of support for the FEPC among "Jewish groups, Negro groups, AF of L [sic], CIO, 'Mexicans,' women's organizations, religion (Jews, Catholics), American Civil Liberties Union, and the like in attendance." In separate correspondence Sánchez wrote to Gonzales, "This is the only federal agency, with the exception of the Department of Justice, that has a direct mandate in the matter of discriminations practiced upon minority groups. As an executive and semi-judicial body, it can wield tremendous influence in improving the status of the minority groups." One scholar refers to Sánchez and other Mexican Americans involved with the

FEPC as "political entrepreneurs" who deliberately chose federal antidiscrimination policy over "seeking the tangible rewards of whiteness and assimilation."[16]

One Mexican American activist involved in the daily grind of the FEPC's efforts was Sánchez's friend and University of Texas colleague Carlos Castañeda. They both believed FEPC gave the federal government the ability to cut across the economic, social, cultural, legal, and political arenas in a comprehensive manner that minority activists on their own could not duplicate. While vitally interested in the FEPC, Sánchez moved on to other efforts by late 1943. Castañeda then filled the vacuum by joining FEPC as an investigator. This cemented Castañeda's activist credentials in an otherwise academic life as a prolific historian of the Spanish Southwest. Likely Sánchez was surprised when he heard his friend was interested in such a difficult bureaucratic job. But though Sánchez had initially recommended others, he quickly sent out new letters and telegrams of support for Castañeda and coordinated others to affirm his friend's suitability. Sánchez personally lobbied the FEPC's Cramer, the ACLU's Baldwin, Congressman Fernández of New Mexico, the CIAA's Victor Borella, and the NAACP's White on Castañeda's behalf. Shortly after the war the two had a misunderstanding over what had transpired to get Castañeda on the FEPC that required some letters to clear the air. Castañeda believed that Mexican Americans did not support his efforts to join the FEPC; his biographer reiterates this belief. But Sánchez supplied Castañeda with dates, letters, and telegrams he wrote and to whom in order to demonstrate that he and others enthusiastically supported him.[17]

OFFICE OF CIVILIAN DEFENSE

In October 1942, not long after Sánchez's thirty-sixth birthday, he received word that his ill father had died, prompting a lengthy visit to New Mexico. This was a restless, reflective time. Sánchez was taking stock of his life and trying to do more for the war effort. He applied to the Office of Civilian Defense (OCD), Eighth District in Dallas and San Antonio (though he worked from Austin) in October 1942 and was hired over the next month on a half-time basis at $12.77 per day with a moderate per diem for travel ($182.77 today). On a yearly full-time basis this would have come to a $4,661.05 salary ($65,739.08 today). While continuing to teach his classes, direct the IARC, and, unbeknownst to everyone but his closest colleagues, work to eliminate racial discrimination against Mexican Americans, Sánchez also continued in this half-time position for just shy of a year, when budget cuts eliminated it in September 1943. He worked several demanding jobs at well over forty hours a week. This was double dipping, as the university paid him full-time for half-time teaching and his IARC work. But Sánchez regarded his OCD work as essential service to his country and after the job was cut offered to continue his part-time efforts for a symbolic amount of $1 a year without any travel reimbursement ($13.47 today).[18]

Sánchez had several roles with OCD. He pushed Good Neighborism, obviously. His work in New Mexico involved consulting on health and hygiene curriculum in adult education. Sánchez developed OCD radio scripts in Spanish. His willingness to offer suggestions for improvement in OCD services and activities, particularly encouraging the inclusion of Mexican Americans, occasionally caused friction with local personnel. But the OCD depended on Sánchez to reach people in ways that localities, often run by segregationist Anglos with little appreciation for or interest in the Mexican Americans in their own backyard, could not. Sánchez was a mediating influence between distracted, hostile government entities and impatient, angry Mexican Americans, as the first epigraph above explains. Sánchez dealt with everything from local draft board discrimination to segregated USO halls to conferring with the Office of War Information about publishing a pamphlet on Mexican Americans.[19]

Sánchez consulted with the State of Texas about prodding local civilian defense boards to include Mexican Americans. In the culture of segregation in South Texas there was a great deal of obduracy on the part of many Anglo officials to allow Chicanas/os to participate even at a token level. Once in Crystal City, a small, segregated farm community in South Texas, Sánchez's activism prompted a letter from the notoriously inert Governor Stevenson to the local defense council requesting they include Mexican Americans. Sánchez encouraged local and state officials to do the most basic things to acknowledge Mexican Americans' sacrifice. He reminded State Defense Coordinator W. L. McGill after one inspection, "You are already aware, of course, that the great majority of the young men who have entered the armed forces from that area are Spanish-speaking citizens. The proportion of young men from this sector of the population in the armed forces is far larger than there [sic] population proportion." He went on, "Local boys have been killed in action, have been decorated, etc. It would do a lot of good if the local daily would give prominence to these events. This is just a suggestion and I did not take it up with the local newspaper pending the conference with you."[20]

In his reports to Robert E. Smith, the director of the eighth regional office of OCD and also a member of Stevenson's Good Neighbor Commission, Sánchez made it clear that his work for OCD and his university's IARC had much in common and boosted wartime morale. They discussed Sánchez's performing such work from within the armed forces. He received high marks in his

OCD evaluations and updated his friend Smith on confidential matters like his FEPC activity. August and September 1943 were difficult months for Sánchez; not only was he downsized from a fulfilling position at OCD, but he took ill for a prolonged period of time, even as Virgie herself experienced more health problems. Smith wrote to Sánchez, "I am terribly sorry to hear of Mrs. Sánchez' illness and I hope that has been changed because I know how terrible that is." Weeks after this correspondence Sánchez moved his wife and children to New Mexico for the duration of the war, while he took a full-time civilian post in Washington (figs. 5.1, 5.2). There was perhaps more to this separation than convenience.[21]

Shortly before Sánchez's OCD position evaporated in the summer of 1943 the Zoot Suit Riots in Los Angeles captured the nation's attention. That summer Mexican American youth and military personnel and law enforcement officials clashed. The explosive situation was inflamed by sensationalist press accounts describing young Mexican Americans as lurid beasts. These disturbances had

5.1. George Eugene as a child in a photograph from the late 1930s or early 1940s. Reproduction by permission of Cynthia Kennedy.

5.2. Connie as a child in a photograph from
the late 1930s or early 1940s. Reproduction
by permission of Cynthia Kennedy.

been building since the Sleepy Lagoon case a year before, when police arrested
a group of supposed gang members with little evidence or due process. This
tinderbox was a concern for local, state, and federal agencies. The U.S. State
Department sent one of its Mexican experts, William Blocker, to Los Angeles
for nearly a week, and, predictably, he produced a lengthy, red-baiting report.
A year after the violence the FBI conducted a study of Mexican Americans who
defended alleged zoot suiters or who complained about discrimination. Like
the State Department and Naval Intelligence, the FBI concluded that Mexican
American groups were rife with communists, singling out alleged Hollywood
radicals like Rita Hayworth, Anthony Quinn, Henry Fonda, Orson Welles, and
Joseph Cotton for their support of the Sleepy Lagoon defense efforts.[22]

Unsurprisingly, Sánchez vigorously disagreed with notions that Chicanas/os
were prone to violent crime. In his essay "Pachucos in the Making" (1943), he
wrote, "The seed for the pachucos was sown a decade or more ago by unintel-
ligent educational measures, by discriminatory social and economic practices,
by provincial smugness and self-assigned 'racial' superiority. Today we reap the

whirlwind in youth whose greatest crime was to be born into an environment which, through various kinds of degrees of social ostracism and prejudicial economic subjugation, made them a caste apart, fair prey to the cancer of gangsterism." One aspect of the situation that most riled Sánchez was the way the media and police used questionable social science to link Mexican Americans with crime, as noted in the second epigraph above. As he wrote this piece in 1943 the zoot suit violence continued. Mexican American youth in Los Angeles were regularly beaten in public, often in front of large crowds, without much more reaction from the Los Angeles police than arresting these victims on fabricated charges.[23]

COORDINATOR OF INTER-AMERICAN AFFAIRS

In the fall of 1943 George I. Sánchez accepted a prestigious offer to serve as an administrator in Rockefeller's CIAA in Washington. At this time his personal life was disintegrating. His father had just passed away, he and Virgie were constantly ill and living apart, and his country repeatedly refused his multiple offers of military service. In a recommendation letter at this time, Embree cryptically alluded to Sánchez as having personal problems; a year earlier Embree had written several unqualifiedly positive recommendations. By summer's end Castañeda praised how Virgie "continued to improve" after a recent visit. In September Sánchez wrote to Gonzales about moving his family away from Austin before embarking on his CIAA job: "I won't be able to leave town until Mrs. Sánchez has returned from the hospital and has gained a little strength." And he himself was not well. Though his commentary on his own health is sparser than that on his spouse, letters to the ACLU, GEB, and a University of Texas administrator indicate that Sánchez suffered from a chronic malady between August and December 1943. He explained a report's tardiness by saying he had "a bad case of malaria during August and September."[24]

The CIAA, run by the thirty-two-year-old Rockefeller, was a federal agency FDR created in 1940 to address inter-American cultural relations. Its formation proved detrimental to the State Department's Division of Cultural Relations, which had been in charge of Good Neighborism since 1938. Sánchez worked directly under Kenneth Holland, the director of the Division of Science and Education. His duties involved planning and administering teacher-training programs for rural Latin America, supervising domestic CIAA efforts in higher education, managing the visits of Latin American figures, training CIAA personnel as educational advisors serving in Latin America, preparing CIAA publications for translation and distribution in Latin America, and serving as a liaison to U.S. educational agencies and foundations. He arrived in Washington in late November and worked very hard for a few months. His salary grade was $5,600 a year with the possibility of $600 in overtime per year ($75,404.16 and $8,079.02 today). This was much higher than his fixed salary of $4,000 at the University of Texas, from which he had been granted an unpaid leave of absence ($53,860.12 today).[25]

Sánchez was a left-leaning activist and educator with ties to Latin American scholars. To argue that he was co-opted by the CIAA in an attempt to burnish its reformist credentials is too one-sided. Sánchez viewed the relationship as mutually beneficial: he got to serve his country by doing what he did best. He regarded CIAA's platform as enhancing his ability to bring Mexican Americans to the forefront. And they were aware that Sánchez had a reputation as a rabble-rousing subversive among segregationist Anglos in the Southwest. While never radical and not always that effective, the CIAA still pushed Sánchez's issues and seemed more interested in Latin American democracy than the State Department. CIAA supported the investigation of discrimination in Texas by subsidizing the state's Good Neighbor Commission; CIAA also supported OCD's efforts at engaging Mexican Americans. So Sánchez joined CIAA in late 1943 looking to serve his country and, perhaps, for an excuse to leave home. It is striking how little he referred to his wife and family during this period. Sánchez lived in an apartment close to Howard University and worked in the Walker Building, then relatively new, near Lafayette Park.[26]

One of Sánchez's CIAA projects was consulting with the Walt Disney Company on educational films for Latin America. This endeavor grew directly out of goodwill tours Rockefeller and Walt Disney took in Latin America in the thirties and forties. Cinema aficionados are familiar with Disney's animated *Saludos Amigos* of 1943, which introduced a new cast of Latin American characters on Donald Duck's sojourn south of the Rio Grande. Less known are the animated educational films Disney produced for Latin America to the tune of $400,000 in 1944 and $375,000 in 1945 ($5,294,204.55 and $4,853,020.83 today). It was on these animated shorts about health, hygiene, and dietary matters, each of which ran around ten minutes in length, that Sánchez lent his expertise. The best known of these films are *The Winged Scourge* (1943), on malaria; *The Unseen Enemy* (1945), on disease prevention; *Planning Good Eating* (1945), on nutrition; *Cleanliness Brings Health* (1944), on washing and hygiene; and *The Grain that Built a Hemisphere* (1943), on corn, a film that was nominated for an Academy Award.[27]

Some of these works were made before Sánchez's CIAA tenure, and although he appears to have consulted on the hygiene and diet films, he was more involved with a series dealing with literacy. Sánchez met with filmmakers for several days at Disney Studios in late January 1944. Despite the assistance and the green light he received from other academic consultants, Mexican educators, including one early collaborator, criticized the final product as insulting and ineffective. Mexican political leaders, though, were quite fond of Disney's productions. Sánchez recalled the literacy films he worked on for Disney as failed experiments. He later claimed to have predicted this failure, though that is unlikely. It is doubtful that Sánchez brought much energy to the project, being ill and working too hard. As he wrote to Walt Disney years later, it was at this very time his life drastically changed: "As a matter of fact, two weeks after I last saw you at your studios in February of 1944 I landed in the hospital for a stay of a year and a half." Though Sánchez could not have known it at the time, his activist war was over.[28]

George I. Sánchez's war of activism sought to more aggressively confront racial discrimination in ways that represented a break from the past. In fact, the postwar surge in Chicana/o civil rights activism, often attributed to returning GIs, can be traced back to Sánchez's wartime efforts. The surprising Bunn Fund explains how he was able to financially sustain such frenetic travel and activity. Sánchez's creation of the Texas Civil Rights Fund with the advice of the ACLU was a precursor to their civil rights collaboration of the 1950s. Sánchez's directorship of the University of Texas's IARC was his most sustained activist role during the war. His support of the Caucasian Race Resolution appears to have been a minor tactical episode, while his FEPC activism was far more important. And his work with OCD and CIAA demonstrated Sánchez's desire to offer ever more of himself to the war effort. Though the world was tearing itself apart, Sánchez was trying to build a movement for equality and justice for Mexican Americans in the United States. His story of sacrifice has been obscured too long.

SÁNCHEZ'S WAR OF SURVIVAL
AND HIS TRANSFORMATIONS
1944–1949

This has been my dream for years. Somehow, I've got to realize it and, now that I've got a new lease on life, I'm determined to "get at" it. The Spanish-speaking child is the only orphan among those representing large minority groups. He needs a kindly and intelligent sponsor. If I pester the GEB about him, the GEB can only blame itself! It started me on this work and I'm sticking to the job.

The Study [of the Spanish-Speaking People] has consistently, and even stubbornly, held to the point of view that the full presentation of all the facts in the case is the *sine qua non* of good human relations. This persistent faith in the scientific method, in objective data, is a product of the conviction that most of the ills of the Spanish-speaking population are the result not of wholesale villainy but of ignorance and misinformation. Whether in the education of migrant children, in politics, in segregatory practices, in health, or in the use of illegal alien labor, the facts in the case— properly presented and widely disseminated—constitute the only safe springboard for action programs.

There is a dearth of biographies in the field of Chicana/o history. But that reality has recently begun to change. Tejano/a literary figures are the subject of outstanding recent works by Leticia Garza-Falcón and John Morán González. A recent volume on Alonso Perales edited by Michael Olivas analyzes the life of a public intellectual involved in the production of books and articles as well as civil rights activism and community leadership. Chicana/o academic biography has recently grown with Félix Almaráz's study of the University of Texas historian Carlos Castañeda, Mario T. García's chapters on Castañeda, George

Sánchez, and Arthur Campa, recent biographies of the University of Texas folk-lorist Américo Paredes by Ramón Saldívar and José Limón, and an edited collection on the University of Notre Dame sociologist and Chicano studies pioneer Julian Samora. This is an academic niche where George I. Sánchez's story has much to contribute. He was an academic's academic. The daily rhythms of Sánchez's work at the University of Texas, his tribulations, his joys, all revolved around a fundamentally academic life in which his sense of morality, ethics, ambition, and the world of ideas converged in a larger quest for social justice.[1]

The period bracketing the spring of 1944 to the end of the decade ushered in monumental transformations for Sánchez. Personally, he dealt with a life-threatening illness, slowly recovered, lost his marriage and daily contact with his children, and remarried. Professionally, Sánchez returned to the University of Texas to an altered administration that no longer was interested in his kind of activist scholarship. Building on his wartime efforts, Sánchez emerged from the conflict as a more forceful, confrontational advocate for civil rights. In this immediate postwar period he experimented with different kinds of civil rights activities that were more policy oriented, collaborative, and diverse.

TUBERCULOSIS

On March 29, 1944, Sánchez wrote to Edwin Embree, "My sins and the doctors caught up with me—I'm laid up at Garfield Memorial Hospital, in Washington, with a case of tuberculosis which looks like bad news. I'll probably have to stay here for a couple of months, then to a sanatorium in New Mexico for several more months in bed. Then, a very light schedule for a few more months and I'll be as good as new. What an outlook! For the next twelve months I am definitely out of circulation. For a guy of my proclivities, the prospect of inaction for months is a body blow—particularly since I've still got to earn a living." Sánchez was incorrect. His case of tuberculosis was not minor enough to be dispatched with some bed rest. It was an aggressive infection that almost killed him. Sánchez was constantly ill between the summer of 1943 and early 1944 as he regularly worked overtime. One of his final CIAA trips was to an Albuquerque Good Neighbor conference in late February 1944 (fig. 6.1). The proceedings were published the next year with photographs. Sánchez appears in one image sitting at the end of a table looking strikingly gaunt and lifeless. Within weeks after that photograph was taken Sánchez learned of his diagnosis. He joked of a previously scheduled meeting, "If that is to happen the mountain will have to come to Mahomet!" He predicted recovery in a couple of months, expressed annoyance with bed rest, and hoped to get some writing done at the

6.1. Sánchez at a conference in Albuquerque on behalf of the Good Neighbor movement through his position as the Office of Coordinator of Inter-American Affairs. Looking gaunt and frail in this photograph, Sánchez, just days or weeks later, would be admitted to the hospital with tuberculosis. Box 75, Folder 2, SP. Reproduction by permission of Benson Latin American Center.

hospital. His friends were shocked. Sánchez had such a reputation for tireless-ness that they suspected the worst. The GEB's Fred McCuistion urged imme-diate relocation to the drier Southwest. Embree's office assistant wrote to Sánchez in his absence that he hoped it was all a terrible mistake. Embree was more helpful, urging his young protégé to take his condition seriously: "These doc-tors cannot be put off forever. As a matter of fact, it is probably good that they caught up with you promptly. Many of my friends who have had to take a few months out—and have chafed under the restraint—have come back to a full life better and stronger than ever." Friends visited Sánchez in the hospital over the next several months when he could endure it. Soon just breathing was dif-ficult enough.[2]

Today in the United States *Tuberculosis bacillus* (TB) no longer strikes the fear it once did thanks to the medical revolution in antibiotic drug treatments. But in the early twentieth century TB was the nation's seventh leading cause of death. There was little treatment outside of bed rest and a change in climate.

TB would have been familiar to Sánchez, as it and silicosis, both deadly lung diseases, were the main killers of miners in the Arizona and New Mexico mines of his youth. While there is no proof his father was infected, he was chronically ill and unable to work for years before dying relatively young in the early 1940s, facts that fit the pattern of TB. The high dust content of the air in the mines, made worse in the twentieth century by more advanced drills, led to silicosis and left miners susceptible to other pulmonary diseases like emphysema, pleurisy, and tuberculosis. TB can lie quietly without symptoms for years until triggered by another illness. Workers in the dust-filled mines of the period commonly died between the ages of thirty-five and forty-five.[3]

Fewer than 5 percent of tuberculosis patients today in the United States have life-threatening problems after a yearlong regimen of antibiotics. Even with the rise of drug-resistant strains of TB since the 1980s, it remains highly treatable. However, an antibiotic treatment geared for it, Streptomycin, would not be readily available for several years. The treatment for aggressive, life-threatening TB in 1944 was a thoracoplasty: a surgical procedure in which several ribs were broken or removed in order to collapse the infected portion of the lung. Thoracoplasty (and similar procedures that used porcelain balls as filler or cut nerves to paralyze and collapse infected lungs) had just caught on by the thirties. Before that, the standard treatment was bed rest at a sanitarium. So in 1944 this barbaric-sounding, disfiguring surgery was state-of-the-art practice in advanced TB cases. Adding to the discomfort of the ghastly procedure (it is still performed where antibiotics are unavailable), most patients received only local anesthesia to allow for continued expectoration of the contagious fluids from the infected parts of the lungs to prevent their building up and secreting into the healthier parts. Most hospitals would not even treat TB patients for fear of spreading the disease. Antibiotics soon caused the general abandonment of this type of surgery in the United States.[4]

Sánchez's case of TB must have advanced quickly since there is a sizeable gap in his correspondence between April and September 1945. Piecing together what happened then, in the absence of medical records, is best done by consulting later references in which Sánchez remembered his illness. In one rather forthcoming, though seemingly inappropriate recollection distributed to his department—an intradepartmental memo about using majority votes in the graduate admissions process—an elderly Sánchez vividly described this bleak time: "During the war I was hospitalized in Washington, D.C. Through sheer luck I came under the hands of a distinguished chest surgeon when I was near death, weighing 75 pounds and drowning in my own blood. The surgeon, who conducted a seminar of other distinguished chest surgeons of the region, used me as a 'guinea pig' case in his seminar. He had tried to collapse my lung by pneumo-thorax (pumping gas between the pleura). That didn't work (too many adhesions). There were three other alternatives: (a) remove the lung, (b) sever the adhesions, and (c) collapse the lung by a series of operations to remove ten ribs." The physicians were divided. His surgeon, E. E. Davis, supported thoracoplasty as having a greater upside, though it was the riskiest option.[5]

By the spring of 1945 Sánchez gloated to anyone who would listen that he was completely recovered. This was bravado. Though he eventually rebuilt some of that enormous reservoir of energy, he suffered from the effects of his successful thoracoplasty. It disfigured his chest and forced him to slump to one side, making the prospect of walking long distances difficult. He had a diminished lung capacity as a result of the surgery and likely endured chronic pain. And though it is impossible to know with certainty, later health problems pertaining to his heart, circulation, ankles, and liver could have had their origins in this life-saving surgery. Whatever health problems it later caused, however, the thoracoplasty undoubtedly extended Sánchez's life decades beyond what was initially thought possible. When he was not coughing up blood, Sánchez prevailed against the wishes of his physicians by working from his sick bed. That fall he sent a lengthy, handwritten report to McCuistion for a White House conference on rural education. Illness did not diminish Sánchez's passion. He confessed to McCuistion his "impatience with the widespread practice of cloaking inferior educational opportunity, segregation, and other unjust, un-American, and unsound practices under the guise of 'pedagogical reasons' ('language handicaps,' 'Mexican (or non-white) race,' 'neighborhood schools,' etc.) not upheld by the facts." He went on, "Educational progress, Americanism, democracy cannot be taught within the confines of the concentration camp or in the atmosphere of special privilege."[6]

By this time Sánchez had recovered to the point that he could be moved. The very day he wrote to McCuistion, he was transferred from Garfield Memorial Hospital to a local sanitarium in Washington. A month later he made his resignation from the CIAA official. His supervisor lamented the illness that cut short their working together, and Rockefeller sent him a complimentary note. However, Sánchez's in-between status of being on unpaid medical leave while putting in occasional hours caused confusion with the CIAA's payroll officials, who unintentionally overpaid him through the summer to the tune of nearly $300 and then asked for the money back as he lay in his sick bed ($3,970.65 today). In November 1944 Sánchez received permission to go back to Albuquerque with his family. The near-death experience reinforced his belief that his time was limited and that he had to strike harder and more often for Mexican

American justice, as the first epigraph above indicates. But in March 1945, when Sánchez went back to work at the University of Texas, he found his activist platform had changed a great deal.[7]

YOU CAN NEVER GO BACK

Sánchez returned to work at the University of Texas in March 1945. Virgie, who he claimed was still in delicate health, remained in New Mexico with the children. Sánchez lived in a bachelor apartment for a while with Elton Hale, a doctoral student at the University of Texas whose committee he served on. It was a lonely existence. The changes at the university accelerated his feelings of isolation. During Sánchez's illness the university's Board of Regents fired President Homer Rainey for his unyielding defense of academic freedom. This took place during an increasingly paranoid and reactionary statewide political context that can best be described as a vicious combination of anticommunist and anti-integration sentiment foreshadowing the red scare of the 1950s. It began with a failed reactionary takeover of the state's Democratic Party in the summer of 1944, resulting in the formation of a brief-lived third party challenge known as the Texas Regulars, an influential knot of reactionary Democrats and right-wing business interests. They were, in the words of one historian, obsessed with "the alleged Negro—New Deal—labor union—communist conspiracy" that long animated anti-Roosevelt forces nationally. By 1944 Rainey was on the defensive with the board, all appointed by the archconservative governors "Pappy" Lee O'Daniel and Coke Stevenson. The board wanted to fire several professors and abolish tenure, and on November 1, 1944, days before the general election, it fired an uncooperative Rainey by a six to two vote. Several regents later pointed to fears of communism, homosexuality, objectionable textbooks, and racial integration as their motivation. This was bad news for a liberal activist-scholar with a name like Sánchez.[8]

The controversy over the University of Texas festered after Rainey ran for the governorship in 1946 as a liberal Democrat. It was into this charged atmosphere that George I. Sánchez reentered the university. He was eager to push civil rights, writing to the ACLU's Baldwin, "Since the Texas Regulars seem to be gaining control of the University administration, it is not far-fetched to think that these activities may result in some embarrassment if they come to the attention of the governing authorities. If the worst comes to the worst, I may one of these days realize my ambition to go back to sheepherding in New Mexico. Seriously, though, this . . . is one way I have of serving notice that I am not abandoning a lifelong fight just to toady to a reactionary administration."[9]

Baldwin anxiously replied, "I hate to add to your burdens, but it is just like you to take this on when you are not really back on your feet and when things at the University are far from secure." During his initial months back Sánchez plotted a new strategy on school segregation. No longer would he use education departments to quietly persuade teachers, parents, and state education bureaucracies of the evils of segregation; he would now confrontationally litigate segregation. He spent a great deal of time attempting to explain to Baldwin how the racial segregation of Mexican Americans was justified pedagogically and why this was important.[9]

Then Sánchez received a rude shock in the summer of 1945 upon discovering that his salary was frozen for yet another year at the same $4,000 level that it had been since the beginning of his third year at the university in 1942–43 ($51,765.56 today). As he explained to Dean B. F. Pittenger, in 1943 he was promised the rate of $5,000 a year, a hefty 25 percent raise, for having taken on the directorship of the university's IARC ($64,706.94). However, Vice President John Alton Burdine prevailed upon Sánchez to perform the added service without an immediate increase with the understanding that his salary would catch up after the next yearly evaluation. Sánchez apparently settled for a gentlemanly understanding along these lines with his dean and vice president. This was a big mistake! Shortly thereafter, in late 1943, he took an unpaid leave of absence for the CIAA job at the higher salary of $6,200 ($80,236.61 today). Most of his work was in fact part-time and conducted in the hospital. Nevertheless, even a part-time Sánchez was good enough for the CIAA to promote him to a yearly rate of $7,500 before his resignation in November ($99,266.34 today). After he returned in March 1945, far poorer as a result of his service to his nation and his school, Sánchez counted on that long-awaited raise. Sánchez disliked having to present his own case, as it might appear self-aggrandizing. Nevertheless, he argued that colleagues of his who worked on the same projects received raises. His research record was extraordinarily good, producing external grants, articles, editorship of a textbook series, and a monograph in 1944, and his extracurricular service at the University of Texas brought the school serious external recognition. Further, he loyally turned down several attractive offers during this period. Sánchez's other employment opportunities included, first, the offer from CIAA to return in the fall of 1944 at an annual rate of $7,500 (99,266.34 today); second, an offer from the American Library Association and the U.S. embassy in 1943 to direct the Benjamin Franklin Library in Mexico City for $6,000 a year ($80,790.17 today); third, an offer from the University of New Mexico to direct its Inter-American School at an unspecified salary; and, fourth, an offer he said he had from the Colorado State College of Education in Greeley (now the University of Northern Colorado) to head the rural education program, also at an unspecified salary. Sánchez felt he was being penalized for having served his country in the CIAA.[10]

Sánchez's salary was not adjusted in the 1945–46 academic year. He was told to wait a year and that he could count on a $400 raise as part of a university-wide adjustment for 1946–47 ($4,778.36 today). But this adjustment was not based on his performance and thus, given his already low salary compared to those of his peers, unsatisfying. Pittenger expressed concern about Sánchez's health and ability to teach. He ultimately agreed that Sánchez's salary, static since 1942, did deserve significant adjustment beyond the standard across-the-board raise, and he promised to put in for a $600 raise ($7,167.54 today) in two installments: $400 for the 1946–47 academic year (on top of the $400 university-wide bump) and another $200 for the 1947–48 academic year. This would have brought Sánchez (after a five-year wait) to the $5,000 level promised by Burdine in 1943. Sánchez was pleased. However, the plan fell apart in the summer of 1946. Pittenger, serving in his last year as dean of the College of Education, had neither the influence over new Vice President James C. Dolley nor the energy to fix one faculty member's grievances built up over several years. Pittenger wrote to Sánchez that the proposed raise had failed. Sánchez was stuck at $4,400 in 1946–47, not a cent more than the university-wide minimum ($52,561.95 today). Pittenger's request to move Sánchez full-time to the History and Philosophy of Education Department also was denied.[11]

But what unfolded in the summer and fall of 1946 was much worse than his salary problems. Sánchez immediately protested to Dean Pittenger and Vice President Dolley over the failure of his salary recommendation and requested a meeting. Sánchez, who had apparently been expecting a discussion of his health and arrived for the meeting on October 2 with records of his chest X-rays, must have been dumbfounded when instead the university president asked to sit in and hold the meeting at his office. President Theophilus Painter and Dean Pittenger informed Sánchez that while the casual understanding he had with former vice president Burdine and his health were problematic for the new administration, his character was a much bigger difficulty. Sánchez was shocked. He wrote later to Dolley, "The other matter, which appears to have weighed heavily in past decisions about promotions for me, involves some vague and unsupported rumors about my personal conduct. These rumors were brought to my attention by Dr. Pittenger in March of 1944 (while I was on leave from the University) and I assumed that the explanation I made to him then (and with which he seemed to be satisfied) had closed the matter satisfactorily. I want to assure you now that, between that time and October 1 of 1946,

I was completely oblivious to the fact that those old rumors were a matter of concern to the administrative authorities of the University, and that those rumors were weighing heavily against me in decisions having to do with promotions for me."[12]

Sánchez continued, "It is impossible, of course, to refute gossip unless a specific accusation is made and supported. I am, therefore, unable to say, specifically, that I have or have not done this or that, unless 'this' or 'that' is defined. I can state, categorically, that any rumor which accuses me of behavior unbecoming of a gentleman or of conduct which is inconsistent with professional propriety or ethics is false. I am fully prepared to defend myself against any formal accusation challenging this statement, no matter who makes the accusation." Sánchez was unbending about it. Three years before, when he desperately tried to get into any kind of military service, when Virgie left with the children for New Mexico, and when he took the CIAA job in Washington, a rumor had gone around in veiled language that, in my opinion, likely refers to a dispute over possible marital infidelity. Sánchez explained to Painter, "Some three years ago, several rumors about me were circulated—rumors having to do with my private, personal life. One of my 'friends' brought these rumors to the attention of my wife, who has been in a very poor state of health for many years and who is, understandably, highly excitable and not prone to be circumspect. It seems that she then wrote a purely private and personal letter to a friend in which she repeated the rumors and stated that I was seeking a divorce. It seems, further, that this friend's husband put the letter in Dean Pittenger's hands."[13]

Wherever the truth lay, little good could come of the way all this unfolded. University officials were concerned with the young professor's personal life and would make no raises available until they were satisfied that it was exemplary. Sánchez admitted to Painter that his marriage was shaky: "On a trip through here (March 1944), [just before Sánchez was hospitalized] Dr. Pittenger called me to his office and told me of the letter and asked about the divorce. I explained about the rumor and indicated that the divorce question was an old one that my wife and I had discussed at various times through the years; but that, at the moment, a divorce was not pending (that was 2 ½ years ago, and there has been no divorce yet!)." This remained true for another two months. Sánchez went on, "He expressed himself as satisfied with my explanation, assured me that his concern was that of a friend (not of the Dean), etc. I assumed the matter was closed."[14]

President Painter came up with a potential solution, but Sánchez refused to go along:

On Saturday, October 19, Dean Pittenger called me to his office to convey to me your request that I obtain from my wife's doctors a statement as to her mental and emotional stability—a letter that, as I told you before, I doubt that a reputable physician would find it within his professional ethics to write. The request seems to carry the implication that, until you are reassured on that score, you will not act on the repeated recommendations of my College that I be given an increase in salary. This request for such a letter is the same one made of me at our conference (Painter, Dolly [sic], Pittenger, and Sánchez) in your office on October 2, 1946—a request which I protested then and which, after further consideration, proves even less palatable now. President Painter, were I to comply with such a request, as a condition to securing a salary increase to which I am entitled by every professional standard, I would be ashamed of myself for the rest of my life. Such an action would be contrary to what I know of professional ethics—and I have been an active member of my profession all over this country and in other countries for 23 years, in a variety of positions of responsibility and prestige, with organizations and institutions of the highest professional standing. That action would not be consonant with my scheme of personal morality, and it would do irreparable damage to my self-respect. To comply with such a request would be, in my estimation, to prostitute my principles.

Sánchez was stunned by the request and felt this form of "protection" was ridiculous. Whatever things he might have said about his wife's emotional state in conversations with his employers, Sánchez was unwilling to commit them to writing in order to obtain a raise.[15]

This did not endear him to the administrators at the University of Texas. Effective November 1, Sánchez's salary rose an extra $400 to a total of $4,800, and the proposal to go full-time in the Department of History and Philosophy of Education went forward ($57,340.31 today). However, when it came to the 1947–48 academic year he was stymied again. By the summer of 1947 Pittenger had left the dean's office and no longer recalled his promise to advance Sánchez by another $200 on top of the across-the-board raise ($2,089.19 today). Neither Dolley nor Painter recalled any such agreement either and were not about to impose on Pittenger to investigate it. By the end of the fall of 1947 the administration officially altered Sánchez's title to professor and consultant in Latin American education and gave him full-time status in the History and Philosophy of Education Department, but his salary was not what had been promised him five years before. In one of the most productive periods of his career, Sánchez received next to nothing for his efforts except a nearly terminal illness, a failed marriage, and grief from gossipy administrators who symbolized to him then (and to most historians since) Jim Crow racism.[16]

DIVORCE

George and Virgie Sánchez's marriage was not always a happy one. Virgie Sánchez filed for divorce on December 6, 1946, arguing that she and her husband had "acquired different likes, dislikes, ideas, and friendships and became unable to live together happily and in harmony as husband and wife and now are incompatible." The part about having different friends set George off in his official response: "That he admits each and all of the allegations contained in the Complaint with the exception of the allegation of incompatibility which he denies and demands strict proof of." George Sánchez's touchy insertion of this small dig in his part of the divorce paperwork must have been an extension, perhaps a final one, of the argument that probably divided them for good. The final divorce decree of December 16 gave Virgie custody of their two children, George Eugene and Julienne Consuelo, sixteen and thirteen, respectively, at the time. It obligated George to pay $120 per month in alimony and $40 per month in child support for each child ($1,433.51 and $477.84 today). George Eugene was sent to military school, for which his father provided. George received relatively open visitation rights.[17]

The divorce documents contain hints of bitterness and personal touches. Later disagreements over alimony resulted in Virgie's submission to the court of George's letters from 1946 about how best to end the marriage and his negotiations with her attorney. George had signed one of the letters with his middle name, Isidore, Virgie's pet name for him, and reassured her that whatever threat he once made of initiating a quick divorce in Mexico had passed and that he would leave it to her to initiate a divorce or not. In the event she did, George quickly rattled off the parameters as he saw them. He gave up custody of the children with visitation rights; he relinquished their home in Albuquerque with the exception of his hand-carved desk, camping and fishing equipment, and other personal items; and he would carry life insurance for Virgie and the children for the next five years and sort through older policies to suggest what to do with them. The document sheds light on their relationship. Except for the daily aspect of raising the children, he was used to authoritatively making decisions to which he expected Virgie to accede.[18]

Virgie had an attorney and George did not. He soon received from this attorney a three-page, single-spaced memo in which the words *community property* appeared in nearly every paragraph. The energetic attorney wanted George to pay his fees and inquired about his book royalties, life insurance policies, and bonds, hinting that husband was cheating wife out of her rightful share. As might be expected, George resented the implication. He explained how little his academic books made and used his tax records to argue that his editor's royalties for the Macmillan series did no more than pay the overhead for the basic academic research so necessary to his ability to meet the proposed $200 a month to his ex-wife and their children ($2,389.18 today). He also protested that his medical bills were high, he could not work as much as before owing to his TB, and their term life insurance had no cash value. Sánchez issued a threat about not getting what he felt was a more equitable settlement: "I don't want to be forced into the position of either contesting the terms of the divorce and/or suing for one myself. In the latter event, I know that I could, if I wanted, obtain terms much more favorable to me, including custody of the children. I don't want to get into that sort of thing, for the children's sake. But neither do I want to be driven to the point where I have to kill myself by overwork in order to pay alimony." Was he prepared to challenge for custody of the children on grounds that Virgie was somehow unfit? There was a menace here.[19]

As in most disputes over a relationship, Virgie and George were right about one another to a certain extent. He was correct that Virgie and her attorney were wildly unrealistic about the financial potential of his academic writings. The University of New Mexico Press had scheduled Sánchez's magnum opus, *Forgotten People*, on a limited printing, and sales were already petering out. In the third quarter of 1943, for example, he cleared a meager $11.37 in royalties ($153.46 today). But her suspicion that their family's financial security declined was also true. Money was tight during the war, and George allowed insurance policies to lapse, sacrificing their cash value for extended coverage. It is unlikely, however, that ex-husband nefariously hid extravagant sums of money from ex-wife.[20]

Sánchez tried to spend time with the children as he and Virgie discussed divorce. In the summer of 1946 Connie accompanied him while he taught a summer session at the University of Southern California. Perhaps she assisted him while his health was still delicate. Or perhaps her father sensed that it might be a while before they would have time together again. He spent less time with his son. The divorce occurred as George Eugene, then sixteen, would have been in his first year at New Mexico Military Institute (NMMI), a rigorous military preparatory academy reputed to be the West Point of the West. In his first year at NMMI George Eugene received a scholarship administered by his father's friend and political ally, Congressman Antonio Fernández. While the official costs of tuition, room and board, and books at NMMI ran to $500 a year, there were many incidental expenses, making the scholarship vital for George Eugene, who was eager to attend the school ($5,972.95 today). Father bore the full cost of his son's next and final year. An NMMI education usually led to military service or to college. It also meant father had less personal contact with son. George Eugene soon joined the navy and served abroad; Connie attended the University of New Mexico and married.[21]

ORGANIZING AND RESEARCHING CIVIL RIGHTS: THE SWCESSP AND SSSP

In the late 1940s George I. Sánchez fully committed himself to civil rights for Mexican Americans. This meant a less purely academic profile for him and thus less professional respect at the University of Texas; it also meant pioneering research to assist Mexican American activists in better understanding the problems facing their community. Sánchez initiated this overlapping activism and research with GEB support. One group of educational experts he created in 1945, the Southwest Council on the Education of Spanish-Speaking People (SWCESSP), was a forum through which like-minded scholars, teachers, and bureaucrats could publicly attack educational discrimination. Sánchez's wartime GEB grant had already produced a statewide survey in Wilson Little's *Spanish-Speaking Children in Texas* and was intended to expand to the entire Southwest until Sánchez fell ill. In an effort to restart that endeavor, Sánchez pushed for GEB funding of a regional body of researchers and activists. Within weeks of arriving back in Austin, Sánchez asked GEB about supporting a conference at the University of Texas to discuss Mexican American educational discrimination with the idea that such an event would be a preliminary step to organizing their interest into an academic field. The GEB encouraged his efforts to create a professional body of educators to publicize what seems obvious today—that the racial segregation of Mexican American schoolchildren occurred and that it was bad.[22]

Sánchez originally envisioned SWCESSP as a regional clearinghouse for research on Mexican American education financed through small research grants to scholars in Arizona, California, Colorado, New Mexico, and Texas. Through the summer of 1945 the GEB considered his idea and signed on after Sánchez rounded up greater interest from outside Texas. By 1946 Sánchez submitted a final grant proposal for the SWCESSP that called for $25,000 for three years ($298,647.44 today). The grant was approved, and the first meeting occurred at the University of Texas on December 13–15 in 1945. The nearly thirty delegates from California, Arizona, Colorado, New Mexico, and Texas recommended establishing a means of communicating findings in the field. So Sánchez organized a small SWCESSP publication series through the University of Texas, the *Occasional Papers of Inter-American Education*, whose goal was an ambitious one: "The assimilation of the Spanish-speaking people of the Southwest, the inevitable cultural contacts and conflicts that occur among them and between them and other groups in this area and a complex of many other issues and problems constitute a situation that should be of serious concern to all. As a matter of fact, however, these issues and problems have not been made the subject of attack upon a large scale by any agency or institution."[23]

The SWCESSP met five times between 1945 and 1951: Austin in 1945, Santa Fe in 1946, Denver in 1948, Albuquerque in 1950, and Los Angeles in 1951. The final meeting was entirely sponsored by the California State Department of Education, as GEB support had run out. SWCESSP garnered local press whenever it met and served as an integrationist bullhorn. While the message might seem a bit one-note to modern observers, it was a note that needed to be heard louder and more often as the racial segregation of Mexican Americans festered in the late forties and fifties. Organizing the SWCESSP conferences was taxing, and Sánchez's friends marveled at his ability to make them happen. A Berkeley colleague pleaded with him to take care: "I hope you are not going to overdo once more because you cannot afford to do this, not only for your own sake but because of your responsibility at a time when persons with your background of training and experience are so greatly needed. You must take care of your health in order that you can continue to make the contributions to intercultural relations and education of which you are capable."[24]

The GEB only lightly funded SWCESSP. It was ultimately a small pressure group that coalesced around a charismatic figure and never developed a wider following. Also, the SWCESSP never had the funds to award research grants or publish a journal. This is not to say the GEB was uninterested in Mexican American research. It simply preferred a more solid institutional base. And Sánchez had the answer. He ultimately obtained from GEB a $41,000 grant for the University of Texas to enact the kind of broad-based studies he had been advocating since the mid-1930s ($428,284.53 today). This effort grew out of Sánchez's own research agenda and the formal recommendations of the SWCESSP in the summer of 1946. In the spring of 1947 Sánchez, the GEB, and President Painter negotiated the terms of the grant. Sánchez gained a half-time secretary, a separate $1,200 internal grant to conduct seed research, a teaching reduction from three to two courses per term, his move to full-time status in the History and Philosophy of Education Department, and greater access to university travel funds ($12,535.16 today). While McCuistion was enthusiastic, other GEB officials were beginning to question the necessity of funding yet another Sánchez project. Jackson Davis, who had been critical of Sánchez before, voiced these doubts, but they were not enough to stop the grant's momentum.[25]

Meeting in early April 1947 with a number of GEB officials in Austin and in San Antonio, Sánchez assembled local experts and educators to support his Study of the Spanish-Speaking People (SSSP) project. Acting on GEB's advice, Sánchez revised his proposal by trimming SSSP's sails to exclusively focus on Texas, a more manageable task. The SSSP focused on civil rights. Sánchez and one of the local participants, Rev. John J. Birch, executive secretary for the U.S. Catholic Church's Bishops' Committee for the Spanish-Speaking, sent reports of the GEB meeting to the Truman administration's President's Committee on Civil Rights as an example of the kind of work being done in Texas with regard to Mexican Americans.[26]

All the studies that flowed from this grant over the next four years reflected Sánchez's historical sensibilities. He viewed the past in terms of the powerful taking advantage of the powerless. In a background report to the GEB he re- marked that Mexican American history was tragic; their acculturation to the United States was hindered by stultifying economic exploitation and racial dis- crimination. To Sánchez, the "consequences of this free-and-easy dipping into the cheap labor reservoir that is Mexico are not too difficult to observe." He called this a form of "cultural indigestion" and designed his SSSP to explain Mexican Americans' disadvantageous position through academic research: "It is my considered opinion that we are now in the early stages of a highly acceler- ated process of acculturation in the Southwest. I am convinced that, given a little time without further major complication, our research and public service agencies can solve the problems presented by our bi-cultural situation." Read in a flat, uncritical manner, this statement seems to desire nothing more than assimilation. The context of his concern for exploited workers and racial prejudice, however, indicates that what Sánchez wanted was less a demolishing of any sense of Chicana/o bicultural identity than acceptance by the Ameri- can public of Mexican Americans as fellow citizens worthy of dignity and respect.[27]

Sánchez believed the way to end this legacy of racism was to marshal facts to enlighten the public. He acknowledged what a difficult task it was to convince people that injustice was a reality that demanded action, as indicated in the second epigraph above. The SSSP grant lasted from 1947 to 1951. Lyle Saunders, a former GEB fellow and highly published assistant professor at the University of New Mexico, took the reins of SSSP at the University of Texas for two years to allow Sánchez more time for his department. The SSSP produced several monographs on education, sociology, racial discrimination, and undocumented labor, and several mimeographed articles. These works were uneven. Some were small pieces of little lasting value, while others, notably the Saunders-Leonard monograph on undocumented labor and Sánchez's own work on school segregation of 1951, stand out.[28]

This was still an impressive outpouring of research over a short period of time. SSSP provided Sánchez with the means to conduct research and fund graduate students; it brought prestige at a critical time for the university as it attempted to distance itself from the black eye of the Rainey firing. Sánchez did not succeed in obtaining a $20,000 grant renewal for an additional five years, however ($179,188.46 today). And unfortunately, the research project, though productive, did not leave the kind of public footprint he had hoped for, perhaps because of its exclusive focus on Texas. This was unfortunate since there was nothing like the SSSP in breadth and scope until the mid-1960s, when the Ford Foundation sponsored the Mexican American Studies Project at UCLA.[29]

Sánchez's struggle to gain respect and advancement at the University of Texas almost got in the way of the grant. His alienation toward the administration and the Board of Regents erupted in August 1947 when he wrote to McCuistion of his plans to leave the university. Making sure he meant business, Sánchez explained, "If, in view of this record, the pending grant of some $40,000 to The University of Texas is in any way contingent upon my participation, I believe that it is well that you know that that participation is problematical." McCuistion warned GEB colleagues that Sánchez was dismayed at what he felt was Painter's disinterest in the study and distrust of activist scholarship. The director of the GEB, Robert Calkins, reported that while Sánchez had no offers yet, he would leave for the West Coast if the opportunity arose. This disagreement did not derail the grant. But a year later the GEB was still playing mediator between the two, who never seemed to agree on whether research (Painter) or activism (Sánchez) came first.[30]

MOVING ON PERSONALLY AND PROFESSIONALLY

By the nebulous criteria of reputation, George I. Sánchez was at the top of his field in the decade after the Second World War. But perversely, at that very same time he lost prestige within the University of Texas. During this period Sánchez flirted with job opportunities in New Mexico, Puerto Rico, Texas, and the South American nation of Colombia. However, he pursued none of them seriously. Why? Sánchez remarried in late August 1947 (fig. 6.2). His second wife, Luisa G. Guerrero, was an intelligent young woman in her mid-twenties. According to her stepgrandchildren, she had a quiet, elegant, regal bearing. Luisa's family, who had immigrated to Texas during the Mexican Revolution, valued education. After graduating from Baylor University during the war,

6.2. George and Luisa Sánchez, the happy
newlyweds in the summer of 1947. Reproduction
by permission of Cynthia Kennedy.

Luisa taught for a short while at an elementary school in the Houston area and
then at the high school in Crockett, a small town in East Texas, from early 1942
to late 1943. She then obtained a position as a translator for the federal government in El Paso for the remainder of the war. She and George never seemed to
be in the same place during the war years. She did, however, enter the University of Texas to pursue a doctorate in education shortly after the war and likely
met him there. A family rumor is that they began dating while he was still
technically married. This is possible.[31]

Whereas George's and Virgie's relationship was turbulent, George's and Luisa's was harmonious. Luisa's family did not come from privilege, as Virgie's
had, but like Virgie she was a teacher with postgraduate training. After marry-
ing, Luisa took a position as a field worker for the Girl Scouts of America and
then taught in the Austin public schools while obtaining her doctorate in education at the University of Texas in 1954. George viewed Luisa as a highly educated professional and represented her that way to others. He seemed comfortable
generally with professional women and always refrained when given the oppor-

tunity by male colleagues to remark on women in an objectifying or misogynist manner in his correspondence. Sánchez's preference for intelligent, educated partners is evidenced by both of his marriages. One immediate concern to Sánchez was whether Luisa and his children would get along. Shortly before their marriage, they entertained his son for a few weeks in Austin. The young George explored a fine arts degree at the University of Texas after his NMMI graduation and before his enlistment in the navy. Sánchez was pleased with his son's aspirations. Also, he and Luisa traveled to New Mexico several months after their marriage on a business trip that was equally a visit to Connie. By all accounts Luisa was fully accepted by her new stepchildren. George had moved on in his personal life.[32]

He also moved on in his professional life, but not without continuing his older academic interests. For example, Sánchez continued championing Good Neighborism. He shaped the history of Good Neighborism in Texas by reviewing a book manuscript for the University of New Mexico Press by his former research assistant Pauline Kibbe, the person who had spied on him for the State Department during the war. Sánchez seemed unaware of this. Perhaps anticipating a genial review given their work together, the editor must have been surprised when Sánchez submitted a scathing report alleging Kibbe had cribbed, and poorly so, from his and others' published works and relied heavily on the racist interpretive tropes of the Black Legend. The book was, Sánchez maintained, a rank apologia for the state. He felt it ludicrously asserted that the Stevenson administration decisively closed the issue of racial discrimination. He also felt that Kibbe had portrayed Mexican American civil rights attorneys irresponsibly enough to tempt them to file libel suits. Yet, ever the generous scholar, Sánchez later reported he was satisfied after a personal meeting in which Kibbe agreed to rewrite the book in a far different tone. One wonders how comfortable Kibbe was in having to gain approval from the former employer she spied on in an effort to discredit the antidiscrimination work they did together and whose support she now needed.[33]

Sánchez branched out to research Native Americans. In the fall of 1945 he and Commissioner of Indian Affairs William Brophy, the chief officer of Native American affairs in the U.S. Department of the Interior, planned a survey of Navajo education in New Mexico and Arizona. Sánchez billed the project in New Deal, service-intellectual terms: an accessible analysis of a problem with recommendations that pulled no punches. Sánchez felt this could be his best book. He conducted his survey from mid-April to mid-June 1946 and spent roughly three months writing it on a rushed deadline of October 1. His basic tenet—that Navajo education needed more funding and reorganization—was

accepted by Brophy's Bureau of Indian Affairs (BIA) staff, except for one longtime bureaucrat. Sánchez solicited the University of New Mexico Press, which
had published *Forgotten People*, to publish the report. The press was interested
if the government would vow to purchase several hundred copies as an informal
subvention. But a problem emerged. The staffer who disagreed with the report
reproduced and circulated certain sections to people who disapproved of the
agency's Navajo policy. Willard Beatty, BIA's director of education, apologized
for the unprofessional conduct and explained that the bureaucrat in question
suffered a mental breakdown and had since been institutionalized. But com-
pounding this sticky situation, Brophy took ill, and his interim replacement,
William Zimmerman Jr., disapproved of the report as too critical of the agency.[34]

Zimmerman and Beatty also disapproved of Sánchez's desire to involve the
University of New Mexico Press. By February 1947, tired of the delay, Sánchez
let Zimmerman know that he planned to pursue publication on his own. Zimmerman acquiesced and, in retrospect, this was unfortunate for Sánchez since
publishing the report through the BIA in a loosely bound paper format meant
its distribution was guaranteed to be small. It also guaranteed that the agency
would not purchase copies of the report were it to be published later by a press,
thereby killing the subvention angle. The report, really a small monograph,
was further delayed until 1948. *"The People": A Study of the Navajos* alleged that
a failed government policy contributed to terrible Navajo poverty. Like Sánchez's discussions of the victimization of Mexicans, Venezuelans, Mexican
Americans, and African Americans in prior works, his comments on the Navajo
can be construed as negative: "The contention that, because the Navajo
was a 'savage' in the last century, his acculturation must proceed at a snail's
pace is a dangerous myth which leads into a tragic vicious circle. That point of
view disregards the lessons of history and is based on an unscientific interpretation of heredity and a fatalistic outlook on culture. It condemns the 'noble red
man' to an ignoble state of permanent inferiority." Sánchez's call to spend over six
million dollars on Navajo schools gave BIA heartburn, and their relationship
soured.[35]

The transformations in George I. Sánchez's life between 1944 and 1949 were
not confined to his personal life—from estranged husband to divorcé to remarriage; from health to near death to surprising recovery—but also involved his
work. Sánchez went from being one of the rising stars at the University of Texas
to one of its most undervalued faculty members. This dramatic story is a unique
and instructive contribution to Chicana/o intellectual biography. Sánchez's activities shifted away from the kind of pure academic research that would have

garnered him raises and professional respect and toward civil rights scholarship and activism. The Sánchez that emerged from the Second World War was edgier and more anxious to directly confront racism and prejudice against his *gente*. This activism, fed by the GEB-funded organizational impetus of his SWCESSP and research impetus of his SSSP, peaked in the 1950s.

Part Three

1950s

7

———•◦⟨∞⟩◦•———

POLITICS AND THE MEXICAN AMERICAN GENERATION

Every night I pray that the Lord may conserve Ike's good health during the next 40 months. Heaven *must* protect us from Nixon! As for the Shivercrats: as you say, they've always been Republican. However, they are now labeling themselves "Independent Democrats" so that they may eat their cake and have it too. Over here, an "independent democrat" is one who, having nursed and grown fat at the breast of their political mother (Democratic Party), now enter into a deal with a Madam to run a House with that mother as one of the principal attractions. I said as much in a radio talk in Spanish during the campaign! So, I don't think I'll be regarded even as one of His Majesty's loyal opposition. But, since the *mexicano* vote was quite solid (for Stevenson), maybe a *modus vivendi* can be arranged.

I could spend a lot of time outlining remedies. But the maladies suggest the cures: if people are hungry, let us go out and see that they eat; if they are sick, let us strive to make them well; if they are ignorant and benighted, let us take enlightenment to them. Some will say: "But that is expensive." True—but misery is not cheap. Others will say: "But we don't know how." That I will not believe, for I have the utmost confidence in our ability to conquer these issues—we have conquered much more difficult ones, once we set our minds to it. Some will ask: "Will the public go with us?" Here again, I have the utmost confidence that the American people are honest, freedom loving, decent people—and we have but to convince them of the justice of the reforms needed and they will be one with us. As you can see, I am highly critical of the past—but I look to the future with optimism and high hope.

George I. Sánchez was a political figure. In addition to partisan politics, he performed a wider kind of political engagement as a public intellectual striving to popularize integrationist notions. All this work was connected to the liberal political ethos of the time that was shaped by two world wars, the Great Depression, and Roosevelt's New Deal as it evolved into a moderated cold war liberalism. The historical literature on Mexican American politics in the 1950s is extensive and advances the point that cold war liberals predominated in this generational cohort. The story of George Sánchez confirms this notion with a consistency and engagement found in few other Mexican American figures of the age. Sánchez was a patriot who believed in America's potential and felt that any fidelity to reactionary aspects of the American past was dangerously wrong. In this, Sánchez was similar to the contemporary historian Richard Hofstadter, who, according to his biographer, abhorred the kind of uncritical devotion to "a culture of capitalism, individualism, and isolationism" inherent in pre-1930s national life. Like Hofstadter, Sánchez supported "a more humane, cosmopolitan, and pluralistic postwar liberalism."[1]

Sánchez's world of politics in the 1950s involved two of the major organizations of the Mexican American Generation: the League of United Latin American Citizens (LULAC) and the American G.I. Forum (AGIF). Liberalism was the vehicle that gave Sánchez broader visibility and an ideological network. His activities were never free of controversy. Sánchez paid a price for his activism by enduring unfair treatment by the University of Texas administration and Board of Regents and being red-baited during the McCarthy era. In this atmosphere, Sánchez and other activists of the Mexican American Generation dialed back the severity of some of their criticisms of American society and were more cautious with the issues they chose to champion. But despite the limitations imposed by a narrower, cold war liberalism, scholars may be surprised at how this Chicano Hofstadter stayed as far left as he believed was possible.

ADMINISTRATIVE SERVICE

But first, George I. Sánchez engaged a different kind of politics. At the beginning of the decade he was pulled into the orbit of administrative service at his university and remained in it for much of the 1950s. It meant shifting away from research. He mentioned to his friend Lyle Saunders in early March 1951, "Professor Arrowood died suddenly the other day, and that means that my work has piled up considerably. I am acting chairman of the department. Then, Professor Hackett [of the Institute for Latin American Studies] committed suicide the day before yesterday—and that has raised some additional administrative problems." Chronically underfunded and understaffed, the Department of History and Philosophy of Education was less than half the size and budget of the

Department of Educational Psychology. It was an early foundations department with a heavy service (teaching) mission within the college. At this time it
consisted of Charles F. Arrowood, the semiretired Frederick Eby (on part-time
status after stepping down as chair), Sánchez (who only taught half-time for the
department until 1947, at which time he moved entirely into it), Newton Edwards,
and one seemingly impermanent assistant professor or lecturer. Sánchez was
made full-time department chair at the next Board of Regents meeting weeks
after he wrote his letter to Saunders. The university administration may have
had problems with George Sánchez, but they had little choice in regard to the
management of the department at that time. He served as chair from the spring
of 1951 to the fall of 1959. Sánchez was proud of his administration and viewed it
as representing continuity with his older, Progressive-era predecessors, Eby and
Arrowood. Though Sánchez lamented that service caused his research to slow,
he nevertheless directed many master's and doctoral students throughout the
decade. And he maintained a full undergraduate teaching load.[2]

His administrative superiors remembered Sánchez as an adversarial department chair. He stood on principle and relished a good fight, usually over departmental autonomy. Whether over his department's recommendations on
faculty salary (often his own), the supervision of graduate students, curriculum,
class size, or admittance standards, Sánchez fought for what his department
wanted. This resulted in inevitable friction. The longtime dean of the College
of Education L. D. Haskew (1947–63) remembered Sánchez as a "Dean's head-
ache." Graduate Dean W. Gordon Whaley in the 1960s regarded Sánchez as an
"acknowledged anti-administration professor." The conflicts with Haskew were
frequent and ugly. In 1955 Sánchez vented to the retired Eby, "I am pretty well
convinced that the Dean has been embarked for several years on a campaign of
persecution by misrepresentation against me because I will not let him run the
department as he would run it. I have taken a good deal of 'pushing around'
administratively, and have not given up in disgust for the sake of the Department." Threatening to resign from the chair and drop his graduate advising,
Sánchez remarked to Eby, "I also resent the omniscient, self-appointed, holier-
than-thou attitude that the Dean has taken towards me and towards matters of
vital consequence to the department." Things got so bad that academic year
that Sánchez did tender his resignation from the chair but then changed his
mind and stayed on another few years. So deep was this animosity that Sánchez
got under Haskew's skin even when genuinely trying to be constructive. The
year after Sánchez stepped down from the department chair, another dispute
between them provoked the mediation of President Harry Ransom.[3]

TERMS OF IDENTITY

It will not surprise readers who work in Latina/o-centered scholarship that George I. Sánchez spent a great deal of time explaining, defending, and advancing various terms of identity. One of the great challenges of scholars who study Latinas/os in the United States is nomenclature. It is not a trivial concern. The U.S. Census has spent the better part of a century grappling with Latina/o identity and has yet to find a consistent term. Are Latinas/os a race, an ethnic group, or a linguistic group? Are they best broken up into national origin groups? The most flippant answer to all these questions is yes. Latinas/os fit into all these groupings, including several at once. In the twentieth century U.S. governing agencies classified Mexican peoples in the United States variously as a *national origin group* from Mexico (a precise subgrouping), as a separate Mexican *race* (controversial and seemingly justifying racial discrimination), as *Spanish-speakers* (a category simultaneously broader, narrower, and imprecise), as *Latin Americans* (more confusing than any other designation for those born in the United States), as *Mexican Americans* (with or without the hyphen, which is a separate issue), as *Hispanics* (a vague product of the 1970s and 1980s), and more recently as *Latinos* (bound by *Caucasian* or *other race* Latino subcategories). As indicated earlier, Sánchez very much preferred *Mexican American*, as did most of his generational cohort. This preference is best explained in Mario T. García's *Mexican Americans: Leadership, Ideology, and Identity, 1930–1960* (1989), the most penetrating study of this group.[4]

Sánchez loved nothing better than to lecture on the many terms his people used to identify themselves and how they all had meaning in some respects and not in others. His sense of humor on the subject resulted in playful discourses. He used any term—*Mexican, Mexican American, Latin American, Spanish American, New Mexican*—provided the context was right. To one curious LULACer who asked what a Latin American was, Sánchez argued that Mexican Americans of the Southwest were of some Spanish and mostly Indian genetic inheritance. But for Sánchez, identity was inherently political. He held that the local use of *Latin American* in the 1930s and 1940s, for example, was simply an effort to avoid being called *Mexican* since that term had become an epithet in Jim Crow Texas. He consistently noted the context of terms of identity as ultimately determinative. Larger political and strategic considerations made Mexican Americans much more self-conscious about what they called themselves, Sánchez remarked to the geographer Richard Nostrand: "You will be interested to know that when asked in Spanish what he is, all of us say, 'Soy mexicano.' Only in English are they 'Spanish,' 'Spanish American,' 'Latin American.' Again, to avoid the oppobrium [*sic*] attached to 'Mexican.'" Scholarly readings of the language used by Mexican Americans for self-definition must account for the context in which terms of identity appear. Like all subaltern peoples struggling against oppression, self-definition was never so internalized as to be unconnected to external considerations. Sánchez's jokes about the malleability of self-definition reaffirm the extent to which he acknowledged a certain amount of ridiculousness to being so carefully attentive to terms.[5]

Another way Sánchez defined his people was through their heterogeneity. The historian David Gutiérrez notes the pains Sánchez took to portray his people as a diverse, heterogeneous population to combat stereotypes. Sánchez lectured on Chicana/o heterogeneity to a wide constituency of scholars and opinion makers. To Charles Marden, a sociologist at Rutgers University, Sánchez argued, "Again, you imply that Mexicans are one ethnic group—also that Indians are one ethnic group. It would be well to emphasize the ethnic heterogeneity of both." Sánchez frequently read the works of others and critically commented on them, always cautioning scholars to avoid attaching too much meaning to any one term for or definition of his people.[6]

Though he shied away from culturally nationalist arguments, Sánchez brooked no slurs against Mexican Americans. He explained to one of his Inter-American Series authors that her uncritical acceptance of Black Legend assumptions damaged her book. He sympathized with this scholar's plight by noting that he too had been led astray by these common interpretive canards. So because this was a very understandable and easy error, he gently chided, it was one that required additional vigilance. Other instances were more frustrating. In 1953 an Anglo schoolteacher in the highly segregated town of Robstown, Texas, asked Sánchez to confirm that he had once said, "The Mexican people are the only race of which I know that under four generations of living in the United States have shown a tendency toward regression rather than progression." This self-avowed friend of Mexican Americans then asked if she could quote that statement in her master's thesis. Though Sánchez discharged his obligation to help, he did so with a two-sentence reply that likely masked his anger: "Under separate cover I am sending you some materials that may help you. I did *not* make the statement you quote—furthermore, it is not a true statement."[7]

Sánchez found sociologists and anthropologists especially troublesome in their imposition of heavy structural explanations for Mexican American culture. He disliked the work of Margaret Mead and John Burma, whose generalizations and overreliance on theory, he thought, flattened the Mexican Americans they studied. He also opposed anyone who justified racial segregation. Sánchez enjoyed anything written by Carey McWilliams, especially his classic history

North from Mexico. He also enjoyed the film *Salt of the Earth.* And he went out of his way to advocate Spanish-language newspapers and radio stations. This might seem contradictory for a figure who stressed linguistic and social assimilation, but to Sánchez, as to most other Mexican American Generation leaders, this was about pride. He regarded bilingualism as a good thing. To a colleague at New York University in 1957, Sánchez laid out a case for bilingual schooling in the Southwest and related the story that when Luisa was working as a visiting teacher in the Austin public schools, a young Mexican American girl once asked if she was white or Mexican. Luisa, sensing a teachable moment, asked the student what she meant. The student replied, "'Oh . . . if you speak two languages, you are Mexican; if you speak only one, you are white.'!!" He went on, "So, since it is well known that to be a Mexican is a misfortune, bilingualism is suspect." Cultural assimilation for George I. Sánchez never meant a denial of who he was.[8]

LULAC AND AGIF

George I. Sánchez may have been first exposed to LULAC in 1930 or 1931, when he spent his master's degree year at the University of Texas, as correspondence with Alonso Perales indicates. Sánchez's friend and ally, the future New Mexico congressman Antonio M. Fernández, preceded him in the national presidency of LULAC for the 1940–41 year. Another New Mexican, Filemon T. Martinez of Albuquerque, was national LULAC president in 1938–39, the first non-Texan to hold the post. The importance of New Mexico to LULAC at this time had to do with the group's successful expansion from its South Texas roots in the late 1930s. Though Sánchez's election to the national presidency occurred after his first year at the University of Texas, he and Virgie were active in New Mexico LULAC during the thirties. In the fall of 1940 Sánchez published an essay for LULAC's newsletter entitled "Americanism" in which he said of America's pluralistic society, "It is only when these differences set class against class, race against race, and sect against sect that they endanger the national creed and undermine the social structure. It is then that level-headed Americans need to muster all their energies and rally around the pennant of tolerance, the spirit of Americanism."[9]

Sánchez continued with LULAC after the war. In the fall of 1945, when the national staff urged him to restart disbanded units there, he served as the governor of district nine of Central Texas. With the exception of the Austin local, which Sánchez had revived in the early 1940s, the LULAC councils in this district (Fayette, Bastrop, Caldwell, Hays, Travis, Blanco, Gillespie, Mason, Llano,

Burnet, Williamson, Bell, Milam, and Lee Counties) had become dormant owing to wartime dislocation. He pushed LULACers working with state agencies such as the Good Neighbor Commission (GNC) to advocate nondiscrimination policies. LULAC officials admired Sánchez's activist scholarship even if the University of Texas did not. Sánchez involved LULAC directly in the planning of his Southwest Council on the Education of Spanish-Speaking People (SWCESSP) and Study of the Spanish-Speaking People (SSSP) projects as well as the wider dissemination of the intellectual products they created. And LULAC appreciated generating public knowledge about their community. In 1946 the president of LULAC, Arnulfo Zamora, of Laredo, tasked with rebuilding the organization after the losses in membership during the war, asked for Sánchez's help in crafting LULAC resolutions commending the SWCESSP, the University of Texas, and Sánchez for their work. Sánchez, never shy about publicity, eagerly complied.[10]

In the late 1940s, when LULAC units in Texas formed a special school desegregation fund administered by Sánchez, a new organization emerged—the American G.I. Forum (AGIF), led by a charismatic founder, the Corpus Christi physician Hector P. Garcia (fig. 7.1). It was not long before liberal LULACers like Sánchez and the San Antonio attorney Gus Garcia (no relation to Hector P.

7.1. Sánchez flanked by the physician and American G.I.
Forum founder Hector P. Garcia (*left*) and the civil rights
attorney Gus C. Garcia (*right*). This photograph is undated but
was perhaps taken in connection with the *Bastrop v. Delgado*
school litigation of the late 1940s. Reproduction by
permission of Cynthia Kennedy.

Garcia) lamented LULAC's comparative stodginess. By 1949 Sánchez was copying AGIF's Hector Garcia on discrimination complaints he forwarded to LULAC. At this time Gus Garcia wrote to the ACLU and Sánchez complaining of LULAC's inertia and envying AGIF's growth. Gus Garcia likened the growing conservatives within LULAC to "blue-bloods" who took no political action except to keep their people in subordinate positions out of economic self-interest or a reactionary desire to maintain colonial hierarchies of the past. Sánchez's role with LULAC became increasingly ceremonial. He was the master of ceremonies at the national LULAC convention of 1948 in Austin. And he was a natural for roping in outside speakers. Sánchez's presence was regarded as something of a coup at local LULAC meetings. And some of Sánchez's continued interest in LULAC simply involved keeping up with friends.[11]

In the 1950s Sánchez encouraged liberal LULACers who were attempting to shake up the organization and reverse its conservative drift. Sánchez supported John J. Herrera, a Houston attorney who had long been active in LULAC and Democratic Party politics. Herrera collaborated with Gus Garcia and the attorney Carlos Cadena in the landmark *Hernández v. Texas* case at the U.S. Supreme Court in 1953. Herrera was LULAC president for the 1952–53 term. Sánchez's fears for LULAC were well founded, as the league seemed to be pulling out of a more active engagement with civil rights by the mid-1950s, just as civil rights began to more forcefully enter the national conversation. For example, Felix Tijerina, the longtime national president of LULAC from Houston in the late 1950s, was a restaurant owner who prized relationships with conservative Anglo politicians for whom the NAACP and other liberal groups were anathema. He supported Eisenhower for president along with conservative segregationist Texas Democrats like Governor Allen Shivers. The liberal Herrera became Tijerina's most vocal enemy within LULAC; the liberal future congressman Henry B. Gonzalez also opposed Tijerina. LULAC at this time lost organizational prestige to AGIF.[12]

While he never formally renounced LULAC, Sánchez gravitated toward AGIF. Though AGIF still subscribed to those same old Mexican American Generation beliefs that LULAC did, historians regard it as a vital civil rights organization that in the 1950s filled a confrontational, activist niche ceded by LULAC. In the early 1950s Sánchez not only merged his own civil rights initiatives with the active and eager AGIF, but also became an honorary member of the organization and took pride in its liberal politics and no-nonsense activism. AGIF's sudden growth was fantastic. As early as the fall of 1948 the nascent AGIF and Hector P. Garcia were developing a reputation in Corpus Christi for their fiery condemnations of racism and poverty, though their original focus was advocating for Mexican American veterans who experienced difficulties from local officials in accessing the health and education benefits due to them. Garcia had already testified to the state's GNC on the unsanitary conditions in Mexican American neighborhoods and migrant labor camps as well as on the dilapidated and segregated public school facilities.[13]

Sánchez and Hector Garcia fed off of each other. Garcia benefited from Sánchez's many years of experience as an activist and his ability to articulate an ideology of reform that went beyond the local. But Sánchez probably benefited more, as Garcia's AGIF gave him an energetic institutional platform. For example, in the fall of 1949 Garcia shared with Sánchez AGIF resolutions decrying the state's lack of enforcement of its own compulsory attendance laws with regard to Mexican Americans, how local school districts avoided the *Delgado* decision through free choice plans, the abuse of Mexican nationals by immigration officials, and the state's tolerance of undocumented farm labor. Sánchez, in turn, pushed for Garcia's inclusion in GNC conferences.[14]

LULAC and AGIF were rivals, especially in South Texas during the early 1950s. Occasionally AGIF officials wondered about Sánchez's loyalties, though they need not have bothered. By 1953 Sánchez's disillusionment with LULAC was almost complete, and his break with the increasingly archconservative Shivers wing of the Democratic Party of Texas was, in fact, ugly. Sánchez and Garcia regularly carped about LULAC's inability to take any decisive action. AGIF found Sánchez's long list of national contacts particularly useful in recruiting speakers. But most of all, George I. Sánchez and Hector P. Garcia were friends who admired one another. Sánchez regarded Garcia as one of the most indispensable Mexican Americans leaders of his time; he recognized greatness in Garcia. Garcia regarded Sánchez as the most ambitious and idealistic Mexican American activist and intellectual in existence and worried that unfulfilled expectations might wound Sánchez.[15]

PARTISAN POLITICS

Sánchez kept up connections with political figures in New Mexico, especially with Congressman Fernández, Lieutenant Governor Tibo Chavez, and the Republican gubernatorial candidate Manuel Lujan Sr., but Texas became his primary arena for partisan politics by the 1950s. It was a southern, one-party state, though that party, the Democrats, was often fractured into multiple factions divided by ideology and the devoted followings of individual politicians who fluidly jockeyed for the next move up in a dizzying array of alliances. In short, Texas politics was messy and confusing. Sánchez staked his turf in it as a liberal. His introduction to Texas politics was through the highly polarized University of Texas during the 1940s. Shortly after Sánchez returned to the university from his convalescence, he contacted his former university president, Homer Rainey, to support his bid to succeed the reactionary governor Coke Stevenson in 1946. Rainey lost a hotly contested Democratic primary to Beauford H. Jester, a conservative, though far more moderate than Stevenson.[16]

At the time one of the greatest divisions within the Democratic Party of Texas was national politics, particularly the presidential campaigns of Adlai Stevenson in 1952 and 1956. They were not so much the cause of the rupture within the state party; rather, they were the flash point over which preexisting tensions erupted with explosive force. Sánchez was a national Democrat who backed Stevenson, the eventual loser in the presidential campaign. He wrote of his disappointment in 1952, "However, the *mexicanos* of this state voted Stevenson by a large majority—the most uneducated group of the state joining the 'eggheads'! Could there be some significance in this?!" Conservatives in the Texas Democratic Party who had effectively controlled the state since the late thirties—what the historian George Norris Green refers to as the establishment in Texas politics—supported Eisenhower in 1952 and 1956. A friend wrote to Sánchez that conservative Democratic support for national Republicans reflected a kind of political honesty that, though depressing, was at least refreshing. But Sánchez took no comfort in such "honesty," as indicated in the first epigraph above. Sánchez and other Texas liberals were disgusted at the moderate Democrats, who spectacularly lost the state party apparatus to Shivers in 1952. Sánchez joined the Democrats of Texas, an intraparty liberal structure arising from Stevenson supporters seeking to align the state party with the national party's more liberal ideological bent. He regularly contributed to the *Texas Observer*, a journalistic beacon for the left in Texas during the 1950s. Sánchez regarded the *Texas Observer* as a good venue in which to raise Mexican American issues with potentially sympathetic Anglo audiences. In this climate a liberal champion emerged in the state judge Ralph W. Yarborough, who unsuccessfully ran for governor in 1952 and 1954 against Shivers and in 1956 against Price Daniel before finally ascending to the U.S. Senate in a special election in 1957.[17]

Sánchez found in the plucky Yarborough a nearly ideal representation of his own political consciousness. In 1954 Yarborough asked Sánchez to join other liberal Mexican American allies in the campaign. Though Yarborough hesitated to ask too much of the professor owing to recent efforts by state legislators to clamp down on university faculty political participation, Sánchez countered, "I have no qualms about legislative limitations, since my interest in politics is as a private and personal matter which has no tie-up in my work at the University—and, of course, no university funds are involved. In other words, I didn't resign my citizenship when I accepted a professorship!" Yarborough replied, "I would to God that all Americans would speak up as you speak up, and determine not to 'resign my citizenship.'"[18]

Sánchez also warmly supported the state senator and later congressman Henry B. Gonzalez of San Antonio. Sánchez regarded Gonzalez as an outstanding champion of Mexican Americans and of liberalism. Gonzalez was one of two state senators who in 1957 led a dramatic filibuster in the legislative session that killed several segregationist bills during the high tide of massive resistance in Texas. Though the legislation was geared to African Americans, Gonzalez and other liberal Mexican Americans (not the increasingly conservative leadership of LULAC) viewed opposing Jim Crow as not only the right position, but also one that would keep overt segregationist impulses from affecting the Mexican American community. Gonzalez made a quixotic run for governor against the incumbent, Price Daniel, in 1958. Though he lost this race, he soon won a congressional seat in San Antonio in the early 1960s that he retained until his death nearly four decades later. Sánchez was a font of advice to Gonzalez, though one suspects it was not always welcome. At one point Sánchez offered a gratuitous suggestion: "You will forgive me for being frank, but I couldn't be of help to you if I were otherwise. I think it would be a mistake to continue the use of guitar players and hoop-la of that sort. You are held in high regard because of your own worth, your integrity, your courage. You are already spectacular. . . . Don't do anything that cheapens your stature." His rant about Gonzalez's use of *mariachis* was less about stodginess than it was his concern that Gonzalez, who had just banked huge liberal credentials through the filibuster, not be perceived as yet another ethnic politician speaking only to his group's issues. In the era before multiculturalism, being a political liberal meant transcending assumed racial and ethnic tribalism.[19]

LIBERALISM

The memory of the New Deal still burned bright for liberal activists like Sánchez. Unlike Hofstadter, Sánchez was more sanguine about connecting Progressivism and the New Deal along the same ideological trajectory. Though the anxiousness of postwar America narrowed the scope of liberalism with regard to policy, the liberal imagination nevertheless expanded with regard to racial justice. The historian Cheryl Greenberg succinctly depicts these changes: "Postwar liberalism, then, embodied both caution and confidence. It endorsed civil rights for those persecuted by race or religion, so long as those rights were pursued legally, were focused on the individual, and did not fundamentally challenge economic relations. Culturally, liberalism embraced what scholars have termed 'cosmopolitanism': elevating tolerance, relativism, and rationalism over parochialisms or provincialism." This definition captures most of Sánchez's liberal, white (nonlabor) allies. They were independent contrarians most concerned with the way the state impinged on individual freedoms. Sánchez prized reform over a more dramatic restructuring of society. Scholars of the Mexican American Generation agree that one of its defining characteristics is that they identified the limits of society and worked within them to bring about necessary reforms. And in the postwar liberal ethos, advocating civil rights was increasingly within the realm of the possible, unlike class-based appeals or cultural nationalism (though they too existed). Mario García argues, "Reform, not revolution, characterized the Mexican American Generation."[20]

Sánchez subscribed to conventional ideas of the era about American politics. He believed the nation was moderately conservative in its sense of self, yet pragmatic and open-minded about reform. In the early 1960s Sánchez contributed a précis on liberalism to *The Nation:* "In a society such as ours, a conservative, middle-of-the-road position on social and economic issues comes as a matter of course. We are a successful, comfortable people by and large and change and self-analysis and self-criticism are not considered urgent. This comfortable state of affairs frequently leads to complacency, to a 'do not rock the boat' philosophy." Sánchez felt that the mission of liberals was to identify deficiencies and agitate for needed reforms, even if unpopular. He believed that only complacency could derail national greatness. Sánchez, like other midcentury intellectuals, believed an informed, intellectualized liberalism could best protect American freedoms from the authoritarian right or left. He often broke his classrooms into interest groups with regard to different issues, taking a page from the contemporary political scientists David Truman and Robert Dahl and the sociologist C. Wright Mills, all of whom argued that American politics functioned through compromises made by overlapping, self-interested, organized constituencies. Sánchez idealized an enlightened democratic process by which American politics mediated competing interests.[21]

While Sánchez's position representing a minority group would always channel his activism in precise directions, it also afforded him the ability to speak to that narrowed spectrum of issues with more passion than the cool, distant, mannered liberalism of white intellectuals. For example, in his outstanding essay "The Default of Leadership," from 1950, Sánchez ends not by addressing Mexican Americans about their deficiencies but by addressing liberals about theirs. It was as if he spoke directly to well-meaning liberals worried about the heat of his rhetoric or bogged down in policy specifics about just relaxing and following their principles, as evidenced in the second epigraph above. Sánchez connected national liberals to what was happening in the Mexican American community. He served on the boards of liberal groups and personally lobbied state officials against literacy requirements for voting and for the right of women to serve on juries. Sánchez lectured to evangelical Protestant missionaries about migrant workers and once spoke to students at a labor-sponsored summer camp on activist citizenship. In short, Sánchez worked long and hard to spread a liberal, tolerant, integrationist message. In 1955 and 1956, for example, he gave nearly twenty addresses to, among others, parent-teacher organizations, local civic clubs, Spanish-language radio spots for the local Planned Parenthood, church groups, foundations, and civil rights groups.[22]

There was constant friction among Mexican American activists over who was too liberal or not liberal enough. Most contemporaries agreed, however, that Sánchez was quite liberal. In one missive, State Representative Maury Maverick Jr., who collaborated with Sánchez on a civil rights case, playfully complained about Tejano conservatives while lauding the liberal Sánchez as "the poor man's Castañeda." In the state's GNC and its short-lived Texas Council on Human Relations (TCHR), Sánchez mixed with a different crowd. The GNC had a well-deserved reputation for being conservative, even more so after Governor Shivers appointed the oilman and Dixiecrat Nevil Penrose as director. In early 1951 Shivers also created a separate TCHR under Robert Sutherland financed entirely by a political supporter, the oilman Robert Smith of Houston. Sánchez had some influence with Smith because of their work together during the war, but little with Penrose. Within a couple of years TCHR was defunct. Though he worked hard to engage conservatives for the good of the Mexican American community, these efforts bore little success and instead bred mutual hostility.[23]

Sánchez took an expansive view of integration, linking the conditions of all oppressed minorities. Discussing the civil rights struggles of Mexican Americans and African Americans to the Truman administration's Committee on Civil Rights in 1947, Sánchez threw in a telling aside: "I realize, of course, that even if the offerings were equal, or even superior, such segregation is indefensible under the laws of Texas and under the constitution of the U.S." Sánchez recognized that the law discriminated against African Americans more directly and formally than against Mexican Americans, but he believed this was all theoretical. Segregation was a moral evil to Sánchez, no matter the legal phrasings. While he did not make a case for ending segregation for African Americans in this letter (he was asked to comment on Mexican Americans), he viewed the treatment of both as unjust, illegal, and deserving of the administration's full attention.[24]

Sánchez also challenged the exclusion of Mexican Americans from historical accounts. This was a different kind of integration, to be sure. He wrote several letters of protest to the editors of *LIFE* magazine's popular series *How the West Was Won*. He lambasted the series for beginning with the nineteenth-century explorers Zebulon Pike and John C. Frémont instead of with the conquistadors from hundreds of years before. Decrying its unwillingness to conceive of the "winning of the West" beyond that "fabulous land grab of the nineteenth century," Sánchez concluded that *How the West Was Won* simply confirmed that Mexican peoples were the "'bad guys' in the script." In another complaint (Sánchez clearly enjoying pestering *LIFE*'s staff), he argued, "You see, we New Mexicans (I have adopted Texas) think of the *gringo* as a comparative new-comer—a nice enough guy, but still a johnnie-come-lately who thinks that time and history begin with him. We like the fellow, but he needs to work on his perspective—and I would like to see *LIFE* help him out a bit." Why did Sánchez waste so much typewriter ribbon on *LIFE* when it was abundantly clear they did not take him seriously? To him, challenging that influential periodical was just as important a public contribution as his academic work, which explains the many essays he published in nonacademic, opinion magazines. Sánchez popularized knowledge. This attitude bled into his academic career. He disliked highly technical writing, and his usual advice to younger scholars was to tone down the jargon and write for broader audiences.[25]

PAYING A PRICE FOR LIBERAL ACTIVISM: SALARY

Sánchez paid a price for his public activism. He was always in a precarious position at the University of Texas as long as reactionary board members controlled it. When Ronnie Dugger, the legendary editor of the *Texas Observer*, researched *Our Invaded Universities*, a stinging account of right-wing politics and corporate influence at the University of Texas, he asked Sánchez to elaborate on the price of being outspoken. Dugger printed Sánchez's reply entirely in the book (after his death) that since 1950 he had been denied raises consistently and estimated the financial loss over twenty or so years to be at $120,000, or roughly $6,000 a year. Sánchez remembered an occasion when administrators, attempting to bring his salary into line with those of other senior peers, failed to do so when a board member redlined the recommendation by commenting that he disliked Sánchez's politics. Sánchez noted with aplomb that while consulting in retirement or a move to another university would probably be financially beneficial, he enjoyed his position and wanted to "thumb my nose at the bastids." However, the lost salary, he lamented, "would buy a lot of Jack Daniels and Falstaff."[26]

State Senator Gonzalez worried about the consequences the professor might suffer for his full-throated political support. Sánchez brushed them aside: "How right you are when you say these are 'dangerously vindictive men'! For years I have been the recipient of their attentions because I have dared to be active out in the field in behalf of minorities, and because I was openly anti-Shivers. I'll tell you about this some day when we can sit down for a while. So be assured that I do not fear their reprisals (since I am already in the doghouse!)." Sánchez brought to Gonzalez's attention the subtle ways in which academics were disciplined through the merit raise process, promotions, and honors—all mechanisms short of dismissal. This was no boast, as there really were forces out to get him. After testifying as an expert witness in 1956 against the segregation of Mexican American schoolchildren in South Texas (the successful *Hernández v. Driscoll* case), Sánchez faced an unwelcome reception on returning to Austin. As he wrote to one of the attorneys, "Today I was 'called on the carpet' by my Dean. He informed me that the Regents, at their recent meeting, gave a lot of discussion to the newspaper stories on the case—a discussion which, I gather, was to the effect that I was a baaad boy." A dispute arose between Sánchez and the administration as to whether or not he was subpoenaed and, thus, had to testify. The frustrated professor proclaimed, "It now develops that any raise that I might have gotten next year, and I expected a substantial one, may well have been washed down the drain by my testimony in the Driscoll case." He concluded, "Now, young man, seence I am escared to death of the Regents, I want to put you on noteece that, hereafter, I will be a weetness only if I am subpoenaed." He reasoned, "As you damn well know, I'll go regardless . . . but it will be well to safeguard every move," since, he noted, he might someday "want to have a showdown on the kicking around that I am getting from Mr. Shivers' appointees."[27]

His salary situation worsened. The disputes Sánchez had with the university administration regarding his compensation, which had eased in the late forties, returned in far worse form in the fifties while he was department chair. In fact, Sánchez was one of the lowest paid members of his department while he was chair. Between 1953 and 1958 his salary was between $500 and $1,700 lower than those of his colleagues, almost all of whom had less seniority and, in some cases, lower rank. The disparities, which had been within hundreds of dollars at the beginning of the 1950s, reached thousands by the 1960s. Sánchez was paid $5,800 in the 1949–50 academic year, $5,900 in 1950–51, $6,300 in 1951–52 (the same as Arrowood at the time of his death the year before), $6,600 for 1952–53, $7,000 for 1953–54 to 1955–56, $7,300 for 1956–57, then $7,900 for 1957–58, and, by the time he left the chair in the fall of 1959, he was earning $8,600 ($56,768.11, $57,028.03, $56,444.37, $58,016.49, $61,071.72, $62,518.33, $65,489.88, and $68,842.85 today). Sánchez wrote to university officials frequently to complain about his salary.[28]

By 1954 his complaints had taken on an edgier tone. That summer he noted to Dean Haskew that while he was pleased the recommendations for raises for his departmental colleagues were enacted, once again his own salary recommendation was disregarded. Sánchez noted that the junior member of the department had been raised to $500 more than the most senior member of the department—himself ($5,329.83 today). He still attempted to maintain an air of civility about the situation. Sánchez must not have gotten any satisfaction from Haskew because he soon sent a formal, lengthy letter explaining his qualifications and describing how his salary suffered from compression (by which more experienced and more productive faculty are surpassed by less experienced but more recent faculty owing to a combination of their own salary stagnation and the rising market value of incoming faculty). For example, the department's recent hire to replace Newton Edwards that fall, Arthur Moehlman, started at $7,200, or $200 more than Sánchez's own salary ($62,349.59 today). And, to add insult to injury, between the time Moehlman signed on and the administration decided on raises for the next year that spring, he had been granted an additional $300, without yet having set foot on campus ($2,597.90 today). Sánchez's department directly appealed the lack of action on its recommendation to advance his salary. Eby wrote a lengthy memo outlining Sánchez's talents, remarking, "It is apparent that the outstanding services and scholarship of Dr. Sánchez have not been adequately evaluated and rewarded," especially since his emergency performance after Arrowood's death represented outstanding leadership. None of this reasoning had any effect. Neither did a resolution in 1955 from AGIF concerning his salary.[29]

It was against this background that Sánchez attempted to resign from the chair and graduate advising. The advising was a more serious threat as far as the college was concerned. Things became much clearer after a conference Sánchez had with President Logan Wilson, Vice President Charles Boner, and Dean Haskew in the summer of 1955. Sánchez's resignation letter observed that all three administrators assured him of their support, but that their recommendations for increasing his salary were denied by the Shivers Board of Regents, which disliked his liberal politics and Mexican American activism. Though he eventually backed down on his threats to abdicate the chair and desist from advising, he received increases of only $300 that year and $600 the year after ($2,607.73 and $5,138.76 today). By the end of the decade Sánchez's salary disparity with his junior peers was growing. By the late fifties and sixties his letters were lengthier and more detailed, comparing his record with what his colleagues made and what they produced. He remarked, "I know that much of the foregoing seems envidious [sic]. This recitation of research and publication, of teaching, of recognition, of field service, and the like could seem to be an attempt to disparage my peers. I do not intend it that way." His point was not that his colleagues were overpaid but that he was underpaid. Haskew and others, however, felt such comparisons were uncollegial. Later, even large raises elicited Sánchez's annual letter of protest.[30]

Sánchez felt strongly enough that, against the advice of President Wilson, Vice President Boner, and Dean Haskew, who intimated to him at their meeting in 1955 that such an action might jeopardize their future support, he took the matter to the university's Committee of Counsel on Academic Freedom and Responsibility. Consisting of top faculty, including the historian Walter Prescott Webb, the law professor Page Keeton, and the economist Clarence Ayres, the committee heard Sánchez's lengthy formal complaint. In this twenty-three-page document of August 26, 1955, Sánchez included correspondence between himself and university administrators. He acknowledged that an agitated Haskew and departmental colleagues talked him out of resigning the chair the morning after he attempted to do so. Clearly, Sánchez and Haskew had a troubled relationship, one that inflamed the entire situation—a point brought out by Boner. Wilson tried to convince Sánchez that his scholarship on Mexican Americans was no longer important and that his salary protests were in poor taste.[31]

The committee was of no help. After having initial difficulty organizing itself, it took the entire fall semester to consider the matter. In December the committee members wrote that it was impossible to determine how Sánchez's academic freedom was harmed since the administration was so vague. Tenure was a simpler issue to handle, they felt, but salary discrimination was too nebulous, and Sánchez's charge of infringement of academic freedom was impossible to weigh one way or another. They criticized Sánchez for not following President Wilson's initiative to protect faculty by limiting their involvement in state races; they criticized the administration for not communicating clearly and promptly; they criticized the regents for singling out budget lines based on politics. So after issuing the holiday tidings of a pox on all houses, they lamely wished that everyone would just try to get along.[32]

This outcome was a letdown for Sánchez. But months later, at the end of the 1956 spring term, President Wilson's efforts to muzzle faculty political involvement went down to defeat at a general faculty meeting. In fact, Sánchez signed the initial protest of the university rule that stimulated the meeting. He gave a rousing speech opposing any denial of his rights as an American citizen. Though he conceded that mixing university work with partisan politics was improper, he added, "I think that I can reconcile my American citizenship and my professional career—if such reconciliation is necessary, which is highly questionable. I do not think that I need to be coerced into these judgments." Shortly after the faculty's public slap at Wilson's policy, Sánchez asked the committee to rehear his case, given that their one criticism of him was that he had not adhered to the now-discredited initiative. Predictably, the committee chair danced around the issue and reiterated the impossibility of demonstrating definitively that Sánchez was or was not discriminated against. He sympathized with Sánchez's plight but did no more.[33]

PAYING A PRICE FOR LIBERAL ACTIVISM: RED SCARE

Sánchez not only paid a price for his liberal activism through his perpetually low salary but also experienced the red scare firsthand. Texas higher education experienced a particularly strident version of the red scare. From the early twentieth century the academy struggled to balance the right of faculty and administrators on college campuses to dissent from the political attitudes of the day with the tendency of many colleges and universities to incentivize political and social conformity. And George I. Sánchez was no radical; like many Mexican American activists in the postwar atmosphere and leaders of other civil rights movements, he embraced anticommunism.[34]

When red-baiting singed an ally of his, Sánchez jumped into the fray. Shortly after the oilman Jack Danciger of Fort Worth, a moderate on race relations, gave a talk on the subject that was picked up by the media, the GNC's Penrose red-baited Danciger in a public address. Sánchez and his assistant, Ed Idar, privately wrote to Danciger expressing their support and submitted an editorial to the *Austin American* decrying Penrose's irresponsibility. But they were soon just as busy defending themselves. One incident occurred in May 1952 when one of Sánchez's activist organizations, the American Council of Spanish-Speaking People (ACSSP) (see chapter 10), was prominently mentioned in a news story in the *Los Angeles Times*. In June the *Daily Worker*, the news organization of the Communist Party USA, carried its own report, which favorably mentioned Sánchez's group, cribbed from the *Los Angeles Times* article. Then the American Legion's newsletter, the *Firing Line*, in July cited the *Daily Worker* article and the organization in another context, never realizing this was based secondhand on the *Los Angeles Times* story. The *Houston Chronicle*, on the basis of the *Firing Line* article, then blasted Sánchez's council as communist-inspired. Sánchez and Idar investigated the trail of articles going back to the original *Los Angeles Times* story and wrote letters of repudiation to the *Firing Line* and the *Houston Chronicle*. They succeeded with *Firing Line*, which ran a corrected story in October noting of the ACSSP that "this organization is 100% American and patriotic in every respect." The retraction went on, "The *Daily Worker* played it a dirty trick and raised some doubts about the American Council by giving it an indirect boost or more correctly, mere mention."[35]

The *Firing Line* editorial borrowed liberally from Sánchez's letter of explanation. Sánchez argued, "The American Council of Spanish-Speaking People takes second place to no one in its condemnation of Communists and Communism." Sánchez and his Mexican American civil rights organizations were cold war liberals. As in the case of the NAACP, this fact narrowed their options in terms of allies and strategies, but it also preserved their viability. By fall the American Legion was praising other Mexican American organizations such as LULAC and AGIF. Sánchez nevertheless complained, "I think that organizations such as yours and ours, should not play into the hands of the Communists by spreading suspicion of, and tainting by implication, organizations or individuals simply because they are mentioned in *The Daily Worker*. What a powerful weapon we would place in their hands thereby! How easy it would become for the Communists to cripple or destroy those organizations that are anti-Communist and which they have been unable to capture or infiltrate!" He could not resist giving a lecture about the perils of anticommunist hysteria. The *Houston Chronicle* refused to disavow its patently discredited charges. In October 1952 Sánchez explored bringing a libel suit with the law firm of Wirin, Rissman, and Okrand of Los Angeles but abandoned the idea by the spring of 1953 owing to a lack of funds.[36]

The red scare reached the Spanish-tiled buildings of the University of Texas as well. In April 1953, a full year before the infamous army–McCarthy hearings that led to the senator's rapid downfall, Sánchez gave a campus talk to the Hillel Foundation attacking Senator Joe McCarthy and his wild, unsubstantiated accusations. Also in the spring of 1953, as Sánchez abandoned his libel case, a curious questionnaire from the right-wing historian J. Evetts Haley and his Institute of Americanism at Texas Technological College in Lubbock circulated among University of Texas faculty. The form asked about duplication in courses, programs, staff, and areas where higher education might be cut. Headed

with the large-type, boldfaced words, "At the request of the Governor of Texas,"
the questionnaire fished for information reflecting poorly on colleges and universities. An extreme opponent of the New Deal, Haley was a failed political
candidate who was actually too far right for Texas voters. President Wilson sent
the faculty a memorandum explaining that he had called Governor Shivers
about the questionnaire and was told it was neither sponsored nor required.
Sánchez quickly fired off a reply criticizing Haley for his biased questions and
pathetic attempt to bully faculty with improperly borrowed authority.[37]

By the early 1960s Sánchez, who had just signed a state-mandated loyalty
oath, penned the short essay "All the Things that I Am Not" as a sarcastic protest. He began, "It has just occurred to me that I am guilty of a heineous [sic]
oversight. When I signed the loyalty oath required of me by act of our 150 percent, red-blooded American legislature—whose wisdom and loyalty are above
question—I forgot to explain that, besides not being a Communist, I am not a
number of other despicable things." Sánchez went on, "I was not a member of
the hoods who perpetrated the Valentine Day Massacre in Chicago. I am not,
and have never been, a landlord who made his millions out of slum housing.
Gee whiz! I didn't even know Fatty Arbuckle, or Dillinger, or even Bill Sol
[Estes]. As for the Ku Klux Klan, I was ruled ineligible. To my ever-lasting
shame, I was not a member of the Legislature that adopted the LOYALTY OATH."[38]

The political life of George I. Sánchez in the long decade of the 1950s was exciting, full, and dangerous. He regularly opposed, in the words of Henry B.
Gonzalez, "powerful and vindictive men" with his liberal politics. He did so
within the confines of cold-war liberalism and its politically necessary, but limiting, acceptance of a destructive kind of anticommunism. Sánchez not only
engaged the political process but also remained active in local, state, and
national Mexican American groups. Sánchez's central goal was to integrate
Mexican Americans into all facets of American life, including political parties,
electoral campaigns, bureaucracy, historical narratives, and academic studies.
He neither feared nor despised his heritage. In fact, he felt he was defending it
by demanding a fuller, fairer integration into American life. The politics of
George I. Sánchez were the politics of integration in all shapes and forms.

8

Mexican Americans and the Immigration Issue

The life of a wetback who escapes the attention of the Immigration Service is not pleasant. He has no rights and no privileges. He must stay off the highways and out of the towns. He must work for whatever is offered under whatever conditions the employer chooses to provide. His home is a shack or a brush shelter, or a blanket thrown beside a ditch. He owns nothing except that which he carries. His wife and his children, when he has them, share his life.

I will want especially to show the relationship between cheap labor invasions from Mexico and the development of slums, of disease, and of ignorance. I will want to make the point that almost from the time this region became a part of the U.S. it has suffered from "cultural indigestion," and that the periodic invasions of cheap labor from Mexico have forestalled cures for that indigestion. I point this out without condemning either Mexico or Mexicans. Rather, I condemn ourselves for failing to recognize that we are doing a disservice to Mexico and her people, to say nothing of our own people, when we permit and, even foster, a dog-eat-dog sort of labor competition in the border states.

If one were to assign to the Mexican American Generation one broadly acknowledged Achilles heel (some would say it had many), it would have to be immigration. Scholars with ample justification accuse the Mexican American Generation of being anti-immigrant. Mexican American Generation activists supported restricting Mexican immigration, including opposing the bracero program of the 1940s and 1950s and supporting crackdowns on undocumented immigrants; they maintained sharp citizenship distinctions that divided organic communities in self-defeating ways and embraced outright nativism on occasion. And George I. Sánchez was in the thick of this activism, a kind of *citizenship sacrifice* by Mexican Americans that would never be honored by society. In this chapter I come to terms with Sánchez on the immigration issue, especially over undocumented immigrants from Mexico to whom he and others often referred as illegal immigrants, wetbacks, or *mojados*. This was an explosive issue in the 1950s. Scholars note that the number of undocumented Mexican immigrants reported by the Immigration and Naturalization Service (INS) from the mid-1920s to the middle of the Second World War, likely a conservative estimate, rarely exceeded the thousands; but between 1944 and 1946 that number moved into the tens of thousands, and from 1947 on it reached the hundreds of thousands, with large spikes in 1949 and 1950. I side here with recent works by David Gutiérrez, Mario García, and Emilio Zamora in concluding that the immigration issue for Mexican Americans was quite tangled. Sánchez believed innocent people were placed entirely at the whim of brutal and potentially deadly economic interests. He organized the study of immigration through his Southwest Council on the Education of Spanish-Speaking People (SWCESSP) and his Study of the Spanish-Speaking People (SSSP) in the late 1940s and 1950s. The major contribution Sánchez made was directing the publication of a small, powerful, and controversial monograph by two sociologists through the SSSP.[1]

ORGANIZING THE STUDY OF IMMIGRATION

Critical race studies demonstrate that the entire citizenship project in the United States is mired in racialist discourses that have a direct bearing on patterns of racial discrimination. The historian Zaragosa Vargas, in his recent *Labor Rights Are Civil Rights*, argues that a period of socioeconomic stagnation for Mexican American workers began in the late forties and fifties as their civil rights movement stalled. In this period Sánchez, through his SWCESSP and especially his SSSP, envisioned studying immigration as a central component of the Mexican American condition. His SSSP published eight studies through the Inter-American Occasional Papers series at the University of Texas: a broader overview of Mexican Americans by Lyle Saunders, four education studies, and three labor and immigration studies. The GEB enthusiastically supported the focus on immigration. Sánchez's ally Rev. John Birch of the U.S. Bishops' Committee for the Spanish Speaking in San Antonio dwelled extensively in his communications with the Truman administration on the connection between economic justice for Mexican Americans and the immigration issue.[2]

Essential to this endeavor was convincing Saunders, a widely published assistant professor of sociology at the University of New Mexico with GEB ties, to serve as director of the SSSP at the University of Texas in 1948 and most of 1949.

Saunders came to Sánchez's attention through Arthur Campa, who had earlier forwarded Sánchez clippings of the troubles Saunders had with a racial prejudice questionnaire at the University of New Mexico. Sánchez must have had a strong sense of déjà vu. He needed a fearless researcher and recruited Saunders in 1947. In 1950 the work they did together on the immigration issue received favorable notice in local newspapers such as the *Austin American* and the university's influential *Daily Texan*. The university's press information office publicized the SSSP and its impressive GEB funding. The moderately conservative governor Beauford H. Jester even sent Sánchez a commendation. In 1947 Sánchez explored relocating to the West Coast, and the GEB grant afforded him the leverage he needed to improve his situation at the University of Texas.[3]

What were the politics of immigration like for Mexican Americans in Texas in the 1950s? By opposing the bracero program and urging stronger action against undocumented immigrants, Mexican Americans opposed the conservative political establishment in Texas. The reactionary governor Shivers and the moderately conservative governor Jester from the late 1940s through the 1950s supported the wishes of growers for cheap, exploitable farm labor. Neither could possibly be confused for a civil rights crusader. Farm interests lived the ultimate Jim Crow dream, enjoying a captive, bound labor force working for pennies a day. Moderates like Senator Lyndon Johnson dared not buck these powerful interests. So with whom did Mexican Americans stand on ending the bracero program and cracking down on undocumented labor? The answer is, with liberals. This is a potentially surprising finding for historians who, in a presentist manner, confuse the parameters of the immigration debate today with the political situation of the 1940s and 1950s. The historian Juan García discovers that a constellation of liberal, pro–civil rights allies supported restrictionism, including the NAACP, the ACLU, the National Education Association, the National Congress of American Indians, the National Consumer's League, and the U.S. Catholic Church's Bishops' Committee for the Spanish Speaking, to say nothing of unions like the AFL, the Congress of Industrial Labor, and the National Farm Labor Union. Sánchez and Ralph Yarborough schemed about immigration restriction as a key issue in Yarborough's campaigns of the 1950s.[4]

As Sánchez's SSSP got under way in the late 1940s, he and other LULAC leaders injected themselves into national politics. In early 1949 Sánchez, LULAC President Raoul A. Cortez, and the attorney Gus Garcia traveled to Washington to lobby against the bracero program and advocate a curtailment of undocumented immigration. They sought to meet with liberals, labor leaders, and President Truman. Through Congressman Fernández, Sánchez managed to get the group on various calendars. Sánchez lobbied a balky Fernández throughout the fall of 1948 over the issue, overheatedly suggesting that communists might also be filtering through the porous border masquerading as immigrants. This trip was controversial among LULAC's membership, however, many wondering why they should pay for it. Though Cortez, the owner of a Spanish-language radio station in San Antonio, financed the trip, he hoped to be reimbursed by LULAC and took the extraordinary step of beseeching the organization to please help cover his expenses.[5]

The trip was a major undertaking for Sánchez, who spent most of January 1949 organizing it. Leading up to the meeting at the White House on January 27, Sánchez wrote to John Steelman, an assistant of Truman, that despite Mexican Americans' having "consistently demonstrated their loyalty to the U.S. and its institutions, in war and in peace, they have been treated as second-class citizens—the Treaty of Guadalupe Hidalgo and the Bill of Rights notwithstanding." Sánchez explained that the "virtual peonage" undocumented farm laborers were subjected to by Southwestern growers forced Mexican Americans "even deeper in the mire of socio-economic underprivelege [sic]." Sánchez stressed that he, Garcia, and Cortez did not hold jobs as full-time activists and represented a people who were by and large unorganized compared to other minorities. They met with neither Truman nor Steelman, but with the presidential aide David Niles, to whom they presented a four-page statement of LULAC's position on undocumented labor, some demographic background, and correspondence they had had with the INS and Attorney General Tom Clark. But the real issue behind immigration was discrimination against Mexican Americans. Sánchez noted that six of the fourteen Texans awarded Congressional Medals of Honor during the Second World War were Mexican Americans who "came back to find themselves converted into second-class citizens, to find their families converted into miserable migrants, themselves ostracized and treated on the same terms as the wetbacks even by veterans' organizations."[6]

They did not persuade Truman, who had already acceded to agricultural interests in 1946 and 1947 by extending the bracero program with Mexico and altering the program's management to filter apprehended undocumented immigrants directly into the bracero program, a process the scholar Julian Samora referred to as "wringing out wetbacks" or "legalizing illegals." Adding insult to injury, Truman agreed to Public Law 78 in 1951, which institutionalized the bracero program. The bracero program existed until 1964, bringing 4.8 million contracted laborers (counted anew each year) into the country. This was slightly less than the 5 million undocumented immigrants apprehended by the INS during the same period. These agricultural policies prioritized the maximization of farm profits and maintenance of abundance; they adjusted the market through crop subsidies, loan programs, and, in this case, inhumane wages for farm labor. The issue was overwhelming for Sánchez, who continued his own lobbying efforts with Serafino Romauldi of the AFL and H. L. Mitchell of the National Farm Labor Union. They wanted even greater levels of activism from him. To Mitchell he remarked, "In the meantime, I don't see how we can possibly do more on this topic. After all, I am supposed to be primarily concerned with education!"[7]

Sánchez's exasperation with Mitchell centered on the SSSP's *"Wetbacks"—A Preliminary Report*, a thirty-nine-page collection of documents with a brief executive summary that he coauthored with Saunders. The collection was addressed to the advisory committee of SSSP on June 12, 1949, and in it Sánchez and Saunders equated the presence of masses of undocumented laborers with a dysfunctional economy. They predicted, "The cotton and citrus industries, vegetable farming, and similar enterprises there [Texas], by the shortsighted dependence on wetback labor, are sowing the wind—and, as a result, the state and the nation will reap a whirlwind of social misery and unrest, of expensive remedial action, of international embarrassment. Those enterprises, by their very dependence on wetbacks and on modified peonage, are exposing themselves to economic disaster." The report expressed sympathy, condescending though it may have been, toward undocumented laborers and their difficulties, as the first chapter epigraph above indicates. While Sánchez and Saunders reviled the conditions forced on the undocumented in *"Wetbacks"—A Preliminary Report*, they regarded the notion of social invisibility—of underground peoples neither seen nor heard by the rest of society with the exception of bullies looking to exploit them—as the real outrage. They estimated the total number of undocumented immigrants in Texas from 100,000 to 500,000 "homeless wanderers." There is little here to suggest animosity toward the people themselves who were crossing. The hatred in *"Wetbacks"—A Preliminary Report* is of the position in which Mexicanos found themselves.[8]

Sánchez's allies were excited. Hector P. Garcia sought to immediately purchase over thirty sets of the preliminary report for his mushrooming AGIF. Sánchez could not keep up with demand, and a week after its release had to run more mimeographs. The *Daily Texan* crafted a lengthy article series on the preliminary report, editorializing about "the cancerous roots of discrimination and social unrest" caused by undocumented immigration. Not everyone agreed, however. The Rio Grande Valley Chamber of Commerce charged that the report was "a damned lie," that its authors had "Communistic leanings," and that it was part of a "highly financed propaganda machine." Immigration was a highly sensitive topic during this period, which in 1948 saw passage of the Displaced Persons Act and in 1952 the McCarran-Walter Act, both of which limited immigration. Governor Shivers, then running for his first full term as governor, was concerned enough about it to create the Texas Council on Human Relations in 1950.[9]

THE WETBACK IN THE LOWER RIO
GRANDE VALLEY OF TEXAS

The years 1951 and 1952 hummed with activity and interest over the undocumented labor issue in the pages of the *Saturday Evening Post,* in *Look* magazine, and in a *New York Times* Pulitzer Prize–winning investigative series by Gladwyn Hill. It was in this environment that the sociologists Saunders and Olen E. Leonard, in July 1951, released *The Wetback in the Lower Rio Grande Valley of Texas* to media buzz. More handily referred to as the Saunders–Leonard report, it reinforced the Sánchez–Saunders preliminary report. Saunders worried that he and Leonard had rushed the study (it took three years of extensive research and writing) and that it was an awkward length—ninety pages, which was too long for an article or report but not quite long enough for a monograph. The Saunders–Leonard report contributed a wealth of statistics indicating that the agricultural, southernmost tip of Texas referred to in the title held over 100,000 undocumented laborers by July 1950; undocumented laborers were paid a differential wage of twenty-five cents an hour as opposed to the forty cents an hour paid to citizen laborers; this wage disparity subsidized the farms in this area, which took in 281 percent of the average state farm income; and infant mortality rates for Mexican and Mexican American children were sixteen times higher than for Anglos. The report explained how rapacious economic interests exploited undocumented immigrants through violence and threatened calls to INS to initiate a swift, potentially dangerous deportation. The lack of legal status meant that the undocumented bore such exploitation in silence, making a mockery of basic human rights.[10]

The Saunders–Leonard report posited a simple explanation for such exploitation: a racist, colonial attitude by local Anglos. Using oral interviews to tease out how ideas of racial superiority contributed to this brutal system, much as had the Paul Taylor interviews of the 1920s, Saunders and Leonard in the 1950s uncovered an embarrassing wealth of racism toward Mexican peoples by Valley Anglos, racism that cut across class, profession, and education. Local Anglos discussed their racism with remarkable frankness. In five pages near the end of the report Saunders and Leonard demonstrated how racism toward Mexicans and Mexican Americans was the social and economic foundation of the entire Rio Grande Valley. They described three people who they claimed were a typical valley farmer, an employee of the Texas Employment Commission (TEC), and a state legislator. They used such descriptions (clumsily, it must be acknowledged) in an attempt to preserve anonymity. The farmer believed one could ruin a Mexican by being too good to him and that Americanization caused Mexican workers to ungratefully ask for higher pay, fewer hours, and better conditions. The TEC employee ranted about Mexican criminality and laziness. The politician stated that alleged filth justified racial segregation and that Mexicans and Mexican Americans were lazy; he then fumed about syphilis, lice, and the horrors of integrated swimming pools. These statements caused no end of controversy for Sánchez.[11]

The first problem was the TEC. Upset that the report attributed such statements to one of its employees, the agency immediately sought confirmation of the person to arrange for a hasty transfer. Sánchez betrayed little inclination to preserve anonymity since he felt that the agency might punish the wrong employee. Saunders disagreed. He felt awkward about a poorly paid bureaucrat being punished for his helpful, even if stupidly racist, honesty. However, he felt no guilt over the state legislator: "I would not mind telling you the name of the legislator, but as long as you don't know it, you have a very valid reason for resisting pressures from those who want you to reveal it." Sánchez replied that a public guessing game had already erupted, bringing a great deal of heat to anyone who talked to the authors. Even the University of Texas Chancellor's Office contacted him after angry legislators questioned the study's financing and sponsorship by the university. Owing to Saunders's qualms about breaking anonymity, he and Sánchez settled on a process in which they endorsed the public pronouncements of South Texas politicians who denied having made such statements. Two—Congressman Joe Kilgore and State Representative Menton Murray—obtained Saunders's and Sánchez's endorsement of statements they made professing their innocence of having made such deplorable comments. State Senator Rogers Kelley did not ask the authors to clear his name. Instead, he issued a press release claiming, "No one has had the depravity, the recklessness or utter disregard for the truth or consequences, to accuse me of making such statements." He then denied the unmade allegations and went further in calling the report a lie and threatening the university with libel. Kelley depended on Mexican American votes and was close to the former state legislator and LULAC cofounder J. T. Canales of Brownsville. And it was Kelley who made the statements.[12]

As these difficulties died down, an entirely different complication arose. This time Sánchez was the focal point of anger. On December 3, 1951, the attorney Alonso S. Perales of San Antonio, a cofounder and early president of LULAC, demanded that Sánchez supply the names of those who spoke so insultingly of Mexican Americans. Not one to be cowed, Sánchez replied, "I am amazed that a lawyer of your experience should presume to act as judge, jury, and executioner on a matter that is not within your competence. I am amused that, after such presumption, you should think that you are thereby entitled to *demand* anything of me. Not even my closest friends do I grant the privilege of making peremptory demands of me." Sánchez asked Perales to give the report more than a cursory glance, and he would then understand that Saunders and Leonard cited racist statements by Anglos as a means of decrying racism, not of seconding them.[13]

For Perales this conflagration afforded a reemergence to prominence. Much remained of the old Mexicanist style in Perales's handling of the affair. Many of his letters were in Spanish, and his media attack against Sánchez and other Chicano liberals generally came in his column in the Spanish-language newspaper *La Prensa* of San Antonio. More important, Perales focused on moral indignation. The subtlety of quoting racists in order to document the racism one decries appeared utterly alien to Perales. Or he was disingenuous. That Perales's *Are We Good Neighbors?* quoted Mexican Americans documenting the racism and hostility they faced makes the idea that he was unfamiliar with this concept dubious. Once Sánchez sent his stinging reply to Perales, the controversy became about Sánchez, whom Perales considered suing. Perales settled on large public meetings that spring in South Texas to vigorously denounce the report and Sánchez.[14]

Saunders was upset that his lack of foresight in designating the precise number of valley political figures he interviewed (three) meant that through an easy process of elimination one could deduce the offender. He and Leonard conducted these interviews without a recording device. Each lasted three or more hours, and the quotations were not verbatim accounts but carefully constructed summaries that, he claimed, were authentic as to the tenor and content of the interviews. They were both present at the interview with Kelley; they took separate notes; they discussed the interview immediately upon leaving his office; and they met that night to combine their separate interview notes into joint field notes. Then each one edited two major drafts of the study at different times, and they double-checked their field notes for all quotations. Though sickened at the vitriol, Saunders retracted nothing. He had already relocated to the University of Colorado's School of Medicine in 1951 and simply ignored Perales's threats.[15]

Mexican American critics of *The Wetback in the Lower Rio Grande Valley of Texas* stuck to several main points. First, they maintained that the comments reflected the authors' personal desire to fan the flames of racism. This tack easily descended into rhetorical invective. The Spanish-language newspaper based in Corpus Christi, *La Verdad*, was a passionate critic of the Saunders–Leonard report. Its editor, Santos de la Paz, almost single-handedly kept the issue in a permanent froth. *La Verdad* referred to Sánchez as an intellectual misfit, a hypocrite, and a Judas among his people. José de la Luz Sáenz, another old-time LULACer in retirement, was almost as hyperbolic. An additional unifying theme was the conservative politics of the critics. M. J. Raymond, a prominent LULACer and political boss in Laredo, formally opposed *The Wetback in the Lower Rio Grande Valley of Texas*. Santos de la Paz's *La Verdad* attacked one defender of the report, the liberal LULACer John Herrera of Houston, as an attorney for wealthy, immoral Anglos. The same article bragged of *La Verdad's* fielding a telephone call from the conservative politician Price Daniel, then state attorney general, who expressed support for the newspaper. One LULACer, the attorney Leo Duran of Corpus Christi, felt the Saunders–Leonard report was a part of a larger problem of well-organized liberals seeking to destroy LULAC. Duran argued that, as a Republican who was certain his party would emerge victorious in that year's presidential election, he would use his influence to investigate liberals like Sánchez and determine where their money came from and why they had it.[16]

Critics of the Saunders–Leonard report engaged in red-baiting. Thomas Sutherland of the Texas Council on Human Relations (TCHR) gave an interview to *La Verdad* to the effect that liberal activists like the University of Texas academics associated with *The Wetback of the Lower Rio Grande Valley of Texas*, and especially Garcia and his growing AGIF, "were sensationalizing even the most insignificant incidents" that emboldened the nation's enemies. Sáenz regularly referred to the report's authors and to Sánchez as Bolsheviks. And Canales dismissively referred to professors at the University of Texas as mentally unfit communists. *La Verdad's* Santos de la Paz called Sánchez and anyone connected with the report stupid, corrupt fanatics and suggested that Joseph Stalin was likely enjoying his copy. *La Verdad* covered the large public meeting in the valley town of Mission in early March 1952, similar to the kinds of *juntas de indignación* of New Mexico that in 1933 had given Sánchez so much trouble, and warned in blaring headlines of a possible FBI inquiry into the report. The meeting produced a document that denounced the report, its authors, and Sánchez; it also denounced the liberal activists in LULAC and AGIF who supported it. This meeting authorized a two-page document arguing that Saunders and Leonard, on hearing such racist tripe, should have immediately reported it to the FBI if they were in fact loyal Americans. Printing the insulting comments, which the committee in Mission doubted were even made, reflected a lack of patriotism and a hatred of Mexicans. It concluded, "The whole procedure has a distinctly pink tinge." The next year the American Legion's *Firing Line* and the *Houston Post* red-baited Sánchez's SSSP.[17]

However, the liberal activist wing of the Mexican American community defended the Saunders–Leonard report as an important examination of social and economic injustice. LULAC and AGIF publicly supported it. The president of LULAC, George Garza of Laredo, who was a doctoral student of Sánchez's, wrote of a rumor that his old professor's job might be imperiled and assured him that "as President of the League of United Latin American Citizens that its national officers and all the members of the League stand behind you 100%" and praised Saunders and Leonard for their courage. Garcia's AGIF offered support at its statewide board of director's meeting held in the valley town of Edinburg, also in December 1951. Garcia took the issue personally and used his newsletter to blast Perales, Sáenz, and especially Santos de la Paz for their name-calling, not just of Sánchez, but of AGIF's state director, Ed Idar, and himself.[18]

Garcia viewed critics of the report as Mexican American elites seeking to protect the racist local politicians on whom they depended. He regarded the incident as highlighting generational tensions within the Mexican American activist community and viewed it as a proxy for the brewing organizational tensions between LULAC and his AGIF. Garcia was furious at Perales, de la Paz, and Sáenz. Sánchez too was frustrated, referring to Perales as "a pathetic figure, a psycho-neurotic with delusions of grandeur." Sánchez continued, "I'm quite hurt and grieved that Perales and *La Verdad* should attack me in such an unwarranted manner. After all, I'm guilty of nothing—unless sticking my neck out for them and for my people generally constitutes guilt. The fact that both of them are notorious fools is no excuse. I'm tempted to sue *La Verdad* for libel, and destroy the sheet." To Idar, who contributed a vigorous public defense of the report, Sánchez replied, "There are some people who may wish to suppress the facts of anti-Mexican prejudice, but it is indeed dismaying that among them are a few *latinos* who are *the very victims of that prejudice!* It is like finding a victim of a hit-and-turn driver who does not want the driver found—or discovering a robbed family campaigning against the police for trying to find the burglar! ¡Qué relajo! ¡Qué escándalo! [What a joke! What a scandal!]" He went on, "I may have 'slipped a cog,' as Raymond puts it; I may be a Judas, as de la Paz has it; and I may even have merited some of the incoherent vituperation heaped on me by Perales—but I know my business. And, my business is helping my people. I'll put my record up against theirs any day—and not the least of my accomplishments is that of directing the program that resulted in the Wetback bulletin. I am proud of that study."[19]

Sánchez's activism on immigration continued after the Saunders–Leonard report. He incorporated SSSP's research on undocumented immigration into an article-length historical overview of Spanish-speaking people in the United States, itself a revised version of a GEB document that was part of his SSSP grant in the late 1940s. It stressed the inability of undocumented immigrants to protest their situations and highlighted how such unfettered capitalism damaged all workers. His efforts on behalf of the TCHR failed, however. Governor Shivers created it to refocus Coke Stevenson's Second World War–era Good Neighbor Commission away from domestic discrimination. By not funding TCHR except through a millionaire campaign donor, Shivers marginalized the agency. Early on, Sánchez and Garcia discussed the possibility that TCHR might be a sham. Yet, for a while, Sánchez hopefully talked up the agency as a fulfillment of his SWCESSP and SSSP. Sánchez ultimately concluded that his presence in the dormant agency was more damaging than any potential it might have once had.[20]

Another setback for Sánchez's restrictionist activism occurred in 1951, when the United States reauthorized the bracero agreement with Mexico. Immigration made strange bedfellows. Liberal activists like Sánchez constantly lobbied for a stronger border patrol with enhanced funding and for punitive measures against the hiring of undocumented laborers. On the other hand, South Texas farming interests argued for less border patrol power out of a professed concern for civil rights. The growers' idea of rights was undoubtedly the farmers' property rights to prevent federal officials from interfering in their unlawful labor recruitment.[21]

The INS cracked down on the undocumented with Operation Wetback in the summer of 1954. It is estimated that the U.S. Border Patrol apprehended over one million persons that summer, including the U.S.-born children of long-time undocumented workers. Scholars note that the 1949–53 period was characterized by a dramatic jump in the number of undocumented laborers apprehended, building up to 1954. In terms of human rights Operation Wetback was a travesty. And it was a failure in terms of Mexican American politics. As many scholars have observed, the fallout from within the Mexican American community over Operation Wetback was severe for restrictionists in LULAC and AGIF. Sánchez's ally Idar had just published his own scathing study of the undocumented, *What Price Wetbacks?* Whereas the Saunders–Leonard report was an academic study focusing on human misery, Idar's *What Price Wetbacks?* disparaged undocumented peoples at a time when the massive deportations invoked a great deal of Chicana/o sympathy and a reevaluation of restrictionism. David Gutiérrez argues that Operation Wetback was indeed a turning point in the immigration issue.[22]

IMMIGRATION CONTRADICTIONS

Sánchez and other Mexican American Generation activists lived in a world of contradiction with regard to their espousal of restrictionism. This is unsurprising. The recent biography of Felix Tijerina, the longtime conservative president of LULAC in the late 1950s, reveals the fascinating contradiction that at the same time Tijerina quietly supported Operation Wetback, he struggled with his own citizenship status. The difference was that this wealthy Houston restaurateur had his attorneys file a suit in federal court for a declaratory judgment of citizenship on his behalf; the million or so deported Mexican peoples that same summer of 1954 had no such opportunity. While Sánchez's contradictions on the immigration issue were not quite so stark, they indicate that, as in Tijerina's case, the issue cut in odd, interesting ways. For example, in 1953 and 1954 a civil rights group Sánchez directed supported the California-based *Galvan v. Press* and *Garcia v. Landon* cases over deported Mexican immigrants. These cases at the U.S. Supreme Court involved red-scare deportations and pushed INS to modify its administration of the McCarran–Walter Act. While Sánchez grumbled about having to defend deported Mexican communists with legal funds earmarked for the civil rights of Mexican American citizens and their decidedly anticommunist organizations, he did ultimately support both. And Sánchez refrained from joining a National Farm Labor Union lawsuit against the U.S. secretary of labor over the bracero program because he wanted to work with the federal government, not sue it over policy.[23]

Sánchez had an expansive view of citizenship. He favored lowering the barriers for Mexican immigrants seeking U.S. citizenship. To the National Council on Naturalization and Citizenship Sánchez wrote, "Most of these people have been solid members of their communities, have raised families here, have sent sons and daughters into our armed forces, and are living as well-respected, permanent residents." However, Sánchez argued that the limited educational opportunities in Mexico made the citizenship exam additionally difficult. He concluded, "These people have no country but this, they would take great pride in citizenship, and have made enough of a contribution to the development of this nation to be awarded citizenship." This does not sound like a nativist. Sánchez complained to the Committee on Slavery of the Economic and Social Council of the United Nations that undocumented Mexican workers needed their attention: "These workers, because of their illegal status and their dire poverty, are at the mercy of employers and are often subjected to conditions that are but little different from serfdom and peonage."[24]

And Sánchez became more personally involved in the immigration issue. In late 1953, between the furor over the Saunders–Leonard report and Operation Wetback, Sánchez worked with INS to solidify the residency status of Luisa's parents, who had resided in Texas since the Mexican Revolution as registered aliens. He supplied the money orders, the application forms, and the passport photographs for new resident alien identification cards. He wrote with familiarity to the INS officials Joseph Reid and John Holland. The next year, as Operation Wetback was ending, Sánchez asked Holland to delay the deportation of the mother of several U.S. citizens who had arrived in Texas in 1916 but lacked proper documentation. Speaking for her son and a son-in-law, Sánchez pleaded that she and her husband were elderly and infirm and that they had been in the United States for so long that deportation represented a serious hardship. He asked, "While I have only a bystander's connection with the matter, I feel that she should be given all the 'breaks' possible and will appreciate anything that you can do to that end." Sánchez requested that his old friend and attorney M. C. Gonzales of San Antonio take the case, confessing to being in a difficult situation after having apparently overextended his friendly offer to help into something more substantial. He paid Gonzales the fifty-dollar flat fee for handling the case, which ultimately dragged on into 1955 before ultimately failing. Sánchez wrote, "P.S. I am not telling anyone that I have paid you a fee in this matter—as far as others are concerned, you are doing the work gratis." As flawed or shortsighted as Sánchez's restrictionism may have been, it was grounded in his sense of morality and humanity. Neither Mexico nor its people were the problem; predatory capitalism was, as evidenced by the second epigraph above. Citizenship did not equate to superiority. People were people. But for him citizenship did convey legal rights and freedom from living in the shadows.[25]

GEORGE'S MARRIAGES

George and Luisa Sánchez's happy marriage, beginning in 1947, involved mutual professional respect (fig. 8.1). Luisa was a career woman. She likely met George when she entered graduate school at the University of Texas in the College of Education, at a time when he and Virgie were separated but not yet

8.1. George and Luisa Sánchez relaxing and enjoying
a casual moment, likely in the 1950s. Reproduction
by permission of Cynthia Kennedy.

divorced. Luisa had a bachelor's degree from Baylor University and worked as a teacher and organizer for civic clubs. Luisa's dissertation advisor was James G. Umstattd, the chair of the Department of Curriculum and Instruction in the College of Education. One of George's colleagues, Newton Edwards, who left for the University of South Carolina shortly before she completed her degree, represented her minor field in the Department of History and Philosophy of Education. The title of her dissertation was "The 'Latin American' of the Southwest—Backgrounds and Curricular Implications" (1954). For the rest of the 1950s and 1960s Luisa taught summer seminars with George at various universities. George and Luisa were a more fully professional, more coequal couple than George and Virgie, though his greater maturity and the fact he had no children with Luisa likely influenced this.[26]

In the summer of 1955 Luisa discovered she had thyroid cancer. After a series of operations at St. David's Hospital in Austin in which the cancer and her thyroid were removed, Sánchez updated concerned friends: "Luisa's illness has kept me so occupied and pre-occupied that I have had to reduce my paper work to the barest minimum—so you will forgive me if I have not been as chatty as heretofore. She is back home again, convalescing—so things will get back to normal soon." The cancer was caught early enough that she avoided extensive treatment. Luisa convalesced for three months before returning to work in late November 1955. They both had serious health problems, and while George's were more lasting, Luisa's caused her husband to constantly link their growing enthusiasm for travel as well as their joint work on projects to the conviction that they had to seize life now and in any way they could. Sánchez offhandedly remarked, "So, as you will gather, I have been very busy (and, consequently, very happy). I can say the same for Luisa. For two fugitives from incurable diseases (she from cancer, I from TB) we have an inordinate amount of fun." Unlike George's first marriage, in which health crises likely contributed to the split, this marriage remained solid and perhaps even deepened after Luisa's health scare.[27]

By 1951 George Eugene had long since joined the U.S. Navy, Connie was a student at the University of New Mexico, and George wanted to lower his alimony payments. This occasioned a last spat with Virgie and was far from his most shining moment. But first, in the spring of 1951, George Sánchez sought to modify the divorce decree of $120 a month toward alimony to Virgie and $40 a month per child by simply sending less money ($1,075.13 and $358.38 today). From April to November 1951, as he suffered the first of his many salary setbacks of the decade, George paid Virgie only $100 total ($895.94 today). Virgie went to court over it. George was in arrears $480 when the complaint reached the district court of Bernalillo County on November 17, 1951 ($4,300.52 today). Virgie acknowledged that while George Eugene was no longer eligible for child support, Connie still lived with her while attending school. Virgie claimed they both were ill and needed the full $120 a month in alimony (Connie's child support was not an issue). She also requested that George reimburse her legal fees. On November 23, 1951, George I. Sánchez was served with a writ to show cause for not meeting his obligations, and on December 6, Virgie's attorney assured the court that George had paid the outstanding balance of $480, including legal fees.[28]

But this clumsy attempt at decreasing his alimony payments was just the first step for Sánchez. The idea that Virgie needed to move on with her life, as he had, had taken root in him. And as the children moved into adulthood, he felt the original divorce decree of December 1946 needed modification. He made such a request on January 18, 1952, through local attorneys, including his friend Tibo J. Chavez, then lieutenant governor of New Mexico. George asked to modify the decree for several reasons: in 1946 he was not represented by an attorney; his doctor now advised him to work less because of his nagging health problems; and he had remarried. He did not ask to be exempted from making the monthly payment of $40 in child support for Connie. But he did ask that he be relieved of the $120 a month in alimony to Virgie. He noted that her health problems had cleared up and that she could now earn a living.[29]

On March 28, 1952, Virgie responded that the divorce terms had largely been set by her ex-husband, that he knew many attorneys and must have unofficially sought their help when negotiating it, and that he was healthy and active, since he was department chair and head of the American Council of Spanish-Speaking People (ACSSP), with a downtown office in Austin. She averred further that since he owned automobiles and boats, had built a lake house in Austin, and used a maid service he must be doing quite well financially. Virgie also claimed she was the one in ill health, producing a note from her physician that she had "hypo tension" and could not work. The part about his downtown office with the ACSSP must have infuriated Sánchez, as Virgie's knowledge of it had stemmed from a letter he wrote Connie in which he bragged a bit about his new civil rights organization, assured her of his health, and then tried to arrange a meeting with her in Albuquerque on his way to Arizona for a professional obligation. He signed it, "Love Daddy." The letter was personal, and it must have angered him to see how Virgie's attorney twisted it in such a way that made his serious health issues seem like a lie and his activism like a lucrative side job.[30]

George's support should have been $960 per year in child support (assuming George Eugene was included) and $1,440 in alimony per year from the beginning of 1947 to the end of 1951, for a total of $2,400 a year (using 1951 calculations; $8,601.05, $12,901.57, and $21,502.62 today). However, George Eugene left for the armed forces in the late forties and no longer qualified, a point both parties agreed on. In those five years (not counting the years of separation during 1945 and 1946, when his support was greater) he spent the following: in 1947, $3,552.57; in 1948, $2,924.14; in 1949, $2,701.59; in 1950, $2,191; and in 1951, $2,614 ($37,110.02, $28,264.06, $26,442.10, $21,177.70, and $23,419.93 today). In total, his support was mostly greater than that stipulated in the decree. George usually sent more to his ex-wife than was required and, perhaps because he paid for military school and college directly, sent less to his children than required. Nineteen fifty was the only year his totals were below what they should have been, although that seems not to have been the subject of any complaint by Virgie. While the record does not show him to be what might today be called a deadbeat dad, George Sánchez's handling of the situation does not show him in the best light. Subsequent events reflected even more poorly on him.[31]

The Bernalillo County District Court disagreed with George's request in a ruling on April 18. In a brief declaratory decision, the district judge simply remarked that the evidence provided did not justify a modification. The court then ordered George to cover Virgie's attorney's fees to the tune of $50 ($439.52 today). At this point, the only thing Sánchez could be accused of is occasionally falling behind or being slightly short with his child support and alimony. But sometime in 1952, perhaps immediately after the verdict against him, though

more likely in the fall of that year, George broke the law by ignoring the decision and stopping all payments. George I. Sánchez's civil rights activism did not
involve civil disobedience. One cannot find evidence of a traffic ticket, much
less an arrest record for him in his voluminous and exhaustive paper collection.
However, in stopping all forms of alimony and child support sometime in 1952
Sánchez broke the law. There was little Virgie could do about it while he was in
Texas. In those days alimony and child support enforcement rarely crossed state
lines. By November 1956 Virgie and her attorney complained to the Bernalillo
district court that George owed $5,760 in alimony over four years ($49,329.53
today). The court ordered George to appear or face contempt of court charges.
There is no evidence he ever did.[32]

At this point the divorce record ends, though the ramifications of this story
came back to haunt him later. Sánchez's high-powered attorney, the sitting
lieutenant governor of New Mexico Tibo Chavez, declined to bill him for services in a losing cause, a generosity Sánchez refused. Perhaps Chavez felt
guilty? The documents prepared by Sánchez and his attorneys were hasty and
perfunctory, as if the parties were assured of an easy victory. They must have
been surprised by the vigorous defense of the original settlement by Virgie and
her attorney. Virgie utilized his personal letters to their children; she twisted his
civil rights activism into a moneymaking enterprise; and she kept up the drum-
beat that he was hiding money. She may not have wanted her ex-husband back,
but she did want him to owe her. The divorce decree meant something to the
wealthy Virgie beyond money. Of less comprehension, however, is how George
justified breaking the law he spent so many years upholding and perfecting in
the pursuit of justice for his people. This was Sánchez at his pettiest.[33]

The immigration issue, whether over contracted workers from Mexico or the
undocumented, was a crucial aspect of George I. Sánchez's activism on behalf
of Mexican Americans. While he pursued civil rights, he also employed sharp
distinctions between citizen and noncitizen. In a way that is perhaps more sophisticated than that of others of his generational cohort, Sánchez always remembered the humanity of Mexican immigrants and the brutal inhumanity of
the conditions in which they worked; and he excoriated those vested interests
that mercilessly exploited them. Nevertheless, his focus on citizenship as the
key principle of Mexican American activism left immigrant brothers, sisters,
and cousins out of the mix. Sánchez opposed the renewal of the bracero agreement and pushed hard against undocumented immigration. While he was not
alone in this, he was a leader in it. Such hard and fast citizenship distinctions in

the long run proved divisive. While the Saunders–Leonard report was controversial, Operation Wetback and other publications demonstrated the divisions
among the Mexican American community more broadly. Did Sánchez's extensive immigration restrictionism alter these exploitive conditions? Did it help
better the lot of Mexican immigrants or Mexican Americans? The answer is
no. This *citizenship sacrifice* that Mexican Americans sought to make would
never be honored by the economic and political powers bent on exploiting
them. This immigration activism was a failure. It was a more complex and prin-
cipled failure than previously thought, but a failure nonetheless.

SEGREGATED SCHOOLS AND PERCEPTIONS OF INEQUALITY

We need to look upon our American minorities objectively. When we do so, we will find that much that we think of as due to ethnic or racial differences are products of a state of mind, of a diseased state of mind, not that of the minority group. Jim Crowism—whether practiced against Negro, Jew, Mexican, or Chinese—is a mass mental aberration, a disease of which we must be cured for our own sakes, if only because of enlightened self-interest. From my point of view, the so-called problem of American minorities is, in reality, the problem of the majority.

To treat a child to genteel segregation because he knows only Spanish is a frightening distortion of good intentions. Then, too, to attach the idea of deficiency and handicap to so beautiful and valuable a language as Spanish hardly fits in with modern educational thought and national policy. For those well-intentioned souls who have endorsed these programs one can only ask forgiveness, for they know not what they do.

So prominent were his civil rights and political activism during the 1950s, one could forget that George I. Sánchez was a professor of education whose primary responsibility at the University of Texas was training future teachers. He studied as well as challenged the unequal and segregated schools provided to Mexican American children. The historical literature on the Chicana/o public school experience is a depressing read of cultural insensitivity, of teaching children to be satisfied with an inferior place in American life, of harsh corporal punishment, and of segregation. Even sympathetic educators taught in ways that would be considered grossly unacceptable today. For example, Sánchez wrote that by the late 1950s about 80 percent of Mexican American students in the public schools of Texas spent more than one year in the first grade, only 25 percent reached the eighth grade, and a mere 8.5 percent reached the twelfth grade. The education historians Guadalupe San Miguel, Gilbert González, Victoria-Maria MacDonald and I have documented a public school system throughout the Southwest that failed Chicana/o children at all levels. It is small wonder the Mexican American Generation made education its marquee issue. Education reform was the life-blood of the Mexican American civil rights movement, and George Sánchez was at the heart of it. Just after his recovery from TB in 1945, Sánchez remarked to M. C. Gonzales, "The more I think about it the more I believe that the time has come to go after the segregated school." He went on, "I think this is the biggest single contribution that anyone can make in this entire field. I can think of no more important a service to our people and our country than to have this issue settled once and for all. Personally, I would be more than satisfied with a lifetime of activity in this field if, when I passed on, I would have on my record the participation in the solution of this matter." Segregated schools that fail to advance opportunity for Mexican Americans linger still.[1]

Sánchez's challenges to educational segregation began during the Second World War but took flight after the war. This led to the *Delgado v. Bastrop* case of 1948. A segregationist backlash against *Delgado* resulted in nearly a decade of delays and bureaucratic red tape leading to the *Hernández v. Driscoll* case of 1957, another ultimately hollow victory for Tejanos. The obfuscation of civil rights by the Texas Education Agency took a toll on Sánchez throughout the fifties as he lost professional influence among them and his own scholarly production slowed. Sánchez nevertheless defended his profession during this decade of harsh antieducation opinion. What separates my treatment here from other educational scholarship is its commitment not just to explain the Chicana/o desegregation effort of the 1950s but also to explore what its foremost educator, George I. Sánchez, actually thought about integration. Sánchez's purist perspective on the topic of integration is very useful to historians seeking to interpret the past; it was not, however, always easy to live with at the time. As I have written elsewhere, Sánchez "could be dogmatically short-sighted in his insistence on the primacy of racial integration as a one-size-fits-all solution to any and all problems." Though Sánchez spent his energy pushing for the desegregation of Mexican American schools, he had a well-developed idea of what the concept of integration was and how it would help not just Mexican Americans' but everyone's educational experience.[2]

POSTWAR PLANS

In 1946 Sánchez ignited new academic research on educational segregation in Texas. Submitting an internal grant application to the Research Council of the University of Texas, he received $1,200 to fund Virgil E. Strickland's doctoral research on the subject ($14,369.48 today). This resulted in an article the two men coauthored in 1948. That the university committed to this research was a feather in Sánchez's cap as he tried to sell the GEB on a much larger grant. This research aided civil rights activists, then beginning to challenge school segregation in the courts, an application of which the university administration and Board of Regents were likely unaware. However, Sánchez needed a larger public podium and base of funding. This is where the GEB came in through the SWCESSP and the SSSP. SWCESSP meetings gave Sánchez an opportunity to unburden himself to a friendly audience about the knotty issue of racism in education beyond just the segregated school. At the SWCESSP meeting of 1951, for example, Sánchez attacked not just bigots spewing obvious hatred, but also the condescension of allegedly sympathetic educators who downplayed the brutality and power of racism, as evidenced by the first epigraph above.[3]

Sánchez was obstinate on the issue. In early 1947 President J. G. Flowers of Southwest Texas State Teachers College in San Marcos, the future president Lyndon Johnson's alma mater, applied for GEB funding for an experimental Mexican school in San Marcos. Sánchez assessed the proposal, and his dialogue with the GEB's Fred McCuistion, who at the time considered the professor's massive SSSP grant, is illuminating as to where Sánchez stood in the eyes of others. Sánchez wrote, "For whatever my opinion is worth, I think it is a serious mistake to give any sort of encouragement to any project which, by commission or omission, encourages the *status quo* of segregated schools. I have consistently refused to participate in any activities in connection with any segregated school unless one of the principal goals of that activity was the elimination of segregation." He continued, "It is exceedingly easy, and therefore particularly dangerous, to want to make the segregated school more efficient and more attractive. Usually, this means that it becomes increasingly difficult to eliminate segregation since the segregated institution has been made more attractive, palliatable [sic], and sometimes has attained a peculiarly prized prestige." "But, as I have said in past addresses," Sánchez concluded with a flourish, "the segregated school is a concentration camp—you may gold plate the fence posts and silver plate the bobbed [sic] wire and hang garlands of roses all the way around it, it is still a concentration camp."[4]

McCuistion countered, "I can understand your anxiety in the matter of elimination of segregation. It is a major and probably a long-time goal but, of course, I suppose there are a number of individuals and institutions anxious to take the next logical steps in the improvement of institutions and agencies serving the minority groups but who are not in a position to take a militant stand on the question of segregation." McCuistion politely characterized Sánchez as militant at the very moment he evaluated his large proposal. Even more striking is that Sánchez continued to pester McCuistion with accusations of Flowers's disingenuousness and hints that San Marcos might be the target of litigation. None of this affected Sánchez's GEB grant, as McCuistion ignored the goading. But it illustrates the degree to which Sánchez pushed his principles and how far out in front of the rest of society he was on desegregation.[5]

Sánchez updated the ACLU's Roger Baldwin on all these developments. With regard to litigation, Baldwin's advice was to get those lawyers working, and Sánchez confided, "I have had so many disappointments in this regard that I am getting almost cynical about it. There are all kinds of individuals whose hearts are in the right place but, somehow, I have not been able to get lawyers to proceed with the actual test of instituting a case. The energy I have expended trying to coax these lawyers would have earned me several law degrees, and then I personally could have done the lawyering!" Sánchez lamented to Baldwin that the best way forward was for Mexican Americans to get outside legal help. Already interested in supporting Mexican American civil rights, Baldwin coyly responded, "You have my sympathy. If you don't get results now I think I can interest what you call an outside agency. Let us know."[6]

DELGADO V. BASTROP

Tejano activists got a boost from southern California. After being denied the opportunity of enrolling their children in the nearby white school for the 1944–45 school year, Mexican American parents sued the Westminster, California, school district in federal court. In 1946 Judge Paul McCormick decided in *Méndez v. Westminster* that Mexican American segregation was illegal. In 1947 a federal appeals court unanimously upheld the ruling. This was a huge win for Sánchez. In 1946 he spoke to the local media about possible legal challenges in Texas and wrote to State Superintendent of Public Instruction L. A. Woods of the initial ruling's applicability. Weeks before the appeals court ratified *Méndez* in 1947, Sánchez wrote to Woods about segregated Mexican schools in Travis County's rural, unincorporated areas. This spurred an agency investigation; Sánchez was copied on the results. In 1947 Tejano activists focused on school segregation in the small community of Bastrop, just east of Austin, in federal court. The *Delgado v. Bastrop Independent School District* case, decided in 1948, was a victory. While more scholars are aware of *Méndez* than of *Delgado*, the latter is also important. Mexican American attorneys tried *Delgado* at the same federal court and at the same time as the NAACP's landmark *Sweatt v. Painter* case over segregation at the University of Texas was under way. In addition, *Delgado* enjoined state officials as potential conspirators, a novel legal tactic. And the Mexican government played a hidden role when the Mexican consulate of San Antonio, Gustavo Ortiz Hernan, connected Sánchez with the attorney Gus Garcia.[7]

In the spring of 1947 Garcia worked on securing a legal opinion of *Méndez* from Attorney General Price Daniel. Aware that Daniel coveted higher office, Garcia and Sánchez correctly surmised that in order to obtain Chicana/o support in the factionalized Texas Democratic Party Daniel might give on Mexican American segregation. Daniel's office refused to defend Mexican American segregation in April 1947, months away from the filing of *Delgado* and weeks from *Sweatt*, when Assistant Attorney General Joe R. Greenhill warned the town of Cuero in Legal Opinion V-128 not to construct separate school facilities for Mexican children. Sánchez and Garcia lobbied Daniel and Greenhill over the matter. But Opinion V-128 hedged that separation for pedagogical reasons remained possible via proper, scientific testing. This resembled the *Salvatierra* decision of 1930 more than anything new. Sánchez had problems with Opinion V-128 that he shared with Greenhill. He wrote, "If, as your opinion indicates, pupils (any pupils, 'Mexican' or other) can be segregated in separate buildings on the basis of 'language deficiencies,' why can't they be segregated on the basis of deficiencies in arithmetic, or ability to draw, or muscular reaction speed, or any other arbitrarily selected subject matter, accomplishment, etc.?" He then asked why the permissible level of segregation was set at the third grade. Sánchez assured Greenhill that permitting schools even limited segregation would "boomerang on the very first instance that the matter is brought to the attention of the federal courts." Sánchez knew of what he spoke: Mexican American activists were then preparing *Delgado*. And he knew to whom he spoke: Greenhill, Attorney General Daniel's civil rights litigator, was also a trusted political advisor who managed Daniel's successful U.S. Senate campaign of 1950 and gubernatorial campaign of 1956.[8]

Sánchez expanded his protests to a wider audience (fig. 9.1). In 1947 he wrote to the governor, comptroller, superintendent of schools, Board of Education, attorney general, and the state's Good Neighbor Commission to complain about Opinion V-128 and note that several communities were already violating it. Sánchez worked with two University of Texas student groups on protests to state authorities. At the state LULAC convention of 1947 in San Antonio,

9.1. Sánchez (*third row, second from right*) and members of the Alba Club in 1947. The
Alba Club was a Mexican American student organization at the University of Texas
that also acted as an activist group with regard to civil rights in the late 1940s and
1950s. Reproduction by permission of Benson Latin American Center.

delegates created the Special School Fund that Sánchez administered. LULAC
claimed ownership of *Delgado:* "Well, it is done. The segregational [*sic*] suit has
been filed in a U.S. Federal District Court, and the money that each one of the
councils pledged at the state convention a short while back is greatly needed. It
is a Lulac fight even though Lulac is not the plaintiff as such in the suit, and it
is our duty to help see it through. So rush the money through, and do not spare
the horses."[9]

The LULAC Special School Fund opens a window into the fascinating reality of Mexican American Generation activism. In 1947 and 1948 LULAC raised
$10,252.26 for the endeavor (in 1947 calculations unless otherwise noted;

$107,094.74 today). Sánchez's public accounting indicates that the fund covered clerical work to the tune of $989.50 and travel for the attorneys at $1,521.24 ($10,336.28 and $15,890.82 today). The bulk, $6,600, went toward attorneys' fees ($68,943.36 today). Sánchez recounted that one prominent Texas attorney requested $20,000 for the job ($208,919.28 today). So he felt very positive about assembling a national team of attorneys for considerably less than half that amount. After *Delgado*, the Special School Fund had $1,141.52 left earmarked for checking on compliance (in 1949 calculations; $11,172.75 today). When Sánchez publicly alluded to spending personal funds on the project, he likely meant $800 of ACLU money left over from the Texas Civil Rights Fund for expert witnesses on the pedagogical unsoundness of segregation ($8,356.77 today). These fund-raising efforts are inspiring. Impoverished people with more basic problems in their lives than segregated schools pitched in for a larger cause. The letters to Sánchez from local groups demonstrate not only the unity of purpose, but also the heterogeneity of the Mexican American community. In towns where LULAC was not organized, other Chicana/o groups contributed, like the Community Club of Bishop, the Nahara, Pavilion, Loanda, Happy Girls, Anahuac, Toros, and Lamplighters groups of Kingsville, and the American Veterans Committee of Laredo; support came from a Woodmen of the World mutual aid society and Spanish-language cinemas in Sinton. New Mexicans pitched in too, led by the national president of LULAC, José Maldonado of Santa Fe. Canuto Ortiz from Orange Grove presented Sánchez nearly $100 in donations from his community (in 1948 calculations; $966.58 today). In Spanish he listed the precise amounts each person gave each collector. Recognizing the incongruity of his usual practice of expressing himself in English out of fidelity to LULAC's official language position, Sánchez here thanked the community in Spanish. Hector P. Garcia, then a LULACer, was in a fund-raising competition with the San Antonio LULACs.[10]

The LULAC Special School Fund was quickly raised and even more quickly spent. It generated conflict between Sánchez, who wanted to preserve the money for desegregation cases, and LULAC officials, who desired the money for other matters. The LULAC lobbying trip of January 1949 to Washington by Sánchez, Gus Garcia, and President Raoul Cortez of LULAC over immigration was financed by a $1,000 loan from the Special School Fund ($9,787.61 today). Sánchez made the loan on the condition LULAC quickly reimburse it. But after membership complained about the necessity of raising funds again, Cortez and his executive secretary broached to Sánchez the idea of reimbursing the fund later. Sánchez, threatening to resign, hotly replied that he never would have signed off on the loan had he known there was any question of their delaying an immediate reimbursement. LULAC immediately backed off and soon repaid the loan. In the meantime Sánchez pestered LULAC locals who had not met their earlier pledges.[11]

Sánchez assembled a body of expert witnesses against educational segregation. Drawn mainly from his SWCESSP, they included two border superintendents, J. W. Nixon of the Laredo Independent School District and H. L. Barber of the Mission Independent School District. Sánchez tapped two highly published, non-Texan schoolteachers in Prudence Bostwick of the Denver public schools and Marie Hughes of the Los Angeles public schools and the American Council of Education. Arthur Campa, then at the University of Denver, contributed a social adjustment statement. Herschel T. Manuel and Frederick Eby of the University of Texas offered arguments drawn from educational psychology, history, philosophy, and anticommunist rhetoric. Lloyd Tireman of the University of New Mexico, despite much hesitancy, also contributed a statement.[12]

Sánchez was a full member of the *Delgado* team. He supplied background material and copies of *Méndez*; he strategized over which schools should be sued; and he conducted firsthand investigations of facilities. Additionally, he good humoredly pointed out the irony that the Perez family, one of the plaintiffs, claimed their children had only learned Spanish in the segregated schools of Elgin after having known just English at their previous abode in Galveston. He failed to get Congressman Fernández and Senator Chávez of New Mexico more involved, however. Abraham L. Wirin, an attorney for the firm Wirin, Rissman and Okrand, regarded Sánchez's contributions as tremendous and remarked, "If the case is lost now, it will certainly be the fault of the lawyers; and if the case is won, the lawyers should send up hosannas." Sánchez was a constant force against compromise. One historian rightly regards Sánchez as "the most militant of the middle class reformers of the 1940s and 1950s." He also schemed to broaden *Delgado* to antidiscrimination legislation.[13]

But *Delgado* ultimately proved to be hollow. Though the pretrial settlement declared unconstitutional the racial segregation of Mexican American schoolchildren, it allowed for the loophole of curricular segregation up to three years. This was, in effect, a continuation of the reality of segregation since most Mexican American children never made it past the early grades anyway. Initially, however, the prosecuting team was enthusiastic about the ruling. Sánchez gushed to Baldwin that *Delgado* was stronger than *Méndez* and represented "a full vindication" of his years of activism. The benefactor Charles Bunn felt *Delgado* settled the matter of Chicana/o educational segregation once and for all. Sánchez effusively congratulated the Mexican consul of San Antonio. It was a happy moment. Wirin continued to represent Sánchez as "the effectual brain trust behind the case" to civil rights activists around the country. This moment of triumph would soon prove illusory, however.[14]

WOODS, DEL RIO, AND GILMER–AIKEN

Before Sánchez and his allies could codify *Delgado* within the public school regulatory apparatus, they turned their attention to several lingering examples of segregation. He remarked to Baldwin, "As you know I am a pragmatist—proof of the pudding is in the eating, and I will not be satisfied simply with a Court decision without full compliance." Yet Sánchez vastly underestimated the widespread societal commitment to preserving racial segregation; he also overestimated *Delgado*'s utility. This was an entrenched guerrila war to preserve Jim Crow. At this point a naïve Sánchez unsuccessfully sounded out Baldwin on creating a professional Mexican American civil rights group to allow the amateurs (himself) to go back to their day jobs. But there was no way out for him. These efforts only went as far as he could spur them. This would always be a severe limitation to the Mexican American civil rights movement of this era, brilliant though Sánchez may have been.[15]

Word of segregation in San Marcos, Cuero, Hondo, and Robstown reached Sánchez and Gus Garcia during and shortly after *Delgado*. A teacher in San Marcos, Felipe de Jesús Reyna, fed Sánchez reports about the situation there and lost his job for it. After Chicanas/os in San Marcos questioned the school setup there in light of *Delgado*, Sánchez advised them to sign a petition protesting segregation; they did so in early July 1948. By the fall Sánchez and Gus Garcia protested to the state education agency. The Special School Fund from LULAC at this point had little money, but only a handful of activists knew that. Sánchez accompanied Superintendent Woods's investigator to San Marcos and noted that the local justification of segregation, based on the alleged filth of Mexican Americans, spelled trouble for the state in a possible trial. But in early 1949 Woods mediated the dispute in a way that gave these schools cover to erect a zoning plan mirroring their designs for racial separation. Though disappointed, Sánchez regarded San Marcos as a temporary setback. He felt Woods was a politician who would work with Mexican Americans to eliminate segregation commensurately with how politically beneficial he found it. Woods had already been of enormous help to Sánchez during the Good Neighbor days of the Second World War and conducted a study of Latin American education in the middle of *Delgado* that aided Mexican Americans. Woods also allowed Sánchez and his allies to investigate schools and send complaints directly to him. In the fall of 1948 Sánchez and Woods even discussed a collaborative partnership between the State Department of Education and the University of Texas College of Education to shape *Delgado*'s policy ramifications.[16]

Ultimately, conflict in Del Rio, a small border city upriver from Laredo, ended this cooperation. The Del Rio complaint came to Superintendent Woods in the first week of 1949. His top assistant, Terrell M. Trimble, investigated and on February 1 confirmed that Del Rio segregated Mexican Americans illegally. Trimble then recommended withdrawing its state accreditation until the situation was corrected. Such a move would have resulted in significantly decreased state funding. The federal judge Ben Rice of Austin, *Delgado*'s author, advised Woods he would not reopen *Delgado* to judicial oversight for each new incident. So, fully on his own, Woods dissolved Del Rio's accreditation on February 12. On April 23, however, he allowed a rehearing of the matter at his office with attorneys from both sides. Del Rio's insistence on a formal legal appeal to a purely administrative process suggests how committed they were to preserve the segregation of brown from white. It was not going to let this go forward without a fight. That same day Woods confirmed his suspension. Soon thereafter, however, the State Board of Education, which oversaw the public schools and was usually a rubber stamp for Woods, reversed the action. This alarmed Mexican American activists. They intended Del Rio to be the one big, post-*Delgado* example to the multitude of little communities not yet in compliance. Instead, their legs were cut out from beneath them.[17]

As further evidence that the immediate *Delgado* afterglow dulled Sánchez's vision, he did not originally regard the state's massive overhaul of public schools in 1949 as adversely affecting civil rights. It did. This overhaul, generally referred to as the Gilmer–Aiken laws, reorganized the state board and agency, increased state support with new funding formulas, enhanced teacher professionalization and pay, lengthened school terms, and bolstered curricular rigor. These educational reforms put Texas in the vanguard of southern states with regard to educational modernization. However, the standard Chicano perspective on Gilmer–Aiken conspiratorially regards it as part of a broader strategy by "Anglo political leaders" who "aimed at undermining *Delgado*'s impact." There is something to this interpretation.[18]

Only by February 1949 did Sánchez begin to worry about Gilmer–Aiken's effect on Mexican Americans' desegregation efforts. He wrote to Hector Garcia that Woods and his office had a good rapport with Mexican American activists and that within a few more years they could end school segregation forever. This hinged on the idea that "as time progresses, *elective* officials will have to cater to us more and more—and that is not necessarily true of *appointive* officials." As Gilmer–Aiken looked more likely to pass, Woods abruptly halted all cooperation on civil rights. Sánchez continued to work with Garcia on back-to-school drives and the election of favorable State Board of Education members. AGIF and LULAC then informed Attorney General Daniel that twenty-four schools across the state were in violation of *Delgado*. Mexican Americans were not complacent. They simply had not yet fully realized that, on the cusp of achieving a triumph, they had just been dealt a crippling blow.[19]

THE KANGAROO COURT

Exchanging an elected state superintendent of public instruction for an appointed commissioner of education and a nine-person, appointed Board of Education for a twenty-one-person, elected Board of Education rendered the newly named Texas Education Agency (TEA) in 1949 more attuned to the dominant societal wish to preserve Jim Crow. Woods's successor, J. W. Edgar, formerly the superintendent of the Austin public schools, took over the reorganized TEA in early 1950 and within a few months crafted an administrative appeals process for racial segregation complaints. This came about as a result of lobbying by Sánchez and Gus Garcia. Hewing strictly to *Delgado*, the state insisted that local school boards first have the opportunity to address complaints before the commissioner heard any appeal. Edgar set himself up as his own federal court overseeing "whether or not in his judgment there has been a violation of the statutes or of constitutional rights." This was a kangaroo court that gave local districts years to perfect segregation, while the real courts refused to interfere in a state agency's regulatory functions.[20]

Sánchez was aware that this process represented a bureaucratic trap. Nevertheless, potential desegregation cases from the towns of Kyle, Nixon, Sanderson, Carrizo Springs, Austin, and Pecos between 1950 and 1957 were mired in this administrative morass. The TEA dropped the Kyle complaint in 1951 since the replacement attorney representing Mexican Americans would not have had proper legal standing were the TEA offices an actual federal court. With regard to Nixon in 1951 Edgar rebuffed Mexican American attempts to avoid the lengthy appeals process and threatened to end all cooperation should the case appear in a federal court. In the Sanderson case of 1952–53, Edgar decreed that the people of Sanderson were wonderful, were technically in the wrong, and would get another year in which to tinker with their segregationist student classification system. A complaint of 1952 from Austin involved how school choice practices reinforced racial separation, and the Pecos complaint of 1953 dealt with district zone boundaries; neither met with decisive action from TEA.[21]

The Carrizo Springs case in 1954 was especially frustrating for Sánchez. Commissioner Edgar's investigators had warned the Carrizo Springs schools they were in violation of *Delgado*, and, despite this damning admission by the school, Mexican Americans were nonetheless forced to begin the mediation process at the local level, chewing up valuable time and resources. It took the entire fall term just to get Edgar to set a hearing for the end of the spring term. Sánchez, whose sister-in-law's family was party to the complaint, was furious with the delay and despised the way this process shifted the burden of proof in a manner inconsistent with courts of law: "I'm convinced that we don't have to go through the rigamarole set up by Edgar and the State Board of Education. . . . Seriously, though, it seems to me that we are sort of friends of the court when we inform Edgar that, apparently, he is participating in segregation. It is up to him, then, to prove or disprove that, and act accordingly." Sánchez elaborated on this unfair burden: "Why should *we* go on trial for pointing out to him that his sub-ordinates have placed him in the position of practicing what he has been enjoined against practicing?" The Carrizo Springs schools offered vague prom-ises of greater inclusion in the future. This weak compromise was the result of over a year of constant mediation, appeals, and local pressure against complain-ing families. Sánchez vented to one attorney that he felt "let down badly in the Carrizo Springs case" as he had encouraged his wife's kin to participate only to have them experience delay and local retaliation.[22]

Commissioner Edgar offers an instructive counterpoint to Sánchez. While Sánchez's position regarding ending racial segregation is something many readers today will readily agree with, such ideas would have been quite radical sixty years ago. Even though Sánchez and Edgar were of the same age, had similar experiences as young professionals, and were high achievers, they made very different choices. Sánchez taught and wrote while a professor at an impor-tant national research university; Edgar administered several large, challenging school districts throughout the state. Sánchez took controversial positions over matters of moral principle, as with segregation; Edgar assiduously skirted con-troversy through careful positioning, deflection, and bureaucratic procedure, especially over segregation. A fawning biography on Edgar makes a virtue of his obsequiousness to segregationists on the elected State Board of Education. He left a nearly quarter-century tenure at the TEA beloved by employees and school officials, who admired his light touch; by the time Sánchez's career ended he was mostly ignored by his colleagues and especially by the TEA. But over racial segregation—one of the great moral issues of their time—Sánchez was right and Edgar was embarrassingly wrong. Edgar did not hate racial mi-norities. He cared, just not enough to risk his job or status. Sánchez, who was

brilliant at most things, might have had more worldly success had he been willing to go along and get along. Yet he made very different choices. That he
could never count on the Edgars of the world, whatever their personal feelings,
made his struggle that much more difficult and lonely.[23]

HERNÁNDEZ V. DRISCOLL

The *Hernández v. Driscoll* case of 1957 was the last major school desegregation case involving Sánchez as a principal player. In 1954 a civil rights group
Sánchez directed (see chapter 10) sponsored several attorneys who protested
before Commissioner Edgar about segregation in the schools of Mathis, Texas,
a small farming community near Corpus Christi. Predictably, Edgar put this
action on hold for a year to allow Mathis to alter its practices. In the fall of 1955
Sánchez and the attorney James DeAnda of Corpus Christi personally inspected the schools and came away unimpressed. Most of the changes were
cosmetic. In his field notes to the attorneys, Sánchez remarked that this was
"a cut-and-dried case." The complaint in Mathis was similar to one from the
nearby town of Driscoll. In 1956 the U.S. Southern District Court of Texas
merged the two cases. Sánchez spread the word to allies throughout the Southwest and made available some money for the attorneys. Previewing his testimony, Sánchez explained to DeAnda, "You see, we would be in a hell of a mess
if we had segregated all the foreign-language groups that have come to the
U.S.—the Italians, Poles, Germans, French, etc. We did not segregate them for
not knowing English—rather, we put them into the *American* school (that does
not tolerate grouping on the basis of class, nationality, language, etc.) and they
became Americans."[24]

Sánchez's testimony in the resulting *Hernández v. Driscoll* victory of 1957 was
ultimately persuasive, despite his obvious romanticizing of the American immigrant educational experience and his own professional evolution away from
accepting limited amounts of pedagogical segregation. Judge James Allred, a
liberal former governor of the state during the Great Depression, did not creatively adjudicate, however. Allred simply applied *Delgado* to the circumstances
in Driscoll, which he separated from Mathis, and found that the school district
illegally segregated Mexican Americans without any testing for alleged language deficiencies. Instead of indicting the entire state, Allred reached a practical, narrow decision that reaffirmed *Delgado*. But in a post–*Brown v. Board of
Education* world, the utility of *Delgado* was questionable. DeAnda felt the narrow *Hernández* case only reaffirmed *Delgado* and worried at its effect on other
cases. This meant that other attorneys had to begin the process of proving all

over again that segregated schools were harmful and that pedagogical justifications for them were misapplied. It did not save Mexican Americans any steps in
the long, winding road toward desegregation.[25]

Sánchez's testimony of 1956 blew up on him. As I documented in chapter 7,
this was the testimony that resulted in his being "called on the carpet" by Dean
Haskew and higher administrators, which resulted, he claimed, in yet another
year of no raise for him. At the time, Sánchez countered his administration
with a forgotten anecdote. Apparently, several years earlier Dean Pittenger had
testified—like Sánchez without being subpoenaed but without a peep from the
Board of Regents—in *Sweatt* on behalf of the university's Jim Crow position.
No matter how righteously justified exposing such hypocrisy might have made
Sánchez feel at the time, it did not help smooth things over with his university
superiors.[26]

THE PROBLEM WITH "SPECIAL" EDUCATION

Sánchez was an integration purist who refused to see his people as less equal
than anyone else. To the SWCESSP meeting in Los Angeles in 1951 Sánchez
spoke presciently: "One of the most important factors in the segregation and
ostracism of population groups in this country is our uncritical use of terms. In
the deceptiveness, the treachery of terminology, in the limitation of words, lies
much of the misunderstanding about American minorities." He went on, "To
assume that all people of the same economic circumstance, or of the same color
of skin, or of the same faith or national origin are culturally homogenous is
absurd. Yet, as with Indians, we have let a term like Negro, or the Jewish faith,
or national origin (Mexican, German, Irish) become determinants in spheres
where the physical features, the religion, or the former homeland have no rel-
evancy except as pegs upon which to hang unscientific biases and generalizations." In other words, Mexican Americans were a problem only in the minds of
people who had difficulty reconciling basic human diversity. Sánchez regarded
any kind of "special" education programs for Spanish-speakers as suspect. But
he was not without sympathy. He knew that language differences in the classroom were challenging: "True, if children are not developing their English at
home, the school has to bear down harder on language development—use
more ingenuity, motivate more assiduously, and so on. But that is not *different*
education but *more and better* education."[27]

By mid-decade Sánchez wrote to Commissioner Edgar of his belief that the
TEA, fearful of the issue of racial segregation, had abdicated its duty to study
Mexican Americans. Edgar had already been thinking the same thing and

asked the professor's help in getting a multiyear study off the ground. Sánchez believed Edgar and the TEA might finally help this time. He even ran interference when local Mexican Americans asked why their children were being singled out with surveys. Sánchez once again found himself extremely disappointed. Why? TEA settled on a large-scale, one-size-fits-all preschool instructional program focusing exclusively on language and conducted in a segregated atmosphere. As indicated in the second epigraph above, Sánchez creatively named the discrimination deriving from such well-intentioned programs as "genteel segregation." As he explained, "I abhor segregation! *And I deny any virtue that may be ascribed to it!* I do not think that either democracy or decency can thrive in the concentration camp. They can silver-plate the camp's barbed wire, gold plate the fence posts, hang garlands all around, and spray the interior with Chanel No. 5—*it still stinks.*"[28]

Sánchez's anger at the years of unofficial support of segregationist school districts by TEA and at its administration of the special preschool instructional program for Mexican American children boiled over into personal animus toward Commissioner Edgar. The inspiration for this program, however, came from the Chicana/o community. This gave Sánchez even more heartburn. In the 1950s, under the direction of Felix Tijerina, the Houston restaurateur and conservative LULAC national president, Texas LULAC began a preschool English language–learning radio program called the Little Schools of the 400, designed to teach four hundred English words to Mexican American children over several broadcasts. This was considered enough English vocabulary to avoid the children's pedagogical segregation when they entered school. Ironically, Edgar's TEA adopted the framework from this program in response to the study Sánchez helped with in the mid-1950s. Many scholars (myself included) have lauded LULAC's efforts here as evidence of Mexican American agency during the heyday of Jim Crow. But Sánchez never saw it that way and made a persuasive argument why not. To the LULACer Albert Armendariz he wrote that at the very moment Mexican Americans had proven in a federal court that pedagogical justifications for segregated classrooms were unconstitutional (an overenthusiastic reading of the 1957 *Hernández* case), the Tijerinas of the community eagerly initiated more segregation. Sánchez argued in a statement to LULAC, "Ladies and gentlemen, I am unalterably opposed to segregation whether that segregation be set up with good intentions or with bad ones, whether in some respects it be beneficial [*sic*] or whether it is all bad. The endorsement of special classes in public schools for our little children who may know only Spanish at the age of six is segregation—genteel segregation, to be sure, but segregation nonetheless."[29]

Was Sánchez so obsessed with integration that he ignored his own community's needs? Possibly. Sánchez was an integration purist. He was more militant about it than his peers. By the late 1950s and 1960s this uncompromising stance put him at odds with Mexican Americans who felt compensatory programs in their communities were beneficial. But for Sánchez, simply gaining a government program was harmful if that program did not meaningfully support the full integration of Mexican Americans in a physical and intellectual sense. In the 1980s David Montejano compellingly argued, "The stability of the segregated order rested on Mexican recognition of their own inferiority." Sánchez's opposition to special education echoed that same idea, just much earlier. What he most objected to in Tijerina's well-meaning, practical program was its acceptance of the premise that something was inherently wrong with the Mexican American child that required abnormal energy and planning from society to fix. To Sánchez, whatever vocabulary was taught in these programs was nothing next to the larger, negative lesson their very existence implied to Anglo officials and to Mexican Americans themselves.[30]

RACIAL JUSTICE OVER ACADEMIC GLORY

Activism hurt George I. Sánchez's academic productivity. In the early 1950s he still published substantially with major GEB support. By the end of the decade, however, he had published only a few book chapters, articles in minor journals, and a coauthored bibliography. In 1948 Carey McWilliams, then an editor at W. W. Norton, solicited from Sánchez a book on the problems of the Southwest through an autobiographical lens. Though flattered at the chance to examine the life of a people and region through the prism of his own life, Sánchez declined owing to his civil rights work. This is a tragedy. On the whole, Sánchez's desire to popularize knowledge compromised subtlety and sophistication. Additionally, he remained a humanist in a discipline becoming increasingly quantitative. One of his central intellectual preoccupations was language. Though another scholar writes of a tension between Sánchez's support for vernaculars and his desire for integration, the commingling of the two is not irreconcilable. By the 1940s Sánchez supported Puerto Rico's bilingual school system as well as vernacular instruction for Native Americans. In 1952 he wrote to a UNESCO committee to support vernacular instruction. And he directed a fascinating dissertation by Sam Frank Cheavens called "Vernacular Languages and Education." In 1954 he published an essay in the *New Mexico School Review* that reframed the issue of language handicap away from notions of disability or dysfunction. The professor still railed against IQ tests. And he remained a social reconstructionist in the classroom despite McCarthyism's chilling effect.[31]

Sánchez enjoyed mentoring graduate students. Between 1940 and 1972 he supervised twenty-eight doctoral dissertations and sixty-five masters theses. Even in a nonchair role, he often exerted great influence in shaping research projects. His students were passionate about their professor. Sánchez also gave of himself to students outside his program. For example, in the forties and fifties he actively supported the young Julian Samora, an early pioneer in Chicano and Latino studies. An extension of Sánchez's mentoring was the John Hay Whitney Foundation's Opportunity Fellowships Program for minority students seeking postgraduate degrees. Sánchez was among the assembly that created them at a meeting in the Waldorf-Astoria Hotel in New York City in December 1949. This group included the Rosenwald Fund's Edwin Embree, Fisk University's Charles Johnson, and the future housing and urban development secretary Robert Weaver. To Sánchez, who remained active in this program into the 1960s, this was another way to find positive, professional validation beyond his depressing existence as a second-class faculty member at the University of Texas.[32]

Sánchez was interested in students with disabilities. A blind student he informally mentored and with whom he shared his office piqued his curiosity over what the university did to support such students. Sánchez had to change offices after stepping down as department chair and asked Dean of Student Life Arno Nowotny about suggestions for continuing to work with the young man, noting that students with such disabilities "need a central coordinator or expediter—to schedule volunteer readers, arrange for space, etc." What Sánchez was leading up to was a student disabilities office. He later joined a university committee called the Faculty–Student Committee on Handicapped Students that called for a greater university commitment. Now walking with a cane and permanently slumped to one side undoubtedly aroused Sánchez's sympathy for those who needed a more level playing field.[33]

The 1950s were a difficult time for his profession. An intellectual reaction against progressive education regarded colleges of education, pedagogical experimentation, and the professors who participated in them as the main problem in education. One historian writes, "Almost without warning, the decade of the 1950s became a period of criticism of American education unequaled in modern times" because of widespread concern over an alleged preoccupation with life adjustment and self-esteem. Colleges of education were accused of ignoring intellectual content as the central goal of schooling. Sánchez, who had his own problems with the profession's disdainful manner of categorizing minorities as well as with its increasing abandonment of corporal punishment, had some sympathy for this attitude. But he also acknowledged that the anti-education mood was dangerous.[34]

What truly annoyed Sánchez was that historians, of which he considered himself one, were so prominent in this trend. To the Latin American historian Lewis Hanke of the University of Texas, Sánchez sarcastically wrote, "Academicians do not know how to teach what they know! How could they? They are not trained as educators—they know virtually nothing about method or the learning process, about classroom organization and administration, etc. They teach as they were taught by other academicians—the blind leading the blind!" For Sánchez it was the piling on he found so offensive, remarking that "generalization, blanket condemnation, and militant yammerings are not only unworthy of scholars but of no avail, except to broaden the breach and crystallize attitudes hitherto only vaguely held." Sánchez continued these arguments with J. Frank Dobie, the famed folklorist, who attempted to soothe Sánchez's irritation: "When I belabor Education, spelled with a capital E, as 'the unctuous elaboration of the obvious,' I am not including George Sánchez. I feel confident you will be on the side of the angels until you die." In 1961 Sánchez voiced pointed opposition to state legislation overhauling teacher certification so as to deemphasize colleges of education. While he acknowledged the abundance of "how to" over "what for" courses, this weakness in his mind did not justify the wholesale disparagement of the discipline. In 1958 Sánchez needled the Ford Foundation's Fund for the Advancement of Education for bringing together a group of prominent U.S. historians such as Richard Hofstadter, Arthur Schlesinger, Merle Curti, and Bernard Bailyn to focus on education as an entirely ignored historical topic. What he found insulting was how history of education specialists in education colleges were left out of Ford's project, which boasted that no one in their group could possibly be described as having had any training in education history, implying that this was to their credit.[35]

George I. Sánchez was an education professor who was proud of his profession's role in shaping the training of teachers. But he was concerned also with the bigger educational picture. From the *Delgado* case in the late 1940s to the promise and ultimate frustration of desegregation throughout the 1950s culminating in *Hernández*, the subject of justice for Mexican Americans and their integration into American society drove Sánchez. He pushed against fellow Mexican Americans as well as sympathetic liberals who, to his mind, only dimly understood the roots of educational injustice and unintentionally contributed to it through "special" education. Sánchez was a unique educational thinker whose insistence on the basic fundamentals of his discipline—well-trained teachers, a sense of professionalism, and a concern for and curiosity about the students they taught—eschewed complex theory while remaining flexible with respect to positive reform and activism. Sánchez's willingness to criticize his profession for mirroring a racist society rather than combating it, to defend his profession when bullied by a range of humanities scholars and politicians, and to hold the line doggedly over principles of justice and fairness still has much to teach us about how to educate our children better and how to train those who do.

Mexican American Racial Identity, Whiteness, and Civil Rights

Here is where the hate words, the emotionally charged phrases, have a field day. Here is where the phrases "nigger lover," "that dirty Mexican," "would you want your daughter to marry a BLANK?," "un-American," and the like—extended to include labor unions, Catholics, Jews, Baptists, educators, ministers, and others—are levers to jack up the status of the self-appointed protector of the faith, and of the nefarious interest which he serves. These tactics must be rewarding in a commercial sense, or the pay-off is in the area of political advantage—or, maybe, these fellows are so perverse and irrational that they derive an unnatural pleasure out of their intellectual and moral depravity.

Let us keep in mind that the Mexican-American can easily become *the front-line of defense* of the civil liberties of ethnic minorities. The racial, cultural, and historical involvements in his case embrace those of *all of the other minority groups.* Yet, God bless the law, he is "White"! So, the Mexican-American can be the wedge for the broadening of civil liberties for others (who are not so fortunate as to be "white" and "Christian"!). Here it is well to note that the *Brown vs. Board of Education* judgment was preceded by two weeks by the *Hernández* judgment—and no one reading the latter could have doubted the outcome of the former. Also, the procedures we have used in the segregation cases involving Mexican-Americans are guides for what the Negroes will have to do.

Race is the most exciting analytical category in U.S. history today. Scholars increasingly see race as a constructed category capable of great variation, not a static one. And race matters, too, as the historian Linda Gordon demonstrates in *The Great Arizona Orphan Abduction:* "But the new awareness of historical and global instability in racial categories—the new critical race theory—does not mean that race isn't 'real.' To the contrary, it is as real as slavery, Auschwitz, the U.S. immigration quotas. . . . Race is a social fact, one with great force. . . . Race is a strong, hot idea—unlike categories such as body type (mesomorph or ectomorph) or temperament (witty or quiet). The categorizing of race seems always to involve power, subordination, and superiority, inclusion and exclusion, and frequently gain." George I. Sánchez would have agreed entirely with this analysis. How most historians now see race—as unstable, nonbinary, discursive categories—owes much to critical race theory, which grew out of the 1970s and 1980s. Critical race theory explains Mexican Americans as a racially indeterminate group whose heterogeneity is seldom recognized. An intriguing subfield is the category of whiteness: How some are classified as white and others not, how and why such notions shift over time, and how the victims of racism dealt with their racialization.[1] Whiteness has enlivened Mexican American history with stimulating studies since the late 1990s. Several scholars argue that the Mexican American Generation's civil rights movement internalized antiblack racism, making it fundamentally racist. Arguing mostly from the perspective of civil rights strategy and well-worn anecdotes, the historian Neil Foley holds that Mexican Americans embraced a "Faustian Pact with whiteness" that internalized antiblack racism. This idea generates scholarly opposition calling for greater nuance in interpreting civil rights strategies and racial identities as well as for focusing on the connections between both civil rights movements. Sánchez's career is a good test of these interpretations.[2]

This chapter examines Sánchez through the prism of race during the 1950s. What did he think of the concept of race? How did he racially identify? How did race shape the Mexican American civil rights movement? What did he think of other civil rights movements? I focus on his most important contribution to civil rights, a little-known group called the American Council of Spanish-Speaking People (ACSSP). Their landmark civil rights case was *Hernández v. Texas* (1954) at the Supreme Court over jury selection and racial classification. I study points of connection between Sánchez and the African American civil rights movement and also investigate Sánchez's attitudes on race and civil rights in Texas politics.

IDEAS OF RACE

George I. Sánchez recognized that while *race* was a term hotly debated in the state and federal courts of Texas, it had little consistent meaning for Mexican Americans on a daily level. The unstable concept could mean anything at any time. One of the most consistent points Sánchez made about race was to deny its legitimacy with regard to human capacity. He viewed race as a tool used by the powerful—wealthy, vested interests—to keep the powerless—racial, ethnic, and religious minorities—in their place. In one SWCESSP talk he explained, "We frequently assign to a minority group—Negro, poor-White, Mexican—characteristics that are not racial or cultural attributes but the attributes of poverty." To Sánchez the brutality of poverty respected no cleverness or novelty in how individual people may have racially classified themselves. As befitted his intellectual debt to the environmentalism and liberal pluralism of the mid-twentieth century, race for Sánchez was uninteresting when separated from racism. His distinction anticipates a current critique of whiteness scholarship by Barbara Fields, who argues that how race relations studies focus on agency and identity is limiting since racism cruelly renders such agency hollow.[3]

Sánchez defined himself variously. It might be said of him and others of this era that their claims of being Spanish, which Sánchez often exercised, reflected a white racial identity and sense of privilege. Scholars believe that Hispanos' late-nineteenth-century propagation of a Spanish identity was a method of separating themselves from indigenous peoples. But George and Luisa, in a letter to a professional journal in 1958, embraced their roots as an "indo-Hispanic people." Sánchez remained fascinated by the intellectual possibilities of the process of *mestizaje* much more than who was or was not a mestizo. To a Californian upset by another author's dwelling on Mexicans' racial mixture, Sánchez tried to defuse what he felt was misplaced anger: "Of course there were Negro slaves in Mexico, who later were absorbed into the mestizaje (primarily in the states of Vera Cruz and Guerrero). So what? You can say the same thing about many thousands of 'white folks' in the U.S.A." What disappointed Sánchez about the work in question was its attribution of laziness to racial mixture. This was racism over race.[4]

One can negatively portray Sánchez in those instances when he discussed group differences. He once wrote to Senator Ralph Yarborough, "I understand that HEW has requested that students be classified as 'white,' 'Negro,' and 'other'—the latter to include 'Latin American.' This is ridiculous! Also, it is contrary to legal definitions—all of which classify Americans of Mexican descent as 'white.' I put the word 'white' in quotes for sociological, biological, and anthropological reasons. Who, indeed, is 'white'!" He went on, "However, in view of a racist oriented culture, we Americans of Mexican descent resent being placed in a category that (improperly) connotes inferiority to the law. We are proud to be 'Latin American,' or 'Mexican American,' or 'Spanish American,' or just plain 'Mexican.' But, as the 'Virginian' said, 'when you call me that, *smile!*' They are not smiling when they look down on us as, unfortunately, they do the Negro, the Indian, the Oriental. I insist that they cut it out."[5]

In a talk to the Austin Commission on Human Relations in 1960, Sánchez admitted to being naïve about racism earlier in his life and explained his evolution on it. This is the sentiment shown in the first epigraph above. That racism enriched some and impoverished others was its dastardly power for Sánchez. There was no agency in negotiating racial identities because minorities' victimization by racists represented powerlessness. For him, racists "murder truth, they desecrate liberty and justice." The only agency to be had was to fight racists with any tool available. He would have been supremely mystified had someone told him that in fighting racism as he did he engaged concepts of race that in turn strengthened racists' racism.[6]

THE ACSSP AND MEXICAN AMERICAN CIVIL RIGHTS

The height of Sánchez's civil rights activism was his American Council on Spanish-Speaking People (ACSSP), an intriguing, underappreciated Mexican American civil rights group. A recent book by Foley criticizes Sánchez and his allies in ACSSP for failing to support African American civil rights and for pursuing a strategy that drove "a wedge even more deeply between blacks and Mexicans" by insisting on rights as white people—the whiteness strategy. I respectfully disagree. For personal or ideological reasons, many today might want to see the African American and Mexican American civil rights movements as the same. They were not. African Americans captured the nation's attention in the 1950s while Mexican Americans generated little interest. And though the results of racial oppression were similar (segregation, economic destitution, hopelessness, violence), each group experienced it through the law differently. For years courts ruled that Mexican peoples were white. So Mexican Americans fought de facto segregation, not the de jure segregation of African Americans. And common allies never regarded the civil rights of Mexican Americans as being equally important as those of African Americans. In 1947 the ACLU staff counsel Clifford Forster advised Mexican Americans to hold off on challenging school segregation until the *Sweatt* case concluded and to defer to NAACP from then on. Sánchez countered, "Please remember that there is no authorization whatsoever in law for the segregation of 'Mexicans,' and the legality or lack of legality of the laws segregating Negroes is immaterial in this other field for the 'Mexicans' are already in the position legally that the Sweatt case would put the Negro in if that case were won." Though the two movements had parallel experiences in a racist society—on a personal level Sánchez recalled that a pipe bomb appeared on his lawn during one desegregation case—the way racial oppression uniquely worked against each remains an underappreciated element of historical comparison.[7]

By early 1951 Roger Baldwin, the founding director of the ACLU, wrote to Sánchez that he felt the time was right to form a Mexican American civil rights superstructure. This occurred as Sánchez's GEB support ended. So with $3,000 of seed money from the ACLU's Marshall Trust, a fund Baldwin oversaw, Sánchez put together a conference in El Paso in May 1951 ($26,878.27 today). Over fifty activists representing Mexican American organizations gathered for this meeting, which was the beginning of the ACSSP. The group's original governing council consisted of Lieutenant Governor of New Mexico Tibo Chavez as chairman, President Arturo Fuentes of the Alianza Hispano-Americana in Arizona as treasurer, the Texas attorney for AGIF and LULAC Gus Garcia as general counsel, the Los Angeles newspaper publisher Ignacio López as vice chairman, President Anthony Rios of the Community Service Organization (CSO) in California as a member, and Director Bernard Valdez of the Colorado Latin American Conference as secretary. Most attendees urged Sánchez to direct the ACSSP. At a later meeting in Austin the governing council produced a budget and named Sánchez director with a full-time assistant, a downtown Austin office, and secretarial help. Within weeks ACSSP was up and running.[8]

Accounting for ACSSP's finances with precision is difficult given the multiple versions of budgets leading up to Marshall Trust approval and because the trust did not always follow the budgets. But the general outlines indicate that between 1951 and 1957 the ACSSP received over $50,000 in funds from the Robert Marshall Civil Liberties Trust (in 1951 calculations; $447,971.15 today). For the first two years Sánchez appears to have accepted a $4,500 salary in the budget, though what he was actually paid is unclear, and by August 1953 Sánchez was doing the job gratis (in 1951 calculations; $40,317.40 today). Such a salary would have represented a brief but significant windfall of roughly 70 percent of Sánchez's university pay. He remarked to an ACLU official in that first year that he could now buy a home with Luisa. The ACSSP was supposed to create a sense of national community among Mexican American activists and lend prestige to shared civil rights work. The ACSSP Newsletter was established to further such a purpose at the cost of a dollar in membership fees. It would appear that at its prime ACSSP only had four hundred dues-paying members. Baldwin and Sánchez got their original wish: a lean, elite, loose collection of activists.[9]

Sánchez's most important ACSSP collaborator was Abraham Lincoln (A. L.) Wirin, who was born in Russia in 1900 and immigrated to the United States in 1908. Raised in poverty, Wirin was awarded scholarships and graduated from Harvard University and Boston University Law School in the 1920s. A lucrative bankruptcy practice in Los Angeles left him unfulfilled, however; in 1931, after the death of his first wife, he became the ACLU's counsel. Sánchez and Wirin often joked about Baldwin's bluestocking background and stinginess. Wirin was a crucial go-between for ACSSP and the Marshall Trust. There were a number of ACSSP-sponsored cases involving police brutality and press hysteria in California, deportation in California, segregated schools and swimming pools in Arizona, Texas, and California, prison segregation in Texas, and public housing segregation throughout the Southwest. The police brutality cases came to the ACSSP through CSO, which was outraged at the beating and arrest in 1951 of one of its leaders, Tony Rios, a founding member of ACSSP's board. ACSSP earmarked up to $1,000 for the effort ($8,959.42 today). The CSO and Alianza organized two other police brutality cases, *Hidalgo v. Biscailuz* and *Bustillos v. Biscailuz*.[10]

Wirin was especially interested in the *Galvan v. Press, Garcia v. Landon,* and *Gonzalez v. Landon* deportation cases. They landed at the U.S. Supreme Court and challenged the stringent, anticommunist provisions for deportation in the McCarran-Walter Act (1952). The ACLU's southern California branch supported the cases while Sánchez approved only limited ACSSP funds. He remarked to Wirin, "Frankly, I do not regard them of great consequence to Mexican-Americans. I think they are worthy as general civil liberties cases, but not in the same class with housing, jury, school, etc. where Mexicans are specifically singled out for discrimination. I'll agree to sweeten the pot for these cases, but with very little sugar." Sánchez jokingly concluded, "OK, so it *is* Rogeritis!" referring to Baldwin's miserliness. *Galvan* was lost in 1954 at the U.S. Supreme Court but generated powerful dissents. So when *Garcia* emerged later that year over similar issues, INS announced plans to alter its administration of McCarran-Walter, thus vacating the deportation of Garcia and others. *Gonzalez* was won at the Supreme Court in 1955 as a summary judgment that did not reach constitutional issues.[11]

In the school desegregation case in Glendale, Arizona, *Ortiz v. Jack*, Sánchez urged Alianza president Fuentes to have his people enter the white school, forcing local officials to keep them out, which would then set up litigation in a federal court. Local school authorities scrambled to institute a free choice plan, and the superintendent worked hard to encourage some Anglos to attend the slightly altered Mexican school. All this lessened segregation by 75 percent, according to Ralph Estrada, Fuentes's second in Alianza. So in 1953 the *Ortiz v. Jack* case was dismissed. It was an odd turn for Sánchez, who commented, "A request for dismissal, based on the fact that segregation has ceased, is probably the thing to do. This case is a remarkable one—victory in defeat!"[12]

The case in Winslow, Arizona, involved a city pool open to whites on some days and Mexicans, African Americans, and Native Americans on other days, whereupon the pool water was replaced. In 1954 Wirin settled *Baca, et al. v. City of Winslow,* though Sánchez wanted a trial. Wirin sent the civil stipulation to Sánchez with the humorous note, "I enclose a copy of the stipulation which I signed, and which is to be filed, closing the Winslow swimming pool case (but opening the swimming pool). It is the best I could do in the circumstances; and I hope it is good enough." To the Marshall Trust Wirin wrote that *Baca* in no way damaged the ability of other groups seeking civil rights.[13]

Prison segregation interested Sánchez in that Jim Crow's existence there occurred in an environment fabricated entirely by the state. Sánchez always sought to make a lie of the usual justifications of Jim Crow, such as the safety of women and children, social harmony, learning environments, and socioeconomic differences. Sánchez wrote to Wirin, "There are three places that this practice is particularly senseless: hospitals, jails, and cemeteries! Yet, it seems, there is where segregation is defended most zealously." He opposed the idea that the inmates' safety necessitated racial segregation. The attorney John Herrera and Wirin tried the Texas-based *Rios et al. v. Ellis et al.* case of 1955 with the assistance of the Alianza field investigator Ralph Guzman. These out-of-state participants raised the hackles of federal judge Ben Connally, who requested a formal statement on Wirin's and Guzman's identities and what they were doing in the Lone Star State. The case went nowhere. Wirin confided that their clients were coerced and, combined with Connally's hostility, made for the attorneys' hasty retreat. This case was ahead of its time. Racial segregation in prisons would become an issue for federal and state courts in the late 1960s.[14]

Segregated public housing was of interest to Sánchez as it too involved a combination of local and federal governing authorities constructing a Jim Crow environment. He investigated this while on the short-lived TCHR in 1951, an effort that resulted in a four-page report concluding that the Housing Authority of Austin blatantly imposed segregation. This minor investigation, which exceeded his undefined authority in the entirely symbolic TCHR, got Sánchez threatened with libel by the housing commissioner Alvin J. Wirtz, a former state senator, New Deal bigwig over public power, and mentor to Lyndon Johnson. Wirin investigated public housing in Los Angeles, but to no avail.

Sánchez reported that his mediations in Austin resulted in some lessening of segregation for Latinos but not for African Americans.[15]

One final area of ACSSP-connected efforts is the *Romero et al. v. Weakley et al.* and *Burleigh et al. v. Weakley et al.* school desegregation cases of 1955 in El Centro in the heart of southern California's agricultural Imperial Valley. The NAACP and the Alianza, legally sponsored by ACSSP, challenged school segregation together. The Southern California ACLU, the Japanese American Citizens League, and the American Jewish Committee submitted amici curiae briefs. This case is another point of connection between the two civil rights movements. Sánchez suggested to Guzman, "In September, have all of the 'Mexicans' and Negroes ask to be transferred out of the segregated schools! Just like the 'whites' do! Then the board will have to rule—and it can't rule one way for 'whites' and another for 'Mexicans' and Negroes." Sánchez advised Guzman to assure the Mexican American and African American plaintiffs that *Brown* put everyone in the same boat. Mexican Americans had to prove racial discrimination in practices of segregation—a double hurdle of intent piled on fact—as the only avenue of civil rights after *Brown* but before the Great Society. In the 1950s Mexican Americans' burdensome racial obscurity as a people resulted in a murky, complicated desegregation process that inched along from mediated half victory to vague stipulation.[16]

ACSSP'S DEMISE

Unfortunately for Sánchez and ACSSP, the Marshall Trust soured on them owing to the displeasure of Baldwin, who, upon stepping down after thirty years, managed the Marshall Trust as continued service. Baldwin was often the sole source of information given to the Marshall trustees, who always approved his recommendations. The seeds of his disappointment were present from the beginning. He wrote in 1951 of his certainty that ACSSP would resemble other civil rights organizations: "We are at last embarked on a movement that promises to give Mexican-Americans the same kind of service in protection of their civil rights which the Negroes, Japanese-Americans and other minorities have." This was an unfair conflation. Sánchez tried to temper expectations about what could be achieved through this support and the existing geography of Mexican American activism. But it was lost on Baldwin.[17]

A year later Baldwin expressed disappointment in the ACSSP's structure and scope, something he had exuberantly signed off on a year earlier. This had to do with his lack of understanding of who Mexican Americans were and what their civil rights movement was about. By June 1952 Wirin warned Sánchez that

Baldwin was unhappy with the ACSSP's small membership. Sánchez was frustratingly aware of Baldwin's feelings and answered, "He is being very unrealistic about our achievements. In the first place, a national organization is not built up over-night—it takes a long period of contact building, of adjustments to existing organizations, etc." Baldwin wanted Texas excluded from ACSSP efforts, which confounded Sánchez, who argued that in one year they had "a jury case in the highest court of Texas, and we will probably appeal the decision to the U.S. Supreme Court," a reference to the *Hernández v. Texas* case. Sánchez exasperatedly asked, "What in the world does he want?"[18]

The answer is easy. Baldwin and the ACLU wanted ACSSP to become a Latino mirror of the NAACP's Legal Defense Fund. And that expectation ran contrary to its 1951 design. To be sure, ACSSP was more than a "think tank," as Foley has recently characterized it, but it was not the NAACP either. Baldwin directly informed Sánchez of his misgivings in late 1952 and early 1953. In urging that Sánchez increase ACSSP's fund-raising and publish a national bulletin as a condition for continued commitment to its already-approved four-year plan—a new demand—Baldwin expressed disappointment: "I had not appreciated how small the chances are for building up an ultimately self-supporting national agency for Mexican Americans, nor did I have before from you so definite a conception of the net result as strong local associations rather than a strong national—or regional. Perhaps I and the trustees entertained false hopes based on the experience of the Negroes and the Japanese-Americans." That Baldwin did not know Mexican Americans or really care to is as tragic as it is inescapable.[19]

From early 1953 on, Sánchez scrambled to keep ACSSP afloat by cutting staff, salaries, and physical space. While the ACLU's Marshall Trust did not withdraw its support immediately, it stepped down its involvement each year and remained doggedly unwilling to support projects in Texas. The Marshall Trust was in the process of liquidating by the mid-1950s, and Sánchez sought access to the leftovers. This dance went on until the summer of 1957, just after Sánchez's positive news on *Hernández v. Driscoll*, when Baldwin confirmed they were dropping ACSSP. Passing over Sánchez's arguments without comment, Baldwin requested he serve as a proposal evaluator for other organizations applying for the leftovers. Then he let fly his disappointments: "The Alianza project is apparently out. The C.S.O. looks pretty limited locally. Is there any prospect of a regional approach, or must we resign ourselves to state and local action? If so, where would any investment produce results and through whom? It's been a long time now that we have wrestled with this problem and we seem no nearer any *general* effort to tackle evils which cover a vast area. I suggest you give us some new thoughts!" Sánchez refused to produce new or different ideas.

Instead, he reiterated ACSSP's successes and mission. This speaks volumes. Sánchez was quite capable of tailoring projects to gain money. But here he steadfastly defended ACSSP as the best possible effort at that time and as ultimately being national in effect.[20]

By 1959 Baldwin wrote an internal memo to the trustees that the Marshall Civil Liberties Trust did not meet expectations. Over nineteen years they spent a third of a million dollars, mostly on Mexican American efforts, several before the ACSSP came into existence. He argued that ACSSP did not nationalize Mexican American civil rights as hoped and had recently expired. In fact, the ACSSP died because the Marshall Trust stopped funding it. Once again refusing to accept the notion that ACSSP had failed, Sánchez replied, "As the years pass, I am more and more convinced that what I have recommended before still holds." He continued, "I cannot imagine how, in this area of endeavor, the Marshall Trust could invest money more profitably than how it has done so far. The ACLU and the NAACP, the AFL-CIO, and lesser organizations are not going to do this kind of a job for Mexican Americans—because they do not have the local connections and the local know-how and the local confidence. I am speaking strictly of the Mexican-American group—for I have the highest regard for the know-how of those organizations on other matters."[21]

There would be no other attempt at an ACSSP-type of organization within the Mexican American community until the founding of the Mexican American Legal Defense and Educational Fund (MALDEF) in the late 1960s with a Ford Foundation grant of $2,200,000 (in 1968 calculations; $14,726,408.05 today). Unlike the ACSSP—founded on a shoestring budget in a more adverse climate by an organization hostile to the existing landscape of Mexican American activism—MALDEF succeeded. Sánchez kept a minuscule remnant of Marshall Trust funds in the bank under ACSSP's name for a couple more years in hopes something might materialize, but nothing did. Valdez, by 1961 the treasurer of a ghost organization, poignantly replied when Sánchez permanently cleared out the account, "The Treasurer of the American Council of Spanish-Speaking People feels very badly to know that he remains the treasurer of an organization without a bank account. Do we need to take any steps to disband the Council, or shall we just let it go by the way of [the] usual Latin-Spanish American Organization?" It was an ignominious end to a visionary effort.[22]

ACSSP'S ALLIES

Sánchez had a bird's-eye view of leading Mexican American organizations through his ACSSP directorship. He had by turns favorable and unfavorable views of LULAC. In the early 1950s Sánchez ruminated, "For the past several years, Lulac has been dominated by a small clique that showed little concern for civil liberties and that was under the misconception that Lulac was above pressure tactics, publicity, and the like." Sánchez supported the liberal Herrera's successful quest for the national presidency but was soon disappointed: "Operating out of the vest pocket of a President who is changed every year or so has kept Lulac to a minimum of effectiveness in national, state, and even local issues. It is nice to organize new councils—but what for? They will soon die out or become apathetic for want of a program of action and for want of an understanding as to how they fit into the state and national picture." He went on, "This has been the history of Lulac, and it will be its future too—unless its current diet is enriched with the vitamins of an information and action program that is intimately related to live issues and to what fellow organizations are doing." Sánchez opined further, "The Lulac mountain labors mightily and, except on very rare occasions, gives birth to a mouse!" AGIF was a point of pride with Sánchez. They took on their own cases with little ACSSP assistance. Sánchez argued from ACSSP's first year that AGIF paid dividends, boasting that they successfully expanded to New Mexico and Colorado and were already eyeing Arizona, California, and Illinois. By 1953 Sánchez believed AGIF was becoming the vanguard of Mexican American activist organizations.[23]

Two groups with more complicated relationships to ACSSP were the CSO, based in Los Angeles, and the Alianza, based in Arizona. In Sánchez's first act as ACSSP director he hired an assistant, Ed Idar Jr., who was an outstanding pick with regard to the Texas milieu. However, tensions arose when CSO and Alianza nominated other candidates. Sánchez got his way after making it clear he would resign if Idar were not hired. López and Rios, after publicly disparaging ACSSP, drifted out of the organization. More damaging were Fuentes's vaguely worded resignation from the board after a few months and the reluctance of Ralph Estrada to replace him. CSO came to the Marshall Trust's attention in early 1950 through A. A. Heist, the director of Southern California ACLU, and Ed Roybal, the Los Angeles city councilor. Saul Alinsky's Industrial Areas Foundation had funded CSO until late 1950. CSO's business manager at the time, Fred Ross, applied for Marshall Trust funds, but the trust was leery of funding efforts in southern California because of its negative experience with the National Farm Labor Union. Sánchez was positive about CSO initially and supported its application for Marshall Trust funds in 1952.[24]

But CSO's fund-raising and its activities soon disappointed him. By 1952 he wrote to Lyle Saunders, his SSSP colleague, that both Rios and López had continual personal feuds and furthered what he felt were "invidious Texas vs. California" attitudes. Most damningly, in Sánchez's opinion, was CSO's failure to turn out the masses in a city with over half a million Chicanos. Sánchez complained, "I would have taken my present course earlier, except that I believed that C.S.O. was a major organization. Actually, it is a small club—with only a few *mexicanos* in it, and no more representative of the local people than the Jewish-Negro-Anglo-Asiatic group we had lunch with!" Sánchez felt CSO was not to be depended on and was shocked that Rios got into a fistfight at a restaurant after one ACSSP meeting.[25]

CSO convinced Wirin to take on Rios's criminal defense and civil action against the Los Angeles Police Department. Sánchez first learned of this when Wirin approached him about his ACSSP payment. This was a surprise to Sánchez. The Marshall Trust had not budgeted ACSSP for this particular litigation, and CSO had already spent an earlier 1952 grant of $1,000 for the case ($8,790.38 today). The CSO could not or would not raise money locally to pay Wirin's fees, which left Sánchez responsible. He agreed to help Wirin out with the $1,000 payment if necessary but insisted Wirin pester CSO about it first. Wirin agreed, lamenting that his efforts to work with the group went nowhere. Sánchez's pessimism about CSO never let up, even in later years.[26]

ACSSP's relationship with Alianza was initially rocky. The memberships of all Mexican American groups at this time were chafing against inequality; those that grew fastest, in line with Sánchez's thinking, used activism as a means of expansion. Alianza, an old-line *mutualista* that ran an insurance business for its members, was new to civil rights activism and in 1952 and 1953 sponsored a couple of cases. Sánchez initially grumbled that Alianza did not even pay the promised legal fees to its own attorney. However, Wirin was more sanguine about Alianza and worked hard on its initiatives throughout 1953 and 1954. In May 1954, following a personal conference with Estrada in Colorado, Sánchez had a change of heart and brainstormed a plan to possibly transfer ACSSP's remaining funds to Alianza. This involved a long-term grant from an enthusiastic Marshall Trust, which offered to match Alianza's civil rights expenditures dollar for dollar. Sánchez felt it would take a final ACSSP board meeting to ratify the shift, disband the board, and transfer the funds to Estrada's new civil rights division within Alianza. Sánchez looked forward to stepping aside, but Alianza preferred to keep him on as trustee of the Marshall funds, even if that meant he had to become a part-time Alianza employee. Sánchez proposed a $30,000 Marshall appropriation over three years with an additional $1,000 for an organizing conference to hammer out the details ($259,789.96 and $8,659.67 today).

But Alianza hesitated at not having complete and immediate control of the funds. This was a blow to the Marshall Trust, as its staff had already begun the process of drawing up the legal documents.[27]

Undaunted, Wirin and Sánchez set to work on a new Alianza–ACSSP arrangement. Wirin valued Sánchez and wanted their collaboration to continue whatever the organizational set up. Wirin went so far as to urge that Sánchez request financial compensation for himself in the next grant, or, failing this, he offered to personally and separately compensate the weary professor out of his own fees. Sánchez and Wirin encouraged Estrada to keep working on the traditionalists on his board. Sánchez explained to the ACLU's Baldwin that all this was very new for an old group like Alianza. The frustration mounted. Alianza wanted money for civil rights; Marshall Trust wanted to give them money; but Marshall Trust also wanted its creation, the ACSSP, to be involved. The final result was Sánchez's earmarking most of the total $5,000 ACSSP grant in 1954–55 to support Alianza ($43,298.33 today). And even this was tested by Alianza's persistent efforts to assume the entire grant at once rather than piece by piece as per Marshall Trust procedure.[28]

In 1955 Alianza inaugurated its civil rights program, led by Estrada, with Wirin as outside council and Ralph Guzman as investigator. This phase of Alianza's aggressiveness resulted in the *Romero v. Weakley* case and spurred them to seek additional external funding. They applied to the Ford Fund for the Republic for $100,000 a year for four years ($869,197.76 today). This met with Sánchez's and Baldwin's hearty approval. Sánchez traveled to Los Angeles to help draft the proposal, and the Marshall Trust offered extended financial support until the Ford grant could take effect. However, Ford balked that fall and instead offered a series of much smaller, declining grants for three years. A big problem for Ford was Alianza's tax status as a fraternal rather than a charitable organization, a status that was necessary for Alianza's insurance business. By 1956 Alianza had scaled back its ambitious civil rights program and dropped the grant application.[29]

HERNÁNDEZ V. TEXAS

The best-known contribution of Sánchez's ACSSP is the *Hernández v. Texas* case of 1954 concerning segregated juries in Texas. It reached the U.S. Supreme Court and was decided shortly before *Brown v. Board of Education* in a unanimous victory against racial segregation. The state of Texas claimed that since Mexican Americans were technically Caucasian, their absence in an all-Anglo jury was not discriminatory; Mexican American civil rights attorneys argued that although they were Caucasian, Mexican Americans were treated as a different class, *a class apart*, that suffered Jim Crow. And then, in the blink of an eye, *Brown* rendered the great victory of *Hernández* obsolete. But it took Mexican Americans well over a decade to come to terms with this basic fact. One historian argues that for Mexican Americans the chimera of *Hernández* "kept them too long on what proved to be an unfruitful constitutional path."[30]

Hernández arose out of the private law practice of Herrera and Garcia. In the lengthy appeals process they added Carlos Cadena, a young law professor in San Antonio. Other attorneys participated, including the future federal judge James DeAnda, the civil rights attorney Cristobal Aldrete, and the liberal state legislator Maury Maverick Jr. By 1952 Sánchez had updated the Marshall Trust on *Hernández* as it worked its way up through state appeals entirely dependent on local LULAC and AGIF funds. Sánchez sought to make funds available for the case if it went to the U.S. Supreme Court. Baldwin was unhappy about earmarking additional money for a Texas case, but Sánchez cut into his own increasingly tight budget for other litigation and office expenses in 1953 to contribute a small but necessary sum of $1,500 for *Hernández* ($13,086.80 today).[31]

Cadena leaned on Sánchez to help him articulate an academically grounded portrayal of Mexican Americans' experience with discrimination. Sánchez's brief essay was a meditation on who Mexican Americans were, what they were treated like, and why: "While the person of Mexican descent is legally white (anthropologically he is predominantly Indian), frequently the term 'white' excludes the 'Mexican' and is reserved for the rest of the non-Negro population. Official forms sometimes call for the 'racial' classifications of 'Negro-White-Mexicans.'" Sánchez then got to the heart of *Hernández:* "In health, wealth, and education, the Mexican-American is far below the rest of the Texas population—even below the Negro. That is, not only is he commonly regarded as a class apart, but by every objective measurement—from biological makeup to deaths from tuberculosis and from infantile diarrhea—he *is* a class apart."[32]

Sánchez was an intermediary between the Mexican American attorneys and Wirin, who worked to soften Baldwin. By this point the Marshall Trust was requesting his approval for all ACSSP legal expenditures. Wirin's eagerness to participate more fully in the case presented a very delicate situation. By October 1953 he offered to take over the writing of the brief and share in oral argument. He wanted to obtain the services of Dean Acheson without fee and proposed to share oral argument with Acheson, presumably with Cadena, Garcia, and Herrera in tow as silent assistants. Cadena did not take well to the suggestion that he step aside in the biggest trial of his life and refused the offer. They won unanimously. For a while everyone was on top of the world.[33]

Sánchez was so happy he approved, without additional whining, Wirin's fee request for the *Rios* and *Galvan* cases. Sánchez argued, "I think that the Hernández decision outlawed the segregation of Negroes in schools, in housing, etc. What do you think? Negroes are a class apart, they are treated differently in law and in practice—ergo, there [sic] constitutional rights have been violated." Wirin cautiously replied that the professor might be making too much out of their victory. That neither Wirin nor Sánchez predicted exactly what *Brown* meant or how it reduced *Hernández* to immediate obsoleteness is no indictment of their intelligence. *Brown's* initial meaning did not go beyond overturning the separate-but-equal precedent of *Plessey v Ferguson*. It took a second *Brown* decision the next year to spell it out. And it took another decade of wrangling to seriously dent the educational status quo. This was a decade in which Mexican American and African American civil rights were blunted by a web of administrative and procedural entanglements. *Brown* was not immediately transformative, but it enabled the long, difficult desegregation process.[34]

The constitutional theory advanced by Cadena, the class apart theory, and Sánchez's role in it have generated debate. One AGIF history credits it to Cadena without mentioning Sánchez or the ACSSP. Sánchez contested this kind of institutional perspective during his lifetime, noting that the class apart theory was "first elaborated upon by myself in a course in which Carlos Cadena was a student. I had long set forth, in my class, that the XIV Amendment protected against discrimination not only on the basis of 'race, creed, color' but also on the basis of recognition and differential treatment against a recognized 'class apart.'" Years later he reiterated this story to Pete Tijerina of MALDEF. Was Sánchez Cadena's muse for the class apart theory? One can reasonably agree or disagree. What this discussion demonstrates is Sánchez's sizeable role in *Hernández* from behind the scenes.[35]

AFRICAN AMERICANS AND COMPARATIVE CIVIL RIGHTS

George I. Sánchez felt that Mexican Americans were ideally positioned to leverage civil rights for others by playing the hand that was dealt them. Such pragmatism was not unknown. African Americans used the tools at hand to challenge Jim Crow, even if those challenges did not loudly denounce segregation as a moral evil, which would make for better reading today. One of the tools at Mexican Americans' disposal was that they were technically white. So while African Americans once sought to make a lie of the effects of separate-but-equal though equalization, Mexican Americans once sought to make a lie of their supposed white status. Responding to ACLU recommendations in 1947 that Mexican Americans demand equalized facilities within segregation, admission to white schools, or "demand that they be admitted to the white schools on the ground that Mexicans are Caucasions [*sic*]," Sánchez retorted, "None of the alternatives that you suggest on page two of your letter are satisfactory"; Mexican American challenges to segregation "need not be argued on racial grounds, but simply on the equal protection of the laws and due process points." In 1958 Sánchez wrote a lengthy note to Baldwin, an excerpt from which appears in the second epigraph above, linking the civil rights movements of Mexican Americans and African Americans. But Sánchez failed to appreciate how *Brown* changed the terrain of civil rights. Most Mexican American activists joined him in this myopia. *Delgado* in 1948 and the creation of the TEA's kangaroo court in 1950 bottled up school desegregation for Mexican Americans in Texas. This failure was too difficult for him to see clearly.[36]

When it came to African Americans and civil rights, Sánchez spoke out often. In April 1948 he addressed the University of Texas chapter of the NAACP over *Sipuel v. Board of Regents of University of Oklahoma*, a Supreme Court case preceding *Sweatt v. Painter* at that state's law school. The Supreme Court telegraphed *Sweatt* with *Sipuel*, which in turn led to *Brown*. Invited by W. Astor Kirk, the NAACP director in Austin, Sánchez spoke at the Texas NAACP conference in 1951. The conference spotlighted Thurgood Marshall, the lead counsel of the NAACP's Legal Defense Fund and later a U.S. Supreme Court justice, and the civil rights activist Walter White. This would have been in the aftermath of *Sweatt* as the NAACP planned its next steps. Sánchez also interjected his civil rights perspective into academia. In 1958 he published an analysis of both the African American and the Mexican American civil rights movements, arguing that *Brown* ended the peculiarity of African Americans' de jure segregation yet did not impact the de facto segregation others had long endured and which African Americans now faced. As a result, the Mexican American experience was now of even greater importance, and all oppressed minorities that fought racism now did so on the same terrain: "We have wasted a lot of time, energy, and money indulging our blind prejudices." He continued, "It is time that we settled down to a full appreciation of our democracy—what it means, and what it can be. We should appreciate fully the value to the nation of what is currently the wasted potential. The Mexican, the Negro, the Jew—the Pole, the Swede, the Japanese—cannot be given differential, discriminatory treatment without great loss and damage to the whole structure."[37]

One important venue for Sánchez's articulation of the Mexican American experience was an annual summer conference at Fisk University's Race Relations Institute. It was a two- to three-week program for students, activists, and academics to engage the subject of racial prejudice in structured seminars with expert speakers. Sánchez attended in 1950, 1957, and 1961 as an invited speaker. In 1950 he gave a forty-five-minute talk titled "The Spanish Speaking People of the Southwest." His talk in 1961, "The Status of Citizenship Rights Among Spanish-Speaking Groups of the Southwest," was delivered a day before Marshall gave two talks on the NAACP and litigation. Sánchez also recommended speakers for the Race Relations Institute in 1955 and 1956; in 1954 he could not speak and instead recommended Julian Samora and Lyle Saunders, who did. These experiences were invaluable for many whom Sánchez recommended. Perhaps the most interesting talk Sánchez gave was in 1957. The renowned civil rights reporter for the *Nashville Tennessean*, Wallace Westfeldt, wrote of the professor's emphasis on economics over culture in Mexican American discrimination.[38]

In addition, Sánchez corresponded on civil rights strategy with Marshall, although the two men were not close, did not always agree, and corresponded infrequently. Marshall initiated their exchange in the late 1940s, and by the late 1950s it was Sánchez who continued it. Because they did not know one another well, third parties often spurred their communication. Despite these qualifications, this association illustrates two related themes: first, the Mexican American and African American civil rights movements did have meaningful points of connection; and second, the so-called whiteness legal strategy of Mexican Americans did not preclude cooperation. Wirin facilitated the men's connection in the summer of 1948 on the heels of *Delgado* when he brought to Marshall's attention the affidavits from expert witnesses that Sánchez had assembled. Marshall was interested is seeing the affidavits and wrote to Sánchez immediately asking if he could examine them in preparation for a case he was investigating in Hearne, Texas. Sánchez felt the affidavits would not be helpful since they dealt with "the pedagogical soundness of segregation that is based on the 'language handicap' excuse." But he nevertheless wanted to meet and review the documents when Marshall visited Austin the next month, supplying his home and office telephone numbers to facilitate a meeting. He wrote, "While the affidavits will probably not be of any help to you, it may be that the plan of attack that we have used may be." Sánchez meant the strategy of enjoining state officials as parties in a lawsuit. The case in Hearne, the trip to Austin, and their planned meeting fizzled, however.[39]

In November of the next year, as the NAACP prepared for *Sweatt*, Wirin sounded out Sánchez on an amicus curiae brief from LULAC's school segregation fund. Sánchez wrote, "I would like to see an amicus brief developed along somewhat different lines from those followed by Thurgood Marshall. In the first place, 'equal protection' should go far beyond mere comparison of professors-books-buildings in [the] law school. The comparison should be one which involves the *whole* of education that has been made available to the white law school graduate and the *whole* of education available to the Negro." He went on, "The whole idea of dichotomous education implies ostracism—and its whole spirit is based on the concept of inequality." Sánchez expressed pessimism about defining race: "Furthermore, the determination as to who is a Negro is subject to so much personal judgment and unscientific formulas that it is in effect arbitrary and capricious. I have known students in southern white institutions who are more negroid than some Negroes in the segregated institutions." Sánchez's response indicates that he did not entirely understand *Sweatt*. Marshall and the NAACP challenged the separate-but-equal doctrine, but they did so in the guise of a traditional equalization case. So in effect Sánchez urged the NAACP to do what it was already doing. He was clearly not attuned to its strategy. And that strategy was still controversial among African American activists. On the other hand, one could claim Sánchez anticipated, however accidentally, the NAACP's actions. Regardless, LULAC's school fund ran out of money, so the brief never materialized.[40]

In 1955 Sánchez vented to Baldwin that he felt Mexican Americans and their civil rights efforts were ignored. He quoted a recent statement by Marshall reported in news accounts to the effect that as more Americans sought to join the growing civil rights momentum, they should know "there is room for *only one driver* on that bandwagon and *that is the NAACP*." Additionally frustrated that the NAACP did not enjoin state officials, the professor exasperatedly wondered if attorneys were more interested in collecting fees than in solving segregation. His experience with the TEA's kangaroo courts was likely on his mind. However, Sánchez did not count on Baldwin sharing his letter with Marshall and the ACLU's counsel Herbert Levy. Marshall patiently explained the enjoinment issue, but Levy was less friendly: "As to this being good business for the lawyers, Mr. Marshall only gets a fixed fee, and neither his salary nor that of his associates depends upon the number of cases handled."[41]

This scolding response and the humiliation of Marshall's having read a letter not written in his usual formal tone embarrassed Sánchez. To Levy (and copied to Marshall) he noted that he had not intended his facetious remarks to be distributed. He defended his position on enjoining local and state officials and concluded, "I should make it clear that I am a 'fan' of Thurgood Marshall. I think that he is doing a fine job—and I admire him for it. I still think that our experience, as Mexican-Americans, would be valuable to the Negroes in their new status (one that we have held for many years). I also think that an entirely new way of thought needs to be worked out—that is, a way that discards the old notion of 'let us make as much of an in-road in the "separate but equal" practice as possible.'" He went on, "'Free choice,' 'transfer policy,' 'gerrymandering,' are old stuff to us. They *are* going to be 'pulled' on the Negroes." The chagrined Sánchez did not wash his hands of the NAACP: "I have my hands full, over and above my professional duties, with the *mexicanos*. Still, I'd like to see the Negroes play their cards the best way possible. And I am still willing to help, in my modest way, in any way that I can." Sánchez may have wanted to establish more of a connection, but he did not expect African Americans to lay down their movement for Mexican Americans or Mexican Americans to lay down theirs for African Americans. Were the two civil rights movements connected? Yes. Were they close? No. Did personal racism divide them? Not in this case.[42]

Continuing their correspondence, Marshall assured Sánchez that they were on good terms. He wrote, "I am sure there is no deep seated problem of personalities involved. At the same time we are always anxious to get constructive suggestions." He went on to give four examples in which the NAACP did and did not enjoin state officials. Sánchez, clearly out of his depth legally, dropped this issue yet continued to pester Marshall on Mexican American strategies. Sánchez's Mexican American civil rights perspective stressed local and state authorities, mediation, and a more regional perspective; Marshall's African American civil rights perspective emphasized a more national, professional, and litigious movement. Marshall directed A. Maceo Smith of the Texas NAACP to confer with Sánchez, and at this point their correspondence ended.[43]

But Sánchez continued to write to Baldwin about wanting a closer relationship between the two movements. That Baldwin had caused the discord in 1955 by sharing Sánchez's ill-considered letter did not stop Sánchez from baring his activist soul to his semiretired, semihostile ACLU colleague. Sánchez noted in 1958 that school segregation was even more difficult to topple in the post-*Brown* environment, as segregationists had hardened considerably during the era of massive resistance after *Brown v. Board.* Sánchez urged the ACLU's Marshall Trust to work harder at connecting the movements, lamenting, "I am sorry that Thurgood Marshall and the NAACP have not seen fit to consult with us in these matters. They are just now facing segregatory measures we faced and solved some time ago. A national office of ours could be very helpful in this respect." The most striking thing about this final comment, notwithstanding the wishful thinking that Mexican Americans had solved anything, is Sánchez's disappointment that there was not more connection between the two civil rights movements.[44]

The constant comparisons with African Americans hurt Mexican Americans. Near the end of their correspondence, Baldwin made it plain to Sánchez what a problem his people were: "Our experiences and yours shows that unlike the NAACP, the Japanese and others, the Mexican-American communities do not readily unite, and tend to think in terms of local problems and interests." Conceding that ACSSP did some good, he argued that it still fell short of creating a national organization. Sánchez replied emphatically that while internal differences within the Chicana/o community were real, racial oppression created a common platform: "The Mexican-Americans *are not* and *do not regard themselves as a homogenous ethnic or cultural group.* This means that resistance to discrimination becomes fragmented, local, and personal; though the discrimination itself is generalized and does not recognize the inherent heterogeneity of the subordinate group." Sánchez may as well have been talking to the wind.[45]

CIVIL RIGHTS IN TEXAS

No Tejano supported African American civil rights more than George I. Sánchez in the 1950s. For example, in 1951 Gus Garcia lobbied Sánchez on formulating an updated version of the Second World War–era Caucasian Race Resolution. But by the 1950s Sánchez was done with this approach. He wrote, "You cannot give privileges to one class of people that are denied to another class. Under this bill, Anglos could be discriminated against and so could Negroes." He went on, "What's the use of picking a fight for something that isn't going to do anybody any good? This is like the old Join [*sic*] Resolution that a legislature pasted [*sic*] several years ago—pretty words with absolutely no application. I don't think that a bill can be drawn up that does not include Anglos and Negroes within its protection." Furthermore, he continued, "personally, I don't want to be put in the position of saying that you must not discriminate against Mexicans, but you can go ahead and discriminate against other classes of people. I just don't think that way, and I don't think that the position is a wise one to take from a great many standpoints." He made the case that "if we are going to lose before the legislature or even before the courts, let us lose supporting a defensible principle. And, lose we will—so let us lose with self-respect instead of without it. I just can't see myself supporting a measure that, on its face, is a violation of the 14th Amendment while at the same time we are yelling loudly that the Amendment should be upheld!"[46]

Sánchez transferred these beliefs to the political realm. While U.S. Senator Ralph Yarborough has gone down in Texas political lore as one of the standout liberals of the twentieth century, his campaigns of the 1950s failed to embrace African Americans. And this neglect came in spite of Sánchez's advice. Yarborough hedged on civil rights in his gubernatorial races of 1952 and 1954, first, by ignoring the issue and then by settling on a vague Jim Crow stance. In 1956 Yarborough hedged yet again, this time without the excuse of being blindsided by a blockbuster Supreme Court decision in the middle of the campaign. The liberal activists like Sánchez remained far ahead of the liberal politicians. Sánchez supplied Yarborough with a two-page refutation of the segregationist constitutional theory of interposition, writing that it allowed the powerful to discriminate against "Mexicans, Jews, Catholics, hill-billies, damyankees [sic], as well as Negroes." In other words, interposition allowed discrimination against any people regarded as a class apart.[47]

The election of 1956 elevated former *Delgado*-era attorney general Price Daniel to the governor's office. It also whipped up an anti-integration hysteria commonly referred to as massive resistance. Late in the legislative session of 1957 a cancerous lump of segregationist bills that had been bottled up by the governor and other fearful moderates broke through the legislative roadblocks. In this highly charged environment two state senators, Henry B. Gonzalez of San Antonio and Abraham Kazen of Laredo, conducted a legendary filibuster on May 2, 1957, killing most of them. Thirty-six hours long, it was reputed to have been the longest filibuster in Texas legislative history. Daniel dutifully signed the three bills that passed, though they were later ruled unconstitutional. The filibuster of these bills ended massive resistance in Texas. But Gonzalez and Kazen were not universally hailed. The president of LULAC at the time, Felix Tijerina, did not support African American civil rights and remained loyal to Daniel. Predictably, Sánchez went the other way. He wrote to Hector Garcia that while the targets of massive resistance were African Americans, Mexican Americans would easily be caught up in the segregationist zeal. He also discussed that while segregation should be opposed, integration was not to be feared: "I have no objection to mixing *mexicanos* and Negroes when a policy of integration has been adopted. However, when Negroes are segregated because of race I don't think we should tolerate the segregation of Mexicans along with them. The objection is not to the Negroes but to the segregation!" Sánchez spoke out publicly in late March 1957 as the bills worked their way through the legislature.[48]

Sánchez was active with labor as a consultant on Mexican Americans, youth, and education. He gave local talks on race relations and served a term on an integrated grand jury, where he predictably found an outlet for his activism (fig. 10.1). In late 1956 the grand jury (likely Sánchez) wrote the county sheriff,

10.1. Sánchez (*far left*) participating in an integrated grand jury in Austin in 1954. Reproduction by permission of Cynthia Kennedy.

"The continued practice of segregating prisoners in the County Jail—as Negroes, 'Mexicans,' 'whites'—is a matter of both embarrassment and chagrin to Jurors of Mexican and Negro antecedents, at least. The practice, in addition, is probably a violation of the constitutional rights of the prisoners. In any case, we do not believe that prisoners should be classified or housed on the basis of race, creed, color, or native language; and we urge the Sheriff to give the matter his most earnest consideration with a view toward the discontinuance of the practice as soon as reasonably feasible." In 1961 he urged the University of Texas Committee of Counsel on Academic Freedom and Responsibility to investigate allegations that law school faculty aiding in desegregation efforts were being punished.[49]

This battle took a toll on him. As a result of his thoracoplasty he walked with a limp, slumped to one side, and used a cane. And he had a bad back. Balance was always an issue. In the spring of 1950 he fell, fracturing a heel and badly spraining an ankle to the extent that it required a cast. Sánchez regularly smoked a pipe, but he quit between the summer of 1954 and at least the spring of 1956. He was too thin, he explained to friends, and giving up smoking allowed him to gain twenty-five to thirty pounds. While the massive resistance bills made their way through the state legislature and his ACSSP circled the drain, Sánchez developed a serious case of high blood pressure. He wrote to Idar, "My health has been giving me a bit of trouble lately, and my doctors have forbidden me to engage in any activity that might raise my blood pressure. We discovered rather suddenly that I had high [blood] pressure, and I will have to take it slow and easy for a while at least. I spent a few days in the hospital, but am operating more or less as usual now. However, I am getting checkups every two or three days and have to avoid all excitement. Why, even when I think of Shivers I must do so in a mellow mood!" Despite all his health problems Sánchez lived his life fully and happily. He assured an old friend, "I still drink it 'neat.'" He enjoyed spicy food, though he ate sparingly. The price Sánchez paid was heavy, but he bore it well and kept his sense of humor.[50]

This chapter examines the ACSSP, the *Hernández v. Texas* Supreme Court case, comparative civil rights with African Americans, and the Texas civil rights scene. One can argue that Sánchez's life experiences are novel compared to those of most Mexican Americans. This is true and, of course, all lives are unique. But his experience was connected to that of so many other figures, groups, and aspects of civil rights in the United States that it is particularly instructive. He cared enough about racial justice to allow it to harm his career and his health. He hated racial prejudice intensely, and his use of the category of race was always directed toward righting that injustice, not toward making discrimination worse for his or any other people. George I. Sánchez is one of the most important and fascinating crusaders for racial justice and civil rights in United States history. His story is that important.

Part Four

1960s–1972

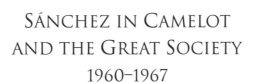

SÁNCHEZ IN CAMELOT
AND THE GREAT SOCIETY
1960–1967

Power lies with the masses of the people, and that power in Latin America can no longer be bought and sold over the counter. Further, the masses in Latin America are very seriously disadvantaged and, by fair means or foul, they will not be denied their heritage much longer. The calamity of Cuba, and reverberations elsewhere, testify eloquently to this. The United States, somehow, must find ways of joining hands with those masses in programs to alleviate their urgent needs—their hunger, their sickness, their lack of education. We need to inject ourselves into their situation in ways which do not infringe on their dignity and self-respect, and which leave no doubts as to our humanitarian motives and our desire for genuine, mutual good will.

What of our current "War on Poverty"? I bleed for Appalachia; but I bleed more profusely for East Austin, for West San Antonio, for the "Magic" Valley. Does our President? Or does he take the position that it can't happen in his native state, good ole Texas?

The 1930s and 1940s were the height of George I. Sánchez's academic production. The 1950s were the height of his civil rights activism. The 1960s brought a little of both and a redoubling of his involvement in electoral politics. Sánchez renewed his scholarly activity—and if it did not quite reach its earlier heights, it was enough to improve his standing at the University of Texas. He still commanded professional prestige but could not maintain the extraordinary pace of prior decades. He was getting older, and his health declined. I explore here Sánchez in Camelot, beginning with the Viva Kennedy movement in 1960 and his renewed emphasis on Latin American research. Sánchez had even greater visibility in Lyndon Johnson's Great Society, continued his activism in issues of integration and education, and became something of an institution at the University of Texas.

Sánchez entered national and state politics more extensively and self-consciously in the sixties. Excellent work by Julie Leininger Pycior and Ignacio García focuses on the transition from Mexican American Generation politics at its zenith through Camelot and the Great Society to the birth of the Chicano movement at the end of this turbulent decade. Sánchez was a crucial figure in this era of political engagement by Mexican Americans. This chapter demonstrates that Sánchez's life sheds a great deal of light on the changing nature of politics and society during the decade of the sixties.[1]

FAMILY

George I. Sánchez wrote to his Berkeley mentor Frank Hart in 1955, "The brash youngster whom you guided to his doctorate is no less brash, though some twenty years older. My daughter presented me with a grandson two years ago, and my son has just returned from the Far East after serving in the Navy for five years as a journalist." George Eugene Sánchez enlisted in the navy in 1950 and served five years in the Pacific, a stint that included participating in the Korean War. Congressman Antonio Fernández of New Mexico hired George Eugene in 1955 as a congressional aide. Sánchez lobbied his friend Fernández on behalf of his son. In one letter Sánchez summarized George Eugene's navy service, promotions, and battle commendations. George was anxious for his son to gain employment that was steadier than his part-time radio jobs in Austin. George Eugene was fluent in Spanish and Japanese, knew some Chinese, and wanted to stay in the Pacific but instead landed in Washington as a staffer for Fernández and then, after the congressman's death, as a member of the Information Branch of the Bureau of Indian Affairs. Sánchez's grandchildren remember George Eugene as being handsome, charming, and talented. He was also troubled.[2]

George Eugene, according to family members, was an alcoholic who could not keep a steady job. Though proud and supportive of his son, his father was also very sensitive about his independence. George Eugene feared he would not live up to his father's legacy. By the late fifties and early sixties he had married, had a daughter, and moved back to New Mexico to explore art. His concerned father kept up with him through his friend Brice Sewell. George Eugene was interested in the folk art of New Mexico, especially *santo* art. He specialized in *retablos*, two-dimensional paintings on wood expressing ethereal religious themes. Sewell, an artist himself before going into educational administration, complimented George Eugene's art and his work at a Spanish radio station. Sewell was as concerned about George Eugene finding his way as his father was. He wrote to Sánchez, "I am still trying to encourage George to go ahead with his folk art, as I still think that eventually it will be his salvation." In 1963 he complimented some examples of George Eugene's work that were being exhibited at an art museum in Santa Fe. George Eugene was then living in the village of Cundiyo in Santa Fe County. Sewell next passed along more delicate news: "He probably has written you that the wife disappeared a couple of weeks ago taking the little girl with her. I had a hunch it was coming after the last time I was there to see them Easter, probably the best thing that could have happened to George. It looks to me like her big trouble is, lazy as hell, probably figures to draw Welfare aid to a dependent mother in some other county." Later Sewell lamented that the wife of "little George" had returned, resulting in continued marital drama. The grandchildren remember that George Eugene worked as a law enforcement official in New Mexico, that he had a troubled marriage, and that he and his spouse were alcoholics.[3]

Sánchez's daughter, Consuelo (Connie), inspired in him more joy. Connie grew up to be a caring, strong figure in the family and maintained a close relationship with her father. After attending college at the University of New Mexico, she married Nelson Sprague and for some time lived in Las Vegas, where Nelson worked as an electrical engineer. In late 1962 Sánchez, his son-in-law, and Connie's father-in-law worked on a computer prototype, he claimed, based on the principles of Mayan mathematics that the professor devised and sought to patent. He worked on this project between visits with his grandchildren, eating and drinking too much, and attending a Las Vegas show, where he reveled in his wife's and daughter's discomfort at the partial nudity of the dancers. By the mid-1960s Connie had relocated to Austin, which greatly pleased her father. It allowed Luisa and him to become more active grandparents.[4]

George I. Sánchez seemed more comfortable being a grandfather than a father. In his curriculum vitae he proudly mentioned that he had five grandchildren. George Eugene had a daughter, Virginia, who was born in 1957. Connie had two daughters and two sons: Mark, born in 1954 (fig. 11.1), George in 1960, Nancy in 1961, and Cindy in 1964. In the 1950s Sánchez purchased a lake cottage outside Austin where he spent weekends with Connie's children. They recall summer days and weekends on the lake as a special time. Accompanied by their grandfather, with his ever-present Falstaff beer in hand, and his beloved dogs, Chino and Airdale, they fished, swam, and played. The youngsters called him Tata. Mark recalls that one day he accidentally startled a rattlesnake that lunged at him; fortunately, his grandfather was carrying his rifle, just in case, and shot it before it could strike (figs. 11.2, 11.3). He also remembered that his grandfather initiated impromptu boxing exercises with a teenage friend; apparently Tata's eye-hand coordination and reflexes were still catlike, as befitted a former boxer. Cindy recalls that he had a more tender side with the girls. They took nature walks with him to look for animal tracks and, though he was not a cuddler, they could sit on his lap anytime they wished. She recalls Tata being a jokester and having a mischievous twinkle in his eye. Luisa was the effective grandmother, not Virgie (fig. 11.4). Connie was closer to her father while George Eugene was closer to his mother.[5]

On Halloween in 1962 George Sánchez's younger brother, Telesforo, died of a heart attack in Santa Fe, where he worked as assistant director of vocational education for the state. It was a sudden blow. He was fifty-three and had a heart condition for which he received treatment. Telesforo was three years younger than George, and he left a wife and two children. George's older brother, Juan,

11.1. Sánchez and his grandson Mark
Sprague relaxing in the mid-1950s with one
of the family dogs. Reproduction by
permission of Cynthia Kennedy.

11.2. Sánchez carrying Mark in the mid-
1950s. Reproduction by permission of
Cynthia Kennedy.

11.3. Mark wearing Tata out in the late 1950s.
Reproduction by permission by Cynthia Kennedy.

11.4. George and Luisa at the cottage in the 1950s or early
1960s. Reproduction by permission of Cynthia Kennedy.

was the only close family relative he had left, and they seem not to have been as
close as he and Telesforo. Friends from New Mexico expressed shock, and Sánchez was quite devastated. He remarked to Campa, who surely remembered
Telesforo as his high school buddy's little brother, "My younger brother, Teles,
died suddenly (in his sleep) last week in Santa Fe. I can't take those things as I
once would, so I stayed here and worked it out."[6]

VIVA KENNEDY

George I. Sánchez's political and academic interests in the early 1960s
revolved around President John F. Kennedy. In the election of 1960 Mexican
Americans made the difference in what was an incredibly narrow margin of
victory for Kennedy in Texas. And George Sánchez was at the heart of it. A year
before, Sánchez wrote of his disgust regarding the stagnant state of Mexican
American political action and sought to create an umbrella organization to
unite the different groups. However, there were too many local rivalries, and he
lacked a single rallying figure that could overcome this balkanization. What
was needed was a charismatic national figure and an opportune moment. This
set the stage for John F. Kennedy. Many Tejanos, especially liberals and inde-
pendents, were drawn to the Kennedy campaign. They were insurgents not tied
to Lyndon Johnson. By the time of the Democratic national convention that
summer, the Los Angeles city councilman Edward Roybal, the San Antonio

state senator Henry B. Gonzalez, and New Mexico's U.S. Senator Dennis Chávez, all of whom supported Kennedy over Johnson, formed the Viva Kennedy clubs. The Kennedy campaign chose Carlos McCormick, a Kennedy volunteer and Alianza official, to run the effort nationally, and McCormick selected the San Antonio attorney and liberal activist Albert Peña to direct the group's efforts in Texas.[7]

Peña tapped Sánchez to draft an essay titled "The American of Mexican Descent: A Statement of Principles by the Viva Kennedy Texas Organization." This document, six pages in length and written in typical Sánchez style with minimal editorial influence by others, made note of the historical legacy of conquest that Mexican Americans experienced, their poverty, discrimination, poor access to health care and education, and lack of opportunity for higher government service. In addition, Angier Biddle Duke, the ambassador to El Salvador under Truman, contacted Sánchez days before the election about forming a pro-Kennedy group of Latin American experts called the Citizens Committee for a New Frontier Policy in the Americas. Sánchez enthusiastically joined. Duke's group issued a partisan broadside blaming Latin American tensions on the Eisenhower administration. Later he solicited ideas for Kennedy's Latin American policy. Sánchez proposed conserving Spanish-speaking ability in the United States as well as increasing the number of Latin American students at American universities through government subsidy as the cheapest, most effective manner of spreading hemispheric goodwill.[8]

Sánchez also thought in electoral terms. He worried that Kennedy's reliance on the Johnson people in Texas would dampen African American and Mexican American enthusiasm. Kennedy won Texas by 46,000 votes out of 2,311,000 cast; Tejanos were estimated to have supported Kennedy with 91 percent of their roughly 200,000 votes. Hence like any group in any close election, the Viva Kennedy clubs claimed that their efforts carried Texas for Kennedy, a fact which, in a tight electoral college split, became nationally important. After the election Sánchez bragged to his old friend Irving Melbo, "I have been up to my ears in the presidential campaign, and we batted very close to 1.000. So, now, what do the *mexicanos* want? Working on that is sheer joy—but, too, it is work."[9]

NEW FRONTIERS FOR LATIN AMERICA

The fullest expression of George I. Sánchez's ideas on Latin America was his essay "A New Frontier Policy for the Americas," the sentiments of which appear in the first epigraph above. It was published in March 1961 in the University of Texas alumni magazine, the *Alcalde*, and inserted into the *Congressional*

Record by Senator Yarborough. Sánchez was a liberal reformer and a cold war devotee. He gave a talk on hemispheric education to the Inter-American Defense College, a Kennedy-inspired training program for U.S. and Latin American military and governmental officials. Cuba was a sore spot for Sánchez, who abhorred the Cuban dictator Fulgencio Batista, yet regarded Fidel Castro as no better. Sánchez conceded that although the Bay of Pigs invasion was a mistake, it was not Kennedy's fault and that, in the final analysis, Castro had "a deranged mind" that demanded some sort of intervention by the United States. But this attitude was tempered by his sympathy for the people suffering the ills Castro sought to rectify.[10]

Sánchez was disappointed at the lack of Mexican American appointments by the Kennedy administration and by Johnson's prominence in that process when it came to Texas, particularly over the appointment of Reynaldo Garza of Brownsville to the federal bench. And he complained bitterly to Yarborough about the State Department's snobbery: "I continue to be angered at the persistent rumors that the Department of State unofficially blackballs Americans of Mexican descent for posts in Latin America, or that it takes a dim view in the matter. I have heard this for years, and it was first attributed (to my knowledge) to Sumner Welles when I worked with Nelson Rockefeller in the office of the Coordinator of Latin American Affairs there in Washington. You made mention of it when I saw you a week ago and I heard it again from a distinguished colleague yesterday." Sánchez continued, "Ask Standard Oil, ask Sears, ask Phillip Morris, ask the philanthropic foundations, etc. The striped pants boys who put out the rumors about the unacceptability of Mexican-Americans are, consciously or otherwise, simply seeking to eliminate competition, and they are victims of their own inadequacy." He was unhappy that the post of assistant secretary of state for Latin America did not go to a Chicana/o.[11]

One way Sánchez advanced Kennedy's New Frontier policy in Latin America was through research. In 1961 he studied Venezuelan education for the Department of Heath, Education, and Welfare (HEW), securing a leave of absence during the middle of the spring term and a lump payment of $6,000 for several weeks of fieldwork ($46,744.82 today). However, the publication of his report foundered in the editing and approval process owing to staff dislocation at HEW and discomfort over his appraisal. Sánchez waited over two years for *The Development of Education in Venezuela* to be published. By that time it was not only out of date but also watered down. He believed that Venezuela's democratic moment of the late 1930s and early 1940s was a flowery façade. He warned his protégé at the University of Notre Dame Julian Samora that "the universities are in a sorry mess down there—student riots, commie politickin', shootings, etc. etc." He further asserted that they were "very disorganized" and had "lots of absenteeism on part of both professors and students, lots of internal politics, pedantic program, etc." Had he published his well-reviewed study unvarnished and with a university press at that time, or in the late thirties when he first discussed such a book, it would have enhanced his reputation. Once again, Sánchez's preferred role as a service intellectual narrowed his options and obscured his professional visibility.[12]

In 1962 Sánchez studied education in Peru for the Agency for International Development (AID), Kennedy's economic bailout program for the developing world. Luisa accompanied him and coauthored the report and their eight-year-old grandson Mark Sprague went with them. George and Luisa secured a $10,000 fee for their two-month stay over the summer ($77,134.11 today). Making this a family venture was important to Sánchez. After his experience in Venezuela he vowed never again to be separated from Luisa for more than a few days at a time and demanded that she be an official investigator. They would long remember this time. Sánchez remarked, "The experience was out of this world (almost literally!). We did 4,000 miles *on the ground*, over the most rugged terrain I've ever seen—narrow dirt roads, dust, precipitous up-grades and down-grades (with maniacal drivers using their trucks and buses in a seeming effort to shove us off the edge of what were really one-lane roads—and that edge dropped off 2–3 or more thousand feet!). Most of the time we spent in the high altitudes—12, 13, 14, 15, 16 thousand feet above sea level. Indians galore. Misery at its most abysmal. Cold and hot. For a while, we were in the below zero high country and, then, on the same day, we were in the tropics of the bottom of a great ravine."[13]

In addition, Sánchez joined the Peace Corps Advisory Board in April 1961, serving on the selection and training committees. He briefly joined President Kennedy in the White House for the inaugural meeting. While not holding a demanding position, Sánchez did help on a variety of issues. The director of the Peace Corps, Robert Sargent Shriver Jr., President Kennedy's brother-in-law, asked Sánchez to help him think through some initial problems. And Sánchez spoke at colleges, provided suggestions for Peace Corps personnel, and gave a personal background report about Venezuela leading up to Shriver's trip there in 1961.[14]

Sánchez offered other assistance as well. He seems to have composed speech lines for President Kennedy's successful visit to Mexico City in July 1962. It is unclear whether Sánchez created these lines at the request of someone or drafted them just in case. The lines are vintage Sánchez, with references to pride in Mexico's history, its leaders, including Miguel Hidalgo y Costilla, José María

Morelos, and Benito Juárez, its educators like Fray de Gante, Bishop Vasco de Quiroga, Justo Sierra, Antonio Caso, and José Vasconcelos, and its colleges dating back to 1553, "one hundred years before the establishment of my *alma mater,* Harvard." He then wrote a line in which Kennedy claimed to being a *primo* [cousin] to the Mexican people. Sánchez at one point wrote to Attorney General Robert Kennedy about the need to replicate the idealism and energy of the Peace Corps in a domestic setting through a national service corps.[15]

Unfortunately for Sánchez, his Peace Corps involvement lessened after he alienated Shriver. On being asked by Shriver in early 1963 to give his impressions of the Peace Corps in Peru, Sánchez replied that while the volunteers were very good, the administrators needed greater Spanish fluency. He felt also that their living quarters were much nicer than those of the native inhabitants and that they suffered from too strong an identification with the U.S. embassy. After defending the linguistic capabilities of the Peru staff and its relationship with the embassy, Shriver thanked Sánchez and must have felt the exchange was over. Yet Sánchez plowed forward with more negative observations. Weeks later Shriver stiffly rejected Sánchez's comments, writing, "There are now more than two hundred Peace Corps Volunteers serving in Peru. I am willing to match them and the staff that supports them, against any group of U.S. citizens serving abroad anywhere, in terms of competence, dedication, spirit and effectiveness. I wish you had a chance to visit them. I know you would be proud and gratified."[16]

Sánchez had pushed his point too far. Some association with the U.S. embassy was necessary in a country experiencing political disturbances. But he distrusted U.S. embassies, which had been a source of humiliation for him— one of the few places where he admitted to experiencing racial discrimination. In one talk he recalled an incident in Peru: "Two years ago, in a U.S. Embassy in a South American country (where we were on official assignment by our government) my wife and I were given a 'dressing-down' by a be-ribboned Marine sargeant [*sic*] when, upon returning from a trip into the interior, we sought to take the elevator up to our office. The rules had been changed, and visitors were supposed to wait for an escort. We received the 'dressing down' (rather, I should say the 'attempted dressing down'—for I do not 'dress down' easily) not because we did not know the rule change but because the all-important sargeant [*sic*] thought that we were natives of that country. I say with sadness that it reminded me of home." Sánchez was sensitive about racial prejudice following the flag. He found the insularity inherent in embassies a breeding ground for damaging, colonial-like attitudes.[17]

But he did eventually work with the State Department. They contacted him in the spring of 1963 to consult with their director of intelligence and research with regard to Mexico. This involved two seminars in Mexico that he and other American academics led in the summer of 1965 for the agency's Bureau of Educational and Cultural Affairs. They offered over one hundred rural, isolated social studies teachers in secondary schools and in teacher training institutes instruction in history, geography, economics, and civic education. Sánchez's expenses were paid, and he received some compensation. He reported afterward that the seminars were nonchalantly slapped together by Mexican officials who had difficulty keeping to the prearranged schedule, although on the whole he felt that it was worthwhile and that the participants were a joy to instruct.[18]

In 1961 Sánchez self-published a book, *Arithmetic in Maya*. In seventy-four pages *Arithmetic in Maya* set out to solve an arcane archeological and mathematical mystery Sánchez had pondered since his youth in the 1920s, when he attended lectures by the great Maya archeologist Sylvanus G. Morley at the University of New Mexico. He later visited Morley's famed Chichén Itzá dig in southern Mexico in the 1930s. Sánchez remarked, "As a rank amateur I tried to draw him out on Maya numbers, for I was curious. So was he, of course. He explained, again, his ideas as to the zero, as to calendrical counts—but we could not get a straight arithmetic." Since the Mayan numbers, a vigesimal system with units of zero, ones, and fives, were religiously symbolic and tied to their calendar, Morley did not believe them to be functional for adding, subtracting, multiplying, and dividing, though the Maya had words for these concepts. Sánchez claimed that in a moment of boredom during a department meeting in the 1950s he doodled the old Mayan symbols on a pad and stumbled on a system to perform math. He enjoyed discussing it with mathematicians and anthropologists throughout the country, and the book generated positive reviews. After having worked on the project for several years in the late fifties, Sánchez submitted an early summary of his work to the *Southwestern Journal of Anthropology*. The editor liked it, but the journal could not cover the printing costs of a lengthy, heavily illustrated article. So Sánchez went back to work and completed it as a book. He intended to publish *Arithmetic in Maya* through the Institute of Latin American Studies and the University of Texas Press. By the fall of 1960 this appeared certain, but there was a snag. A reviewer who recommended publication changed his mind, objecting to Sánchez's lack of formal credentials as a mathematician, anthropologist, or archeologist. So Sánchez impatiently withdrew his manuscript, believing he had to move quickly to protect what he felt was his method's application for computer technology.[19]

Another book Sánchez published, this time with the commercial press Ginn, was *Mexico*, one in a series of brief surveys of foreign countries. Between signing the advance contract in April 1962 to the revisions he sent the company in

April 1964, Sánchez and the editors at Ginn constantly discussed two issues—
Sánchez's penchant for history and the length of the book. Much is packed into
the brief *Mexico*, but it is undeniably shallow. Today it reads as a serviceable,
well-written but ultimately dated survey that is something of a public relations
piece for the Institutional Revolutionary Party (PRI). Sánchez was chummy
with the ruling elite in Mexico and, while he had many private criticisms, at
least in print he was deferential. The PRI at this time was becoming increasingly
autocratic. Between Sánchez's first draft of *Mexico* and its eventual publication,
the government initiated a brutal crackdown, resulting in the kidnapping, tor-
ture, and killing of perhaps thousands of students and dissenters.[20]

In addition to a couple of book chapters, the New Frontier spurred Sánchez's
graduate advising. Of the first fifteen dissertations he directed at the University
of Texas between 1942 and 1962, only three were on Latin American education;
from 1962 to 1966, however, three of six dissertations he directed were on Latin
America, while a fourth dealt with the Trust Territory of the Pacific Islands.
Sánchez's students became an outlet for his interests, especially in Latin America. Perhaps his greatest student was Thomas P. Carter, whom Sánchez met
while in Peru. Carter wrote a dissertation on Peruvian education in short order
and became a leading scholar on Chicana/o education through the 1970s and
1980s. Efforts to capitalize on this synergy with an edited volume on comparative Latin American education came to naught, however. Such a book would
have endured longer than the little, uncritical *Mexico*.[21]

PASSO AND MEXICAN AMERICAN POLITICS

One aspect of Sánchez's activism in the 1960s was his involvement in high-
level Mexican American political maneuverings through the Political Association of Spanish-Speaking Organizations (PASSO, sometimes called PASO),
which grew out of the Viva Kennedy experience nationally and the Mexican
American Political Association in California. Tejanos in PASSO first met in
Victoria, Texas, in February 1961. They were immediately pulled into Senator
Gonzalez's primary race for Lyndon Johnson's vacant U.S. Senate seat. Gonzalez lost, and angry PASSO members declined to support the winner, the LBJ-
backed conservative Democrat and interim senator Bill Blakely. John Tower, a
Republican, eventually won the seat by nine thousand votes largely owing to
Mexican American apathy. In this negative but effective manner PASSO ob-
tained some influence within the Texas Democratic Party.[22]

One touchstone of this emergence was Sánchez's essay called "The American of Mexican Descent." The essay grew out of organizational principles he

wrote for PASSO and later sent to Carey McWilliams, then the editor of *The Nation*. McWilliams could not publish it at the time and sent it to the *Chicago Jewish Forum*. The essay was redistributed by the *American G.I. Forum News Bulletin* in 1961 and in the newsletters of the Alianza and the Colorado Anti-Discrimination Commission in 1962. It was debated in the pages of the *Texas Observer* in 1961 and 1962. Sánchez argued that policy decisions about Mexican Americans were based on "opinions of individuals poorly qualified to make far-reaching judgments about the Mexican-American." What was different about this essay was Sánchez's nibbling around the edges of cultural nationalism, a practice usually associated with young, militant Chicanas/os later in the decade. Sánchez claimed, "It is my purpose, however, to underline the fact that only the *mexicanos* can speak for the *mexicanos*, and that it would be well to assess very carefully the claims of any individual, *mexicano* or otherwise, who would speak for us." That idea horrified white liberals.[23]

Twin forces of dissatisfaction—Mexican American conservatives' anger toward Texas liberal Democrats and Mexican American liberals' anger toward Texas conservative Democrats—formed a combustible mood in the gubernatorial race of 1962. The moderately conservative incumbent Daniel sought a fourth term, while the Houston liberal Don Yarborough and the former LBJ aide and Kennedy's secretary of the navy, John B. Connally, challenged him. Carlos McCormick backed the conservative Connally because of his connections to LBJ; Idar and Hector P. Garcia of AGIF backed Daniel after flirting with Connally; Sánchez and other liberals backed Yarborough. The PASSO convention had a polarizing choice and ended up narrowly backing Daniel over Yarborough, with Connally a distant third. Sánchez was incensed and walked out. Some local PASSO units broke ranks and endorsed Yarborough. Garcia was the object of a great deal of vituperation for backing a segregationist incumbent governor over a liberal challenger. Sánchez argued that no candidate but Yarborough could possibly meet PASSO's statement of principles: "We certainly cannot improve ourselves by prostituting our principles or by being *alcahuetes* [a gossip or enabler of bad things] to attain some little advantages." Daniel did not finish with enough votes to make the runoff election, and PASSO quickly endorsed Yarborough, who then lost the runoff to Connally. They then tried to endorse Connally, who at this point refused to commit himself to anything. It was a disaster for PASSO. Sánchez wrote a circular about supporting Yarborough and pestered Idar and Garcia about their support of Daniel. These letters went unanswered and, in Garcia's opinion, Sánchez crossed a line by writing, "I can take political disagreement and not have my feelings hurt. What I cannot take is political hypocrisy. Please forgive me if I hurt your feelings, but you are exemplifying political hypocrisy as you go all out for a Governor and a political record that contradicts everything that you and I have worked for in behalf of our people. Yes, Hector, I am saddened by your actions." Sánchez eventually apologized, but while things between them mended somewhat the relationship was never quite as close as before.[24]

But this was not the end of Sánchez's apostasy. He worked hard for Jack Cox, Connally's Republican opponent in the general election. A former Democratic state legislator, Cox ran a tough race against Connally. This should not be surprising given how internally rent the Democratic Party was in 1962 and the fact that in 1961 Tower, a little-known Republican candidate, won Johnson's Senate seat. Kennedy barely carried Texas in the presidential election of 1960, even with Johnson on the ticket. Cox was reactionary and anti–civil rights. But a Connally defeat offered the chance of a liberal takeover of the party the next election cycle. Sánchez backed Cox for that strategic reason. He used his Yarborough mailing list of over fifty people, worked on a Spanish language radio spot, wrote a position paper on academic freedom, and justified his actions in the *Texas Observer*. Meanwhile, Hector Garcia and the active remnants of PASSO desperately backed Connally as individuals. Cox narrowly lost to Connally, yet many liberal Democrats viewed the situation as Sánchez did: "Jack knew my purpose—I did not sail under any false colors with him, and he agreed with my position and, in addition, promised certain reforms that the *mexicanos* need badly." Then Sánchez made a prediction: "Just watch what Mr. Connally does! He, and his mentor, are no slouches in politics. They will come around with reforms that we need—whether I voted for Cox or Connally! Maybe, because many of us voted for Cox!" Sánchez updated Senator Ralph Yarborough on these activities. It was in Yarborough's interests for the party establishment to suffer a blow in 1962 so that liberals would be in a stronger position to help him survive an expected primary challenge from the right in 1964.[25]

This disaster for PASSO set the stage for a crucial year in 1963. The association had to find a way to preserve its viability. Albert Peña looked for local races in which they could make an impact and determined that the Anglo-dominated agricultural town of Crystal City, southwest of San Antonio, was a good test. Mexican Americans there were already involved in a voter registration drive sponsored by the Teamsters union. PASSO recruited a slate of candidates, five of whom won election for mayor and city council. Sánchez spread the word about this revolt in the brush country to journalists and published a letter in the *San Antonio Express News* pushing back against a columnist's castigation of PASSO as being tainted by its association with the Teamsters. He defensively explained to Yarborough that Anglo racism in Crystal City—he did not include all whites—justified bloc voting along ethnic lines, something he normally opposed.[26]

Crystal City worried Texas liberals. Sánchez commented to Ronnie Dugger, the editor and founder of the *Texas Observer*, about a recent article in its pages, stating, "The *Observer*, through inadvertence, has been guilty of alienating some of the *mexicanos* who, fundamentally, are liberals. Labor has made its mistakes in its treatment of the 'minority' groups. If memory serves me right, the *Observer* (among others) has taken me to task for saying (cryptically, really) that only the *mexicanos* can speak for the *mexicanos*. I will reiterate that seeming chauvinism by saying that only the Negro can speak for the Negro." He concluded to Dugger, "If the liberals have the gift of leadership, they had better begin using it *now*—and not play the last-minute game of 'after all, under the skin, we are brothers.' Hell!" Dugger rebuked Sánchez by countering that the logical meaning of his statement was that "in politics, mexicanos should elect only mexicanos." He lashed out: "Inherently, there is a danger in this work—the danger that righteousness against economic oppression that is undeniably racial in part may metamorphose into retaliatory racism."[27]

Sánchez was not used to being called a racist. He replied, "This is the unkindest cut that I have received from a friend!" He continued, "I have been fighting racism since you were wearing three-cornered pants—in Georgia, in Alabama, in Louisiana, in Texas, in Illinois, in New Mexico, and elsewhere. Don't go holier than thou on me at this late date; for I can give you aces and spades on this matter and still win, hands down. I have numerous scars that attest to my fight against racism, in this and other countries. Have you?" He regarded Maury Maverick Jr., the San Antonio state legislator, and Edwin Embree of the Rosenwald Fund as outstanding agents for the minority populations within their professional competencies because they dedicated themselves to understanding them; but this was an act of will on their part, not unearned deference. Sánchez closed as follows: "And for Pete's sake, do not call me a racist!" He then added, "P.S. Oh, yes. How my heart bleeds for the Crystal City 'Anglo' politicians!" Dugger published Sánchez's letter but remained hostile toward the assertiveness of minorities.[28]

PRESIDENT JOHNSON AND MEXICAN AMERICANS

In the fall of 1963 Sánchez was consumed with politics. On November 14 he participated in a conference in Los Angeles on behalf of the President's Committee on Equal Employment Opportunity. He was invited by Vice President Johnson and spoke about education and job training as part of a panel chaired by the secretary of Health, Education, and Welfare, Anthony Celebrezze. Several days later things changed dramatically. Like many men of his generation, Sánchez did not dwell on traumatic events. There is little evidence to indicate what he personally felt about Pearl Harbor, the mass murder committed on his campus by Charles Whitman in 1966, or the Kennedy assassination. One ramification of the Kennedy assassination that demonstrably affected Sánchez was an essay by the University of Texas sociologist Reece McGee published in the *Nation* weeks later. "Texas: The Roots of the Agony" offered five reasons the assassination simply had to occur in Texas: intellectual absolutism, the institutionalization of violence, the proliferation of guns, the respectability of the radical right, and the absence of any countervailing left. McGee portrayed a state full of dangerous, extremist, self-righteous, well-armed fanatics.[29]

Sánchez assigned the essay to one of his spring classes, which prompted former governor Daniel to write that he doubted the professor had read the essay. Along with the letter he supplied a marked-up version of McGee's piece and also a lengthy address, "Christian Principles in the Political Process," that he had delivered to a YMCA youth banquet that December, filling in for the originally scheduled LBJ. In his lengthy discussion of God in the affairs of government, Daniel dwelled on the assassination, Kennedy's legacy, and the godlessness of Communists like Lee Harvey Oswald. Likely faced by stupefied children who were wondering when this scary old man would stop talking, Daniel pivoted to lambaste Reece's article, professors at the University of Texas, and other communists. Not one to be pushed around, especially by a man he had long regarded as gutless, the slumped, wizened Professor Sánchez replied forcefully that the ousted governor was as badly misinformed on this as he was about Mexican American school segregation and his badly dashed hopes for a fourth term. He welcomed Daniel in his classroom anytime. Daniel quickly backed off his insinuations, hoping he had given no offense, thereby confirming Sánchez's character assessment.[30]

Sánchez blind-copied this correspondence to McGee and to McWilliams at *The Nation*. He and his colleague William Drake also wrote supportive letters to *The Nation*. This touched McGee, who replied that he and his colleague were the only ones to publicly defend his right to speak. McGee soon left the University of Texas after being told by his department chair that he no longer had a future there. In November 1964 the philosophy professor David Miller requested that the university Counsel on Academic Freedom and Responsibility consider this situation. Sánchez, who was on the committee, supplied additional information, including the fact that McWilliams had originally asked him to write the article. He had declined and suggested Dugger, who then suggested McGee. While not in agreement with the entire essay, Sánchez was concerned that McGee was forced out.[31]

Sánchez disliked Connally viscerally. As the Yarborough–Connally political feud simmered in the summer of 1963, in part prompting the tragic presidential campaign swing through Texas, Sánchez entered the fray on behalf of Yarborough in the *Texas Observer*, castigating Connally's proclamation of the first week of July 1963 as G.I. Forum week. Connally had mentioned AGIF's role in aiding Mexican Americans' assimilation, a comment which drew the professor's ire. "We have never accepted the accusation," he wrote, "that we were anything but Americans—in fact, that some of us have been here, in what is now the good old U.S.A., long before Mr. Connally's folks came to Texas or even the Western Hemisphere." Sánchez viewed Connally as LBJ's lackey. His feelings toward LBJ were more complex. In this, Sánchez was like most mortals in the presence of the titan-like Johnson, who inspired awe, intimidation, humor, admiration, and puzzlement, often at the same time. There is little to suggest, however, that Sánchez and LBJ had any meaningful connections over their years of occasional dealings. Sánchez wanted to dislike LBJ despite having supported him. In 1964 Sánchez ambivalently wrote to Campa, "I turned in your name as an outstanding Texas Mexican! LBJ is in need of help. *Me choca* [he irks me] but Barry [Goldwater] is intolerable. Yes, no?" It was the role Johnson played in the Texas Democratic Party, not his national profile, that most raised Sánchez's ire. He knew where he stood with LBJ. To a friend asking for help in obtaining an appointment to a minor federal board, Sánchez warned, "While LBJ has invited me to several top level sessions in Washington (and I have accepted), I have no illusions as to where I stand with him. A recommendation from me would do more harm than good. My 'in' with him is just window dressing!"[32]

Sánchez really was, in his words, "window dressing" to the Great Society. He did not let up on criticizing Johnson's programs, as indicated by an essay from 1965 in the *Texas Observer*, an excerpt of which appears as the second epigraph above. But he criticized the Great Society not for its goals or methods but for the fact that it left out Mexican Americans. Much like LBJ, Sánchez still saw the improvement of education as the key to economic justice; he favored equalizing opportunity over more direct income redistribution. Much as Sánchez rhetorically and conceptually looked backward to the New Deal for inspiration, his liberalism by the 1960s was oriented toward that of the Great Society in its emphasis on specific groups such as the elderly, Mexican Americans, and African Americans, all of whose continuing disadvantage mocked the pretensions of an affluent nation. And he favored Great Society centralization: "We are not at all frightened by the dire predictions of 'federal control.' We are much more

frightened by the demonstrated irresponsibility of local control in the education of our children!"[33]

The Equal Employment Opportunity Commission (EEOC) was an important element of the Great Society for Mexican Americans. In the spring of 1966
EEOC held a conference on Mexican American issues in Albuquerque, and an
hour after convening, Mexican American delegates staged a highly publicized
walkout protest. Sánchez wrote to Franklin D. Roosevelt Jr., the chairman of
the EEOC, that although he did not attend the conference he agreed in principle with the walkout. Roosevelt, who resigned from the commission a month
later to run for office in New York State, regarded it as a public relations stunt.
His departure along with that of another official left openings at the EEOC,
and Sánchez emerged as a possible replacement. On May 14 Yarborough recommended to LBJ that Sánchez be considered for the job, arguing, "I realize it
is difficult for you to nominate Texans to high office without facing charges of
'discrimination,' but I am confident you will give this recommendation the
consideration that Dr. Sánchez's qualifications deserve." Sanchez's supporters
included Congressman John Brademas of Indiana, leaders of the Mexican
American Political Association in California such as Bert Corona and Eduardo
Quevedo, President Hank Brown of the Texas AFL-CIO, Bexar County Commissioner Albert Peña, Jesus Perez of the San Antonio AGIF, Julian Samora of
the University of Notre Dame (who elicited Brademas's letter), and the attorneys Manuel Velasco of Victoria and Bob Sánchez of McAllen. Two detractors
chimed in. Punctuating a frosty two-decade relationship, CSO President Albert Piñon wrote that at one point Sánchez would have been ideal, but that his
age, time commitments, and health were now concerns. While negative, the
letter still expressed respect.[34]

The other negative evaluation of Sánchez created sparks. On June 7, 1966, at
about the time Sánchez privately urged Yarborough to concede defeat on the
effort, the Corpus Christi LULACer William D. Bonilla wrote to President
Johnson that Sánchez was in no way deserving or fit for such an important post.
Bonilla claimed, correctly, that Sánchez was inactive in LULAC and, incor-
rectly, that he was minimally active in PASSO. Bonilla raised eyebrows by charg-
ing, "I would like to further point out that Dr. George I. Sánchez has been ill
and is unfortunately almost senile." Had the letter been kept private between
Bonilla and the president's staff, Sánchez would never have known, but Bonilla
made it public by sending a copy to Yarborough and to LULAC President Alfred J. Hernandez.[35]

Yarborough was angry and wrote to Sánchez and to Johnson loyalist Hector
Garcia, an occasional Bonilla ally, of his outrage. Sánchez wrote to Bonilla di-

rectly, "I am amazed and shocked at the untruthful and slanderous letter that you wrote to the President about me. I am puzzled as to your motivation, for not only have I not had any disagreement with you, or been associated with you in any way, but you know virtually nothing of me." This was inaccurate as they were clearly on opposite sides of PASSO in 1963. Sánchez went on, "I do not need to describe or to justify my participation in civic affairs to you. You do not have the stature to merit such attention." Secure that Bonilla, then flirting with Tower's senatorial reelection campaign, was no intimate of LBJ either, Sánchez replied as follows with calculated insults: "If the purpose of your letter was to bring yourself to the attention of the President, you may have done so—to your own detriment. Certainly, libeling your betters is the worst sort of procedure in getting attention from intelligent, responsible officials." To Yarborough, Sánchez explained the dispute as a political one. Apparently, Garcia had proposed Bonilla for PASSO's presidency while Sánchez favored Peña for another term. Sánchez wrote, "The battle was between Hector and me! I won, and Hector walked out. Later, we laughed about it and have been good friends again for a long time." He reiterated that, in any case, he did not want the EEOC position and asked Yarborough to nominate someone else.[36]

Bonilla replied with what might colloquially be regarded as a nonapologetic apology. In a confusing letter full of passive aggressive inference and stagey deference, he wrote that he had neither major disagreements nor associations with Sánchez and that, while no intellectual, he too was interested in the welfare of his people. Had the nomination been official, he explained, he would have kept quiet. Bonilla claimed he respected Sánchez as an individual. He then quoted resolutions from the ephemeral 1952 Rio Grande Valley protest group over the Saunders–Leonard report condemning Sánchez as having allegedly authorized the publication of racism directed against Mexican Americans; he had a problem with this, he said, though he then contradictorily wished not to "cast any reflection on your record." Bonilla admitted, "Since I did not read the pamphlet discussed in the report, I do not know whether that statement or those statements were contained therein, but I do have the report I have quoted from in my possession." Bonilla then passed along something falling just shy of an apology: "I wrote a personal letter and I am sorry if you feel I was wrong in doing so but in my heart, I felt it was a necessity."[37]

There is no record of a response by Sánchez or that Bonilla's letter had any effect on the White House, which throughout 1966, in a reaction to the walkout in Albuquerque, desperately searched for some Chicana/o to place on the EEOC. The longtime president of the Civil Service Commission John W. Macy created for Johnson brief biographies of eight Mexican Americans—four

Republicans and four Democrats—with Sánchez as one of the Democrats. Macy remarked of Sánchez, "I have been informed that you know him" and that "Sánchez looks attractive and is in our preliminary thinking for the National Commission on Rural Poverty, unless you believe that the EEOC would be more appropriate." Macy remarked that Bonilla "raised a question of Sánchez's health which I have not yet had an opportunity to explore." After this, Sánchez was still under active consideration. In another internal memo from the White House aide Lou Schwartz to Macy about Latinos being considered for ambassadorial positions, Sánchez was named as one of three possibilities, though someone scribbled on the margins of the memo next to Sánchez's name, "Uncle Tom."[38]

From that point on, things moved quickly. On August 18 at 8:00 p.m. Macy sent President Johnson a brief memo with the subject line "George I. Sánchez." Macy wrote, "In response to your inquiry of this morning concerning the identity of those who recommended Sánchez for appointment to the Equal Employment Opportunity Commission, I find that letters of endorsement were received in my office from Senator Yarborough and Congressman Brademas. These letters combined with favorable comments from Harry McPherson about him prompted me to include his name in a list of Spanish-American candidates in my memorandum of June 29. In light of your evaluation of Sánchez, his name will receive no further consideration." Perhaps the mere identity of Sánchez's supporters told Johnson all he needed to know in order to make a negative decision. Perhaps he remembered Sánchez's sharp criticism of him. Whatever the case, Sánchez's years of suspicion and hostility toward LBJ were repaid in full after one morning conversation the president had with his staff. The search for a Mexican American EEOC commissioner dragged on into 1967. It involved fourteen names in four distinct periods with half under repeat consideration. Sánchez's name was in the first flight of possible candidates from June 1966 but not in the next wave of October 1966. On the advice of Hector Garcia, LBJ eventually picked Vicente Ximenes of the AGIF in the spring of 1967.[39]

Another sore spot among Mexican American activists was the long-planned White House conference on Mexican Americans. Sánchez participated in a White House planning meeting for it in October 1966 (fig. 11.5). He gave a ringing speech that was carried in AGIF's newsletter, saying, "Personally, I am tired of these (I am sure) well-intentioned conferences—and I would have stayed away from this one were it not that the White House called it. I didn't want conferences; I want action." But the White House continued to delay. Sánchez was invited to the eventual conference in El Paso in October 1967, but did not

11.5. Sánchez at a White House Planning Conference on Mexican Americans and the Great Society, December 1966. He is obscured, leaning back on the table to the right. Reproduction by permission of Benson Latin American Center.

attend. It was a fiasco for the White House with loud protests by Chicana/o youth that generated heavy, negative media coverage.[40]

INTEGRATION PURIST

Sánchez was an integration purist, a stance that colored his prickly relationship with trends in educational and social science theory in the 1960s. His commitment to integration was controversial. He despised cultural deprivation theory, for example, viewing it as a rationalization for Mexican American segregation via "special" education. Work on the culturally deprived child held that poverty-stricken minority children were culturally isolated, understimulated by their environment, and underdeveloped as a result. Thus, the schools had to develop completely new ways of teaching. Sánchez fumed, "I find it absurd that otherwise intelligent educators and statesmen should find a foreign home-language such an insuperable hurdle. *They* impose retardation on such children, and *they* add to that imposition throughout the educational process—by having the children repeat grades, by 'genteel segregation,' by watering down the curriculum, by using improper criteria for measuring progress, by suppressing Spanish, and by a great many other professional shameful malpractices." Sánchez thought that sympathetic educators often indulged in assumptions of low Mexican American educability and cultural exoticism.[41]

Integrating Mexican Americans with other schoolchildren and according their language and culture respected status, though in theory simpler than developing all new compensatory programs, was harder to enact. Jim Crow school systems had already pioneered specialized programs through which de facto segregation took place. Sánchez sent in more complaints about the state's migrant program and found little sympathy from liberal allies. The Texas ACLU was incredulous that migrant education could be seen as racial discrimination. As for the TEA, in late 1963 a rattled J. W. Edgar shared Sánchez's heated complaints with a member of the State Board of Education. This official, R. W. Byram of Austin, copied Sánchez on his note to Edgar recommending that TEA sever contact with him. Sánchez relished that Edgar's being formally and publicly dictated to by a state board member undercut Edgar and reinforced the impression of him as being spineless. Sánchez rubbed his nose in it: "It was not only amateurish, but officious. It was also inexcusable in that he recommended to you that I be 'blacklisted' with the TEA. I am sure that you did not intend to have him try to pressure me; for, as you well know, I do not pressure worth a damn."[42]

Soon after this episode Sánchez took his complaints to the Department of Commerce's Community Relations Service, headed by the former governor of Florida LeRoy Collins and Commerce Secretary Luther Hodges. This was a citizen's advisory committee that the White House had put Sánchez on months before the election of 1964 to stress volunteerism and the mediation of disputes as part of the Civil Rights Act of 1964. It gave the professor another platform from which to express his extreme pessimism over federally approved compensatory education. At this time another member of the State Board of Education, the attorney and former educator at Texas Technological College William H. Evans, excitedly replied to Sánchez of his amazement that Mexican American education could possibly be thought of as a civil rights issue. Sánchez replied, "I applaud the intentions of those who would improve the education of migratory workers. I insist, Mr. Evans, that segregation (call it 'separation' or 'pilot programs' or what have you) is not the answer."[43]

In the spring of 1965 Sánchez complained to the Community Relations Service of Austin's adoption of Head Start as part of its war on poverty, a move which he felt "would bring about the establishment of segregated schools for pre-school children, *de facto* or by official regulation (both procedures have been proposed)." This practice of de facto segregation, assured Sánchez, was a widespread phenomenon in Texas, though easily fixed with minor rezoning. His final letter to the Community Relations Service noted, "Segregation, even that that is well-intentioned, makes me angry—and ashamed of the official agencies charged with corrective efforts." He sent more complaints to AGIF officials, to Yarborough, and to local Mexican Americans who wondered why Sánchez was so negative about the federally funded programs in their towns that they thought helped a great deal.[44]

BILINGUAL EDUCATION

Despite having worked firmly within an English-only model as a teacher in the 1920s and as a researcher in the 1930s and 1940s, Sánchez made the shift toward vernacular education for language-minority children by the 1950s. To a colleague at Columbia University Sánchez wrote, "A foreign home-language is not a handicap, unless the educational process (informal and formal) makes it so. A foreign mother-tongue can be, and is for many, a decided advantage if properly cultivated—and for centuries we have known that a second language is learned best if the vernacular is developed. . . . Please, do not fall into the common error of attributing all ills of people with a non-English vernacular to 'language handicap.' I remember meeting Albert Einstein—his English left a bit to be desired!" To a California teacher he argued that vernacular education was not about reinforcing ethnicity but about making Mexican American children "Americans-plus." Sánchez never assumed integration and bilingual education were incompatible.[45]

A modern reader with some knowledge of Chicana/o history might regard Sánchez's qualifications regarding bilingual education as weak tea. But it is important to note that supporting bilingual education in the early 1960s was unpopular in academia. For example, in 1961 Sánchez submitted a lengthy essay, "Bilingualism in the Southwest—a Tragi-Comedy," to the *National Conference on Research in English Bulletin*. He warned Richard Alm, who solicited the article, that language justified massive failure rates for Mexican Americans. The next year a sheepish Alm confirmed that while he approved the article, as did the unnamed reviewer, the association's executive committee had the final say. One committee member, Constance McCullough of San Francisco State

College, accused the paper of betraying "emotional overtones." Though Mc-Cullough conceded to making no evaluation of the actual research, she dismissed the very premise of the bilingual approach. Alm apologized, and Sánchez withdrew his essay. Once again Sánchez experienced frustration with academic publishing owing to the progressiveness of his ideas and the passion with which he expressed them. He also fostered the interest of Monroe Sweetland of the National Education Association in early bilingual instruction for Spanish-speakers.[46]

But as much as Sánchez supported bilingual education as a concept, he could not divorce it from his hard-bitten activist perspective of language as a segregation trap. This experience and his academic profile did not always coexist harmoniously. Sánchez found himself intellectually isolated from two foundational scholars of the bilingual education movement: Joshua A. Fishman, then at the University of Pennsylvania, and Theodore Andersson, his colleague at the University of Texas. Directing the major research project called the Survey of Language Resources of American Ethnic Groups, which was sponsored by the Office of Education, Fishman in the spring of 1961 asked for Sánchez's expertise on how Mexican Americans maintained their vernaculars. To Fishman, lingering vernaculars and ethnicity represented submerged resistance to the ethnocentrism of white Anglo-Saxons. Sánchez was confused over Fishman's positive perceptions of native language retention. For Sánchez they were proof that the schools were not doing their jobs and that the dominant society wanted to keep Mexican Americans poor, ignorant, and on the farms as economically and racially exploited groups. Fishman prevailed upon Sánchez to write an essay on Mexican Americans and language retention for the project's eventual book. Sánchez turned in his lengthy historical analysis, and Fishman, a few months later, rejected it as not being interpretively in step with the rest of the essays. Sánchez complained to Campa, "Maybe I am wrong, but I am convinced that Spanish has been maintained in the Southwest not because of any positive measures, but rather because the schools have been so bad and have not taught English!" The resulting *Language Loyalty in the United States* was a key early text in the emerging bilingual education movement. And Sánchez's ideas were not in it.[47]

Andersson collaborated not with his campus neighbor Sánchez but with Fishman on bilingual education. At a conference on the bilingual child in Austin in the summer of 1964, Andersson was listed on the program as an outstanding educator in the field along with Fishman, a former Sánchez student named Pauline Rojas, the HEW official A. Bruce Gaarder, and Thomas Horn, a curriculum instructor in Sánchez's college. Sánchez, on the other hand, appeared on the program as a session chair. When Andersson and the education professor Joseph Michel applied for federal funds for a foreign language research center at the university, Sánchez contributed only a few comments. Sánchez's involvement in bilingual education instead came from his political activism. He helped Senator Yarborough with his bilingual education bill, which made its way through Congress in 1967. Bilingual education was good politics for Yarborough, who needed solid Mexican American support in his bid for a third term in 1970. In one campaign speech Yarborough echoed Sánchez on vernaculars: "This bill would make both languages first languages and first-class languages." Sánchez felt that the bilingual education push afforded Mexican Americans a deserving niche within the Great Society and was entirely due to Yarborough.[48]

Yarborough's bill initially targeted Mexican Americans of the Southwest. It was widened, however, to include other languages. His revised bill passed the House 294–122 in May 1967 and the Senate 71–7 in December as Title VII of the Elementary and Secondary Education Act (ESEA); President Johnson signed it into law in January 1968, even as his Great Society slumped under the weight of the unpopular war in Vietnam. Bilingual education's strongest opponents were not in the Congress, however, but in the executive branch. In particular, Commissioner of Education Harold Howe felt the bilingual education act was unnecessary.[49]

Sánchez shaped Yarborough's opinions on Mexican American education over the years. They were friends and neighbors in the same Austin subdivision. Yarborough publicly lauded Sánchez as the most idealistic Mexican American leader he knew. During the legislative process Sánchez wrote for Yarborough's staff a three-page, single-spaced memo full of speech lines and arguments favoring bilingual education. He adduced influential Canadian studies on cognition and bilingualism, the national self-interest involved in language resources, hemispheric relations, and how this bill demonstrated the Great Society's first real interest in Mexican Americans. The professor ended in Yarborough's voice: "Whether my proposed legislation passes or not, I urge you to insist to your local authorities to do everything within their power to provide a bilingual education for your children, whether their home language is Spanish or English, whether the foreign language to be taught is Spanish, French, German, or Chinese. Bilingualism, *per se*, is the gift of the educated man. Let us be educated Americans. Let us be bilingual."[50]

During these years Sánchez wrote "History, Culture, and Education," one of his finest essays. This keynote chapter in a collection called *La Raza: Forgotten Americans*, edited by Samora, grew out of the essay rejected for Fishman's *Language Loyalty* collection and for the *National Conference on Research in*

English Bulletin. Sánchez presented a version of this work at Occidental College in Los Angeles in 1963 and in San Francisco in 1965, both at conferences sponsored by the Rosenberg Foundation. Though slated for only thirty minutes at Occidental, Sánchez must have gone considerably over that limit given that a published version of the address in another collection is far more elaborate than his conference notes. Sánchez was, by all accounts, a marvelous lecturer. Samora directed the San Francisco conference and put the talks together for an edited collection. Sánchez was fussy about keeping the essay copyrighted in his name, as he later hoped to write a more general book on Mexican American education. He never got to it, however, and "History, Culture, and Education" stands as one of his final published works on the subject. It is well written and begins with the conundrum, Why did Mexican Americans retain their vernacular? Here Sánchez went beyond the failure of the schools and into the nature of socioeconomic and racial exploitation. He discussed demographic realities, history, the need for cultural acceptance, educational theory, the defectiveness of Texas schools, the segregationist trap that language and "special" education held for Chicana/o children, and principles by which bilingual-bicultural education could be enacted. The essay was his swan song in academic publishing.[51]

BECOMING AN INSTITUTION

By the 1960s Sánchez had achieved an exalted status at the University of Texas as a voice of protest. This rise in prestige was reflected in his salary, as in the middle of the 1960s he received substantial raises. Ironically, this was about the time his scholarly productivity tapered off. Was this the school's attempt to correct an embarrassing example of salary compression for a once highly productive but outspoken professor? Stuck at $8,600 since his final year as department chair, Sánchez received a $500 raise shortly after the beginning of the fall term of 1960 to make his total $9,100 ($68,842.85, $3,934.88, and $71,614.85 today). The next academic year, 1961–62, he received a $900 raise to bring his salary to an even $10,000 ($7,011.72 and $77,908.03 today). His salary remained at that level until the 1963–64 academic year, when it was raised $1,000 to $11,000 ($7,612.58 and $83,738.40 today). While they do not seem like terribly much today, the two raises in 1961–62 and 1963–64 individually represent, respectively, a 9.8 percent and 10 percent adjustment—quite a bump in any era. They should have been cause for celebration. But in 1962 Sánchez protested to President Joseph Smiley and Dean Clyde Colvert that the accumulation of so many years of salary discrimination made the prior year's raise of $900 inadequate. Sánchez mostly blamed ex-President Wilson and Dean Haskew. "What their prejudice was based upon," he wrote, "I can't say—maybe it was simply that I had no respect for either of them and told them so! And this I did on several occasions, under due provocation—and I would not take back a single action or word if I were offered the tower [of the University of Texas] as a personal paper-weight."[52]

Weeks after finding out he had received another large raise of $1,000, Sánchez protested being shortchanged again ($7,612.58 today). The originally recommended raise was $2,000, or 20 percent of his salary ($15,225.16 today). He objected again in the 1964–65 budget cycle, when he was supposed to receive the missing $1,000 from the 1963–64 cycle that was instead cut in half to a $500 raise for a total of $11,500 ($7,514.35, $3,757.18, and $86,415.08 today). Now Sánchez was hopping mad. Colvert urged that he communicate directly with Vice Chancellor Norman Hackerman, assuring the angry professor that the perception of him by administrators had changed for the better. Sánchez argued that Shivers's appointees on the board red-penciled his salary after "pressure was put on me to remain in Shivers' camp to organize the 'Mexican' leadership." He reported being "openly threatened 'with the Regents' if I did not cooperate (by John Van Cronkite). I pled respect for the Regents, and ignorance of organizational politics. Then my troubles began." His salary protests ceased after the 1964–65 cycle. In the 1965–66 cycle he received a $2,500 raise, over 20 percent of his prior salary, to $14,000 ($18,487.70 and $103,531.11 today). That amount increased by $500 to $14,500 in the 1966–67 school year, by $1,000 to $15,500 (6.8 percent) in the 1967–68 year, and by $3,300 to $18,800 (21 percent) for the 1971–72 year, which Sánchez did not live to complete ($3,594.83, $104,250.08, $6,974.40, $108,103.22, $18,980.70, and $108,132.49 today). If one were to compile just those instances where a specific dollar amount of raises recommended by his department or college was denied to him at one level or another (these were seldom disputed) in the 1940s, 1950s, and 1960s and add the amounts together, one would get a total of $4,300, or 22.8 percent of his final year's salary ($24,732.43 today). However, if one took each amount and multiplied it by the number of years until his final 1971–72 year at the university and then added the adjusted amounts, the result is $55,800, a steep price to pay for civil rights activism and liberal politics (using 1971 calculations; $320,946.44 today).[53]

In the 1960s Sánchez spoke out on academic freedom. In a well-publicized lecture at the university in April 1965, Sánchez complained of the lack of respect shown educators by noneducators sitting on boards of governance. Sánchez drew on his experience of Latin American higher education and of how the pervasive influence of politics harmed academic freedom. Yarborough wrote to Sánchez the next week to congratulate him for his courage in speaking out and to remark that he was "filling the role formerly filled by Don Pancho Dobie [the folklorist J. Frank Dobie] and Dr. Webb [the historian Walter Prescott Webb]." The *Texas Observer* published the address. In December 1965 Sánchez participated in a local television debate over academic freedom. In addition, in 1963 Sánchez was elected to the board of a proposed junior college in Travis County, but the bond to fund the institution did not pass. He opposed his college's initiative on mandating psychological screenings for doctoral candidates, wrote to the *Daily Texan* of his distress over tuition hikes, and corresponded with angry alumni over efforts by faculty, including himself, to make their opposition to the Vietnam War known through news outlets. His cantankerous reputation, however, was a double-edged sword. After one dispute Sánchez's colleague Robert Peck wrote, "If I may, George, let me comment on your final paragraph where you quite honestly express the fact that you are mad. It has been remarked by a great many people that you usually are." Peck closed with a cutting aside: "Next time, if you'll just call me on the phone, we probably could obviate the need for letters. I don't want to spoil your fun, though; so write if you must."[54]

Sánchez kept up his public speaking, averaging fifteen talks a year outside the university between 1960 and 1964. He spoke, seemingly, to anyone who asked him to, in junior highs and high schools, professional societies, and academic groups and in radio and television spots. A few were given at prestigious venues (figs. 11.6, 11.7). But by 1965 he gave only half the number of external addresses, none for several years after, and only three in 1970, the last year records were kept. Sánchez was disturbed that education scholars ignored his work, particularly a major UCLA–Ford Foundation project. He became somewhat hostile to change regarding his department and the College of Education. He regarded education professors as general humanists, opposed specialization, and rigidly regarded *his* kind of research—wide-ranging, interdisciplinary studies based on interviews, visits, and field reports, and intended for a general audience—as the best kind of research.[55]

PRIVATE HELL

Sánchez's good friend Lyle Saunders once coined the phrase "terrible tempered George" to describe him. It was a term of endearment following a blowup. Since being diagnosed with serious high blood pressure in the mid-1950s, Sánchez was under orders from doctors to take it easy. This was not just about rest but also about stepping away from the drama of work. He explained to a colleague why he did not attend brown bag lunches: "First: I'm under orders to

11.6. Sánchez about to give an address at the
University of Texas in the early 1960s.
Reproduction by permission of Cynthia Kennedy.

take a *siesta* at noon. Second: I do not eat lunch. Third: I work mostly in my study at home. Too far from U. Fourth: I am a-social! My years, I guess." This was a far cry from the workaholic who came to the University of Texas in 1940 brimming with self-confidence, enthusiasm, and vigor, proud of his young family, and holding the future in the palm of his hand. The image of a tempestuous crank who taught his courses and stayed away from his colleagues is this older Sánchez. For the people who worked with him by the later sixties, particularly his younger colleagues, he must have been someone to avoid.[56]

Though he was more financially comfortable than ever during this period, Sánchez never stopped working. He and Luisa often taught summer school at different locales as subsidized vacations, and they were always a hit. But these jobs were, above all, about the extra income. To an academic friend who had just purchased a house, Sánchez confided, "With Luisa and me, mortgages are a way of life. We would be lost and feel like we had lost one of the mainstays of life if we weren't mortgaged." In the fall of 1961 George and Luisa remortgaged

11.7. Sánchez speaking at Union City, California, to a group of educators in 1963.
He is in the middle, flanked by Union City school administrators. Reproduction
by permission of Benson Latin American Center.

their home for $11,000 from the Austin Savings and Loan Association with an-
other $2,000 loan from the Capital National Bank in Austin ($85,698.83 and
$15,581.61 today). At this time George Sánchez entered into a long-running dis-
pute with the Internal Revenue Service (IRS) over his taxes. It hinged on their
summer teaching at the University of Alaska in 1960. The IRS did not accept
their sizeable deductions as legitimate business expenses, placing them in arrears by $545.27 for 1960 ($4,306.89 today). Sánchez disputed his 1960 tax bill in
the summer of 1961, hiring a tax attorney after failed mediation with an IRS
official in Austin. In 1962, at a special appeal hearing at the Houston offices of
the IRS, he was able to eliminate $222.07 of the taxes the IRS claimed he owed
(using 1962 calculations; $1,712.92 today). While he accepted the adjustment, he
was unhappy about it and complained to Yarborough of the discriminatory
treatment he and other university professors received at the hands of the IRS.

The dustup resulted in a flurry of letters involving Senator Yarborough, IRS personnel, and Sánchez's tax attorney.[57]

George I. Sánchez was never the picture of great vigor. He was a small, slumped man, 5 feet 6 inches in height and weighing 130 pounds. His friends constantly worried about him. His struggle with TB continued to plague him. He felt a special connection to those who suffered from it. Furthermore, he suffered from kidney stones, and in the winter of 1961 battled pneumonia in his one good lung. In 1963 he experienced a burst blood vessel high in his nose, likely due to his blood pressure, resulting in complications that required hospitalization. The same malady struck him again in February 1967 as Sánchez was at a speaking engagement and required a doctor to monitor him in his hotel room between talks.[58]

In another instance Sánchez seriously injured himself. Even though he was suffering from a slipped disc and three broken ribs, he gave a talk at UCLA on October 8, 1964. Sánchez left the engagement immediately after his talk and was in pain. A few days later he was invited to the White House to attend a bill-signing ceremony for some amendments made to the National Defense of Education Act. He attended, and things turned scary: "That night, however, I did a Harry Truman: I slipped on the bathroom floor and, to prevent crashing my good ribs on the edge of the bathtub, I (I can't imagine how I did it) flipped myself over the edge of the tub, landing on my right shoulder, hip, and head—knocking myself out! Then, and this is ludicrous, I had a hell of a time getting out of the tub when I came to. My left arm couldn't pull me up, neither could my right (they were momentarily incapacitated) and my damned back wouldn't cooperate. It took sheer genius to get on my knees and flip myself out of the tub! Believe it or not, I lay on the floor and laughed! So would have anyone else, it was such a damned funny situation."[59]

Sánchez unsurprisingly had other slips and falls. He was prone to a loss of balance and mobility owing to the aftereffects of his thoracoplasty. Drinking to excess likely exacerbated the problem. Sánchez always enjoyed celebrating with friends and could polish off a variety of drinks at one sitting. He consumed large quantities of beer at his lake cottage on the weekends. His grandchildren remember that he drank constantly. His drinking became more prominent as his health problems increased and his research productivity slowed; by the mid- to late 1960s Sánchez was probably an alcoholic, and in fact he may have been a highly functional alcoholic for years. His grandchildren and a contemporary activist I interviewed believe he was an alcoholic. There is no smoking gun to prove this. Drinking makes only minor appearances in Sánchez's letters until the 1960s but then takes a heightened prominence. For example, when ordered by physicians to use oxygen bottles and avoid alcohol while in the highlands of Peru, Sánchez bragged to anyone about his ability to consume his normal amount despite doctor's orders. The episode indicates that his addiction to alcohol perhaps grew to the point that Sánchez felt compelled to share his problem with others, even if in a forced, inappropriate way. He began to brag about his drinking even to people he did not know very well. These later letters get stranger, less predictable; their tone is erratic and overexuberant. By the late 1960s Sánchez's drinking was getting out of hand.[60]

As the 1960s began, numerous opportunities opened for George I. Sánchez. A revival of his research agenda coincided with a dramatic rise in his political activity through PASSO. He was ambivalent about Lyndon Johnson, loyal to Ralph Yarborough, and disdainful of John Connally. Sánchez influenced the Great Society, especially the Bilingual Education Act, from behind the scenes. But by the mid- to late 1960s, just as he became something of an institution at the University of Texas, his national profile dipped. He was getting old and increasingly sick, he had little energy, and his drinking likely began to exert a heavier and more obvious toll on him. This period marked the beginning of the end.

CHICANISMO AND OLD AGE
1967–1972

I can sympathize whole-heartedly with your sense of frustration, but do not sell us short. There have been many *mexicanos* who have fought the good fight, and many are still doing it. . . . Don't expect an oldtimer like myself to hold your hand; I've fought, bled, and died in this game. Go out and fight your own fight. I started more than forty years ago, and am still at it. My head has been bloodied, my soul has been injured. Go out and do the same. What else? Thanks for your very nice letter. I am attaching a copy of my biography, where my writings are listed. Most of them are out of print. I sometimes think that I am out of print!

In the mid-1960s George I. Sánchez received a lengthy handwritten letter from a graduate student at the University of New Mexico. This young man lamented the community's poor organization and asked why Sánchez did not try to form a national group of leaders to get the attention of authorities. Conscientious, passionate young men and women like this student would soon call themselves Chicanos and Chicanas and initiate more confrontational activism to transform the Mexican American community. Sánchez responded with a hasty, frustrated letter represented in the epigraph above. Feeling out of print and with a dented soul, Sánchez by the late 1960s and early 1970s could diagnose the problems but could not satisfy young people with the means by which to combat them. He was one of them, but he was a stranger. Like many liberals who came of age before and during the Second World War, Sánchez found that the protest and counterculture movements of the 1960s gave him pause. He worked hard to embrace the new ethos of Chicanismo and in some respects succeeded. But in other ways he could not. During this period Sánchez's professional and activist profile declined as he spent more time at home with his family, enduring poor health. He died in the spring of 1972 at the age of sixty-five.[1]

More critical interpretations of the 1960s and the Chicano movement have abounded of late. The older triumphalism attendant to the birth of Chicano Studies during *el movimiento* in the late sixties and seventies and somewhat institutionalized in the teaching of Chicana/o history ever since has given way to more critical perspectives by historians who question, among many things, the movement's reliance on cultural nationalism. This new scholarship also explores interethnic coalitions and activist collaboration. Recent work by Ernesto Chávez, Laura Pulido, Lorena Oropeza, David Montejano, Maylei Blackwell, and Ramón Gutiérrez have led the way in this direction. George I. Sánchez offers a fascinating perspective of the early days of the movement from a veteran of Mexican American activism whose heart was willing but whose mind was hesitant over a full embrace of all that Chicanismo offered.[2]

CHICANISMO

Sánchez accrued a new academic role as an elder statesman to a younger generation anxious to develop Chicano studies as a field. It is impossible to untangle this academic movement from the activism practiced throughout the country. A part of this ferment was a series of school boycotts by high school students throughout the Southwest from 1967 to 1970. This excited Sánchez. As he remarked in an interview with a journalist, "These young people are not going to take any more of the nonsense that their parents have put up with." Sánchez was in vogue at Chicano studies conferences at the University of Texas in 1970 and at the University of California, Riverside in 1971. And his talks *sounded* Chicano as well. They were full of musings on his and his people's mixed racial background and laced with profanity and off-color jokes to demonstrate his willingness to dispense with formality. In the Los Angeles conference he pointedly referred to then–Texas Governor Preston Smith, who had remarked that Mexicans enjoyed living in slums, as a "son of a bitch!" In these talks he drew a direct line from his activism of the 1930s to that of the 1970s. He wrote about the etymology of Chicana/o slang, discussed the concepts of *mestizaje* and *la raza*, and outlined how his people defined themselves over time. In this light Sánchez appears to be fully steeped in Chicanismo, pushing boundaries in ways that must have felt incredibly liberating. One connection he had with *el movimiento* was the republication of his *Forgotten People* in 1967. Early scholars in the field had to contend with a dearth of published material for the new courses they were creating. And *Forgotten People* filled that void for some of the first Chicano studies classes in existence. It was re-reviewed positively and seen as a manifestation of the gathering movement. Sánchez was a resource to the first wave of Chicano scholarship.[3]

Sánchez was not ensconced in an ivory tower. He kept tabs on the Los Angeles school walkouts through internal documents from the Los Angeles City Board of Education. Someone fed him material from the separatist La Raza Unida political party. Sánchez greatly admired César Chávez's United Farm Workers (UFW) as well as Rodolfo (Corky) González, the poet and activist from Denver; in 1967 he criticized González, however, for supporting the New Mexico firebrand Reies Lopez Tijerina. Sánchez had known about Tijerina since 1963, when he asked the professor for permission to reprint a Spanish translation of *Forgotten People* through his New Mexico organization Alianza Federal de Mercedes, a group later embroiled in a violent effort to wrest land away from the federal government. After a phone conversation, Sánchez replied to Tijerina's request in writing as if he were getting his response on record for the FBI, claiming to have "no desire to be associated, or to have my works associated, with organizations of questionable reputation or association." He announced his willingness to defend his authorial rights if necessary.[4]

The nation's ethnic revival of the 1960s and 1970s eroded a basic underlying premise of twentieth-century liberalism: pluralistic politics in which ideology and national interest subsumed ethnicity. How would Texas liberals react to the rising ethnic consciousness? Senator Ralph Yarborough went left. Perhaps because he never had as solid a relationship with Mexican Americans as he desired owing to LBJ's presence, the senator embraced the Chicano movement as a manifestation of liberalism within the community. In 1967 he made speeches about how LULAC and AGIF had lost connection with the masses and recklessly praised Sánchez as one of the only Mexican American figures who never sold out. Congressman Henry B. Gonzalez, however, pivoted to the right during the late sixties, disturbed by ethnic separatism and protests against the Vietnam War. Gonzalez initially opposed Yarborough's bilingual education bill as smacking of reverse discrimination. Sánchez disagreed, and the two engaged in a testy debate. It is a measure of the respect Sánchez had for Congressman Gonzalez that he backed down, trying not to further inflame his friend's seething anger at how the world was changing. Few merited Sánchez's backing away from a position he felt was correct, but Gonzalez was one of them.[5]

Sánchez was proud to be involved in what activists called La Marcha, La Causa, or La Huelga of 1966. This was a three-month march of over four hundred miles from the Rio Grande Valley to the capitol in Austin by striking farmworkers (fig. 12.1). It began on Independence Day and culminated on Labor Day.

12.1. Sánchez (*left*), surrounded by exuberant Chicano supporters of the farmworkers'
march to Austin on Labor Day in 1966, often known as La Marcha. He wears his
United Farm Workers pin. A nearby participant is less eager to have his picture taken.
Reproduction by permission of Benson Latin American Center.

On the long trek north La Marcha picked up a number of supporters, including
AGIF's Hector P. Garcia, who, despite his more moderate politics, always supported better wages and health care for farmworkers. Governor Connally,
Attorney General Waggoner Carr, and Speaker of the House Ben Barnes, riding
together in a Cadillac, intercepted the marchers on the side of the road near
New Braunfels, a town just north of San Antonio, to inform them their protest
would have no effect in moving the state legislature to adopt the $1.25 hourly
minimum wage bill they supported. The striking workers endured harassment
from law enforcement officials in South Texas before making it to the state-
house steps for a Labor Day rally, where Sánchez enthusiastically joined them.[6]

Months later Sánchez created the last activist organization of his life, the
unfortunately named Joint Conference of Mexican Americans. It brought lib-

eral Chicanas/os from Texas organizations such as LULAC, AGIF, and PASSO to agitate as a separate pressure group over common policy goals. They supported a statewide voter registration system, a $1.25 per hour minimum wage, increased government services for farmworkers, studying the effects of temporary Mexican workers on the border, and opposing college tuition hikes, a return to the bracero program, and sales tax increases. Sánchez kicked off the Joint Conference in Austin on January 7, 1967. At the next meeting in Laredo that May the participants proposed the abolition of the Texas Rangers and expressed support for organized labor. Sánchez and the student Lupe Zamarripa sent bellicose exhortations for members to heighten their activism. The group tapered off in 1968 as Sánchez had to step aside for health reasons.[7]

One of the final university conflicts George I. Sánchez was embroiled in was the student-inspired establishment of a Center for Mexican American Studies (CMAS), directed by the literature and anthropology professor Américo Paredes. Sánchez was a fan of Paredes and felt his book, the classic *"With His Pistol in His Hand": A Border Ballad and Its Hero* (1958), was a breathtaking work of scholarly creativity, passion, and bravery. Modern scholars regard Paredes's work as a blend of anticolonial and modernist literary themes. Paredes charts an older way of Tejano life in transition at the turn of the century; through *corridos*, or traditional Mexican folk songs, he produces a counternarrative to the traditional themes of Anglo dominance and Chicano defectiveness. When the CMAS situation prompted Paredes to explore leaving the university, Sánchez offered assistance. This focused on the desire of the University of Texas to combine CMAS with a center for African American studies in one broad ethnic studies program. Despite vehement student protests from both groups the university did just that in 1969 under the direction of the African American scholar Henry A. Bullock. Sánchez agreed with student efforts at autonomy and resigned in protest from the faculty committee in the fall of 1970 and again just before his death in 1972. Chicano protesters had to make clear that their demands for a separate Mexican American Studies Center did not imply hostility to African Americans or to Bullock, a Bancroft Prize–winning professor of history who knew little about Mexican Americans. How does one express racial/ethnic pride or solidarity or both without crossing into chauvinism? This was (and is) a challenge to all minority activists.[8]

Bullock, however, took the criticism as a personal affront, regarding it as racist in nature. In a lengthy memo of 1970 announcing his resignation, Paredes vehemently denied Bullock's charges: "Color has never been that important to us. What matters most to us is our bilingual, bicultural heritage." To the likely bewildered administrators, Sánchez sought to contextualize the situation. He took pains not to directly address Bullock's allegations. Sánchez's writing here, because he discusses group differences, veers into uncomfortable territory: "Mexican Americans in Texas are going to resent bitterly being classed along-side Negroes. This is not a matter of race prejudice, notably absent among Mexican Americans, but one of association with a people, the blacks, to whom the 'Anglos' have traditionally assigned a position of inferiority. I think it will be resented, also, by the Negro because he does not want to borrow the prejudices directed against 'Mexicans' in Texas tradition." The focus for Sánchez was on *racism*, not *race*. He later quipped that ethnic studies should "set up a program for the study of gringos, a truly difficult bad lot!"[9]

NOT CHICANO ENOUGH

Sánchez's eager embrace of Chicanismo would never go far enough. To some young radicals, Sánchez's insistence on working within the system, his discomfort with cultural nationalism, and his overly complex formulations of racial identity marked him as too moderate, too academic, too inhibited. Sánchez was in a position similar to that of other older, left-leaning, American intellectuals. The recent biography of the historian Richard Hofstadter paints an analogous picture of an increasingly pessimistic professor who, by the end of his life, lamented what he felt was the younger generation's lack of constructive protest. Like Hofstadter, Sánchez was hurt by the criticism of students. By the late sixties and early seventies young Chicanos were emboldened enough to badger Chicana/o faculty in campus job talks for their insufficient Chicanismo or for being *vendidos* (sellouts), a crossing of professional boundaries that the respect-driven Sánchez could never countenance.[10]

Such criticism from young Chicano activists had to do with the mustier content of Sánchez's ideas. For example, race remained tricky for him. By the end of the 1960s Sánchez claimed a more modern-sounding identity: "I am of Spanish-Mexican descent (that means that I am part Indian, in addition to the complexity of genes that came from Europe, the Middle East, and North Africa). I am a *chicano* (please note the orthography)." But as the Chicano movement stressed racial separateness—a sense of being brown and not white—Sánchez's delicate dance around race seemed ever more old-fashioned. Even interracial activism, something he practiced his entire career, brought out distinctions on Sánchez's part owing to his discomfort with assertions of Brown Power and Black Power. He felt that coalitions were about identifying shared goals and contingency, not creating new or different peoples. Sánchez awkwardly utilized the saying "Una mano lava la otra, y las dos la cara" (one hand washes the other and both wash the face) to encapsulate his version of interracial activism.[11]

Sánchez's vision of history was revisionist. He refused to engage in sentimental notions, believing that "we, Mexican Americans, were betrayed. Screwed, that is," by the United States, an oppression its history celebrated. One idea that never failed to animate Sánchez was his belief that social scientists assumed all manner of defectiveness regarding Mexican Americans. To Sánchez such interpretive constructions conflated the brutal conditions of poverty with culture. As something of an antidote, he often recommended the impish satire of Oscar Lewis's *Children of Sánchez* called *Los Hijos de Jones* by the Mexican economist Victor Urquidi. Sánchez excoriated the mushrooming investigation of machismo by social scientists as an academic snipe hunt. He felt that the word could just as easily be assigned to women, gays and lesbians, a family, a town, or a specific class of people as to male, heterosexual prowess. He insisted that *machismo* "refers to 'guts,' not 'nuts'!"[12]

The bulk of Sánchez's dissent from the deficiency models of social scientists, however, was directed at education scholars. From 1967 to 1970 Sánchez wrote numerous protests to Commissioner Edgar of the TEA, to state and national legislators, to newspapers, to bureaucrats, and to civil rights allies about how he felt the state perpetuated the segregation of Mexican American and Mexican immigrant children through its migrant program. By the late 1960s Sánchez was more familiar with the new educational jargon and began referring to it explicitly: "I resent the term 'culturally deprived.'" He went on, "If there is any deprivation it is that imposed by the dominant group and retardation is a function of inferior education." To Sánchez there was no blaming the victim for what he felt was the school's responsibility. And he became alarmed at the zombie-like resurgence of those IQ testing and heritability arguments he had regarded as long since dead and buried.[13]

Sánchez never really altered his immigration restrictionism. Hewing to the specific issues of temporary work visas, wages, and migrant segregation did represent, however, a softening of his hard-line restrictionism of the fifties. Why? In general the Mexican American community abandoned restrictionism for the Johnson era's immigration liberalization. Even long-running holdouts such as César Chávez and the UFW, who were the most damaged by the importation of Mexican scab labor during disputes, changed their tune by the mid-1970s. Though some Mexican Americans stuck with restrictionism, the emerging Chicano position was one of fewer restrictions and a freer border economy. The world was slipping farther away from Sánchez on this issue. His continued harping on it, even if somewhat moderated, must have made him seem ancient to the young.[14]

In politics Sánchez remained steadfastly loyal to his friend Yarborough. And as early as 1967 he sensed danger: "I have a dirty, suspicious Mexican mind. From way out in my political left field I sense a concerted move to scrag you in 1970." Seeking his third term in 1970, Yarborough faced a Democratic primary challenge from the conservative, former congressman Lloyd Bentsen of South Texas. Sánchez offered to help, despite his infirmities. Yarborough lost his reelection bid, however, ending his career. The split between Congressman Gonzalez and Sánchez grew wider. And Sánchez continued flirting with the increasingly competitive Texas Republican Party. Though he engaged the congressman and future president George H. W. Bush and Senator John Tower in 1968 on policy, this was still a means of defeating conservative, establishment Democrats. Sánchez continued to despise Richard Nixon. As he explained in 1970 in a letter to Hector Garcia, "I see some strange people around: Bentsen, Smith, etc. I may try Bush and Eggers. Smelly—but we can beat them next go-around." There would not be another election for George I. Sánchez.[15]

Sánchez continued his work in civil rights. In the spring of 1968, at about the time he stepped away from directing the Joint Conference, he vehemently protested an incident in Austin in which local police shot and killed a Mexican American teenager. Calling it a cold-blooded murder, he was appalled at the city's lackluster response. On the whole, however, Sánchez's local profile was as something of a mediator between the growing Mexican American community and the city. With regard to the Austin public schools, Sánchez called attention to their lack of compliance with the bilingual education act and warned of specific schools that put the district in danger of bringing on a lawsuit. Superintendent Irby Carruth, a friend, at one point brought him in to mediate a row between Spanish-speaking and English-speaking cafeteria workers over the use of Spanish in the kitchens.[16]

Sánchez engaged in a spirited correspondence with the U.S. Civil Rights Commission and the Justice Department, mostly over his continued complaints about the TEA's migrant education program. He also testified to the U.S. Civil Rights Commission in December 1968 and consulted on civil rights with other sectors of the federal government into the last year of his life. Sánchez had trouble accepting the fact that the most important civil rights achievement of his career, the *Hernández* case of 1954, was so clearly obsolete. On the other hand, he was very up to date on the Supreme Court's decision in the *Hobsen v. Hansen* case of 1967, which limited schools' ability to justify classification policies over performance on IQ tests. And he informally consulted with civil rights attorneys and activists throughout the country.[17]

Sánchez was directly involved with the *Chapa v. Odem* case of 1967, which arose out of a small town near Corpus Christi. His civil rights collaborator from the 1950s, James DeAnda, tried the case. The historian Steven Wilson remarks that, though a decade removed from *Hernández v. Driscoll*, DeAnda curiously used traditional tactics, including testimony and advice from George Sánchez and the *class apart* strategy. As in *Hernández v. Driscoll*, a federal judge ordered the town of Odem to cease its tracking system. So DeAnda won, again. And once again he faced the same obfuscation after the schools tinkered with their classification system just enough to pass judicial muster. Had DeAnda sought recourse from *Brown's* completely different legal basis instead of the narrower reading of due process entailed in the class apart strategy, claims Wilson, the result might have been different. A few years later DeAnda did just that, without Sánchez, in a much bigger case against the Corpus Christi public schools, the landmark *Cisneros v. Corpus Christi ISD* case of 1970. Sánchez's prominent role in *Chapa* represented the end of an older legal strategy and the beginning of a newer one for Mexican Americans.[18]

Chicana/o legal activists regarded Sánchez with awe as a civil rights pioneer. George Sánchez was involved in the brainstorming that resulted in the Mexican American Legal Defense and Educational Fund (MALDEF) in 1968 with a $2,200,000 start-up grant from the Ford Foundation ($14,726,408.05 today). The attorney Pete Tijerina was in contact with NAACP's Legal Defense Fund in 1967, which linked Mexican Americans to the Ford Foundation and contributed key staff. In 1966 Sánchez had written to others about the need for a new, well-funded civil rights organization. Tijerina asked Sánchez in early 1967 about developing MALDEF with the help of the Legal Defense Fund's organizational know-how and Ford funds. Sánchez responded that while he was enthusiastic about a new civil rights group, he was against subsuming their efforts as an extension of the African American civil rights movement. He wrote, "I have always felt that though we should make common cause with the Negroes from time to time, we should not blend their issues with ours. Don't misunderstand, I was a pioneer among the champions for Negro rights—and I am still on their side. However, while the effects of discrimination against Negro and 'Mexican' are essentially the same, the causes, the history, and the remedies differ broadly." Likely reflecting on his own painful efforts to educate the ACLU on who Mexican Americans were, Sánchez made the case to Tijerina that "riding the coat tails of the NAACP" was far less preferable than gaining autonomy.

Sánchez strategized with Tijerina and other MALDEF attorneys about specific cases in his final years.[19]

PROFESSIONAL EBBING

Infirmity rapidly diminished Sánchez as a scholar during his final years. Yet this narrowing of professional activity was also a choice. He wrote one labor ally that he was tempted to retire and run for political office, but he never tested this fanciful inclination. In addition to writing some book reviews, Sánchez had several higher-profile service commitments. The most interesting professional assignment he undertook was as a member of an investigation team formed by the American Association of University Professors (AAUP) and dispatched to San Francisco State University in 1969. Extreme acrimony among students, faculty, and the administration rocked the campus. Sánchez felt that the university administration and the governor of California, Ronald Reagan, were mostly to blame. He and the rest of the team reluctantly recommended that AAUP blacklist the school. When it came to the administration at the University of Texas, Sánchez continued to protest but with less frequency than before. He was still concerned with free speech. Sánchez supported early efforts by the university in what might today be called affirmative action; he opposed strict admissions qualifications determined by standardized testing as discriminatory to minority students, who often came from schools with less overall opportunity. In the fall of 1971, his last season as a fan of the university football team, which had won back-to-back national champion rankings, Sánchez once again received seats in the end zone that he protested publicly.[20]

Sánchez inhabited a dysfunctional department in his final years. In late 1969 his Department of History and Philosophy of Education agreed to change its name to the Department of Cultural Foundations of Education, in line with the disciplinary trends of the time. Sánchez had become a malcontent in an unhealthy work climate. An external evaluation of his department conducted in 1970 unanimously concluded that "the most serious problem confronting the Department is the deep-seated divisions within the staff of the Department" and that these divisions were "so enervating and crippling that normal processes of compromise and orderly change and improvement appear to have broken down." Another striking aspect of this report was the degree to which the evaluators felt senior faculty bullied junior faculty. Though he claimed to be the junior faculty's biggest supporter, Sánchez in fact chastised junior members directly and indirectly for disagreeing with him. He was also willing to make negative remarks about junior colleagues in formal, professional channels well after they had left for greener pastures. William Drake usually sided with Sánchez in departmental conflicts in the late sixties and early seventies. Sánchez was department chair for much of the 1950s and Drake for much of the 1960s. They were frequently in opposition to the next chair, John Rich, as well as their colleagues Arthur Moehlman and John Laska and especially Dean of Graduate Studies W. Gordon Whaley.[21]

Sánchez still taught a heavy load. Though the classroom was becoming increasingly difficult for him to manage owing to his physical limitations, he took a great deal of pride in his ability to handle the biggest teaching responsibilities in a department whose faculty carried onerous teaching loads. He originally hoped to teach his popular undergraduate courses full-time until 1976, when he turned seventy. However, these plans proved difficult to realize as his health declined. Sánchez remarked to his dean in 1969 that shortages in teaching assistants caused him to minimize his enrollments: "I do not propose to carry the over-load that I have carried before." He went on, "Our Ed. H. student load per full Professor is and always has been the highest in the College. I am tired of 'carrying' other faculty members."[22]

Sánchez endured quite a bit of interference from Dean Whaley. James H. Boren, a longtime graduate student of Sánchez's who had been writing his dissertation since 1953 while he worked in academia, for Senator Yarborough, and for the USAID mission in Peru, experienced trouble (understandably, it should be noted) in obtaining Whaley's signature for his completed work in 1969. Boren had a dogged champion in Sánchez, who protested that Whaley's actions were "tantamount to a vote of no confidence" in his graduate student direction and that he would "not be second-guessed in the field of my professional competence by anyone" or tolerate being "made to appear incompetent." He protested when Whaley attempted to torpedo a dissertation committee directed by William Drake because the topic examined the life of the former university president Homer P. Rainey, still regarded with hostility in some university quarters. Sánchez was generous with his time when it came to his graduate students, including those of other professors and former students.[23]

In fact, Sánchez had the reputation of being somewhat easygoing with graduate students, but by the late 1960s they were getting under his skin. Like many faculty, he disliked the confrontational tone of graduate students' demands to be afforded an increased voice in departmental affairs. Despite his desire to be seen as young at heart, Sánchez brooked no dispute as to who was really in charge. As the years went on he became rigid about professional boundaries. In 1969 he addressed one group of students that had publicly protested a recent departmental hiring decision. "I am very disappointed," he said. "Your naiveté is shocking. Your implied lack of trust is distressing. Your procedure is inexcusable and childish. Yours are not the acts of mature scholars but of spoiled children. I accept my part of the responsibility for your acting like spoiled children. I'll beat my breast and say 'mea culpa' many times. But I will also say, 'don't get delusions of grandeur.'" He concluded, "If you don't like it here, go elsewhere. We are staying and we will continue to be in charge. I will not argue the points I have made, except with my peers. I will be glad to clarify and expand on them to you. I am ready to hear your ideas."[24]

His anger boiled over again in 1971. The graduate students were distressed at a decrease in summer funds because of higher than usual faculty participation in summer school. They were also unhappy at carrying an ill professor's coursework that term (not Sánchez). This complaint drew an angry response from the department chair, John Rich, and with whom Sánchez agreed: "Their competence as responsible scholars is not yet established. And they are impertinent when they presume to judge my decisions. If they don't like it here, they can go elsewhere. They are not indispensable to my enrollments or to my professional stature, whatever it may be. In brief, they can go to hell." The number of people who irritated Sánchez grew constantly in his final years as his body fell apart and just making it through the day was an ordeal.[25]

PRIVATE LIFE IN THE FINAL YEARS

The last few years of Sánchez's life were financially secure. George and Luisa earned a very comfortable joint income of over $20,000 during this period (1967 calculations; $139,488.02 today). Tax records indicate that the Sánchezes gave small amounts to the AGIF and LULAC, a local Primitive Baptist church, the United Farm Workers' Organizing Committee, the American Cancer Society, the March of Dimes, the United Fund, Planned Parenthood, local schools and parent-teacher groups, and local charities whose causes pertained to tuberculosis, cerebral palsy, and muscular dystrophy. They assumed payments on a note to an Austin bank for Connie's husband, Nelson Sprague, and sent George Eugene money. Sánchez was proud of his children. Connie became a librarian at the Texas State Library, the research center next door to the capitol and several blocks away from his office. He regarded George Eugene as an important artist. Whatever angst George might have once had in his relationship with his children, he was an involved, supportive, and devoted grandparent to their children.[26]

Sánchez was not one who made friends easily, but he kept those he had close to him to the end. He remained particularly close to Brice Sewell. Near the end of his life George joked that his successful cataract surgery had improved his vision enough that he could notice the profusion of miniskirts on campus, while Sewall groused about his inability to intellectually connect with the hippies of Santa Fe. Sánchez also kept in close touch with Arthur Campa. Much of their contact was now by telephone, but the letters between the two show glimpses of a warm friendship dating back decades. Sánchez protected the memory of departed friends with alacrity. To two authors working on a biography of the late Gus Garcia that he distrusted, he falsely claimed not only that the legendary attorney was not an alcoholic but also that he had never personally seen Garcia drunk. While Sánchez was willing to confide to his near friends and allies about Garcia's condition, to strangers he kept mum out of a misplaced care for his friend's memory.[27]

Many approaching their later years embrace religion. George Sánchez did not. Though he claimed to be a deeply spiritual person, he regarded organized religion as hypocritical. He was most connected to church officials and missions that had an activist dimension. He remained somewhat connected to Catholicism through liberal church activists and especially through Luisa, who, according to family tradition, remained stubbornly Catholic. And he lauded the role of Protestant missions as progressive forces within the Mexican American community. But personally, Sánchez labeled himself an agnostic, agnosticism being, he claimed, just as much of a religion as any other. In his final letter to the editor at the *Texas Observer* over his opposition to the tax-exempt status of churches, he blasphemously related, "If I put a bed of thorns in my study, does that make my home a tax-exempt church? Or, maybe I could use a picture of Mephistopholes [*sic*]. I could, (as I do) hold services (cocktail parties) there, with due reverence from my parishioners (guests). I could, coyly, suggest that my devotees help pay off that nagging mortgage, and give generously to support me in the style to which I have become accustomed." He ended with the sarcastic coup de grâce, "Some of my best friends are Christians."[28]

Virgie Sánchez lived in Albuquerque and never remarried, still considering George her rightful husband. That she initiated the divorce proceedings made no difference to her. As we have seen, in the mid-1950s she had taken legal action against her ex-husband over his nonpayment of alimony. Like a landmine long after the war, lying in wait, this situation blew up on Sánchez in the late 1960s, causing the last professional disaster of his career. By 1966 his violation of the court's order to pay alimony must have reached a new level of danger since he cryptically remarked to his friend Tom Wiley at the University of New Mexico that legal difficulties made visiting in New Mexico impossible. This was the first time he ever mentioned such a thing to his New Mexico friends. In February 1967, Tom Popejoy, the president of the University of New

Mexico, wrote to Sánchez that he had been selected by the faculty to receive an honorary doctor of laws degree at the university's upcoming spring commencement. Sánchez enthusiastically accepted, ordered his regalia, and made travel arrangements. Then the bottom fell out.[29]

Behind the scenes Sánchez must have tried to convince Virgie to drop the complaint and perhaps entice her to do so by offering to settle what was by then a large bill. How much did an honorary doctorate from his alma mater matter to Sánchez? Quite a bit, one suspects, but not as much as jail time for fifteen years of back alimony. On May 4 Sánchez wrote to Popejoy, "There is a legal judgement against me in New Mexico that I cannot, in all conscience honor. I've tried every way to get this matter settled and, up until yesterday, felt that it was settled. Upon conferring with my lawyer here I learn that I would be putting myself in jeopardy if I placed myself within the jurisdiction of the District Court of Albuquerque, and he advises me not to do so. This leaves me no choice but, with deep regret, to advise you that I will not be present." He did not realize Popejoy had a policy of not awarding honorary degrees in absentia. Sánchez's friends in New Mexico were hurt and puzzled at his nonappearance. To one he wrote, "When Drurie [John Durrie, Popejoy's assistant] wrote me that degress [sic] are not granted in absentia I almost vomited." To Sewell he wrote the only truly ugly thing about his ex-wife to be found in his writings: "However, it seems that, though I was cleared at first, it would be unwise for me to expose my frail body to the rigorous climate of God's country. So, for 'reasons of health,' I'll not be there (confidential). A big disappointment, but bitches will be bitches."[30]

He explained the situation to his disappointed New Mexico friends over the next few years. Popejoy left the presidency in 1968, and Frank Angel, then a dean of education at the University of New Mexico and later president of New Mexico Highlands University, became Sánchez's champion. Angel prodded Durrie, who sent the degree along with his compliments in 1970. Apparently it had been ordered and was sitting in a closet for three years. Sánchez was ecstatic and related to Durrie how he "fought-bled-and-died" to support the University of New Mexico in the 1930s. He also mentioned his own educational odyssey, writing, "I struggled through seven and one-half years as a part-time student to get a degree there." He shared a little more with Durrie about his legal problem: "I have not challenged the alimony judgment in deference to the feelings of my children and grandchildren. I could overturn it easily. I prefer just not to honor it."[31]

The belated honorary doctor of laws degree in 1970 was a spot of good news in an otherwise dismal time for Sánchez. His health went from bad to worse.

Already by the mid-1960s he was consulting a team of doctors for his lifelong problems associated with tuberculosis, high blood pressure, a bad back, and creaky ankles and hips owing to his balance and mobility issues. He also developed serious eye problems. Sometime in the spring of 1969 cataracts impaired his vision so much that he lost the ability to read. By summer he was completely blind and needed the assistance of a graduate student to get through his summer class. He was scheduled for cataract surgery for one eye later that summer and the other eye that fall. His inability to see kept him from reading and writing and should have kept him from teaching, though he continued to work. He did not recover until well into 1970. And when he did he made it a habit of not parking in unfamiliar places or driving at night, indicating that perhaps his night vision and depth perception remained limited. But something else was not quite right with Sánchez. He seemed to have little energy. Late in 1971 Sánchez complained to a prospective consulting client, "Lately I've been sort of 'run down,' and a schedule such as you propose seems exhausting at the moment." And he started acting as though he might not have much time left. In the fall of 1970 he wrote his chairman that it would be wise to hire his replacement immediately. He volunteered to mentor this replacement, a major concession for the increasingly reclusive Sánchez. He even offered to give away several hundred copies of his *Arithmetic in Maya* to the *Texas Observer* for a fund-raising book sale.[32]

Was his drinking beginning to get out of control, or reaching the point at which it was physically hurting him? At some level this explanation is likely. As his grandchildren recall, Sánchez drank large quantities of beer on the weekends at the cottage, and his letters indicate he also had a fondness for stronger spirits, a fact that an activist colleague confirmed. By 1968 Sánchez was forced by his doctors to cancel a conference paper to the American Ethnological Society owing to exhaustion. He indicated in this letter that the doctors not only told him to cease all activity, but also asked that he limit himself to "beer only" until he could get a complete physical sometime the next month. Sánchez increasingly felt the need to discuss his drinking habits with people he had just met. To a representative of the John Hay Whitney Foundation with whom he evidently struck up a conversation after one meeting, Sánchez noted that on his flight back, "I drank only half of my allotted embalming fluid (saved a bottle as a peace offering for Luisa, my Board of Control)." Sánchez's notes to a group of teachers and administrators in the spring of 1971 indicate his compulsion to utilize a strained analogy calling attention to his fondness for straight bourbon and other cocktails. The consumption of alcohol was appearing more regularly in his talks and letters as he became sicker.[33]

By the spring of 1972 George I. Sánchez was dying. He was losing weight and
energy. His liver was failing. The situation was serious enough that it necessitated at least one lengthy stay in the hospital (fig. 12.2). Professionally he had
already cut back on everything beyond his courses. One letter of protest, likely
written shortly before the final hospital stay, was vintage Sánchez. He complained that the administration was giving CMAS and Paredes the runaround.
He wrote, "I will not serve on any committee whose sole purpose is 'window-
dressing'—and certainly not as a front for blatant neglect and discrimination."
He went on, "This double, hypocritical talk that Dr. Paredes misunderstood
the Administration's position is a lot of male bovine manure. Both he and I
understand the English language very well (though it is, indeed, a 'barbarous
tongue')." Paredes deeply appreciated Sánchez's protest and told him so at his
home shortly before the hospitalization. This was his last protest.[34]

While Sánchez was very ill and either at St. David's Hospital in Austin or at
home waiting to die, only a few political allies and colleagues seemed aware.
MALDEF's new general counsel, Mario Obledo of San Francisco, wrote to

12.2. Sánchez in old age, in a photograph
likely from the very late 1960s or early
1970s. Reproduction by permission of
Cynthia Kennedy.

Sánchez at his hospital room in what reads like a final tribute. In two of his final letters, brief ones, Sánchez indicated to a representative of the Kennedy School of Communications at Harvard and to a very young Gonzalo Barrientos, later a longtime state legislator from Austin, that he was discharged from the hospital, was going home, and hoped to be back at work soon. His grandchildren remember no such optimism. Was it just Sánchez's public face? or did he perhaps believe it? Whatever the case, he was immediately set up in his bed at home and never got out of it. Sánchez continued to lose weight and energy. His legs swelled, and he appeared increasingly jaundiced. His grandchildren were very upset, as they were still young and their beloved Tata's death was the first they experienced. He was never alone. Luisa cared for him throughout his final days, and one day near the end when he was ready to die, Connie's children came in one by one to say goodbye to the family patriarch. George I. Sánchez passed away on April 5, 1972, a Wednesday night. Hepatic coma and portal cirrhosis were the official causes of death. He was sixty-five years old.[35]

Death comes to us all. When it does it usually ravages the body—life's final ordeal. Death does not respect what we have done or what we could have done. That is for the living. Some believe, even if unconsciously, that how a life ends represents the ultimate meaning of that life. In the Christian tradition there is a tendency to look for judgment in someone's final days as the price of that persons' sin. Sánchez's colleagues were not immune to this. His department chair, John Martin Rich, in a pedestrian, dry memo, clumsily mentioned liver failure as the cause of death in the first sentence. Did this indiscretion on Rich's part reflect past disagreements? Or was it perhaps simply thoughtlessness? Other colleagues soon memorialized him in words that painted a fuller, appreciative portrait. They concluded that in assessing Sánchez's life, "one comes to a general conclusion, that here was a truly great man, great in his sensitivity toward the needs of the underprivileged mass of humanity; great in the quality of his sacrificial service to his fellow man; and great in his scholarship and ability to interpret and evaluate our common human needs. Ralph Waldo Emerson once said that a scholar is a man of action. George I. Sánchez was such a man." However his life ended, these words of praise more adequately encapsulate its meaning. The alcoholism that killed him was not even remotely the sum of his life. Instead, the search for the meaning of his life would occupy the minds of scholars for the next forty years.[36]

George I. Sánchez, up until the end, tried to connect with the Chicano movement and its young activists. He also continued advocating older ideas. And though his career ebbed and a myriad of health problems made life difficult in the end, he received some belated recognition for his life's work and basked in the adoration of his loved ones. He fought injustice constantly, regardless of the personal price to be paid, and never lost sight of the struggle to integrate Mexican Americans to their rightful, proud place in the nation. His example lives on in the lives of countless Americans of true civic virtue who fight some good fight every day.

EPILOGUE

What does the study of George I. Sánchez's life say about Chicana/o history? about the broader sweep of U.S. history? What does it have to offer us in our lives here and now? These questions were first posed in the immediate aftermath of his death by his loved ones, students, and colleagues. People he had never met found ways to remember him and assign meaning to his life. They continue to do so. Scholars, in particular, remain fascinated by Sánchez.

Several obituaries were the first to analyze Sánchez's life. Writing to Carey McWilliams of *The Nation*, Sánchez's old friend and colleague William Drake listed Sánchez's accomplishments and discussed who he was as a person: "Wanted—more men like George I. Sánchez, but where shall we find this quality of mind and of humanity in our war-torn ravished world?" Drawing heavily from Drake's letter, McWilliams's obituary on June 5, 1972, in *The Nation* was laudatory. He remarked that the kind of monument Washington, D.C., most needed was a "People's Pantheon" for virtuous citizens who persistently and without fanfare made their world a better place and those with whom they came into contact better people. He felt Sánchez would be a perfect candidate to be enshrined in such a place. The *Journal of Mexican American Studies* quickly published an editorial on Sánchez's passing, providing a positive academic outlook on his career as an "outstanding pioneer" and perhaps even "'the father' of Chicano studies." Congressman Jake Pickle of Austin inserted brief remarks and a news account of Sánchez's life in the *Congressional Record*. The *Daily Texan* drew heavily from CMAS personnel in their story on his life, and the *Texas Observer* published a poem titled "Dr. George I. Sánchez, Don Quixote of the Texas Range" in his honor.[1]

Other efforts at memorializing Sánchez took root. Elementary schools in Austin and Houston were named after him in 1977 and 1985, respectively. The

Austin school was the old Palm Elementary, a mostly segregated Mexican American school in which he was involved over segregation. In 1978 a work section at the U.S. Office of Education was named after him. But the most important memorial of the decade was the publication of *Humanidad: Essays in Honor of George I. Sánchez*, edited by Américo Paredes. Paredes's essay communicates the personal knowledge of a friend. It is a warm, engaging, and enduring projection of Sánchez's memory. This memorial volume eventually was published through the Chicano Studies Center Publications of UCLA in 1977. Luisa Sánchez was involved in advising Paredes as to the volume's contributors and other aspects of the publication.[2]

The University of Texas spent the next two decades remembering Sánchez. The library put together a tribute to Sánchez and Carlos Castañeda in 1975. In 1983 the university began a fund-raising effort to create an endowed professorship in Sánchez's honor. Led by the historian Ricardo Romo, later the president of the University of Texas at San Antonio, this chair rewarded outstanding faculty in either the College of Liberal Arts or the College of Education. In the 1980s the University of Texas sponsored student scholarships in honor of Sánchez. But the biggest commitment to Sánchez's institutional memory occurred in 1995, when it named the new College of Education building after him. An article at the time indelicately quoted a school official to the effect that the university's motivation was anxiousness to affix a Hispanic surname to some building, though the testimonials at the dedication ceremony were warm and enthusiastic. It is a shame that Sánchez did not live longer. If he had, he would have been lionized during his lifetime. Already by the 1980s his memory manifested as a potent ingredient in how the University of Texas defined itself. After years of fighting marginalization and harassment from university regents and administrators, and likely countless microaggressions, lost to time, from insensitive or dismissive colleagues, Sánchez became at least as much of an institutionalized fixture of the University of Texas as any professor of his era.[3]

As indicated at the beginning of this book, too often scholars have studied Sánchez from the viewpoint of one interest or another, one discipline or another, and one or another set of narrow questions. Unfortunately, such endeavors overlook the fascinating whole. This book, in examining all aspects of Sánchez's record as an intellectual and an activist, takes a different approach. A decade of research and writing on George I. Sánchez has taught me that his was a singularly American life. In the heroic tradition of American biography, George I. Sánchez's life exemplifies hard work, perseverance, and success; however, it also shares the more pessimistic, critical aspects of modern biography. Sánchez's life communicates how Mexican Americans of his era faced direct discrimination and failed institutions and fought a depressing battle for the most basic recognition. This tension between what was and what should be drove Sánchez throughout his life. It drove him past the dim horizons of his upbringing in poverty, beyond the restraints of societal prejudice, out of the lives of loved ones and colleagues who could not support his sacrifice, and past the very endurance of his body. Sánchez fought for justice for his people, for their integration into American life. He did so as if he had nothing to lose, though he often did. This civic and intellectual struggle to integrate the Mexican American defines George I. Sánchez's life.

This biography also addresses major questions and issues in the rapidly developing field of Chicana/o history. The first chapter demonstrates the universe of limited social and educational possibilities for Mexican American youth. The second and third chapters contribute to the ignored legacy of the New Deal in the Mexican American mind as well as opening a window into the fascinating, long-obscured role of internationalism among early Mexican American Generation leaders. The fourth and fifth chapters on the wartime experience analyze the role of Good Neighborism on Mexican Americans' domestic home front as well as the popular topic of wartime civil rights activism; Sánchez's war of ideas and his war of activism were two sides of an organic whole. The sixth chapter more self-consciously addresses Sánchez as a unique, one-of-a-kind early Chicano academic and what that experience was like in a Jim Crow state and university. The seventh chapter treats the well-worn topic of liberalism and the Mexican American Generation. Likewise, the eighth chapter deals with the subject of immigration restrictionism and, like the politics chapter, finds that Sánchez, more than most of his activist peers, was surprisingly committed to it. The ninth chapter offers a unique take on the much-studied topic of education by focusing on what Sánchez meant by integration, not just his commitment to desegregation. The tenth chapter definitively contextualizes the recent debate on whiteness and comparative civil rights. The eleventh and twelfth chapters on the 1960s and early 1970s—from Camelot to the Great Society to the Chicano movement—shed a different kind of light on the crucial decade filtered through Sánchez's age, experience, passion, and hesitancy.

But this biography is more than just an introductory primer on several important topics in Chicana/o history. It is also the story of an iconoclastic American life. George I. Sánchez, born in 1906 the middle son of a poor mining family, became, by the 1930s, one of the only Mexican Americans in the country to hold a doctoral degree, attaining the status of a leading intellectual of his community while in his late twenties. Fortunate to be supported by wealthy foundations and powerful Anglo patrons in New Mexico and beyond, he had a burning zeal to reclaim his ancient New Mexico family's tarnished honor. This belief in reclaiming a lost status occupied Sánchez throughout the thirties as he transitioned from an Albuquerque public school teacher and administrator, to graduate school in Texas and California, and then to the New Mexico State Department of Education as a crusading bureaucrat in the middle of the Great Depression. Even as Sánchez lost his state job, he would broaden his horizons by working for philanthropies in the U.S. government and for foreign governments. This was also his first taste of academic writing, something he enjoyed immensely. After moving to the University of Texas, Sánchez experienced the Second World War in two ways: as a war of ideas and as a war of activism. He burned to make a difference and succeeded in doing so through governmental service and activism that have remained mostly obscured until now, but his repeated attempts to join the military service were turned away. Sánchez almost lost his life to tuberculosis and did lose his marriage while dealing with an administration at the University of Texas that no longer regarded his work as highly as before. Though he remarried in 1947, this was an anxious time for Sánchez. By the 1950s he was a cold war liberal, a thoughtful restrictionist, and an integration purist. He dealt with other civil rights movements with nuance and sophistication. Many scholars remember Sánchez primarily for his life and career during the 1960s, though in many ways that decade was a less effective extension of what had come before. Despite his greater proximity to power during this period, Sánchez was increasingly on the outside looking in, especially as Lyndon Johnson's Great Society emerged. Though Sánchez sought to embrace the Chicano movement, it sometimes left him cold and seemingly very old before he succumbed to his numerous ailments in the spring of 1972.

This book plumbs one unique, outstanding, compelling life in search of meaning. What does it mean to be Mexican American? What does it mean to be an activist-scholar? What does it mean to sacrifice oneself over the course of a lifetime for a larger cause? Several conclusions stand out. First, George I. Sánchez is one of the most important intellectuals and activists of the Mexican American Generation. Second, his life is instructive to all historians of the United States as to notions of race, identity, the academy, and the theme of integration in American life. Third, the successes and failures, personal and professional, of older generations of civil rights activists touch our lives today in profound ways—their struggles, regardless of who we are or where we are or how we define ourselves, are our struggles, and we can learn from their experience to make our world a better place. Not only *can* we do this, but we *should* do it. Sánchez's career is a primer for understanding an entire generation of activism based on the notion that Mexican Americans are as American as any other group. This is such an obvious, seemingly moderate claim that it seems hardly worth making. Yet, in reading Sánchez's story, one knows that for too long the nation did not acknowledge such notions and resented having attention called to them. Given the recent resurgence of controversies over Latina/o IQ, criminality, and acculturation, and the battle over ethnic studies, one could easily conclude that not much has changed. Sánchez's lifetime mission of integrating his people so that they might claim their rightful, equal place at the table of American life continues. All students of history, intellectuals, activists, and engaged citizens can stand to benefit from learning more about George I. Sánchez. His struggle is that important.

NOTES

INTRODUCTION

1. When referring to the Chicano movement of the late 1960s and 1970s and its creation of Chicano studies, I drop my usual gender inclusiveness of "-a/o" for the masculine "o" as true to common usage at that time. Chicanos in that era would have argued that the "o" ending was inherently inclusive and respectful, though the work of Chicana feminists over several decades has demonstrated otherwise. See Orozco, "Sexism in Chicano Studies and the Community," in *Chicana Voices*, 11–18; Blackwell, *¡Chicana Power!*, 28–34.

2. D. Gutiérrez, "Significant to Whom?," 527–29; R. Gutiérrez, "Internal Colonialism," 287–92, 293 (first quotation); Chávez, "¡Mi Raza Primero!," 4–7, 4 (second quotation); Mariscal, *Brown-Eyed Children of the Sun*, 9 (remaining quotations); Soldatenko, *Chicano Studies*, chap. 1.

3. Saragoza, "Recent Chicano Historiography," 9 (first quotation); Chavarria, "On Chicano History," in *Humanidad*, 44 (remaining quotations); Blackwell, *¡Chicana Power!*, 29–30.

4. Gutiérrez, "Significant to Whom?," 525–27; Chavarría, "On Chicano History," in *Humanidad*, 42, 44; M. García, *Mexican Americans*, chaps. 9–11; Saragoza, "Recent Chicano Historiography," 10–11.

5. Kreneck, *Mexican American Odyssey*; I. García, *Hector P. Garcia*; Kells, *Hector P. Garcia*; Almaráz, *Knight Without Armor*; Saldívar, *The Borderlands of Culture*; Limón, *Américo Paredes*. For the most recent *testimonio*, see García and Castro, *Blowout!*

6. Leff, "George I. Sánchez"; Mowry, "Educational Thought and Action."

7. Gutiérrez, "Significant to Whom?"; Gutiérrez, *Walls and Mirrors*; Getz, *Schools of Their Own*; San Miguel, *"Let All of Them Take Heed"*; I. García, *Viva Kennedy*; I. García, *White But Not Equal*; Pycior, *LBJ and Mexican Americans*.

8. M. García, *Mexican Americans*; M. García, "Foreword," in *Forgotten People*.

9. Schlossman, "Self-Evident Remedy?"; Romo, "George I. Sánchez and the Civil Rights Movement"; Welsh, "Prophet Without Honor"; Murillo, "The Works of George I. Sánchez"; Getz, "The Quaker, the Primitivist, and the Progressive."

10. Blanton, "From Intellectual Deficiency to Cultural Deficiency"; Blanton, *Strange Career of Bilingual Education*; Blanton, "George I. Sánchez, Ideology, and Whiteness"; Blanton, "The Citizenship Sacrifice"; Blanton, "A Legacy of Neglect."

11. The current understanding of the generational theme owes much to the discussion in chapter 1 of Mario García's *Mexican Americans*, where he fleshes out a convincing, enduring portrait of the Mexican American Generation that is attentive to exceptions within the generational patterns and how they are important.

12. Zamora, *World of the Mexican Worker*, chap. 4. For other works expanding on this aspect of the generational theme, see G. Sánchez, *Becoming Mexican American*; F. Arturo Rosales, ¡*Pobre Raza!*

13. García, *Mexican Americans*, chap. 1. For other works on the Mexican American Generation, see Alvarez, *The Power of the Zoot*; Garza-Falcón, *Gente Decente*; R. García, *Rise of the Mexican American Middle Class*; I. García, *White But Not Equal*; González, *Border Renaissance*; D. Gutiérrez, *Walls and Mirrors*; and G. Sánchez, *Becoming Mexican American*.

14. I. García, *Chicanismo*. For studies on the Chicano Generation with a local or thematic focus, see Montejano, *Quixote's Soldiers*; Chávez, "*Mi Raza Primero!*"; Pulido, *Black, Brown, Yellow, and Left*; Oropeza, *Raza Sí, Guerra No!*; Blackwell, *Chicana Power!*; and San Miguel, *Brown, Not White*.

15. Orozco, *No Mexicans, Women, or Dogs Allowed*, 4, 5 (first quotation); Hinojosa, "¡Medicina Sí, Muerte No!," 36 (second quotation). For other studies emphasizing continuity that take issue with or downplay the generational theme, see Quiroz, *Claiming Citizenship*; Gómez-Quiñones, *Chicano Politics*; Chávez, *The Lost Land*.

16. González, *Border Renaissance*, 221, n. 3.

17. For recent work on LULAC and AGIF, see Orozco, *No Mexicans, Women, or Dogs Allowed*; Zamora, *Claiming Rights and Righting Wrongs*; Kaplowitz, *LULAC, Mexican Americans, and National Policy*; Ramos, *The American G.I. Forum*; Carroll, *Felix Longoria's Wake*.

CHAPTER 1. EARLY LIFE AND EDUCATION

Epigraph. GIS, "I, Mexican American," November 19–21, 1971, box 70, folder 26, SP, 1. (All epigraphs in the book are taken from the writings of George I. Sánchez.)

1. Simmons, *New Mexico*, 156–60.

2. Perales, ed., *Are We Good Neighbors?*, 147, 157, 164–65, 169–70, 181–82, 200–201, 207, 210–11. For some educational histories, see San Miguel and Valencia, "From the Treaty of Guadalupe Hidalgo to *Hopwood*," 353–412; San Miguel, "*Let All of Them Take Heed*"; Blanton, *Strange Career of Bilingual Education*; MacDonald, *Latino Education in the United States*; Gonzalez, *Chicano Education in the Era of Segregation*.

3. Paredes, "Jorge Isidoro Sánchez y Sánchez (1906–1972)," in *Humanidad*, 121; GIS to Raymond Teske, February 23, 1971, box 33, folder 16, SP; GIS to P. Knowlton, October 20, 1943, box 23, folder 8, SP; GIS, "Biographical Data . . . To December 31, 1949,"

box 1, folder 10, SP; GIS, "Biographical Data . . . To September 1, 1966," University of New Mexico Archives, GISFF, folder 1.

4. Gómez, *Manifest Destinies*, 114–15; Maria Montoya, "Dennis Chávez and the Making of Modern New Mexico," in *New Mexican Lives*, ed. Etulain, 245; McWilliams, *North from Mexico*, 44 (first quotation); Sánchez, *Forgotten People*, 3 (remaining quotations); Gutiérrez, "Significant to Whom?," 527.

5. GIS to Virginia Familathe, May 23, 1964, box 15, folder 12, SP; GIS to John Houk, October 29, 1964, box 5, folder 1, SP; Standard Form 86, "Security Investigation Data for Sensitive Information for Sánchez, George Isidoro," undated, box 36, folder 1, SP. Much on Sánchez's childhood derives from recollections, particularly in his later years. The concern that these anecdotes may be exaggerated is not unfounded. However, if they are inflated, it is remarkably consistent from the 1940s through the early 1970s. He was inconsistent, however, in the spelling of his middle name.

6. GIS to L. Halvorson, January 19, 1962, box 18, folder 17, SP (quotation); Sánchez, "Community Power Structure," December 8, 1966, box 14, folder 11, SP; Leff, "George I. Sánchez, 37.

7. GIS to Lupe Ramírez, April 12, 1971, box 30, folder 19, SP; GIS to William Ramírez, May 9, 1969, box 30, folder 19, SP (quotation); GIS, "Biographical Data . . . To December 31, 1952," box 1, folder 11, SP; GIS to J. Jones, March 28, 1957, box 26, folder 2, SP.

8. GIS to Hank Brown, March 18, 1968, box 2, folder 7, SP; Dubofsky, *We Shall Be All*, 384–86; Clements, *After the Boom*, 50; Bird, Georgakas, and Shaffer, *Solidarity Forever*, 126–27; Green, *Grass-Roots Socialism*, 359; Rosenbaum, *Mexicano Resistance*, 139; Arrieta, "La Alianza Hispano-Americana, 1894–1965: An Analysis of Collective Action and Cultural Adaptation," in *Nuevomexicano Cultural Legacy*, ed. Lomelí et al., 118; Meeks, *Border Citizens*, 99.

9. GIS to Taiei Miura, December 4, 1953, box 25, folder 13, SP; GIS to Alan Exelrod, June 27, 1969, box 25, folder 1, SP; Blanton, "The Rise of English-Only Pedagogy: Immigrant Children, Progressive Education, and Language Policy in the United States, 1900–1930," in *When Science Encounters the Child*, ed. Beatty et al., 56–76; Gordon, *The Great Arizona Orphan Abduction*.

10. *The Mucker, 1919–1920 Yearbook*, Jerome High School, SP; Clements, *After the Boom*, 50–51; GIS to John Houk, October 29, 1964, box 5, folder 1, SP; GIS to V. Richards, July 6, 1948, box 31, folder 3, SP; Leff, "George I. Sánchez," 37; GIS to *Texas Observer*, May 16, 1969, box 34, folder 16, SP; GIS to Samuel M. Ortegón, January 14, 1961, box 13, folder 16, SP.

11. Annual Report, "Education and Honors," January 13, 1949, box 1, folder 16, SP; Nancy Neff, "Sánchez Engaged in Lifelong Struggle Against Injustice," *On Campus*, October 11, 1994, GISVF–UT.

12. GIS to *Texas Observer*, October 17, 1967, box 34, folder 16, SP; "The Gateway Gear," Laredo Rotary International Club, July 30, 1941, box 1, folder 4, SP; GIS, "Commencement, West Oso High School, Exposition Hall, Corpus Christi, Texas, May 24, 1965," box 14, folder 10, SP; GIS to Eunice Myrick, undated [between June 9 and October 1, 1964], box 26, folder 6, SP (quotation).

13. "University Honors UT Prof," *Austin Statesman*, January 7, 1971, GISVF–UT; GIS to Alfredo Griego, May 11, 1971, box 27, folder 17, SP; GIS, "Community Power Structure," December 8, 1966, 1–3, box 14, folder 11, SP. For LBJ's experience, see Blanton, *Strange Career of Bilingual Education*, 82–84, 132–33; Preuss, "Cotulla Revisited," 20–37.

14. GIS, "Community Power Structure," December 8, 1966, box 14, folder 11, SP, 4, 5 (quotation). The "white mule" Sánchez mentioned is moonshine or white lightning, illegal and potent alcohol.

15. Ibid., 6–7; biographical data on GIS for Julius Rosenwald Fund, March 23, 1937, box 127, folder 2, JRF; Mowry, "Educational Thought and Action," 25.

16. "GEB, Fellowship Application Blank, 1930–1931," box 245, folder 2465, GEBC, 2; GIS to J. Jones, March 28, 1957, box 26, folder 2, SP (quotation); GIS, "Community Power Structure," December 8, 1966, box 14, folder 11, SP, 6.

17. GIS to P. Knowlton, October 20, 1943, box 23, folder 8, SP; University of New Mexico Transcript of Record, George Isidoro Sánchez, July 21, 1930, box 1, folder 5, SP; Annual Report, "Education and Honors," January 13, 1949, box 1, folder 16, SP; "GEB, Fellowship Application Blank, 1933–1934," box 245, folder 2465, GEBC, 5–6.

18. University of New Mexico, Transcript of Record, Sánchez, George Isidoro, July 21, 1930, box 1, folder 5, SP; State University of New Mexico, Permanent Record Sheet, Sánchez, George Isidoro, November 9, 1942, box 1, folder 5, SP. For more on Sánchez and psychometric research, see Blanton, "Intellectual Deficiency to Cultural Deficiency," 39–62.

19. "GEB, Fellowship Application Blank, 1930–1931," box 245, folder 2465, GEBC, 1; GIS to P. Knowlton, October 20, 1943, box 23, folder 8, SP (quotation); GIS to Max Rafferty, September 15, 1966, box 30, folder 19, SP; Tom Wiley to GIS, July 7, 1969, box 27, folder 17, SP.

20. GIS to Gerald Freund, February 5, 1964, box 14, folder 6, SP; University of Texas, Official Transcript, Sánchez, George Isidoro, November 7, 1942, box 1, folder 5, SP; University of New Mexico, Summer Session 1930, Certificate of Record, Sánchez, George I., August 11, 1930, box 1, folder 5, SP; "GEB, Fellowship Application Blank, 1930–1931," box 245, folder 2465, GEB, 3.

21. GIS to John Harrison, January 3, 1964, box 52, folder 15, SP; Herschel Manuel to GIS, October 17, 1968, box 54, folder 9, SP (quotation); Davis, *A Culture of Neglect*, 86; GIS to Carlos Castañeda, August 13, 1931, box 38, folder 3, CP; Carlos Castañeda to GIS, August 20, 1931, box 38, folder 3, CP; GIS to Alonso Perales, April 30, 1931, box 2, folder 19, APP.

22. GIS to James Zimmerman, August 24, 1933, box 10, folder "Sánchez, George I., 1933–35," ZP; James Zimmerman to GIS, March 1, 1934, box 10, folder "Sánchez, George I., 1933–35," ZP; GIS to James Zimmerman, March 2, 1934, box 10, folder "Sánchez, George I., 1933–35," ZP; "Programme of the Final Examination for the Degree of Doctor of Education of George Isidoro Sánchez," April 30, 1934, box 1, folder 2, SP; "University of California, The Seventy-First Commencement, May 1934," box 1, folder 2, SP; Mowry, "Educational Thought and Action," 28; Sánchez, "The Educa-

tion of Bilinguals"; "GEB, Fellowship Application Blank, 1933–1934," box 245, folder 2465, GEBC, 3 (quotation).

23. University of California, Department at Berkeley, Transcript of Record for Sánchez, George Isidoro, November 2, 1942, box 1, folder 5, SP; Standard Form 86, "Security Investigation Data for Sensitive Information for Sánchez, George Isidore [*sic*]," undated, box 36, folder 1; SP; Irving Melbo to GIS, March 8, 1949, box 24, folder 21, SP; GIS to Virginia Familathe, May 25, 1964, box 15, folder 12, SP (quotation); Virginia Familathe to GIS, May 16, 1964, box 15, folder 12, SP.

CHAPTER 2. NEW MEXICO SCHOOLS AND NEW DEAL POLITICS

Epigraph. Sánchez, "Bilingualism and Mental Measures," 770.

1. Cohen, *Making a New Deal*; Garcia, *Rise of the Mexican American Middle Class*, 305 (quotation); Yolanda Romero, "Migrant Housing and Labor Camps in Northwest Texas, 1930s–1940s," in *Tejano Epic: Essays in Honor of Félix D. Amaráz*, ed. De León, 91–93; Barrera, *Race and Class in the Southwest*, 112; Weber, *Dark Sweat, White Gold*; Gonzalez, *Labor and Community*; Dinwoodie, "Deportation," 193–206.

2. Kliebard, *Struggle for the American Curriculum*, 27–29, 189.

3. Ibid., 189; Evans, *Social Studies Wars*, 49–51; Evans, *This Happened in America*, 138–40; Andra Makler, "'Problems of Democracy' and the Social Studies Curriculum During the Long Armistice," in *Social Education in the Twentieth Century*, ed. Woyshner et al., 32–33; "Members of the New Mexico Educational Association, 1929–1930," box 5, folder "New Mexico Education Association, 1929–1933," ZP, 4; GIS to John Grosshans, April 3, 1946, box 18, folder 7, SP; Wiley, *Politics and Purse Strings*, 58–78.

4. Kirkendall, *Social Scientists and Farm Politics*, 1–6; Jackson Davis, internal memorandum, "Interviews: JD; Re: George I. Sanchez [*sic*]," October 11, 1943, box 286, folder 2983, GEBC (quotations); Sánchez, "Scores of Spanish-Speaking Children"; Davis, *Exposing a Culture of Neglect*, 78; "Professor Raps School Policies: University Man Says No Basis Exists for Segregation of Children," undated [likely summer of 1930], LULACVF; Manuel, *Education of Mexican and Spanish-Speaking Children in Texas*. Sánchez's thesis built on the then recently published work of Manuel, who believed the segregation of Mexican American schoolchildren was a social evil and attacked the psychometric evaluations justifying it.

5. Sánchez, "Study of the Scores of Spanish-Speaking Children," 3, 5–13, 23, 25–29, 67–70; García, *Mexican Americans*, 258; GIS to David Macpherson, February 27, 1963, box 23, folder 1, SP.

6. Sánchez, "Bilingualism and Mental Measures," 770; Sánchez, "Scores of Spanish-Speaking Children," 223–31.

7. Sánchez, "Group Differences," 555; Sánchez, "Implications of a Basal Vocabulary," 401; Blanton, "Intellectual Deficiency to Cultural Deficiency," 59; Schlossman, "Self-Evident Remedy?," 885; Lozano, "Managing the 'Priceless Gift,'" 277–84.

8. Welsh, "Prophet Without Honor," 21–22; Getz, "Extending the Helping Hand," 502–3; Bachelor, *Educational Reform in New Mexico*, 132 n. 9.

9. Mowry, "Educational Thought and Action," 45 (quotation); Leff, "George I. Sánchez," 171.

10. Sánchez, "Southwest Spanish-Americans Prepare to Challenge Power-Structure Forcing Second-Class Citizenship," 21; Sprague interview; Welsh, "Prophet Without Honor," 24–25; Sánchez and Sánchez, "Education in Mexico," 190–92.

11. James Zimmerman to Leo Favrot, January 29, 1931, box 100, folder 900, GEBC; GIS to James Zimmerman, January 22, 1931, box 100, folder 900, GEBC; James Zimmerman to Leo Favrot, February 11, 1931, box 100, folder 900, GEBC; Leo Favrot to GIS, March 3, 1931, box 100, folder 900, GEBC; GIS to Leo Favrot, March 6, 1931, box 100, folder 900, GEBC; Leo Favrot to James Zimmerman, February 2, 1931, box 100, folder 900, GEBC; Georgia Lusk, John Milne, and James Zimmerman to GEB, March 6, 1931, box 100, folder 900, GEBC; W. Brierley to Georgia Lusk, April 24, 1931, box 100, folder 900, GEBC; W. Brierley, David Stevens, and Trevor Arnett, internal memorandum no. 27, "I-2483, Division of Information and Statistics—New Mexico," May 22, 1931, box 100, folder 900, GEBC; GIS to James Zimmerman, January 22, 1931, box 100, folder 900, GEBC; Sánchez, "Educational Research in New Mexico," 321–22; GIS to James Zimmerman, November 14, 1931, box 6, folder "St. Dept. of Education, 1928–34," ZP; James Zimmerman to GIS, December 9, 1931, box 6, folder "St. Dept. of Education, 1928–34," ZP; GIS to James Zimmerman, March 14, 1934, box 6, folder "St. Dept. of Education, 1928–34," ZP; James Zimmerman to Georgia Lusk, February 21, 1933, box 6, folder "St. Dept. of Education, 1928–34," ZP; Getz, "Extending the Helping Hand," 511–12; Division of Information and Statistics, *New Mexico Common Schools Annual Financial and Statistical Report, 1932–1933*, box 100, folder 901, GEBC.

12. Fickinger and Sánchez, "A Source of School Revenue Fails Us," 32–33; Sánchez, "Teachers' Salaries Cost Less Today," 31; Fickinger and Sánchez, "Analysis of Teachers' Salaries in New Mexico," 1–2.

13. GIS to W. Brierley, July 16, 1932, box 100, folder 900, GEBC; Jackson Davis to GIS, July 21, 1932, box 100, folder 900, GEBC; GIS to W. Brierley, July 12, 1933, box 100, folder 900, GEBC; A. Armour to GIS, July 18, 1933, box 100, folder 900, GEBC.

14. GIS to Leo Favrot, October 17, 1932, box 100, folder 900, GEBC, 1–2 (first quotation); GIS to Leo Favrot, October 22, 1932, box 100, folder 900, GEBC (second and third quotations).

15. GIS to Leo Favrot, April 26, 1933, box 100, folder 900, GEBC; Fred McCuistion to GIS, April 29, 1933, box 100, folder 900, GEBC; Sánchez, "Southwest Spanish-American Prepare to Challenge Power-Structure Forcing Second-Class Citizenship," 21 (quotation).

16. Richard Page to GIS, April 7, 1933, box 1, folder 1, PP; GIS to Richard Page, April 10, 1933, box 1, folder 1, PP (first quotation); Richard Page to GIS, April 12, 1933, box 1, folder 1, PP (second quotation); GIS to Frank Angel, September 19, 1970, box 5, folder 6, SP.

17. Richard Page, "Attitude Toward Natively Spanish-Speaking People of the Southwest," in Richard Page, "Brief Prepared for Investigating Committee in Defense of the Race Study," box 1, folder 1, PP, 34 (quotations).

18. Getz, "Politics, Science, and Education," 51–54; Gonzales, *Forced Sacrifice as Ethnic Protest*, 114, 130, 218, 244; "Give Governor 24 Hours to Oust Those Responsible for Racial Questionnaire," *Albuquerque Journal*, April 28, 1933, box 1, folder 1, PP (quotation).

19. Lowitt, *Bronson M. Cutting*, 195–96; Getz, "Politics, Science, and Education," 54 (first quotation); Bronson Cutting to James Zimmerman, May 8, 1933, box 12, folder "U.S. Senator Bronson Cutting," ZP (second quotation).

20. James Zimmerman to Bronson Cutting, May 1, 1933, box 12, folder "U.S. Senator Bronson Cutting," ZP (first and second quotations); Page, "Brief Prepared for 'Investigative Committee' in Defense of the Race Study," box 1, folder 1, PP, 42 (third quotation); "Racial Report Urges Page Be Fired; Condemns Sánchez and Criticizes Zimmerman," *Albuquerque Journal*, May 9, 1933, box 1, folder 4, ASP; "The Committee Report," *Albuquerque Tribune*, May 10, 1933, box 1, folder 4, ASP.

21. GIS to Leo Favrot, April 27, 1933, box 100, folder 900, GEBC (first quotation); Leo Favrot to GIS, May 8, 1933, box 100, folder 900, GEBC (second quotation); GIS to Leo Favrot, May 11, 1933, box 100, folder 900, GEBC; Leo Favrot to GIS, May 15, 1933, box 100, folder 900, GEBC; Welsh, "Prophet Without Honor," 24–25; Gonzales, "'La Junta de Indignación,'" 161–86; GIS to Frank Angel, September 19, 1970, box 5, folder 6, SP (third quotation); Carlos Castañeda to GIS, May 2, 1933, box 38, folder 3, CP; GIS to Carlos Castañeda, May 18, 1933, box 38, folder 3, CP; Getz, "Politics, Science, and Education in New Mexico," 57–60, 67; GIS to Richard Page, May 10, 1933, box 1, folder 1, PP (fourth quotation).

22. Fellowship Reader Card for George I. Sánchez, 1930–1951, folder "Fellowship Reader Cards," GEBC; GIS, "My Dear Citizen," box 6, folder "St. Department of Education, 1928–1934," ZP; GIS, "Future Legislative Program for Financing Public Education in New Mexico," box 10, folder "Sánchez, George I., 1933–1935," ZP; GIS, "Management and Mismanagement in a State Business—Education," box 100, folder 901, GEBC; GIS, "Equitable Distribution Needed for New School Revenue," box 10, folder "Sánchez, George I., 1933–1935," ZP.

23. Cohen, *Making a New Deal*; Cohen, *When the Old Left Was Young*, 199, 211–12, 275–76; Sánchez, "Education of Bilinguals," 27–36.

24. Sánchez, "Education of Bilinguals," 103–6.

25. GIS to James Zimmerman, November 1, 1933, box 10, folder "Sánchez, George I., 1933–35," ZP, 2 (quotations).

26. James Zimmerman to GIS, November 10, 1933, box 10, folder "Sánchez, George I., 1933–35," ZP; James Zimmerman to GIS, December 4, 1933, box 10, folder "Sánchez, George I., 1933–35," ZP; James Zimmerman to Bronson Cutting, December 5, 1933, box 12, folder "U.S. Sen. Bronson Cutting," ZP; Bronson Cutting to James Zimmerman, December 8, 1933, box 12, folder "U.S. Sen. Bronson Cutting," ZP; James Zimmerman to Leo Favrot, December 4, 1933, box 12, folder "U.S. Sen. Bronson Cutting," ZP.

27. GIS to Leo Favrot, November 30, 1933, box 10, folder "Sánchez, George I., 1933–35," ZP; Leo Favrot to James Zimmerman, December 13, 1933, box 10, folder "Sánchez, George I., 1933–35," ZP; Leo Favrot to GIS, December 13, 1933, box 10, folder "Sánchez, George I., 1933–35," ZP, 1–2 (quotation).

28. James Zimmerman to GIS, January 10, 1934, box 10, folder "Sánchez, George I., 1933–35," ZP; James Zimmerman to Leo Favrot, January 10, 1934, box 10, folder "Sánchez, George I., 1933–35," ZP; Leo Favrot to James Zimmerman, January 20, 1934, box 10, folder "Sánchez, George I., 1933–35," ZP; GIS to James Zimmerman, January 23, 1934, box 10, folder "Sánchez, George I., 1933–35," ZP; GIS to James Zimmerman, January 28, 1934, box 10, folder "Sánchez, George I., 1933–35," ZP; James Zimmerman to Sánchez, February 15, 1934, box 10, folder "Sánchez, George I., 1933–35," ZP; James Zimmerman to GIS, March 13, 1934, box 10, folder "Sánchez, George I., 1933–35," ZP; GIS to Bronson Cutting, March 2, 1934, box 10, folder "Sánchez, George I., 1933–35," ZP.

29. GIS to James Zimmerman, March 20, 1934, box 10, folder "Sánchez, George I., 1933–35"; James Zimmerman to GIS, April 17, 1934, box 10, folder "Sánchez, George I., 1933–35," ZP; GIS to W. Brierley, May 14, 1934, box 10, folder "Sánchez, George I., 1933–35," ZP; James Zimmerman to GIS, June 19, 1934, box 10, folder "Sánchez, George I., 1933–35"; GIS to Georgia Lusk, July 11, 1934, box 10, folder "Sánchez, George I., 1933–35," ZP; Virgie Sánchez to James Zimmerman, telegram, September 4, 1934, UNM, ZP, box 10, folder "Sánchez, George I., 1933–35," ZP; Lowitt, *Bronson M. Cutting*, 270–78, 308–9.

30. James Zimmerman to Virgie Sánchez, September 6, 1934, box 10, folder "Sánchez, George I., 1933–35," ZP; GIS, "Rural Education," 1937, box 286, folder 2983, GEBC (quotation).

31. GIS to James Zimmerman, January 3, 1938, GISFF, 2 (quotations). For the southern regionalist school, see Odum, *Southern Regions of the United States*; Odum and Moore, *American Regionalism*; Embree, Alexander, and Johnson, *The Collapse of Cotton Tenancy*; Vance, *Human Geography of the South*; Singal, *The War Within*.

32. GIS to Leo Favrot, August 8, 1934, box 100, folder 901, GEBC; "'U' Alumnus Recognized by Yale: Dr. George I. Sanchez of Santa Fe, Gives Series of Lectures Because of Achievements in Bi-lingual Research Work," *The Alumnus* (September 1934), 7; Virgie Sánchez to James Zimmerman, August 17, 1934, box 10, folder "Sánchez, George I., 1933–35," ZP (quotations); James Zimmerman to Virgie Sánchez, August 21, 1934, box 10, folder "Sánchez, George I., 1933–35," ZP; James Zimmerman to GIS, November 6, 1934, box 6, folder "State Department of Education, 1928–34," ZP.

33. GIS to James Zimmerman, November 9, 1934, box 10, folder "Sánchez, George I., 1933–35," SP; GIS to Jackson Davis, November 9, 1934, box 100, folder 901, GEBC (quotation); GIS to Leo Favrot, November 9, 1934, box 100, folder 901, GEBC; Leo Favrot to GIS, November 20, 1934, box 10, folder 901, GEBC; Jackson Davis to GIS, November 26, 1934, box 10, folder 901, GEBC.

34. "Bi-Lingual Problems Must Be Solved, Says Dr. George I. Sánchez. Teachers Association Head Urges Increased Educational Advantages," *Silver City Enterprise*, December 14, 1934, box 1, folder 18, SP; GIS to W. Brierley, December 27, 1934, box 100, folder 901, GEBC; W. Brierley to GIS, January 2, 1935, box 100, folder 901, GEBC.

35. Leo Favrot to GIS, March 16, 1935, box 100, folder 901, GEBC; GIS to Leo Favrot, March 20, 1935, box 100, folder 901, GEBC; GIS to New Mexico State Board of Education, March 19, 1935, box 100, folder 901, GEBC; Leo Favrot to GIS, March 25, 1935, box 100, folder 901, GEBC.

36. GIS to Leo Favrot, March 20, 1935, box 100, folder 901, GEBC (first quotation); Lowitt, *Bronson M. Cutting*, 307–9; Dinwoodie, "Indians, Hispanos, and Land Reform,"
300–301; James Zimmerman to Leo Favrot, March 13, 1935, box 100, folder 901,
GEBC (second quotation); Leo Favrot to James Zimmerman, March 20, 1935, box
100, folder 901, GEBC.

37. James Zimmerman to Leo Favrot, March 13, 1935, box 100, folder 901, GEBC (quotation); Russell Contreras, "Celebrated Scholar Remains Unrecognized in Home State,"
Santa Fe New Mexican, February 11, 2012, http://www.santafenewmexican.com.

CHAPTER 3. EXILE, RECOGNITION, AND UNDEREMPLOYMENT

Epigraph. Sánchez, *Forgotten People*, 98.

1. For some recent studies of Mexican immigrant populations, their identities, and the
   role of Mexican consulates, see Sánchez, *Becoming Mexican American*; Gonzalez,
   Mexican Consuls and Labor Organizing; Wiese, "Mexican Nationalisms, Southern
   Racisms," 749–77. For recent work connecting these ideas more directly to the found-
   ers of LULAC, see Johnson, "The Cosmic Race in Texas," 404–19; Zamora, *The
   World of the Mexican Worker in Texas*.

2. James Zimmerman to Leo Favrot, March 13, 1935, box 100, folder 901, GEBC; Leo
   Favrot to James Zimmerman, March 20, 1935, box 100, folder 901, GEBC; Delpar,
   The Enormous Vogue of Things Mexican, 74–76; GIS to Walter Hill, March 19, 1935,
   box 100, folder 901, GEBC (first quotation); Walter Hill to GIS, March 26, 1935, box
   100, folder 901, GEBC; Edwin Embree to Trevor Arnett, March 6, 1935, box 100,
   folder 901, GEBC (second quotation); Trevor Arnett to Edwin Embree, March 8,
   1935, box 100, folder 901, GEBC; "People met and interviewed during New Mexico
   Trip: 1935," undated [likely late spring of 1935], box 309, folder 24, JRFA.

3. Edwin Embree to Leo Favrot, March 7, 1935, box 212, folder 2042, GEBC (quotations);
   Walter Hill to Leo Favrot, March 12, 1935, box 212, folder 2042, GEBC; Leo Favrot to
   Edwin Embree, March 16, 1935, box 212, folder 2042, GEBC; Edwin Embree to James
   Zimmerman, March 26, 1935, box 8, folder "Organizations and Associations-Julius
   Rosenwald Fund, 1934–35/41/44," ZP; James Zimmerman to Edwin Embree, April 6,
   1935, box 8, folder "Sánchez, George I., 1933–35," ZP; Edwin Embree to James Zimmerman, April 10, 1935, box 8, folder "Sánchez, George I., 1933–35," ZP; Edwin Embree
   to Leo Favrot, September 20, 1935, box 212, folder 2042, GEBC. Tannenbaum wrote
   of the glories of revolutionary Mexico and its schools, taught at Columbia University,
   and helped create the New Deal's Farm Security Administration. See Velasco,
   "Reading Mexico, Understanding the United States," 646–49.

4. Embree and Waxman, *Investment in People*, 80, 193, 277–78; GIS to Carlos Castañeda, March 11, 1935, box 38, folder 3, CP; Carlos Castañeda to GIS, March 15, 1935,
   box 38, folder 3, CP; Fred McCuistion, "A Peep at Mexico," and George I. Sánchez,
   "A Brief Review of the New Education in Mexico: Including Interpretations by
   George I. Sánchez and Moisés Sáenz," 22–27, box 213, folder 2045, GEBC; Hale,
   "Frank Tannenbaum and the Mexican Revolution," 244–45. Sánchez recalled that
   the minister turned one challenging question around on his visitors: "How can you

be critical of our educational policy when you segregate Negroes?" See George I. Sánchez, "Past and Present Inter-American Educational Relations," in *Inter-American Educational Relations: Proceedings of the Fourth Western Regional Conference on Comparative Education, School of Education, University of California at Los Angeles*, 4.

5. GIS to Leo Favrot, May 23, 1935, box 212, folder 2042, GEBC (quotation); GIS to Leo Favrot, March 5, 1935, box 212, folder 2042, GEBC.

6. GIS to Maurice Ries, April 1, 1963, box 31, folder 3, GEBC; and GIS to W. Anderson, April 22, 1969, box 5, folder 4, GEBC; Brunhouse, *Sylvanus G. Morley*, 218; Sánchez, *Arithmetic in Maya*, pgs. 1, 5, 7; GIS to James Zimmerman, June 18, 1935, box 10, folder "Sánchez, George I., 1933–35," ZP; James Zimmerman to GIS, July 5, 1935, box 10, folder "George I. Sánchez, 1933–35," ZP; GIS to James Zimmerman, September 20, 1935, box 10, folder "Sánchez, George I., 1933–35," ZP (first quotation); Sánchez, "Challenges to Inter-American Educational Relations" 4; James Zimmerman to GIS, September 4, 1935, box 10, folder "George I. Sánchez, 1933–35," ZP; GIS to James Zimmerman, September 20, 1935, box 10, folder "George I. Sánchez, 1933–35," ZP; GIS to James Zimmerman, September 23, 1935, box 10, folder "George I. Sánchez, 1933–35," ZP (second quotation).

7. James Zimmerman to Leo Favrot, May 10, 1935, box 598, folder 6355, GEBC; notes of Leo Favrot of conversation with James Zimmerman, May 16, 1935, box 598, folder 6355, GEBC; W. Armour to James Zimmerman, August 12, 1935, box 598, folder 6355, GEBC; Frances Mathis to W. Armour, August 15, 1935, box 598, folder 6355, GEBC; Leo Favrot to James Zimmerman, September 16, 1935, box 598, folder 6355, GEBC; James Zimmerman to Jackson Davis, December 6, 1935, box 598, folder 6355, GEBC; Jackson Davis to James Zimmerman, December 16, 1935, box 598, folder 6355, GEBC; James Zimmerman to Edwin Embree, October 25, 1935, box 309, folder 24, JRFA; GIS to James Zimmerman, October 2, 1935, box 127, folder 3, JRFA.

8. GIS to James Zimmerman, October 17, 1935, box 10, folder "Sánchez, George I., 1933–35," ZP; Edwin Embree to James Zimmerman, October 17, 1935, box 8, folder "Organizations and Associations—Julius Rosenwald Fund, 1934–35/41/44," ZP; James Zimmerman to Edwin Embree, October 25, 1935, UNM, ZP, box 8, folder "Organizations and Associations—Julius Rosenwald Fund, 1934–35/41/44," ZP; Sánchez, *Mexico: A Revolution by Education*, 95 (quotation).

9. Sánchez, *Mexico: A Revolution by Education*, 91, 105–9, 106 (quotation); Vaughan, *Cultural Politics in Revolution*, 28–31, 46; Sol Tax, review of *Mexico: A Revolution by Education*, 446; Eyler Simpson, review of *Mexico: A Revolution by Education*, 256–57.

10. George I. Sánchez, activities list, October 7, 1936, to July 22–23, 1937, box 127, folder 3, JRFA; Edwin Embree to Leo Favrot, January 16, 1936, box 212, folder 2042, GEBC; Washington, "Educar es Redimir," 203–5; GIS to P. Knowlton, October 20, 1943, box 23, folder 8, SP. See also Hoffschwelle, *The Rosenwald Schools*.

11. Dunne, "Next Steps," 8–9; Charles S. Johnson, "Section 8—The Negro Public Schools," in *Louisiana Educational Survey, Volume 4*, 185, 216, JP; A. Lewis to GIS, October 14, 1936, folder 13, box 207, JRFA; A. Lewis and C. Barrow to Edwin Embree, September 16, 1936, folder 13, box 207, JRFA; GIS to R. Todd, September 28,

1936, folder 13, box 207, JRFA; GIS to Clyde Mobley, September 28, 1936, folder 13, box 207, JRFA; GIS to J. Bateman, September 28, 1936, folder 13, box 207, JRFA; GIS to A. Lewis, September 28, 1936, folder 13, box 207, JRFA; Edwin Embree to A. Lewis, September 29, 1936, folder 13, box 207, JRFA; GIS to A. Lewis, September 30, 1936, folder 13, box 207, JRFA; Dorothy Elvidge to A. Lewis, November 27, 1936, folder 13, box 207, JRFA; A. Lewis to GIS, July 9, 1937, folder 14, box 207, JRFA; GIS, "The Rural Normal School's Teacher Education Program Involves . . . ," September 17, 1936, folder 16, box 207, JRFA; GIS, "Brief Outline with Recommendations," September 17, 1936, folder 13, box 207, JRFA; GIS, "Suggested Budget—Grambling," April 9, 1937, folder 16. box 207, JRFA; GIS, "Recommendations," December 9, 1936, folder 16, box 207, JRFA.

12. "Memorandum of the January meeting of the Rosenwald Council on Rural Education," January 29, 1937, box 213, folder 2047, GEBC; Charles Johnson to Edwin Embree, January 21, 1937, box 335, folder 5, JRFA; Charles Johnson to Edwin Embree, February 25, 1937, box 335, folder 5, JRFA; Charles Johnson to Dorothy Elvidge, June 23, 1937, box 335, folder 5, JRFA; Robert Park, "Memorandum on Rote Learning," March 4, 1937, 1–17, JRFA. Park founded the Chicago School of sociology and taught during his last years at Fisk. Redfield, also a University of Chicago product, studied rural Mexican villages. Bond was an education historian at Fisk, later the president of Lincoln University, and a contributor to the NAACP's *Brown v. Board* research.

13. Johnson, "The Education of the Negro Child," 272; Dunne, "Next Steps," 23–26; Johnson, "The Cultural Environment of the Negro Child and Its Educational Implications," February 15, 1939, box 160, folder 5, JP, 1 (quotation).

14. GIS, "Community Power Structure," December 8, 1966, box 14, folder 11, SP, 9 (first quotation), 14 (second and third quotations). This was an address delivered in New Mexico in the fall of 1966 that thereafter appeared in a community newspaper. See "Southwest Spanish-Americans Prepare to Challenge Power Structure Forcing Second-Class Citizenship," *Southwesterner* 6 (December 1966), 21–23. I recently discovered that this newspaper left out or garbled portions of Sánchez's talk in a manner far more negative to African Americans than the talk he wrote. As a result, my previous essay touching on this, "George I. Sánchez, Ideology, and Whiteness," is more condemnatory of Sánchez than these passages. For more on this shift in the language used to discuss African Americans and their plight, see Gutman, *The Black Family*, xvii–xxii; Scott, *Contempt and Pity*, chaps. 6 and 9. For an African American scholar in this vein, see Frazier, *Black Bourgeoisie*.

15. GIS, activities list, October 7, 1936, to July 22–23, 1937, box 127, folder 3, JRFA; Bartley, *The New South*, 15; Ross, "Mary McLeod Bethune," 1–6; McCuistion and Bond, "School Money in Black and White," box 213, folder 2046, GEBC.

16. George I. Sánchez, "Community Power Structure," December 8, 1966, box 14, folder 11, SP, 9 (quotation). For such racial violence at that time, see Martin, *The Angelo Herndon Case*; Carter, *Scottsboro*; Goodman, *Stories of Scottsboro*; Kelly, *Hammer and Hoe*. For black–brown relations of this period, see García, "Mexican Americans and the Politics of Citizenship," 187–204; Weise, "Mexican Nationalisms, Southern Racisms," 749–77.

17. GIS to James Zimmerman, September 30, 1936, box 10, folder "Sánchez, George I., 1933–35," ZP (quotation); GIS to Leo Favrot, March 23, 1937, box 286, folder 2983, GEBC; Leo Favrot to GIS, March 25, 1937, box 286, folder 2983, GEBC; Leo Favrot to GIS, March 31, 1937, box 286, folder 2983, GEBC; GIS to Leo Favrot, April 5, 1937, box 286, folder 2983, GEBC; Leo Favrot to GIS, April 7, 1937, box 286, folder 2983, GEBC.

18. GIS to Leo Favrot, March 23, 1937, box 286, folder 2983, GEBC; "Interviews: LMF, Dr. George I. Sánchez, Julius Rosenwald Fund, Chicago, Illinois," July 27, 1937, box 286, folder 2983, GEBC; Leo Favrot to GIS, box 286, folder 2983, GEBC; GIS to Edwin Embree, May 22, 1937, box 127, folder 3, JRFA; GIS to Leo Favrot, October 22, 1936, box 514, folder 5490, GEBC (first quotation); GIS to Carlos Castañeda, June 14, 1937, box 38, folder 3, CP (second quotation); Carlos Castañeda to GIS, June 16, 1937, box 38, folder 3, CP (third quotation).

19. Leo Favrot to Virgie Sánchez, May 28, 1937, box 286, folder 2983, GEBC (quotation); GIS to Leo Favrot, July 9, 1937, box 212, folder 2043, GEBC; GIS to Edwin Embree, undated, [likely late July], 1937, box 127, folder 3, JRFA; GIS to J. Dixon, July 14, 1937, box 127, folder 3, JRFA; Ruth Warren to Carl Ross, July 21, 1937, box 127 folder 3, JRFA; Ruth Warren to GIS, July 23, 1937, box 127, folder 3, JRFA; "The Fundlings" [i.e., Rosenwald employees] to GIS, July 28, 1937, box 127, folder 3, JRFA; GIS to Julius Rosenwald Fund, July 28, 1937, box 127, folder 3, JRFA; Ruth Warren to Virgie Sánchez, July 30, 1937, box 127, folder 3, JRFA; Ruth Warren to GIS, September 17, 1937, box 127, folder 3, JRFA; Ruth Warren to GIS, September 20, 1937, box 127, folder 3, JRFA; Ruth Warren to Carl Van Ness, October 6, 1937, box 127, folder 3, JRFA; Carl Van Ness to Ruth Warren, October 12, 1937, box 127, folder 3, JRFA.

20. GIS to Edwin Embree, October 17, 1937, box 127, folder 4, JRFA (first and second quotations); GIS to Carlos Castañeda, September 21, 1937, box 38, folder 3, CP (third quotation); GIS to Leo Favrot, September 21, 1937, box 286, folder 2983, GEBC (fourth quotation); Sánchez, "Past and Present Inter-American Educational Relations," 3.

21. Pedro Grases to GIS, March 29, 1947, box 18, folder 8, SP; GIS to Pedro Grases, July 14, 1947, box 18, folder 8, SP; GIS to Fredrick Pike, January 10, 1958, box 30, folder 4, SP; Charles Hauch to GIS, October 26, 1960, box 61, folder 7, SP; GIS to Charles Hauch, October 31, 1960, box 61, folder 7, SP (quotation).

22. GIS to Edwin Embree, December 21, 1937, box 127, folder 4, JRFA (first quotation); GIS to Edwin Embree, October 17, 1937, box 127, folder 4, JRFA; GIS to Leo Favrot, September 21, 1937, box 286, folder 2983, GEBC; GIS to Edwin Embree, May 12, 1938, box 127, folder 4, GEBC; GIS to Edwin Embree, June 28, 1938, box 127, folder 4, JRFA; GIS to Jackson Davis, May 16, 1938, box 286, folder 2983, GEBC; GIS to Edwin Embree, August 19, 1938, box 127, folder 4, JRFA (second quotation).

23. GIS to Edwin Embree, June 28, 1938, box 127, folder 4, JRFA (first quotation); Edwin Embree to GIS, June 29, 1938, box 127, folder 4, JRFA; GIS to Jackson Davis, May 16, 1938, box 286, folder 2983, GEBC (second quotation); GIS to James Zimmerman, May 10, 1938, "George I. Sánchez Faculty File, 1838–41," folder 1, GISFF (third quotation); James Zimmerman to GIS, May 24, 1938, folder 1, GISFF; GIS to Ruth Warren, November 29, 1938, box 127, folder 4, JRFA.

24. GIS to Carlos Castañeda, September 21, 1937, box 38, folder 3, CP; GIS to Edwin Embree, August 19, 1938, box 127, folder 4, JRFA (first quotation); Virgie Sánchez, "Travel Impressions" and "Dont's for Globe-Trotters," 50 (second quotation).

25. GIS to Edwin Embree, July 12, 1938, box 127, folder 4, JRFA; Edwin Embree to GIS, July 15, 1938, box 127, folder 4, JRFA; GIS to Edwin Embree, August 19, 1938, box 127, folder 4, JRFA; GIS to Edwin Embree, October 17, 1937, box 127, folder 4, JRFA; Edwin Embree to GIS, October 29, 1937, box 127, folder 4, JRFA.

26. GIS to Ruth Warren, November 29, 1938, box 127, folder 4, JRFA (first quotation); James Zimmerman to GIS, May 24, 1938, folder 1, GISFF; J. Dixon to Leo Favrot, June 3, 1938, box 286, folder 2983, GEBC; Leo Favrot to J. Dixon, June 11, 1938, box 286, folder 2983, GEBC; GIS to Leo Favrot, December 19, 1938, box 286, folder 2983, GEBC (second quotation); Rupert Vance, "Planning the Southern Economy (1935)" in *Regionalism in the South*, ed. Reed and Singal, 75; Leo Favrot to GIS, December 27, 1938, box 286, folder 2983, GEBC (third quotation).

27. Sánchez, "The Community School in the Rural Scene," in *The Community School*, 164, 178; Sánchez, "Theory and Practice in Rural Education," 596; GIS, "Minority Groups and Democracy," box 73, folder 10, SP, 10–11 (quotation); Welsh, "Prophet Without Honor," 29; Orozco, "Regionalism, Politics, and Gender"; F. Kercheville to Ben Cherrington, May 10, 1939, RG 59, CDF 1930–39, box 4688, 810.42711/1061, SDRCF; GIS to Ben Cherrington, May 9, 1939, RG 59, CDF, 1930–39, box 4688, 810.42711/1068, SDRCF; Ben Cherrington, May 18, 1939, RG 59, CDF 1930–39, box 4688, 810.42711/1068, SDRCF; George Frasier to Ben Cherrington, RG 59, CDF 1930–39, box 4688, 810.42711/1150, SDRCF; Ben Cherrington to George Frazier, August 3, 1939, RG 59, CDF, 1930–39, box 4688, 810.42711/1150, SDRCF; Lyndon Johnson to Cordell Hull, November 1, 1939, RG 59, CDF 1930–39, box 4689, 810.42711/1317, SDRCF; Cordell Hull to Lyndon Johnson, November 30, 1939, RG 59, CDF 1930–39, box 4589, 810.42711/1317, SDRCF; James Zimmerman to Warren Kelchner, April 30, 1940, RG 59, CDF 1940–44, box 1584, 592.A8 Personnel/1283, SDRCF.

28. GIS to Louis Adamic, April 17, 1945, box 2, folder 4, SP; GIS to Archibald Gillies, September 25, 1970, box 60, folder 2, SP; García, *Mexican Americans*, 145–50; Orozco, "Beyond Machismo, La Familia, and Ladies Auxiliaries," 17.

29. GIS to Leo Favrot, December 19, 1938, box 286, folder 2983, GEBC (quotation); Leo Favrot to GIS, December 27, 1938, box 286, folder 2983, GEBC; Sánchez, "State Public School Equalization Fund," box 286, folder 2983, GEBC, 1–12; Tom Wiley to GIS, September 24, 1964, box 62, folder 13, SP; GIS to Tom Wiley, September 29, 1964, box 62, folder 13, SP; Minutes to "Special Meeting of State Board of Education Held January 20, 1939," box 6, folder "New Mexico State Department of Education, 1935–42," SP; Wiley, *Politics and Purse Strings*, 71–75; Sánchez, "The Equalization of Educational Opportunity," 3–47.

30. Sánchez, *Forgotten People*, 27 (quotation), 29–35.

31. Ibid., 28 (quotation), 98; Stitler, review of *Forgotten People*, 364–66; Saldívar, *The Borderlands of Culture*, 229–30.

32. Sánchez, *Forgotten People*, xvi; University press release, "*Albuquerque Tribune*, October 9, 1939," GISVF–UNM; University biographical statement, "Dr. George I. Sánchez," GISVF–UNM.

33. Sánchez, *Forgotten People*, xvi–xvii; Blanton, "George I. Sánchez," 575; GIS to the University of New Mexico, the American Association for Adult Education, and the Carnegie Corporation, January 5, 1940, GISVF–UNM; George I. Sánchez, "Community Education in Taos County: A Critical Review and a Proposal," UNM, Zimmerman Reading Room, 1–26; GIS to Edwin Embree, April 3, 1940, box 127, folder 5, JRFA; GIS to Ralph Yarborough, March 25, 1959, box 63, folder 10, SP.

34. GIS to Philip Ortego, April 22, 1968, box 28, folder 6, SP.

35. Richardson, "Reds, Race, and Research," 139; GIS to Carlos Castañeda, May 22, 1939, box 38, folder 3, CP; Carlos Castañeda to GIS, May 27, 1939, box 38, folder 3, CP; GIS to Carlos Castañeda, November 22, 1939, box 38, folder 3, CP; Carlos Castañeda to GIS, November 24, 1939, box 38, folder 3, CP; GIS to Carlos Castañeda, December 1, 1939, box 38, folder 3, CP; Carlos Castañeda to GIS, December 4, 1939, box 38, folder 3, CP; GIS to Carlos Castañeda, December 6, 1939, box 38, folder 3, CP; Carlos Castañeda to GIS, December 11, 1939, box 38, folder 3, CP; Carlos Castañeda to GIS, January 22, 1940, box 38, folder 3, CP; GIS to Carlos Castañeda, April 1, 1940, box 38, folder 3, CP; GIS to Frederick Eby, October 21, 1964, box 12, folder 18, SP; B. Pittenger to Homer Rainey, November 29, 1939, box 4R26, folder "ED: Fac.-Sánchez, 1939–40, 43, 45," BPP; Leo Haynes to Clarence Gray, March 22, 1940, box 4R26, folder "ED: Fac.- Sánchez, 1939–40, 43, 45," BPP.

36. Davis, *A Culture of Neglect*, 81, 83–88; Schlossman, "Self-Evident Remedy?," 890; GIS to L. Haskew, September 27, 1948, box 50, folder 3, SP (quotation); GIS to Stanley Ross, March 2, 1970, box 31, folder 5, SP; "Venezuelan Prof Joins Faculty," October 9, 1940, *Daily Texan*, GISVF–UT; University press release, May 28, 1940, GISVF–UT; Homer Rainey to GIS, December 30, 1940, box 54, folder 13, SP; GIS to Homer Rainey, undated [likely early January 1941], box 54, folder 13, SP; Anderson, "Race, Meritocracy, and the Academy," 151–75.

37. "Resolution Adopted By The LULAC Council No. 34, May 7, 1940," folder 1, GISFF (first quotation); "We, members of the student body . . . ," folder 1, GISFF; University press release, "George I. Sánchez," undated [likely from April, May, or early June 1940]; An Anglo, "Since Everybody is throwing brickbats . . . ," *Albuquerque Tribune*, April 30, 1940, box 1, folder 18, SP (second quotation); James Zimmerman to GIS, January 18, 1941, folder 1, GISFF; James Zimmerman to GIS, February 6, 1941, folder 1, GISFF; GIS to James Zimmerman, February 13, 1941, folder 1, GISFF; James Zimmerman to GIS, February 26, 1941, folder 1, GISFF.

CHAPTER 4. SÁNCHEZ'S WAR OF IDEAS

Epigraph. GIS to Nelson Rockefeller, February 7, 1942, box 31, folder 9, SP.

1. For recent works touching significantly on Mexican American educational activism during the Second World War, see San Miguel, "*Let All of Them Take Heed*," chap. 4; Blanton, *Strange Career of Bilingual Education*, chap. 6.

2. GIS to Edwin Embree, September 14, 1940, box 127, folder 5, JRFA; GIS to Edwin Embree, October 25, 1940, box 127, folder 5, JRFA; Edwin Embree to GIS, October 1, 1940, box 127, folder 4, JRFA; GIS to Edwin Embree, November 11, 1940, box 127, folder 4, JRFA; Edwin Embree to GIS, November 14, 1940, box 127, folder 4, JRFA.

3. Newsletter, "Memorial Edition. In Memory of an Illustrious Scholar and Educator This Edition Is Most Gratefully Dedicated: Frederick Eby, 1874–1968," Department of History and Philosophy of Education, University of Texas, April 18, 1968, SP, 2 (quotations); GIS to A. Brogan, April 23, 1942, box 51, folder 10, SP; Leo Haynes to GIS, July 14, 1941, box 60, folder 7, SP; Leo Haynes to GIS, July 7, 1942, box 60, folder 7, SP; Leo Haynes to GIS, July 29, 1943, box 60, folder 7, SP; Leo Haynes to GIS, October 20, 1943, box 60, folder 7, SP; Leo Haynes to GIS, December 1, 1943, box 60, folder 7, SP; Florence Reiboldt to GIS, April 6, 1945, box 60, folder 8, SP; Rivera, "Interview with George I. Sánchez," 9, 19.

4. GIS to James Shotwell, November 4, 1941, box 9, folder 21, SP; GIS to Edwin Embree, October 21, 1941, box 127, JRFA; GIS to Pedro Cebollero, December 2, 1941, box 10, folder 8, SP; Pedro Cebollero to GIS, December 15, 1941, box 10, folder 8, SP; GIS to Pedro Cebollero, January 14, 1942, box 10, folder 8, SP; Pedro Cebollero to GIS, August 21, 1942, box 10, folder 8, SP.

5. Coordinator of Inter-American Affairs, "Approved Projects Under the Cultural Relations Program, November 7, 1940," box 5, folder 35, RP; *New Mexico Quarterly Review* staff, "The School for the Rio Grande," 295–300.

6. Sitkoff, *A New Deal for Blacks*, 324; GIS to Nelson Rockefeller, December 31, 1941, box 31, folder 9, SP (quotations); GIS, "Latin American Research and Policies Commission," December 31, 1941, box 31, folder 9, SP, 1–9.

7. GIS, "Teacher's Report, 1940–1941," box 48, folder 1, SP; GIS, "Teacher's Report, 1941–1942," box 48, folder 1, SP; GIS, "Teacher's Report, 1942–1943," box 48, folder 1, SP, 1–2; Leo Haynes to GIS, October 20, 1943, box 60, folder 7, SP; Leo Haynes to GIS, December 1, 1943, box 60, folder 7, SP; Leo Haynes to GIS, December 8, 1943, box 60, folder 7, SP.

8. Mickenberg, *Learning from the Left*, 94–95; Schurz, "How Cultural Contacts are Winning Accord for the Americas," in *Cultural Relations Among the Democracies*, 15; Cole, "Intercultural Education," 25–26; Doyle, "Some Intellectually Dishonest Arguments," 179; Andersson, *Foreign Languages*, 86–87; P. Knowlton to GIS, April 25, 1941, box 23, folder 7, SP (quotation); GIS to P. Knowlton, April 30, 1941, box 23, folder 7, SP.

9. P. Knowlton to GIS, July 28, 1941, box 23, folder 7, SP; P. Knowlton to GIS, October 3, 1941, box 23, folder 7, SP; Brett et al., *The Role of Books in Inter-American Relations*, 42; GIS to P. Knowlton, July 30, 1941, box 23, folder 7, SP; GIS to P. Knowlton, August 3, 1941, box 23, folder 7, SP; P. Knowlton to GIS, August 6, 1941, box 23, folder 7, SP; James Michener to GIS, September 9, 1941, box 23, folder 11, SP; GIS to James Michener, September 24, 1941, box 23, folder 11, SP; Publicity material, box 24, folder 1, SP; Willis Jones to GIS, box 21, folder 4, SP; Bowden, de Porter, Cutright, and Charters, *The Day Before Yesterday in America*; Castañeda and Delaney, *The Lands of Middle America*; Delaney, Sánchez, Cutright, and Charters, *Spanish Gold*; Barr,

Jones, Delaney, *Our Friends in South America*; Inman and Castañeda, *A History of Latin America for Schools*; Cutright, Charters, Sánchez, *Latin America: Twenty Friendly Nations.*

10. Cutright, Charters, Sánchez, *Latin America: Twenty Friendly Nations*, 415–516, 436; Ben Cherrington, "The Role of Education in International Cultural Relations," in *Inter-American Cultural Relations: Department of State Publication 1369*, 3–14; Delaney, Sánchez, Cutright, Charters, *Spanish Gold*, 406; P. Knowlton to GIS, August 6, 1941, box 23, folder 7, SP; GIS to Aurelia Habekost, January 16, 1942, box 23, folder 5, SP.

11. GIS to Edmundo Mireles, September 22, 1941, box 24, folder 3, SP; Edmundo Mireles to GIS, September 24, 1941, box 24, folder 3, SP; GIS to P. Knowlton, September 25, 1941, box 23, folder 7, SP; P. Knowlton to GIS, October 3, 1941, box 23, folder 7, SP; Arthur Campa to GIS, undated [early August 1942], box 9, folder 9, SP; GIS to Arthur Campa, August 10, 1942, box 9, folder 9, SP; Arthur Campa to GIS, August 27, 1942, box 9, folder 9, SP; GIS to James Michener, August 11, 1942, box 23, folder 12, SP; James Michener to GIS, October 13, 1942, box 23, folder 12, SP; James Michener to GIS, November 4, 1942, box 23, folder 12, SP; James Michener to GIS, November 16, 1942, box 23, folder 12, SP; GIS to James Michener, November 18, 1942, box 23, folder 12, SP; James Michener to GIS, January 28, 1943, box 23, folder 13, SP; GIS to Samuel Inman, August 13, 1942, box 20, folder 2, SP; GIS to Carlos Castañeda, January 6, 1942, box 10, folder 4, SP; Carlos Castañeda to GIS, January 7, 1942, box 10, folder 4, SP; GIS to Carlos Castañeda, October 16, 1942, box 10, folder 4, SP; Zamora, *Claiming Rights and Righting Wrongs*, 122–23, 134; James Michener to GIS, December 9, 1941, box 23, folder 11, SP; GIS to A. Bowden, February 19, 1942, box 8, folder 13, SP; Aurelia Habekost to GIS, January 29, 1942, box 23, folder 4, SP; P. Knowlton to GIS, March 21, 1945, box 23, folder 8, SP; Albright, review of *Latin America: Twenty Friendly Nations*, 118–19.

12. Márquez, *LULAC*, 10, 38–39; Orozco, "Regionalism, Politics, and Gender," 477.

13. Rivas-Rodríguez, ed., *Mexican Americans and World War II*, xvi–xviii; Zamora, *Claiming Rights and Righting Wrongs*, 121–22; GIS to Nelson Rockefeller, December 31, 1941, box 31, folder 9, SP; GIS to Nelson Rockefeller, February 7, 1942, box 31, folder 9, SP; Santiago Vargas, Jose Hernandez, and Alejos Lara to GIS, February 1, 1942, box 31, folder 9, SP.

14. Sánchez, "A New Pan-Americanism," 32, 39 (quotation); Emilio Zamora, "Fighting on Two Fronts: José de la Luz Sáenz and the Language of the Mexican-American Civil Rights Movement," in *Recovering the U.S. Hispanic Literary Heritage*, ed. Aranda and Torres-Saillant, 4:226–27; GIS to Dennis Chávez, October 17, 1941, box 22, folder 11, SP; "Benefit Tea," undated, box 1, folder 18, SP; "Puerto Rico Graduates to Hear U.T. Professor," undated, box 1, folder 18, SP; "Mrs. Sánchez Is Speaker, Women's Defense Work Discussed," undated, box 1, folder 18, SP; "LULAC Hears Dr. Sánchez, Latin American Council Elects," *Austin Statesman*, March 2, 1942, 5, box 1, folder 18, SP; "LULAC Plans Benefit Tea, Sánchez Home to Be Opened," undated, box 1, folder 18, SP.

15. Emilio Zamora, "Mexico's Wartime Intervention on Behalf of Mexicans in the United States: A Turning of Tables," in *Mexican Americans and World War II*, ed.

Rivas-Rodríguez, 230–32; William Blocker to Secretary of State, September 4, 1943, 811.4016/687, box 3806, CDF, 1940–44, RG 59, SDRCF; G. Palacios Roji to GIS, June 23, 1943, box 28, folder 9, SP.

16. Adolf Berle to William Blocker, September 20, 1943, 811.4016/687, box 3806, CDF 1940–44, RG59, SDRCF (first quotation); William Blocker to State Department, September 2, 1943, 811.4016/687, box 3806, CDF 1940–44, SDRCF (remaining quotations).

17. Coke Stevenson to Adolf Berle, October 7, 1943, 811 4016/712, box 3806, CDF 1940–44, RG 59, SDRCF; Manuel Gonzales to Cordell Hull, September 18, 1943, 811.4016/700, box 3806, CDF 1940–44, RG 59, SDRCF; John Herrera to Manuel Gonzales, September 16, 1943, 811.4016/700, box 3806, CDF 1940–44, RG 59, SDRCF; Paul Daniels to Manuel Gonzales, September 29, 1943, 811.4016/700, box 3806, CDF 1940–44, RG 59, SDRCF; Adolf Berle to Coke Stevenson, September 29, 1943, 811.4016/700, box 3806, CDF 1940–44, RG 59, SDRCF; Adamic, *A Nation of Nations*, 68; Welles, *Sumner Welles*, 320–23.

18. Henry Waterman to State Department, September 24, 1943, 811.4016/705, box 3806, CDF 1940–44, RG 59, SDRCF; William Blocker to State Department, October 1, 1943, 811.4016/706, box 3806, CDF 1940–44, RG 59, SDRCF (quotation); William MacLean to Carrigan, Bonsal, and Duggan, October 8, 1943, 811.4016/706, box 3806, CDF 1940–44, RG 59, SDRCF; William MacLean to McGurk, October 11, 1943, 811.4016/706, box 3806, CDF 1940–44, RG 59, SDRCF.

19. William Blocker to State Department, October 1, 1943, 811.4016/711, box 3806, CDF 1940–44, RG 59, SDRCF; Pauline Kibbe to William Blocker, September 28, 1943, 811.4016/711, box 3806, CDF 1940–44, RG 59, SDRCF (quotations); Pauline Kibbe, "Report to Dr. Sánchez on Trip to El Paso and Del Rio, Texas, May 19–26, 1943," box 32, folder 14, SP; GIS to Otey Scruggs, November 29, 1955, box 32, folder 11, SP.

20. Felix Montoya to GIS, October 30, 1941, box 22, folder 11, SP; David Herrera, Raul Torres, Solomon Alba, Manuel Mendoza, Julian Ramos to GIS, February 7, 1941, box 22, folder 11, SP; J. Ruytal to GIS, May 24, 1942, box 31, folder 15, SP; Richard Garza to Alonso Perales, March 3, 1943, box 16, folder 12, SP.

21. "Justice for Mexicans in U.S.," *Washington Post*, May 6, 1942, 13 (first quotation); GIS to Eugene Katz, September 12, 1942, box 21, folder 11, SP (remaining quotations); Francisco Flores to GIS, May 1, 1943, box 22, folder 11, SP; GIS to R. Thorp, February 1942, box 35, folder 1, SP; Theodore Chacon to GIS, July 12, 1941, box 22, folder 11, SP; GIS to Theodore Chacon, July 31, 1941, box 22, folder 11, SP.

22. Sánchez, "Problems in Education in Mexico," 321–27; Sánchez, "Higher Education in Modern Mexico," 32; GIS to James Shotwell, April 22, 1941, box 9, folder 21, SP; James Shotwell to GIS, May 21, 1941, box 9, folder 21, SP; GIS to James Shotwell, May 24, 1941, box 9, folder 21, SP; James Shotwell to GIS, June 2, 1941, box 9, folder 21, SP; GIS to James Shotwell, June 9, 1941, box 9, folder 21, SP; GIS to Frederick Eby, July 27, 1941, box 45, folder 3, SP; GIS to Homer Rainey, August 11, 1941, box 54, folder 13, SP; Herbert Bursley to Notter and Duggan, May 10, 1941, NARA II, RG 59, CDF 1940–44, box 2110, 711.12/1608, SDRCF; Nettie Benson to GIS, July 8, 1943, box 8, folder 5, SP.

23. GIS to Homer Rainey, January 19, 1942, box 54, folder 13, SP (quotations).

24. GIS to James Shotwell, May 8, 1942, box 9, folder 22, SP; James Shotwell to GIS, May 14, 1942, box 9, folder 22, SP; Irving Kandel to James Shotwell, May 2, 1942, box 9, folder 22, SP; George Sánchez to James Shotwell, May 19, 1942, box 9, folder 22, SP; GIS to James Shotwell, June 27, 1942, box 9, folder 22, SP; GIS to James Shotwell, November 23, 1942, box 9, folder 22, SP; Patricia O'Quin to GIS, December 3, 1942, box 9, folder 22, SP; GIS to James Shotwell, February 6, 1943, box 9, folder 22, SP; Patricia O'Quin to GIS, February 10, 1943, box 9, folder 22, SP; Patricia O'Quin to GIS, February 17, 1943, box 9, folder 22, SP, F. Boardman to James Shotwell, February 4, 1943, box 9, folder 22, SP; W. Stewart to GIS, May 14, 1943, box 21, folder 19, SP.

25. Sánchez, *Development of Higher Education in Mexico*, 123 (quotations); Barth, review of *The Development of Higher Education in Mexico*, 306–8.

26. James Shotwell to GIS, December 9, 1941, box 9, folder 21, SP; GIS to Robert Smith, December 1, 1942, box 28, folder 14, SP; Arthur Campa to GIS, April 24, 1969, box 9, folder 13, SP; Arthur Campa to GIS, undated [early August 1942], box 9, folder 9, SP (quotation); GIS to U.S. Naval Office of Naval Officer Procurement, September 16, 1942, box 38, folder 9, SP; W. Kirkland to GIS, September 29, 1942, box 38, folder 9, SP; GIS to Director, Naval Officer Procurement, October 2, 1942, box 38, folder 9, SP; GIS to U.S. Office of Naval Officer Procurement, November 12, 1942, box 38, folder 9, SP.

27. Friedman, *Nazis and Good Neighbors*, 59–65; Woodward, *Thinking Back*, 45–47.

28. Charles Arrowood to Office of Naval Officer Procurement, October 31, 1942, box 44, folder 15, SP (first quotation); James Shotwell to GIS, November 4, 1942, box 44, folder 15, SP; GIS to Edwin Embree, October 26, 1942, box 127, folder 5, JRFA; Edwin Embree to GIS, October 28, 1942, box 127, folder 4, JRFA; Edwin Embree to Office of Naval Officer Procurement, October 28, 1942, box 127, folder 4, JRFA; GIS to Edwin Embree, November 1, 1942, box 127, folder 4, JRFA; Z. Steakley to GIS, November 23, 1942, box 38, folder 9, SP; Z. Steakley to GIS, November 23, 1942, box 38, folder 9, SP; GIS to Z. Steakley November 27, 1942, box 38, folder 9, SP; E. Walbridge to GIS, December 1, 1942, box 38, folder 9, SP (remaining quotations).

29. GIS to E. Walbridge, December 4, 1942, box 38, folder 9, SP; GIS to E. Walbridge, December 8, 1942, box 38, folder 9, SP (quotations); GIS to H. McBride, December 24, 1942, box 38, folder 9, SP. While racism cannot be ruled out, it should be noted that the Mexican American activist Bob Sánchez (no relation to GIS) from Texas, then a very young man, served in ONI during the war. See Sánchez interview.

30. GIS to J. Steakley March 11, 1943, box 38, folder 9, SP; Randall Jacobs to GIS, March 8, 1943, box 38, folder 9, SP (first quotation); Donald Bowles to GIS, March 13, 1943, box 38, folder 9, SP; Z. Steakley to GIS, March 13, 1943, box 38, folder 9 SP; GIS to Naval Officer Procurement, March 23, 1943, box 38, folder 9, SP; E. Walbridge to GIS, April 1, 1943, box 38, folder 9, SP; E. Walbridge to GIS, May 18, 1943, box 38, folder 9, SP (second quotation).

31. Allen Gullion to GIS, April 6, 1943, box 38, folder 9, SP; Thomas Horn to GIS, April 22, 1943, box 38, folder 9, SP (quotation); GIS to Thomas Horne, Jr., April 28, 1943, box 38, folder 9, SP; F. Crosley to GIS, May 6, 1943, box 38, folder 9, SP; Frank Bowles to SP, October 19, 1943, box 38, folder 9, SP; Irving Melbo to GIS, October 28,

1943, box 38, folder 9, SP; GIS to Irving Melbo, October 29, 1943, box 38, folder 9, SP; Irving Melbo to GIS, November 2, 1943, box 38, folder 9, SP.

32. GIS to R. Thomason, May 2, 1962, box 37, folder 11, SP; GIS to Charles Bunn, April 3, 1943, box 8, folder 19, SP (quotation); Monnett Davis to GIS, February 16, 1944, box 287, folder 121.67/4229n, CDF 1940–44, RG 59, SDRCF; Brice Sewell to GIS, November 11, 1942, box 8, folder 23, SP; GIS to Brice Sewell, November 11, 1942, box 8, folder 23, SP [possibly November 14, 1942]; GIS to Henry Gonzalez, November 14, 1942, box 8, folder 23, SP; Arthur Campa to GIS, October 21, 1945, box 56, folder 13, SP.

CHAPTER 5. SÁNCHEZ'S WAR OF ACTIVISM

First epigraph. GIS to Elmore Torn, March 31, 1943, box 28, folder 15, SP.
Second epigraph. Sánchez, "Pachucos in the Making," 14.

1. For these recent studies focusing on Mexican American civil rights during the war, see Zamora, *Claiming Rights, Righting Wrongs*; Guglielmo, "Fighting for Caucasian Rights," 1212–37; Ramos, "A Class Apart," chap. 5.

2. Charles Bunn to GIS, undated [likely late January or early February], box 8, folder 19, SP; GIS to Charles Bunn, February 4, 1942, box 8, folder 19, SP; Harriet and Charles Bunn to GIS, February 19, 1942, box 8, folder 19, SP; GIS to Charles Bunn, February 27, 1942, box 8, folder 19, SP; Charles Bunn to GIS, March 2, 1942, box 8, folder 19, SP; GIS to Charles Bunn, March 6, 1942, box 8, folder 19, SP; Charles Bunn to GIS, March 10, 1942, box 8, folder 19, SP; GIS to Charles Bunn, March 14, 1942, box 8, folder 19, SP; Charles Bunn to GIS, March 19, 1942, box 8, folder 19, SP; GIS to Charles Bunn, April 24, 1942, box 8, folder 19, SP; GIS to J. Burdine, March 30, 1942, box 8, folder 24, SP; J. Burdine to GIS, April 1, 1942, box 8, folder 24, SP; GIS to Charles Bunn, September 15, 1942, box 8, folder 19, SP; GIS to Charles Bunn, November 16, 1942, box 8, folder 19, SP; GIS to Charles Bunn, November 30, 1942, box 8, folder 19, SP; Charles Bunn to GIS, December 21, 1942, box 8, folder 19, SP; GIS to Norman Hackerman, July 8, 1968, box 55, folder 4, SP (quotation). The program grew to include trainees from Mora, New Mexico, as well as men. For more on the topic, see Ruiz, *Cannery Women*; Santillán, "Rosita the Riveter."

3. GIS to Charles Bunn, September 15, 1942, box 8, folder 19, SP; Charles Bunn, September 27, 1942, box 8, folder 19, SP; Charles Bunn to SP, September 3, 1943, box 8, folder 19, SP; GIS to Charles Bunn, November 3, 1943, box 8, folder 19, SP; GIS to Charles Bunn, March 29, 1945, box 8, folder 19, SP; Charles Bunn to GIS, April 22, 1945, box 8, folder 19, SP; GIS to Charles Bunn, April 9, 1946, box 8, folder 19, SP. For the amounts at the end of the paragraph, which span several years during the war, I have calculated the modern dollar amounts from the year 1942.

4. J. Canales to GIS, May 22, 1943, box 9, folder 19, SP (first quotation); Hector Valdez, Hector Benitez, Jose Garza, J. Robles, Manuel Cirilio, and Johnny Leal to J. Canales, May 22, 1943, box 9, folder 19, SP; GIS to Victor Rotnem, May 8, 1943, box 37, folder 7, SP: GIS to Melecio Garcia, May 14, 1943, box 37, folder 7, SP; GIS to M. Gonzales, May 14, 1943, box 37, folder 7, SP: GIS to Victor Rotnem, May 12, 1943, box 37, folder 7, SP; Wendell Berge to GIS, May 15, 1943, SP (third quotation); Victor

Rotnem to GIS, May 18, 1943, box 37, folder 7, SP; Wendell Berge to GIS, July 12, 1943, box 37, folder 7, SP (second quotation); GIS to Charles Bunn, April 3, 1943, box 8, folder 19, SP. That a Mexican American leader who received death threats in 1919 for initiating an investigation of the Texas Rangers' crimes against humanity could be so shocked at the existence of racial discrimination is most odd. See Johnson, *Revolution in Texas*, 169–75.

5. GIS to Roger Baldwin, September 15, 1942, box 2, folder 17, SP; Roger Baldwin to GIS, September 18, 1942, box 2, folder 17, SP (quotation). Whiteness scholars argue— Foley directly, Guglielmo indirectly—that Mexican Americans cut themselves off from the African American civil rights experience by believing in their *whiteness*. While certainly a tidy assertion, it is hardly supported by the primary archival record here and elsewhere. See Ramos, "A Class Apart"; Zamora, *Claiming Rights and Righting Wrongs*; Blanton, "Mexican Americans, Ideology, and Whiteness."

6. GIS to Roger Baldwin, September 21, 1942, box 2, folder 17, SP; Roger Baldwin to GIS, September 29, 1942, box 2, folder 17, SP; Roger Baldwin to GIS, December 17, 1942, box 2, folder 17, SP; GIS to Roger Baldwin, December 21, 1942, box 2, folder 17, SP (first quotation); Roger Baldwin to GIS, December 28, 1942, box 2, folder 17, SP; "Minutes of the Meeting Held at the Stephen F. Austin Hotel of the Texas Civil Rights Funds," November 4, 1943, box 34, folder 4, SP; GIS to Roger Baldwin, March 17, 1943, box 2, folder 17, SP; GIS to Roger Baldwin, January 4, 1943, box 2, folder 17, SP (second quotation); GIS to Roger Baldwin, August 23, 1943, box 2, folder 17, SP; Roger Baldwin to GIS, August 26, 1943, box 2, folder 17, SP; GIS to Roger Baldwin, September 18, 1943, box 2, folder 17, SP; Roger Baldwin to GIS, September 22, 1943, box 2, folder 17, SP; Texas Civil Rights Fund Minutes, January 12, 1944, box 34, folder 4, SP.

7. GIS to Roger Baldwin, September 18, 1943, box 2, folder 17, Sp; GIS to Roger Baldwin, August 23, 1943, box 2, folder 17, SP; M. Gonzales to Clifford Forster, November 1, 1943, box 21, folder 10, SP; GIS to Simon Gross, June 1, 1943, box 34, folder 1, SP; GIS to M. Gonzales, February 23, 1943, box 17, folder 10, SP; M. Gonzales to GIS, March 1, 1943, box 17, folder 10, SP; M. Gonzales to GIS, August 10, 1942, box 17, folder 10, SP: GIS to M. Gonzales, September 3, 1943, box 32, folder 15, SP; GIS to G. Joughin, November 27, 1943, box 34, folder 1, SP; M. Gonzales to G. Joughin, January 19, 1944, box 34, folder 1, SP; J. Loftin to GIS, May 7, 1945, box 34, folder 1, SP; M. Gonzales to G. Joughin, March 21, 1944, box 34, folder 2, SP; G. Louis Joughin to M. Gonzales, March 22, 1944, box 34, folder 2, SP; M. Gonzales to G. Joughin, March 23, 1944, box 34, folder 2, SP; Harry Moore to G. Joughin, March 28, 1944, box 34, folder 2, SP; M. Gonzales to Clifford Forster, November 1, 1943, box 21, folder 10, SP; M. Gonzales to GIS, December 30, 1942, box 17, folder 10, SP; GIS to M. Gonzales, May 17, 1943, box 17, folder 10, SP; M. Gonzales to GIS, August 30, 1943, box 17, folder 10, SP. For more on these long-forgotten cases, see Ramos, "A Class Apart," chap. 5.

8. Elizabeth Gardner to GIS, February 22, 1945, box 54, folder 2, SP; Elizabeth Gardner, "Inter American Relations in Texas at the University of Texas: Report of Activities, 1943–1945," 1–12; "Division of Inter-American Activities in the United States: Spanish and Portuguese-Speaking Minorities," September 23, 1942, 1–6, box 5, folder 36, NAR, RG4, RP; Leo Haynes to GIS, June 4, 1943, box 54, folder 13, SP; Frederick

Eby to Homer Rainey, September 15, 1943, box 54, folder 13, SP; GIS to Homer
Rainey, October 21, 1943, box 54, folder 13, SP; GIS to Homer Rainey, November 6,
1943, box 54, folder 13, SP; Homer Rainey to Frederick Eby, April 7, 1943, box 4R 26,
folder "ED: Fac.–Sánchez, 1939–40, 43, 45," BPP; Elizabeth Gardner, "Inter-American
Relations in Texas at the University of Texas: Report of Activities, 1943–1945," 9–11,
box 54, folder 2, SP. The original committee lineup was Sánchez as director, the
historians Carlos Castañeda and Charles W. Hackett, the sociologists W. E. Gettys
and R. D. Hopper, the educational psychologist Herschel T. Manuel, the University
of Texas Hogg Foundation's Robert L. Sutherland, and Dean T. H. Shelby of
the university's extension service. Later replacements for Sánchez and Castañeda
were Harry E. Moore of the Sociology Department and Loren Mozley of the Art
Department.

9. Herschel Manuel to David Stevens, December 8, 1942, box 513, folder 5478, GEBC;
Herschel Manuel to GEB, December 21, 1942, box 513, folder 5478, GEBC; William Berrien to Herschel Manuel, December 29, 1942, box 513, folder 5478, GEBC;
William Berrien to David Stevens, December 29, 1942, box 513, folder 5478, GEBC;
David Stevens and Jackson Davis, inter-office memo, January 4, 1943, box 513, folder
5478, GEBC; William Berrien, inter-office memo, January 20, 1943, box 513,
folder 5478, GEBC; Jackson Davis to Herschel Manuel, January 9, 1943, box 513,
folder 5478, GEBC; Jackson Davis, inter-office memo, February 6, 1943, box
513, folder 5478, GEBC; Herschel Manuel to Jackson Davis, January 12, 1943, box 513,
folder 5478, GEBC; Jackson Davis to Herschel Manuel, January 14, 1943, box 513,
folder 5478, GEBC; GIS to Fred McCuistion, March 22, 1943, box 513, folder 5478,
GEBC; D. Taylor to Fred McCuistion, March 22, 1943, box 513, folder 5478, GEBC;
Jackson Davis to Fred McCuistion, April 2, 1943, box 513, folder 5478, GEBC; Fred
McCuistion, inter-office memo, April 7, 1943, box 513, folder 5478, GEBC; GIS to
Fred McCuistion, April 10, 1943, box 513, folder 5478, GEBC; Fred McCuistion and
Gordon Worley, inter-office memo, April 19 and 27, 1943, box 513, folder 5478, GEBC;
Fred McCuistion to GIS, April 30, 1943, box 513, folder 5478, GEBC; Fred McCuistion to GIS, May 4, 1943, box 513, folder 5478, GEBC; GIS to Fred McCuistion,
May 6, 1943, box 513, folder 5478, GEBC; Fred McCuistion to GIS, May 13, 1943,
box 513, folder 5478, GEBC; GIS to Fred McCuistion, May 19, 1943, box 513, folder
5478, GEBC; Fred McCuistion, inter-office memo, May 24, 1943, box 513, folder
5478, GEBC.

10. Fred McCuistion, inter-office memo, June 3, 1943, box 513, folder 5478, GEBC;
Homer Rainey to GEB, June 8, 1943, box 513, folder 5478, GEBC; GIS to GEB, June
10, 1943, box 513, folder 5478, GEBC; GIS, "The Education of Spanish-Speaking
Children in the Southwest. A Proposal to be Submitted to the General Education
Board. The Situation in Texas," June 10, 1943, box 513, folder 5478, GEBC, 1–8; L.
Woods to GEB, June 4, 1943, box 513, folder 5478, GEBC; GEB to Homer Rainey,
June 23, 1943, box 513, folder 5478, GEBC; Myrtle Tanner and L. Woods, "Statewide
Survey of Enumeration, Enrollment, Attendance, and Progress of Latin American
Children in Texas Public Schools, 1943–44," box 34, folder 12, SP, 1–10; L. Woods,
"Superintendent's Report on Texas Children of Latin-American Descent, undated

[estimated August through October 1943], box 514, folder 5479, GEBC, 1–4; Little, *Spanish-Speaking Children in Texas*; Fred McCuistion, inter-office memo, August 25, 1943, box 513, folder 5478, GEBC; Homer Rainey to W. Brierley, September 7, 1943, box 513, folder 5478, GEBC; GIS to Fred McCuistion, September 9, 1943, box 513, folder 5478, GEBC; GIS to Fred McCuistion, September 21, 1943, box 513, folder 5478, GEBC; Jackson Davis, inter-office memo, October 11, 1943, box 513, folder 5478, GEBC; Fred McCuistion, inter-office memo, October 8, 1943, box 513, folder 5478, GEBC; GIS to Fred McCuistion, November 3, 1943, box 513, folder 5478, GEBC; Wilson Little to Fred McCuistion, January 3, 1944, box 513, folder 5478, GEBC; Davis, *A Culture of Neglect*, 102–4; University of Texas, "Study of the Education of Spanish-Speaking Children in the Southwest, General Education Board Grant, Statement of Income and Expenses," April 30, 1945, box 513, folder 5478, GEBC; Fred McCuistion, inter-office memo, July 4, 1944, box 513, folder 5478, GEBC; Robert Sutherland, July 12, 1944, box 513, folder 5478, GEBC; Homer Rainey and Robert Sutherland to GEB, July 24, 1944, box 513, folder 5478, GEBC; W. Brierley to Homer Rainey, July 26, 1944, box 513, folder 5478, GEBC; Fred McCuistion to Robert Sutherland, July 28, 1944, box 513, folder 5478, GEBC; Wilson Little to Fred McCuistion, August 2, 1944, box 513, folder 5478, GEBC; Robert Sutherland to Fred McCuistion, August 4, 1944, box 513, folder 5478, GEBC; A. Mann to Robert Sutherland, August 15, 1944, box 513, folder 5478, GEBC; A. Mann, inter-office memo, August 9, 1944, box 513, folder 5478, GEBC; Robert Sutherland to Fred McCuistion, October 11, 1944, box 513, folder 5478, GEBC; Fred McCuistion to Robert Sutherland, October 20, 1944, box 513, folder 5478, GEBC.

11. House Concurrent Resolution, H.C.R. No. 105, May 7, 1943, 1 (quotation). For a contrasting interpretation, see Guglielmo, "Fighting for Caucasian Rights," 1212–37.

12. GIS to R. Smith, April 30, 1943, box 28, folder 14, SP (first two quotations); GIS to Roger Baldwin, August 23, 1943, box 2, folder 17, SP (third quotation); J. Loftin to Roger Baldwin, November 9, 1943, box 2, folder 17, SP; Roger Baldwin to G. Joughin, December 2, 1943, box 2, folder 17, SP; G. Joughin to Roger Baldwin, December 8, 1943, box 2, folder 17, SP.

13. Lawrence Cramer to GIS, July 15, 1942, box 38, folder 13, SP; GIS to Lawrence Cramer, July 20, 1942, box 38, folder 13, SP; Lawrence Cramer to GIS, July 25, 1942, box 38, folder 13, SP; GIS to Lawrence Cramer, July 31, 1942, box 32, folder 13, SP; Lawrence Cramer to GIS, August 10, 1942, box 32, folder 13, SP; Ernest Trimble to Lawrence Cramer, December 29, 1943, NARA II, PI 147, entry 19, box 339, folder "Hearing Background Material." For recent scholarship on the FEPC, see Zamora, *Claiming Rights and Righting Wrongs*; and Gritter, *Mexican Inclusion*.

14. Lawrence Cramer to GIS, February 9, 1943, box 32, folder 13, SP; GIS to Lawrence Cramer, February 9, 1943, box 32, folder 13, SP; Lawrence Cramer to GIS, February 10, 1943, box 32, folder 13, SP; Thurman Dodson to GIS, February 16, 1943, box 32, folder 13, SP; Paul McNutt to GIS, February 19, 1943, box 32, folder 13, SP; GIS to Lawrence Cramer, February 12, 1943, box 32, folder 13, SP; Lawrence Cramer to GIS, February 17, 1943, box 32, folder 13, SP.

15. Office for Emergency Management, Division of Central Administrative Services, Minutes and Reports Section, "Verbatim Transcript: Conference on Scope and Powers of Committee of Fair Employment Practice," February 19, 1943, box 38, folder 14, SP, 56–57 (first quotation), 56 (second quotation).

16. Walter White to GIS, March 11, 1943, box 38, folder 13, SP; GIS to Smith, Eby, Gray, Sutherland, and Gonzales, undated [likely enclosed with letter of March 1, 1943], box 38, folder 13, SP (first quotation); GIS to M. Gonzales, March 1, 1943, box 37, folder 7, SP (second quotation); Lawrence Cramer to GIS, March 22, 1943, box 37, folder 7, SP; GIS to Alonso Perales, March 29, 1943, box 37, folder 7, SP; Gritter, *Mexican Inclusion*, 3 (remaining quotations).

17. Carlos Castañeda to GIS, September 3, 1943, box 38, folder 13, SP; Carlos Castañeda to GIS, September 23, 1943, box 38, folder 13, SP, Carlos Castañeda to GIS, March 23, 1945, box 10, folder 4, SP; Carlos Castañeda to GIS, May 12, 1945, box 10, folder 4, SP; GIS to Roger Baldwin, May 31, 1943, box 38, folder 13, SP; GIS to Lawrence Cramer, May 31, 1943, box 38, folder 13, SP; GIS to Antonio Fernández, May 31, 1943, box 38, folder 13, SP; GIS to Victor Borella, May 31, 1943, box 38, folder 13, SP; GIS to Walter White, May 31, 1943, box 38, folder 13, SP; Antonio Fernández to GIS, June 1, 1943, box 38, folder 13, SP; Antonio Fernández to Lawrence Cramer, June 1, 1943, box 38, folder 13, SP; Antonio Fernández to Francis Haas, June 1, 1943, box 38, folder 13, SP; Lawrence Cramer to GIS, June 2, 1943, box 38, folder 13, SP; GIS to Carlos Castañeda, November 22, 1946, box 38, folder 13, SP; Carlos Castañeda to GIS, December 5, 1946, box 38, folder 13, SP. For Castañeda's perspective, see Almaráz, *Knight Without Armor*.

18. GIS to Frederick Eby and C. Gray, October 16, 1942, box 45, folder 3, SP; GIS to Robert Smith, October 16, 1942, box 28, folder 14, SP; GIS to Robert Smith, October 27, 1942, box 28, folder 14, SP; GIS to Robert Smith, November 10, 1942, box 28, folder 14, SP; Robert Smith to GIS, November 12, 1942, box 28, folder 14, SP; Frederick Eby and C. Gray to J. Burdine, December 10, 1942, box 55, folder 8; SP; Milton Gregory to GIS, December 8, 1942, box 28, folder 6, SP; Milton Gregory to GIS, November 6, 1942, box 28, folder 12, SP; J. Kastor to GIS, December 16, 1942, box 28, folder 12, SP; GIS to J. Kastor, June 3, 1943, box 28, folder 12, SP; J. Kastor to GIS, August 26, 1943, box 28, folder 12, SP; J. Kastor to GIS, October 1, 1943, box 28, folder 12, SP; B. Marshall to GIS, September 15, 1943, box 28, folder 11, SP; B. Marshall to GIS, September 16, 1943, box 28, folder 11, SP; GIS to B. Marshall, September 22, 1943, box 28, folder 11, SP; GIS to Robert Smith, October 5, 1943, box 28, folder 14, SP.

19. GIS to Edward Oakley, January 20, 1943, box 28, folder 10, SP; Dorothy Hanny to Edward Oakley, January 27 1943, box 28, folder 10, SP; Edward Oakley to Department of Justice, February 4, 1943, box 28, folder 10, SP; Edward Oakley to Dorothy Hanny, February 11, 1943, box 28, folder 10, SP; GIS to Edward Oakley, February 8, 1943, box 28, folder 10, SP; Edward Oakley to GIS, February 13, 1943, box 28, folder 10, SP; GIS to Phillip Sánchez, March 8, 1943, box 28, folder 14, SP; GIS to Edward Oakley, May 12, 1943, box 28, folder 10, SP; Edward Oakley to Esquipula Naranjo, May 24, 1943, box 28, folder 10, SP; Edward Oakley to GIS, May 28, 1943, box 28, folder 10, SP; Edward Oakley to Helen Nolan, August 12, 1943, box 28, folder 10, SP;

GIS to Edward Oakley, August 16, 1943, box 28, folder 10, SP; Edward Oakley to G. Wilmoth, August 25, 1943, box 28, folder 10, SP; GIS to Elmore Torn, January 2, 1943, box 28, folder 15, SP; GIS to Elmore Torn, box 28, folder 15, SP; GIS to Elmore Torn, February 2, 1943, box 28, folder 15, SP; SP to Elmore Torn, March 31, 1943, box 28, folder 15, SP; Elmore Torn to GIS, April 9 1943, box 28, folder 15, SP; GIS to Elmore Torn, May 5, 1943, box 28, folder 15, SP; GIS to Elmore Torn, June 3, 1943, box 28, folder 15, SP; GIS to Elmore Torn, June 24, 1943, box 28, folder 15, SP; Morse Cartwright to Members of the National Committee of Educational Advisers, Bureau of Special Operations, Office of War Information, February 1, 1943, box 28, folder 11, SP; GIS to J. Page, May 3, 1943, box 29, folder 1, SP. For the influence of wartime radio among Latinos, see Maggie Rivas-Rodríguez, "Embracing the Ether: The Use of Radio by the Latino World War II Generation," in *Beyond the Latino World War II Hero*, ed. Rivas-Rodríguez and Zamora, 21–37.

20. J. Page to Coke Stevenson, January 29, 1943, box 28, folder 11, SP; R. Crawford to Coke Stevenson, February 5, 1943, box 28, folder 11, SP; GIS to William McGill, January 7, 1943, box 28, folder 13, SP (quotation); GIS to William McGill, January 12, 1943, box 28, folder 13, SP; William McGill to GIS, January 14, 1943, box 28, folder 13, SP; GIS to William McGill, January 20, 1943, box 28, folder 13, SP; GIS to William McGill, February 8, 1943, box 28, folder 13, SP.

21. GIS to Robert Smith, February 8, 1943, box 28, folder 14, SP; GIS to Robert Smith, February 11, 1943, box 28, folder 14, Sp; GIS to Robert Smith, March 1, 1943, box 28, folder 14, SP; Robert Smith to GIS, March 4, 1943, box 28, folder 14, SP; "Office of Emergency Management Notice of Efficiency Rating," March 31, 1943, box 28, folder 17, SP; GIS to Robert Smith, September 3, 1943, box 28, folder 14, SP; Robert Smith to GIS, September 7, 1943, box 28, folder 14, SP (quotation); Robert Smith to GIS, September 25, 1943, box 28, folder 14, SP; GIS to Robert Smith, October 5, 1943, box 28, folder 14, SP; Robert Smith to GIS, October 9, 1943, box 28, folder 14, SP.

22. William Blocker to Secretary of State, August 3, 1943, NARA II, RG59, CDF, 1940–44, box 3806, 811.4016/651, SDRCF, 1–17; Dean Heathman, "Confidential Counter-Intelligence Summary, 11 ND: Zoot-Suit Riots (B7M)," June 1943, NARA II, RG59, CDF, 1940–44, box 3806, 811.4016/651, SDRCF, 1–9; J. McGurk to Bonsal and Shaw, August 11, 1943, NARA II, RG59, CDF, 1940–44, box 3806, 811.4016/651, SDRCF 1–2; Frederick Roderick, "Racial Conditions (Spanish-Mexican Activities) in Los Angeles Field Division," FBI Report, NARA II, RG 59, CDF 1940–44, box 3806, 811.4016/807, SDRCF, 115; Gutiérrez, *Walls and Mirrors*, 127–28. There is a great deal of new work coming out on this period and topic. See Mazón, *The Zoot Suit Riots*; Pagán, *Murder at the Sleepy Lagoon*; Alvarez, *The Power of the Zoot*; Ramírez, *The Woman in the Zoot Suit*; Bernstein, *Bridges of Reform*.

23. GIS to Robert Smith, April 30, 1943, box 28, folder 14, SP; Sánchez, "Pachucos," 13 (quotations); McWilliams, *North from Mexico*, 211–16; Sánchez, *Becoming Mexican American*, 267.

24. Edwin Embree, letter of recommendation, October 28, 1942, box 127, folder 4, JRFA; Betty Bares to Edwin Embree, November 12, 1943, box 127, folder 4, JRFA; Edwin Embree to Betty Bares, undated [likely the same day as the last telegram], box 127,

folder 5, JRFA; GIS to J. Burdine, October 26, 1943, box 55, folder 8, SP; Carlos Castañeda to GIS, August 30, 1943, box 38, folder 13, SP; Carlos Castañeda to GIS, September 3, 1943, box 38, folder 13, SP (first quotation); GIS to M. Gonzales, September 3,
1943, box 32, folder 15, SP (second quotation); GIS to Carlos Castañeda, October 25,
1943, box 38, folder 13, SP; GIS to Roger Baldwin, August 23, 1943, box 2, folder 17, SP;
GIS to Fred McCuistion, September 9, 1943, box 513, folder 5478, GEBC; GIS to A.
Brogan, December 26, 1943, box 51, folder 10, SP (third quotation); Dave Cheavens,
"Soft-Spoken UT Professor Loaned to Coordinator of Latin American Affairs," *Austin
Statesman*, December 3, 1943, GISVF–UT.

25. Espinosa, *Inter-American Beginnings*, 159–61; Ninkovich, *The Diplomacy of Ideas*,
36–41; Coordinator of Inter-American Affairs, *Our American Neighbors*; *The Program
of the Department of State in Cultural Relations. Department of State Publication
1594*; *The Program of the Department of State in Cultural Relations. Department of
State Publication 1441*, 1; *Official Exchange of Professors, Teachers, and Graduate Students Under the Convention for the Promotion of Inter-American Cultural Relations.
Department of State Publication 1612*, 4–5; Frances Iversen, inter-office memo, October
9, 1945, box 38, folder 4, SP; Kenneth Holland to GIS, February 15, 1943, box 28, folder
11, SP; Kenneth Holland to GIS, October 23, 1943, box 19, folder 9, SP; Kenneth Holland to GIS, October 29, 1943, box 19, folder 9, SP; GIS to James Zimmerman, October 29, 1943, box 63, folder 21, Sp; GIS to U.S.O., Ross, May 31, 1943, box 22, folder 11, SP.

26. James Young to Nelson Rockefeller, May 6, 1942, NARA II, RG 229, entry 1, box 57,
folder "Spanish and Portuguese Speaking Minorities," OIAACF; Nelson Rockefeller
to John Clark, May 9, 1942, NARA II, RG 229, entry 1, box 57, folder "Spanish and
Portuguese Speaking Minorities," OIAACF; Nelson Rockefeller to James Young,
May 11, 1942, NARA II, RG 229, entry 1, box 57, folder "Spanish and Portuguese
Speaking Minorities," OIAACF; Schwarz, *Liberal*, 260–263; "Pan-Americanism Must
Begin at Home, Sánchez Tells Parent-Teacher Congress," May 6, 1942, *Albuquerque
Journal*, NARA II, RG 229, entry 1, box 57, folder "Spanish and Portuguese Speaking
Minorities," OIAACF; William Blocker to State Department, October 27, 1943,
NARA II, RG 59, CDF 1940–44, box 3806, 811.4016/724, SDRCF; William Blocker to
State Department, November 8, 1943, NARA II, RG 59, CDF 1940–44, box 3806,
811.4016/733, SDRCF; "Memorandum (Confidential)," January 12, 1944, box 5, folder
35, RG4, RP; GIS to Roger Baldwin, October 27, 1943, box 2, folder 17, SP; Texas Civil
Rights Fund addresses, undated [November 1943 to March 1944], box 3, folder 4, SP;
GIS to G. Joughin, January 19, 1944, box 34, folder 1, SP; Iriye, *Cultural Internation-
alism*, 143–44.

27. Gabler, *Walt Disney*, chap. 8; Kahn, *Jock*, 134–37; de Usabel, *High Noon of American
Films in Latin America*, 157, 163–66; Shale, *Donald Duck Joins Up*, chap. 5; Halfdan
Gregersen to Board of Directors, Inter-American Educational Foundation, Inc., un-
dated [likely in 1945 or 1946], RG4, box 5, folder 40, RP.

28. GIS to Ben Sharpsteen, January 22, 1944, Walt Disney Company Archives, Burbank,
California; Halfdan Gregersen to Board of Directors, Inter-American Educational
Foundation, Inc., undated [likely 1945 or 1946], RG4, box 5, folder 40, RP; Hernane
Tavares to Nelson Rockefeller, March 21, 1943, RG4, box 5, folder 40, RP; Nelson

Rockefeller to Hernane Tavares, March 26, 1943, RG4 box 5, folder 40, RP; Donald Rowland to Frank Waring, October 6, 1944, NARA II, RG 229, entry 1, box 216, folder "Misc. Disney File," OIAACF; Seth Fein, "Everyday Forms of Transnational Collaboration," in *Close Encounters of Empire*, ed. Joseph et al., 405–7; GIS to Richard Whittington, August 26, 1963, box 62, folder 9, SP; GIS to Ralph Long, August 7, 1958, box 22, folder 24, SP; GIS to Walt Disney, February 10, 1947, box 11, folder 14, SP (quotation); Carl Nater to GIS, February 24, 1947, box 11, folder 14, SP.

CHAPTER 6. SÁNCHEZ'S WAR OF SURVIVAL
AND HIS TRANSFORMATIONS

First epigraph. GIS to Fred McCuistion, November 29, 1944, box 286, folder 2983, GEBC.
Second epigraph. Sánchez, "Study of Spanish-Speaking People," August 28, 1950, box 515, folder 5493, GEBC, 1–2.

1. Garza-Falcón, *Gente Decente*; González, *Border Renaissance*; Olivas, ed., *In Defense of My People*; Almaráz, *Knight Without Armor*; M. García, *Mexican Americans*, chaps. 9, 10, and 11; Saldívar, *The Borderlands of Culture*; Limón, *Américo Paredes*; Pulido et al., eds., *Moving Beyond Borders*.

2. GIS to Edwin Embree, March 29, 1944, box 127, folder 5, JRFA (first quotation); School of Inter-American Affairs, *Mexico's Role in International Intellectual Cooperation*, photographic insert between 28 and 29; GIS to Queenie Bilbo, March 19, 1944, box 11, folder 18, SP; GIS to Edwin Embree, March 29, 1944, box 127, folder 5, JRFA; GIS to Fred McCuistion, March 23, 1944, box 286, folder 2983, GEBC (second quotation); Fred McCuistion to GIS, March 28, 1944, box 236, folder 2983, GEBC; Sumiko Oura to GIS, April 5, 1944, box 127, folder 4, JRFA; Edwin Embree to GIS, April 20, 1944, box 127, folder 4, JRFA (third quotation); GIS to Paul Fickinger, April 7, 1959, box 15, folder 16, SP.

3. Gordon, *Arizona Orphan Abduction*, 218; Center for Disease Control and Prevention, "Questions and Answers About TB," http://www.cdc.gov; Newman, "Olden Days," 161.

4. Naef, "The 1900 Tuberculosis Epidemic," 1376; Newman, "Olden Days," 162; Melick, "Surgical Therapy of Pulmonary Tuberculosis," 158; Potts, "Surgery in Pulmonary Tuberculosis," 54–60; Bayne, "I'm Afraid It's Bad News," 258.

5. GIS to Departmental Faculty, March 18, 1971, box 49, folder 2, SP (quotation); GIS to James Dolley, October 28, 1946, box 55, folder 9, SP. Another physician in this consultation was J. W. Peabody, then president of the American College of Chest Physicians.

6. Huang and Lyons, "Cardiorespiratory Failure," 409–17; Phillips, Kinnear, and Shneerson, "Late Sequelae of Pulmonary Tuberculosis," 445–51; Unknown to GIS, August 11, 1944, box 19, folder 19, SP; GIS to Fred McCuistion, September 27, 1944, box 286, folder 2983, GEBC (quotations); National Education Association, *The White House Conference on Rural Education*, 176–77; GIS to Robert Jones, April 8, 1947, box 21, folder 2, SP.

7. GEBC; Kenneth Holland to GIS, December 29, 1944, box 19, folder 9, SP; Nelson Rockefeller to GIS, December 23, 1944, box 31, folder 9, SP; J. Hisle to GIS, June 30, 1944, box 38, folder 4, SP; Advice of Personnel Action, Inter-American Educational Foundation to GIS, November 18, 1944, box 20, folder 5, SP; GIS to Fred McCuistion, November 29, 1944, box 286, folder 2983, GEBC, 4; GIS to J. Dolley, October 28, 1946, box 55, folder 9, SP; Carlos Castañeda to A. Hunt, December 20, 1944, box 339, folder "Hearing Background Material," entry 19, PI 147, FEPCP.

8. GIS to Roger Baldwin, March 8, 1945, box 2, folder 17, SP; GIS to Guy West, March 8, 1954, box 62, folder 3, SP (quotation); B. Pittenger to GIS, July 30, 1946, box 50, folder 1, SP; GIS to J. Umstattd, December 20, 1945, box 59, folder 5, SP; Green, *Establishment in Texas Politics,* 46–57, 56 (quotation), 86–89.

9. GIS to Roger Baldwin, March 8, 1945, box 2, folder 17, SP (first quotation); Roger Baldwin, March 12, 1945, box 2, folder 17, SP (second quotation); M. Gonzales to GIS, November 3, 1945, box 17, folder 11, SP; M. Gonzales to GIS, May 21, 1946, box 17, folder 11, SP; GIS to Roger Baldwin, March 21, 1945, box 2, folder 17, SP; GIS to Roger Baldwin, May 28, 1945, box 2, folder 17, SP; Roger Baldwin to GIS, June 4, 1945, box 2, folder 17, SP; GIS to Roger Baldwin, July 7, 1945, box 2, folder 17, SP.

10. GIS to B. Pittenger, July 19, 1945, box 50, folder 1, SP; B. Pittenger to GIS, July 20, 1945, box 50, folder 1, SP; GIS to B. Pittenger, September 10, 1945, box 50, folder 1, SP; Florence Reiboldt to GIS, April 6, 1945, box 60, folder 8, SP; C. Gray to Theophilus Painter, February 15, 1945, box 4R 26, folder "ED: Fac.—Sánchez, 1939–40, 43, 45," BPP; GIS to Charles Arrowood, July 28, 1945, box 44, folder 15, SP; GIS to B. Pittenger, July 19, 1945, box 50, folder 1, SP (quotations).

11. B. Pittenger to GIS, July 30, 1946, box 50, folder 1, SP; GIS to Charles Arrowood, March 28, 1947, box 44, folder 12, SP; College of Education Budget, July 26, 1945, box 60, folder 7, SP; College of Education Budget, July 20, 1946, box 60, folder 7, SP; Betty Thedford to GIS, July 26, 1946, box 60, folder 7, SP.

12. GIS to James Dolley, September 30, 1946, box 55, folder 9, SP; GIS to James Dolley, October 28, 1946, box 55, folder 9, SP (quotations).

13. GIS to James Dolley, October 28, 1946, box 55, folder 9, SP, 2 (first quotation); draft letter of GIS to Theophilus Painter, box 54, folder 14, SP, 4 (second quotation).

14. GIS to Theophilus Painter, undated letter draft [soon after October 19, 1946], box 54, folder 14, SP (quotation).

15. Ibid. (quotations).

16. B. Pittenger to James Dolley, October 4, 1946, box 50, folder 1, SP; GIS to Charles Arrowood, November 5, 1946, box 49, folder 15, SP; GIS to Charles Arrowood, March 28, 1947, box 44, folder 12, SP; GIS to James Dolley, July 23, 1947, box 55, folder 9, SP; James Dolley to GIS, July 29, 1947, box 55, folder 9, SP; GIS to James Dolley, August 1, 1947, box 55, folder 9, SP; James Dolley to GIS, August 5, 1947, box 55, folder 9, SP; GIS to James Dolley, August 9, 1947, box 55, folder 9, SP; GIS to James Dolley, August 18, 1947, SP: James Dolley to GIS, August 23, 1947, SP; Betty Thedford to GIS, July 29, 1947, box 60, folder 7, SP; Betty Thedford to GIS, December 6, 1947, box 60, folder 7, SP; College of Education Budget, June 24, 1948, box 50, folder 7, SP. Painter

and Dolley were at that time central figures in the university's resistance to desegregating its law school.

17. *Sánchez v. Sánchez*, December 6 (first quotation), 10 (second quotation), and 16, 1946, BC. The packet of legal documents begins with the initial filing from 1946 and includes child support and alimony documents stretching to 1956.

18. *Sánchez v. Sánchez*, April 2, 1952, GIS to Virgie Sánchez, November 7, 1946, BC.

19. *Sánchez v. Sánchez*, April 2, 1952, Claude Mann to GIS, November 19, 1946, GIS to Claude Mann, November 22, 1946 (quotation), BC.

20. Maxine Prince to GIS, November 10, 1943, box 40, folder 5, SP; GIS to New England Mutual Life Insurance Company, November 2, 1943, box 27, folder 16, SP; Roland Dow to GIS, September 21, 1942, box 27, folder 16, SP.

21. Afton Nance to GIS, April 6, 1950, box 26, folder 8, SP; GIS to Antonio Fernández, December 17, 1945, box 15, folder 15, SP; Antonio Fernández to D. Pearson, box 28, folder 1, SP; GIS to D. Pearson, February 27, 1946, box 28, folder 1, SP; D. Pearson to GIS, March 2, 1946, box 28, folder 1, SP; GIS to Antonio Fernández, March 5, 1946, box 28, folder 1, SP; D. Pearson to Virgie Sánchez, March 5, 1946, box 28, folder 1, SP; Miers Johnson to Antonio Fernández, March 10, 1946, box 28, folder 1, SP; Antonio Fernández to Miers Johnson, March 13, 1946, box 28, folder 1, SP; GIS to NMMI, August 11, 1947, box 28, folder 1, SP.

22. GIS to Charles Bunn, December 21, 1945, box 8, folder 19, SP; GIS to Fred McCuistion, March 6, 1945, box 514, folder 5490, GEBC; Fred McCuistion to GIS, March 2, 1945, box 514, folder 5490, GEBC; Fred McCuistion, internal memo, March 26, 1945, box 514, folder 5490, GEBC; Fred McCuistion, internal memo, March 26, 1945, box 514, folder 5490, GEBCC.

23. GIS to Fred McCuistion, April 3, 1945, box 514, folder 5490, GEBC; GIS to Fred McCuistion, June 1, 1945, box 514, folder 5490, GEBC; Fred McCuistion to GIS, June 12, 1945, box 514, folder 5490, GEBC; GIS to Fred McCuistion, July 7, 1945, box 514, folder 5490, GEBC; Fred McCuistion to GIS, July 17, 1945, box 514, folder 5490, GEBC; Sánchez, *Inter-American Education Occasional Papers*, I, 1–11, 7 (quotation).

24. George Kyte to GIS, May 7, 1946, box 21, folder 23, SP (quotation).

25. GIS to Fred McCuistion, May 31, 1946, box 515, folder 5491, GEBC; GIS to Fred McCuistion, June 1, 1946, box 515, folder 5491, GEBC; GIS to Fred McCuistion, June 17, 1946, box 514, folder 5490, GEBC, 1; Fred McCuistion to GIS, June 24, 1946, box 514, folder 5490, GEBC; Fred McCuistion to GIS, July 11, 1946, box 514, folder 5490, GEBC; GIS to Fred McCuistion, July 20, 1946, box 514, folder 5490, GEBC; GIS to Fred McCuistion, November 15, 1946, box 514, folder 5490, GEBC; Fred McCuistion to GIS, October 14, 1946, box 515, folder 5491, GEBC; Fred McCuistion to GIS, November 27, 1946, box 515, folder 5491, GEBC; GIS to Fred McCuistion, January 30, 1947, box 515, folder 5491, GEBC; Fred McCuistion to GIS, February 7, 1947, box 515, folder 5491, GEBC; Theophilus Painter to Fred McCuistion, February 5, 1947, box 515, folder 5491, GEBCC; GIS to Fred McCuistion, February 4, 1947, box 515, folder 5491, GEBC; GIS to Fred McCuistion, February 19, 1947, box 515, folder 5491, GEBC; Jackson Davis to Fred McCuistion, March 6, 1947, box 515, folder 5491, GEBC.

26. Fred McCuistion to GIS, February 28, 1947, box 515, folder 5491, GEBC; "Report of the Texas Trip of Trustees and Officers of the General Education Board, April 5–13, 1947," box 515, folder 5491, GEBC; GIS to Fred McCuistion, April 18, 1947, box 515, folder 5491, GEBC; Fred McCuistion to GIS, May 19, 1947, box 515, folder 5491, GEBC; W. Brierley to Theophilus Painter, June 19, 1947, box 515, folder 5491, GEBC; Theophilus Painter to W. Brierley, June 24, 1947, box 515, folder 5491, GEBCC; John Birch to GIS, May 27, 1947, box 8, folder 8, SP; GIS to John Birch, June 4, 1947, box 8, folder 8, SP; GIS to Robert Carr, November 8, 1947, box 3, folder 2, SP.

27. Sánchez, "Spanish-Speaking People in the Southwest: A Brief Historical Review," undated [likely sometime late in 1948 or early in 1949], box 515, folder 5494, GEBC, 4 (first and second quotations), 8 (third quotation).

28. Sánchez, "Study of Spanish-Speaking People," August 28, 1950, box 515, folder 5493, GEBC, 1–10; GEB Personal History Record and Application for Fellowship, Lyle Saunders, March 23, 1945, box 245, folder 2465, GEBC; GIS to Gus Garcia, March 18, 1948, box 16, folder 48, SP; GIS to Arthur Campa, October 1, 1951, box 9, folder 11, SP; GIS to Lyle Saunders, June 30, 1947, box 32, folder 5, SP; Lyle Saunders, "Tentative Outline for a Study of the Spanish-Speaking People of Texas," February 23, 1948, box 32, folder 5, SP; Saunders and Leonard, *Wetback in the Lower Rio Grande Valley*; Sánchez, *Concerning Segregation*.

29. Richardson, "Reds, Race, and Research," 162–63; Fred McCuistion to GIS, March 2, 1951, box 515, folder 5492, GEBC; Edouard Eller to Fred McCuistion, May 22, 1951, box 515, folder 5492, GEBC; Edouard Eller to Theophilus Painter, May 23, 1951, GEBC; Theophilus Painter to Edourd Eller, May 31, 1951, box 515, folder 5492, GEBC; Edouard Eller to GIS, July 26, 1951, box 515, folder 5492, GEBCC. For the Ford project, see MacDonald and Hoffman, "Compromising *La Causa*," 251–81.

30. GIS to Fred McCuistion, August 7, 1947, box 56, folder 2, SP (quotation); Fred Mc-Cuistion, internal memorandum, July 26, 1947, box 515, folder 5491; Robert Calkins, internal memorandum, September 4, 1947, box 515, folder 5491, GEBC; Theophilus Painter to GIS, August 23, 1947, box 515, folder 5491, GEBC; GIS to Theophilus Painter, August 20, 1947, box 515, folder 5491, GEBC; Robert Calkins, internal memorandum, September 10, 1948, box 515, folder 5491, GEBC.

31. Antonio Fernández to GIS, April 17, 1945, box 15, folder 15, SP; GIS to Antonio Fernández, April 21, 1945, box 15, folder 15, SP; Pedro Cebollero to GIS, May 5, 1945, box 10, folder 8, SP; Louis Montoya to Antonio Fernández, September 30, 1946, box 15, folder 15, SP; GIS to Antonio Fernández, October 11, 1946, box 15, folder 15, SP; GIS to Mariano Villaronga, December 9, 1946, box 61, folder 6, SP; GIS to Pedro Cebollero, January 14, 1949, box 10, folder 8, SP; Lewis Fraser to GIS, November 29, 1948, box 16, folder 9, SP; GIS to Lewis Fraser, December 3, 1948, box 16, folder 9, SP; GIS to Charles Arrowood, December 19, 1950, box 44, folder 15, SP; Millan Egert to GIS, December 11, 1950, box 44, folder 15, SP; GIS to Millan Egert, December 22, 1950, box 44, folder 15, SP; Luisa Sánchez to U.S. Civil Service Commission, February 21, 1949, box 11, folder 2, SP; Luisa Sánchez to Superintendent of Crockett Independent Schools, February 21, 1949, box 11, folder 2, SP; GIS to Lila Pfeufer, August 7, 1947,

box 29, folder 7, SP; Brice and Judy Sewall to GIS, September 25, 1947, box 32, folder 18, SP; Sprague interview; Kennedy interview.

32. Ruth Landes to GIS, October 27, 1947, box 22, folder 3, SP; GIS to Ruth Landes, November 25, 1947, box 22, folder 3, SP; Sprague interview; Kennedy interview; GIS to Lila Pfeufer, August 7, 1947, box 29, folder 7, SP; GIS to Rufus Sedillo, February 24, 1948, box 32, folder 12, SP; Telesforo Sánchez to GIS, February 24, 1948, box 31, folder 19, SP; GIS to Telesforo Sánchez, March 2, 1948, box 31, folder 19, SP.

33. Dudley Wynn to GIS, December 19, 1945, box 63, folder 4, SP; GIS to Dudley Wynn, December 31, 1945, box 63, folder 4, SP, 1–5; Dudley Wynn to GIS, January 4, 1946, box 63, folder 4, SP; GIS to Dudley Wynn, January 29, 1946, box 63, folder 4, SP; Dudley Wynn to GIS, February 1, 1946, box 63, folder 4, SP; GIS to Dudley Wynn, March 8, 1946, box 63, folder 4, SP.

34. George I. Sánchez to William Brophy, October 31, 1945, box 27, folder 8, SP; Willard Beatty to GIS, February 13, 1946, box 27, folder 8, SP; GIS to Willard Beatty, February 18, 1946, box 27, folder 8, SP; Willard Beatty to GIS, March 6, 1946, box 27, folder 8, SP; Willard Beatty to GIS, June 5, 1946, box 27, folder 8, SP; GIS to William Brophy, October 1, 1946, box 27, folder 8, SP; GIS to William Brophy, October 21, 1946, box 27, folder 8, SP; Willard Beatty to GIS, November 15, 1946, box 27, folder 8, SP; GIS to Willard Beatty, November 18, 1946, box 27, folder 8, SP; GIS to Fred Harvey, October 29, 1946, box 18, folder 20, SP; Fred Harvey to GIS, November 7, 1946, box 18, folder 20, SP; Fred Harvey to GIS, December 5, 1946, box 18, folder 20, SP; GIS to Fred Harvey, December 12, 1946, box 18, folder 20, SP; Ruth Kirk to Joaquin Ortega, November 24, 1946, box 27, folder 8, SP; Joaquin Ortega to GIS, November 27, 1946, box 27, folder 8, SP; GIS to Joaquin Ortega, December 3, 1946, box 27, folder 8, SP; GIS to Willard Beatty, December 3, 1946, box 27, folder 8, SP; Willard Beatty to GIS, December 6, 1946, box 27, folder 8, SP; GIS to George Boyce, December 11, 1946, box 27, folder 8, SP; George Boyce to GIS, December 12, 1946, box 27, folder 8, SP; GIS to Willard Beatty, December 16, 1946, box 27, folder 8, SP; GIS to Antonio Fernández, December 17, 1946, box 15, folder 15, SP; Ruth Kirk to GIS, December 16, 1946, box 21, folder 20, SP; Ruth Kirk to Antonio Fernández, December 16, 1946, box 21, folder 20, SP; GIS to Ruth Kirk, December 17, 1946, box 21, folder 20, SP.

35. William Zimmerman to GIS, January 10, 1947, box 27, folder 9, SP; GIS to William Zimmerman January 14, 1947, box 27, folder 9, SP; GIS to William Zimmerman February 19, 1947, box 27, folder 9, SP; William Zimmerman to GIS, February 27, 1947, box 27, folder 9, SP; Paul Sears to GIS, February 28, 1947, box 27, folder 9, SP; GIS to Willard Beatty, March 4, 1947, box 27, folder 9, SP; Willard Beatty to GIS, March 10, 1947, box 27, folder 9, SP; Willard Beatty to GIS, April 2, 1947, box 27, folder 9, SP; Sánchez, *"The People,"* 70 (quotation), 87; GIS to Willard Beatty, December 8, 1947, box 27, folder 9, SP; Willard Beatty to GIS, December 23, 1947, box 27, folder 9, SP; "Dr. Sánchez's Study Reveals Navajo Needs," April 25, 1948, *Daily Texan*, GISVF–UT; GIS to Antonio Fernández, September 23, 1948, box 15, folder 15, SP; GIS to Ruth Kirk, October 19, 1948, box 21, folder 20, SP; Ruth Kirk to GIS, October 26, 1948, box 21, folder 20, SP; GIS to Ruth Kirk, December 16, 1948, box 21, folder 20, SP.

CHAPTER 7. POLITICS AND THE MEXICAN
AMERICAN GENERATION

First epigraph. GIS to Lyle Saunders, November 11, 1952, box 32, folder 9, SP.
Second epigraph. Sánchez, "The Default of Leadership," 7.

1. Brown, *Richard Hofstadter*, xiv (quotations). For more on the liberal politics of Mexican
American Generation leaders in the 1940s and 1950s generally, see García, *Mexican
Americans*; García, *Viva Kennedy*.

2. GIS to Lyle Saunders, March 1, 1951, box 32, folder 8, SP (quotation); College of Education budget, July 26, 1945, box 60, folder 7, SP; College of Education Budget, July
20, 1946, box 60, folder 7, SP; College of Education Budget, July 24, 1948, box 60,
folder 7, SP; College of Education Budget, July 21, 1949, box 60, folder 7, SP; College
of Education Budget, June 8, 1950, box 60, folder 7, SP; GIS, annual report for 1950,
box 60, folder 4, SP; Maryvenice Stewart to GIS, March 17, 1951, box 60, folder 7, SP;
GIS Annual Reports for 1951, 1952, 1953 1954, 1955, 1959, box 60, folder 4, SP; GIS to
Pedro Cebollero, December 6, 1958, box 10, folder 8, SP; "Sunday Reception Will
Honor University Professor, Sánchez," March 13, 1960, *Daily Texan*, GISVF–UT;
GIS to Julian Samora, April 7, 1955, box 31, folder 21, SP; GIS to L. Haskew, June 3,
1952, box 50, folder 5, SP.

3. Leff, "George I. Sánchez," 481–86, 482 (first and second quotations); GIS to Freder-
ick Eby, June 17, 1955, box 45, folder 3, SP (remaining quotations); GIS to Logan
Wilson, February 20, 1956, box 43, folder 1, SP; GIS to William Drake, November 20,
1964, box 41, folder 18, SP; L. Haskew to GIS, November 18, 1958, box 43, folder 7, SP;
GIS to L. Haskew, November 21, 1958, box 43, folder 7, SP; GIS to Committee on
Graduate Studies in Education, undated [near September 20, 1960], box 50, folder 8
SP; L. Haskew to GIS, September 23, 1960, box 50, folder 8, SP; GIS to Harry Ran-
som, September 27, 1960, box 50, folder 8, SP; GIS to L. Haskew, September 27, 1960,
box 50, folder 8, SP; GIS to L. Haskew, October 6, 1960, box 50, folder 8, SP; GIS to
William Drake, October 6, 1960, box 50, folder 8, SP; Harry Ransom to GIS, October
5, 1960, box 50, folder 8, SP; GIS to Harry Ransom, October 11, 1960, box 50, folder 8,
SP; GIS to L. Haskew, October 20, 1960, box 50, folder 8, SP.

4. García, *Mexican Americans*, chap. 1.

5. E. Luna to GIS, August 15, 1956, box 22, folder 29 SP; GIS to E. Luna, August 21,
1956, box 22, folder 29, SP; Richard Nostrand to GIS, September 24, 1969, box 28,
folder 5, SP; GIS to Richard Nostrand, September 29, 1969, box 28, folder 5, SP (quotation); Orozco, *No Mexicans, Women, or Dogs*, 223. Sánchez further quipped to
Luna of Mexican Americans, "In English they are called by many names (some not
very complimentary!). But, as we say in Spanish, *Llámeme lo que me llamen; pero,
llámeme [a] comer* [Call me what you will; but call me for dinner]." He added, "Since
I am all of the things designated by the terms used for our people—Mexican,
Spanish-American, Latin-American, Mexican-American—all that I can say is that:
Call what you will, but smile when you call me that, podner!"

6. Gutiérrez, "Significant to Whom?," 526–27; Charles Marden to GIS, July 18, 1950, box
24, folder 7, SP; GIS to Charles Marden, July 25, 1950, box 24, folder 7, SP (quotation);

Marden, *Minorities in American Society*, 128–54; GIS to Julian Samora, February 20, 1952, box 31, folder 21, SP; Julian Samora, "Changing Patterns of Leadership Among the Spanish-speaking People," February 15, 1952, box 31, folder 21, SP.

7. GIS to Prudence Cutright, September 18, 1942, box 11, folder 18, SP; James Michener to Prudence Cutright, September 30, 1942, box 11, folder 18, SP; Prudence Cutright to GIS, October 2, 1942, box 11, folder 18, SP; Maurine Huffstutler to GIS, June 18, 1953, box 19, folder 16, SP (first quotation); GIS to Maurine Huffstutler, July 16, 1953, box 19, folder 16, SP (second quotation).

8. Sánchez, review of *North from Mexico*, 530–31; Ruth Morton to GIS, October 29, 1954, box 26, folder 4, SP; GIS to Ruth Morton, November 3, 1954, box 26, folder 4, SP; Allen Broyles to GIS, February 26, 1957, box 8, folder 14, SP; GIS to Allen Broyles, March 4, 1957, box 8, folder 14, SP; GIS to J. Rivera, March 31, 1960, box 31, folder 3, SP; GIS to Ralph Yarborough, March 4, 1964, box 22, folder 2, SP; Leo Resnick to GIS, March 5, 1964, box 22, folder 2, SP; John Flache to GIS, May 17, 1964, box 22, folder 2, SP; GIS to Ralph Yarborough, June 1, 1964, box 22, folder 2, SP; GIS to Frederick Redefer, March 8, 1957, box 30, folder 21, SP (quotations).

9. Orozco, "Regionalism, Politics, and Gender," 459–83; George J. Garza, "Founding and History of LULAC," *LULAC News* 21:8 (February 1954) (El Paso), 65–69; Carlos Castañeda to GIS, June 12, 1940, box 38, folder 3, CP; Sánchez, "Americanism" (quotation); GIS to Alonso Perales, April 30, 1931, box 2, folder 19, APP.

10. Jane Pijoan, "General Memorandum #2," April 18, 1946, box 2, folder 5, SP [old system]; Francisco Flores to GIS, October 16, 1945, box 22, folder 11, SP; Manuel Vela to GIS, May 31, 1948, box 61, folder 6, SP; GIS to Manuel Vela, June 4, 1948, box 61, folder 6, SP; "Editorial from Council 85," *LULAC News* 12:8 (February 1946) (Laredo) 5, 15; GIS to Arnulfo Zamora, May 21, 1948, box 63, folder 21, SP; Arnulfo Zamora to GIS, May 10, 1946, box 22, folder 12, SP; Arnulfo Zamora to GIS, April 26, 1948, box 63, folder 21, SP; GIS to Arnulfo Zamora, May 4, 1948, box 63, folder 21, SP.

11. GIS to Raoul Cortez, September 17, 1949, box 10, folder 19, SP; Gus Garcia to George Rundquist, March 3, 1949, box 16, folder 19, SP (quotation); Gus Garcia to GIS, March 4, 1949, box 16, folder 19, SP; Program to annual banquet, "1948 National Convention of the League of United Latin American Citizens, Austin, Texas," June 11, 1948, box 22, folder 11, SP; GIS to Henry Moreno, May 6, 1948, box 26, folder 4, SP; GIS to Harold Medina, February 25, 1954, box 24, folder 19, SP; Harold Medina to GIS, March 16, 1954, box 24, folder 19, SP; Arthur Campa to GIS, April 4, 1954, box 9, folder 12, SP; John Herrera to GIS, undated [likely early November 1950], box 19, folder 5, SP; John Herrera to GIS, November 8, 1950, box 19, folder 5, SP; "A History of Council 296 at the University of Texas," *LULAC News* (February 1957) (Houston); M. Gonzales to GIS, November 15, 1956, box 17, folder 11, SP; M. Gonzales to GIS, February 16, 1961, box 17, folder 11, SP.

12. John Herrera to GIS, June 18, 1951, box 19, folder 5, SP; Garza, "Founding and History of LULAC," *LULAC News* 21:8 (February 1954), (El Paso), 71, 76; Blanton, "The Citizenship Sacrifice," 318–19; Kreneck, *Mexican American Odyssey*, 203–8, 222–24.

13. Carroll, *Felix Longoria's Wake*, 35–53; Rosales, "Fighting the Peace at Home," 612–16; Hector Garcia to GIS, November 13, 1948, box 4, folder 9, SP; GIS to Hector Garcia, November 18, 1948, box 4, folder 9, SP. For more on AGIF, see Allsup, *American G.I. Forum*; Ramos, *The American G.I. Forum*; Carroll, *Felix Longoria's Wake*; I. García, *Hector P. Garcia*; Kells, *Hector P. Garcia*.

14. Hector Garcia to GIS, October 4, 1949, box 4, folder 9, SP; American G.I. Forum, resolutions September 26, 1949, box 4, folder 9, SP; GIS to Hector Garcia, October 7, 1949, box 4, folder 9, SP; Hector Garcia to GIS, October 10, 1949, box 4, folder 9, SP; GIS to Hector Garcia, October 18, 1949, box 4, folder 9, SP; Ed Edar to GIS, June 27, 1951, box 4, folder 11, SP; GIS to Ed Idar, June 29, 1951, box 4, folder 11, SP.

15. Ed Idar to Hector Garcia, August 24, 1953, box 214, folder 17, GP; Hector Garcia to Gus Garcia, box 4, folder 9, SP; "An Editorial," *Laredo Times*, March 14, 1951, box 4, folder 9, SP; Rogers Kelley, "On Blending of Heritages," *LULAC News* 23:6 (January 1956) (El Paso), 6, 20; Ed Idar, "Forum Objects to Speech," *LULAC News* 23:6 (January 1956) (El Paso), 9; Oscar Laurel, "Laurel Makes Statement," *LULAC News* 23:6 (January 1956) (El Paso), 9; Ramon Garces, "Editorial," *LULAC News* 23:6 (January 1956) (El Paso), 3; Arthur Campa to GIS, April 4, 1958, box 9, folder 12, SP; GIS to Arthur Campa, May 5, 1958, box 9, folder 12, SP; GIS to Hector Garcia, May 16, 1958, box 174, folder 2, GP; Ted Estrada to GIS, August 31, 1960, box 4, folder 10, SP; GIS, toast to Hector Garcia, undated [likely read at AGIF convention in September 1960], box 4, folder 10, SP; Hector Garcia to GIS, September 21, 1960, box 4, folder 10, SP; Hector Garcia to GIS, March 19, 1956, box 4, folder 10, SP; GIS to Hector Garcia, March 23, 1956, box 4, folder 10, SP.

16. LULAC Council No. 34 in Politics," *LULAC News* 5:9 (December 1938) (El Paso), 59–60; Manuel Luján to GIS, January 23, 1948, box 22, folder 28, SP; GIS to Manuel Luján, January 30, 1948, box 22, folder 28, SP; GIS to Manuel Luján, February 12, 1948, box 22, folder 28, SP; Manuel Luján to GIS, February 16, 1948, box 22, folder 28, SP; Manuel Luján to GIS, March 10, 1948, box 22, folder 28, SP; GIS to Manuel Luján, July 28, 1948, box 22, folder 28, SP; Manuel Luján to GIS, March 16, 1951, box 22, folder 28, SP; GIS to Tibo Chavez, June 18, 1952, box 5, folder 3, SP; GIS to Antonio Fernández, May 8, 1946, box 15, folder 15, SP, 1–2; GIS to Antonio Fernández, January 17, 1946, box 15, folder 15, SP; Antonio Fernández to GIS, January 22, 1946, box 15, folder 15, SP; GIS to Antonio Fernández, April 24, 1946, box 15, folder 15; Antonio Fernández to GIS, May 18, 1951, box 15, folder 15, SP; GIS to Antonio Fernández, June 11, 1951, box 15, folder 15, SP; Robert McConnell to GIS, November 20, 1956, box 24, folder 15, SP; Robert McConnell to GIS, January 4, 1957, box 24, folder 15, SP; Antonio Fernández to GIS, March 18, 1947, box 15, folder 15, SP; GIS to Antonio Fernández, March 24, 1947, box 15, folder 15, SP; Robert Cole to GIS, November 8, 1956, box 15, folder 15, SP; GIS to Mrs. Antonio Fernández, November 14, 1956, box 15, folder 15, SP; Joseph Julien to GIS, June 20, 1952, box 21, folder 1, SP; GIS to Joseph Julien, July 7, 1952, box 21, folder 1, SP; García, *Viva Kennedy*, 140–44; GIS to Homer Rainey, May 7, 1945, box 54, folder 13, SP; Homer Rainey to GIS, June 6, 1945, box 54, folder 13, SP; Green, *Establishment in Texas Politics*, 94–99.

17. GIS to Lyle Saunders, November 4, 1952, box 32, folder 9, SP; GIS to Newton Edwards, November 21, 1952, box 49, folder 6, SP (quotation); Lyle Saunders to GIS, November 8, 1952, box 32, folder 9, SP; GIS to Lyle Saunders, November 11, 1952, box 32, folder 9, SP; Green, *Establishment in Texas Politics*, 141–48, 162–65, 178–80; Pycior, *LBJ and Mexican Americans*, 91–93; Keith, *Eckhardt*, 115–21, 124–25; Cox, *Ralph W. Yarborough*, 100; Frankie Randolph to GIS, undated [September 1958], box 30, folder 19, SP; GIS to Frankie Randolph, box 30, folder 19, SP; GIS to Ronnie Dugger, August 18, 1959, box 34, folder 16, SP; Ronnie Dugger to GIS, February 21, 1963, box 34, folder 16, SP; GIS to Ronnie Dugger, February 28, 1963, box 34, folder 16, SP.

18. Ralph Yarborough to GIS, April 10, 1954, box 63, folder 10, SP; GIS to Ralph Yarborough, April 12, 1954, box 63, folder 10, SP (first quotation); Ralph Yarborough to GIS, April 19, 1954, box 63, folder 10, SP (second quotation); Ralph Yarborough to GIS, October 20, 1954, box 63, folder 10, SP. For more on the highly masculine rhetoric of Texas liberals of the era, see Lauchlan, "The Texas Liberal Press," 486–512.

19. GIS to Henry Gonzalez, May 9, 1958, box 17, folder 12, SP (quotation); "Wooldridge Is Rally Site of Gonzalez," *Austin American*, July 11, 1958, GISVF–UT.

20. Alan Brinkley, "Richard Hofstadter's *The Age of Reform*," in *American Retrospectives*, ed. Kutler, 58; Cheryl Greenberg, "Twentieth Century Liberalisms: Transformations of an Ideology," in *Perspectives on Modern America*, ed. Sitkoff, 72 (first quotation); Davies, *From Opportunity to Entitlement*, 32–34; Brown, *Richard Hofstadter*, 94–95; García, "Americans All," 279 (second quotation); Gutiérrez, *Walls and Mirrors*, 213–14.

21. Carey McWilliams to GIS, September 3, 1964, box 24, folder 18, SP; GIS to Carey McWilliams, "On the Centennial of *The Nation*," undated [September 1964], box 24, folder 18, SP (quotation); Brown, *Richard Hofstadter*, 136–37; Harl Douglass to GIS, October 11, 1954, box 40, folder 2, SP; GIS to Harl Douglass, October 14, 1954, box 40, folder 2, SP; Berry, *Interest Group Society*, 8–12.

22. Sánchez, "The Default of Leadership," 7 (quotation); H. Mitchell to GIS, October 25, 1949, box 25, folder 13, SP; Erie Dasuael to GIS, November 17, 1952, box 12, folder 1, SP; GIS to Erie Dasuael, November 21, 1952, box 12, folder 1, SP; GIS to Price Daniel, December 8, 1948, box 12, folder 3, SP; Price Daniel to GIS, January 6, 1949, box 12, folder 3, SP; Adelfa Guerrero to GIS, September 16, 1953, box 18, folder 13, SP; Texas AFL-CIO, "Texas AFL-CIO Summer Citizenship Conference at St. Edward's University," June 14–28, 1965, box 14, folder 10, SP; GIS speaking engagements, July 1955 to December 1956, undated, box 13, folder 3, SP.

23. Maury Maverick to Hector Garcia, September 9, 1954, box 6, folder 4, SP (quotation); Green, *Establishment in Texas Politics*, 110–11, 140–41; GIS, "Address to Texas Good Neighbor Commission—Austin, March 26, 1948," box 17, folder 15, SP, 1–6; Neville Penrose to GIS, November 7, 1950, box 34, folder 7, SP; GIS to Nevill G. Penrose, December 15, 1950, box 34, folder 7, SP; GIS to Theophilus Painter, January 15, 1951, box 34, folder 7, SP; Theophilus Painter to Robert Smith, January 17, 1951, box 34, folder 7, SP; Ross Clinchy to GIS, May 29, 1953, box 10, folder 17, SP; GIS to Ross Clinchy, June 9, 1953, box 10, folder 17, SP.

24. Robert Carr to GIS, April 29, 1947, box 3, folder 2, SP; GIS to Robert Carr, May 6, 1947, box 3, folder 2, SP (quotation); Robert Carr to GIS, May 14, 1947, box 3, folder 2, SP.

25. GIS to *LIFE* editors, April 13, 1959, box 22, folder 20, SP (first two quotations), 2; Mary Frere to GIS, May 7, 1959, box 22, folder 20, SP; GIS to Mary Frere, May 13, 1959, box 22, folder 20, SP (remaining quotations); GIS to *LIFE*, May 18, 1959, box 22, folder 20, SP; Mary Frere to GIS, June 24, 1959, box 22, folder 20, SP; GIS to *LIFE*, September 4, 1959, box 22, folder 20, SP; Mary Frere to GIS, October 6, 1959, box 22, folder 20, SP; GIS to Lloyd Cook, August 4, 1947, box 10, folder 21, SP, 1–2.

26. Dugger, *Our Invaded Universities*, 118 (quotation). See also GIS to Ronnie Dugger, October 21, 1971, box 34, folder 16, SP. In chapter 11 I present a fuller analysis of these dollar estimations by Sánchez about his lost salary.

27. Henry Gonzalez to GIS, May 7, 1958, box 17, folder 12, SP; GIS to Henry Gonzalez, May 9, 1958, box 17, folder 12, SP (first quotation); GIS to James de Anda, November 8, 1956, box 12, folder 6, SP (remaining quotations). Sánchez ended his letter by including an off-color Spanish saying: "Pobre del pobre que al cielo no va—Lo joden aquí y lo chingan allá" (How poor are the poor who cannot get to Heaven—they get fucked there the way they get screwed here).

28. Leff, "George I. Sánchez," 484–86; GIS to Leo Crespi, February 15, 1949, box 11, folder 12, SP; GIS to L. Haskew, June 3, 1952, box 50, folder 5, SP; GIS to Harry Ransom, box 55, folder 11, SP; History and Philosophy of Education Budget for 1949–50 and 1950–51, June 8, 1950, box 60, folder 7; Arthur Holt to GIS, June 16, 1950, box 50, folder 9, SP; Maryvenice Stewart to GIS, July 19, 1951, box 50, folder 9, SP; Maryvenice Stewart to GIS, June 5, 1952, box 50, folder 9, SP; Maryvenice Stewart to GIS, July 10, 1953, box 50, folder 9, SP; Maryvenice Stewart to GIS, May 17, 1954, box 50, folder 9, SP; Betty Thedford to GIS, July 11, 1955, box 50, folder 9, SP; Betty Thedford to GIS, July 1, 1957, box 50, folder 9, SP; Betty Thedford to GIS, August 18, 1959, box 50, folder 9, SP.

29. GIS to L. Haskew, May 26, 1954, box 44, folder 13, SP; GIS to Logan Wilson, June 5, 1954, box 55, folder 1, SP; Budget Council of the Department of History and Philosophy of Education to L. Haskew, C. Boner, and Logan Wilson, undated [May or June 1954], box 55, folder 1, SP; "Statement Prepared by Professor Eby—Reference to Professor Sánchez Concurred in by Professors Moehlman and Wegener," undated [May or June 1954], box 55, folder 1, SP (quotation); Ed Idar to L. Haskew, July 6, 1955, box 50, folder 7, SP.

30. GIS to Logan Wilson, February 20, 1956, box 43, folder 1, SP; GIS to Harry Ransom, undated [likely late spring 1959], box 55, folder 11, SP (quotation); GIS to Harry Ransom, August 21, 1959, box 55, folder 11, SP.

31. GIS to W. Keeton, August 26, 1955, box 44, folder 13, SP; GIS, Complaint to Committee of Counsel on Academic Freedom and Responsibility, August 26, 1955, box 44, folder 13, SP, 1–23.

32. W. Keeton to GIS, September 2, 1955, box 44, folder 13, SP; Clarence Ayres to Committee of Counsel on Academic Freedom and Responsibility, undated [likely November 1955], box 44, folder 14, SP; Clarence Ayres to GIS, December 20, 1955, box 44, folder 13, SP; GIS to Clarence Ayres, January 17, 1956, box 44, folder 14, SP.

33. GIS to Clarence Ayres, May 15, 1956, box 43, folder 1, SP; "Council Ruling Hit by Sánchez," *Daily Texan*, May 9, 1956, GISVF–UT; GIS, speech to faculty, May 8, 1956, box 43, folder 1, SP; Committee of Counsel on Academic Freedom and Responsibility to GIS May 21, 1956, box 44, folder 14, SP.

34. Gruber, *Mars and Minerva*, 210–12; Berg, "Black Civil Rights and Liberal Anticommunism," 96.
35. Ed Idar to Jack Danciger, October 27, 1953, box 12, folder 2, SP; Ed Idar to Editor, *Austin American*, October 27, 1953, box 12, folder 2, SP; GIS to Jack Danciger, October 28, 1953, box 12, folder 2, SP; Nicholas Nonnenmacher to GIS, September 10, 1952, box 3, folder 5, SP; GIS to Nicholas Nonnenmacher, September 17, 1952, box 3, folder 5, SP; GIS to Fred Okrand, October 15, 1952, box 3, folder 5, SP; Ed Idar to Nicholas Nonnenmacher, October 16, 1952, box 3, folder 9, SP; Ed Idar to G. Moody, October 16, 1952, box 3, folder 9, SP; Nicholas Nonnenmacher, editorial, October 1, 1952, *Firing Line*, box 3, folder 9, SP (quotations).
36. GIS to Nicholas Nonnenmacher, September 17, 1952, box 3, folder 5, SP (quotations); Berg, "Black Civil Rights and Liberal Anticommunism, 75–96; Fred Okrand to GIS, September 26, 1952, box 28, folder 18, SP; GIS to Fred Okrand, October 15, 1952, box 3, folder 5, SP; A. Wirin to GIS, October 20, 1952, box 62, folder 17, SP; Fred Okrand to GIS, October 23, 1952, box 28, folder 18, SP; Fred Okrand to GIS, November 18, 1952, box 28, folder 18, SP; GIS to Fred Okrand, December 6, 1952, box 28, folder 18, SP; GIS to Fred Okrand, December 16, 1952, box 28, folder 18, SP; Fred Okrand to GIS, December 18, 1952, box 28, folder 18, SP; Fred Okrand to GIS, February 6, 1953, box 28, folder 18, SP; GIS to Fred Okrand, March 26, 1953, box 28, folder 18, SP.
37. "'Prove Charges, Sen. McCarthy,' Sánchez Urges: UT Teachers Says an Accused Person Can't Clear Himself," *Daily Texan*, April 22, 1953, GISVF–UT; J. Haley, "At the request of the Governor of Texas," [undated, sent to the University of Texas in February 1953], box 55, folder 1, SP; Logan Wilson, "Memorandum RE Institute of Americanism Questionnaire," February 19, 1953, box 55, folder 1, SP; GIS to J. Haley, February 25, 1953, box 55, folder 1, SP; Green, *Establishment in Texas Politics*, 174–75, 185.
38. Sánchez, "All the Things that I Am Not," undated [likely from the early 1960s], box 68, folder 3, SP (quotations); Dugger, *Our Invaded Universities*, 64–67.

CHAPTER 8. MEXICAN AMERICANS AND THE IMMIGRATION ISSUE

First epigraph. Sánchez and Saunders, *"Wetbacks"—A Preliminary Report*, June 12, 1949, box 515, folder 5494, GEBC, 3.
Second epigraph. GIS to Ruth Wasson, March 8, 1955, box 62, folder 1.
1. Gutiérrez, *Walls and Mirrors*; García, *Mexican Americans*, 52–53; Zamora, *Claiming Rights and Righting Wrongs*, 221–22; Blanton, "The Citizenship Sacrifice," 299–320; Samora, ed., *Los Mojados*, 46–47. This chapter employs the terms *undocumented* and *immigrant*. I use the offensive terms *mojado* and *wetback* only as they appear in quoted sources or titles. I will not employ variations of the term *illegal*, though this is trickier, as it is common in scholarship. Mae W. Ngai's *Impossible Subjects: Illegal Aliens and the Making of Modern America*, for example, is an outstanding, award-winning study. My reasons are personal. I do not believe any human beings are inherently illegal or that the migration of peoples seeking better lives deserves classification on par with assault and murder. I believe common use of *illegal* in dis-

cussing immigration desensitizes us to the fact that exploitation occurs regularly and undergirds our national affluence. Nevertheless, there are good administrative, juridical, and vernacular reasons to use *illegal*. And I acknowledge my own perspective may not seem at all persuasive or even relevant. I note, however, that as of the spring of 2013 journalistic outlets such as the Associated Press have abandoned use of the term *illegal* in their immigration reporting.

2. Martínez, "Immigration and the Meaning of United States Citizenship," 335–44; Vargas, *Labor Rights Are Civil Rights*, 278–79; Curriculum vitae for GIS from 1948 to 1954, undated, box 1, folder 6, SP; J. Burks memorandum, April 30, 1948, box 515, folder 5492, GEBC; Lyle Saunders to Fred McCuistion, June 10, 1948, box 515, folder 5492, GEBC; Fred McCuistion, memorandum, January 25, 1949, box 515, folder 5492, GEBC; GIS to Fred McCuistion, February 16, 1949, box 515, folder 5492, GEBC; GIS to Fred McCuistion, February 21, 1951, box 515, folder 5492, GEBC; J. Burks memorandum, December 8, 1952, box 515, folder 5492, GEBC; John Birch to GIS, May 27, 1947, box 8, folder 8, SP; John Birch, "The Spanish Speaking People in the United States," May 14, 1947, box 8, folder 8, SP, 1–7.

3. Arthur Campa to GIS, April 26, 1947, box 9, folder 10, SP; Lyle Saunders to Robert Calkins, July 21, 1948, box 515, folder 5492, GEBC; GIS to Fred McCuistion, February 16, 1949, box 515, folder 5492, GEBC; GIS to Robert Sutherland, December 5, 1947, box 52, folder 10, SP; GIS to Arthur Campa, January 26, 1948, box 9, folder 10, SP; Stewart Cole to GIS, April 11, 1950, box 10, folder 20, SP; "Saturday Banquet to Honor Dr. Sánchez," *Daily Texan*, April 24, 1950, GISVF–UT; "Problems of Texas Latinos Under Study," *Austin Statesman*, June 27, 1950, GISVF–UT; William Keys to GIS, December 17, 1958, box 21, folder 11, SP; Beauford Jester to GIS, September 30, 1948, box 20, folder 13, SP; GIS to Beauford Jester, October 5, 1948, box 20, folder 13, SP; Irving Melbo to GIS, undated [late August or early September], 1947, box 24, folder 21, SP; Irving Melbo to GIS, September 15, 1947, box 24, folder 21, SP; GIS to Irving Melbo, October 17, 1947, box 24, folder 21, SP.

4. García, *Operation Wetback*, 140–41; Dobbs, *Yellow Dogs and Republicans*, 55–58; Keith, *Eckhardt*, 84; Jay Stilley to Texas Ginners, Bulletin no. 45 on "Mexican Labor Situation," June 29, 1948, box 33, folder 12, SP; Lois Sager, "Action, Not Promises, Necessary on Mexican Labor, Expert Says," *Dallas Morning News*, July 22, 1948, 6, box 33, folder 12, SP; GIS to Antonio Fernández, December 13, 1948, box 15, folder 15, SP; GIS to Ralph Yarborough, April 12, 1954, box 63, folder 10, SP; Ralph Yarborough to GIS, April 19, 1954, box 63, folder 10, SP.

5. Cortez, "A Monthly Message from the President General," *LULAC News* 15:5 (February 1949) (San Antonio); Raoul Cortez, memorandum to LULAC, October 18, 1948, box 22, folder 12, SP; GIS to Antonio Fernández, November 4, 1948, box 15, folder 15, SP; Antonio Fernández to GIS, November 8, 1948, box 15, folder 15, SP; GIS to Antonio Fernández, October 23, 1948, box 15, folder 15, SP; GIS to Antonio Fernández, December 13, 1948, box 15, folder 15, SP; telegram, Antonio Fernández to GIS, December 9, 1948, box 5, folder 6, SP; telegram, Antonio Fernández to GIS, December 10, 1948, box 5, folder 6, SP; GIS to Antonio Fernández, December 9, 1948, box 5, folder 6, SP.

6. GIS to John Steelman, January 23, 1949, box 62, folder 4, SP (first quotation); Raoul Cortez, Gus Garcia, and Sánchez, "The 'Wetback' Problem of the Southwest," January 27, 1949, box 515, folder 5492, GEBC, 3 (second quotation); "Editorial," *LULAC News* 16:4 (April 1950) (San Antonio).

7. Samora, *Los Mojados*, 18–20, 47 (first quotation), 48 (second quotation); Matusow, *Farm Policies and Politics*, 118–19; GIS to Antonio Fernández, December 13, 1948, box 15, folder 15, SP; GIS to Serafino Romauldi, February 23, 1949, box 62, folder 4, SP; Serafino Romauldi to GIS, March 18, 1949, box 62, folder 4, SP; H. Mitchell, July 26, 1949, box 62, folder 4, SP; GIS to H. Mitchell, September 20, 1949, box 62, folder 4, SP (third quotation).

8. GIS and Lyle Saunders, *"Wetbacks"—A Preliminary Report*, June 12, 1949, 9 (first quotation), 1 (second quotation), box 515, folder 5494, GEBC.

9. Hector Garcia to GIS, June 18, 1949, box 4, folder 9, SP; GIS to Hector Garcia, June 20, 1949, box 4, folder 9, SP; Dick Elam, "Stop Wetback Flow, Texans Warned," *Summer Texan*, June 12, 1949, GISVF–UT (first quotation); "Facts, Not Propaganda," *Valley Evening Monitor*, June 14, 1949, box 4, folder 9, SP; "25 Cents Per Day? Report on Abusing Webacks Called 'Lie' by Washmon," *Valley Evening Monitor*, June 14, 1949, box 4, folder 9, SP (remaining quotations); GIS to Gus Garcia, July 12, 1949, box 16, folder 19, SP; Gus Garcia to GIS, July 21, 1949, box 16, folder 19, SP; Ngai, *Impossible Subjects*, 236–39; Raymond Brooks, "Isolate Problems First, Relations Group Advised," *Austin American*, January 28, 1950, GISVF–UT; Raymond Brooks, "Human Relations Council Outlines Work Objectives," *Austin American*, June 27, 1950, GISVF–UT; "Dr. G. I. Sánchez Appointed to Human Relations Council," *Daily Texan*, May 9, 1950, GISVF–UT; Martha Cole, "Texans Make Good Neighbors to Fight Red Propaganda," *San Antonio Express*, September 24, 1950, box 5, folder 2, JSP; Roy Roddy, "Bracero Troubles Traced to Lulacs," *Dallas News*, October 19, 1951, LULACVF; "Article Raps Texas' Treatment of Latins," *Valley Evening Monitor*, March 12, 1951, box 4, folder 10, JSP; GIS to H. Mitchell, July 7, 1949, box 62, folder 4, SP; GIS to Robert Jones, December 19, 1950, box 21, folder 2, SP; GIS to Carey McWilliams, July 8, 1949, box 24, folder 18, SP.

10. Thomas Sutherland, "Texas Tackles the Race Problem," *Saturday Evening Post*, January 12, 1952, box 215, folder 4, GP; Keith Davis to GIS, March 14, 1951, box 12, folder 1, SP; GIS to Keith Davis, March 16, 1951, box 12, folder 1, SP; "Lulac President Hits Reports on Latin-American Status," *San Antonio Express*, March 15, 1951, box 4, folder 10, JSP; "National LULAC President's Outburst Over 'Look' Article Ridiculous," *La Verdad*, March 23, 1951, box 4, folder 10, JSP, 1; "'Post' Article by Texan Explains State's Race Relations Progress," *Daily Texan*, January 11, 1952, GISVF–UT; GIS to Lyle Saunders, April 4, 1951, box 32, folder 8, SP; Lyle Saunders to GIS, April 6, 1951, box 32, folder 8, SP; Gladwin Hill to GIS, March 30, 1951, box 19, folder 7, SP; Gladwin Hill to GIS, April 14, 1951, box 19, folder 7, SP; GIS to Gladwin Hill, April 26, 1951, box 19, folder 7, SP, Gladwin Hill to GIS, April 24, 1951, box 19, folder 7, SP; Gladwyn Hill, "Million a Year Flee Mexico Only to Find Peonage Here," *New York Times*, March 25, 1951; Gladwyn Hill, "Peons Net Farmer a Fabulous Profit," *New York Times*, March 26, 1951; Gladwyn Hill, "Peons in the West Lowering Culture,"

New York Times, March 27, 1951; Gladwyn Hill, "Southwest Winks at 'Wetback' Jobs," *New York Times*, March 28, 1951; Gladwyn Hill, "Interests Conflict on 'Wetback' Cure," *New York Times*, March 29, 1951; Lyle Saunders to GIS, April 12, 1950, box 32, folder 7, SP; GIS to Lyle Saunders, April 28, 1950, box 32, folder 7, SP; Lyle Saunders to GIS, May 2, 1951, box 32, folder 8, SP; GIS to Lyle Saunders, July 5, 1951, box 32, folder 8, SP; Saunders and Leonard, *Wetback in the Lower Rio Grande Valley*, 3, 17, 20, 22–25, 38, 43, 48, 54–55, 70, 72, 83. For more on this controversy, see Blanton, "The Citizenship Sacrifice," 299–320.

11. Saunders and Leonard, *Wetback in the Lower Rio Grande Valley*, 66–70.

12. GIS to Lyle Saunders, October 24, 1951, box 32, folder 8, SP; GIS to Lyle Saunders, October 30, 1951, box 32, folder 8, SP; Lyle Saunders to GIS, October 29, 1951, box 32, folder 8, SP (first quotation); Lyle Saunders to GIS, October 30, 1951, box 32, folder 8, SP; GIS, November 2, 1951, box 32, folder 8, SP; Harry Crozier to Hilton Richardson, November 15, 1951, box 62, folder 8, SP; Ed Idar to Harry Crozier, November 20, 1951, box 63, folder 8, SP; Lyle Saunders to GIS, November 1, 1951, box 32, folder 8, SP; GIS to Lyle Saunders, November 2, 1951, box 32, folder 8, SP; Menton Murray to GIS, November 6, 1951, box 32, folder 8, SP; GIS to Lyle Saunders, November 9, 1951, box 32, folder 8, SP; Lyle Saunders to GIS, box 32, folder 8, SP; GIS to Joe Kilgore, telegram, November 2, 1951, box 63, folder 8, SP; Rogers Kelley to GIS, September 22, 1950, box 21, folder 11, SP; GIS to Lyle Saunders, November 2, 1951, box 32, folder 8, SP; GIS to Lyle Saunders, November 9, 1951, box 32, folder 8, SP; GIS to Rogers Kelley, November 9, 1951, box 32, folder 8, SP; Lyle Saunders to GIS, November 13, 1951, box 32, folder 8, SP; GIS to Lyle Saunders, November 27, 1951, box 32, folder 8, SP; Lyle Saunders to GIS, undated [possibly from November or December 1951], box 32, folder 9, SP; Idar interview, October 24, 1991, box 6, tape 9, IP; Rogers Kelley to GIS, November 16, 1951, box 62, folder 8, SP; Rogers Kelley, "Statement of Rogers Kelley," November 15, 1951, box 62, folder 8, SP (second quotation). Saunders eventually affirmed Kelley's identity to Sánchez, and decades later Idar confirmed it in an interview.

13. Alonso Perales to GIS, December 3, 1951, box 62, folder 8, SP; GIS to Alonso Perales, December 5, 1951, box 62, folder 8, SP (quotation); Alonso Perales to GIS [undated, likely from December 1951], box 62, folder 8, SP.

14. Alonso Perales to J. Luz Sáenz, May 9, 1946, box 2, folder 1, JSP; Alonso Perales, "Un Decidido Defensor de Nuestra Raza en Texas en 1859," *La Prensa*, December 2, 1951, box 5, folder 17, JSP; Alonso Perales, "En Defensa de mi Raza," *La Prensa*, December 9, 1951, 8; Alonso Perales, "¿Elogios Para Los Que Injurian a los Mexicanos?," *La Prensa*, December 16, 1951; Alonso S. Perales to J. Sáenz, November 21, 1951, box 2, folder 1, JSP; Alonso Perales to J. Sáenz, November 30, 1951, box 2, folder 1, JSP; Alonso Perales to J. Luz Sáenz, December 4, 1951, box 2, folder 1, JSP; Ed Idar to Lyle Saunders, December 12, 1951, box 32, folder 8, SP; Martínez, "Alonso S. Perales and the Effort to Establish the Civil Rights of Mexican Americans as Seen through the Lens of Contemporary Critical Legal Theory," in *In Defense of My People*, ed. Olivas, 124–27. See Perales, ed., *Are We Good Neighbors?*

15. Saunders and Leonard, *Wetback in the Lower Rio Grande*, 66; Lyle Saunders to GIS, November 13, 1951, box 32, folder 8, SP; GIS to Lyle Saunders, November 27,

1951, box 32, folder 8, SP; Lyle Saunders to GIS, December 14, 1951, box 32, folder 8, SP; Lyle Saunders to GIS, undated [likely from November or December 1951], box 32, folder 8, SP.

16. J. Canales to J. Sáenz, March 6, 1952, box 1, folder 11, JSP; J. Sáenz, essay draft, November 17, 1951, box 3, folder 10, JSP; "Honorosa Distinción y Horrible Contraste . . . ," *La Verdad*, December 14, 1951; Santos de la Paz, "Editor Attacks Censoriousness of Wet-Back Pamphlet's Distribution in Texas," *La Verdad*, December 28, 1951; J. Sáenz, *El Mañana*, May 11, 1952 (Reynosa, Mexico), box 7, scrapbook A, JSP; "El Lic. Raymond Censura el Folleto 'Los Mojados,'" *La Prensa*, December 13, 1951; "Filling's," January 25, 1952, *La Verdad*; Leo Duran to J. Sáenz, box 1, folder 11, JSP.

17. Garcilazo, "McCarthyism, Mexican Americans," 295; J. Sáenz to J. Canales, April 2, 1952, box 1, folder 11, JSP; J. Canales to Ed Idar, January 18, 1952, box 215, folder 4, GP; "Filling's," *La Verdad*, January 18, 1952, CAH (first quotation); "Filling's," *La Verdad*, December 21, 1951, CAH; "Fillings," *La Verdad*, December 28, 1951; "Posiblemente Una Investigación del F.B.I. a Los Simpatizadores del Folleto," *La Verdad*, March 14, 1952; Santos de la Paz, R. E. Austin, Luis Alvarado, and O. T. Salinas, resolutions of the Mission meeting of March 9, 1952, box 4, folder 2, JSP (second quotation).

18. Lyle Saunders to GIS, December 14, 1951, box 32, folder 8, SP; GIS to Lyle Saunders, February 25, 1952, box 32, folder 9, SP; George Garza to GIS, January 14, 1952, box 16, folder 22, SP (quotation); GIS to George Garza, January 31, 1952, box 16, folder 22, SP; AGIF, "Resolution," undated [likely December 1951 or shortly afterward in 1952], box 44, folder 11, SP; AGIF, "Resolutions Adopted," December 9, 1951, box 4, folder 1, JSP; "University Praised by GI Forum Board," *Daily Texan*, December 11, 1951, GISVF–UT; Hector Garcia to AGIF, "Important," undated [likely December 1951], box 173, folder 33, GP.

19. Hector Garcia to Editor of *La Prensa*, December 13, 1951, box 214, folder 16, GP; Hector Garcia to GIS, December 31, 1951, box 4, folder 9, SP; GIS to Hector Garcia, December 20, 1951, box 214, folder 15, GP (first and second quotations); "Study Attack Draws Retorts," *San Antonio Light*, December 9, 1951, GISVF–UT; Ed Idar to GIS, January 14, 1952, box 4, folder 11, SP; GIS to Ed Idar, January 18, 1952, box 4, folder 11, SP (third quotation).

20. Sánchez, "Spanish-Speaking People," 111; Green, *Establishment in Texas Politics*, 140–41; Dobbs, *Yellow Dogs and Republicans*, 56–57; GIS, October 12, 1950, box 224, folder 13, GP; GIS to Fred McCuistion, February 21, 1951, box 56, folder 5, SP; Theophilus Painter to GIS, April 30, 1951, box 34, folder 8, SP; GIS to Theophilus Painter, June 20, 1951, box 34, folder 9, SP; Theophilus Painter to GIS, June 27, 1951, box 34, folder 9, SP; Thomas Sutherland to Robert Smith, August 1, 1951, box 34, folder 9, SP; Robert Smith to GIS, November 29, 1951, box 34, folder 9, SP; Ed Idar to GIS, May 9, 1952, box 34, folder 10, SP; Ed Idar to Allan Shivers, May 8, 1952, box 34, folder 10, SP; Robert Smith to GIS, May 20, 1952, box 34, folder 10, SP; GIS to Robert Smith, May 22, 1952, box 34, folder 10, SP; Robert E. Smith to GIS, May 23, 1952, box 34, folder 10, SP; GIS to Robert Smith, June 18, 1952, box 34, folder 10, SP; GIS to Allan Shivers, June 30, 1952, box 34, folder 10, SP; "Resignation of Sánchez May Wreck Human Relations Council's Program," *Valley Evening Monitor*, July 6, 1952, box 7, scrapbook A, JSP.

21. Antonio Fernández to GIS, June 28, 1951, box 15, folder 15, SP; GIS to Antonio Fernández, July 5 1951, box 15, folder 15, SP; Antonio Fernández to GIS, February 6, 1952, box 15, folder 15, SP; GIS to Antonio Fernández, February 20, 1952, box 15, folder 15, SP; Antonio Fernández to GIS, February 23, 1952, box 15, folder 15, SP; GIS to Antonio Fernández, February 27, 1952, box 15, folder 15, SP; GIS to Antonio Fernández, March 4, 1952, box 15, folder 15, SP.

22. Hernández, "The Crimes and Consequences of Illegal Immigration," 421–22; "Wetback Round-Up Needs Support of LULAC," *LULAC News* 22:1 (July 1954) (El Paso); "Editorial," *LULAC News* 22:2 (August 1954) (El Paso); Idar and McLellan, *What Price Wetbacks?*; Joseph Robison to GIS, June 30, 1955, box 31, folder 5, SP; GIS to Joseph Robison, July 7, 1955, box 31, folder 5, SP; Gutiérrez, *Walls and Mirrors*, 178.

23. Kreneck, *Mexican American Odyssey*, 155–60; A. Wirin to James Marshall, September 2, 1954, box 62, folder 19, SP; GIS to A. Wirin, December 11, 1953, box 62, folder 9, SP; *Galvan v. Press*, 347 U.S. 522 (1954); *Garcia v. Landon*, 348 U.S. 866 (1954); GIS to Simon Gross, April 3, 1952, box 31, folder 6, SP.

24. GIS to National Council on Naturalization and Citizenship, March 8, 1954, box 27, folder 1, SP (first and second quotations); Sonia Smick to GIS, April 13, 1954, box 27, folder 1, SP; Albert Murphy to GIS, June 30, 1954, box 27, folder 1, SP; John Humphrey to GIS, April 21, 1950, box 35, folder 16, SP; GIS to John Humphrey, May 3, 1950, box 35, folder 16, SP (final quotation).

25. Joseph Reid to GIS, October 28, 1953, box 31, folder 1, SP; GIS to Joseph Reid, December 11, 1953, box 31, folder 1, SP; Hortencia Holguin to Joseph Reid, December 11, 1953, box 31, folder 1, SP; GIS to John Holland, November 9, 1954, box 17, folder 11, SP; (first quotation); GIS to M. Gonzales, December 12, 1954, box 17, folder 11, SP; GIS to M. Gonzales, January 7, 1955, box 17, folder 11, SP (second quotation); M. Gonzales to GIS, January 17, 1955, box 17, folder 11, SP; Ruth Wasson to GIS, March 4, 1955, box 62, folder 1, SP; GIS to Ruth Wasson, March 8, 1955, box 62, folder 1, SP.

26. GIS to Irving Melbo, August 25, 1947, box 24, folder 21, SP; GIS to Newton Edwards, March 8, 1954, box 49, folder 6, SP; Newton Edwards to GIS, March 12, 1954, box 49, folder 6, SP; GIS to James Umstattd, March 16, 1954, box 5, folder 5, SP [old system]; Luisa Sánchez, "The 'Latin American' of the Southwest."

27. GIS to A. Wirin, September 12, 1955, box 63, folder 1, SP; A. Wirin to GIS, October 12, 1955, box 63, folder 1, SP; GIS to A. Wirin, October 17, 1955, box 63, folder 1, SP (first quotation); A. Wirin to GIS, November 15, 1955, box 63, folder 1, SP; Dorothy Carpenter to GIS, January 9, 1965, box 9, folder 18, SP; GIS to Dorothy Carpenter, January 15, 1965, box 9, folder 18, SP; GIS to Eva Borrego, November 14, 1955, box 5, folder 2, SP; GIS to Clarice Whittenburg, November 29, 1955, box 62, folder 11, SP; GIS to Arthur Campa, August 24, 1956, box 9, folder 12, SP; Arthur Campa to GIS, August 31, 1956, box 9, folder 12, SP; GIS to Keats McKinney, November 17, 1961, box 2, folder 5, SP (second quotation).

28. *Sánchez v. Sánchez*, November 17, 23, December 6, 1951, BC.

29. *Sánchez v. Sánchez*, January 18, 1952, BC.

30. *Sánchez v. Sánchez,* February 7, March 25, April 2, 1952, BC. The evidence included Sánchez's letter to Connie of November 9, 1951 (second quotation) and E. Brentan's to the court of March 27, 1952 (first quotation).
31. *Sánchez v. Sánchez,* November 7, 22, 1946; GIS Memorandum of Cash Contributions, undated [probably January–April 1952], BC.
32. *Sánchez v. Sánchez,* April 18, 1952, November 9, 1956, BC.
33. GIS to Tibo J. Chavez, June 18, 1952, box 10, folder 12, SP.

CHAPTER 9. SEGREGATED SCHOOLS AND
PERCEPTIONS OF INEQUALITY

First epigraph. Sánchez, "Concerning American Minorities," *Proceedings, Fifth Annual Conference, SWCESSP, George Pepperdine College, Los Angeles, California, January 18–20, 1951,* box 57, folder 8, SP, 54.

Second epigraph. Sánchez, "Pre-School for All," *Texas Observer,* September 4, 1959, 7.

1. Sánchez, "History, Culture, and Education," 18; GIS to M. Gonzales, April 25, 1945, box 31, folder 20, SP (quotation). For educational histories, see San Miguel, *"Let All of Them Take Heed";* Gonzalez, *Chicano Education in the Era of Segregation;* Blanton, *Strange Career of Bilingual Education;* MacDonald, *Latino Education in the United States.* For how schools continue to fail Chicanas/os and Latina/o immigrants, see Valenzuela, *Subtractive Schooling;* Valenzuela, ed., *Leaving Children Behind;* Valencia, *Chicano School Failure and Success.*
2. Blanton, "A Legacy of Neglect," 22 (quotation).
3. GIS to Research Council, May 13, 1946, box 51, folder 10, SP; Charles Arrowood to GIS, May 28, 1946, box 51, folder 10, SP; GIS to Charles Arrowood, May 29, 1946, box 51, folder 10, SP; A. Brogan to GIS, July 20, 1946, box 59, folder 8, SP; Betty Thedford to GIS, September 15, 1946, box 59, folder 8, SP; A. Brogan to GIS, May 9, 1947, box 59, folder 8, SP; GIS to A. Brogan, September 25, 1947, box 51, folder 10, SP; GIS to Fred McCuistion, January 30, 1947, box 56, folder 2, SP; GIS to Roger Baldwin, October 3, 1946, box 2, folder 1, SP; Strickland and Sánchez, "Spanish Name Spells Discrimination," 22–24; Sánchez, "The Default of Leadership," *SWCESSP Fourth Regional Conference, Albuquerque, New Mexico, January 23–25, 1950. Summarized Proceedings IV,* box 23, folder 34, GP, 6; Sánchez, "Concerning American Minorities," *Proceedings, Fifth Annual Conference, SWCESSP, George Pepperdine College, Los Angeles, California, January 18–20, 1951,* box 57, folder 8, SP, 54.
4. J. Flowers to GIS, January 3, 1947, box 15, folder 19, SP; GIS to J. Flowers, January 7, 1947, box 15, folder 19, SP; J. Flowers to GIS, January 13, 1947, box 15, folder 19, SP; GIS to Fred McCuistion, January 14, 1947, box 56, folder 2, SP (quotations).
5. Fred McCuistion to GIS, January 22, 1947, box 56, folder 2, SP (quotation); GIS to Fred McCuistion, January 30, 1947, box 56, folder 2, SP; Fred McCuistion to GIS, February 7, 1947, box 515, folder 5491, GEBC; GIS to Fred McCuistion, April 18, 1947, box 56, folder 2, SP; GIS to Fred McCuistion, April 18, 1947, box 56, folder 2, SP; Fred McCuistion to GIS, April 25, 1947, box 515, folder 5491, GEBC.

6. GIS to Roger Baldwin, February 14, 1946, box 2, folder 18, SP; Roger Baldwin to GIS, February 18, 1946, box 2, folder 18, SP; GIS to Roger Baldwin, March 5, 1946, box 2, folder 18, SP; Roger Baldwin to GIS, March 11, 1946, box 2, folder 18, SP; GIS to Roger Baldwin, April 10, 1946, box 2, folder 18, SP; Roger Baldwin to GIS, April 15, 1946, box 2, folder 18, SP; GIS to Roger Baldwin, April 18, 1946, box 2, folder 18, SP; GIS to Roger Baldwin, May 24, 1946, box 2, folder 18, SP; GIS to Roger Baldwin, May 31, 1946, box 2, folder 18, SP; GIS to Roger Baldwin, February 13, 1947, box 2, folder 18, SP (first quotation); Roger Baldwin to GIS, February 17, 1947, box 2, folder 18, SP (second quotation).

7. Valencia, *Chicano Students and the Courts*, 22–37; Gilbert G. Gonzalez, "Segregation and the Education of Mexican Children, 1900–1940," in *The Elusive Quest for Equality*, ed. Moreno, 72–73; Goldstone, *Integrating the 40 Acres*, 22–37; Olivas, "The Arc of Triumph and the Agony of Defeat;" *Westminster School District, et al. vs. Gonzalo Méndez, et al.*, No. 11,310, April 14, 1947, United States Circuit Court of Appeals for the Ninth Circuit, box 32, folder 15, SP; GIS to L. Woods, March 22, 1946, box 34, folder 19, SP; L. Woods to GIS, March 26, 1946, box 34, folder 19, SP; GIS to L. Woods, February 11, 1947, box 34, folder 9, SP; John Olsen to L. Woods, February 14, 1947, box 34, folder 9, SP; GIS to L. Woods, February 18, 1947, box 34, folder 9, SP; "Segregation Bad for Education Says Sánchez," *Daily Texan*, June 22, 1947, GISVF–UT; GIS to Gustavo Hernan, October 29, 1946, box 28, folder 22, SP; GIS to Gustavo Hernan, January 20, 1947, box 28, folder 22, SP; Gustavo Hernan to GIS, March 13, 1947, box 28, folder 22, SP; GIS to Gustavo Hernan, April 15, 1947, box 28, folder 22, SP; GIS to Gustavo Hernan, April 17, 1947, box 28, folder 22, SP; GIS to Gustavo Hernan, May 1, 1947, box 28, folder 22, SP; GIS to Gustavo Hernan, May 8, 1947, box 28, folder 22, SP; Rubén Riestra to GIS, May 12, 1947, box 28, folder 22, SP; GIS to Gustavo Hernan, June 6, 1947, box 28, folder 22, SP; GIS to Gustavo Hernan, July 24, 1947, box 28, folder 22, SP; Gustavo Hernan to GIS, August 6, 1947, box 28, folder 22, SP.

8. Joe Greenhill to Wayne Hartman, Opinion No. V-128, April 8, 1947, box 32, folder 15, SP; GIS to Henry Gonzalez, January 16, 1958, box 17, folder 12, SP; GIS to Joe Greenhill, May 8, 1947, box 56, folder 7, SP (quotations); Goldstone, *Integrating the 40 Acres*, 23–24; Brands, *A Texas Supreme Court Trilogy*, 2:14–17, 24–27. Daniel appointed Greenhill to the state supreme court in 1957.

9. GIS to Beauford Jester, May 15, 1947, box 32, folder 15, SP; GIS to Price Daniel et al., August 15, 1947, box 32, folder 15, SP; GIS to T. Trimble, October 4, 1947, box 35, folder 5, SP; Cristobal Aldrete to Price Daniel, July 28, 1947, box 32, folder 15, SP; Cristobal Aldrete to faculty, undated [shortly before August 7, 1947], box 32, folder 15, SP; Rafael Flores to GIS, August 14, 1947, box 32, folder 15, SP; Cristobal Aldrete to GIS, August 12, 1947, box 2, folder 9, SP; "Facts and Opinions on Segregation," *LULAC News* 14:5 (November 1947) (Laredo, Texas), 7, 18; Olivas, "Arc of Triumph and the Agony of Defeat," 5; "Around the Lulac Shield: All Texas Lulac Councils," *LULAC News* 14:5 (November 1947) (Laredo, Texas), 21 (quotation); George I. Sánchez to A. Wirin, August 12, 1947, box 62, folder 15, SP.

10. GIS, "Special School Fund Report," *LULAC News* 15:4 (January 1949) (San Antonio, Texas); GIS to Gus Garcia, June 22, 1948, box 15, folder 18, SP; Raul Perez to GIS,

January 9, 1949, box 22, folder 13, SP; GIS to Raul Perez, January 13, 1949, box 22, folder 13, SP; GIS to Raoul Cortez, January 13, 1949, box 22, folder 13, SP; GIS to Roger Baldwin, April 15, 1948, box 2, folder 18, SP; C. Valverde to GIS, March 26, 1948, box 61, folder 1, SP; Andres Salinas to GIS, June 3, 1948, box 31, folder 19, SP; Edmundo Nora to GIS, January 31, 1948, box 28, folder 5, SP; Raoul Cortez to GIS, November 17, December 22, 1947, box 22, folder 11, SP; Arnulfo Rios to GIS, November 28, 1947, box 22, folder 11, SP; Ana Velasquez to GIS, December 1, 1947, box 22, folder 11, SP; Joe Garza to GIS, December 2, 1947, box 22, folder 11, SP; José Maldonado to GIS, December 1, 16, 1947, box 22, folder 11, SP; A. Sánchez to GIS, January 28, 1948, box 22, folder 12; E. Longoria to GIS, February 7, 1948, box 22, folder 12; Joe Garza to GIS, box 22, folder 12, SP; Louis Wilmot to GIS, April 6, June 7, 1948, box 22, folder 12, SP; Canuto Ortiz to GIS, May 3, 12, June 2, 1948, box 22, folder 12, SP; GIS to Canuto Ortiz, May 12, 1948, box 22, folder 12, SP; Armando Flores to GIS, undated, box 22, folder 12, SP; Carlos Garcia to GIS, May 24, 1948, box 22, folder 12, SP; Trine Perez to GIS, June 16, 1948, box 22, folder 12; Pedro Candelaria to GIS, June 29, 1948, box 22, folder 12, SP; Raul Rivera and Rita Esquivel to GIS, July 8, 1948, box 22, folder 12, SP; GIS to Hector Garcia, April 1, 1948, box 99, folder 26, GP; Hector Garcia to GIS, May 26, 1948, box 172, folder 47, GP; GIS to Hector Garcia, June 4, 1948, box 172, folder 47, GP.

11. GIS to Raoul Cortez, February 3, 1949, box 10, folder 19, SP; GIS to Raoul Cortez, March 11, 1949, box 10, folder 19, SP; GIS to Raoul Cortez, April 14, 1949, box 10, folder 19, SP; Jacob Rodriguez to GIS, April 17, 1949, box 22, folder 13, SP; GIS to Jacob Rodriguez, April 19, 1949, box 22, folder 13, SP; Jacob Rodriguez to GIS, April 20, 1949, box 22, folder 13, SP; GIS to Joe Castañuela, May 10, 1949, box 22, folder 13, SP; Jacob Rodriguez to GIS, May 13, 1949, box 22, folder 13, SP; GIS to Jacob Rodriguez, May 16, 1949, box 22, folder 13, SP; Daniel Valdés to GIS [undated, likely shortly before February 24, 1948], box 61, folder 1, SP; GIS to Daniel Valdés, February 24, 1948, box 61, folder 1, SP.

12. J. Nixon to GIS, May 20, 1948, box 28, folder 5, SP; GIS to J. Nixon, May 22, 1948, box 28, folder 5, SP; J. Nixon to GIS, May 24, 1948, box 28, folder 5, SP; H. Barber, statement, undated [likely late 1947 or early 1948], box 7, folder 15, SP; GIS to H. Barber, November 22, 1947, box 7, folder 15, SP; H. Barber to GIS, November 26, 1947, box 7, folder 15, SP; GIS to Prudence Bostwick, November 14, 1947, box 8, folder 11, SP; GIS to Marie Hughes, November 13, 1947, box 19, folder 17, SP; GIS to Marie Hughes, December 16, 1947, box 19, folder 17, SP; GIS to Marie Hughes, February 20, 1948, box 19, folder 17, SP; Marie Hughes to GIS, March 3, 1948, box 19, folder 17, SP; Arthur Campa to GIS, November 17, 1947, box 32, folder 15, SP; Herschel Manuel, "A Statement Concerning Segregation in the Education of Children of Mexican Descent," December 10, 1947, box 32, folder 15, SP; Frederick Eby, statement, undated [likely late 1947 or early 1948], box 32, folder 15, SP; GIS to Lloyd Tireman, January 30, 1948, box 35, folder 2, SP; Lloyd Tireman to GIS, February 3, 1948, box 35, folder 2, SP; GIS to Lloyd Tireman, February 5, 1948, box 35, folder 2, SP.

13. GIS to Robert Eckhardt, June 16, 1947, box 12, folder 18, SP; GIS to A. Wirin, August 12, 1947, box 62, folder 15, SP; GIS to A. Wirin, October 3, 1947, box 62, folder 15, SP;

GIS to A. Wirin, October 17, 1947, box 62, folder 15, SP; GIS to A. Wirin, November 1, 1947, box 62, folder 15, SP; GIS to A. Wirin, December 5, 1947, box 62, folder 15, SP; GIS to A. Wirin, December 6, 1947, box 62, folder 15, SP; GIS to A. Wirin, April 20, 1948, box 62, folder 15, SP; A. Wirin to GIS, March 24, 1948, box 62, folder 15, SP (first quotation); García, *White But Not Equal*, 108 (second quotation).

14. GIS to Roger Baldwin, June 16, 1948, box 2, folder 18, SP (first quotation); Roger Baldwin to GIS, June 18, 1948, box 2, folder 18, SP; Charles Bunn to GIS, July 5, 1948, box 8, folder 9, SP; GIS to Miguel Calderón, July 9, 1948, box 9, folder 3, SP; A. Wirin to GIS, June 18, 1948, box 15, folder 15, SP; GIS to A. Wirin, June 22, 1948, box 62, folder 15, SP; A. Wirin to GIS, June 24, 1948, box 62, folder 15, SP; A. Wirin to Joseph Robison, August 3, 1948, box 62, folder 15, SP (second quotation).

15. GIS to editor of *The Cotulla Record*, November 3, 1947, box 10, folder 19, SP; A. Wirin to GIS, September 4, 1951, box 62, folder 16, SP; George I. Sánchez to A. Wirin, October 18, 1948, box 62, folder 15, SP; GIS to Roger Baldwin, June 29, 1948, box 2, folder 18, SP (quotation); Roger Baldwin to GIS, July 6, 1948, box 2, folder 18, SP.

16. Guadalupe Hernandez et al. to Fred Kaderli, July 1, 1948, box 32, folder 2, SP; GIS to L. Woods, July 1, 1948, box 32, folder 2, SP; Felipe Reyna, November 12, 1948, box 32, folder 2, SP; GIS to Felipe Reyna, November 17, 1948, SP; Felipe Reyna to GIS, November 18, 1948, SP; GIS to Gus Garcia, July 2, 1948, box 16, folder 18, SP; GIS to Gus Garcia, August 20, 1948, box 16, folder 18, SP; GIS to Gus Garcia, August 20, 1948, box 16, folder 18, SP; Gus Garcia to L. Woods, November 22, 1948, box 32, folder 2, SP; GIS to Gus Garcia, December 21, 1948, box 32, folder 2, SP; Gus Garcia to L. Woods, January 6, 1949, box 32, folder 2, SP; Terrell Trimble to Price Daniel, January 27, 1949, box 32, folder 2, SP; GIS to Gus Garcia, February 11, 1949, box 32, folder 2, SP; GIS to Arnulfo Martinez, June 8, 1949, box 32, folder 2, SP; "School Board Sets Up Three Zones Within San Marcos Independent School District," *San Marcos Record*, January 28, 1949, box 32, folder 2, SP; Gus Garcia to E. Morrison, January 20, 1949, box 16, folder 19, SP; Hans Richards, "New High School Planned," *Hondo Anvil Herald*, January 7, 1949, box 16, folder 19, SP; Lyle Saunders to L. Woods, September 16, 1948, box 32, folder 5, SP; Blanton, *Strange Career of Bilingual Education*, 114–15; Lyle Saunders to GIS, October 7, 1949, box 32, folder 6, SP; Myrtle Tanner to GIS, March 17, 1948, box 34, folder 9, SP; GIS to L. Woods, July 1, 1948, box 32, folder 2, SP; Lyle Saunders to L. Woods, September 16, 1948, box 32, folder 5, SP; GIS to L. Woods, July 16, 1948, box 34, folder 9, SP; L. Woods to GIS, July 27, 1948, box 34, folder 9, SP; L. Woods, "Instructions and Regulations," undated [likely July 1948], box 34, folder 9, SP; GIS to L. Woods, September 23, 1948, box 34, folder 9, SP.

17. Cristobal Aldrete to L. Woods, January 5, 1949, box 12, folder 7, SP; L. Woods, "Statement," April 23, 1949, box 12, folder 7, SP, 1–8; GIS to Gus Garcia, March 8, 1949, box 16, folder 19, SP; San Miguel, *"Let All of Them Take Heed,"* 128–29; GIS to Gus Garcia, April 23, 1949, box 16, folder 19, SP; Gus Garcia to GIS, April 26, 1949, box 16, folder 19, SP; GIS to A. Wirin, October 18, 1948, box 62, folder 15, SP; Gus Garcia to GIS, July 21, 1949, box 16, folder 19, SP; Gus Garcia to L. Woods, July 21, 1949, box 16, folder 19, SP; Ed Idar to GIS, September 10, 1949, box 19, folder 2, SP; GIS to Ed Idar September 14, 1949, box 19, folder 2, SP.

18. Preuss, *To Get a Better School System*, 79–104; John Milne to GIS, December 10, 1948, box 25, folder 13, SP; GIS to John Milne, December 16, 1948, box 25, folder 13, SP; San Miguel, *"Let All of Them Take Heed,"* 129–30 (quotations); GIS to Gus Garcia, April 20, 1949, box 16, folder 19, SP.

19. GIS to Hector Garcia, February 10, 1949, box 4, folder 9, SP (quotation); GIS to Hector Garcia, April 14, 1949, box 4, folder 9, SP; Hector Garcia to GIS, April 25, 1949, box 4, folder 9, SP; notes by Hector Garcia for speech to AGIF, September 25, 1949, box 223, folder 5, GP; Hector Garcia to Alfred Garza, December 24, 1948, box 110, folder 29, GP; GIS to Hector Garcia, September 28, 1949, box 4, folder 9, SP; Raoul Cortez and Hector Garcia to Price Daniel, undated [in late April or May 1949], box 4, folder 10, SP.

20. Schlossman, "Self-Evident Remedy?," 895; San Miguel, *"Let All of Them Take Heed,"* 129–30; Anderson, *J. W. Edgar*, 41–56; Preuss, *To Get a Better School System*, 77–93; J. Edgar to GIS, April 26, 1950, box 34, folder 12, SP; J. Edgar to GIS, May 15, 1950, SP; TEA, "Agenda: State Board of Education," April 14, 1950, box 34, folder 17, SP; TEA, "Statement of Policy Pertaining to Segregation of Latin-American Children," May 8, 1950, box 34, folder 12, SP (quotation).

21. GIS to Gus Garcia, May 18, 1950, box 16, folder 20, SP; J. Edgar to GIS, March 8, 1951, box 34, folder 12, SP; GIS to J. Edgar, March 16, 1951, box 34, folder 12, SP; Ed Idar to Hector Garcia, October 22, 1950, box 224, folder 13, GP; Ed Idar to GIS, November 12, 1950, box 4, folder 11, SP; Ed Idar to Hector Garcia, November 17, 1950, box 224, folder 13, GP; San Miguel, *"Let All of Them Take Heed,"* 131–32; J. Edgar to Gus Garcia, October 9, 1950, box 16, folder 20, SP; Gus Garcia to GIS, October 11, 1950, box 16, folder 20, SP; J. Edgar to Gus Garcia, October 3, 1951, box 34, folder 12, SP; GIS to Cristobal Aldrete, February 4, 1952, box 2, folder 9, SP; Cristobal Aldrete to GIS, June 20, 1953, box 2, folder 9, SP; Cristobal Aldrete to D. Watkins, August 15, 1952, box 34, folder 12, SP; J. Edgar, "Mrs. Refugio Perez et al v. Terrell County Common School District No. 1," July 10, 1953, box 34, folder 12, SP; ACSSP, *Civil Liberties Newsletter No. 2*, December 17, 1951, box 515, folder 5493, GEBC; GIS to Bascom Hayes, June 26, 1952, box 34, folder 12, SP; Bascom Hayes to GIS, July 1, 1952, box 34, folder 12, SP; GIS to Carlos Cadena, May 5, 1955, box 9, folder 2, SP; GIS to Carlos Cadena, May 31, 1955, box 9, folder 2, SP; J. Edgar to W. McCree, August 12, 1953, box 34, folder 12, SP; J. Edgar, "Marcos Barraza, et al. v. Board of Trustees, Pecos ISD," July 28, 1953, box 34, folder 12, SP; Frank Pinedo to J. Edgar, July 7, 1953, box 34, folder 12, SP.

22. Cristobal Aldrete to J. Edgar, September 18, 1954, box 2, folder 9, SP; Cristobal Aldrete to GIS, November 9, 1954, box 2, folder 9, SP; GIS to Cristobal Aldrete, November 10, 1954, box 2, folder 9, SP; GIS to Cristobal Aldrete, November 19, 1954, box 2, folder 9, SP; Murry Garner to J. Edgar, November 9, 1954, box 2, folder 9, SP; Cristobal Aldrete to J. Edgar, December 1, 1954, box 2, folder 9, SP; J. Edgar to Cristobal Aldrete, December 3, 1954, box 2, folder 9, SP; GIS to Carlos Cadena, September 22, 1954, box 9, folder 2, SP (first and second quotations); GIS to J. Edgar, November 29, 1954, box 34, folder 12, SP; Cristobal Aldrete to J. Edgar, December 31, 1954, box 2, folder 9, SP; GIS to Cristobal Aldrete, April 20, 1955, box 2, folder 9, SP; GIS to Cris-

tobal Aldrete, May 3, 1955, box 2, folder 9, SP; GIS to Cristobal Aldrete, May 25, 1955, box 10, folder 1, SP; Robert Oman to Cristobal P. Aldrete, June 10, 1955, box 10, folder 1, SP; Cristobal Aldrete to GIS, June 25, 1955, box 10, folder 1, SP; George Sánchez to Carlos Cadena, April 15, 1955, box 9, folder 2, SP (third quotation); Carlos Cadena to GIS, April 20, 1955, box 9, folder 2, SP; GIS to Carlos Cadena, April 22, 1955, box 9, folder 2, SP; GIS to A. Wirin, February 8, 1955, box 63, folder 1, SP.

23. Anderson, *J. W. Edgar*, 14–15, 92–95, 107–9, 115–22, 152, 164–74.

24. GIS to Albert Peña, October 23, 1954, box 29, folder 20, SP; Albert Peña to Carlos Cadena, October 23, 1954, box 29, folder 20, SP; GIS to Albert Peña, November 10, 1954, box 29, folder 20, SP; Albert Peña, to J. Edgar, November 8, 1954, box 29, folder 20, SP; Albert Peña, to J. Edgar, November 29, 1954, box 29, folder 20, SP; Albert Peña to GIS, September 21, 1955, box 29, folder 20, SP; J. Edgar to T. Harbin, undated [likely on or shortly after May 11, 1955], box 29, folder 20, SP; GIS to Albert Peña, October 3, 1955, box 29, folder 20, SP; GIS to James DeAnda, October 28, 1955, box 12, folder 6, SP; GIS to James DeAnda, October 11, 1956, box 12, folder 6, SP; GIS to James De-Anda, November 3, 1956, box 12, folder 6, SP; GIS, undated notes [likely shortly after October 27, 1955], box 61, folder 14, SP (first quotation); T. Harbin to GIS, October 27, 1955, box 61, folder 14, SP, Sánchez, "Grouping on Basis of Tests," undated [likely summer of 1956], box 61, folder 14, SP, 1–8; James DeAnda to Richard Casillas, November 4, 1955, box 61, folder 14, SP; GIS to Richard Casillas, October 3, 1955, box 61, folder 14, SP; Casillas, Peña and DeAnda, Civil Action No. 1384, "Pre-Trial Memorandum" on *Hernández v. Driscoll* and *Villareal v. Mathis*, undated, box 63, folder 2, SP; A. Wirin to GIS, September 14, 1956, box 62, folder 2, SP; A. Wirin to GIS, October 29, 1956, box 63, folder 2, SP; James DeAnda, Richard Casillas, and Albert Peña, Civil Action 1384, "Complaint to Enjoin Violation of Federal Civil Rights and Action for Damages" on *Hernández v. Driscoll* and *Villareal v. Mathis*, box 61, folder 14, SP; Ralph Guzman to GIS, February 7, 1956, box 18, folder 13, SP; GIS to Ralph Guzman, February 9, 1956, box 18, folder 13, SP; James DeAnda to GIS, February 28, 1956, box 61, folder 14, SP; GIS to James DeAnda, May 1, 1956, box 61, folder 14, SP (second quotation).

25. "Education, Public Schools—Texas," *Race Relations Law Reporter* 2:2 (April 1957), 329–34; Blanton, *Strange Career of Bilingual Education*, 115–16; James DeAnda to GIS, January 16, 1957, box 61, folder 14, SP; A. Wirin to James DeAnda, January 23, 1957, box 63, folder 2, SP; Manuel Velasco to GIS, November 6, 1957, box 4, folder 13, SP; GIS to Manuel Velasco, November 15, 1957, box 4, folder 13, SP; GIS to Simon Gross, August 19, 1957, box 31, folder 8, SP.

26. GIS to James DeAnda, November 8, 1956, box 12, folder 6, SP (quotation); Dugger, *Our Invaded Universities*, 117–19; Paredes, "Jorge Isidoro Sánchez," 125; GIS to L. Haskew, November 8, 1956, box 50, folder 7, SP.

27. GIS, "Concerning American Minorities," in *Proceedings of the Fifth Annual Conference, Southwest Council on the Education of Spanish-Speaking People at George Pepperdine College, Los Angeles, California, January 18–20, 1951*, box 57, folder 8, SP, 51–52 (first quotation), 52–53 (second quotation); J. Jones to GIS, March 22, 1957, box

21, folder 1, SP; GIS to J. Jones, box 9, folder 2, SP [old system] (third quotation); Clotilde de Náñez to GIS, February 24, 1948, box 26, folder 8, SP; GIS to Clotilde de Náñez, March 11, 1948, box 26, folder 8, SP. For more on this topic, see Blanton, "'A Legacy of Neglect.'"

28. GIS to J. Edgar, April 1, 1954, box 34, folder 12, SP; J. Edgar to GIS, May 11, 1954, box 34, folder 12, SP; Bascom Hayes to GIS, June 8, 1954, box 34, folder 12, SP; GIS to Bascom Hayes, June 9, 1954, box 34, folder 12, SP; Bascom Hayes to GIS, June 21, 1954, box 34, folder 12, SP; Porfirio Flores to GIS, September 16, 1955, box 15, folder 16, SP; GIS to Porfirio Flores, September 20, 1955, box 15, folder 16, SP; Division of Research, TEA, "Report of Pupils in Texas Public Schools Having Spanish Surnames, 1955–1956," August, 1957, box 34, folder 13, SP; J. Hitt to GIS, box 34, folder 13, SP; GIS to J. Hitt, March 12, 1958, box 34, folder 13, SP; Lee Wilborn to GIS, February 10, 1960, box 26, folder 2, SP; GIS to Lee Wilborn, February 16, 1960, box 26, folder 2, SP; GIS to Lee Wilborn, April 11, 1960, box 26, folder 2, SP; GIS to Lawrence Rutledge, September 22, 1960, box 31, folder 15, SP; GIS to Ronnie Dugger, August 10, 1959, box 34, folder 16, SP; Ronnie Dugger to GIS, August 14, 1959, box 34, folder 16, SP; GIS to Ronnie Dugger, August 18, 1959, box 34, folder 16, SP; GIS to Ronnie Dugger, December 12, 1958, box 34, folder 16, SP (quotation).

29. Bascom Hayes to GIS, December 18, 1961, box 34, folder 14, SP; GIS to J. Edgar, December 16, 1963, box 34, folder 14, SP; J. Edgar to GIS, January 8, 1946, box 34, folder 14, SP; Blanton, *Strange Career of Bilingual Education*, 122–23; San Miguel, *"Let All of Them Take Heed,"* 139–63; Kaplowitz, *LULAC*, 63–67; GIS to Albert Armendariz, June 23, 1959, box 22, folder 14, SP; Sánchez, "A Message to LULAC," undated [likely June 23, 1959], box 22, folder 14, SP, 2 (quotation).

30. I. García, *White But Not Equal*, 108; Montejano, *Anglos and Mexicans*, 233 (quotation).

31. Carey McWilliams, May 7, 1948, box 24, folder 18, SP; GIS to Carey McWilliams, May 18, 1948, box 24, folder 18, SP; GIS to William Belt, December 15, 1955, box 7, folder 16, SP; Sánchez and Putnam, *Materials Relating to the Education of Spanish-Speaking People in the United States*; Sánchez, "Quantitative and Objective Criteria in Education"; Schlossman, "Self-Evident Remedy?," 901; Pedro Cebollero to GIS, April 9, 1947, box 10, folder 8, SP; GIS to Elaine Eastman, May 6, 1948, box 12, folder 18, SP; U.S. National Commission for UNESCO, Panel of Fundamental Education, Summary Minutes of the Second Meeting, September 8, 1952, box 32, folder 8, SP, 1–15; GIS to William Madsen, October 12, 1959, box 23, folder 1, SP; Margaret Longridge to GIS, March 14, 1960, box 22, folder 22, SP; GIS to Margaret Longridge, March 17, 1960, box 22, folder 22, SP; Cheavens, "Vernacular Languages and Education"; W. O'Donnell to GIS, May 14, 1953, box 28, folder 6, SP; GIS to W. O'Donnell, May 27, 1953, box 28, folder 6, SP; W. O'Donnell to GIS, June 3, 1953, box 28, folder 6, SP; W. O'Donnell to GIS, January 27, 1954, box 28, folder 6, SP; GIS to W. O'Donnell, February 2, 1954, box 7, folder 2, SP; Sánchez, "The Crux of the Dual Language Handicap," 38; GIS to James Cooper, September 23, 1961, box 8, folder 3, SP; James Cooper to GIS, December 1, 1961, box 8, folder 3, SP; Evans, *Social Studies Wars*, 113; Ravitch, *The Troubled Crusade*, 111–13.

32. Paredes, "Jorge Isidoro Sánchez," 121–22; Juan Lujan to GIS, April 30, 1952, box 22, folder 8, SP; GIS to Juan Lujan, May 7, 1952, box 22, folder 8, SP; GIS to Marjorie Johnston, October 19, 1953, box 20, folder 14, SP; Pedro Cebolleros to GIS, October 14, 1952, box 10, folder 8, SP; GIS to Pedro Cebolleros, September 17, 1952, box 10, folder 8, SP; Cowart, "The Educational Philosophy of Jaime Torres Bodet," v–vi; Cowart interview; Koenig, "Julia Mellenbruch," 310–11; George Garza to GIS, May 26, 1954, box 16, folder 22, SP; Aurelio M. Montemayor, "Su Palabra es Oro—His Word Is Gold," *IDRA Newsletter* 38:9 (October 16, 2011), 3–4; Carmen Samora, "Grace and Redemption: Julian Samora, 1920–1996," in *Moving Beyond Borders*, ed. Pulido et al., 33–37; Julian Samora to GIS, March 4, 1948, box 31, folder 21, SP; GIS to Julian Samora, March 11, 1948, box 31, folder 21, SP; Julian Samora to GIS, March 23, 1948, box 31, folder 21, SP; GIS to Julian Samora, April 15, 1948, box 31, folder 21, SP; Julian Samora to GIS, April 21, 1948, box 31, folder 21, SP; GIS to Julian Samora, May 5, 1948, box 31, folder 21, SP; Julian Samora to GIS, September 25, 1948, box 31, folder 21, SP; GIS to Julian Samora, October 19, 1948, box 31, folder 21, SP; GIS to Fred McCuistion, June 27, 1949, box 31, folder 21, SP; GIS to Julian Samora, June 27, 1949, box 31, folder 21, SP; Julian Samora to GIS, July 8, 1950, box 31, folder 21, SP; Kahn, *Jock*, 176–80; Pritchett, *Robert Clifton Weaver*, 161–63; minutes, "Attendants at Conference, Opportunity Fellowships–John Hay Whitney Foundations, Waldorf-Astoria Hotel, New York, December, 2–3, 1949," 1–12; GIS to Robert Weaver, December 5, 1950, box 59, folder 15, SP; Robert Weaver to GIS, December 12, 1950, box 59, folder 15, SP.

33. GIS to Arno Nowotny, May 22, 1959, box 49, folder 5, SP (quotation); GIS to Harry Ransom, October 23, 1959, box 51, folder 7, SP; Harry Ransom to GIS, October 31, 1959, box 51, folder 7, SP; Jack Holland to GIS, November 11, 1959, box 51, folder 7, SP; Arno Nowotny to GIS, November 11, 1959, box 51, folder 7, SP; GIS to Ed Price, November 11, 1959, box 51, folder 7, SP; Ed Price to GIS, November 12, 1959, box 51, folder 7, SP; "Faculty-Student Committee on Handicapped Students, minutes, December 4, 1959, box 51, folder 7, SP, 1–3.

34. Kliebard, *Struggle for the American Curriculum*, 228–33, 259–60, 261 (quotation); Redefer, "A Blow for Education," 303–4; GIS to Henry Otto, August 9, 1961, box 28, folder 23, SP; Peter Cranford to GIS, March 31, 1962, box 11, folder 13, SP; GIS to Peter Cranford, April 5, 1962, box 11, folder 13, SP.

35. GIS to Secretary of the Committee on Graduate Studies in Education, May 14, 1953, box 43, folder 7, SP; GIS to Lewis Hanke, December 16, 1952, box 53, folder 16, SP (first and second quotations); J. Dobie to GIS, July 20, 1960, box 13, folder 13, SP (third quotation); GIS to Malcolm McGregor, March 22, 1961, box 24, folder 15, SP (remaining quotations); GIS to Bob Eckhart, March 7, 1961, box 34, folder 15, SP; GIS to Clarence Faust, September 26, 1958, box 16, folder 2, SP; Clarence Faust to GIS, October 1, 1958, box 16, folder 2, SP; Buck et al., *The Role of Education in American History*; Sánchez, "Prospect for the Department of the History and Philosophy of Education," undated [likely 1951 or 1952], box 47, folder 4, SP; GIS to William Drake, November 23, 1959, box 45, folder 2, SP.

CHAPTER 10. MEXICAN AMERICAN RACIAL IDENTITY,
WHITENESS, AND CIVIL RIGHTS

First epigraph. Sánchez, "Discrimination in High Places," *Balance* 3:4 (Austin, Texas), 2, box 13, folder 14, SP.
Second epigraph. GIS to Roger Baldwin, August 27, 1958, box 31, folder 8, SP.

1. Gordon, *Great Arizona Orphan Abduction*, 99 (quotation); Delgado and Stefancic, *Critical Race Theory*, 1–9; López, *White by Law*, 1–36; Sheridan, "'Another White Race,'" 109–44; Wilson, "Brown Over 'Other White,'" 145–94; Gross, "Texas Mexicans and the Politics of Whiteness," 195–205. For foundational studies of whiteness, see Roediger, *The Wages of Whiteness* and *Towards the Abolition of Whiteness*; Jacobson, *Whiteness of a Different Color*; Ignatiev, *How the Irish Became White*; Lipsitz, *The Possessive Investment in Whiteness*. For critiques of whiteness, see Arnesen, "Whiteness and the Historians' Imagination," 3–32; Fields, "Whiteness, Racism, and Identity," 48–56; Kolchin, "Whiteness Studies," 154–73; Wickberg, "Heterosexual White Male," 136–57; Bayor, "Another Look at 'Whiteness,'" 13–30.

2. For support of the internalization thesis, see Foley, *The White Scourge*; Foley, "Becoming Hispanic: Mexican Americans and the Faustian Pact with Whiteness," in *Reflexiones 1997*, ed. Foley, 53–70; Foley, "Partly Colored or Other White: Mexican Americans and Their Problem with the Color Line," in *Beyond Black and White*, ed. Cole and Parker, 123–44; Foley, *Quest for Equality*; Carroll, *Felix Longoria's Wake*; Phillips, *White Metropolis*; Guglielmo, "Fighting for Caucasian Rights," 1212–37. For opposition to it, see Blanton, "George I. Sánchez, Ideology, and Whiteness," 569–604; Weise, "Mexican Nationalisms, Southern Racisms," 749–77; Zamora, *Claiming Rights and Righting Wrongs*; Orozco, *No Mexicans, Women, or Dogs*; Johnson, "The Cosmic Race in Texas," 404–19; Max Krochmal, "Black and Brown at Work: Chicano Labor and Multiracial Politics in Post–World War II Texas," in *Life and Labor in the New South*, ed. Zieger, 133–76.

3. Sánchez, "Concerning American Minorities," box 515, folder 5493, GEBC, 53 (quotation); Fields, "Whiteness, Racism, and Identity," 48–49.

4. Hilde Reitzes to GIS, July 11, 1947, box 31, folder 13, SP; Gómez, *Manifest Destinies*, 64–71; Sánchez and Sánchez, "An Experience in Texas," 464 (first quotation); Teodoro Estrada to GIS, March 8, 1963, box 15, folder 9, SP; GIS to Teodoro Estrada, March 12, 1963, box 15, folder 9, SP (second quotation).

5. GIS to American Council on Race Relations, October 14, 1946, box 2, folder 1, SP; GIS to Ralph Yarborough, September 26, 1967, box 174, folder 1, GP (quotations).

6. Sánchez, "Discrimination in High Places," box 73, folder 38, SP, 1 (quotation); GIS to John McMahon, March 6, 1947, box 1, folder 13, SP. For the published version of this talk see Sánchez, "Discrimination in High Places," *Balance* 3:4 (November 14, 1960), box 13, folder 14, SP, 2–4.

7. Romo, "George I. Sánchez," 342–62; Blanton, "George I. Sánchez, Ideology and Whiteness," 569–604; Foley, *Quest for Equality*, 123–35, 147, 131 (first quotation); Clifford Forster to GIS, May 19, 1947, box 3, folder 2, SP; GIS to Clifford Forster, May 24, 1947, box 3, folder 2, SP (second quotation); Fairclough, *Race and Democracy*, xviii.

8. Theophilus Painter to GIS, July 20, 1950, box 56, folder 6, SP; GIS to Roger Baldwin, January 24, 1951, box 2, folder 19, SP; GIS to Roger Baldwin, February 2, 1951, box 2, folder 19, SP; Roger Baldwin to GIS, February 6, 1951, box 2, folder 19, SP; GIS to Roger Baldwin, February 22, 1951, box 2, folder 19, SP; Roger Baldwin to GIS, March 22, 1951, box 2, folder 19, SP; Roger Baldwin to Fred Ross, March 22, 1951, box 2, folder 19, SP; GIS to George Rundquist, May 29, 1951, box 3, folder 1, SP; George Rundquist to GIS, May 31, 1951, box 3, folder 1, SP; George Rundquist to GIS, June 7, 1951, box 3, folder 1, SP; Roger Baldwin to Robert Marshall Civil Liberties Trust, August 16, 1951, box 31, folder 6, SP; GIS to George Rundquist, May 29, 1951, box 3, folder 1, SP; A. Wirin to GIS, May 22, 1951, box 62, folder 16, SP; Roger Baldwin to A. Wirin, June 8, 1951, box 62, folder 15, SP; Roger Baldwin to A. Wirin, June 14, 1951, box 62, folder 16, SP; GIS to Roger Baldwin, June 22, 1951, box 62, folder 16, SP; A. Wirin to GIS, June 25, 1951, box 62, folder 16, SP; A. Wirin to Roger Baldwin, June 25, 1951, box 62, folder 16, SP; Roger Baldwin to Robert Marshall Civil Liberties Trust, August 16, 1951, box 31, folder 6, SP; GIS to Robert Marshall Civil Liberties Trust, August 28, 1951, box 31, folder 6, SP.

9. GIS to George Rundquist, May 29, 1951, box 3, folder 1, SP; Ed Idar to GIS, September 13, 1954, box 31, folder 7, SP; GIS to Simon Gross, September 15, 1954, box 31, folder 7, SP; GIS to Robert Marshall Civil Liberties Trust, August 28, 1951, box 31, folder 6, SP; GIS to Simon Gross, March 26, 1953, box 31, folder 6, SP; Simon Gross to GIS, March 31, 1953, box 31, folder 6, SP; Roger Baldwin to Simon Gross, April 22, 1954, box 31, folder 7, SP; Roger Baldwin to GIS, May 19, 1954, box 31, folder 7, SP; Roger Baldwin to Simon Gross, July 7, 1952, box 31, folder 6, SP; Simon Gross to GIS, August 4, 1952, box 31, folder 6, SP; GIS to ACSSP Board of Directors, October 9, 1953, box 3, folder 6, SP; GIS to Robert Marshall Civil Liberties Trust, October 2, 1952, box 31, folder 6, SP; GIS to Simon Gross, August 12, 1953, box 31, folder 6, SP; Simon Gross to GIS, August 24, 1953, box 31, folder 6, SP; GIS to Simon Gross, September 3, 1953, box 31, folder 6, SP; GIS to Robert Marshall Civil Liberties Trust, October 2, 1952, box 31, folder 6, SP; *ACSSP Newsletter* 1:1 (March 1, 1953), box 3, folder 13, SP; *ACSSP Newsletter* 1:2 (April 1, 1953), box 3, folder 13, SP; *ACSSP Newsletter* 1:3 (May 1, 1953), box 3, folder 13, SP; GIS to Ed McDonald, February 6, 1952, box 6, folder 3, SP [old system]; GIS to ACSSP Board of Directors, July 1, 1952, box 3, folder 6, SP; Foley, *Quest for Equality*, 131–32.

10. ACLU of Southern California, "Biographical Data: A. Wirin," undated [likely sometime in the 1960s], box 55, folder 15, collection 900, SCACLUP; Murray Fromson, "He Champions the Underdogs: Peoples' Lawyer Abraham Wirin Defends Unpopular Causes," *Pasadena Star-News*, November 29, 1959, box 112, folder 4, collection 900, SCACLUP; Clore Warne to Eason Monroe, September 16, 1952, box 74, folder 3, collection 900, SCACLUP; Phil Kerby, "A. Wirin: Gentle Voice of Reason," *Los Angeles Times*, February 7, 1978, C3; Myrna Oliver, "A. Wirin, First Full-Time ACLU Lawyer, Dies at 77," *Los Angeles Times*, February 5, 1978, A3, A21; A. Wirin to GIS, June 14, 1951, box 62, folder 16, SP; A. Wirin to GIS, September 15, 1953, box 62, folder 18, SP; A. Wirin to Roger Baldwin, September 29, 1953, box 62, folder 18, SP; A. Wirin to Carlos Cadena, September 19, 1953, box 62, folder 18, SP; A. Wirin to GIS, October

5, 1953, box 62, folder 18, SP; GIS to A. Wirin, September 18, 1952, box 62, folder 17, SP; Kutulas, *The ACLU,* 50–52, 60–61; A. Wirin to GIS, February 9, 1959, box 63, folder 2, SP; A. Wirin to GIS, February 11, 1959, box 63, folder 2, SP; GIS to A. Wirin, February 26, 1959, box 63, folder 2, SP; John Finerty to GIS, October 1, 1953, box 62, folder 18, SP; A. Wirin to Robert Marshall Trust, September 22, 1953, box 52, folder 18, SP; A. Wirin to GIS, October 12, 1953, box 62, folder 18, SP; A. Wirin to GIS, December 7, 1953, box 62, folder 18, SP; A. Wirin to GIS, March 23, 1954, box 62, folder 19, SP; GIS to A. Wirin, April 8, 1954, box 62, folder 19, SP; A. Wirin to GIS, April 9, 1954, box 62, folder 19, SP; A. Wirin to James Marshall, February 24, 1956, box 63, folder 2, SP; "ACLU Counsel's Report," May, 17, 1955, box 74, folder 3, collection 900, SCACLUP; "ACLU Counsel's Report," January 17, 1956, box 74, folder 3, collection 900, SCACLUP; "ACLU Counsel's Report," February 21, 1956, box 74, folder 3, collection 900, SCACLUP; "ACLU Counsel's Report," March 17, 1956, box 74, folder 3, collection 900, SCACLUP; "ACLU Counsel's Report," March 20, 1956, box 74, folder 3, collection 900, SCACLUP; "ACLU Counsel's Report," May 15, 1956, box 74, folder 3, collection 900, SCACLUP; Ralph Guzman and Ralph Estrada, "Court Refuses to Hear Charges of Race Prejudice and Adverse Publicity Surrounding L.A. Murder Conviction," March 4, 1955, box 63, folder 1, SP; GIS to Ed Idar, May 4, 1954, box 19, folder 20, SP; Escobar, "Bloody Christmas," 184–85; Bernstein, *Bridges of Reform,* 152, 157; Kenneth C. Burt, "The Battle for Standard Coil: The United Electrical Workers, the Community Service Organization, and the Catholic Church in Latino East Los Angeles," in *American Labor and the Cold War,* ed. Cherney et al., 128–29.

11. John Finerty to GIS, October 1, 1953, box 62, folder 18, SP; A. Wirin to Robert Marshall Trust, September 22, 1953, box 62, folder 18, SP; A. Wirin to GIS, December 7, 1953, box 62, folder 18, SP; A. Wirin to GIS, March 23, 1954, box 62, folder 19, SP; GIS to A. Wirin, December 11, 1953, box 62, folder 18, SP (quotations); A. Wirin to James Marshall, undated [likely on or shortly before September 2, 1954], box 62, folder 19, SP; A. Wirin to GIS, May 25, 1954, box 62, folder 19, SP; A. Wirin to GIS, December 20, 1955, box 63, folder 1, SP; A. Wirin to James Marshall, December 20, 1955, box 63, folder 1, SP; *Galvan v. Press,* 347 U.S. 522 (1954); *Garcia v. Landon,* 348, U.S. 866 (1954); Roger Baldwin to GIS, March 26, 1952, box 31, folder 6, SP; GIS to Simon Gross, April 3, 1952, box 31, folder 6, SP; Blanton, "George I. Sánchez, Ideology, and Whiteness," 588–89.

12. GIS to Arturo Fuentes, May 2, 1952, box 31, folder 6, SP; Ralph Estrada to A. Wirin, September 22, 1952, box 28, folder 18, SP; Fred Okrand to GIS, September 29, 1952, box 28, folder 18, SP; GIS to Fred Okrand, October 7, 1952, box 28, folder 18, SP (quotation); A. Wirin to GIS, October 12, 1953, box 62, folder 18, SP.

13. John Finerty to GIS, October 1, 1953, box 62, folder 18, SP; A. Wirin to Robert Marshall Trust, September 22, 1953, box 62, folder 18, SP, 2–3; GIS to A. Wirin, May 4, 1954, box 62, folder 19; A. Wirin to GIS, May 28, 1954, box 62, folder 19, SP; A. Wirin to GIS, June 22, 1954, box 62, folder 19, SP (quotation); A. Wirin to James Marshall, June 22, 1954, box 62, folder 19, SP; *Mollie Baca, et al., vs. City of Winslow, et al.,* Stipulation No. Civ-294-pct, U.S. District Court, Arizona, undated [likely around June 22, 1954], box 62, folder 19, SP.

14. GIS to A. Wirin, February 19, 1954, box 62, folder 19, SP (quotation); John Herrera to GIS, May 5, 1955, box 19, folder 5, SP; GIS to John Herrera, May 13, 1955, box 19, folder 5, SP; A. Wirin to Ben Connally, August 12, 1955, box 63, folder 1, SP; Ralph Guzman to Ben Connally, August 12, 1955, box 63, folder 1, SP; *Rios et al. v. Ellis et al.*, Plaintiffs' Answer to Defendants' Motion to Dismiss and Motion to Make a More Definite Statement, U.S. District Court, Southern District of Texas, undated [on or shortly before August 24, 1955], box 63, folder 1, SP; A. Wirin to Ralph Estrada, August 24, 1955, box 63, folder 1, SP; Trulson and Marquart, "Racial Desegregation and Violence in the Texas Prison System," 233–36, 240–41.

15. Mark Adams, "Confidential—Not for Publication. Public Housing Projects in Austin, Texas. A Report to the Texas Council on Human Relations," undated [likely on or shortly before April 18, 1951], 1–4; Alvin Wirtz to GIS, April 21, 1951, box 34, folder 8, SP; Alvin Wirtz to GIS, May 3, 1951, box 34, folder 11, SP; GIS to A. Wirin, September 27, 1951, box 62, folder 16, SP; GIS to A. Wirin, October 30, 1951, box 62, folder 16, SP; A. Wirin to GIS, November 5, 1951, box 62, folder 16, SP; John Finerty to GIS, October 1, 1953, box 62, folder 18, SP; A. Wirin to Robert Marshall Trust, September 22, 1953, box 62, folder 18, SP; A. Wirin to GIS, April 16, 1954, box 62, folder 19, SP; A. Wirin to John Herrera, April 16, 1954, box 62, folder 19, SP; GIS to A. Wirin, April 20, 1954, box 62, folder 19, SP; Philip Sadler to A. Wirin, May 6, 1954, box 62, folder 19, SP; A. Wirin to Philip Sadler, May 13, 1954, box 62, folder 19, SP; GIS to A. Wirin, May 17, 1954, box 62, folder 19, SP; Philip Sadler to A. Wirin, January 7, 1954, box 62, folder 19, SP; GIS to A. Wirin, June 8, 1954, box 62, folder 19, SP; Warren Cochrane to Will Maslow, November 18, 1952, box 62, folder 19, SP; A. Wirin to GIS, March 20, 1955, box 63, folder 1, SP; GIS to A. Wirin, April 5, 1955, box 63, folder 1, SP; A. Wirin to GIS, April 13, 1955, box 63, folder 1, SP; GIS to A. Wirin, April 18, 1955, box 63, folder 1, SP; A. Wirin to GIS, April 20, 1955, box 63, folder 1, SP; GIS to A. Wirin, April 22, 1955, box 63, folder 1, SP. Local officials literally piled Anglo, African American, and Mexican American applications in separate stacks.

16. Ralph Guzman to GIS, March 6, 1955, box 2, folder 11, SP; Ralph Guzman, "Preliminary Report on the El Centro School Segregation Problem," February 14, 1955, box 2, folder 11, SP, 1–7; GIS to Ralph Guzman, March 8, 1955, box 2, folder 11, SP (quotation); "ACLU Counsel's Report," July 19, 1955, box 74, folder 3, collection 900, SCACLUP; "ACLU Counsel's Report," May 17, 1955, box 74, folder 3, collection 900, SCACLUP; "ACLU Counsel's Report," October 18, 1955, box 74, folder 3, collection 900, SCACLUP; A. Wirin to GIS, February 3, 1955, box 63, folder 1, SP; "Segregation Charged in Southland: Suits Hit El Centro, Imperial County School Officials," *Los Angeles Times*, February 8, 1955, box 63, folder 2, SP; A. Wirin to GIS, June 27, 1955, box 63, folder 1, SP; *Joe R. Romero, et al. v. Guy Weakley et al.* and *R. J. Burleigh et al. v. Guy Weakley, et al.*, 131 Federal Supplement, 818 (SD California, May 5, 1955); *Joe R. Romero, et al. v. Guy Weakley, et al.* and *R. J. Burleigh, et al. v. Guy Weakley, et al.*, box 63, folder 3, SP; Blanton, "George I. Sánchez, Ideology, and Whiteness," 601–2; Powers and Patton, "Between *Mendez* and *Brown*," 164–65.

17. Roger Baldwin to James Marshall, June 8, 1951, box 2, folder 19, SP (quotation); GIS to Roger Baldwin, September 7, 1951, box 2, folder 19, SP; Foley, *Quest for Equality*, 131–33.

18. A. Wirin to GIS, June 20, 1952, box 62, folder 17, SP; GIS to A. Wirin, June 25, 1952, box 62, folder 17, SP (quotations).

19. Foley, *Quest for Equality*, 131 (first quotation); Roger Baldwin to GIS, December 18, 1952, box 3, folder 5, SP; GIS to Roger Baldwin, January 7, 1953, box 3, folder 5, SP; Roger Baldwin to GIS, January 15, 1953, box 3, folder 5 (second quotation).

20. Ed Idar to Bernard Valdez, April 10, 1953, box 61, folder 2, SP; GIS to A. Wirin, June 25, 1952, box 62, folder 17, SP; A. Wirin to GIS, September 2, 1954, box 62, folder 19, SP; A. Wirin to GIS, September 16, 1954, box 62, folder 19, SP; GIS to Roger Baldwin, September 10, 1954, box 31, folder 7, SP; A. Wirin to GIS, June 3, 1955, box 63, folder 1, SP; A. Wirin to GIS, March 4, 1955, box 63, folder 1, SP; GIS to A. Wirin, September 24, 1955, box 63, folder 1, SP; GIS to A. Wirin, October 20, 1955, box 63, folder 1, SP; GIS to A. Wirin, January 3, 1956, box 63, folder 2, SP; A. Wirin to GIS, January 4, 1956, box 63, folder 1, SP; GIS to A. Wirin, January 25, 1956, box 31, folder 8, SP; GIS to Bernard Valdez, August 21, 1956, box 61, folder 2, SP; GIS to Bernard Valdez, April 24, 1957, box 61, folder 2, SP; GIS to Bernard Valdez, August 5, 1957, box 61, folder 2, SP; GIS to Bernard Valdez, November 13, 1957, box 61, folder 2, SP; Henry Bain to GIS, May 31, 1956, box 31, folder 8, SP; GIS to Henry Bain, June 26, 1956, box 31, folder 8, SP; GIS to Simon Gross, August 22, 1956, box 31, folder 8, SP; GIS to Roger Baldwin, April 25, 1957, box 2, folder 20, SP; Roger Baldwin to GIS, May 3, 1957, box 2, folder 20, SP (quotation); GIS to Roger Baldwin, May 7, 1957, box 2, folder 20, SP.

21. Roger Baldwin to Marshall Civil Liberties Trust, March 17, 1959, box 31, folder 8, SP; GIS to Roger Baldwin, March 24, 1959, box 31, folder 8, SP (quotation).

22. O'Connor and Epstein, "Legal Voice for the Chicano Community," 248–49; GIS to Bernard Valdez, May 30, 1961, box 61, folder 2, SP; Bernard Valdez to GIS, June 5, 1961, box 61, folder 2, SP (quotation).

23. Romo, "George I. Sánchez and the Civil Rights Movement," 355; Blanton, "George I. Sánchez, Ideology, and Whiteness," 590–91, 601–2; Foley, *Quest for Equality*, 125–26, 131–32; GIS to ACSSP Board of Directors, July 1, 1952, box 3, folder 6, SP (first quotation); Roger Baldwin to GIS, June 23, 1954, box 31, folder 7, SP; GIS to Roger Baldwin, July 16, 1954, box 31, folder 7, SP; Roger Baldwin to GIS, July 23, 1954, box 31, folder 7, SP; GIS to John Herrera, June 16, 1953, box 19, folder 5, SP (remaining quotations); GIS to ACSSP Board of Directors, July 1, 1952, box 3, folder 6, SP; Roger Baldwin to GIS, June 23, 1954, box 31, folder 7, SP; GIS to Roger Baldwin, July 16, 1954, box 31, folder 7, SP; Roger Baldwin to GIS, July 23, 1954, box 31, folder 7, SP; GIS to Simon Gross, July 27, 1953, box 31, folder 6, SP.

24. GIS to Roger Baldwin, June 15, 1951, box 2, folder 19, SP; GIS to Tibo Chavez, December 14, 1951, box 3, folder 5, SP; Roger Baldwin to GIS, October 25, 1951, box 2, folder 19, SP; GIS to Roger Baldwin, October 31, 1951, box 2, folder 19, SP; GIS to Roger Baldwin, December 5, 1951, box 2, folder 19, SP; Roger Baldwin to GIS, December 17, 1951, box 2, folder 19, SP; GIS to Roger Baldwin, December 21, 1951, box 2, folder 19, SP; Ralph Estrada to A. Wirin, July 16, 1951, box 62, folder 16, SP; A. Wirin to Ralph Estrada, July 18, 1951, box 62, folder 16, SP; GIS to ACSSP Board of Directors, August 22, 1951, box 3, folder 6, SP; Ignacio López, August 25, 1951, box

3, folder 5, SP; GIS to Ignacio López, August 28, 1951, box 3, folder 5, SP; GIS to Tibo Chavez, September 10, 1951, box 3, folder 5, SP; GIS to A. Wirin, October 30, 1951, box 62, folder 16, SP; Lino Lopez to GIS, undated [likely summer or fall of 1951] box 22, folder 22, SP; GIS to Lyle Saunders, November 4, 1952, box 32, folder 9, SP; A. Heist to Edward Roybal, January 31, 1950, box 74, folder 11, collection 900, SCACLUP; Roger Baldwin to A. Heist, April 27, 1950, box 74, folder 11, collection 900, SCACLUP; Fred Ross to A. Heist, May 24, 1950, box 74, folder 11, collection 900, SCACLUP; A. Heist to George Rundquist, June 15, 1950, box 74, folder 11, collection 900, SCACLUP; George Rundquist to A. Heist, June 21, 1950, box 74, folder 11, collection 900, SCACLUP; A. Heist to George Rundquist, November 6, 1950, box 74, folder 11, collection 900, SCACLUP; Fred Ross to A. Heist, November 7, 1950, box 74, folder 11, collection 900, SCACLUP; A. Heist to Fred Ross, November 8, 1950, box 74, folder 11, collection 900, SCACLUP; Roger Baldwin to Fred Ross, December 21, 1950, box 74, folder 11, collection 900, SCACLUP; A. Heist to Roger Baldwin, December 27, 1950, box 74, folder 11, collection 900, SCACLUP; Roger Baldwin to A. Heist, January 2, 1951, box 74, folder 11, collection 900, SCACLUP; A. Heist to Roger Baldwin, January 5, 1951, box 74, folder 11, collection 900, SCACLUP; Roger Baldwin to A. Heist, January 12, 1951, box 74, folder 11, collection 900, SCACLUP; Roger Baldwin to Fred Ross, March 22, 1951, box 74, folder 11, collection 900, SCACLUP; GIS to Roger Baldwin, January 24, 1951, box 2, folder 19, SP; Roger Baldwin to GIS, February 6, 1951, box 2, folder 19, SP; GIS to Roger Baldwin, February 22, 1951, box 2, folder 19, SP; GIS to A. Wirin, September 27, 1951, box 62, folder 16, SP; Ed Idar to A. Wirin, December 4, 1951, box 62, folder 16, SP; "L.A. Spanish Group Gives $1,000 Boost," *Los Angeles Daily News*, May 16, 1952, box 3, folder 16, SP.

25. Tibo Chavez to Earl Warren, December 10, 1951, box 10, folder 12, SP; GIS to Tibo Chavez, December 14, 1951, box 10, folder 12, SP; GIS to Roger Baldwin, December 21, 1951, box 2, folder 19, SP; GIS to Anthony Rios, January 21, 1952, box 31, folder 3, SP; GIS to Lyle Saunders, November 4, 1952, box 32, folder 9, SP (quotations). Foley wrongly implies that the Sánchez quotation "the Jewish-Negro-Anglo-Asiatic group we had lunch with" indicates his disparagement of those peoples rather than the paucity of Chicanas/os in CSO. For whatever it is worth, the ACLU agreed with Sánchez. Foley, *Quest for Equality*, 132, 147.

26. Fred Okrand to GIS, November 18, 1952, box 28, folder 18, SP; GIS to Fred Okrand, December 6, 1952, box 28, folder 18, SP; A. Wirin to GIS, September 28, 1953, box 62, folder 18, SP; A. Wirin to Roger Baldwin, September 29, 1953, box 62, folder 18, SP; A. Wirin to GIS, October 5, 1953, box 62, folder 18, SP; GIS to A. Wirin, October 9, 1953, box 62, folder 18, SP; A. Wirin to GIS, December 7, 1953, box 62, folder 18, SP; GIS to Fred Ross, April 28, 1953, box 31, folder 5, SP; Lyle Saunders to GIS, January 12, 1953, box 32, folder 9, SP; Howard Bindelglass to GIS, July 19, 1960, box 31, folder 8, SP; GIS to Howard Bindelglass, July 28, 1960, box 31, folder 8, SP.

27. GIS to ACSSP Board of Directors, July 1, 1952, box 3, folder 6, SP; A. Wirin to GIS, October 12, 1953, box 62, folder 18, SP; GIS to A. Wirin, April 8, 1954, box 62, folder

19, SP; A. Wirin to GIS, April 9, 1954, box 62, folder 19, SP; "Alianza Group Files Suit on Racial Matter," *Arizona Daily Star*, December 3, 1953 (Tucson), box 28, folder 18, SP; GIS to A. Wirin, May 4, 1954, box 62, folder 19, SP; GIS to Simon Gross, May 12, 1954, box 31, folder 7, SP; GIS to Roger Baldwin, May 26, 1954, box 31, folder 7, SP; Ralph Estrada to GIS, August 25, 1954, box 2, folder 11, SP; GIS to Ralph Estrada, July 20, 1954, box 2, folder 11, SP; Ralph Estrada to GIS, February 25, 1954, box 2, folder 11, SP; Ralph Estrada to GIS, September 3, 1953, box 2, folder 11, SP.

28. A. Wirin to GIS, August 26, 1954, box 62, folder 19, SP; A. Wirin to GIS, September 16, 1954, box 62, folder 19, SP; A. Wirin to Roger Baldwin, September 16, 1954, box 62, folder 19, SP; GIS to A. Wirin, September 24, 1954, box 62, folder 19, SP; GIS to A. Wirin, September 30, 1954, box 62, folder 19, SP; GIS to Roger Baldwin, October 1, 1954, box 31, folder 7, SP; A. Wirin to GIS, October 5, 1954, box 62, folder 19, SP; GIS to A. Wirin, October 8, 1954, box 62. folder 19, SP; GIS to Roger Baldwin, October 19, 1954, box 31, folder 7, SP; Roger Baldwin to GIS, October 10, 1954, box 31, folder 7, SP; Roger Baldwin to GIS, October 22, 1954, box 31, folder 7, SP; Simon Gross to GIS, November 11, 1954, box 31, folder 7, SP; GIS to Roger Baldwin, October 26, 1954, box 31, folder 7, SP; GIS to Ralph Estrada, November 18 1954, box 2, folder 11, SP; Ralph Estrada to GIS, November 18, 1954, box 2, folder 11, SP; GIS to Ralph Estrada, November 17, 1954, box 2, folder 11, SP; A. Wirin to GIS, November 23, 1954, box 62, folder 19, SP; Ralph Estrada to A. Wirin, November 23, 1954, box 62. folder 19, SP; Ralph Estrada to GIS, November 23, 1954, box 2, folder 11, SP.

29. A. Wirin to GIS, February 3, 1955, box 63, folder 1, SP; A. Wirin to GIS, February 3, 1955, box 63, folder 1, SP; A. Wirin to GIS, February 3, 1955, box 63, folder 1, SP; A. Wirin to GIS, August 12, 1955, box 63, folder 1, SP; Ralph Estrada, "A Civil Liberties Program in the southwest for Mexican-Americans Under the Auspices of Alianza Hispano-Americana," undated draft [shortly before or on August 12, 1955], box 63, folder 1, SP, 1–11; GIS to Simon Gross, September 15, 1955, box 31, folder 7, SP; GIS to Simon Gross, November 19, 1954, box 31, folder 7, SP; Simon Gross to GIS, October 28, 1955, box 31, folder 7, SP; Simon Gross to Ralph Estrada, October 28, 1955, box 31, folder 7, SP; Simon Gross to GIS, November 7, 1955, box 31, folder 7, SP; GIS to Simon Gross, July 20, 1954, box 31, folder 7, SP; Simon Gross to GIS, July 9, 1954, box 31, folder 7, SP; A. Wirin to GIS, September 29, 1955, box 63, folder 1, SP; GIS to A. Wirin, November 1, 1955, box 63, folder 1, SP; Ralph Estrada to James Marshall, November 17, 1955, box 63, folder 1, SP; A. Wirin to GIS, June 6, 1956, box 63, folder 2, SP; A. Wirin to GIS, May 17, 1956, box 63, folder 2, SP.

30. Olivas, ed., *"Colored Men" and "Hombres Aquí"*; García, *White But Not Equal*; Wilson, *Rise of Judicial Management*, 38–39, and "Brown Over 'Other White,'" 164 (quotation); Sheridan, "Another White Race," 109–44; Gross, "Texas Mexicans and the Politics of Whiteness," 195–205; *Hernández v. State of Texas*, Supreme Court Reporter, Volume 74, 347 U.S., 667–73.

31. García, *White But Not Equal*, 54–57, 120–23; GIS to Robert Marshall Trust, January 9, 1952, box 31, folder 6, SP; GIS to A. Wirin, October 21, 1953, box 63, folder 18, SP.

32. GIS to Carlos Cadena, October 2, 1953, box 9, folder 2, SP; Carlos Cadena to GIS, undated, Thursday [likely soon after October 16, 1953], box 9, folder 2, SP; GIS to Carlos Cadena, October 21, 1953, box 9, folder 2, SP; Sánchez, untitled brief [for *Hernández*], undated [likely late 1953], box 9, folder 19, SP, 2–3 (first quotation), 3 (second quotation); GIS to A. Wirin, October 14, 1953, box 62, folder 18, SP.

33. GIS to Carlos Cadena, October 2, 1953, box 9, folder 2, SP; Carlos Cadena to GIS, undated, Thursday [likely soon after October 16, 1953], box 9, folder 2, SP; GIS to Carlos Cadena, October 21, 1953, box 9, folder 2, SP; Carlos Cadena to GIS, undated, Sunday [likely shortly before December 7, 1953], box 9, folder 2, SP; A. Wirin to Carlos Cadena, September 29, 1953, box 62, folder 18, SP; A. Wirin to GIS, October 15, 1953, box 62, folder 18, SP; A. Wirin to Carlos Cadena, October 15, 1953, box 62, folder 18, SP; A. Wirin to GIS, October 16, 1953, box 62, folder 18, SP; A. Wirin to GIS, October 24, 1953, box 62, folder 18, SP; A. Wirin to GIS, November 6, 1953, box 62, folder 18, SP; A. Wirin to GIS, December 7, 1953, box 62, folder 18, SP; GIS to A. Wirin, December 11, 1953, box 62, folder 18, SP; A. Wirin to GIS, box 62, folder 19, SP; García, *White But Not Equal*, 120; GIS to Ed Idar, May 4, 1954, box 19, folder 20, SP; GIS to Carlos Cadena, May 4, 1954, box 9, folder 2, SP Carlos Cadena to GIS, May 6, 1954, box 9, folder 2, SP; GIS to Carlos Cadena, May 8, 1954, box 9, folder 2, SP; GIS to Carlos Cadena, May 13, 1954, box 9, folder 2, SP.

34. GIS to A. Wirin, May 13, 1954, box 62, folder 19, SP; GIS to A. Wirin, May 25, 1954, box 62, folder 19, SP (quotation); A. Wirin to GIS, May 28, 1954, box 62, folder 19, SP; GIS to John Herrera, November 8, 1954, box 19, folder 5, SP; John Herrera to GIS, May 31, 1954, box 19, folder 5, SP; GIS to John Herrera, December 13, 1954, box 19, folder 5, SP; John Herrera to GIS, December 14, 1954, box 19, folder 5, SP; GIS to Ed Idar, November 8, 1955, box 4, folder 11, SP; Tushnet, *Making Civil Rights Law*, 218–22; Peltason, *Fifty-Eight Lonely Men*.

35. GIS to Hector Garcia, July 23, 1970, box 4, folder 10, SP (quotation); American G.I. Forum, "The Hernandez Case," May 3, 1954, box 4, folder 10, SP, 1–10; GIS to Pete Tijerina, June 3, 1971, box 25, folder 1, SP; Ramos, *The American G.I. Forum*, 75–77; García, *White But Not Equal*, 177–78, 224 nn 32, 33; García, *Hector P. Garcia*, 190–92; Romo, "George I. Sánchez," 357; Olivas, "*Hernández v. Texas*: A Litigation History," in "*Colored Men*" and "*Hombres Aquí*," ed. Olivas, 216–17; James DeAnda, "*Hernández* at Fifty, A Personal History," in "*Colored Men*" and *Hombres Aquí*," ed. Olivas, 204.

36. Tushnet, *The NAACP*, 34, 82–83, 88, 104, 129–37, 159–66; GIS to Gustavo Hernán, January 17, 1946, box 28, folder 22, SP; Clifford Forster to GIS, May 19, 1947, box 3, folder 2, SP (first quotation); GIS to Clifford Forster, May 24, 1947, box 3, folder 2, SP (remaining quotations); GIS to Roger Baldwin, August 27, 1958, box 31, folder 8, SP; Fred Okrand to GIS, November 24, 1953, box 62, folder 18, SP; A. Wirin to GIS, May 19, 1954, box 62, folder 19, SP; A. Wirin to Ralph Estrada, May 19, 1954, box 62, folder 19, SP; GIS to Simon Gross, April 28, 1954, box 31, folder 7, SP; Hart Stilwell to GIS, February 18, 1957, box 33, folder 9, SP; GIS to Hart Stilwell, February 18, 1957, box 33, folder 9, SP; Maury Maverick, Jr. to GIS, January 6, 1954, box 24, folder 6, SP.

37. Ramos, *The American G.I. Forum*, 77–78; "Anti-Bias Gain Here Is Praised," *Albuquerque Journal*, November 25, 1951, box 3, folder 15, SP; Tushnet, *The NAACP*, 120–25; "Sánchez to Discuss Negro Education," *Daily Texan*, April 28, 1948, GISVF–UT; W. Kirk to GIS, September 7, 1951, box 21, folder 18, SP; "Sánchez to Speak at NAACP Meet," *Daily Texan*, October 7, 1951, GISVF–UT; Sánchez, "School Integration and Americans of Mexican Descent," 14 (quotation).

38. Gilpin and Gasman, *Charles S. Johnson*, 183–200; Charles Johnson to GIS, March 18, 1950, box 36, folder 2, JP; GIS to Charles Johnson, March 28, 1950, box 36, folder 2, JP; Charles Johnson to GIS, March 31, 1950, box 36, folder 2, JP; GIS to Charles Johnson, June 3, 1950, box 36, folder 2, JP; Charles Johnson to GIS, June 8, 1950, box 36, folder 2, JP; GIS to Charles Johnson, July 6, 1950, box 36, folder 2, JP; Charles Johnson to GIS, July 19, 1950, box 36, folder 2, JP; program schedule, Seventh Annual Institute of Race Relations, June 26–July 8, 1950, box 37, folder 9, JP, 1–13; Herman Long to GIS, May 17, 1961, box 13, folder 15, SP; Herman Long to GIS, May 25, 1961, box 13, folder 15, SP; GIS to Herman Long, June 14, 1961, box 13, folder 15, SP; GIS to Herman Long, June 28, 1961, box 13, folder 15, SP; program notes, 18th Annual Race Relations Institute, box 13, folder 15, SP, 1–4; Charles Johnson to GIS, March 13, 1954, box 20, folder 16 SP; GIS to Charles Johnson, April 1, 1954, box 20, folder 16, SP; Charles Johnson to GIS, April 10, 1954, box 20, folder 16, SP; Galen Weaver to GIS, April 20, 1954, box 62, folder 3, SP; Julian Samora to GIS, April 14, 1954, box 31, folder 21, SP; Charles Johnson, "Meeting the Challenge of Integration: Summary Report of the Eleventh Annual Institute of Race Relations," undated [likely summer or fall of 1954], box 38, folder 8, JP, 1–7; Galen Weaver to GIS, March 15, 1955, box 62, folder 3, SP; GIS to Galen Weaver, March 21, 1955, box 62, folder 3, SP; Vicente Ximenes to GIS, June 23, 1955, box 63, folder 6, SP; Herman Long to GIS, June 7, 1956, box 62, folder 3, SP; Galen Weaver to GIS, May 1, 1956, box 62, folder 3, SP; GIS to Galen Weaver, May 3, 1956, box 62, folder 3, SP; Arnulfo Martinez to GIS, May 26, 1956, box 24, folder 11, SP; Vicente Ximenes to Hector Garcia, undated [likely July or August 1955], box 222, folder 2, GP; Herman Long to GIS, May 4, 1957, box 9, folder 4, SP [old system]; GIS to Herman Long, May 13, 1957, box 9, folder 4, SP [old system]; Brochure for 1957, "New Dimension in Human Relations," box 9, folder 4, SP [old system]; Herman Long to GIS, May 24, 1957, box 13, folder 9, SP; GIS to Herman Long, June 17, 1957, box 13, folder 9, SP; GIS to Herman Long, July 30, 1957, box 13, folder 9, SP; Galen R. Weaver to GIS, March 29, 1957, box 62, folder 3, SP, 1–3; GIS to Galen Weaver, April 9, 1957, box 62, folder 3, SP; Galen Weaver to GIS, April 24, 1957, box 7, folder 8, SP; Wallace Westfeldt, "Institute Studies Indians, Latins: Fisk Panel Reviews Racial Problems of U.S. Southwest," *Nashville Tennessean*, July 5, 1957, box 39, folder 5, JP.

39. A. Wirin to GIS, July 1, 1948, box 62, folder 15, SP; Thurgood Marshall to GIS, July 1, 1948, box 24, folder 8, SP; GIS to Thurgood Marshall, July 6, 1948, box 24, folder 8, SP (quotations); Thurgood Marshall, July 14, 1948, box 24, folder 8, SP; A. Wirin to GIS, October 14, 1948, box 62, folder 15; Shabazz, *Advancing Democracy*, 57–59.

40. A. Wirin to GIS, November 16, 1949, box 62, folder 15, SP; GIS to A. Wirin, November 18, 1949, box 62, folder 15, SP (quotations); A. Wirin to GIS, November 28, 1949,

box 62, folder 15, SP; GIS to A. Wirin, December 14, 1949, box 62, folder 15, SP; Tushnet, *The NAACP*, 125–35; Goldstone, *Integrating the 40 Acres*, 26–27.

41. GIS to Roger Baldwin, June 20, 1955, box 2, folder 1, SP (first quotation); Thurgood Marshall to GIS, July 11, 1955, box 24, folder 8, SP; Herbert Levy to GIS, August 18, 1955, box 3, folder 2, SP (second quotation); A. Wirin to GIS, June 3, 1955, box 63, folder 1, SP; GIS to Roger Baldwin, August 26, 1955, box 2, folder 20, SP.

42. GIS to Herbert Levy, August 26, 1955, box 3, folder 2, SP (quotations).

43. Herbert Levy to GIS, September 7, 1955, box 3, folder 2, SP; Thurgood Marshall to GIS, September 12, 1955, box 24, folder 8, SP (quotation); GIS to Thurgood Marshall, September 24, 1955, box 24, folder 8, SP; Thurgood Marshall to GIS, October 7, 1955, box 24, folder 8, SP; Thurgood Marshall to A. Smith, October 7, 1955, box 24, folder 8, SP.

44. GIS to Roger Baldwin, August 8, 1958, box 31, folder 8, SP; Roger Baldwin to GIS, August 14, 1958, box 31, folder 8, SP; GIS to Roger Baldwin, August 27, 1958, box 31, folder 8, SP (quotation); Roger Baldwin to GIS, September 2, 1958, box 31, folder 8, SP.

45. Roger Baldwin to GIS, August 14, 1958, box 31, folder 8, SP (first quotation); GIS to Roger Baldwin, August 27, 1958, box 31, folder 8, SP (second quotation).

46. Ramos, *The American G.I. Forum*, 77; Gus Garcia to GIS, February 22, 1951, box 16, folder 20, SP; "A Bill, To Be Entitled," undated, box 16, folder 20, SP; GIS to Gus Garcia, February 23, 1951, box 16, folder 20, SP (quotations).

47. Green, *Establishment in Texas Politics*, 155–62, 174–76; Dobbs, *Yellow Dogs and Republicans*, 108–13; Keith, *Eckhardt*, 118; GIS to Creekmore Fath, May 26, 1954, box 63, folder 19, SP; Sánchez, "Yo voy a votar por el Juez Yarborough . . . ," undated [likely spring of 1954], box 63, folder 17, SP; Cox, *Ralph W. Yarborough*, 136–37; GIS to Ralph Yarborough, February 27, 1956, box 63, folder 10, SP; Sánchez, "Interposition," undated [likely around February 27, 1956], box 63, folder 10, SP, 2 (quotation).

48. Green, *Establishment in Texas Politics*, 190; Kreneck, *Mexican American Odyssey*, 205–6; GIS to Hector Garcia, undated, [likely February or March 1957], box 174, folder 5, GP; GIS to Hector Garcia, March 7, 1957, box 4, folder 10, SP (quotation); GIS to Hector Garcia, April 30, 1957, box 4, folder 10, SP; Ramon Garces, "Segregation Bills Termed Threat to Latin Americans," *Laredo Times*, March 24, 1957, box 19, folder 21, SP.

49. Vargas, *Labor Rights Are Civil Rights*, 273–74; "Dr. Sánchez Warns Against 'Zoning' Culture Groups," *Daily Texan*, February 8, 1951, GISVF–UT; Lorraine Barnes, "Anglo-Latin Groups Pool Ideas in Cultural Study," *Austin American*, November 25, 1957, GISVF–UT; Travis County Grand Jury to T. O Lang, September 28, 1956, box 22, folder 1, SP (quotation); GIS to D. Reddick, December 4, 1961, box 43, folder 2, SP; Goldstone, *Integrating the 40 Acres*, 106–9.

50. GIS to C. Simmons, March 5, 1947, box 33, folder 1, SP; Paul Wassenich to GIS, April 14, 1950, box 62, folder 1, SP; GIS to Newton Edwards, October 30, 1954, box 49, folder 9, SP; GIS to V. Beggs, January 3, 1956, box 7, folder 16, SP; GIS to Group Hospital Services, Inc., January 27, 1955, box 18, folder 18, SP; GIS to C. Hardwicke, January

27, 1955, box 18, folder 18, SP; GIS to Ed Idar, Jr., March 25, 1957, box 19, folder 21, SP (first quotation); GIS to Robert Morrison, May 20, 1957, box 26, folder 4, SP; GIS to V. Thomas, June 4, 1957, box 35, folder 1, SP; GIS to Henry David, August 11, 1959, box 13, folder 12, SP; GIS to Rice Ober, February 10, 1955, box 28, folder 7, SP (second quotation); Sprague interview; Kennedy interview; George I. Sánchez, "Twice Wounded," *Texas Observer* 51 (October 30, 1959), 7.

CHAPTER 11. SÁNCHEZ IN CAMELOT AND THE GREAT SOCIETY

First epigraph. Sánchez, "A New Frontier Policy for the Americas," 9–10.
Second epigraph. Sánchez, "The American of Mexican Descent," 27. This article from 1965 in the *Texas Observer* is a different piece from his essay of 1962 of the same title in the *Chicago Jewish Forum*.

1. Pycior, *LBJ and Mexican Americans*; García, *Viva Kennedy*.
2. Frank Hart to GIS, undated [likely soon before November 9, 1955], box 18, folder 19, SP; GIS to Frank Hart, November 9, 1955, box 18, folder 19, SP (quotation); GIS to Dennis Chávez, October 27, 1955, box 10, folder 11, SP; GIS to Antonio Fernández, October 27, 1955, box 15, folder 15, SP; Robert McConnell to GIS, November 1, 1955, box 15, folder 15, SP; GIS to Antonio Fernández, December 20, 1955, box 15, folder 15, SP; Helen Peterson to GIS, July 24, 1958, box 29, folder 21, SP; Sprague interview; Kennedy interview.
3. GIS to Helen Peterson, August 1, 1958, box 29, folder 21, SP; Michael Candelaria, "Images in *Penitente* and *Santo* Art: A Philosophical Inquiry into the Problem of Meaning," in *Nuevomexicano Cultural Legacy*, ed. Lomelí et al., 272–73; GIS to Brice Sewell, February 14, 1963, box 32, folder 18, SP; Brice Sewell to GIS, March 28, 1963, box 32, folder 18, SP (first quotation); Brice Sewell to GIS, May 23, 1963, box 32, folder 18, SP (second quotation); Brice Sewell to GIS, September 17, 1963, box 32, folder 18, SP (third quotation); Sprague interview; Kennedy interview.
4. GIS to Ralph Yarborough, November 29, 1962, box 63, folder 10, SP; GIS to Brice and Judy Sewell, December 5, 1962, box 32, folder 18, SP; GIS to Consuelo Sprague, October 15, 1964, box 33, folder 5, SP. Sprague interview; Kennedy interview.
5. Sprague interview; Kennedy interview; George I. Sánchez y Sánchez, curriculum vitae, undated [between 1967 and 1972], box 1, folder 6, SP; Arthur Campa to GIS and Luisa Sánchez, July 30, 1964, box 9, folder 13, SP; GIS to B. Lovely, September 12, 1962, box 3, folder 2, SP.
6. "State Education Official Succumbs," *Albuquerque Journal*, November 1, 1962, box 1, folder 18, SP; "Mr. Sánchez Dies Suddenly," *Albuquerque Tribune*, November 1, 1962, box 1, folder 18, SP; Telesfor Sánchez, obituary, *Albuquerque Journal*, November 3, 1962, box 1, folder 18, SP; Brice Sewell to GIS, box 32, folder 18, SP; Alfredo Galaz to GIS, box 8, folder 7, SP [old system]; GIS to Arthur Campa, November 6, 1962, box 9, folder 12, SP (quotation).
7. GIS to Ed Idar, October 30, 1959, box 19, folder 21, SP; Ed Idar to GIS, November 2, 1959, box 19, folder 21, SP; GIS to Ed Idar, November 16, 1959, box 19, folder 21, SP;

GIS to Ed Idar, December 3, 1959, box 19, folder 21, SP; Ed Idar to GIS, December 29, 1959, box 19, folder 21, SP; Pycior, *LBJ and Mexican Americans*, 112–21, 117; García, *Viva Kennedy*, 43–45.

8. GIS to Members of Viva Kennedy Committee on "Statement of Principle," undated [likely late summer of 1960], box 61, folder 15, SP; GIS to Members of Viva Kennedy Committee on "Statement of Principle," undated [likely late summer of 1960], box 61, folder 15, SP; García, *Viva Kennedy*, 74–84; Angier Duke to GIS, telegram, October 23, 1960, box 21, folder 16, SP; GIS to Angier Duke, telegram, October 25, 1960, box 21, folder 16, SP; GIS to Angier Duke, October 25, 1960, box 21, folder 16, SP; Angier Duke to GIS, November 1, 1960; Citizens Committee for a New Frontier Policy in the Americas, "Time Is Running Out to Reestablish the Bonds of the Americas," print advertisement, box 21, folder 16, SP; Angier Duke to GIS, November 18, 1960, box 21, folder 16, SP; GIS to Angier Biddle Duke, December 2, 1960, box 21, folder 16, SP.

9. GIS to E. Goldstein, October 27, 1960, box 61, folder 15, SP; García, *Viva Kennedy*, 105; GIS to Irving Melbo, December 16, 1960, box 24, folder 21, SP (quotation); GIS to John Kennedy, January 18, 1962, box 21, folder 14, SP.

10. Stephen M. Streeter, "The Myth of Pan Americanism: U.S. Policy Toward Latin America During the Cold War, 1954–1963," in *Beyond the Ideal*, ed. Shenan, 167–81; GIS to Angier Duke, December 2, 1960, box 21, folder 16, SP; GIS to Angier Duke, October 25, 1960, box 21, folder 16, SP; Jon Bauman, "Sánchez on US Committee," *Daily Texan*, December 7, 1960, GISVF–UT; Sánchez, "A New Frontier Policy," 9–11; "Dr. George I. Sánchez, Noted University of Texas Professor, Writes Brilliant New Frontier Policy for the Americas," *Congressional Record*, March 8, 1961 (107:41), box 63, folder 10, SP; Peter Barr, "Dr. Sánchez Asks Consideration of Latin American Masses," *Daily Texan*, March 15, 1961, GISVF–UT; GIS to Roland del Mar, July 16, 1963, box 14, folder 2, SP; John Howell to GIS, July 23, 1963, box 14, folder 2, SP; GIS to John Howell, July 30, 1963, box 14, folder 2, SP; Roland del Mar to GIS, August 12, 1963, box 14, folder 2, SP; GIS to Glenn Smiley, November 5, 1962, box 33, folder 3, SP (quotation); G. Solis to GIS, October 22, 1963, box 33, folder 3, SP; GIS to G. Solis, October 29, 1963, box 33, folder 3, SP.

11. Pycior, *LBJ and Mexican Americans*, 122–24; García, *Viva Kennedy*, 107–20; GIS to Ralph Yarborough, June 6, 1961, box 63, folder 10, SP (quotations); GIS to Vicente Ximenes, June 14, 1961, box 63, folder 6, SP; Vicente Ximenes to GIS, June 22, 1961, box 63, folder 6, SP.

12. Venezuelan passport and visa materials, George I. Sánchez, March 28, 1961, box 61, folder 11, SP; GIS to Pedro Grases, January 31, 1961, box 18, folder 18, SP; GIS to Joseph Smiley, June 12, 1962, box 55, folder 3, SP; GIS to Charles Hauch, November 8, 1960, box 61, folder 7, SP; Charles Hauch to GIS, December 8, 1960, box 61, folder 7, SP; GIS to Charles Hauch, December 15, 1960, box 61, folder 7, SP; Charles Hauch to GIS, January 9, 1961, box 61, folder 7, SP; GIS to Charles Hauch, January 17, 1961, box 61, folder 7, SP; GIS to Charles Hauch, January 20, 1961, box 61, folder 7, SP; Charles Hauch to GIS, April 11, 1961, box 61, folder 7, SP; Charles Hauch to GIS,

November 22, 1961, box 61, folder 7, SP; Bess Goodykoontz to GIS, November 28, 1961, box 61, folder 7, SP; GIS to Bess Goodykoontz, November 22, 1961, box 61, folder 7, SP; GIS to Francis Keppel, January 10, 1962, box 61, folder 7, SP; Charles Hauch to GIS, April 2, 1961, box 61, folder 7, SP; GIS to Charles Hauch, April 4, 1961, box 61, folder 7, SP; Charles Hauch to GIS, April 6, 1962, box 61, folder 7, SP; GIS to Charles Hauch, April 12, 1962, box 61, folder 7, SP; GIS to Charles Hauch, May 9, 1962, box 61, folder 7, SP; Charles Hauch to GIS, May 14, 1962, box 61, folder 7, SP; GIS to Charles Hauch, September 6, 1962, box 61, folder 7, SP; GIS to Charles Hauch, September 24, 1962, box 61, folder 7, SP; GIS to S. Herrell, February 2, 1963, box 61, folder 7, SP; GIS to Francis Keppel, February 4, 1963, box 61, folder 7, SP; Oliver Caldwell to GIS, April 5, 1963, box 61, folder 7, SP; GIS to Oliver Caldwell, April 10, 1963, box 61, folder 7, SP; David Getter to GIS, October 30, 1969, box 17, folder 1, SP; GIS to David Getter, November 14, 1969, box 17, folder 1, SP; GIS to George Hall, March 1, 1962, box 18, folder 17, SP; George Hall to GIS, March 1, 1962, box 18, folder 17, SP; Julian Samora to GIS, undated [likely in the spring of 1961], box 31, folder 22, SP; GIS to Julian Samora, May 11, 1961, box 31, folder 22, SP (quotations); Sánchez, *The Development of Education in Venezuela*; Alessandro, review of *Education and Social Change in Chile* and *The Development of Education in Venezuela*, 605–6.

13. James Boren to GIS, January 16, 1962, box 36, folder 1, SP; GIS to James Boren, January 30, 1962, box 36, folder 1, SP; GIS to James Boren, March 22, 1962, box 36, folder 1, SP; James Boren to GIS, April 21, 1962, box 36, folder 1, SP; GIS to Robert Culbertson and James Boren, September 9, 1962, box 36, folder 1, SP; GIS to James Boren and Robert Culbertson, February 4, 1963, box 36, folder 2, SP; GIS to Joseph Smiley, June 12, 1962, box 55, folder 3, SP; Charles Ray to GIS, December 11, 1962, box 9, folder 10, SP; Charles Ray to GIS, February 2, 1962, box 9, folder 10, SP; GIS to Charles Ray, February 20, 1963, box 9, folder 10, SP (quotation).

14. "Kennedy Appoints 2 UT Professors," *Daily Texan*, April 6, 1961, GISVF–UT; GIS to John Boyd, February 3, 1964, box 8, folder 11, SP; roster for Peace Corps, National Advisory Council and Career Planning Board, undated, box 29, folder 12, SP, 1–5; Pycior, *LBJ and Mexican Americans*, 122–23. Robert Shriver to GIS, March 27, 1961, box 29, folder 8, SP; GIS to Robert Shriver, undated [likely shortly after March 27, 1961], box 29, folder 8, SP; Robert Shriver to GIS, June 21, 1961, box 29, folder 8, SP; Robert Shriver to GIS, June 29, 1961, box 29, folder 8, SP; GIS to Robert Shriver, June 29, 1961, box 29, folder 8, SP; Robert Shriver to GIS, July 12, 1961, box 29, folder 8, SP; GIS to Robert Shriver, October 6, 1961, box 29, folder 8, SP; program, International Relations Conference on Latin America, International Relations Club at Wayland Baptist College, March 1–3, 1962, box 14, folder 1, SP; "The Common People Must Be Reached, Says Speaker," *Plainview Daily Herald*, March 4, 1962, box 14, folder 1, SP; Eugene Jones to GIS, March 6, 1962, box 14, folder 1, SP; Eugene Jones to Bill Moyers, March 6, 1962, box 14, folder 1, SP; Joe Wilkinson to GIS, May 19, 1964, box 10, folder 22, SP; GIS to Joe Wilkinson, May 28, 1964, box 10, folder 22, SP; Arthur Campa to GIS and Luisa Sánchez, July 30, 1964, box 9, folder 13, SP.

15. Sánchez, "'Punch Lines' for the President's Talks in Mexico," undated [likely in the spring of 1962], box 38, folder 11, SP (quotations); Sánchez, "Underdeveloped Peoples at Home (An Idea for a Domestic Peace Corps)," March 8, 1962, box 72, folder 18, SP; GIS to Robert Kennedy, December 7, 1962, box 21, folder 15, SP.

16. GIS to Robert Shriver, October 29, 1962, box 29, folder 9, SP; Robert Shriver, November 27, 1962, box 29, folder 9, SP; GIS to Robert Shriver, December 12, 1962, box 29, folder 9, SP; Robert Shriver to GIS, January 3, 1963, box 29, folder 9, SP (quotation); Thomas Carter to GIS, November 29, 1962, box 36, folder 3, SP; GIS to Thomas Carter, December 5, 1962, box 36, folder 3, SP.

17. Sánchez, "Past and Present Inter-American Educational Relations," 2 (quotation).

18. Wiliam Nagle to GIS, March 25, 1963, box 37, folder 15, SP, SP; Notification of Personnel Action, March 18, 1963, box 37, folder 15, SP; GIS to William Nagle, April 9, 1964, box 37, folder 15, SP; William Nagle to GIS, April 21, 1964, box 37, folder 15, SP; Thomas Hughes to GIS, May 7, 1964, box 37, folder 15, SP; Robert Person to GIS, September 22, 1954, box 37, folder 15, SP; Notification of Personnel Action, September 17, 1964, box 37, folder 15, SP; Optional Form 8 of U.S. Civil Service Commission, undated, box 37, folder 15, SP; Elizabeth Brinton to GIS, June 11, 1965, box 37, folder 13, SP; GIS to Elizabeth Brinton, June 15, 1965, box 37, folder 13, SP; George I. Sánchez to Elizabeth Brinton, June 23, 1965, box 37, folder 13, SP; GIS to Elizabeth Brinton, August 23, 1965, box 37, folder 13, SP; GIS, "The Jalapa Seminar, July 12–24," August 23, 1965, box 37, folder 13, SP, 1–3; GIS, "The 'Mexico City Seminar'," August 23, 1965, box 37, folder 13, SP, 1–4; GIS to William Brickman, June 29, 1965, box 10, folder 10, SP.

19. Sánchez, *Arithmetic in Maya*, 1–10, 7 (quotation); Brunhouse, *Sylvanus G. Morley*, 112–47; GIS to Bruce Meador, December 14, 1962, box 24, folder 19, SP; GIS to Carter Zeleznik, January 3, 1962, box 63, folder 21, SP; Bruce Vogeli to GIS, October 31, 1963, box 61, folder 6, SP; Bruce Vogeli to GIS, November 26, 1963, box 61, folder 6, SP; GIS to Maurice Ries, April 1, 1963, box 31, folder 3, SP; GIS to W. French Anderson, April 22, 1969, box 5, folder 4, SP; Satterthwaite, review of *Arithmetic in Maya*, 256; Carpenter, review of *Arithmetic in Maya*, 108; Kelley, review of *Arithmetic in Maya*, 1104; H. Ettlinger to GIS, December 13, 1956, box 19, folder 9, SP; H. Ettlinger to GIS, January 7, 1957, box 19, folder 9, SP; GIS to H. Ettlinger, January 9, 1957, box 19, folder 9, SP; GIS to Leslie Spier, February 25, 1957, box 33, folder 5, SP; Leslie Spier to GIS, March 17, 1957, box 33, folder 5, SP; GIS to Eastin Nelson, October 20, 1960, box 52, folder 15, SP; GIS to Eastin Nelson, March 10, 1961, box 52, folder 15, SP; GIS to Eastin Nelson, March 22, 1961, box 52, folder 15, SP.

20. GIS to Ben DeLuca, April 5, 1962, box 17, folder 2, SP; GIS to Lindley Stiles, April 6, 1962, box 17, folder 2, SP; Ben DeLuca to GIS, April 10, 1962, box 17, folder 2, SP; GIS to Lindley Stiles, June 5, 1963, box 17, folder 3, SP; Ben DeLuca to GIS, June 13, 1963, box 17, folder 3, SP; Lindley Stiles to GIS, June 14, 1963, box 17, folder 3, SP; GIS to Lindley Stiles, September 11, 1963, box 17, folder 3, SP; Ben DeLuca to GIS, September 17, 1963, box 17, folder 3, SP; GIS to Ben DeLuca, September 20, 1963, box 17, folder 3, SP; GIS to James Lohman, March 11, 1964, box 17, folder 4, SP; GIS to James

Lohman, March 13, 1964, box 17, folder 4, SP; GIS to James Lohman, April 8, 1964, box 17, folder 4, SP; Sánchez, *Mexico*, 71.

21. Sánchez, "The United Mexican States," in *Comparative Educational Administration*, ed. Reller, 151–65; Sánchez, "Education in Mexico," and "Venezuela: Contradictions and Political Factionalism," in *The Caribbean, Mexico Today*, ed. Wilgus, 145–51, 375–76; Curriculum Vitae of George I. Sánchez, up to 1966, box 1, folder 14, SP, 18–19; Valencia, "A Tribute to Thomas P. Carter," 239–40; Wayne Barcomb to GIS, January 19, 1966, box 3, folder 5, SP [old system]; GIS to Wayne Barcomb, January 25, 1966, box 7, folder 14, SP; Wayne Barcomb to GIS, February 9, 1966, box 7, folder 14, SP; GIS to Jim Rogers, February 2, 1966, box 7, folder 14, SP; Jim Rogers to GIS, December 1, 1965, box 3, folder 5, SP [old system].

22. García, *Viva Kennedy*, 123–32; Pycior, *LBJ and Mexican Americans*, 124–26; GIS to Albert Peña, January 11, 1961, box 61, folder 15, SP; Albert Peña to GIS, January 27, 1961, box 61, folder 15, SP.

23. GIS to Albert Peña, January 11, 1961, box 61, folder 15, SP; Carey McWilliams to GIS, July 24, 1961, box 24, folder 18, SP; García, *Viva Kennedy*, 134–35; Sánchez, "The American of Mexican Descent," 124 (quotations); Curriculum Vitae for George I. Sánchez, undated [likely 1965 or 1966], box 1, folder 14, SP, 9; "Prof. Sánchez' Paper Adopted by PASSO Unites U.S. Latins Political Interests," *American G.I. Forum News Bulletin* 8:10 (October 1961), 1; Dugger, "Political Interests of Latins United," 1, 3; Sánchez, "The Latin Citizen," 6; Sánchez, "Proposals on Latins," 7; García, *Hector Garcia*, 239–40; GIS to Ronnie Dugger, April 19, 1963, box 34, folder 16, SP.

24. Ed Idar to GIS, January 23, 1962, box 30, folder 9, SP; Ed Idar to GIS, January 25, 1962, box 30, folder 9, SP; Ed Idar to *Texas Observer*, January 25, 1962, box 30, folder 9, SP; GIS to Ed Idar, January 29, 1962, box 30, folder 9, SP; Hector Garcia to GIS, February 7, 1962, box 4, folder 10, SP; García, *Viva Kennedy*, 138–42, 144–46; Pycior, *LBJ and Mexican Americans*, 134; John Wagner to GIS, February 12, 1962, box 30, folder 9, SP; GIS to John Wagner, April 12, 1962, box 30, folder 9, SP; Manuel Velasco to GIS, February 13, 1962, box 30, folder 9, SP; Gregorio Coronado to GIS, February 13, 1962, box 30, folder 9, SP; GIS to Gregorio Coronado, February 17, 1962, box 30, folder 9, SP; press release by Don Yarborough gubernatorial campaign, February 22, 1962, box 30, folder 9, SP; GIS to Oscar Phillips [forwarded to Hector Garcia with a note], March 6, 1962, box 174, folder 1, GP; GIS to PASSO, undated [around February 9, 1962], box 30, folder 9, SP (first quotation); García, *Hector Garcia*, 241–43; GIS to Hector Garcia, March 6, 1962, box 30, folder 10, SP; GIS, circular letter for Don Yarborough gubernatorial campaign, undated [likely February or March 1962], box 30, folder 10, SP; GIS to Hector Garcia, April 24, 1962, box 30, folder 10, SP (second quotation); GIS to Albert Peña, May 11, 1962, box 30, folder 10, SP; GIS to Hector Garcia, May 16, 1962, box 89, folder 30, GP; GIS to Ed Idar, May 16, 1962, box 89, folder 30, GP; Ed Idar to Hector Garcia, May 17, 1962, box 89, folder 30, GP; Ed Idar to GIS, May 17, 1962, box 30, folder 10, SP; Hector Garcia to GIS, May 25, 1962, box 4, folder 10, SP; GIS to Hector Garcia, May 27, 1962, box 174, folder 11, GP.

25. García, *Viva Kennedy*, 145–46; GIS to Judy Breck, September 15, 1962, box 11, folder 11, SP; GIS, circulars for Don Yarborough and Jack Cox gubernatorial campaigns and telephone lists, undated, box 11, folder 11, SP, 1–5; GIS to *Texas Observer*, October 22, 1962, box 11, folder 11, SP; GIS, position paper for higher education and the University of Texas, undated, box 11, folder 11, SP; Hector Garcia, circular for John Connally gubernatorial campaign, undated, box 11, folder 11, SP; GIS to Josey Y'Barbo, undated [likely on or around September 15, 1962]; Angie Guerrero to GIS, June 14, 1962, box 18, folder 13, SP; GIS to *Texas Observer*, October 22, 1962, box 11, folder 11, SP; GIS to Judy Breck, September 15, 1962, box 11, folder 11, SP; Ramiro Casso to GIS, November 10, 1962, box 10, folder 3, SP; GIS to Ramiro Casso, November 19, 1962, box 10, folder 3, SP (quotations); GIS to Ralph Yarborough, November 20, 1962, box 63, folder 10, SP.

26. García, *Viva Kennedy*, 146–51; Pycior, *LBJ and Mexican Americans*, 136–37; Gladwyn Hill to GIS, September 20, 1963, box 19, folder 7, SP; Blandina Cardenas, "Dr. Sánchez Exposes Misery of Mexicans in 'Look' Article," *Daily Texan*, September 24, 1963, GISVF–UT; GIS to Carey McWilliams, January 7, 1965, box 24, folder 18, SP; GIS to Ralph Yarborough, May 3, 1963, box 63, folder 11, SP; GIS, "PASO Not Outside-Controlled," *San Antonio Express News*, June 11, 1963, box 30, folder 11, SP.

27. GIS to Ronnie Dugger, December 21, 1962, box 34, folder 16, SP (first and second quotations); GIS to Ronnie Dugger, February 4, 1963, box 34, folder 16, SP; Dugger, "A Comment," 10 (remaining quotations).

28. Sánchez, "A Re-phrasing," 13 (quotations); Ronnie Dugger to GIS, undated [likely days after April 19, 1963], box 34, folder 16, SP.

29. García, *Viva Kennedy*, 152–57; Lyndon Johnson to GIS, October 22, 1963, box 20, folder 17, SP; GIS to Lyndon Johnson, October 30, 1963, box 20, folder 17, SP; Philip Des Marais to GIS, October 25, 1963, box 38, folder 12, SP; Hobart Taylor to GIS, November 4, 1963, box 33, folder 14, SP; GIS to Hobart Taylor, November 7, 1963, box 33, folder 14, SP; GIS to Hobart Taylor November 25, 1963, box 33, folder 14, SP; Hobart Taylor to GIS, December 9, 1963, box 38, folder 12, SP; Hobart Taylor to GIS, December 10, 1963, box 38, folder 12, SP; program, Regional Conference of Community Leaders on Equal Employment Opportunity, November 14, 1963, box 38, folder 12, SP, 1–12; Sánchez, untitled talk to EEO Conference, Los Angeles, November 14, 1963, box 38, folder 12, SP; Davies, *From Opportunity to Entitlement*, 32–34; McGee, "Texas: The Roots of the Agony," 427–31.

30. Price Daniel to GIS, December 20, 1963, box 12, folder 3, SP; Price Daniel, "Christian Principles in the Political Process," address to YMCI HI-Y Youth and Government Banquet, Austin, Texas, December 14, 1963, box 10, folder 4, SP, 1–5; GIS to Price Daniel, January 3, 1964, box 12, folder 3, SP (quotations); Price Daniel to GIS, January 13, 1964, box 12, folder 3, SP.

31. Gideon Sjoberg, "Intellectual Risk Taking, Organizations, and Academic Freedom and Tenure," in *Edgework*, ed. Lyng, 258; Reece McGee to GIS and William Drake, January 4, 1964, box 10, folder 4, SP [old system]; Reece McGee to GIS, undated [likely January 4, 1964], box 10, folder 4, SP [old system]; Sánchez and Drake, "The State of Texas," 20; David Miller to W. Keeton, November 16, 1964, box 43, folder 3,

SP; W. Keeton to Counsel on Academic Freedom and Responsibility, November 20, 1964, box 43, folder 3, SP; GIS to Counsel on Academic Freedom and Responsibility, November 24, 1964, box 43, folder 3, SP; Orville Wyss to counsel on Academic Freedom and Responsibility, November 25, 1964, box 43, folder 3, SP; John Silber to Counsel on Academic Freedom and Responsibility, December 9, 1964, box 43, folder 3, SP; W. Keeton to Counsel on Academic Freedom and Responsibility, December 9, 1964, box 43, folder 3, SP.

32. GIS to John Connally, May 2, 1963, box 11, folder 8, SP; GIS to John Connally, March 12, 1965, box 11, folder 8, SP; John Connally to GIS, March 18, 1965, box 11, folder 8, SP; GIS to Ronnie Dugger, June 27, 1963, box 34, folder 16, SP (first quotation); Arthur Perry to GIS, September 3, 1963, box 163, folder 234, JSP; Lyndon Johnson to GIS, February 22, 1954, box 163, folder 234, SP; GIS to Arthur Campa, October 6, 1964, box 9, folder 13, SP (second quotation); Arthur Campa to GIS, November 2, 1964, box 9, folder 13, SP; GIS to Arthur Campa, November 11, 1964, box 9, folder 13, SP; GIS to Concha DeKleven, May 23, 1966, box 28, folder 6, SP; Irving Melbo to GIS, April 15, 1965, box 24, folder 21, SP; GIS to Irving Melbo, May 5, 1965, box 24, folder 21, SP (third quotation); Lawrence O'Brien, invitation list, October 13, 1964, box 46, folder "Sánchez, George I.," WHCF; David North, invitation list, October 11, 1966, box 45, folder "Sánchez, George I.," WHCF; Lawrence O'Brien to GIS, October 13, 1964, box 38, folder 11, SP; W. Watson to GIS, June 8, 1967, box 38, folder 11, SP; Robert Wood to Terrence Scanlon, April 1, 1966, box 513, folder "Sánchez, George I.," OFJM; Terrence Scanlon to Mike Manatos and Henry Hall Wilson and Cliff Carter, April 25, 1966, box 513, folder "Sánchez, George I.," OFJM; John Macy to Harry McPherson, August 12, 1966, box 513, folder "Sánchez, George I.," OFJM; Terrence Scanlon to John Macy, September 13, 1966, box 513, folder "Sánchez, George I.," OFJM; Lyndon Johnson to GIS, August 5, 1964, box 36, folder 14, SP; press release, University of Texas, August 8, 1964, box 36, folder 14, SP; press release, University of Texas, October 14, 1964, box 36, folder 14, SP; "Sánchez Named to Trade Board," *Daily Texan*, January 31, 1967, GISVF–UT.

33. Sánchez, "The American of Mexican Descent," 26–27; "UTEP Lecturer Calls for New Deal for Spanish Speaking E.P. People," *El Paso Herald-Post*, December 9, 1966, box 20, folder 26, SP; Sánchez, untitled talk to EEO Conference, Los Angeles, November 14, 1963, box 38, folder 12, SP, 3 (quotation); Davies, *From Opportunity to Entitlement*, 32–34.

34. Kaplowitz, *LULAC*, 87–88, 94–104; GIS to Franklin Roosevelt, Jr., March 18, 1966, box 38, folder 1, SP; GIS to participants who "walked out," undated [likely late March or early April 1966], box 38, folder 1, SP; GIS to Franklin Roosevelt, Jr., April 5, 1966, box 38, folder 1, SP; Franklin Roosevelt, Jr. to GIS, April 26, 1966, box 38, folder 1, SP; GIS to Franklin Roosevelt, Jr., May 5, 1966, box 38, folder 1, SP; Luther Holcomb to GIS, April 26, 1966, box 38, folder 1, SP; Herman Edelsberg to GIS, June 6, 1966, box 15, folder 9, SP; "UT Professor Proposed for U.S. Job," *Dallas Times Herald*, May 20, 1966, GISVF–UT; Robert Baskin, "Yarborough Snubs Holcomb for Post," *Dallas Morning News*, May 21, 1966, GISVF–UT; Ralph Yarborough to Lyndon Johnson,

May 14, 1966, box 63, folder 13, SP (quotation); GIS to Ralph Yarborough, May 16, 1966, box 63, folder 13, SP; Ralph Yarborough to GIS, May 20, 1966, box 63, folder 13, SP; Mike Manatos to Ralph Yarborough, May 18, 1966, box 63, folder 13, SP; press release by Ralph Yarborough, May 19, 1966, box 63, folder 13, SP; GIS to Ralph Yarborough, June 9, 1966, box 63, folder 13, SP; John Brademas to Lyndon B. Johnson, June 6, 1966, box 63, folder 13, box 513, folder "Sánchez, George I.," OFJM; Henry H. Wilson, Jr. to John Brademas, June 8, 1966, box 513, folder "Sánchez, George I.," OFJM; Eduardo Quevedo et al. to Lyndon B. Johnson, June 19, 1966, box 513, folder "Sánchez, George I.," OFJM; Robert P. Sánchez to Lyndon B. Johnson, June 23, 1966, box 513, folder "Sánchez, George I.," OFJM; John W. Macy, Jr. to Robert P. Sánchez, July 9, 1966, box 513, folder "Sánchez, George I.," OFJM; Albert A. Peña, Jr. to Lyndon B. Johnson, June 9, 1966, box 29, folder 20, SP; Julian Samora to John Brademas, May 23, 1966, box 31, folder 22, SP; Hank S. Brown to Lyndon B. Johnson, May 24, 1966, box 38, folder 1, SP; John B. Clinton to Hank S. Brown, May 26, 1966, box 46, folder "Sánchez, George I.," WHCF; Jesus Perez to Lyndon B. Johnson, undated [likely late May or early June 1966], box 46, folder "Sánchez, George I.," WHCF; John B. Clinton to Jesus Perez, June 13, 1966, box 46, folder "Sánchez, George I.," WHCF; John B. Clinton to Albert A. Peña, June 16, 1966, box 46, folder "Sánchez, George I.," WHCF; Manuel A. Velasco to Lyndon B. Johnson, June 11, 1966, box 46, folder "Sánchez, George I.," WHCF; John B. Clinton to Manuel A. Velasco, June 20, 1966, box 46, folder "Sánchez, George I.," WHCF; Albert Piñon, June 9, 1966, box 513, folder "Sánchez, George I.," OFJM.

35. William Bonilla to Lyndon Johnson, June 7, 1966, box 513, folder "Sánchez, George I.," OFJM (quotation).

36. Ralph Yarborough to GIS, June 10, 1966, box 63, folder 13, SP; Ralph Yarborough to Hector Garcia, June 10, 1966, box 63, folder 13, SP; GIS to William Bonilla, June 14, 1966, box 63, folder 13, SP (first three quotations); Pycior, *LBJ and Mexican Americans*, 177; GIS to Ralph Yarborough, June 16, 1966, box 63, folder 13, SP (fourth quotation); Ralph Yarborough to Lyndon Johnson, November 1, 1966, box 513, folder "Sánchez, George I.," OFJM.

37. William Bonilla to GIS, June 16, 1966, box 63, folder 13, SP (quotations).

38. John Macy to Lyndon Johnson, June 26, 1966, box 513, folder "Sánchez, George I.," OFJM (first, second, and third quotations); John Macy to Lyndon Johnson, June 29, 1966, box 513, folder "Sánchez, George I.," OFJM; Lou Schwartz to John Macy, August 8, 1966, box 513, Sánchez, George I.," OFJM (fourth quotation).

39. John Macy to Lyndon Johnson, August 18, 1966, box 513, folder "Sánchez, George I.," OFJM (quotation); James Falcon to John Macy, March 3, 1967, box 774, folder "Equal Employment Opportunity Commission," OFJM; John Macy, March 10, 1967, box 774, folder "Equal Employment Opportunity Commission," OFJM; Jake Jacobsen to Lyndon Johnson, March 13, 1967, box 774, folder "Equal Employment Opportunity Commission," OFJM; Cristobal Aldrete to Louis Martin, March 20, 1967, box 774, folder "Equal Employment Opportunity Commission," OFJM; Pycior, *LBJ and Mexican Americans*, 196–98.

40. Kaplowitz, *LULAC*, 106–7; Pycior, *LBJ and Mexican Americans*, 178–81, 207–14; Summary of George I. Sánchez talk to EEOC seminar, "Understanding Minority Groups Members—Spanish-American," undated [likely September 1966], box 36, folder 13, SP; list, "Pre-planning for White House Conference on Problems of Spanish-Speaking Peoples, Planning Session—October 26, 1966, Mexican-Americans," October 26, 1966, box 513, folder "Sánchez, George I.," OFJM; "Editorial," *The Forumeer*, November 1966, box 14, folder 11, SP (quotation); Sánchez, "White House Conference on the Spanish-Speaking," October 26, 1966, box 37, folder 3; Ralph Guzman to GIS, November 2, 1966, box 18, folder 13, SP; GIS, November 10, 1966, box 18, folder 13, SP; Vicente Ximenes to Lyndon Johnson, July 14, 1967, box 39, FG 687 "Interagency Committee on Mexican American Affairs," WHCF; David North to GIS, October 3, 1967, box 39, folder 6, SP; GIS to David North, October 4, 1967, box 39, folder 6, SP; Albert Cruz and Robert Hayden to GIS, October 16, 1967, box 39, folder 6, SP.

41. Kahlenberg, *Tough Liberal*, 9–10; Sánchez, "A Communication," 5 (quotation); Manuel, *Spanish-Speaking Children of the Southwest*, 34–41, 195; Hardgrave and Hinojosa, *The Politics of Bilingual Education*, 1; San Miguel, *"Let All of Them Take Heed,"* 186. See also Blanton, "A Legacy of Neglect."

42. Price Ashton to GIS, November 27, 1962, box 31, folder 8, SP; GIS to Robert Marshall Civil Liberties Trust, November 30, 1962, box 31, folder 8, SP; GIS to Robert Marshall Civil Liberties Trust, May 26, 1966, box 31, folder 8, SP; Howard Bindelglass to GIS, June 2, 1966, box 31, folder 8, SP; Brandoch Lovely to GIS, January 14, 1965, box 33, folder 20, SP; GIS to Brandoch Lovely, January 18, 1965, box 33, folder 20, SP; Elizabeth Burba to GIS, January 28, 1965, box 33, folder 20, SP; GIS to J. Edgar, December 16, 1963, box 34, folder 14, SP; J. Edgar to GIS, January 8, 1946, box 34, folder 14, SP; GIS to J. Edgar, January 13, 1964, box 34, folder 14, SP; R. Byram to J. Edgar, January 13, 1964, box 34, folder 14, SP; GIS to R. Byram, January 16, 1964, box 34, folder 14, SP; GIS to J. Edgar, January 21, 1964, box 34, folder 14, SP (quotation).

43. Lyndon Johnson to GIS, August 5, 1964, box 36, folder 14, SP; press release, University of Texas News and Information Service, August 6, 1964, box 36, folder 14, SP; press release, University of Texas News and Information Service, October 14, 1964, box 36, folder 14, SP; Matusow, *The Unraveling of America*, 183–84, 187–88; GIS to J. Edgar, October 23, 1964, box 34, folder 14, SP: J. Edgar to GIS, November 16, 1964, box 34, folder 14, SP; GIS to J. Edgar, November 19, 1964, box 34, folder 14, SP; GIS, "A Position Paper on Education for Preliminary Conference, Reality and Potential in State Affairs of Americans of Mexican Descent in Texas," undated [around November 19, 1964], box 34, folder 14, SP; William Evans to GIS, November 18, 1964, box 34, folder 14, SP; GIS to William Evans, November 24, 1964, box 34, folder 14, SP (quotation), 2; GIS to LeRoy Collins, November 19, 1964, box 34, folder 14, SP; LeRoy Collins to GIS, September 28, 1964, box 36, folder 14, SP; GIS to William Bonilla, September 8, 1964, box 34, folder 14, SP; GIS to William Bonilla, October 22, 1964, box 34, folder 14, SP.

44. GIS to LeRoy Collins, April 7, 1965, box 36, folder 14, SP (first quotation); Jay Janis to GIS, May 10, 1965, box 36, folder 14, SP; GIS to Jay Janis, May 26, 1964, box 36, folder

14, SP (second quotation); GIS to Rudy Ramos, June 10, 1964, box 4, folder 12, SP; Rudy Ramos to Hector Garcia, June 28, 1964, box 4, folder 12, SP; GIS to Ralph Yarborough, January 16, 1967, box 20, folder 19, SP; Hector Garcia to GIS, June 12, 1968, box 4, folder 10, SP; GIS to Hector Garcia, June 17, 1968, box 4, folder 10, SP; Efrain Dominguez to GIS, November 2, 1967, box 12, folder 11, SP; Efrain Dominguez, "Letter to the Editor," *Valley Evening Monitor,* October 31, 1967, box 12, folder 11, SP, 4; GIS to Efrain Dominguez, November 7, 1967, box 12, folder 11, SP; Efrain Dominguez to GIS, November 9, 1967, box 12, folder 11, SP.

45. A. Gaarder to GIS, December 4, 1959, box 37, folder 4, SP; GIS to A. Gaarder, December 15, 1959, box 37, folder 4, SP; A. Gaarder to GIS, December 28, 1959, box 37, folder 4, SP; GIS, to A. Gaarder, January 5, 1960, box 37, folder 5, SP; GIS to Richard Renner, January 6, 1960, box 37, folder 5, SP; GIS to Eduardo Barrera, January 26, 1960, box 37, folder 5, SP; Richard Renner to GIS, February 2, 1960, box 37, folder 5, SP; GIS to A. Gaarder, February 5, 1960, box 37, folder 5, SP; GIS to A. Gaarder, February 24, 1960, box 37, folder 5, SP; A. Gaarder to GIS, March 25, 1960, box 37, folder 5, SP; A. Gaarder to GIS, March 30, 1960, box 37, folder 5, SP; GIS to A. Gaarder, April 12, 1960, box 37, folder 5, SP; GIS to Henry David, March 6, 1961, box 26, folder 2, SP (first quotation); Kathryn Williamson to GIS, February 26, 1964, box 62, folder 12, SP; GIS to Kathryn Williamson, March 4, 1964, box 62, folder 12, SP (second quotation); GIS to Arthur Campa, February 27, 1963, box 9, folder 12, SP; Schlossman, "Self-Evident Remedy?," 901; Caridad Gutiérrez to GIS, February 2, 1962, box 18, folder 13, SP; GIS to Cardiad Gutiérrez, April 5, 1962, box 18, folder 13, SP.

46. Richard Alm to GIS, September 12, 1961, box 2, folder 14, SP; GIS to Richard Alm, September 23, 1961, box 2, folder 14, SP; GIS to Richard Alm, December 15, 1961, box 2, folder 14, SP; Constance McCullough to Richard Alm, February 9, 1962, box 2, folder 14, SP (quotation); Richard Alm to GIS, April 30, 1962, box 2, folder 14, SP; GIS to McCullough, April 30, 1962, box 2, folder 14, SP; Monroe Sweetland to GIS, May 5, 1965, box 27, folder 4, SP; Lawrence Darthick to Roy Archibald and Monroe Sweetland, May 4, 1965, box 27, folder 4, SP; GIS to Monroe Sweetland, May 13, 1965, box 27, folder 4, SP; Monroe Sweetland to GIS, May 28, 1965, box 27, folder 4, SP.

47. Joshua Fishman to GIS, January 6, 1959, box 15, folder 18, SP; GIS to Joshua Fishman, January 16, 1959, box 15, folder 18, SP; Joshua Fishman to GIS, May 15, 1961, box 15, folder 18, SP; GIS to Joshua Fishman, May 30, 1961, box 15, folder 18, SP; Joshua Fishman to GIS, June 5, 1961, box 15, folder 18, SP; GIS to Joshua Fishman, June 20, 1961, box 15, folder 18, SP; Joshua Fishman to GIS, October 10, 1961, box 15, folder 18, SP; GIS to Joshua Fishman, October 17, 1961, box 15, folder 18, SP; Joshua Fishman to GIS, October 19, 1961, box 15, folder 18, SP; GIS to Joshua Fishman, May 4, 1962, box 15, folder 18, SP; GIS to Joshua Fishman, May 11, 1962, box 15, folder 18, SP; Joshua Fishman to GIS, August 23, 1962, box 15, folder 18, SP; GIS, September 6, 1962, box 15, folder 18, SP; Joshua Fishman to GIS, September 11, 1962, box 15, folder 18, SP; GIS to Joshua Fishman, September 21, 1962, box 15, folder 18, SP; GIS to Arthur Campa, September 21, 1962, box 9, folder 12, SP (quotation); Arthur Campa to GIS,

September 27, 1962, box 9, folder 12, SP; Arthur Campa to GIS, October 29, 1962, box 9, folder 12, SP; GIS to Arthur Campa, November 6, 1962, box 9, folder 12, SP; Theodore Andersson to GIS, June 11, 1963, box 5, folder 5, SP; Chester Christian to Theodore Andersson, July 5, 1963, box 5, folder 5, SP; GIS to Theodore Andersson, July 17, 1963, box 5, folder 5, SP; Joshua Fishman to GIS, June 4, 1963, box 15, folder 18, SP; GIS to Joshua Fishman, June 17, 1963, box 15, folder 18, SP; Fishman, ed., *Language Loyalty in the United States.*

48. Theodore Andersson to GIS, May 1, 1957, box 5, folder 5, SP; GIS to Theodore Andersson, May 10, 1957, box 5, folder 5, SP; program, "Conference for the Teacher of the Bilingual Child," June 8–10, 1964, University of Texas at Austin, box 14, folder 6, SP, 1–2; Joseph Michel, "Proposal for Establishing Foreign Language Education Center in the College of Education, Department of Curriculum and Instruction, January 12, 1966, box 25, folder 13, SP, 1–13; GIS to Joseph Michel, December 16, 1965, box 25, folder 13, SP; Theodore Andersson to GIS, June 22, 1966, box 5, folder 5, SP; GIS to Theodore Andersson, June 28, 1966, box 5, folder 5, SP; Theodore Andersson to GIS, box 5, folder 5, SP; Schlossman, "Self-Evident Remedy?," 873; Pycior, *LBJ and Mexican Americans,* 184–86; Cox, *Ralph W. Yarborough,* 232–35; Blanton, *Strange Career of Bilingual Education,* 135–36; Dugger, "Senator Yarborough," 11–12; Ralph Yarborough, "Equality of Economic Opportunity for the Spanish-Speaking of the Southwest: Myth Today But Reality Tomorrow," February 11, 1967, box 29, folder 1, SP, 2 (quotation); GIS to Ronnie Dugger, May 1, 1967, box 34, folder 16, SP.

49. Blanton, *Strange Career of Bilingual Education,* 124–40; San Miguel, "Conflict and Controversy," 506; Hardgrave and Hinojosa, *Politics of Bilingual Education,* 3–5; S. 428, "A Bill to Amend the Elementary and Secondary Education Act of 1965 in Order to Provide Assistance to Local Educational Agencies in Establishing Bilingual American Education Programs . . . ," box 63, folder 17, SP, 1–11; Ralph Yarborough, "Two Proposals for a Better Way of Life for Mexican-Americans of the Southwest," *Congressional Record* 113:5 (January 17, 1967), box 63, folder 17, SP, 1–2; press release by Ralph Yarborough, August 8, 1967, box 63, folder 17, SP; Ralph Yarborough, "Harold Howe II: A Perceptive Speech on Bilingual Education," *Congressional Record— Senate,"* April 30, 1968, box 772, folder "Education on Bilingual Children, Advisory Committee on the," OFJM, 4655–57.

50. Pycior, *LBJ and Mexican Americans,* 184; Dugger, "Senator Yarborough," 11; GIS to Joe Alaniz, box 63, folder 14, SP (quotation); Blanton, *Strange Career of Bilingual Education,* 136.

51. GIS to Paul Sheldon, March 12, 1963, box 14, folder 3, SP; GIS to Paul Sheldon, March 22, 1963, box 14, folder 3, SP; Sánchez, "Spanish Influences in the Southwest," box 14, folder 3, SP, 1–5; program, "Southwest Conference, 1963—Social and Educational Problems of Rural and Urban Mexican American Youth," April 6, 1963, box 14, folder 3, SP, 1–4; Sánchez, "Spanish in the Southwest," in *Educating the Mexican American,* ed. Hernández-M. and Johnson, 24–32; Julian Samora to GIS, December 23, 1964, box 14, folder 10, SP; GIS to Julian Samora, January 4, 1965, box 14, folder 10, SP; GIS to Julian Samora, January 29, 1965, box 14, folder 10, SP; Julian Samora to GIS, May 10, 1966, box 31, folder 22, SP; GIS to Julian Samora, May 13,

1966, box 31, folder 22, SP; Sánchez, "History, Culture, and Education," in *La Raza*, ed. Samora, 1–26.

52. Betty Thedford to GIS, May 18, 1960, box 60, folder 10, SP; Betty Thedford to GIS, October 24, 1960, box 60, folder 10, SP; Betty Thedford to GIS, August 22, 1961, box 60, folder 10, SP; Betty Thedford to GIS, May 18, 1962, box 60, folder 10, SP; Betty Thedford to GIS, August 1, 1963, box 60, folder 10, SP; GIS to Joseph Smiley, June 12, 1962, box 55, folder 3, SP; GIS to Clyde Colvert, December 12, 1962, box 50, folder 9, SP (quotation).

53. GIS to Clyde Colvert, August 15, 1963, box 50, folder 9, SP; GIS to Clyde Colvert, May 8, 1964, box 50, folder 9, SP; Clyde Colvert to GIS, May 12, 1964, box 50, folder 9, SP; GIS to Norman Hackerman, June 23, 1964, box 42, folder 15, SP (quotations); Betty Thedford to GIS, July 20, 1965, box 60, folder 7, SP; Betty Thedford to GIS, May 20, 1966, box 60, folder 7, SP; Betty Thedford to GIS, July 29, 1967, box 60, folder 7, SP; Stephen Spurr to GIS, August 5, 1971, box 60, folder 7, SP; Dugger, *Our Invaded Universities*, 118.

54. Anita Brewer, "UT Prof. Scores Board's Makeup," *Austin American*, undated [likely April 29, 1965], box 1, folder 18, SP, A-1, A-6; Faculty Annual Report for Fiscal Year Ending August 31, 1965, GIS," box 60, folder 5, SP, 1–9; newsletter, Department of History and Philosophy of Education, University of Texas, April 1964, box 47, folder 2, SP, 1–3; Ralph Yarborough to GIS, May 4, 1965, box 63, folder 12, SP (first quotation); Beulah Hodge to GIS, December 16, 1965, box 14, folder 10, SP; Sánchez, "Colleges and Democracy," 12; E. Jackson to GIS, September 3, 1963, box 35, folder 6, SP; E. Jackson to GIS, November 11, 1963, box 35, folder 6, SP; J. Williams to I. Davis, January 18, 1967, box 35, folder 6, SP; GIS to Donald Yarborough, October 4, 1963, box 63, folder 8, SP; Oliver Brown, Gordon Anderson, William Drake, and Ben Harris, undated [October 1964], box 59, folder 11, SP; GIS to Ben Harris, November 10, 1964, box 59, folder 11, SP; GIS to *Daily Texan*, March 19, 1963, box 8, folder 4, SP; Dudley Woodward to GIS, March 14, 1960, box 63, folder 4, SP; GIS to Dudley Woodward, March 17, 1960, box 63, folder 4, SP; R. E. L. Gowan, "UT-Ex Hits Profs," *Daily Texan*, March 3, 1967, box 17, folder 8, SP; GIS to R. Gowan, March 6, 1967, box 17, folder 8, SP; GIS to Clyde Colvert, September 24, 1964, box 44, folder 4, SP; Robert Peck to GIS, September 24, 1964, box 44, folder 4, SP (second and third quotations); GIS to Robert Peck, box 44, folder 4, October 2, 1964, box SP.

55. Ernesto Galarza to GIS, August 12, 1963, box 16, folder 14, SP; GIS to Ernesto Galarza, August 19, 1963, box 16, folder 14, SP; Ralph Guzman to GIS, October 11, 1960, box 18, folder 13, SP; GIS to Ralph Guzman, October 19, 1960, box 18, folder 13, SP; GIS, annual reports to the University of Texas for 1960–71, box 60, folder 5, SP, 1–39; Paul Sheldon to GIS, February 19, 1964, box 28, folder 8, SP; GIS to Mexican-American Study Project, April 6, 1966, box 25, folder 5, SP; GIS to Leo Grebler, April 13, 1964, box 25, folder 5, SP; Grebler, Moore, and Guzman, *The Mexican-American People*, v–xiv; GIS to Bert Corona, July 21, 1966, box 41, folder 24, SP; GIS to Wayne Holtzman, September 21, 1965, box 50, folder 11, SP; Wayne Holtzman to GIS, October 4, 1965, box 50, folder 11, SP; GIS to Jackson Reid, March 7, 1966, box 30, folder 21, SP; Sánchez, "Some of My Best Friends Are Optometrists: A Few Notes," undated [likely spring of

1966], box 44, folder 1, SP, 1–5; GIS to Committee on Graduate Studies in Education, March 8, 1956, box 44, folder 1, SP; William Brickman to GIS, September 24, 1963, box 8, folder 16, SP; GIS to William Brickman, October 2, 1963, box 8, folder 16, SP.

56. Lyle Saunders to GIS, July 21, 1955, box 32, folder 9, SP (first quotation); GIS to Wendell Gordon, April 30, 1965, box 17, folder 8, SP (second quotation); GIS to Louis Slattery, February 12, 1964, box 33, folder 1, SP.

57. Charles Ray to GIS, April 17, 1963, box 39, folder 10, SP; GIS to Charles Ray, April 24, 1963, box 39, folder 10, SP (quotation); GIS, Application for Federal Employment, Standard Form 57, March 5, 1962, box 37, folder 11, SP, 1–6; GIS to U.S. Treasury Department, August 2, 1961, box 38, folder 6, SP; Robert Phinney to GIS and Luisa Sánchez, October 26, 1961, box 38, folder 6, SP; Roland Jones to GIs and Luisa Sánchez, February 5, 1962, box 38, folder 6, SP; GIS to Ralph Yarborough, April 17, 1963, box 63, folder 11, SP; Ralph Yarborough to GIS, April 26, 1963, box 63, folder 11, SP; Ralph Yarborough to GIS, June 11, 1963, box 63, folder 11, SP; Sander Shapiro to Ralph Yarborough, June 4, 1963, box 32, folder 19, SP; GIS to Sander Shapiro, June 7, 1963, box 32, folder 19, SP; Ralph Yarborough to Sander Shapiro, undated [shortly before June 17, 1963], box 63, folder 11; GIS to Ralph Yarborough, June 17, 1963, box 63, folder 11, SP; GIS to Robert Phinney, July 30, 1963, box 38, folder 6, SP; Robert Phinney to GIS, August 6, 1963, box 38, folder 6, SP.

58. GIS, Application for federal employment, Standard Form 57, March 5, 1962, box 37, folder 11, SP, 1–6; Hector Garcia to Manuel Avila, March 11, 1961, box 82, folder 7, GP; Hector Garcia, diet sheet, undated [early 1960s], box 89, folder 30, GP; "TB Workshop Scheduled for Monday," *San Antonio Express News*, November 30, 1962, box 14, folder 1, SP; "First Annual Tuberculosis Nursing Workshop Series," October 22–23, 1962, December 3–4, 1962, February 7–8, 1963, box 14, folder 1, 1–3; Stella McCullough to GIS, December 14, 1962, box 14, folder 1, SP; Stella McCullough to GIS, March 1, 1963, box 14, folder 1, SP; James Boren to GIS, January 16, 1962, box 36, folder 1, SP; GIS to James Boren, January 30, 1962, box 36, folder 1, SP; Charles Ray to GIS, January 20, 1962, box 39, folder 10, SP; GIS to Lindley Stiles, June 5, 1963, box 17, folder 3, SP; Lindley Stiles to GIS, June 14, 1963, box 17, folder 2, SP; GIS to Lindley Stiles, September 11, 1963, box 17, folder 2, SP; GIS to James Cox, February 23, 1967, box 39, folder 3, SP; program, Southwest Regional VISTA In-service Education Program for Volunteers from South Texas, February 16–19, 1967, box 39, folder 3, SP, 1–3.

59. Program, *Fourth Western Regional Conference on Comparative Education, Inter-American Educational Relations, School of Education, UCLA, October 8–10, 1964,* box 14, folder 9, SP, 1–2; GIS to Gordon Ruscoe, October 12, 1964, box 14, folder 9, SP; GIS to Connie Sprague, October 15, 1964, box 33, folder 5, SP; GIS to Lyle Saunders, October 21, 1964, box 41, folder 20, SP (quotations); Lyle Saunders to GIS, October 26, 1964, box 41, folder 20, SP.

60. Lyle Saunders to GIS, May 22, 1956, box 32, folder 9, SP; GIS to Keats McKinney, November 17, 1961, box 2, folder 5, SP; Sprague interview; Kennedy interview; Sánchez interview; GIS to Lyle Saunders, December 11, 1963, box 32, folder 9, SP; GIS to *True Magazine*, October 24, 1963, box 35, folder 10, SP; GIS to *True Magazine*,

October 24, 1963, box 35, folder 10, SP; GIS to John Buchanan, March 25, 1966, box 8, folder 18, SP.

CHAPTER 12. CHICANISMO AND OLD AGE

Epigraph. GIS to Manuel Salas, February 16, 1965, box 31, folder 19, SP.

1. Manuel Salas to GIS, February 13, 1965, box 31, folder 19, SP; GIS to Manuel Salas, February 16, 1965, box 31, folder 19, SP; Manuel Salas to GIS, undated [likely late February or early March], box 31, folder 19, SP; GIS to Manuel Salas, March 5, 1965, box 31, folder 19, SP.

2. Blackwell, *¡Chicana Power!*; Chávez, *"¡Mi Raza Primero!"*; Gutiérrez, "Internal Colonialism," 281–95; Montejano, *Quixote's Soldiers*; Oropeza, *Raza Sí, Guerra No!*; Pulido, *Black, Brown, Yellow, and Left.*

3. "An Interview with George I. Sánchez," 103 (first quotation); program for the Mexican-American Studies Institute for the State of Texas, November 19–21, 1970, University of Texas—Austin, box 14, folder 5, SP; Sánchez, "I, Mexican American," University of Texas, November 20, 1970, box 70, folder 26; program, Mexican Americans and Educational Change Symposium, May 21–22, 1971, University of California-Riverside; Sánchez, "Educational Change in Historical Perspective," undated [May 21 or 22, 1971], box 15, folder 7, SP, 3 (second quotation); Carlos Cortés to GIS, June 11, 1971, box 15, folder 7, SP; GIS to Carlos Cortés, June 21, 1971, box 15, folder 7, SP; GIS to Editor, *Daily Texan*, February 20, 1970, box 4, folder 1, SP; GIS to Norris Hundley, September 1, 1970, box 29, folder 1, SP; GIS to John Pierce-Jones, August 29, 1966, box 30, folder 4, SP; García, "Foreword," in Sánchez, *Forgotten People*, xi; GIS to Carey McWilliams, April 2, 1968, box 24, folder 18, SP; Ortego, "People of Sánchez," 482–83; Padilla, review of *Forgotten People*, 561–62; Guadalupe Salinas to GIS, October 22, 1970, box 31, folder 19, SP; GIS to Guadalupe Salinas, October 27, 1970, box 31, folder 19, SP; Octavio Romano to GIS, April 27, 1967, box 31, folder 5, SP; GIS to Octavio Romano, May 2, 1967, box 31, folder 5, SP; Rudy Acuña to GIS, August 2, 1967, box 2, folder 1, SP; Rudy Acuña to GIS, September 16, 1967, box 2, folder 1, SP. For more on the school blowouts, see San Miguel, *Brown, Not White*; and García and Castro, *Blowout!*

4. Everette Chaffee to Los Angeles City Board of Education, March 13, 1968, box 3, folder 9, SP [old system]; Reymundo Marin and Antonia Castañeda, undated 1970, box 30, folder 19, SP; José Gutiérrez, "Todos Differentes, Todos Unidos, Raza Unida Party," undated, box 30, folder 19, SP; Nathalie Gross to GIS, December 26, 1966, box 18, folder 7, SP; GIS to Nathalie Gross, January 3, 1967, box 18, folder 7, SP; GIS to Rodolfo González, November 8, 1967, box 17, folder 8, SP; "Crusade News Flashes!," *El Gallo* 1:5 (November 1967), 2, SP; Jim McCulloch to GIS, undated [likely early October 1967], box 24, folder 15, SP; GIS to Jim McCulloch, October 17, 1967, box 24, folder 15, SP; Reies Tijerina to GIS, June 26, 1963, box 22, folder 22, SP; GIS to Reies Tijerina, July 1, 1963, box 22, folder 22, SP (quotation); GIS to Dan Chavez, July 22, 1964, box 10, folder 10, SP; Dan Chavez to GIS, December 6, 1964, box 10, folder 10, SP; Dan Chavez to GIS, October 26, 1966, box 10, folder 10, SP; GIS to Dan Chavez,

November 12, 1966, box 10, folder 10, SP; Dan Chavez to GIS, November 15, 1966, box 10, folder 10, SP; GIS to *The Nation*, June 17, 1968, box 26, folder 8, SP; Clark Knowlton to GIS, December 18, 1968, box 21, folder 22, SP.

5. Kymlicka, *Multicultural Citizenship*, 61–69; Dugger, "Senator Yarborough," 11–12; Kells, *Hector P. García*, 150; Hector Garcia to GIS, July 15, 1968, box 4, folder 10, SP; Ralph Yarborough to Hector Garcia [copied with note in margins to GIS], July 19, 1968, box 4, folder 10, SP; press release, "Gonzalez Comments on Yarborough Proposals," January 18, 1967, box 17, folder 12, SP; GIS to Henry Gonzalez, February 6, 1967, box 20, folder 9, SP; Henry Gonzalez to GIS, February 8, box 17, folder 12, SP; GIS to Henry Gonzalez, February 14, 1967, box 17, folder 12, SP; Henry Gonzalez to GIS, March 7, 1967, box 17, folder 12, SP.

6. Leonard Cardenas to GIS, February 23, 1967, box 9, folder 18, SP; Leonard Cardenas to *The Reporter*, February 23, 1967, box 9, folder 18, SP; GIS, address to White House Conference on the Spanish-Speaking, October 26, 1966, box 37, folder 3, SP, 3.

7. Minutes, Mexican American Joint Conference, January 7, 1967, box 20, folder 22, SP, 1–8; GIS to Mexican American Joint Conference, February 23, 1968, box 89, folder 30, GP; Lupe Zamarripa to Mexican American Joint Conference, May 13, 1967, box 89, folder 30, GP; Resolutions of the Mexican American Joint Conference Committee, May 13, 1967, box 89, folder 30, GP, 1–3; GIS to Harry Ransom, May 18, 1967, box 20, folder 20, SP; GIS to Mexican American Joint Conference, May 20, 1967, box 20, folder 20, SP; Ralph Yarborough to GIS, June 19, 1967, box 20, folder 20, SP; William Macomber, Jr. to Ralph Yarborough, June 15, 1967, box 20, folder 20, SP; GIS to Raymond Telles, June 28, 1967, box 20, folder 20, SP; GIS to David North, October 4, 1967, box 20, folder 21, SP; GIS to William Crook, December 6, 1967, box 20, folder 21, SP; James Cox to GIS, December 18, 1967, box 38, folder 10, SP; GIS to James Cox, January 10, 1968, box 38, folder 10, SP; GIS to Mexican American Joint Conference, undated [likely spring of 1968], box 20, folder 21, SP; GIS to Texas State Board of Public Welfare, June 1, 1968, box 173, folder 29, GP; GIS to Ralph Yarborough, June 1, 1968, box 173, folder 29, GP; GIS to Lupe Zamarripa, May 16, 1969, box 54, folder 10, SP.

8. GIS to Frank Wardlaw, April 30, 1959, box 62, folder 1, SP; Dean McHenry to GIS, July 13, 1971, box 29, folder 5, SP; Américo Paredes to GIS, July 15, 1971, box 29, folder 5, SP; González, *Border Renaissance*, 129–30; Saldívar, *The Borderlands of Culture*, 399–401; Goldstone, *Integrating the 40 Acres*, 143–45; GIS to Joe Bernal, March 18, 1970, box 7, folder 16, SP; GIS to Norman Hackerman, March 19, 1970, box 55, folder 4, SP; GIS to Henry Bullock, March 23, 1970, box 8, folder 17, SP; Henry A. Bullock to GIS, April 1, 1970, box 8, folder 17, SP; José Limón to GIS, October 6, 1970, box 22, folder 19, SP; GIS to José Limón, October 8, 1970, box 22, folder 19, SP; Américo Paredes to Ethnic Studies Committee Members, October 13, 1970, box 42, folder 14, SP; GIS to Américo Paredes, October 16, 1970, box 42, folder 14, SP; GIS to Américo Paredes, September 29, 1971, box 42, folder 14, SP; GIS to Américo Paredes, January 31, 1972, box 29, folder 5, SP; GIS to James Roach, January 31, 1972, box 29, folder 5, SP; Américo Paredes to GIS, February 7, 1972, box 42, folder 14, SP; Limón, "Gentlemen," 5; San Miguel, *Brown, Not White*, 105–6.

9. Américo Paredes to Ethnic Studies Committee Members, October 13, 1970, box 42, folder 14, SP; GIS to Américo Paredes, October 16, 1970, box 42, folder 14, SP; GIS to Gardner Lindsey, April 10, 1970, box 55, folder 4, SP (first quotation); GIS to Gardner Lindsey, April 24, 1970, box 55, folder 4, SP (second quotation); GIS to Robert Sánchez, April 7, 1970, box 32, folder 4, SP; Robert Sánchez to Harry Ransom, April 10, 1970, box 32, folder 4, SP; GIS to Hector Garcia, April 24, 1970, box 4, folder 10, SP.

10. Gutiérrez, "Significant to Whom?," 527; Brown, *Richard Hofstadter*, 172; Nathan Murillo, "The Works of George I. Sánchez: An Appreciation," in *Chicano Psychology*, ed. Martinez and Mendoza, 24; Nathan Murillo, "George I. Sánchez and Mexican American Educational Practices," in *Multicultural Education*, ed. Banks, 130; José E. Limón, "El Meeting: History, Folk Spanish, and Ethnic Nationalism in a Chicano Student Community," in *Spanish in the United States*, ed. Amastae and Elías-Olivares, 317–18.

11. GIS to *Saga*, February 26, 1969, box 31, folder 19, SP (first quotation); Fred Huston to GIS, June 10, 1970, box 19, folder 1, SP; GIS to Fred Huston, June 19, 1970, box 19, folder 1, SP; GIS to Ralph Yarborough, September 26, 1967, box 63, folder 14, SP; Peter Libassi to Ralph Yarborough, undated [shortly before October 23, 1967], box 63, folder 14, SP; Peter Libassi to J. Edgar, October 20, 1967, box 63, folder 14, SP; John Castillo to GIS, January 10, 1968, box 9, folder 18, SP; GIS to John Castillo, March 26, 1968, box 9, folder 18, SP (second quotation).

12. Ruben Cortez to GIS, May 17, 1970, box 21, folder 1, SP; GIS to Ruben Cortez, June 17, 1970, box 21, folder 1, SP (first quotation); George Rivera, "Interview with Dr. George I. Sánchez," 9, 19; GIS to Tom Taylor, May 1, 1968, box 33, folder 16, SP; Tom Taylor to GIS, May 10, 1968, box 33, folder 16, SP; GIS to Tom Taylor, May 15, 1968, box 33, folder 16, SP; GIS to Janie Vega, March 27, 1968, box 61, folder 6, SP; Sánchez, *Los Hijos de Jones*; Olen Leonard to GIS, May 26, 1966, box 37, folder 1, SP; GIS to Olen Leonard, June 1, 1966, box 37, folder 1, SP; Olen Leonard to GIS, June 9, 1966, box 37, folder 1, SP; GIS to Robert Hayden, November 10, 1966, box 37, folder 3, SP (second quotation); Robert Hayden to GIS, December 2, 1966, box 18, folder 18, SP; GIS to Robert Hayden, December 6, 1966, box 18, folder 18, SP.

13. GIS to J. Edgar, March 21, 1967, box 34, folder 14, SP; GIS to Joe Bernal, March 21, 1967, box 20, folder 19, SP; GIS to J. Edgar, March 21, 1967, box 20, folder 19, SP; GIS to Ralph Yarborough, April 26, 1968, box 20, folder 20, SP; Hart Stilwell to GIS, April 19, 1968, box 22, folder 19, SP; GIS to Hart Stilwell, April 24, 1968, box 22, folder 19, SP; Robert Sánchez to GIS, April 23, 1969, box 32, folder 4, SP; GIS to Robert Sánchez, May 24, 1968, box 32, folder 4, SP; GIS to Bill Reeves, April 2, 1970, box 30, folder 21, SP; GIS to Edward Hindsman, July 11, 1968, box 33, folder 5, SP; Joseph Michel to GIS, May 26, 1969, box 25, folder 13, SP; GIS to Joseph Michel, June 3, 1969, box 25, folder 13, SP; GIS to Armando Rodríguez, December 9, 1970, box 34, folder 6, SP; Dean Bistline to GIS, December 23, 1970, box 34, folder 6, SP; GIS to Mrs. Sid Smith, July 26, 1968, box 7, folder 6, SP (quotations); Sánchez, "Classroom Reality," 490; Sánchez, "Right to Challenge," 682; GIS to *Life*, June 17, 1970, box 22, folder 20, SP; A. Scott to GIS, July 2, 1970, box 22, folder 20, SP.

14. Christ Aldrete to GIS, February 14, 1967, box 2, folder 9, SP; GIS to Christ Aldrete, February 23, 1967, box 2, folder 9, SP; Lupe Zamarripa, "Mexican American Conference Probes Educational Problems," *Daily Texan*, January 8, 1967, box 15, folder 1, SP; Samora, *Los Mojados*; Portes, "Return of the Wetback," 40–46; Gutíerrez, "Sin Fronteras?," 5–37.

15. GIS to Ralph Yarborough, February 27, 1967, box 63, folder 14, SP (first quotation); Lupe Zamarripa, "Yarborough Bombs Leaders: LULAC Director Obledo Opposes Labor Conference," *La Fuerza*, April 20, 1967, box 197, folder 6, SP; GIS to Ralph Yarborough, April 2, 1970, box 63, folder 16, SP; Ralph Yarborough to GIS, July 9, 1970, box 63, folder 16, SP; GIS to Wilbur Mills, April 22, 1969, box 36, folder 16, SP; GIS to Roy Elizondo, March 8, 1968, box 30, folder 12, SP; George Bush to GIS, January 29, 1968, box 8, folder 25, SP; George Bush, "For the Mexican-American Texan—A Future of Fair Play and Progress," undated [likely January 1968], box 8, folder 25, SP, 1–3; GIS to George Bush, February 2, 1968, box 8, folder 25, SP; GIS to John Tower, May 24, 1968, box 63, folder 15, SP; GIS to John Tower, March 6, 1969, box 35, folder 1, SP; GIS to Carey McWilliams, December 9, 1968, box 24, folder 18, SP; GIS to Frank Angel, November 9, 1970, box 5, folder 6, SP; GIS to Hector Garcia, July 23, 1970, box 4, folder 10, SP (final quotation).

16. Harry Akin to GIS, April 11, 1968, box 2, folder 4, SP; GIS to Harry Akin, April 16, box 2, folder 4, SP; GIS to Irby B. Carruth, May 29, 1968, box 7, folder 10, SP; GIS, "Palm, The School Building—A Report," undated [around June 13, 1971], box 7, folder 10, SP; Civil Subpoena to GIS, U.S. District Court for the Western District of Texas, Civil Action File No. A-70-CA-80, *United States vs. Austin ISD*, June 13, 1971, box 7, folder 10, SP; GIS to Irby Carruth, April 23, 1969, box 7, folder 10, SP; Irby Carruth to GIS, February 23, 1967, box 20, folder 19, SP; GIS to Irby Carruth, February 28, 1967, box 20, folder 19, SP.

17. Valencia, *Chicano Students and the Courts*, 122; GIS to U.S. Commission on Civil Rights, July 12, 1967, box 36, folder 13, SP; GIS to U.S. Department of Justice, September 25, 1967, box 36, folder 37, SP; Annie Reid to GIS, October 16, 1967, box 36, folder 13, SP; Walter Lewis to GIS, October 17, 1967, box 36, folder 13, SP; GIS to John Doar, November 8, 1967, box 37, folder 8, SP; John Doar to GIS, December 4, 1967, box 37, folder 8, SP; Carol Kummerfeld to GIS, January 23, 1968, box 36, folder 13, SP; Peter Libassi to Walter Lewis, January 11, 1968, box 36, folder 13, SP; Lawrence Glick to GIS, June 7, 1968, box 36, folder 13, SP; GIS to J. Avena, January 13, 1971, box 36, folder 14, SP; "Civil Rights Commission Subpoenas UT Professor," *Daily Texan*, December 6, 1968, GISVH; GIS to Carlos Conde, August 12, 1970, box 11, folder 7, SP; GIS to Carlos Conde, January 12, 1971, box 11, folder 7, SP; Charles Ehlert to GIS, March 21, 1969, box 12, folder 22, SP; Vilma Martinez to GIS, April 10, 1968, box 24, folder 6, SP; GIS to Vilma Martinez, April 16, 1968, box 24, folder 6, SP; GIS to Gerald Lopez, November 19, 1968, box 25, folder 1, SP; GIS, deposition on civil action with regard to minority culture in California schools, undated [likely late June or early July 1969], box 9, folder 4, SP, 1–4; Fred Hiestand to GIS, July 7, 1969, box 9, folder 4, SP; Hector Garcia to GIS, June 12, 1968, box 4, folder 10, SP; GIS to Hector Garcia, June 17, 1968, box 4, folder 10, SP; White House press release, November 4, 1968, box 4, folder 10, SP.

18. Wilson, *Rise of Judicial Management*, 190–92; Wilson, *"Brown* over 'Other White,'" 172–73, 180–90; GIS to James DeAnda, July 7, 1967, box 12, folder 6, SP; GIS to James DeAnda, August 7, 1967, box 12, folder 6, SP; GIS to James DeAnda, August 10, 1967, box 12, folder 6, SP; *Diego Chapa, A Minor, et al., vs. Odem Independent School District*, Civil Action No. 66-C-92, District Court of the U.S., Southern District of Texas, Corpus Christi Division, July 28, 1967, box 12, folder 6, SP; Fred Bonavita, "Judge Orders Halt to Discrimination in Odem Schools," *Corpus Christi Caller Times*, July 31, 1967, box 12, folder 6, SP, 1, 12.

19. San Miguel, *"Let All of Them Take Heed,"* 169–72; O'Connor and Epstein, "Legal Voice for the Chicano Community," 248–49; GIS to John Martinez, January 27, 1966, box 1, folder 5, SP; Pete Tijerina to GIS, February 22, 1967, box 25, folder 1, SP; Betty Elder to Pete Tijerina, December 12, 1966, box 25, folder 1, SP; Jack Greenberg to Pete Tijerina, January 23, 1967, box 25, folder 1, SP; Leroy Clark to Pete Tijerina, January 24, 1967, box 25, folder 1, SP; Alfred Hernandez to Pete Tijerina, February 4, 1967, box 25, folder 1, SP; GIS to Pete Tijerina, February 28, 1967, box 25, folder 1, SP (quotations); Pete Tijerina to GIS, May 26, 1967, box 25, folder 1, SP; Pete Tijerina to GIS, January 29, 1968, box 25, folder 1, SP; GIS to Pete Tijerina, February 2, 1968, box 25, folder 1, SP; GIS to Pete Tijerina, August 19, 1968, box 25, folder 1 SP; GIS to Ed Idar, July 15, 1971, box 25, folder 1, SP; Ed Idar to GIS, July 19, 1971, box 25, folder 1, SP.

20. Henry Muñoz to GIS, April 1, 1968, box 2, folder 7, SP; GIS to Henry Muñoz, April 3, 1968, box 2, folder 7, SP; Sánchez, review of *Simón Bolívar: Educator*, 144–45; Sánchez, review of *The Spanish-Americans of New Mexico*, 394–95; GIS to Archibald Gillies, July 21, 1970, box 60, folder 2, SP; Archibald Gillies to GIS, September 21, 1970, box 60, folder 2, SP; Amelia Hostein to GIS, March 30, 1971, box 60, folder 2, SP; GIS to Esther Raushenbush, April 2, 1971, box 60, folder 2, SP; Bertram Davis to AAUP review team, February 7, 1969, box 32, folder 1, SP; GIS to Bertram Davis, February 26, 1969, box 32, folder 1, SP; Julian Samora to Bertram Davis, February 27, 1969, box 32, folder 1, SP; Channing Phillips to GIS, February 28, 1969, box 32, folder 1, SP; GIS to Julian Samora, March 4, 1969, box 32, folder 1, SP; GIS, notes on San Francisco State, undated [likely late February 1969], box 32, folder 1, SP, 1–8; GIS to John Silber, June 28, 1970, box 33, folder 1, SP; Bob Adams to GIS, May 6, 1967, box 2, folder 4, SP; GIS to Bob Adams, May 16, 1967, box 2, folder 4, SP; GIS to *Daily Texan*, April 24, 1968, box 51, folder 3, SP; GIS to *Daily Texan*, May 3, 1967, box 4, folder 1, SP; GIS to *Daily Texan*, November 3, 1969, box 51, folder 3, SP; Norman Hackerman to GIS, July 1, 1968, box 55, folder 4, SP; GIS to Norman Hackerman, July 8, 1968, box 55, folder 4, SP; GIS to Harry Ransom, May 18, 1967, box 42, folder 15, SP; GIS to Jackson Reid, March 13, 1968, box 30, folder 21, SP; GIS to Department of Intercollegiate Athletics, September 3, 1971, box 59, folder 11, SP.

21. William Harmer, "Proposal for Name Change of Department of History and Philosophy of Education to Department of Cultural Foundations of Education," December 19, 1969, box 49, folder 1, SP; John Rich to Members of the Administrative Council, December 8, 1969, box 49, folder 1, SP; Department of History and Philosophy of Education report, "Departmental Titles: History and Philosophy of

Education, 1966," undated [likely in 1966], box 47, folder 6, SP, 1–7; GIS to Department of Cultural Foundations of Education, December 2, 1970, box 49, folder 1, SP; R. Butts, Philip Smith, and William Stanley, "Report of the External Evaluators to the Department of Cultural Foundations of Education at the University of Texas at Austin," undated [likely early in 1971], box 49, folder 1, SP, 2 (quotations); Carl Riggs to GIS, March 24, 1967, box 40, folder 6, SP; GIS to Carl Riggs, April 10, 1967, box 40, folder 6, SP; Carl Riggs to GIS, February 15, 1968, box 40, folder 6, SP; GIS to Carl Riggs, February 19, 1968, box 40, folder 6, SP; GIS to William Drake, October 10, 1967, box 45, folder 2, SP; GIS to John Laska, December 9, 1970, box 49, folder 1, SP; GIS to William Drake, December 9, 1970, box 45, folder 9, SP; W. Whaley to William Drake, April 22, 1970, box 12, folder 16, SP; William Drake to John Rich, April 27, 1970, box 12, folder 16, SP; William Drake to John M. Rich, June 29, 1970, box 12, folder 16, SP; William Drake to W. Whaley, September 30, 1970, box 12, folder 16, SP; William Drake to W. Whaley, December 7, 1970, box 12, folder 16, SP.

22. George I. Sánchez to William Drake, October 10, 1967, box 45, folder 9, SP; GIS to John Whitney, March 19, 1970, box 60, folder 2, SP; GIS to Wayne Holtzman, February 25, 1969, box 50, folder 13, SP (quotation).

23. W. Whaley to GIS, June 5, 1969, box 51, folder 14, SP; GIS to W. Whaley, June 10, 1969, box 51, folder 14, SP; W. Whaley to GIS, June 18 1969, box 51, folder 14, SP; GIS to W. Whaley, June 19, 1969, box 51, folder 14, SP (quotations); GIS to Graduate Assembly and Whaley Committee, undated [likely summer or fall of 1969], box 51, folder 14, SP; GIS to W. Whaley, April 27, 1970, box 51, folder 14, SP; W. Whaley to GIS, April 30, 1970, box 51, folder 14, SP; Billy Cowart to GIS, January 26, 1968, box 10, folder 19, SP; Harvie Branscomb to GIS, August 25, 1971, box 8, folder 14, SP; GIS to Harvie Branscomb, August 31, 1971, box 8, folder 14, SP; GIS to Thomas Carter, October 11, 1966, box 9, folder 18, SP; Theodore Brown to GIS, February 1, 1968, box 12, folder 18, SP; GIS to Theodore Brown, February 6, 1968, box 12, folder 18, SP; Irving Melbo to GIS, March 19, 1968, box 24, folder 21, SP; GIS to Irving Melbo, March 27, 1968, box 24, folder 21, SP; Cowart interview.

24. GIS to Department of Cultural Foundations of Education, December 2, 1970, box 49, folder 1, SP; "Preliminary Required Reading List, Doctoral Candidates, Department of History and Philosophy of Education, Fall 1968," undated, box 45, folder 2, SP; GIS, Statement to the faculty and graduate students, January 23, 1969, box 49, folder 1, SP (quotations).

25. Graduate Students to the Faculty, April 29, 1971, box 49, folder 2, SP; John Rich to Department of Cultural Foundations of Education, undated [likely soon after April 29, 1971], box 49, folder 2, SP; GIS to John Rich, undated [likely soon after April 29, 1971], box 49, folder 2, SP (quotation).

26. Wade, Barton, and Marsh to GIS, March 21, 1967, box 1, folder 26, SP, 1–19; Sprague interview; Kennedy interview; J. Hawkins to GIS, December 28, 1961, box 1, folder 26, SP; GIS to Capital National Bank, June 20, 1969, box 9, folder 18, SP; Lyle Saunders to Julienne Sprague, June 20, 1969, box 16, folder 2, SP; GIS to Marian Trahan, May 19, 1966, box 35, folder 5, SP; GIS to Alba Moesser, May 20, 1969, box 26, folder 4, SP.

27. Brice Sewell to GIS, May 15, 1969, box 32, folder 18, SP; Brice Sewell to GIS, June 5, 1969, box 32, folder 18, SP; GIS to Brice Sewell, November 9, 1970, box 32, folder 18, SP; John Johnson to GIS, June 25, 1969, box 9, folder 13, SP; "'Hispanic Traditions' Lecture Is Wednesday," *Albuquerque Journal*, November 10, 1969, box 9, folder 13, SP; Arthur Campa to GIS, April 24, 1969, box 9, folder 13, SP; Guillermo Pérez and Luis de Leon to GIS, August 7, 1971, box 29, folder 7, SP; GIS to Guillermo Pérez, October 22, 1971, box 29, folder 7, SP.

28. Sánchez, "The Mexican-American in Texas," 18–19; GIS to Kay Northcott, December 13, 1971, box 34, folder 16, SP (quotations); Kennedy interview; Sprague interview.

29. GIS to Tom Wiley, September 16, 1966, box 40, folder 5, SP; Tom Popejoy to GIS, February 15, 1967, box 40, folder 5, SP; GIS to Tom Popejoy, February 23, 1967, box 40, folder 5, SP; John Durrie to GIS, February 27, 1967, box 40, folder 5, SP; John Durrie to GIS, undated, box 40, folder 5, SP; GIS to John Durrie, March 3, 1967, box 40, folder 5, SP; John Durrie to GIS, April 24, 1967, box 40, folder 5, SP; Tom Wiley to GIS, April 26, 1967, box 40, folder 5, SP; Commencement program, University of New Mexico, 1967, box 40, folder 5, SP; "Honorary Degree Recipients Chosen," *University of New Mexico Campus News* 3:5 (May 1967), 1, 4.

30. GIS to Tom Popejoy, May 4, 1967, box 40, folder 5, SP (first quotation); John Durrie to GIS, May 12, 1967, box 40, folder 5, SP; John Durrie to GIS, May 31, 1967, box 40, folder 5, SP; Frank Angel to GIS, June 23, 1967, box 40, folder 5, SP; GIS to Frank Angel, September 19, 1970, box 5, folder 6, SP (second quotation); Brice Sewell to GIS, May 16, 1967, box 32, folder 18, SP; GIS to Brice Sewell, May 25, 1967, box 32, folder 18, SP (third quotation).

31. GIS to Frank Angel, September 19, 1970, box 5, folder 6, SP; Frank Angel to GIS, September 21, 1970, box 5, folder 6, SP; Frank Angel to GIS, October 6, 1970, box 40, folder 5, SP; John Durrie to GIS, November 3, 1970, box 40, folder 5, SP; GIS to John Durrie, November 6, 1970, box 40, folder 5, SP (quotations); John Durrie to GIS, November 11, 1970, box 40, folder 5, SP; GIS to Frank Angel, December 11, 1970, box 40, folder 5, SP; "University Honors UT Prof," *Austin American*, January 7, 1971, box 1, folder 18, SP.

32. GIS to Dana Little, April 24, 1969, box 22, folder 19, SP; GIS to Donald Weismann, June 6, 1969, box 62, folder 3, SP; Donald Weismann to GIS, June 13, 1969, box 62, folder 3, SP; Julius Rivera to GIS, August 13, 1969, box 31, folder 3, SP; Luisa Sánchez to Julius Rivera, August 18, 1969, box 31, folder 3, SP; Julius Rivera to GIS, September 23, 1969, box 31, folder 3, SP; GIS to Julius Rivera, October 3, 1969, box 31, folder 3, SP; Edwin Stanfield to GIS, December 16, 1969, box 33, folder 5, SP; GIS to Edwin Stanfield, January 7, 1970, box 33, folder 5, SP; GIS to Américo Paredes, September 29, 1971, box 42, folder 14, SP; William Turnbull to GIS, December 16, 1971, box 12, folder 21, SP; GIS to William Turnbull, undated [likely late 1971 or very early 1972], box 12, folder 21, SP (quotation); GIS to John Rich, November 18, 1970, box 49, folder 1, SP; GIS to Kay Northcott, June 7, 1971, box 34, folder 16, SP; Cliff Olofson to GIS, June 20, 1971, box 34, folder 16, SP.

33. Sprague interview; Kennedy interview; Dugger, *Our Invaded Universities*, 118, 427; GIS to William Madsen, April 23, 1968, box 3, folder 9, SP [old system] (first quotation);

GIS to Florence Dickerson, September 15, 1970, box 60, folder 2, SP (second quotation); Laura Williams to GIS, April 21, 1971, box 15, folder 6, SP; GIS, notes to "Mexican American Children," May 13, 1971, box 15, folder 6, SP, 1–5.

34. Lupe Zamarripa to GIS, January 3, 1972, box 63, folder 21, SP; GIS to Lupe Zamarripa, January 17, 1972, box 63, folder 21, SP; José Limón to GIS, December 3, 1971, box 52, folder 15, SP; GIS to José Limón, December 17, 1971, box 52, folder 15, SP; GIS to James R. Roach, January 31, 1972, box 29, folder 5, SP (quotations); GIS to Américo Paredes, January 31, 1972, box 29, folder 5, SP; Américo Paredes to GIS, February 7, 1972, box 42, folder 14, SP; Paredes, "Jorge Isidoro Sánchez y Sánchez," in *Humanidad: Essays in Honor of George I. Sánchez*, ed. Paredes, 123.

35. Ralph Yarborough to GIS, February 28, 1972, box 63, folder 16, SP; Ralph Yarborough to GIS, February 29, 1972, box 63, folder 16, SP; Frank Angel to GIS, March 21, 1972, box 5, folder 6, SP; Mario Obledo to GIS, March 17, 1972, box 25, folder 1, SP; GIS to Hugo Morales, March 14, 1972, box 26, folder 4, SP; GIS to Gonzalo Barrientos, March 16, 1972, box 7, folder 14, SP; "Sánchez Services Pending," *Austin Statesman*, April 6, 1972, box 95, folder 1, SP; Sprague interview; Kennedy interview; Leff, "George I. Sánchez," 556.

36. John Rich, undated [likely April 1972], GISVF–UT; William Drake et al., "In Memoriam: George I. Sánchez (Jorge Isidoro Sánchez y Sánchez)," undated, GISVF–UT, 1 (quotation).

EPILOGUE

1. Lelevier and Rodriguez, A *Portfolio of Outstanding Americans of Mexican Descent;* William Drake to Carey McWilliams, April 27, 1972, box 23, folder 20, collection 1319, MP (first quotation); Luisa Sánchez to Carey McWilliams, May 4, 1972, box 23, folder 20, collection 1319, MP; Carey McWilliams to Luisa Sánchez, May 26, 1972, box 23, folder 20, collection 1319, MP; McWilliams, "George Sánchez," 709 (second quotation), 710; "Prof. G. I. Sánchez—Educator, Leader, Humanitarian," *Congressional Record*, May 2, 1972, box 23, folder 20, collection 1319, MP; Carey McWilliams to William Drake, May 25, 1972, box 23, folder 20, collection 1319, MP; Gomez, "Editorial. Jorge Isidoro Sánchez y Sánchez (1904–1972)," 122 (third and fourth quotations); Sheila Francis, "Professor Called 'Historical Figure,'" *Daily Texan*, April 13, 1972, GISVF–UT; Homer Barrera, "Dr. George I. Sánchez, Don Quixote of the Texas Range," *Texas Observer*, June 29, 1973, GISVF–UT (final quotation).

2. "George I. Sánchez Elementary School: Dedication—Open House," May 1, 1977, box 1, folder 23, SP, 1–4; "Work Section Named for Texas Educator," *Dallas Morning News*, October 13, 1978, box 95, folder 1, SP; Julian Samora to Carey McWilliams, March 28, 1973, box 23, folder 20, collection 1319, MP; Carey McWilliams to Julian Samora, April 4, 1973, box 23, folder 20, collection 1319, MP; Américo Paredes to Carey McWilliams, June 14, 1973, box 23, folder 20, collection 1319, MP; Carey McWilliams to Américo Paredes, June 18, 1973, box 23, folder 20, collection 1319, MP; Luisa Sánchez to Carey McWilliams, July 1, 1977, box 29, folder 3, collection 1319, MP; Tevis, "SANCHEZ."

3. Angie Quiros, "Tentative Schedule" for tribute to George I. Sánchez and Carlos E. Castañeda, February 21, 1975, box 100, folder 23, GP; Kathy Glover, "UT News press release," October 25, 1983, GISVF–UT, 1–2; Richard Bonnin, "UT Regents Honor Renowned Hispanic Educator, Scholar George I. Sánchez," *On Campus*, October 11, 1994, box 95, folder 1, SP, 1, 3; Andrea Buckley, "Building Renamed for Former UT Professor," *Daily Texan*, October 10, 1994, GISVF–UT; Melanie Gerik, "Education Building Named After UT Civil Rights Leader," *Daily Texan*, May 3, 1995, box 95, folder 1, SP; program, "Dedication of the George I. Sánchez Building," May 2, 1995, box 95, folder 1, SP.

BIBLIOGRAPHY

ARCHIVAL SOURCES

Center for American History,
University of Texas at Austin

George I. Sánchez Vertical File (GISVF–UT)
LULAC Vertical File (LULACVF)
Benjamin Franklin Pittenger Papers (BPP)
La Verdad

Center for Southwest Research,
University of New Mexico at Albuquerque

Antonio A. Sedillo Papers (ASP)
George I. Sánchez Faculty File, 1938–41 (GISFF)
George I. Sánchez Vertical File (GISVF–UNM)
James F. Zimmerman Papers (ZP)
Richard M. Page Papers (PP)

Fisk University Franklin Library,
Special Collections–Archives, Nashville

Charles Spurgeon Johnson Papers (JP)
Julius Rosenwald Fund Archives (JRFA)

Lyndon Baines Johnson Presidential Library, Austin

Lyndon Johnson Senate Papers (LBJSP)
White House Central Files (WHCF)
Office Files of John Macy (OFJM)

Mary and Jeff Bell Library, Texas A&M University at Corpus Christi

Hector P. Garcia Papers (GP)

National Archives and Records Administration II, College Park, Maryland

State Department Records, Central Files (SDRCF)
Fair Employment Practices Commission Papers (FEPCP)
Office of Inter-American Affairs, Central Files (OIAACF)

Nettie Lee Benson Latin American Collection, University of Texas at Austin

Carlos E. Castañeda Papers (CP)
George I. Sánchez Papers (SP)
José de la Luz Sáenz Papers (JSP)
Ed Idar Jr. Papers (IP)
LULAC News

Rockefeller Archive Center, Sleepy Hollow, New York

General Education Board Collection (GEBC)
Rockefeller Family Collection, Nelson A. Rockefeller Papers (RP)

University of Houston Libraries, Special Collections, Houston

Alonso S. Perales Papers (APP)
Virgie R. Sánchez, Plaintiff, vs. George I. Sánchez, Defendant, December 6, 1946, DR
  36,5131946, Second Judicial District Court (Domestic Relations Division), Bernalillo
  County, State of New Mexico (BC).

Walt Disney Company Archives, Burbank, California

Young Research Library, University of California at Los Angeles

Southern California ACLU Papers (SCACLUP)
Carey McWilliams Papers (MP)

ORAL INTERVIEWS

Cowart, Billy Frank. Interview by author, October 13, 2011, digital recording, residence,
  Belton, Texas.
Idar, Eduardo (Ed), Jr. Interview by Margo Gutiérrez, 1991–2000, tape recording, Benson
  Latin American Collection, University of Texas at Austin.

Kennedy, Cynthia. Interview by author, December 11, 2011, digital recording, Holiday Inn Express, Georgetown, Texas.

Sánchez, Roberto P. (Bob). Interview by author, December 6, 2012, digital recording, visitors lobby of M. D. Anderson Cancer Center, Houston.

Sprague, Mark. Interview by author, April 24, 2009, digital recording, business, Austin.

THESES AND DISSERTATIONS

Cheavens, Sam Frank. "Vernacular Languages and Education." Ph.D. diss., University of Texas at Austin, 1957.

Cowart, Billy Frank. "The Educational Philosophy of Jaime Torres Bodet and Its Implications for Mexican and World Education." Ph.D. diss., University of Texas at Austin, 1963.

Leff, Gladys R. "George I. Sánchez: Don Quixote of the Southwest." Ph.D. diss., North Texas State University, 1976.

Mowry, James Nelson. "A Study of the Educational Thought and Action of George I. Sánchez." Ph.D. diss., University of Texas at Austin, 1977.

Ramos, Lisa Y. "A Class Apart: Mexican Americans, Race, and Civil Rights." Ph.D. diss., Columbia University, 2008.

Sánchez, George I. "A Study of the Scores of Spanish-Speaking Children on Repeated Tests." M.A. thesis, University of Texas, 1931.

Sánchez, George I. "The Education of Bilinguals in a State School System." Ph.D. diss., University of California at Berkeley, 1934.

Sánchez, Luisa G. Guerrero. "The 'Latin American' of the Southwest—Backgrounds and Curricular Implications." Ed.D. diss., University of Texas, Austin, 1954.

PUBLICATIONS OF GEORGE I. SÁNCHEZ

Cutright, Prudence, W. W. Charters, and George I. Sánchez. *Latin America: Twenty Friendly Nations.* New York: Macmillan, 1944.

Delaney, Eleanor C., George I. Sánchez, Prudence Cutright, and W. W. Charters. *Spanish Gold.* New York: Macmillan, 1946.

Fickinger, Paul L., and George I. Sánchez. "Analysis of Teachers' Salaries in New Mexico with a Comparison of Salaries Paid Other Public Servants." *New Mexico School Review* (March 1932): 18–25.

———. "A Source of School Revenue Fails Us." *New Mexico School Review* (March 1932): 32–33.

Sánchez, George I. "A Communication." *Texas Observer,* August 23, 1963, 4–5.

———. "A New Frontier Policy for the Americas." *Alcalde* 49:7 (March 1961), 9–11.

———. "A Re-phrasing." *Texas Observer,* May 16, 1963, 13.

———. *Arithmetic in Maya.* Privately published, 2201 Scenic Drive, Austin, 1961.

———. "Bilingualism and Mental Measures: A Word of Caution." *Journal of Applied Psychology* 18:6 (December 1934): 765–72.

———. "Classroom Reality." *Nation* 206:16 (April 15, 1968): 490.

———. "Colleges and Democracy." *Texas Observer*, May 14, 1965, 12.

———. *Concerning Segregation of Spanish-Speaking Children in the Public Schools. Inter-American Education Occasional Papers IX*. 1951; reprint New York: Arno Press, 1974.

———. "Discrimination in High Places." *Balance* 3:4 (November 14, 1960): 2–4.

———. "Educational Research in New Mexico." *Journal of Educational Research* 25:4–5 (April-May, 1932): 321–22.

———. *Forgotten People: A Study of New Mexicans*. 1940; reprint Albuquerque: University of New Mexico Press, 1996.

———. "Fundamental Problems in Education in Mexico." *Educational Forum* 7:4 (May 1943): 321–27.

———. "Group Differences and Spanish-speaking Children—A Critical Review." *Journal of Applied Psychology* 16:5 (October 1932): 549–58.

———. "Higher Education in Modern Mexico." *The Nation's Schools* 35:6 (June 1945): 32.

———. *Mexico: A Revolution by Education*. 1936; reprint Boston: Ginn, 1966.

———. "Pachucos in the Making." *Common Ground* 4:1 (Autumn 1943): 13–20.

———. "Past and Present Inter-American Educational Relations: A Personal Memoir." *Inter-American Educational Relations: Proceedings of the Fourth Western Regional Conference on Comparative Education, School of Education, University of California at Los Angeles* (October, 1964): 1–7.

———. "Pre-School for All." *Texas Observer*, September 4, 1959, 7.

———. "Proposals on Latins." *Texas Observer*, March 16, 1962, 7.

———. "Quantitative and Objective Criteria in Education—A Delusion." *Texas Journal of Secondary Education* 13:3 (Spring 1960): 1–5.

———. "Review of *North from Mexico* by Carey McWilliams." *Pacific Historical Review* 18:4 (November 1949): 530–31.

———. "Review of *Simón Bolívar: Educator* by Luis B. Prieto." *Hispanic American Historical Review* 51:1 (February 1971): 144–45.

———. "Review of *The Spanish-Americans of New Mexico: A Heritage of Pride* by Nancie L. González." *Pacific Historical Review* 39:3 (August 1970): 394–95.

———. "Right to Challenge." *Nation* 206:22 (May 27, 1968): 682.

———. "School Integration and Americans of Mexican Descent." *American Unity: A Monthly Manual of Education* 16:3 (March-April 1958): 9–14.

———. "Scores of Spanish-Speaking Children on Repeated Tests." *Journal of Genetic Psychology* 40 (March 1932): 223–31.

———. "Spanish-Speaking People in the Southwest—A Brief Historical Review." *California Journal of Elementary Education* 12:2 (November 1953): 106–11.

———. "Teachers' Salaries Cost Less Today Than They Did a Decade Ago." *New Mexico School Review* (March 1932): 30–31.

———. "The American of Mexican Descent." *Texas Observer*, December 31, 1965, 26–27.

———. "The American of Mexican Descent." *Chicago Jewish Forum* 20:2 (Winter 1961–62): 120–24.

———. "The Crux of the Dual Language Handicap." *New Mexico School Review* 38 (March 1954): 13–15.

——. *The Development of Education in Venezuela.* Washington, D.C.: Government Printing Office, 1963.

——. *The Development of Higher Education in Mexico.* 1944; reprint Westport, Conn.: Greenwood Press, 1970.

——. "The Equalization of Educational Opportunity—Some Issues and Problems." *University of New Mexico Bulletin,* no. 347, *Education Series* vol. 10, no. 1. Albuquerque: University of New Mexico Press, 1939.

——. "The Implications of a Basal Vocabulary to the Measurement of the Abilities of Bilingual Children." *Journal of Social Psychology* 5 (1934): 395–402.

——. "The Latin Citizen: His Hardship, His Promise." *Texas Observer,* March 9, 1962, 6.

——. "The Mexican-American in Texas: An Educator Speaks Out." *Home Missions* 18:7 (July 1967): 18–19.

——. *"The People": A Study of the Navajos.* Washington, D.C.: United States Indian Service, 1948.

——. "The State Public School Equalization Fund in Law and in Practice." *New Mexico Business Review* 8 (January 1939).

——. "Theory and Practice in Rural Education." *Progressive Education* 13:8 (1936).

——. "Twice Wounded." *Texas Observer* 51 (October 30, 1959), 7.

Sánchez, George I., ed. *Inter-American Education Occasional Papers, I. First Regional Conference on the Education of Spanish-Speaking People in the Southwest.* Austin: University of Texas Press, 1946.

Sánchez, George I., and William E. Drake. "The State of Texas." *Nation* 198:2 (January 6, 1964): 20.

Sánchez, George I., and Howard Putnam. *Materials Relating to the Education of Spanish- Speaking People in the United States: An Annotated Bibliography* 1959; reprint, Westport, Conn.: Greenwood Press, 1971).

Sánchez, George I., and Virgie R. Sánchez. "Education in Mexico in the Sixteenth Century." *New Mexico Quarterly* 4:3 (August 1934): 184–92.

Sánchez, Luisa, and George I. Sánchez. "An Experience in Texas." *Educational Leadership* 15:8 (May 1958): 464–65.

Strickland, Virgil E., and George I. Sánchez. "Spanish Name Spells Discrimination." *The Nation's Schools* 41:1 (January 1948): 22–24.

SECONDARY SOURCES

Adamic, Louis. *A Nation of Nations.* New York: Harper and Brothers, 1945.

Albright, Frank S. "Review of *Latin America: Twenty Friendly Nations* by Cutright, Charters, and Sánchez." *Elementary School Journal* 45:2 (October 1944): 118–19.

Alessandro, Joseph V. "Review of *Education and Social Change in Chile* and *The Development of Education in Venezuela.*" *Hispanic American Historical Review* 47:4 (November 1967): 604–6.

Allsup, Carl. *The American G.I. Forum: Origins and Evolution.* Austin: University of Texas Center for Mexican American Studies, 1982.

Almaráz, Félix D. *Knight Without Armor: Carlos Eduardo Castañeda.* College Station: Texas A&M University Press, 1999.

Alvarez, Luis. *The Power of the Zoot: Youth Culture and Resistance during World War II.* Berkeley: University of California Press, 2008.

Amastae, Jon, and Lucía Elías-Olivares, eds. *Spanish in the United States: Sociolinguistic Aspects.* New York: Cambridge University Press, 1982.

Anderson, James D. "Race, Meritocracy, and the American Academy During the Immediate Post–World War II Era." *History of Education Quarterly* 33:2 (Summer 1993): 151–75.

Anderson, Stephen C. *J. W. Edgar: Educator for Texas.* Austin: Eakin Press, 1984.

Andersson, Theodore. *Foreign Languages in the Elementary School: A Struggle Against Mediocrity.* Austin: University of Texas Press, 1969.

"An Interview with George I. Sánchez." *National Elementary Principal* 50:2 (November 1970): 102–4.

Aranda, José F., Jr., and Silvio Torres-Saillant, eds. *Recovering the U.S. Hispanic Literary Heritage.* Volume 4. Houston: Arte Público Press, 2002.

Arnesen, Eric. "Whiteness and the Historians' Imagination." *International Labor and Working- Class History* 60:1 (Fall 2001): 3–32.

Bachelor, David L. *Educational Reform in New Mexico: Tireman, San José, and Nambé.* Albuquerque: University of New Mexico Press, 1991.

Banks, James A., ed. *Multicultural Education, Transformative Knowledge, and Action: Historical and Contemporary Perspectives.* New York: Teachers College Press, 1996.

Barr, Glenn Ross, Willis K. Jones, and Eleanor C. Delaney. *Our Friends in South America.* New York: Macmillan, 1950.

Barrera, Mario. *Race and Class in the Southwest: A Theory of Racial Inequality.* Notre Dame: University of Notre Dame Press, 1979.

Barth, Pius J. "Review of *The Development of Higher Education in Mexico* by George I. Sánchez." *School Review* 53:5 (May 1945): 306–8.

Bartley, Numan V. *The New South, 1945–1980.* Baton Rouge: Louisiana State University Press, 1995.

Bayne, Ronald. "I'm Afraid It's Bad News." *Canadian Medical Association Journal* 159:3 (August 11, 1998): 258.

Bayor, Ronald H. "Another Look at 'Whiteness': The Persistence of Ethnicity in American Life." *Journal of American Ethnic History* 29:1 (Fall 2009): 13–30.

Beatty, Barbara, Emily D. Cahan, and Julia Grant, eds. *When Science Encounters the Child: Education, Parenting, and Child Welfare in 20th-Century America.* New York: Teachers College Press, 2006.

Berg, Manfred. "Black Civil Rights and Liberal Anticommunism: The NAACP in the Early Cold War." *Journal of American History* 94:1 (June 2007).

Berry, Jeffrey M. *The Interest Group Society.* 2d ed. New York: HarperCollins Press, 1989.

Berstein, Shana. *Bridges of Reform: Interracial Civil Rights Activism in Twentieth-Century Los Angeles.* New York: Oxford University Press, 2011.

Bird, Stewart, Dan Georgakas, and Deborah Shaffer. *Solidarity Forever: An Oral History of the IWW.* Chicago: Lake View Press, 1985.

Blackwell, Maylei. *¡Chicana Power! Contested Histories of Feminism in the Chicano Movement*. Austin: University of Texas Press, 2011.

Blanton, Carlos Kevin. "A Legacy of Neglect: George I. Sánchez, Mexican American Education, and the Idea of Integration." *Teachers College Record* 114:6 (June 2012): 1–34.

———. "From Intellectual Deficiency to Cultural Deficiency: Mexican Americans, Testing, and School Policy in the American Southwest, 1920–1940." *Pacific Historical Review* 72:1 (February 2003): 39–62.

———. "George I. Sánchez, Ideology, and Whiteness in the Making of the Mexican American Civil Rights Movement, 1930–1960." *Journal of Southern History* 72:3 (August 2006): 569–604.

———. "The Citizenship Sacrifice: Mexican Americans, the Saunders–Leonard Report, and the Politics of Immigration, 1951–1952." *Western Historical Quarterly* 40:3 (Autumn 2009): 299–320.

———. *The Strange Career of Bilingual Education in Texas, 1836–1931*. College Station: Texas A&M University Press, 2004.

Bowden, A. O., Carmen González de Porter, Prudence Cutright, and W. W. Charters. *The Day Before Yesterday in America*. New York: Macmillan, 1946.

Brett, George P., Jr., Burr L. Chase, Robert F. deGraff, Malcolme Johnson, and Jared S. Thompson. *The Role of Books in Inter-American Relations*. New York: Book Publishers Bureau, 1943.

Brown, David S. *Richard Hofstadter: An Intellectual Biography*. Chicago: University of Chicago Press, 2006.

Brunhouse, Robert L. *Sylvanus G. Morley and the World of the Ancient Mayas*. Norman: University of Oklahoma Press, 1971.

Buck, Paul H. *The Role of Education in American History*. New York: Fund for the Advancement of Education, 1957.

Burma, John H. *Spanish-Speaking Groups in the United States*. Durham: Duke University Press, 1954.

Brands, H. W., interviewer. *A Texas Supreme Court Trilogy*. Volume 2: *Oral History Interview with the Honorable Joe R. Greenhill, Sr*. Austin: Jamail Center for Legal Research, University of Texas School of Law, 1998.

Carpenter, D. H. "Review of *Arithmetic in Maya* by George I. Sánchez." *Man* 62 (July 1962): 108.

Carroll, Patrick J. *Felix Longoria's Wake: Bereavement, Racism, and the Rise of Mexican American Activism*. Austin: University of Texas Press, 2003.

Carter, Dan. T. *Scottsboro: A Tragedy of the American South*. Baton Rouge: Louisiana State University Press, 1969.

Castañeda, Carlos E., and Eleanor C. Delaney. *The Lands of Middle America*. New York: Macmillan, 1947.

Chávez, Ernesto. *"¡Mi Raza Primero!" Nationalism, Identity, and Insurgency in the Chicano Movement in Los Angeles, 1966–1978*. Berkeley: University of California Press, 2002.

Chávez, John R. *The Lost Land: The Chicano Image of the Southwest*. Albuquerque: University of New Mexico Press, 1984.

Cherny, Robert W., William Issel, and Kieran Walsh Taylor, eds. *American Labor and the Cold War: Grassroots Politics and Postwar Political Culture.* New Brunswick: Rutgers University Press, 2004.

Clements, Eric L. *After the Boom in Tombstone and Jerome, Arizona.* Reno: University of Nevada Press, 2003.

Cohen, Lizbeth. *Making a New Deal: Industrial Workers in Chicago, 1919–1939.* New York: Cambridge University Press, 1991.

Cohen, Robert. *When the Old Left Was Young: Student Radicals and America's First Mass Student Movement, 1929–1941.* New York: Oxford University Press, 1993.

Cole, Stephanie, and Alison M. Parker, eds. *Beyond Black and White: Race, Ethnicity, and Gender in the U.S. South and Southwest.* College Station: Texas A&M University Press, 2004.

Cole, Stewart G. *Intercultural Education.* New York: American Jewish Committee, 1941.

Contreras, Russell. "Celebrated Scholar Remains Unrecognized in Home State." *Santa Fe New Mexican,* February 11, 2012.

Coordinator of Inter-American Affairs. *Our American Neighbors.* Washington, D.C.: Public Affairs Press, 1945.

Cox, Patrick. *Ralph W. Yarborough, the People's Senator.* Austin: University of Texas Press, 2001.

Davies, Gareth. *From Opportunity to Entitlement: The Transformation and Decline of Great Society Liberalism.* Lawrence: University Press of Kansas, 1996.

Davis, Mathew D. *Exposing a Culture of Neglect: Herschel T. Manuel and Mexican American Schooling.* Greenwich: Information Age Publishing, 2005.

De León, Arnoldo, ed. *Tejano Epic: Essays in Honor of Félix D. Almaráz.* Austin: Texas State Historical Association Press, 2005.

Delgado, Richard, and Jean Stefancic. *Critical Race Theory: An Introduction.* New York: New York University Press, 2001.

Delpar, Helen. *The Enormous Vogue of Things Mexican: Cultural Relations Between the United States and Mexico, 1920–1935.* Tuscaloosa: University of Alabama Press, 1992.

Department of State. *Inter-American Cultural Relations: Department of State Publication 1369.* Washington, D.C.: Government Printing Office, 1939.

———. *The Program of the Department of State in Cultural Relations. Department of State Publication 1441.* Washington, D.C.: Government Printing Office, 1940.

———. *Official Exchange of Professors, Teachers, and Graduate Students Under the Convention for the Promotion of Inter-American Cultural Relations. Department of State Publication 1612.* Washington, D.C.: Government Printing Office, 1941.

———. *The Program of the Department of State in Cultural Relations. Department of State Publication 1594.* Washington, D.C.: Government Printing Office, 1941.

———. *Cultural Relations Among the Democracies: Department of State Publication 1714.* Washington, D.C.: Government Printing Office, 1942.

Dinwoodie, David H. "Deportation: The Immigration Service and the Chicano Labor Movement in the 1930s." *New Mexico Historical Review* 52:3 (1977): 193–206.

———. "Indians, Hispanos, and Land Reform: A New Deal Struggle in New Mexico." *Western Historical Quarterly* 17:3 (July 1986): 300–301.

Division of Information and Statistics. *New Mexico Common Schools Annual Financial and Statistical Report of the State Superintendent of Public Instruction, 1932–1933.* Santa Fe: Division of Information and Statistics, 1933.

Dobbs, Ricky F. *Yellow Dogs and Republicans: Allen Shivers and Texas Two-Party Politics.* College Station: Texas A&M University Press, 2005.

Doyle, Henry Gratta. "Some Intellectually Dishonest Arguments—And Some that Are 'Plain Dumb'–Against the Study of Foreign Languages." *Hispania* 26:2 (May 1943).

Dubofsky, Melvyn. *We Shall Be All: A History of the Industrial Workers of the World.* Chicago: Quadrangle Books, 1969.

Dugger, Ronnie. "A Comment." *Texas Observer*, April 18, 1963, 10.

———. *Our Invaded Universities: Form, Reform, and New Starts.* New York: W. W. Norton, 1974.

———. "Political Interests of Latins United." *Texas Observer*, September 15, 1961, 1, 3.

———. "Senator Yarborough and Texas' 'No-Surrender' Conference." *Texas Observer*, April 28, 1967, 11–12.

Dunne, Matthew William. "Next Steps: Charles S. Johnson and Southern Liberalism." *Journal of Negro History* 83:1 (Winter 1998): 1–34.

"Education, Public Schools—Texas." *Race Relations Law Reporter* 2:2 (April 1957): 329–34.

Embree, Edwin R., William W. Alexander, and Charles S. Johnson. *The Collapse of Cotton Tenancy.* Chapel Hill: University of North Carolina Press, 1935.

Embree, Edwin R., and Julia Waxman. *Investment in People: The Story of the Julius Rosenwald Fund.* New York: Harper and Brothers, 1949.

Escobar, Edward J. "Bloody Christmas and the Irony of Police Professionalism: The Los Angeles Police Department, Mexican Americans, and Police Reform in the 1950s." *Pacific Historical Review* 72:2 (May 2003): 171–99.

Espinosa, J. Manuel. *Inter-American Beginnings of U.S. Cultural Diplomacy, 1936–1948. Cultural Relations Programs of the U.S. Department of State, Historical Studies: No. 2.* Washington, D.C.: Department of State Publication, 1976.

Etulain, Richard W., ed. *New Mexican Lives: Profiles and Historical Stories.* Albuquerque: University of New Mexico Press, 2002.

Evans, Ronald W. *The Social Studies Wars: What Should We Teach the Children?* New York: Teachers College Press, 2004.

———. *This Happened in America: Harold Rugg and the Censure of Social Studies.* Charlotte: Information Age Publishing, 2007.

Everett, Samuel, ed. *The Community School.* New York: D. Appleton-Century, 1938.

Fairclough, Adam. *Race and Democracy: The Civil Rights Struggle in Louisiana, 1915–1972.* Athens: University of Georgia Press, 1995.

Fields, Barbara J. "Whiteness, Racism, and Identity." *International Labor and Working-Class History* 60:1 (Fall 2001): 48–56.

Fishman, Joshua, ed. *Language Loyalty in the United States: The Maintenance and Perpetuation of Non-English Mother Tongues by American Ethnic and Religious Groups.* The Hague: Mouton, 1966.

Foley, Neil, ed. *Reflexiones 1997: New Directions in Mexican American Studies.* Austin: Center for Mexican American Studies of the University of Texas, 1998.

———. *Quest for Equality: The Failed Promise of Black–Brown Solidarity.* Cambridge: Harvard University Press, 2010.

———. *The White Scourge: Mexicans, Blacks, and Poor Whites in Texas Cotton Culture.* Berkeley: University of California Press, 1997.

Frazier, E. Franklin. *Black Bourgeoisie.* Glencoe, Ill.: Free Press, 1957.

Friedman, Max Paul. *Nazis and Good Neighbors: The United States Campaign Against the Germans of Latin America in World War II.* New York: Cambridge University Press, 2003.

Gabler, Neal. *Walt Disney: The Triumph of the American Imagination.* New York: Vintage Press, 2006.

García, Ignacio M. *Chicanismo: The Forging of a Militant Ethos among Mexican Americans.* Tucson: University of Arizona Press, 1997.

———. *Hector P. Garcia: In Relentless Pursuit of Justice.* Houston: Arte Público Press, 2003.

———. *Viva Kennedy: Mexican Americans in Search of Camelot.* College Station: Texas A&M University Press, 2000.

———. *White But Not Equal: Mexican Americans, Jury Discrimination, and the Supreme Court.* Tucson: University of Arizona Press, 2009.

García, Juan Ramon. *Operation Wetback: The Mass Deportation of Mexican Undocumented Workers in 1954.* Westport, Conn.: Praeger Press, 1980.

García, Mario T. "Americans All: The Mexican American Generation and the Politics of Wartime Los Angeles, 1941–1945." *Social Science Quarterly* 65:2 (June 1984): 278–89.

———. "Mexican Americans and the Politics of Citizenship: The Case of El Paso, 1936." *New Mexico Historical Review* 59:2 (Spring 1984): 187–204.

———. *Mexican Americans: Leadership, Ideology, and Identity, 1930–1960.* New Haven: Yale University Press, 1989.

García, Mario T., and Sal Castro. *Blowout! Sal Castro and the Chicano Struggle for Educational Justice.* Chapel Hill: University of North Carolina Press, 2011.

Garcia, Richard A. *Rise of the Mexican American Middle Class: San Antonio, 1929–1941.* College Station: Texas A&M University Press, 1991.

Garcilazo, Jeffrey M. "McCarthyism, Mexican Americans, and the Los Angeles Committee for Protection of the Foreign-Born, 1950–1954." *Western Historical Quarterly* 32:3 (Fall 2001): 273–95.

Garza-Falcón, Leticia M. *Gente Decente: A Borderlands Response to the Rhetoric of Dominance.* Austin: University of Texas Press, 1998.

Getz, Lynne Marie. "Extending the Helping Hand to Hispanics: The Role of the General Education Board in New Mexico in the 1930s." *Teachers College Record* 93:3 (Spring 1992): 500–515.

———. "Politics, Science, and Education in New Mexico: The Racial-Attitudes Survey of 1933." *History of Higher Education Annual* 10 (1990): 51–68.

———. "The Quaker, the Primitivist, and the Progressive: Three Cultural Brokers in New Mexico's Quest for Multicultural Harmony." *Journal of the Gilded Age and Progressive Era* 9:2 (April 2010): 243–56.

———. *Schools of Their Own: The Education of Hispanos in New Mexico.* Albuquerque: University of New Mexico Press, 1997.

Gilpin, Patrick J., and Marybeth Gasman. *Charles S. Johnson: Leadership Beyond the Veil in the Age of Jim Crow.* Albany: State University of New York Press, 2003.

Goldstone, Dwonna Naomi. *Integrating the 40 Acres: The Fifty-Year Struggle for Racial Equality at the University of Texas.* Athens: University of Georgia Press, 2006.

Gomez, Daniel J. "Editorial. Jorge Isidoro Sánchez y Sánchez (1904–1972)—A Man for All Seasons." *Journal of Mexican American Studies* 1:3/4 (Spring/Summer, 1972): 122.

Gómez, Laura E. *Manifest Destinies: The Making of the Mexican American Race.* New York: New York University Press, 2007.

Gómez-Quiñones, Juan. *Chicano Politics: Reality and Promise, 1940–1990.* Albuquerque: University of New Mexico Press, 1990.

Gómez-Quiñones, Juan, and Luis Leobando Arroyo. "On the State of Chicano History: Observations on Its Development, Interpretations, and Theory, 1970–1974." *Western Historical Quarterly* 7:2 (April 1976): 155–85.

Gonzales, Phillip B. [Felipe]. *Forced Sacrifice as Ethnic Protest: The Hispano Cause in New Mexico and the Racial Attitude Confrontation of 1933.* New York: Peter Lang, 2001.

———. "'La Junta de Indignación': Hispano Repertoire of Collective Protest in New Mexico, 1884–1933." *Western Historical Quarterly* 31:2 (Summer 2000): 161–86.

Gonzalez, Gilbert G. *Chicano Education in the Era of Segregation.* Philadelphia: Balch Institute Press, 1990.

———. *Labor and Community: Mexican Citrus Worker Villages in a Southern California County, 1900–1950.* Urbana: University of Illinois Press, 1994.

———. *Mexican Consuls and Labor Organizing: Imperial Politics in the American Southwest.* Austin: University of Texas Press, 1999.

González, John Morán. *Border Renaissance: The Texas Centennial and the Emergence of Mexican American Literature.* Austin: University of Texas Press, 2009.

Goodman, James E. *Stories of Scottsboro.* New York: Vintage Books, 1995.

Gordon, Linda. *The Great Arizona Orphan Abduction.* Cambridge: Harvard University Press, 1999.

Grebler, Leo, Joan W. Moore, and Ralph C. Guzman. *The Mexican-American People: The Nation's Second Largest Minority.* New York: Free Press, 1970.

Green, George Norris. *The Establishment in Texas Politics: The Primitive Years, 1938–1957.* Norman: University of Oklahoma Press.

Green, James R. *Grass-Roots Socialism: Radical Movements in the Southwest, 1895–1943.* Baton Rouge: Louisiana State University Press, 1978.

Gritter, Matthew. *Mexican Inclusion: The Origins of Anti-Discrimination Policy in Texas and the Southwest.* College Station: Texas A&M University Press, 2012.

Gross, Ariela J. "Texas Mexicans and the Politics of Whiteness." *Law and History Review* 21:1 (Spring 2003): 195–205.

Gruber, Carol S. *Mars and Minerva: World War I and the Uses of the Higher Learning in America.* Baton Rouge: Louisiana State University Press, 1975.

Guglielmo, Thomas A. "Fighting for Caucasian Rights: Mexicans, Mexican Americans, and the Transnational Struggle for Civil Rights in World War II Texas." *Journal of American History* 92:4 (March 2006), 1212–37.

Gutiérrez, David G. "Significant to Whom? Mexican Americans and the History of the American West." *Western Historical Quarterly* 24:4 (November 1993): 519–39.

———. "Sin Fronteras? Chicanos, Mexican Americans, and the Emergence of the Contemporary Mexican Immigration Debate, 1968–1978." *Journal of American Ethnic History* 10:4 (Summer 1991): 5–37.

———. *Walls and Mirrors: Mexican Americans, Mexican Immigrants, and the Politics of Ethnicity.* Berkeley: University of California Press, 1995.

Gutiérrez, Ramón A. "Internal Colonialism: An American Theory of Race." *Du Bois Review* 1:2 (2004): 281–95.

Gutman, Herbert G. *The Black Family in Slavery and Freedom 1750–1925.* New York: Pantheon Books, 1976.

Hale, Charles A. "Frank Tannenbaum and the Mexican Revolution." *Hispanic American Historical Review* 75:2 (May 1995): 215–46.

Hardgrave, Robert L., Jr., and Santiago Hinojosa. *The Politics of Bilingual Education: A Study of Four Southwest Texas Communities.* Manchaca, Tex.: Sterling Swift, 1975.

Hernández, Kelly Lytle. "The Crimes and Consequences of Illegal Immigration: A Cross-Border Examination of Operation Wetback, 1943 to 1954." *Western Historical Quarterly* 37:4 (Winter 2006): 421–44.

Hernández, M., William J., and Henry Sioux Johnson, eds. *Educating the Mexican American.* Valley Forge, Penn.: Judson Press, 1970.

Hinojosa, Felipe D. "¡Medicina Sí, Muerte No!": Race, Public Health, and the 'Long War on Poverty' in Mathis, Texas, 1948–1971." *Western Historical Quarterly* 44:4 (Winter 2013): 437–58.

Hoffschwelle, Mary S. *The Rosenwald Schools of the American South.* Gainesville: University Press of Florida, 2006.

Huang, Chin Tang, and Harold A. Lyons. "Cardiorespiratory Failure in Patients with Pneumonectomy for Tuberculosis." *Journal of Thoracic and Cardiovascular Surgery* 74:3 (September 1977): 409–17.

Idar, Ed, Jr., and Andrew C. McLellan. *What Price Wetbacks?* Austin: American G.I. Forum and Texas State Federation of Labor, 1954.

Ignatiev, Noel. *How the Irish Became White.* New York: Routledge, 1995.

Inman, Samuel Guy, and Carlos E. Castañeda. *A History of Latin America for Schools.* New York: Macmillan, 1944.

Iriye, Akira. *Cultural Internationalism and World Order.* Baltimore: Johns Hopkins University Press, 1997.

Jacobson, Matthew Frye. *Whiteness of a Different Color: European Immigrants and the Alchemy of Race.* Cambridge: Harvard University Press, 1998.

Jerome High School. *The Mucker, 1919–1920 Yearbook.* Jerome, Ariz., 1920.

Johnson, Benjamin H. "The Cosmic Race in Texas: Racial Fusion, White Supremacy, and Civil Rights Politics." *Journal of American History* 98:2 (September 2011): 404–19.

———. *Revolution in Texas: How a Forgotten Rebellion and Its Bloody Suppression Turned Mexicans into Americans.* New Haven: Yale University Press, 2003.

Johnson, Charles S. "The Education of the Negro Child." *American Sociological Review* 1:2 (April 1936): 264–72.

Joseph, Gilbert M., Catherine C. LeGrand, and Ricardo D. Salvatore, eds. *Close Encounters of Empire: Writing the Cultural History of U.S.–Latin American Relations.* Durham: Duke University Press, 1998.

Kahlenberg, Richard D. *Tough Liberal: Albert Shanker and the Battles Over Schools, Unions, Race, and Democracy.* New York: Columbia University Press, 2007.

Kahn, E. J., Jr. *Jock: The Life and Times of John Hay Whitney.* New York: Doubleday, 1981.

Kaplowitz, Craig A. *LULAC, Mexican Americans, and National Policy.* College Station: Texas A&M University Press, 2005.

Keith, Gary A. *Eckhardt: There Once Was a Congressman from Texas.* Austin: University of Texas Press, 2007.

Kelley, David H. "Review of *Arithmetic in Maya* by George I. Sánchez." *American Anthropologist* 64:5 (October 1962): 1104.

Kells, Michelle Hall. *Hector P. Garcia: Everyday Rhetoric and Mexican American Civil Rights.* Carbondale: Southern Illinois University Press, 2006.

Kelly, Robin D. G. *Hammer and Hoe: Alabama Communists During the Great Depression.* Chapel Hill: University of North Carolina Press, 1990.

Kirkendall, Richard S. *Social Scientists and Farm Politics in the Age of Roosevelt.* Columbia: University of Missouri Press, 1966.

Kliebard, Herbert M. *The Struggle for the American Curriculum, 1893–1958.* New York: Routledge, 1986.

Koenig, Rodney. "Julia Mellenbruch: Maestra de Español." *Journal of the German-Texan Heritage Society* 29:3 (Fall 2007): 310–11.

Kolchin, Peter. "Whiteness Studies: The New History of Race in America." *Journal of American History* 89:1 (June 2002): 154–73.

Kreneck, Thomas H. *Mexican American Odyssey: Felix Tijerina, Entrepreneur and Civic Leader, 1905–1965.* College Station: Texas A&M University Press, 2001.

Kutler, Stanley I., ed. *American Retrospectives: Historians on Historians.* Baltimore: Johns Hopkins University Press, 1995.

Kutulas, Judy. *The ACLU and the Making of Modern Liberalism, 1930–1960.* Chapel Hill: University of North Carolina Press, 2006.

Kymlicka, Will. *Multicultural Citizenship: A Liberal Theory of Minority Rights.* New York: Oxford University Press, 1995.

Lauchlan, Angus. "The Texas Liberal Press and the Image of White Texas Masculinity, 1938–1963." *Southwestern Historical Quarterly* 110:4 (April 2007): 486–512.

Lelevier, Benjamin, and David Rodriguez. *A Portfolio of Outstanding Americans of Mexican Descent.* Menlo Park, Calif.: Educational Consulting Associates, 1970.

Lewis, Oscar. *The Children of Sánchez: An Autobiography of a Mexican Family.* New York: Random House, 1961.

Limón, José E. *Américo Paredes: Culture and Critique.* Austin: University of Texas Press, 2012.

———. "Gentlemen." *La Luz* 3:5 (1974): 5.

Lipsitz, George. *The Possessive Investment in Whiteness: How White People Profit from Identity Politics.* Philadelphia: Temple University Press, 1998.

Little, Wilson. *Spanish-Speaking Children in Texas.* Austin: University of Texas Press, 1944.

Lomelí, Francisco A., Victor A. Sorrell, and Genaro M. Padilla, eds. *Nuevomexicano Cultural Legacy: Forms, Agencies, and Discourse.* Albuquerque: University of New Mexico Press, 2002.

López, Ian F. Haney. *White by Law: The Legal Construction of Race.* New York: New York University Press, 1996.

Louisiana Educational Survey Commission. *Louisiana Educational Survey.* Volume 4. Baton Rouge: Louisiana Educational Survey Commission, 1942.

Lowitt, Richard. *Bronson M. Cutting: Progressive Politician.* Albuquerque: University of New Mexico Press, 1992.

Lozano, Rosina A. "Managing the 'Priceless Gift': Debating Spanish Language Instruction in New Mexico and Puerto Rico, 1930–1950." *Western Historical Quarterly* 44:3 (Autumn 2013): 271–93.

Lyng, Stephen, ed. *Edgework: The Sociology of Risk-Taking.* New York: Routledge, 2005.

MacDonald, Victoria-María. *Latino Education in the United States: A Narrated History from 1513–2000.* New York: Palgrave Macmillan, 2004.

MacDonald, Victoria-María, and Benjamin Polk Hoffman. "'Compromising *La Causa?*' The Ford Foundation and Chicano Intellectual Nationalism in the Creation of Chicano History, 1963–1977." *History of Education Quarterly* 52:2 (May 2012): 251–81.

Madsen, William. *Society and Health in the Lower Rio Grande Valley.* Austin: Hogg Foundation for Mental Health, University of Texas, 1961.

———. *The Mexican-Americans of South Texas.* New York: Holt, Rinehart, and Winston, 1964.

Manuel, Herschel T. *Spanish-Speaking Children of the Southwest: Their Education and the Public Welfare.* Austin: University of Texas Press, 1965.

———. *The Education of Mexican and Spanish-Speaking Children in Texas.* 1930; reprint, New York: Arno Press, 1974.

Marden, Charles F. *Minorities in American Society.* New York: American Book Company, 1952.

Mariscal, George. *Brown-Eyed Children of the Sun: Lessons from the Chicano Movement, 1965–1975.* Albuquerque: University of New Mexico Press, 2005.

Márquez, Benjamín. *LULAC: The Evolution of a Mexican American Political Organization.* Austin: University of Texas Press, 1993.

Martin, Charles H. *The Angelo Herndon Case and Southern Justice.* Baton Rouge: Louisiana State University Press, 1976.

Martínez, George A. "Immigration and the Meaning of United States Citizenship: Whiteness and Assimilation." *Washburn Law Journal* 46:2 (Winter 2007): 335–44.

Martinez, Joe L., Jr., and Richard H. Mendoza, eds. *Chicano Psychology.* 2d ed. New York: Academic Press, 1984.

Matusow, Allen J. *Farm Policies and Politics in the Truman Years.* Cambridge: Harvard University Press, 1967.

——. *The Unraveling of America: A History of Liberalism in the 1960s.* New York: Harper and Row, 1984.

Mazón, Mauricio. *The Zoot-Suit Riots: The Psychology of Symbolic Annihilation.* Austin: University of Texas Press, 1984.

McGee, Reece. "Texas: The Roots of the Agony." *Nation* (December 21, 1963): 427–31.

McWilliams, Carey. "George Sánchez." *Nation* (June 5, 1972): 709–10.

——. *North from Mexico: The Spanish-Speaking People of the United States.* 1949; reprint New York: Greenwood Press, 1990.

Meeks, Eric V. *Border Citizens: The Making of Indians, Mexicans, and Anglos in Arizona.* Austin: University of Texas Press, 2007.

Melick, Dermont W. "Surgical Therapy of Pulmonary Tuberculosis—A Rare Necessity of the 1980s. An Historical Review." *Arizona Medicine* 40:3 (March 1983): 158–59.

Mickenberg, Julia L. *Learning from the Left: Children's Literature, the Cold War, and Radical Politics in the United States.* New York: Oxford University Press, 2006.

Montejano, David. *Anglos and Mexicans in the Making of Texas.* Austin: University of Texas Press, 1986.

——. *Quixote's Soldiers: A Local History of the Chicano Movement, 1966–1981.* Austin: University of Texas Press, 2011.

Montemayor, Aurelio M. "Su Palabra es Oro—His Word Is Gold." *IDRA Newsletter* 38:9 (October 16, 2011): 3–4.

Moreno, José F., ed. *The Elusive Quest for Equality: 150 Years of Chicano/Chicana Education.* Cambridge: Harvard Educational Review, 1999.

Morris, Willie. "Major Defection to GOP in Texas." *Texas Observer*, September 15, 1961, 1, 3.

Naef, Andreas P. "The 1900 Tuberculosis Epidemic—Starting Point of Modern Thoracic Surgery." *Annals of Thoracic Surgery* 55:6 (June 1993): 1375–78.

National Association for Chicano Studies, Editorial Committee: Teresa Córdova, Norma Cantú, Gilberto Cardenas, Juan García, and Christine M. Sierra. *Chicana Voices: Intersections of Class, Race, and Gender.* Albuquerque: University of New Mexico Press, 1990.

National Education Association. *The White House Conference on Rural Education: October 3, 4, and 5, 1944.* Washington, D.C.: National Education Association, 1945.

Newman, Melvin M. "The Olden Days of Surgery for Tuberculosis." *Annals of Thoracic Surgery* 48:2 (August 1989): 161–62.

New Mexico Quarterly Review staff. "The School for the Rio Grande. A Symposium." *New Mexico Quarterly Review* 12:3 (August 1942): 295–300.

Ngai, Mae M. *Impossible Subjects: Illegal Aliens and the Making of Modern America.* Princeton: Princeton University Press, 2004.

Ninkovich, Frank A. *The Diplomacy of Ideas: U.S. Foreign Policy and Cultural Relations, 1938–1950.* New York: Cambridge University Press, 1981.

O'Connor, Karen, and Lee Epstein. "A Legal Voice for the Chicano Community: The Activities of the Mexican American Legal Defense and Educational Fund, 1968–82." *Social Science Quarterly* 65:2 (June 1984): 245–56.

Odum, Howard W. *Southern Regions of the United States*. Chapel Hill: University of North Carolina Press, 1936.

Odum, Howard W., and Harry Estill Moore. *American Regionalism: A Cultural-Historical Approach to National Integration*. New York: Henry Holt, 1938.

Olivas, Michael A. "The Arc of Triumph and the Agony of Defeat: Mexican Americans and the Law." *Historia Chicana*, August 17, 2010, 1–12.

Olivas, Michael A., ed. *"Colored Men" and "Hombres Aquí": Hernández v. Texas and the Emergence of Mexican-American Lawyering*. Houston: Arte Público Press, 2006.

———, ed. *In Defense of My People: Alonso S. Perales and the Development of Mexican-American Public Intellectuals*. Houston: Arte Público Press. 2012.

Oropeza, Lorena. *Raza Sí, Guerra No! Chicano Protest and Patriotism During the Viet Nam War Era*. Berkeley: University of California Press, 2005.

Orozco, Cynthia E. "Beyond Machismo, La Familia, and Ladies Auxiliaries: A Historiography of Mexican-Origin Women's Participation in Voluntary Associations and Politics in the United States, 1870–1990." *Perspectives in Mexican-American Studies* 5 (1993): 1–34.

———. *No Mexicans, Women, or Dogs Allowed: The Rise of the Mexican American Civil Rights Movement*. Austin: University of Texas Press, 2009.

Ortego, Phillip Darraugh. "People of Sánchez," *Nation* 15:206 (April 8, 1968): 482–83.

Padilla, Amado M. "Review of *Forgotten People* by George I. Sánchez." *Sociological Quarterly* 11:4 (Autumn 1970): 561–62.

Pagán, Eduardo Obregón. *Murder at the Sleepy Lagoon: Zoot Suits, Race, and Riot in Wartime L.A.* Chapel Hill: University of North Carolina Press, 2003.

Paredes, Américo, ed. *Humanidad: Essays in Honor of George I. Sánchez*. Los Angeles: Chicano Studies Center Publications of the University of California, Los Angeles, 1977.

Peltason, J. W. *Fifty-Eight Lonely Men: Southern Federal Judges and School Desegregation*. Urbana-Champaign: University of Illinois Press, 1971.

Perales, Alonso S., ed. *Are We Good Neighbors?* 1948; reprint, New York: Arno Press, 1974.

Phillips, M. S., W. J. M. Kinnear, and J. M. Shneerson. "Late Sequelae of Pulmonary Tuberculosis Treated by Thoracoplasty." *Thorax* 42 (1987): 445–51.

Phillips, Michael. *White Metropolis: Race, Ethnicity, and Religion in Dallas, 1841–2001*. Austin: University of Texas Press, 2006.

Portes, Alejandro. "Return of the Wetback." *Society* 11:3 (March–April 1974): 40–46.

Potts, William L. "Surgery in Pulmonary Tuberculosis." *Diseases of the Chest* 8 (February 1942): 54–60.

Powers, Jeanne M., and Lirio Patton. "Between *Mendez* and *Brown*: *Gonzales v. Sheeley* (1951) and the Legal Campaign Against Segregation." *Law and Social Inquiry* 33:1 (Winter 2008): 127–71.

Preuss, Gene B. "Cotulla Revisited: A Reassessment of Lyndon Johnson's Year as a Public School Teacher." *Journal of South Texas* 10 (1997): 20–37.

———. *To Get a Better School System: One Hundred Years of Education Reform in Texas*. College Station: Texas A&M University Press, 2009.

Pritchett, Wendell E. *Robert Clifton Weaver and the American City: The Life and Times of an Urban Reformer.* Chicago: University of Chicago Press, 2008.

Pulido, Alberto López, Barbara Driscoll de Alvarado, and Carmen Samora, eds. *Moving Beyond Borders: Julian Samora and the Establishment of Latino Studies.* Urbana: University of Illinois Press, 2009.

Pulido, Laura. *Black, Brown, Yellow, and Left: Radical Activism in Los Angeles.* Berkeley: University of California Press, 2006.

Pycior, Julie Leininger. *LBJ and Mexican Americans: The Paradox of Power.* Austin: University of Texas Press, 1997.

Quiroz, Anthony. *Claiming Citizenship: Mexican Americans in Victoria, Texas.* College Station: Texas A&M University Press, 2005.

Ramírez, Catherine S. *The Woman in the Zoot Suit: Gender, Nationalism, and the Cultural Politics of Memory.* Durham: Duke University Press, 2009.

Ramos, Henry A. J. *The American G.I. Forum: In Pursuit of the Dream, 1948–1983.* Houston: Arte Público Press, 1998.

Ravitch, Diane. *The Troubled Crusade: American Education, 1945–1980.* New York: Basic Books, 1985.

Redefer, Frederick L. "A Blow for Education: Death of the P.E.A." *Nation* 15:181 (October 8, 1955): 303–4.

Reed, John Shelton, and Daniel Joseph Singal, eds. *Regionalism in the South: Selected Papers of Rupert Vance.* Chapel Hill: University of North Carolina Press, 1982.

Reller, Theodore Lee, ed. *Comparative Educational Administration.* Englewood Cliffs: Prentice- Hall, 1962.

Richardson, Susan R. "Reds, Race, and Research: Homer P. Rainey and the Grand Texas Tradition of Political Interference, 1939–1944." *Perspectives on the History of Higher Education* 24 (2005): 125–71.

Rivas-Rodríguez, Maggie, ed. *Mexican Americans and World War II.* Austin: University of Texas Press, 2005.

Rivas-Rodríguez, Maggie, and Emilio Zamora, eds. *Beyond the Latino World War II Hero: The Social and Political Legacy of a Generation.* Austin: University of Texas Press, 2009.

Rivera, George, Jr. "Interview with Dr. George I. Sánchez." *La Luz* (May 1976): 9, 19.

Roediger, David, *The Wages of Whiteness: Race and the Making of the American Working Class.* London: Verso, 1991.

———. *Towards the Abolition of Whiteness: Essays on Race, Politics, and Working-Class History.* London: Verso, 1994.

Romo, Ricardo. "George I. Sánchez and the Civil Rights Movement: 1940–1960." *La Raza Law Journal* 1 (1986): 342–62.

Rosales, F. Arturo. *¡Pobre Raza! Violence, Mobilization, and Justice Among Mexico Lindo Immigrants, 1900–1936.* Austin: University of Texas Press, 1999.

Rosales, Steven. "Fighting the Peace at Home: Mexican American Veterans and the 1944 GI Bill of Rights." *Pacific Historical Review* 80:4 (November 2011): 597–627.

Rosenbaum, Robert J. *Mexicano Resistance in the Southwest.* Austin: University of Texas Press, 1981.

Ross, B. Joyce. "Mary McLeod Bethune and the National Youth Administration: A Case Study of Power Relationships in the Black Cabinet of Franklin D. Roosevelt." *Journal of Negro History* 60:1 (January 1975): 1–28.

Ruiz, Vicki L. *Cannery Women, Cannery Lives: Mexican Women, Unionization, and the California Food Processing Industry, 1930–1950*. Albuquerque: University of New Mexico Press, 1987.

Saldívar, Rámon. *The Borderlands of Culture: Américo Paredes and the Transnational Imaginary*. Durham: Duke University Press, 2006.

Samora, Julian, ed. *La Raza: Forgotten Americans*. Notre Dame: University of Notre Dame Press, 1966.

———. *Los Mojados: The Wetback Story*. Notre Dame: University of Notre Dame Press, 1971.

San Miguel, Guadalupe, Jr. *Brown, Not White: School Integration and the Chicano Movement in Houston*. College Station: Texas A&M University Press, 2001.

———. "Conflict and Controversy in the Evolution of Bilingual Education in the United States—An Interpretation." *Social Science Quarterly* 65:2 (June 1984): 505–18.

———. *"Let All of Them Take Heed:" Mexican Americans and the Campaign for Educational Equality in Texas, 1910–1981*. Austin: University of Texas Press, 1987.

San Miguel, Guadalupe, Jr., and Richard R. Valencia. "From the Treaty of Guadalupe Hidalgo to *Hopwood*: The Educational Plight and Struggle of Mexican Americans in the Southwest. *Harvard Educational Review* 68 (Fall 1998): 353–412.

Sánchez, George J. *Becoming Mexican American: Ethnicity, Culture and Identity in Chicano Los Angeles, 1900–1945*. New York: Oxford University Press, 1993.

Sánchez, Luis Oscar [Victor Urquidi]. *Los Hijos de Jones*. Austin: Institute of Latin American Studies, University of Texas at Austin, 1969.

Sánchez, Virgie. "Travel Impressions" and "Dont's for Globe-Trotters," *LULAC News* 6:5 (May 1939): 50.

Santillán, Richard. "Rosita the Riveter: Midwest Mexican American Women During World War II, 1941–1945." *Perspectives in Mexican American Studies* 2 (1989): 115–47.

Saragoza, Alex M. "Recent Chicano Historiography: An Interpretive Essay." *Aztlán* 19:1 (Spring 1988–1990): 1–77.

Satterthwaite, Linton. "Review of *Arithmetic in Maya* by George I. Sánchez." *American Antiquity* 28:2 (October 1962): 256.

Saunders, Lyle, and Olen E. Leonard. *The Wetback in the Lower Rio Grande Valley of Texas*. Inter-American Education Occasional Papers VII. Austin: University of Texas Press, 1951.

Schlossman, Steven. "Self-Evident Remedy? George I. Sánchez, Segregation, and Enduring Dilemmas in Bilingual Education." *Teachers College Record* 84:4 (Summer 1983): 871–907.

School of Inter-American Affairs. *Mexico's Role in International Intellectual Cooperation: Proceedings of the Conference Held in Albuquerque, February 24–25, 1944*. Inter-Americana, Short Papers VI. Albuquerque: University of New Mexico Press, 1945.

Schwarz, Jordan A. *Liberal: Adolf A. Berle and the Vision of an American Era.* New York: Free Press, 1987.

Scott, Daryl Michael. *Contempt and Pity: Social Policy and the Image of the Damaged Black Psyche, 1880–1996.* Chapel Hill: University of North Carolina Press, 1997.

Shabazz, Amilcar. *Advancing Democracy: African Americans and the Struggle for Access and Equity in Higher Education in Texas.* Chapel Hill: University of North Carolina Press, 2004.

Shale, Richard. *Donald Duck Joins Up: The Walt Disney Studio During World War II.* Studies in Cinema, no. 16. Ann Arbor: UMI Research Press, 1982.

Shenin, David, ed. *Beyond the Ideal: Pan Americanism in Inter-American Affairs.* Westport, Conn.: Greenwood Press, 2000.

Sheridan, Clare. "'Another White Race': Mexican Americans and the Paradox of Whiteness in Jury Selection." *Law and History Review* 21:1 (Spring 2003): 109–44.

Simmons, Marc. *New Mexico: A Bicentennial History.* New York: W. W. Norton, 1977.

Simpson, Eyler N. "Review of *Mexico: A Revolution by Education* by George I. Sánchez." *Annals of the American Academy* 190 (March 1937): 256–57.

Singal, Daniel J. *The War Within: From Victorian to Modernist Thought in the South, 1919–1945.* Chapel Hill: University of North Carolina Press, 1982.

Sitkoff, Harvard. *A New Deal for Blacks: The Emergence of Civil Rights as a National Issue.* Volume 1: *The Depression Decade.* New York: Oxford University Press, 1978.

———. *Perspectives on Modern America: Making Sense of the Twentieth Century.* New York: Oxford University Press, 2001.

Soldatenko, Michael. *Chicano Studies: The Genesis of a Discipline.* Tucson: University of Arizona Press, 2009.

Stiler, Harry G. "Review of *Forgotten People* by George I. Sánchez." *Journal of Farm Economies* 24:1 (February 1942): 364–66.

Tax, Sol. "Review of *Mexico: A Revolution by Education.*" *American Sociological Review* 2:3 (June 1937): 446.

Tevis, Martha. "Sánchez, George Isidore." *Handbook of Texas Online.* http://www.tsha online.org. Published by the Texas State Historical Association.

Trulson, Chad, and James W. Marquart. "Racial Desegregation and Violence in the Texas Prison System." *Criminal Justice Review* 27:2 (Autumn 2002): 233–55.

Tushnet, Mark V. *Making Civil Rights Law: Thurgood Marshall and the Supreme Court, 1936–1961.* New York: Oxford University Press, 1994.

———. *The NAACP: Legal Strategy Against Segregated Education, 1925–1950.* Chapel Hill: University of North Carolina Press, 1987.

Usabel, Gaizka S. de. *The High Noon of American Films in Latin America.* Studies in Cinema, no. 17. Ann Arbor: UMI Research Press, 1982.

Valencia, Richard R. "A Tribute to Thomas P. Carter (1927–2001): Activist Scholar and Pioneer in Mexican American Education." *Journal of Latinos and Education* 5:4 (2006): 237–52.

———. *Chicano Students and the Courts: The Mexican American Legal Struggle for Educational Equality.* New York: New York University Press, 2008.

Valencia, Richard R., ed. *Chicano School Failure and Success: Past, Present, and Future.* 3d ed. New York: Routledge, 2011.

Valenzuela, Angela, ed. *Leaving Children Behind: How "Texas Style" Accountability Fails Latino Youth.* Albany: State University of New York Press, 2005.

——. *Subtractive Schooling: U.S.–Mexican Youth and the Politics of Caring.* Albany: State University of New York Press, 1999.

Vance, Rupert B. *Human Geography of the South.* Chapel Hill: University of North Carolina Press, 1932.

Vargas, Zaragosa. *Labor Rights Are Civil Rights: Mexican American Workers in Twentieth-Century America.* Princeton: Princeton University Press, 2005.

Vaughan, Mary Kay. *Cultural Politics in Revolution: Teachers, Peasants, and Schools in Mexico, 1930–1940.* Tucson: University of Arizona Press, 1997.

Velasco, Jesus. "Reading Mexico, Understanding the United States: American Transnational Intellectuals in the 1920s and 1990s." *Journal of American History* 86:2 (September 1999): 641–67.

Washington, Alethea H. "Educar es Redimir." *Journal of Negro Education* 6:2 (April 1937): 203–5.

Weber, Devra. *Dark Sweat, White Gold: California Farm Workers, Cotton, and the New Deal.* Berkeley: University of California Press, 1996.

Weise, Julie M. "Mexican Nationalisms, Southern Racisms: Mexicans and Mexican Americans in the U.S. South, 1908–1939." *American Quarterly* 60:3 (September 2008): 749–77.

Welles, Benjamin. *Sumner Welles: FDR's Global Strategist.* New York: St. Martin's Press, 1997.

Welsh Michael. "A Prophet Without Honor: George I. Sánchez and Bilingualism in New Mexico." *New Mexico Historical Review* 69:1 (1994): 19–34.

Wickberg, Daniel. "Heterosexual White Male: Some Recent Inversions in American Cultural History." *Journal of American History* 92:1 (June 2005): 136–57.

Wiley, Tom. *Politics and Purse Strings in New Mexico's Public Schools.* Albuquerque: University of New Mexico Press, 1968.

Wilgus, A. Curtis, ed. *The Caribbean, Mexico Today.* Gainesville: University of Florida Press, 1964.

Wilson, Steven H. "Brown Over 'Other White': Mexican Americans' Legal Arguments and Litigation Strategy in School Desegregation Lawsuits." *Law and History Review* 21:1 (Spring 2003): 145–94.

——. *The Rise of Judicial Management in the U.S. District Court, Southern District of Texas, 1955–2000.* Athens: University of Georgia Press, 2002.

Woodward, C. Vann. *Thinking Back: The Perils of Writing History.* Baton Rouge: Louisiana State University Press, 1986.

Woyshner, Christine, Joseph Watras, and Margaret Smith Crocco, eds. *Social Education in the Twentieth Century: Curriculum and Context for Citizenship.* New York: Peter Lang, 2004.

Zamora, Emilio. *Claiming Rights and Righting Wrongs in Texas: Mexican Workers and Job Politics During World War II.* College Station: Texas A&M University Press, 2009.

——. "The Failed Promise of Wartime Opportunity for Mexicans in the Texas Oil Industry." *Southwestern Historical Quarterly* 95:2 (January, 1992): 221–36.

——. *The World of the Mexican Worker in Texas.* College Station: Texas A&M University Press, 1993.

Zieger, Robert H., ed. *Life and Labor in the New South: Essays in Southern Labor History since 1950.* Gainesville: University of Florida Press, 2012.

INDEX

Note: Italic page numbers refer to illustrations. The abbreviation GIS refers to George I. Sánchez.